Sport in Society:
Readings in the Sociology of Sport

SECOND EDITION

JOSEPH G. WEIS

Sport in Society, Second Edition
Joseph G. Weis

Custom Editor:
Tom Tucker

Project Development Editor:
Spring Greer

Marketing Coordinators:
Lindsay Annett and Sara Mercurio

Production/Manufacturing Supervisor:
Donna M. Brown

Sr. Project Coordinator:
K.A. Espy

Pre-Media Services Supervisor:
Dan Plofchan

Rights and Permissions Specialist:
Kalina Hintz

Senior Prepress Specialist:
Kim Fry

Cover Design:
Krista Pierson

Cover Image:
© Getty Images

Compositor:

Printer:
Globus Printing and Packaging

© 2006 the Thomson Corporation. Thomson and the Star logo are trademarks used herein under license.

Printed in the
United States of America
1 2 3 4 5 6 7 8 9 08 07 06

For more information, please contact Thomson Custom Solutions, 5191 Natorp Boulevard, Mason, OH 45040.
Or you can visit our Internet site at www.thomsoncustom.com

ALL RIGHTS RESERVED. No part of this work covered by the copyright hereon may be reproduced or used in any form or by any means — graphic, electronic, or mechanical, including photocopying, recording, taping, Web distribution or information storage and retrieval systems — without the written permission of the publisher.

The Adaptable Courseware Program consists of products and additions to existing Thomson products that are produced from camera-ready copy. Peer review, class testing, and accuracy are primarily the responsibility of the author(s).

For permission to use material from this text or product, contact us by:
Tel (800) 730-2214
Fax (800) 730 2215
www.thomsonrights.com

Sport in Society / Joseph G. Weis – Second Edition
p. 456
ISBN 0-759-35225-9

SPORT IN SOCIETY:
Readings in the Sociology of Sport

Joseph G. Weis

Table of Contents

I. INTRODUCTION TO THE SOCIOLOGY OF SPORT

1. Frey, J. H. and D. S. Eitzen. "Sport and Society." Annual Review of Sociology 17:503-522, 1991.

II. HISTORY OF SPORT

2. Day, Jane S. "Performing on the Court." Pp. 65-77 in The Sport of Life and Death: The Mesoamerican Ballgame. E. Michael Whittington (ed.). N.Y.: Thames and Hudson, 2001.

3. Hill, W. D. and J. E. Clark. "Sports, Gambling, and Government: America's First Social Compact?" American Anthropologist 103/2: 331-345, 2001.

4. Conover, A. "Little Brother of War: Lacrosse Sticks Were Tools of the Trade in a Rugged Indian Game…" Smithsonian 28/9: 32-34, December 1997

5. Veblen, Thorstein. "Modern Survivals of Prowess," pp. 170-183, in The Theory of the Leisure Class. Mentor Books, 1953.

III. FUNCTIONS OF SPORT

6. Birrell, S. "Sport as Ritual: Interpretations from Durkheim to Goffman." Social Forces 60/2: 354-376, 1981

7. Segrave, J. O. "Sport as Escape." Journal of Sport and Social Issues 24/1: 61-77, 2000.

8. Giamatti, A. Bartlett. "Baseball and the American Character." In Giamatti, A Great and Glorious Game. Chapel Hills: Algonquin Books, 1998, p. 41-65.

9. Eitzen, P. Stanley. "Upward Mobility Through Sport? The Myths and Realities." Z Magazine 12/March: 14-19, 1999

IV. SOCIALIZATION AND SPORT

10. Woolger, C. and T. G. Power. "Parent and Sport Socialization: Views from the Achievement Literature." Journal of Sport Behavior 16/3: 171-190, 1993.

11. Linder, K., Johns, D., and J. Butcher. "Factors in Withdrawal from Youth Sport: A Proposed Model." Journal of Sport Behavior 14/1: 3-18, 1991

12. Eccles, Jacquelynne and Bonnie Barber. "Student Council, Volunteering, Basketball, or Marching Band?" Journal of Adolescent Research 14/1: 10-43, 1999

V. ACADEMIC ACHIEVEMENT AND INVOLVEMENT IN SPORTS

13. Fejgin, Naomi. "Participation in High School Competitive Sports." Sociology of Sport Journal 11: 211-230, 1994

14. Broh, B. A. "Linking Extracurricular Programming to Academic Achievement: Who Benefits and Why?" Sociology of Education 75: 69-91, 2002.

15. Purdy, D., Eitzen, S., and R. Hufnagel. "Are Athletes Also Students?" Social problems 29: 439-448, 1982

16. Rishe, P. J. "A Reexamination of How Athletic Success Impacts Graduation Rates: Comparing Student-Athletes to All Other Undergraduates." American Journal of Economics and Sociology 62/2: 408-427

VI. GENDER ISSUES IN SPORT

17. Rhoads, S. E. "Sports, Sex, and Title IX." Public Interest 154: 86-98, 2004.

18. Ryan, J. "Female Gymnasts and Ice Skaters: The Dark Side." Pp. 3-15 in Little Girls in Pretty Boxes. New York: Doubleday, 1996.

VII. RACE AND SPORT

19. Sage, George. "Racial Inequality and Sport." From Power and Ideology in American Sport (Sage), pp. 8-98, Champaign, IL: Human Kinetics, 1998
20. Gonzalez, G. Letitia. "The Stacking of Latinos in Major League Baseball: A Forgotten Minority?" Journal of Sport and Social Issues 20: 134-160, 1996

21. Churchill, Ward. "Crimes Against Humanity." Z Magazine 6: 43-47, 1993

22. Brown, T. N. et al. "There's No Race on the Playing Field: Perceptions of Racial Discrimination Among White and Black Athletes." Journal of Sport & Social Issues 27/2: 162-183, 2003.

VIII. DEVIANCE IN SPORT

23. Langbein, L. and R. Bess. "Sports in School: Source of Amity or Antipathy?" Social Science Quarterly 83/2: 436-454, 2002.

24. Hughes, Robert and Jay Coakley. "Positive Deviance Among Athletes: The Implications of Overconformity to the Sport Ethic." Sociology of Sport Journal 8/3: 307-325, 1991

25. Sack, A. "The Underground Economy of College Football." Sociology of Sport Journal 8/March: 1-15, 1991

26. Nixon, Howard L. "Gender, Sport, and Aggressive Behavior Outside Sport." Journal of Sport and Social Issues 21/4: 379-391, 1997

IX. SPORT SUBCULTURES

27. Donnely P. and K. Young. "The Construction and Confirmation of Identity in Sport Subcultures." Sociology of Sport Journal 5: 223-240, 1988

28. Heino, R. "What is So Punk About Snowboarding?" Journal of Sport & Social Issues 24/1: 176-191, 2000.

29. Gauthier, D. K. and C. J. Forsyth. "Buckle Bunnies: Groupies of the Rodeo Circuit." Deviant Behavior 21: 349-365, 2000.

X. SPORT ECONOMICS AND BUSINESS

30. Zimbalist, Andrew. "Unpaid Professionals: The Student as Athlete." From Unpaid Professionals (Zimbalist), pp. 16-20, Princeton University Press, 1999

31. Baade, R. and R. Dye. "The Impact of Stadiums and Professional Sport on Metropolitan Area Development." Growth and Change 21/2: 1-14, 1990

XI. MEDIA AND SPORT

32. Messner, M., M. Dunbar, and D. Hunt. "The Televised Sports Manhood Formula." Journal of Sport & Social Issues 24/4: 380-394, 2000.

33. Colangelo, J. and L. Sherman. "Sports and the Media: Synergy is the Key to Winning Success." Management Review May: 44-46.

Section I

Introduction to the Sociology of Sport

Sport and Society

James H. Frey & D. Stanley Eitzen

Sport is an arena of patterned behaviors, social structures, and interinstitutional relationships that holds unique opportunities to study and understand the complexities of social life. Sport is an activity that commands a degree of primary or secondary involvement unsurpassed by other institutionalized settings. Sport offers an opportunity for research on "highly crystallized forms of social structure not found in other systems or situations" (Luschen 1990:59). That is, field research in sport provides, for example, structured conflict and competitiveness in controlled settings rarely found in other aspects of social life. Group dynamics, goal attainment by social organizations, subcultures, behavioral processes, social bonding, structured inequality, socialization, and organizational networks are just a few sociological topics that can be studied in sport settings. This view presupposes that the structure or forms of behavior and interaction found in sport settings are similar to those found in other societal settings. In other words, sport like other institutions is a microcosm of society.

At the same time that sport is a product of social reality, it is also unique. No other institution, except perhaps religion, commands the mystique, the nostalgia, the romantic ideational cultural fixation that sport does. No other activity so paradoxically combines the serious with the frivolous, playfulness with intensity, and the ideological with the structural.

The purposes of this review are twofold: first, to describe the current understanding of sport and society through the work of sport sociologists in selected areas, and, second, to assess the adequacy of the research and theorizing in these fields. The paper is divided into five parts. The first part presents the theoretical perspectives guiding research in sport sociology. The next two sections examine sport and two social processes: socialization and social change. The fourth section looks at an institution—the polity—and its relationship to sport. The final section demonstrates how sport reinforces racial and gender inequality. Except for the section on the polity, the discussion focuses on North America, especially the United States.

THEORETICAL PERSPECTIVES

At the macro level, the focus of this paper, three theoretical perspectives—structural functionalism, conflict theory, and cultural studies—are prominent in the works of sport sociologists. The sociology of sport emerged in the 1960s and 1970s. The earliest contributions to the field were efforts to delineate and justify this new subfield as a scholarly and important field of inquiry, and they tended to be informed by structural functionalism. The structural-functional paradigm focuses on social organizations, how they work, and how they are maintained. The functions (i.e. consequences) of patterned behaviors for the organizations in question, are emphasized (Frey 1986). Guided by the tenets of structural functionalism, these and subsequent works focused on socialization of youth through sport, sport as a vehicle for assimilation, sport as a social system, the relationship of sport to other institutions, and the integrating functions of sport for participants, observers, and social organizations.

These works appeared at a time in American history when society was undergoing rapid changes, popular American beliefs were being challenged, and authority questioned. Many sport sociologists reacted against structural functionalism with its bias for accepting and rationalizing what is; they adopted, rather, a theoretical perspective—conflict theory—which argues that sport reflects and reinforces the hegemony of societal arrangements, thereby perpetuating class and power differentials (Haerle 1974, Brohm 1978, Gruneau 1983, Hargreaves 1986, Sage 1990). Those guided by conflict theory also focused on social problems in sport such as sexism, racism, classism, oppression, organizational conflict, and deviance.

Recently, a number of sport sociologists have embraced a cultural studies approach to sport-related phenomena. From this perspective both functional and conflict perspectives are challenged because they are deterministic, that is, they tend to ignore or dismiss human agency in social change. Also, both theoretical perspectives are considered faulty because they omit the significance of cultural imperatives, where sport is seen as a cultural expression. In this view, sport is a socially constructed arena where developmental and emergent features are of central significance. Canadian and European scholars have taken the lead in writing from this perspective (Gruneau 1983, Hargreaves 1986), followed recently by American scholars (MacAloon 1987, Harris 1989, Birtell 1989).

Cultural studies theorists reject the natural science model as the best means to know a phenomenon. Rather, a phenomenological approach is preferred. A leading proponent asserts:

> The replication of so-called scientific studies of sport has done little to enhance either our knowledge or understanding of the nature and meaning of sporting practices. By separating sport from its developmental features, the 'variable' approach completely ignores the socio-historical and political dimensions of cultural life.
>
> The specific contribution of cultural studies has been to link up the lived experience of human actors, and cultural meanings, texts, representations (culture as interpretation) with broader political and economic structures of modern industrial societies (Hollands 1984:70–71).

The existence of sport must be explained in terms of something more than simply the needs of the social system or the production needs of a capitalist economy. Sport is created by people interacting, using their skills and interests to make sport into something that meets their interests and needs (Coakley 1990).

Change is also important to cultural studies theorists. Sport is "produced" out of everyday life (Gruneau 1983). Thus, people act to create their institutions; they are not simply passive responders. At times, however, the design of sport is not always desirable (e.g. athletes cannot always transfer schools) because some of those involved are adversely affected, and they do not usually have sufficient resources to resist organizational change. For example, college athletes can do little or nothing about the way the NCAA runs college sports. Sport and any vestiges of culture can be forms of resistance (Fiske 1989, Foley 1990, although for the most part existing class relations, including those of gender and race, are reproduced (Foley 1990, Hargreaves 1986, Gruneau 1989, Adelman 1986).

SPORT AND SOCIALIZATION

The involvement of youth, particularly male children, in sport is typically encouraged by parents, school administrators, and community leaders because this activity is viewed as a very effective setting for learning acceptable values and beliefs and for acquiring desirable character traits. Despite a barrage of criticism, very strong societal support exists for sport participation because of the belief that sport teaches proper values such as self-discipline, sportsmanship, and an appreciation for hard work, competition, and goal attainment.

Most claims about the value of sport participation focus on sport as an agent of socialization. But despite strong cultural beliefs, there is little evidence to support the claims made for the contribution of sport to the socialization process. Studies comparing male athletes and male nonathletes (there are very few studies comparing women) yield little evidence to support the idea that sport is necessary for complete and adequate socialization, or that involvement in sport results in character building, moral development, a competitive or team orientation, good citizenship, or valued personality traits (Dubois 1986, Fine 1987, Coakley 1987, McPherson et al 1989, Rees et al 1990). Sport seems to make little difference. Athletes and non-athletes are comparable on various personality traits and value orientations. Sport participation has no general effect on self-image; it does not reduce prejudice; it is not necessary for leadership development; and social adjustment is not necessarily enhanced (Fine 1987). The widespread conclusion by sport sociologists is that when an apparent socialization effect is found, it is actually the result of a selection process that attracts and retains children and youth in sport who already have or are comfortable with the values and behavioral traits that coaches demand and that lead to success in sport. Those without these desired values and traits either show no interest in sport, or they leave sport voluntarily (i.e. they drop out) or involuntarily (i.e. they are removed by coaches) (Stevenson 1975, 1985).

The debate over the experience of youth in sport stems largely from cultural myths rather than from empirical studies. The content is not so critical; the reaction and definitions of the child's significant others are what make a difference (Sherif 1976, Fine 1987). Continued participation is likely if support and perception are positive; participation will not continue if the socializing influence from significant others is absent. Withdrawal takes place if the sport role is no longer crucial to identity, and non-sport activities and peers become more attractive (Ball 1976, Brown 1985). Aversive socialization or a dramatic negative experience can also stimulate withdrawal. Brown (1985) found that many swimmers, age 10–12, dropped out of the sport to protect their self-esteem in the face of declining success and reduced rewards for participation.

Finally, the socialization of youth and adults, whether participants or not, occurs through the media's presentation of sport. The mass media socialize through image management, the manipulation of symbols, and commentary (Prisuta 1979, Jhally 1989, Wenner 1989, Sage 1990). The mediated sports product that reflects conservative, authoritarian, and nationalistic values is warmly received by the audience; it is not forced upon them (Wenner 1989, Prisuta 1979). There is implicit political content in the form of value messages in the mediated presentation of sport. For example, Wenner's (1986) study of Super Bowl pregame commentary found that the value content strongly endorsed hard work, rugged individualism, and national pride. Media are in a sense the creators of culture, conveying information about what is acceptable and unacceptable. Thus, the media reinforce established order and value consensus by virtue of the presentation, by commentary and pictures of sport events. These media presentations can influence our ideas about sport, our perceptions of gender, race, social relations, and proper behaviors, and our adherence to certain values.

SOCIAL CHANGE: FROM PLAY TO CORPORATE SPORT

Although typologies are not intended to be accurate representations of reality, they are useful for analytical purposes. One such typology is that used to distinguish play from sport in the transformation of *ludic*, playful activity pursued for its own sake, to physical activity that is used for extrinsic purposes. Historically, this transformation has produced what Page (1973), Guttman (1988), and others have described as the secularization, commodification, rationalization, bureaucratization, quantification, and commercialization of modern sport.

Huizinga (1949), Stone (1955), Caillois (1961), Edwards (1973), McPherson et al (1989), Coakley (1990), and many others who study sport have found useful the analytic distinction between play and sport. Play is viewed as an activity where entry and exit are free and voluntary, rules are emergent and temporary, fantasy is permitted, utility of action is irrelevant, and the result is uncertain. Play has no formal history nor organization; motivation and satisfaction are intrinsic; and the outcome does not have serious impact beyond the context of the activity. On the other hand, modern sport as represented by the Olympic Games, big-time college athletics, and professional sports exhibits the opposite profile. This type of sport is hardly voluntary; rules are formal, generalizable, and enforced by formal regulatory bodies (e.g. National Collegiate Athletic Association—NCAA); the outcome is serious for individuals and organizations not actually participating in the physical activity, and winning (the outcome) is more important than participation (the process).

As sport becomes institutionalized, particularly at the highest levels of amateur and professional competition, it has come to reflect the corporate commodity model. Sport is more like work than play.

The locus of control has moved from the player/participant to the manager and audience. Morality and ennoblement are replaced by spectacle and entertainment. Play is replaced by display (Stone 1955). Attracting spectators and media sponsorships becomes more important than the playing process because sport is now driven by profit and the market. The ethics of the business and corporate world tend to guide sport, not the principles of play and enjoyment (Eitzen & Sage 1989:16–18, Sage 1990). We should not be surprised that high-level sport has been transformed into a commercialized, commodified, and massified phenomenon. Since the business organization has replaced the family as the basic unit coordinating economic activity, and monopoly capital has promoted consumer markets as the preeminent factor in economic organization, many institutions, including sport, in America have been rationalized and corporatized. The commercial factor is so prominent that even a Gross National Sports Product (GNSP) has been calculated. In 1988 the GNSP was $63.1 billion (Comte & Stogel 1990). This places the sport GNP twenty-second on the list of the top 50 industry GNP, ahead of the automobile, petroleum, and airline industries.

The consequences of the commercialization of sport are significant. First, changes may be made in the game format or rules. In football, for example, the forward pass and the narrowing of the hash marks were changes designed to make football more appealing to viewers and spectators. Second, the orientation or values of the participants may change from those based on self-development and satisfaction to those of entertainment and self-interest. Coakley (1990) has described this as a change from an *aesthetic orientation* that emphasizes the beauty and pleasure of movement, skill and ability, and lifelong activity to a *heroic orientation* that emphasizes danger and excitement, style, and a short-term commitment to victory. There is a developing industry of sport sciences for the primary goal of performance enhancement. The emphasis is on strategies, technical improvement, nutritional and psychological intervention, or any technique to manipulate or engineer the athlete to perform better. This has been called the "scientization" of athletic sport; it is a trend consistent with the instrumental goals of corporate sport (Brohm 1978). Third, control and influence are largely in the hands of persons and organizations who are not direct participants. Leagues, regulatory groups like the NCAA, media, event sponsors, owners in professional sports, athletic departments and alumni in collegiate programs are examples of the centers of influence. This has forced professional athletes to take measures to enhance their own impact on decision-making; these include labor unionization, representation by agents, and recourse to legal challenges. The fourth consequence of commercialization is the decline of amateurism and the rise of professionalism (Sewart 1985, Eitzen 1989). Elite amateur sport is corporate sport, whether it is related to the Olympic Games or to collegiate sports. True, amateur sport is characterized by participation for the love of the sport, not the extrinsic rewards. Intrinsic motivation and reward are still relevant, but their significance seems to be devalued by the rising importance of monetary rewards (legal and illegal) for athletes, the exaggerated importance of winning that translates into treating athletes as interchangeable parts, the increase in the incidence of athletes using performance enhancing drugs, and the association of athletic success with outcome goals of profit, visibility, entertainment, and community/organization prestige.

Section I: Introduction to the Sociology of Sport

The commercialization of sport is strongly influenced by the role of the media, particularly television, in programming the sports product and in the monies paid to sports organizations for broadcasting rights. The role of the media has increased rapidly in recent years. For instance, in 1980 the three major television networks broadcast live sports programming only 787 hours, In 1989, however, the three networks plus ESPN, SCA, and TBS channels broadcast 7341 hours of live sports programming (Stogel 1990:48), an increase of nearly 900% in the last decade. The influx of media money is obviously substantial. The National Football league, for example, sold rights to its games from 1990 through 1993 for a total of $3.6 billion, increasing the league's yearly income from television about 90% over 1989.

The athletic establishment covets television coverage of its events because of the contribution the media make to profits and to exposure to a mass audience. The media pursue sports programming because it is cheaper to produce than other types of programs and it enables the media to reach a normally difficult-to-reach audience of young, college-educated males with disposable income (Coakley 1990:281). This makes sports programming attractive to certain advertisers. Thus, the media and sport emerge in a symbiotic relationship, particularly economically. It is important to understand that the media play a dominant role because sport is primarily directed by commercial guidelines.

> Television simply expands the commercial interests that are already an inherent part of spectator sports in capitalist societies. Although some changes are uniquely linked to the special needs of television coverage, the real reason for most of the changes occurring over the past 3 decades has been the desire to produce more marketable entertainment for all spectators and a more attractive commercial package for sponsors and advertisers (Coakley 1990:280).

However, once a sports entity has been displayed on television and received the financial support from television, the sports organization is forever changed (Parente 1977, Altheide & Snow 1978).

The nature of sport has been changed by the media with its emphasis on display or what has been called "entertainmentization." Many changes in the nature of sport have resulted from media's influence and the desire of *both* media entrepreneurs and representatives of the sport establishment to enhance the appeal of their sport product to maintain profit margins. Thus, the media sometimes glorify violence, create heros and heroines, demand that athletic schedules be shifted, and that rule changes be made to enhance the product, increase the audience, and generate greater revenues from advertisers.

The preeminent role of media in sport means that TV media's presentation of sport is "mediated." That is, viewers see a representation of sport as it is depicted by commentary, shot or scene selection, and editorialization (Comisky et al 1977, Coakley 1990). Because the public rarely questions the media's construction of reality, particularly that treated by the press and television, the media play a role in shaping images and opinions regarding sport (Greendorfer 1983, Tuchman 1978). The media's representation of an event is taken as reality, overlooking the reality that it is a staged event mediated by commentary. What is presented is generally consistent with the commercial and entertainment agendas of media and sport establishment.

One of the sport-related behaviors that has been projected as a result of media's definition of sport is gambling. Not only do media outlets provide the information a gambler needs, they also are a source of legitimation of gambling. The inclusion of point-spreads and injury reports in descriptions of upcoming games and the promotion of gambling celebrities and analysts together communicate the message that gambling is an acceptable activity and that gambling on sport is a natural accompaniment of sport, even though it is legal in only two states. Thus, the symbiotic relationship of sport and the media is enhanced by the provision of gambling information that appeals to viewers and readers (D'Angelo 1987).

As an activity, gambling is widespread and essentially a legitimate activity to most (Rosecrance 1988). The dated (1974) but very comprehensive study of America's gambling behavior reported that just under two thirds of Americans had gambled in the previous twelve months. Over 40 million persons had bet on sport. A 1984 Gallup Poll and the 1983 Miller Lite Sport Survey reported, respectively, that 17% and 23% of the population bet on sport (Frey 1985). In 1989, Americans gambled $290 billion on all types of games, an increase of nearly 100% from 1982. Of this amount $43 billion was bet illegally, and nearly 70% of that was bet on sports. Sports betting in 1989 represents approximately 11% of all gambling, an increase of 42% over 1982 (Christianson 1990:8). Sports betting is very popular, and this popularity is promoted by the fact that the natural association of sport and gambling is frequently part of the content of the media's presentation of and commentary on sport events.

SPORT AND THE POLITY: INTERNATIONAL RELATIONS

Two major motives govern a country's political and economic activity. The first is that of building an efficient but dynamic modern state. In other words, the country should exhibit an acceptable standard of living, a stable political order, an equitable system of social justice, and social behavior governed by controlled, rational, not impulsive, procedures. The second national motive is to be recognized as a responsible actor in the international community of nations (Geertz 1963). In other words, nations seek internal stability and external status. Sport is commonly viewed as a vehicle to achieve both.

The integrative role of sport for a nation is similar to the structural-functional role assigned to sport in communities, in the classic studies by the Lynds (1929), Hollingshead (1949) and Stone (1981) and the recent study by Wilkerson & Dodder (1987). Integration to counteract internal racial, ethnic, regional and class diversity and conflict is a major reason that nations promote participation in highly visible international events. Lever's study of soccer in Brazil documented the way that sport gave a diverse population something to share in the name of national solidarity (1983:19). Thus, sport can contribute to a national identity or sense of nationalism that temporarily overrides differences. The world rugby championships provide an interesting example. Annually when national teams are selected, the warring factions in Ireland and Northern Ireland lay aside their bitter animosities, combining players to form the Irish national team which members of both nations cheer. Governments will often encourage international competition in acknowledgment of the unifying role of sport (Anthony 1969, Frey 1984, Riordan 1986). However, critics employing a conflict perspective assert that the use of sport to encourage the homogenization of a population represents an effort to control that population by instilling certain dominant values, which reduce the likelihood of a challenge against those in power (Klein 1989).

Section I: Introduction to the Sociology of Sport

Involvement in international sport requires participation in networks of organizations that are transnational in scope. Before this participation can be effective, an organizational base staffed by competent personnel must be developed. Sport provides a mechanism to link organizations and to develop managerial and administrative skills among the local population. Several Latin American countries, including Cuba, have done this (Arbena 1985). Nicaragua used baseball as a mechanism to rebuild internal institutions after a revolution and to reinstitute regional and intranational communication and coordination. In some cases, Cuba and the Dominican Republic, for example, the use of sport to enhance the human capital of an indigenous population serves to reduce the dependency of a nation of smaller size and limited resources on the larger nations (Frey 1988, Klein 1989).

The primary role of sport in international relations is one of public diplomacy. That is, sport serves to articulate secondary national interests (e.g. visibility, ideological expression, status enhancement, legitimacy), to test foreign relations initiatives (e.g. ping-pong diplomacy between the United States and China), to enhance cultural exchange and understanding, and to reduce the potential for actual conflict by playing out hostilities in a restricted and controlled setting (Reich 1974, Frey 1984, Riordan 1986). Thus, sport is an activity of international cooperation and interaction, but it is peripheral to the survival of a state political system (Frey 1984:72). Olympic record performances are irrelevant to hard-core negotiations over primary national interests that if unresolved could lead to war.

Nevertheless, status in the community of nations is ultimately related to success in athletic events. The gold medal count in the Olympics is important precisely because that count becomes a measure of political legitimacy, of modernization, or of a people's resolve (Espy 1979, Frey 1984, Heinila 1985).

The motivation to achieve acceptable status in a community of nations and thus to translate this status into political advantage is not limited to developing countries. Eastern bloc nations have spent enormous resources to achieve success in international competitions. The United States and other western nations have been reluctant to admit their keen interest in international sports success, but it is there nonetheless. International sports success is a very serious goal in the United States, for success is interpreted internally and externally as "proof" of the superiority of a nation's social, economic, and political systems. Thus, the only difference between the United States and the nations of the Eastern bloc and the Third World is that the United States does not admit that its international sporting efforts are serious (Frey 1984, Riordan 1986).

SPORT AND INEQUALITY: RACE

American sport sociologists have devoted considerable attention to the examination of racial discrimination in sport. The major conclusion of this work, devoted for the most part to comparing whites and blacks, is that just as racial discrimination exists in society, it exists in sport. Blacks do not have equal opportunity; they do not receive similar rewards for equal performance when compared to whites; and their prospects for a lucrative career beyond sport participation are dismal.

Americans remain comfortable with the cultural myth that the United States is an open society and that athletic excellence is an avenue of upward social mobility. Black subcultures reinforce this belief

(Edwards 1984). The myth seemingly is supported by two facts. First, although blacks make up 11–12% of the US population, they are vastly overrepresented in sport, with (1988 data) blacks comprising 21% of major league baseball players, 57% of professional football players, and 73% of professional basketball players. Second, many black athletes receive very high pay, some the highest in their sport. Research by sport sociologists, however, provides irrefutable evidence that blacks are the objects of discrimination in sport.

To begin, while blacks are overrepresented in some sports, they are underrepresented in others. Phillips (1976) argues that the reason blacks excel and are disproportionately found in some sports lies in what he calls the "sports opportunity structure." Blacks are found in those sports in which facilities, coaching, and competition are available to them: in the schools and community recreation programs. They are rarely found, however, in those sports that require the facilities, coaching, and competition usually provided only in private clubs or that are otherwise too expensive or exclusive to obtain.

Once blacks enter the ranks of sport, at whatever level or whatever sport, discriminatory practices continue. These take three forms: position allocation, analysis of performance differentials, and reward structures. One of the best documented forms of discrimination at both the college and professional levels is popularly known as "stacking." This term refers to situations in which minority group members are relegated to specific team positions and typically excluded from competing for others. Thus, sport reproduces the race relations found in society. Blacks tend to be "stacked" in those team positions that match racial and ethnic stereotypes, that is, they are placed into positions that require physical skills while whites are disproportionately found in positions that require intelligence, leadership, and that have greater outcome control.

In an early analysis Grusky (1963) observed that the importance of a position in an organization depends upon that position's spatial location or relevance to outcome, and the degree of interaction associated with that position. He said the more central one's spatial location: (a) the greater the likelihood dependent or coordinative tasks will be performed; and (b) the greater the rate of interaction with the occupants of other positions (Grusky 1963:345–46). Centrality has become a significant concept in analyzing the allocation of blacks and whites to positions on sport teams (Loy & McElvogue 1970). Racial segregation in sport is positively related to position centrality. Whites are typically found in central positions that require intelligence, coordinative and decision-making skills, and high rates of interaction, and thus greater outcome control—positions such as offensive center, quarterback, and middle linebacker in football, pitcher and catcher in baseball, and point guard in basketball. Blacks are channeled to noncentral positions that require physical skill such as speed and quickness, less interaction, and that have less impact on outcome—positions such as running back, receiver, defensive line, and corner back in football, the outfield in baseball, and forward in basketball (Loy & McElvogue 1970, Scully 1974, Yetman & Eitzen 1984, Leonard 1988).

Since Loy & McElvogue first noted the stacking phenomenon in team sports (1970), research ongoing to the present finds these patterns for college sport (Schneider & Eitzen 1979) and women's sport (Eitzen & Furst 1989), as well as for professional sport, although it is no longer found in professional basketball where blacks have such a numerical superiority. Moreover, this pattern of racial stacking has also been found in other sports such as rugby, soccer, cricket, and hockey in other societies such as Canada, England, and Australia (Best 1987, Maguire 1988, Lapchick 1989, Lavoie 1989).

Biological explanations of stacking, which are reflections of racial stereotypes, have been refuted (Eitzen & Sanford, 1975). Another explanation focuses on modeling, arguing that blacks choose to play certain positions because they desire to emulate role models (McPherson 1975a). This makes the exclusionary system self-perpetuating since most role models tend to fill noncentral positions. Economic explanations assert that the economic costs of developing play skills at certain positions such as quarterback are greater than for others (e.g. outfield); because blacks occupy lower socioeconomic status in American society, they will choose to play noncentral positions where the development of required skills is less costly. As black education improves, the proportion found in central positions will improve (Medoff 1986). Presumably, improving SES is the result of better education and improved experience in decision making and developing intellectual skills. However, no evidence supports this trend in the broader society (Yetman 1987, Phillips 1988). In fact, black economic income, defined as a percentage of white income, has declined over the years.

Moreover, the economic hypothesis presumes that blacks will enhance their human capital through educational achievement. It is well documented, however, that on every measure of educational progress blacks score less well than whites. Eitzen & Purdy's study (1986) of college recruiting confirmed that sports tend to recruit the academically marginal blacks, thereby projecting a higher failure rate. Black athletes are exploited for their skill and given a scholarship, but they receive no education. The higher academic failure rate perpetuates the myth that blacks have superior physical skills, but inferior intellectual skills.

Another mechanism of discrimination is called the "the unequal opportunity for equal ability" hypothesis. Blacks must be better than whites to be admitted to college and to remain on athletic teams. Research has shown consistently that blacks are disproportionately found as starters and "stars" on the team, whereas whites are found disproportionately as nonstarters. After an elaborate study of baseball, Scully concluded, "Not only do blacks have to outperform whites to get into baseball, but they must consistently outperform them over their playing careers in order to stay in baseball" (Scully 1974:263). In Jonathan Brower's words, "mediocrity is a white luxury" (1973). This interesting relationship has been found in professional baseball and basketball, where the detailed statistics in those sports make such studies possible. This pattern also exists at the college level, where it is manifested in two additional ways. First, blacks must exhibit higher athletic skills than most of their white teammates in order to receive a scholarship (Evans 1979). And, second, blacks are more likely than whites to be recruited from community colleges, which means that universities make a relatively smaller investment in blacks, and that the universities are relatively assured of getting athletes with proven athletic abilities (Tolbert 1975).

Blacks are underrepresented in sports journalism, in officiating, and in sports administrative positions (Lapchick, 1990). Most visible is the paucity of blacks as head coaches or managers. Black women who aspire to coaching and management positions are victims of double jeopardy—their race and their gender. The lack of black coaches and managers is likely the result of two forms of discrimination. Overt discrimination occurs when owners ignore competent blacks because of their prejudices or because they fear the negative reaction of fans to blacks in leadership positions. The other form of discrimination is more subtle. Blacks are not considered for coaching positions because they did not, during their playing days, play at positions requiring leadership and decision-making due to stacking.

Most Americans believe that participation in sport is a mechanism to improve race relations (Miller Lite 1983). This view is an expression of the contact hypothesis which suggests that exposure to other racial groups through interaction reduces prejudice. Although one study (McClendon & Eitzen 1975) has found some support for this hypothesis in limited situations (when both races on a team contribute to winning and the team is successful), most research does not find that interracial contact in sport reduces racial prejudice (Chu & Griffey 1989, Lapchick 1989, McPherson et al 1989).

The history of desegregation in American sport shows clearly that owners and coaches integrated teams when they realized that winning leads to profits and that skin color does not matter if teams win (Coakley 1990:209). Thus, the commercial interests of those who control sport override cultural views. This is substantiated further by the finding that attendance at sports events is not responsive to the racial composition of teams (Koch & Vander Hill 1988).

SPORT AND INEQUALITY: GENDER

Most of what is known about sport is based on studies of white males. Sport and the values associated with sport have traditionally been those relevant to males not females. Any research that did include gender typically assumed that there was an inherent conflict between being a woman and participating in sport (Hall 1988). Thus, sport has tended to celebrate the achievements of men while marginalizing the status of women by placing women in expressive, supportive roles such as cheerleaders, or relegating participation by women to a secondary status. Sport has been as a result largely a "male preserve" supported by institutional practices of discrimination against women.

In a manner similar to the experiences of blacks in sport women have been prohibited from full and equal participation because of formal restrictions and cultural predispositions.

Several myths have evolved with respect to the participation of women in sport. These include the idea that sport is harmful to the female reproductive system and thus a threat to child bearing; that sport masculinizes a female in appearance; that the development of male masculinity is threatened if girls outperform adolescent boys in sport; that human and economic resources are wasted because the performance levels of females are significantly lower than those of males; and that sport is not important for the social development of women because the values of achievement, aggressiveness, and competition are irrelevant to the life experience of women. Even though all of the above have been refuted by evidence (for a summary, see McPherson et al 1989), these myths remain influential, causing stigma and role conflict for some women athletes. Although women athletes may experience role conflict, research shows that for most it is a positive experience. Data comparing women athletes and non-athletes from the United States, Australia, and India suggest, for example, that women athletes have a better self-image, a better body image, and a better outlook toward life than nonathletes (Snyder & Kivlin 1975). However, these results could be the product of selection, not socialization, and the outcome of strong in-group bonds formed by a subculture of athletes who acknowledge their differences from most women.

The most serious problems women face in sport involve discrimination. Title IX or Affirmative Action Legislation (1972) was designed to rectify discrimination, particularly in access to facilities, financial aid, and opportunity for participation. Some improvement was made, but when the US Supreme Court ruled in *Grove City v. Bell* (1984) that Title IX language applied only to programs receiving federal funds, progress was stalemated, with some 800 federal investigations involving possible sexist practices dropped or narrowed (Sabo 1988). The original broader interpretation of Title IX was restored by the Civil Rights Restoration Act of 1988, but the pace of investigations has not resumed, since it depends on the will of the Justice Department.

A dramatic example of discrimination by denying access to the control of sport is found in Acosta & Carpenter's (unpublished) analysis of the participation of women in the administration of athletic programs. Since Title IX, schools are offering more sports for women, and participation by women as athletes has shown a dramatic increase. However, the proportion of women who are coaches or admininstrators has declined significantly. In 1972, 90% of women's teams were coached by women; in 1989, 47% were coached by women. Similarly, the non-coach administrators of women's sports programs tend to be men, and the few women administrators in place are supervised by men.

The discrimination against women in sport has been documented in many areas and continues. The greatest promise of scholarship in this area, however, is theoretical. Feminist social theorists assert that sport is one of many social systems dominated by patriarchal value systems and dominance patterns (Birreli 1984, Hall 1988). The starting point of feminist social theory is the understanding of the dominance patterns found in patriarchal social structures (Hall 1984:88). Since sport is a cultural form, emergent, changing, and subject to the influence of gender and class, the meanings attached to sport participation cannot be properly assessed with traditional empirical methods. In the view of most feminist theorists, a feminist view must be cultural, humanist, interpretive, phenomenological, and value oriented. Thus, there is an affinity for the incorporation of the cultural studies approach by feminist scholars.

An interesting variant of gender scholarship and theoretical development has been through the study of masculinity and sport. Two of these developments appear to be especially fruitful (Messner 1990). Some pro-feminist, male scholars have used their own biographies to understand masculine worlds from a feminine viewpoint that emphasizes institutional patriarchy (Sabo 1986, Kimmel 1987). Thus, the emphasis is on the links between the costs and privileges of masculinity. The other approach is called "inclusive feminism." Messner, a leading proponent of this approach, summarizes:

> Through an inclusive feminism that recognizes the importance of working from multiple standpoints, we can begin to build an understanding of how class, racial, and sexual struggles within hierarchies of intermale dominance serve to construct men's global subordination of women (1990:149).

Just as scholars in other subfields in sociology, scholars in the sociology of sport are beginning to describe dominance and subordination and to analyze their complexity as they are simultaneously structured along racial, gender, and class lines (Birrell 1989).

CONCLUSION

Over a decade ago Gunther Luschen summarized the status of sport sociology as a subdiscipline of sociology in volume 6 of the *Annual Review of Sociology* (Luschen 1980). He asserted that sport sociology had garnered some followers who published sport-related articles in over 100 different scholarly journals. It appeared that sport sociology was on the verge of expanding as a field of social inquiry and of gaining acceptance in mainstream sociology. This promise, however, has not been realized.

Even with the formation of the North American Society for the Sociology of Sport (NASSS) and the publication of its *Sociology of Sport Journal*, sport sociology remains somewhat of an orphan speciality. The critical mass of theorists and researchers required to promote collaborative efforts, network formation, and professional identity has not emerged (Kenyon 1986, Coakley 1987). Even with the routine inclusion of sport sociology sessions on regional, national, and international conference programs, the profession of sociology has not accepted the study of sport into its mainstream. Neither has sport sociology attained high status in physical education where there are more physical educators claiming sport sociology as an area of study than there are such members of the American Sociological Association. Few graduate programs are available, and fewer courses are found in standard undergraduate curriculums. Sport research is often an "after-thought," pursued as an academic interest only after "serious" work is done.

The most serious charge against sport sociology is that the theoretical development is relatively weak (Luschen 1980, Kenyon 1986, Coakley 1987 , MacAloon 1987). Coakley summarizes this criticism:

> Unfortunately, much of the research in sociology of sport has been neither cumulative or theory-based, nor has it been dedicated to theory development (Kenyon 1986). More often, research has been designed to describe sport in ways that call popular beliefs into question, or to document the existence for an issue or problem. This is true of the field as a whole, but it is especially true of work done in the U.S. This is not to say that theory has not informed some of the work done by American sport sociologists, but little of their research has grown directly out of concern for theory testing or theory development in sociology (1987:14).

As a subdiscipline the sociology of sport is only 25 years old, and its professional association has been in existence just over a decade. This subdiscipline has the same problems found in the rest of sociology. While much of the research in sport sociology is not guided by theory, some very important work is. Leaders in the field are calling for theoretically based studies (see, Kenyon 1986, Birrell 1989), and some exemplars are leading the way. The work of gender theorists appears especially promising not only for the sport sociology but for sociology in general. This is because sport is such a fruitful arena in which "to take into account the contours of the particular relations of dominance and subordination that exist among groups located at the intersection of class and racial conflicts" (Birrell 1989:221).

Section II

History of Sport

Performing on the Court

JANE STEVENSON DAY

Games are a means, through make-believe, of coping with the world.

The birthplace of the first team sports played with a rubber ball was not Europe, nor Asia, but the ancient Americas. While the rest of the world was caught up in contests of individual athletic skills such as jousting, footraces, swimming, and wrestling, New World cultures were fielding teams of ballplayers who competed against each other on specially designed stone courts. Beginning possibly around 1500 B.C., these teams were the first to play with a ball made of rubber—as opposed to the wooden or leather spheres used in other parts of the world—and it was the elastic, bouncing nature of solid rubber balls combined with the concept of team play that made the New World games unique.

In the late 15th and early 16th centuries, when the Spanish arrived in the Americas, they witnessed this dramatic game, first on the islands of the Caribbean, then, in 1519, in the great Aztec capital city of Tenochtitlan. Rubber was unknown in Europe and Asia, and the astonished Spanish soldiers thought the bouncing rubber ball must be magic or the work of the devil. From that time on, lively rubber balls began to replace their leaden wood and leather European counterparts.

There was an immense enthusiasm for team competition among the indigenous peoples of the New World, particularly in Mesoamerica, an enthusiasm unrivaled in any other place until recent times. Today team games have become a phenomenal feature of American life and a hallmark of contemporary culture around the world. The modern games of football, basketball, soccer, and volleyball perpetuate traditions established 3,500 years ago in the New World. Teams and heroes, music and rituals, gambling, and rubber balls of various sizes were all part of sports long ago just as they are today.

PUTTING THE GAME IN CONTEXT

The ballgame was first played around 1500 B.C. on the Gulf Coast of Mexico by the Olmec—Mesoamerica's first great civilization. This hot, tropical setting formed the backdrop for the evolution of formalized teams, rubber balls, standardized protective equipment, religious rituals, and ballcourt architecture (see both Bradley and Taladoire). Eventually, these concepts spread throughout Mesoamerica and into the American Southwest and the Caribbean Islands, becoming one of the true hallmarks of pre-Columbian civilization. More than 1,500 ballcourts have been found in Mesoamerica, and many more probably still lie undiscovered beneath the streets and buildings of modern cities in Mexico and Guatemala. Together with the art associated with them, such as ceramic figurines and vessels, stone sculptures, carved monuments, wall murals, and specialized gaming equipment, these ballcourts provide the fundamental evidence for this ceremonial sport.

Between 1500 B.C. and A.D. 1521, with some notable exceptions (a few ballcourts were as large as a football field; others big enough for only two players), courts averaged 120 by 30 ft (36.5 by 9 m). They were shaped like a capital "I" with parallel masonry walls enclosing a long narrow playing alley that connected two end zones. Made of cut stones, originally whitewashed and painted with vivid colors, the courts were impressive, costly structures designed for ritual performances. Stone sculptures of the gods and small temples dedicated to them were frequently incorporated into the walls. On the interior, courts were often decorated with tenoned stone heads, carvings of jaguars, serpents, or raptors; and at some sites, life-sized stone friezes depict post-game rituals of human sacrifice. According to the location where the game was played, the rubber ball itself also varied in size. In Central Mexico, the Aztecs played a game with a ball about the size of a softball. From southern Mesoamerica, in some depictions of the Maya game, it appears to be as large as a beach ball.

PLAYING THE GAME

The ritual ballgame was played throughout Mesoamerica for more than three thousand years. Not surprisingly, it varied somewhat in both method of play and in meaning. We know from the early Spanish chronicles (beginning with the Conquest in 1519) that in the Aztec form of the game, for example, only the buttocks and knees could make contact with the ball. Eyewitnesses record that the ball was made of heavy, solid rubber, weighed 6 to 8 lb (3 to 4 kg), and was bounced against the walls of the court and from player to player at a fast pace. Points were scored when a ballplayer either missed a shot at one of the two vertical stone hoops set opposite each other at center court, was unable to return the ball to the opposing team before it bounced twice, or allowed the ball to bounce outside the boundaries of the court.

Although basic elements of the game appear consistent throughout Mesoamerica, the Aztecs probably played only one form of the sport and depictions of games in painted wall murals, and ceramic images of ballplayers dressed for the court, suggest there were other ways of playing. Figurines are particularly illustrative, portraying contestants wearing various combinations of attire and gear, including yokes, *hachas*, knee- and elbow-pads, arm bands, helmets, and heavy gloves. In addition, objects carried by players—bats, sticks, *manoplas* or handstones—imply numerous methods by which the ball may have been manipulated on the courts (for descriptions of this equipment, see Scott).

THE MEANING OF THE GAME
The significance of the complex Mesoamerican ballgame has been the focus of research and speculation by many scholars. A basic interpretation is that the ball and its movement in the court symbolize the movement of heavenly bodies in the sky, the game being seen as a battle of the sun against the moon and stars. The universal struggle between the opposing forces of day and night, good and evil, life and death was symbolically enacted by opposing teams on the ballcourt.

Clearly associated with this view of the game is the cult of fertility. Agricultural communities everywhere depend upon earth's bounty for survival; and agricultural productivity, in turn, requires the warmth and light of the sun and the timely occurrence of seasonal rains. Human sacrifice by decapitation is a recurring theme in ballgame imagery. Streams of blood spurting from the neck of a decapitated victim may be seen as watering the earth or as an offering to sustain the sun in its daily battle against the forces of the night.

Although this analysis of the ballgame's significance is somewhat simplistic, it underlies many more complex explanations of the elaborate religious and secular rites associated with the sport and illuminates its broad appeal to diverse audiences. The ballgame and its accompanying ceremonies clearly satisfied the innate needs of pre-Columbian cultures for more than 3,000 years. At its most basic level, ritual activities such as the reenactment of myth and sacrificial offerings were an attempt to impose order on an inexplicable universe and to tame the unruly cosmos for the benefit of humankind.

This essay will focus on two aspects of the game: the concept and continuity of team sports in pre-Hispanic societies and the dramatic, theatrical events that took place on the ballcourts of ancient Mesoamerica.

PLAYING AS A TEAM
Mesoamerican Pre-Columbian Pop Culture: The Team

> To play alone is a primary move
> of mind,
> but to learn the rules
> For playing with another
> is a partnership of mind and spirit
> An identifying of body and soul to win
> not as one
> but as a team.

Seeing oneself as a member of a group rather than as an independent individual is socially significant within a society. Personal sacrifice for overall good, a shared adherence to a set of common rules, and participation in team ritual serve to bond members of a group into a functioning unit. Historian William

Section II: History of Sport

McNeill asserts that, beginning very early in the human record, group activities such as dancing, singing, hunting, work teams, military drills, and eventually team games were integrating factors in human development. The use of music, chanting, and song to inspire work groups; the close cooperation among hunters to increase their success in the chase; and the almost hypnotic impact of extended periods of rhythmic dancing are examples of activities that facilitate physical and emotional unity.

Nowhere was the power of group coherence more evident than in Mesoamerica, where a ritual team sport was credited with the regeneration of life and the maintenance of cosmic order. The playing of the game promoted human bonding and emphasized the qualities of cooperation and obedience to rules as a means to achieve success. This ritual game of chance, with its focus on the concept of a team rather than on an individual, both reflected and influenced the societies in which it developed and surely contributed to the unique culture and worldview of pre-Columbian Mesoamerica.

To date, the first documented evidence for this association of teams and games can be found in a group of eight ceramic figurines recovered in an archaeological context from a tomb at the site of El Opeño in the modern Mexican state of Michoacán. Results of radiocarbon dating places these figurines at around 1500 B.C., Mesoamerica's Early Formative Period. They were found as a group and represent a ballgame scene. Five of the figures are male; they stand as if ready to hit a ball with the rectangular *manoplas* or heavy mitts in their hands and wear padding around the knee and lower leg. The other three figures are females, who recline or sit as if watching the game. Aside from protective padding on the males, all eight are nude except for a helmet-like head covering. The figures are clearly intended as a *scene*. Numbers of other figurines dressed as ballplayers are known from contemporaneous Formative Period sites in Tlapacoya and Tlatilco in the Valley of Mexico and Xochipala in the western state of Guerrero. The figures wear a variety of ballgame padding and carry gaming equipment. Like the El Opeño figurines, these may originally have been part of mortuary ballgame scenes, but any evidence for contextual association is lost.

More very early evidence supporting the use of sculpture to compose dramatic scenes comes from San Lorenzo in Veracruz, the first great Olmec site (1500–900 B.C.). This site specifically, and Olmec culture generally, exerted strong influence on succeeding cultures, thus data from excavations there are particularly significant. Ann Cyphers has recently concluded from her work at the site, that many, if not all, of the immense stone sculptures found at San Lorenzo and outliers were once positioned in scenes on the terraces of public buildings where they could be viewed by the populace from afar. These scenes, in Cypher's opinion, depicted an assortment of religious myths and served to validate the ruling elite. The large stone monuments may even have been rearranged periodically in order to illustrate different stories.

One set of figures from the El Azuzul Acropolis, in the San Lorenzo area, is particularly interesting: a pair of identical male stone figures, almost life size, were discovered there in association with two stone jaguar sculptures. The two seated young men are dressed alike in matching yokes, headdresses, and loincloths. They lean forward facing the jaguars and grasp a horizontal baton or bat with both hands. It is obvious that some myth or story is reflected in this dramatic scene. Even more tantalizing is the possibility that the *Popol Vuh*, the Maya creation myth concerning the Hero Twins who play a ballgame against the Lords of the Underworld (here represented by the jaguars), may well have originated with the Olmec.

At the Middle Formative Olmec site of La Venta (900–400 B.C.) the tradition of dramatic grouping of figures continues. A group of figurines, known as Offering Number 4, were recovered in a cache at the site. They were arranged in a scene consisting of 16 male figurines made of stone grouped in front of six miniature incised jade columns, or stelas. One figure stands alone, facing the other 15, with his back to the stelas. Unfortunately, the significance of the grouping is lost to us.

Ceramic groups or teams are also found in West Mexican shaft tombs, dating from the slightly later Late Formative and Protoclassic periods (400 B.C.–A.D. 300). These figures wear various types of diagnostic protective gear and depict ballgame activities. Most obvious and best known are the miniature models of actual ballcourts, all but one complete with players, balls, and spectators. The exception depicts two men fighting in the middle of the playing field, suggesting activities other than ballgames may have taken place on the courts.

In addition to these models we also find evidence of the ballgame in miniature ceramic groupings from burials in the West Mexican state of Colima. One such group is modeled fully in the round and the tiny figures wear heavy ballgame yokes with either a false phallus or an animal-head *hacha* attached at the front. Some of the West Mexican figures blow conch-shell trumpets, while others dance or perform acrobatics. It is difficult to document whether all these figurines were really ballplayers; more likely, some were performers participating in ballgame rituals. There is little doubt that entertainment formed part of the colorful events at a ballgame, so such groups wearing ballgame yokes may actually be related to the other activities of a team. Another set of figures, also dressed as ballplayers, appear at first glance to be warriors. They carry weapons and are posed in aggressive stances, but the spears and clubs in their hands may instead be bats and paddles used in playing the ballgame. In fact, the roles of warrior and ballplayer may often have been identical, with participants for either drawn from the same groups or teams of young men.

Closely related to the Colima groups are miniature figurines from tombs at the Middle Formative site of Chupícuaro in Michoacán. Hundreds of solid ceramic male and female figurines were recovered at that site during a hurried salvage operation before the construction of a dam. Like their Colima counterparts, certain groups of the figurines are very stylized, wearing ballgame yokes, arm bands, and leg guards; many hold balls, play musical instruments or wear phallic yokes.

It is easy to imagine that these various groups of early Western Mexican figurines were once arranged in scenes depicting rituals or festive events associated with the ballgame. In each of the groups described above, the ballgame-related figures fall into sets that visually appear to have been made by the hand of a single artist or workshop. Their costumes and accoutrements are distinct from those of other figures in the same region and certainly suggest they were intended to be participants in ballgame scenes. Although there is not sufficient evidence to be certain of such arrangements, the grouped figurines from the El Opeño tombs and the platform models of ballcourts and village life from tombs in Nayarit and Jalisco indicate that this may have been the case.

Other groups of stylized ballgame figures dating from the Early Classic Period (A.D. 300–600) were found in the Huastec region of Veracruz. All of these slender figurines, both male and female, wear heavy, padded ballgame yokes. In addition, some wear protective arm- and kneepads or carry balls, but most simply stand erect with arms hanging at both sides. Again, there has not been sufficient excavation in this region to document the arrangement of these figures in the tombs. However, they form a distinctive, standardized group within the figurine tradition of the Veracruz region. Their great number and their padded yokes and equipment suggest that entire teams may have been made to compose ritual ballgame scenes in burials.

During the Classic Period (A.D. 300–900) finely made individual ballgame figurines with the appropriate gear are present throughout Mesoamerica, but generally we lack evidence that they were once grouped as sets or teams. An exception to this are several ceramic groups found in tombs in the Mexican state of Oaxaca.

One such group scene, now in the collection of the Denver Art Museum, comes from the Isthmus of Tehuantepec in southern Oaxaca. The figures were found as a group, and each is associated with elements of the ballgame. The scene consists of six ceramic figurines, two removable masks, and a throne. There are four male figures, one seated and three standing, and two female figures, one seated and one standing. The eyes of all six figures, as well as those on the two masks, are closed, as if dead, suggesting the scene is taking place in the Underworld.

The throne, or possibly a litter, could have been occupied by either of the two seated figurines. All the male figures wear a wide textile yoke-like belt, protective bands on their arms, and elaborate jewelry consisting of nose rings, ear ornaments, and bead necklaces. Two of the standing males hold balls in their upraised right hands; the seated male figure probably also held a ball, but the hand is broken off from the upraised right arm. The fourth male holds a handstone, or manopla, in his left hand and what may be an atlatl (a type of spearthrower) in his right. The females wear skirts, wrist bands, and elaborate jewelry. The seated female has a rectangular implement strapped to her right hand, perhaps a manopla. The heads of both females are rudimentary, as the full head masks were meant to cover them.

The masking suggests performance; perhaps the two masked women played specific parts in a mythic drama. Interestingly the standing female figurine carries a large netted turtle (or turtle shell) on her back, held by a tumpline. The giant turtle often symbolizes the earth in Mesoamerican iconography. This scene, in particular, may relate to an episode in the Popol Vuh when the Hero Twins assist the Maize God (their resurrected father) to emerge from a split in a giant turtle shell. In these resurrection scenes we commonly see the twins and the Maize God wearing ballgame yokes as they ascend to earth after defeating the Lords of the Underworld in a ballgame.

It is interesting that certain elements such as ballgame yokes, protective arm and leg padding, manoplas, rubber balls, and the presence of females dressed as ballplayers, link the oldest group of figurines from the El Opeño ballgame scene with those that follow. The West Mexican miniatures, the simple, yet elegant figures from the Huastec region, and the ritual ballgame scenes from Oaxaca and Campeche all have similar characteristics. The teams or scenes represented are separated from each other by several thousand years, yet the continuity of ritual and equipment is clear. Perhaps many more ceramic groupings once existed, but the figurines that composed the scenes have been dispersed and removed from their original mortuary context. Probably only the most aesthetically pleasing figures were preserved for museums and the art market. In spite of this, the few known groups give us a concrete glimpse of teams and ritual events associated with the ballgame.

The ballgame continued to be a major ritual activity in Mesoamerica until the time of the Spanish Conquest in 1521. Maya pottery and stone sculpture, Teotihuacan wall murals, and the carved ballcourt walls at El Tajín all attest to the game's importance throughout the Classic Period. During the Terminal Classic (A.D. 800–1000), ballcourts proliferate at many sites; El Tajín has 18, Chichén Itzá 13, and Cantona 24. At the Terminal Classic Maya site of Chichén Itzá the side walls of the immense ballcourt are carved with two complete teams standing in long lines behind their captains. The captains face each other over the image of a large ball decorated with a human skeleton head. The standing captain holds in one hand the decapitated head of his kneeling opponent. From the beheaded captain's neck issue streams of blood represented by twining serpents. In the Middle Classic Period, the same scene is incised on the sides of tripod cylinder pots from Tiquisate on the Pacific coast of Guatemala, and similar decapitated figures with twined serpents representing blood are carved on ballgame stelae from the contemporary site of El Aparicio (cat. 132 and 133) in the state of Veracruz.

In the Late Postclassic Period (A.D.1200–1519), scenes with players, patron deities, ballcourts, and sacrificial victims are frequently painted on the pages of the Mixtec codices (screenfold books) and, beginning in 1519, the Aztec form of the game starts to be well described by the first Spanish chroniclers. During the Postclassic Period the game seems to change from a mainly religious to a more secular form, but the teams, rituals, and bouncing rubber ball remain as constant and significant elements of Mesoamerican culture.

PERFORMANCE ON THE COURT

Ballcourt construction in Mesoamerica entailed a major commitment of resources by a community or an individual ruler. As far as we know, the courts were primarily dedicated to the playing of a ceremonial game of chance by two opposing teams. Nonetheless, I think we can speculate that other events might also have taken place there; surely the expensive stadiums were used more than the few times a year required for ceremonial games associated with seasonal and astronomical activities. Undoubtedly, the game was also played for fun and exercise by men, boys, and possibly some females, either in the courts or local fields. Perhaps aspiring athletes practiced on the ballcourts; and certainly some form of professional training or apprenticeship must have taken place. From the colorful Tepantitla Palace murals at Teotihuacan (see Uriarte) depicting a range of ballgames played with bats, sticks, and paddles, and from figurines carrying various types of playing equipment and wearing protective padding on different parts of the body (see Scott), we can assume that diverse forms of the game must have existed. Particular games may have been linked with specific gods and played on the ballcourts during rituals honoring them.

The courts may also have been used for non-ballgame-related events. As mentioned above, one ballcourt model from Nayarit does not depict a ballgame; instead two figures are shown wrestling at center court and a third figure, not seen in the illustration of the model, stands behind the court wall as if waiting to be called onto the playing field. Also known from West Mexico are a number of pairs of fighting figures. Colima figurines sometimes depict pairs of ballplayers locked in combat with one player pinning the other to the ground ready to deliver a death blow. It is interesting to speculate that these figures might represent gladiators or scenes of punishment, or perhaps human sacrifice.

What other ways might ballcourts have been utilized in the ceremonial life of kings and commoners during the pre-Columbian period? Obviously, the courts were intended above all for playing a ritual ballgame, but we should also consider the possibility of their use as stages for pageantry, festivals, and drama. Thought-provoking comparisons can be made to events in other parts of the world. For example, in the Roman empire gladiators fought wild animals and each other to a bloody death in order to entertain the public. Spectators spent entire days at these sporting festivals diverted by rich feasting, music, drama, markets, and politics. The many sports arenas of the empire pulsed with the excitement and activity that tied the masses to Rome. Medieval Europe invites another comparison. As in ancient Mesoamerica, the general population was illiterate. Religious pageants brought the passion of Christ and the stories of the Bible out of the churches and into the streets. Usually referred to as "Mystery" plays, these dramas, sometimes involving whole villages in their production, were an important ecclesiastical method of instructing people in the lessons and stories of the New Testament. Their vivid imagery provided both education and escape for the local masses. A modern-day example of this is the Bavarian town of Oberammergau, where the whole population still joins in acting out the story of the Passion of Christ for large groups of spectators and pilgrims. Not unlike ancient Mesoamerica, the reassuring iconography of a familiar tale helped medieval communities make sense of a confusing world and brought them a feeling of spiritual and political unity.

DRAMA ON THE COURTS

Mesoamerica's ancient ballcourts may also have served as theaters or locales for theatrical events. A number of scholars have argued convincingly that among the Maya, the games, as well as other public events, were frequently more like stylized drama than sport—with music, dance, colorful ceremonies, and human sacrifices (see Miller). The ballcourts were seen as entrances to the Underworld, that dark region where the Hero Twins were called to play ball against the Lords of Death. The story of this legendary game, often painted on ceramic vessels or carved on stone panels, was dramatically acted out on the courts by Maya kings dressed as ballplayers. In the reenactment the kings played against captives taken in battle then tortured and weakened in preparation for the staged contest against royal protagonists. The competition ended with the death of the captive players.

Other myths were also acted out on Maya ballcourts. As discussed earlier, relief carvings on the immense ballcourt at Chichén Itzá clearly illustrate a different ritual, one concerned with decapitation rites and fertility of the earth. On the great Chichén Itzá court, large teams competed against each other on a playing alley with stone ballgame rings on the walls at the center. The game ended with human sacrifice by decapitation. Both at Chichén Itzá and at Central Mexican sites, *tzompantli* (skull racks) were placed in the plaza outside the courts to hold the decapitated heads. The display must have provided a constant reminder of the basic significance of the ballgame, a dramatic debt offering to the gods of a human life in exchange for an orderly universe.

Elegant figurines have been recovered from burials on Jaina Island and nearby sites in the modern state of Campeche. These figures suggest other mythic dramas. Many of the Jaina-style figurines are costumed as warriors, kings, gods, and ballplayers, dressed perhaps to perform in a theatrical event; some of them have removable head masks, indicating they may have played more than one role in a dramatic presentation. A number of other figures in the Jaina tradition are depicted as hunters with blowpipes, or as dancers wearing a variety of human and animal masks. These surely reflect the mythic stories of the Hero Twins and recall their many adventures in the Underworld as they battled the gods of darkness and pestilence on the ballcourt. Figurines of Jaina women most frequently depict Ixchel, goddess of the moon, weaving, and fertility. Though considered the consort of the sun, in her role as the moon, ruler of the night sky, she was seen as his opponent who must be defeated to allow the sun to rise each morning. Perhaps when dressed as a female ballplayer she performed on the ballcourt in the reenactment of this cosmic drama. All of these dramatic rituals would have been accompanied by elaborate colorful parades of dancers, musicians, priests, and costumed attendants. The magnificent processional murals from the site of Bonampak in Chiapas, Mexico, clearly illustrate such performances, recording for us their importance in ceremonial activities at the royal courts of the Maya region.

Another example worth consideration is carved on the walls of the South Ballcourt at the Terminal Classic/Early Postclassic (A.D. 800–1200) site of El Tajín in the modern state of Veracruz. Beginning around A.D. 800, this city experienced a population explosion. Numerous satellite communities sprang up around the central polity, probably as the result of an influx of emigrants from the Valley of Mexico after the fall of the massive city of Teotihuacan. The changing demographics at the site produced a need to solidify new alliances and legitimize the power of El Tajín's rulers. In light of this, several scholars have addressed the complicated iconography of the South Ballcourt. Among them, Rex Koontz has interpreted a related complex of powerful images, positing that the El Tajín ballcourts were not only used for games but were venues for forging alliances between diverse groups of warriors, for legitimizing rulership, for enacting ceremonial pre- and post-warfare rituals, and for subsequent human sacrifices. The images depicting this ceremony are found on six carved panels on the playing field walls of the main (South) ballcourt. According to Koontz, the sequence presents two men dressed as ballplayers meeting on the court to form an alliance. This is followed by one of these warrior/ballplayers receiving weapons (*atlatl* darts) from a deity that is associated with a feathered serpent image. This gift legitimizes his elite position as well as the pending battle. On his return from the successful battle, a victim is offered as a sacrifice to the gods. In exchange for the severed head of the ballgame sacrifice, the human receives the symbolic implements of rulership. These rituals, carried out on the ballcourt, presented a lavish spectacle, documented by the scenes of elaborate costumes, music, and dance shown on the ballcourt panels.

In addition to the reenactment of the above drama, it is also probable that the 18 ballcourts at El Tajín served as arenas for playing out pent-up aggression. Certainly the influx of new ethnic populations gave rise to new social pressures, tensions, and conflicts that may have been played out in ritual violence on the ballcourt. In this instance, ballgames may have acted as a catharsis for an ethnically diverse community, minimizing the possibility of internal warfare.

An elaborately carved pair of shell bracelets, also from the Gulf Coast region of Veracruz, echoes the warfare iconography of the El Tajín ballcourt. While size prohibits the depiction of the entire story, the delicately incised design on the bracelets clearly shows a warrior/ballplayer receiving weapons, probably *atlatl* darts, from a seated female who emerges from the maw of a twining feathered serpent deity. These thematic elements are comparable, in shorthand version, with those portrayed on the sculptured walls at El Tajín's South Ballcourt.

Until recently, the 18 ballcourts at El Tajín were considered the largest number at any one site, but now excavations at the city of Cantona in the modern state of Puebla have revealed 24. This amazing site flourished between A.D. 600–1000 and, like El Tajín, it appears to have received an influx of new populations during the Terminal Classic Period. Cantona sits midway on an ancient trade route running between the Central Highlands of Mexico and the Gulf Coast. What little has so far been published indicates that the site was located in dry desert country (*malpais*) and covered 12 sq. km (almost 5 sq. miles). It was a heavily fortified military citadel with access limited by stone fortifications and a moat. The numerous ballcourts at the site were enclosed within and among 3,000 elite living compounds, pyramids, and ceremonial plazas on a mountainside in the south unit of the city. Situated as it was on an important trade route, Cantona controlled commercial activities over a wide region. The presence of the 24 ballcourts, however, is still amazing and unexplained. Nevertheless, we can speculate that, like El Tajín, the city must have been occupied, or at least used in transit, by diverse groups of people who were probably different ethnically, linguistically, and certainly culturally. Conspicuous social differences among the elite personages of Cantona, wealthy traders, soldiers, porters, and slaves must also have been glaringly evident and, consciously or unconsciously, in such a situation it seems likely that escalating tensions and aggression between groups may have been addressed on the ballcourts rather than the battlefield. We can also speculate that in a large military trading center in the middle of the *malpais* both residents and transients would have looked to the ballgame for entertainment as well as for colorful ceremonies and rituals. As a result, the traditional gambling associated with ballgames during the Postclassic Period may have been a particularly attractive pastime in such an isolated situation.

Finally, let us look at the Aztec ballgame that took place on the great court in the central plaza of the capital city of Tenochtitlan. By the Aztec period (c. A.D. 1400) the game seems to have become largely secular, though religious pageantry still surrounded the event. From Spanish descriptions we know that the nobility of the Aztec world took great delight in the ballgame and either played it themselves or fielded professional competitive teams. Betting formed a major aspect of the sport, and both spectators and players gambled heavily on the outcome of this ritual game of chance. The nobility never seemed to lack the wealth to pay their gambling debts, but addictive gambling by people of low status could bring disaster. In an early 16th-century chronicle, Fray Diego Durán reports:

> They…gambled their homes, their corn granaries, their maguey plants. They sold their children in order to bet and even staked themselves and became slaves to be sacrificed later if they were not ransomed.

The stakes of the game were also high for the players. Blows from the heavy rubber ball could leave them badly injured, or even dead, but the dangers apparently paled in comparison to the glory enjoyed by the greatest heroic athletes. According to the Spanish chronicles, these professional players were awarded honors and special privileges at court, often becoming the intimates of kings. The most lauded player was he who actually managed to send the ball through one of the stone rings placed at the center of each wall of the ballcourt—a rare occurrence. Usually the game was won by the accumulation of points, as the passing of the ball through the ring was so difficult that as soon as it happened the game was over and

> The man who sent the ball through the stone ring was surrounded by all. They honored him, sang songs of praise to him, and joined him in dancing. He was given a very special award of feathers or mantles and breechcloths, something very highly prized. But what he most prized was the honor involved: that was his great wealth. For he was honored as a man who had vanquished many and had won a battle.

The ballcourt spectacle in the city center of the Aztec capital of Tenochtitlan must have been noisy and colorful, and, as is indicated in the above quote, ceremonies surrounding the sport and its heroes must have included music and dancing by both the spectators and the players. This use of music, dance, and song at ritual events was recorded by Fray Bernardino de Sahagún, who tells of long lines of colorfully attired dancers moving through the city streets, and describes ceremonies in the sacred precincts as being accompanied by chanting and singers. This relationship is reinforced by caches found buried near the court. One cache, found in the plaza near the main ballcourt, included a stone statue of Xochipilli, the god of flowers, music, springtime, and the ballgame. Associated with the deity figure were a group of miniature stone musical instruments, two small stone models of a ballcourt, two highly polished stone balls—one black and one white—and an obsidian knife. These symbolic objects clearly indicate that despite a more secular approach to the game during the Late Postclassic Period, the rituals and original intent of the team sport remained intact: the black and white balls still reflecting the cosmic battle of the diurnal sun and the nocturnal sun, and the knife continuing to link the theme of human sacrifice to the sacred and political needs of the more secular Aztec empire.

It is evident that the ancient Mesoamerican ballgames expressed religious beliefs, were an arena for secular activities, and perhaps fulfilled psychological needs as well. Through drama and pageantry the team sport both reflected and influenced the culture from which it sprang—a stratified theocracy, rich with colorful ritual. This is particularly true in the area of human relationships where teams, or by extension Mesoamerican societies, committed themselves to group cooperation and strict governance according to set rules. In various roles, team games served as a substitute for war, as a showcase for the wealth and power of kings, as a vehicle for athletic contests, and as an outlet for gambling. In addition, the ballcourt itself was a stage for drama, music, dance, and entertainment.

Over its 3,000-year history however, the pre-Columbian ballgame always remained a ceremonial game of chance—a human team symbolically pitted against the gods and the frightening powers of the natural world. Through the reenactment of myths, cyclical rituals, and human sacrifice the people of pre-Hispanic Mesoamerica battled desperately to influence the universe and control the cosmic forces. At times, it was probably difficult to be certain where ritual ended and entertainment began. Although often unrecognized, this is still true in modern ballgames that also allow aggressive tendencies and unrestricted feelings to be acted out within the confines of the playing field.

Both today and long ago athletic heroes were so admired that they become the comrades of kings (or presidents) and wealth and honor are, and were, awarded to the winning teams. Even symbolic activities remain intrinsic in modern games, as songs and chants echo through the stadiums, and dancers and vendors of food and memorabilia vie with players on the field for the spectators' attention. Unlike pre-Columbian Mesoamerica, where the inherent religious significance of the game was clearly understood, modern audiences are less apt to recognize the ancient ceremonies lurking beneath the surface of sporting events. Nevertheless, the sacred and secular aspects still blend, and our human need for ritual and order, for spectacle and for bonding, is dramatically acted out on the ballcourts of both yesterday and today.

Sport, Gambling and Government: America's First Social Compact?

Warren D. Hill & John E. Clark

Enlightenment philosophers got it wrong; pleasure rather than hardship was the downhill slope leading to primitive government. The earliest, clear evidence for government in the Americas, for example, implicates ritual drinking, feasting, gambling, competitive team sports, and other proffered entertainments in the primary governmental process, with war and her sister deprivations nowhere to be seen. We have discussed some of this evidence from southern Mexico elsewhere (Blake and Clark 1999; Clark 1994, 1997; Clark and Blake 1994) and so will restrict attention here to possible connections between sports and government—an improbable possibility only recently suggested by discovery of a 3,600-year-old ballcourt. Both the ballcourt's location and date constitute strong circumstantial evidence that its construction and/or use was important in and for the development of hereditary inequality and formal ascribed leadership. Data from later Mesoamerican civilizations further add to the circumstantial case that the ballgame played a notable role in the origins and perpetuation of the first formal community governments in Mesoamerica and, hence, the Americas. We explore here connections between this competitive sport, its collateral competitive activities such as gambling, and the origins of government. By government we mean formal, community leadership recruited by ascription or, in short, the type of hereditary rulership typical of chiefdom societies.

In the following discussion we address possible significant associations between competitive games and the emergence of ascribed leadership positions and social ranks. We still do not have many answers, but we hope to raise important questions and provide some plausible possibilities for connections between the two. We first outline the circumstantial case for a connection between the Mesoamerican ballgame and the emergence of simple chiefdoms in the Mazatan region of southern Mexico. After a brief description of the archaeological evidence of principal interest, and an overview of the Mesoamerican ballgame as understood in late time periods, we explore four likely connections between the game and early government. We consider a range of ethnographic information from American tribal societies in trying to understand the social roles of competitive games and their possible deleterious effects on egalitarian social structures. If there was indeed a significant relationship between playing the ballgame and the emergence of heritable political power and government in early Mesoamerica, the logical possibilities are that it concerned either the primary activity of the game itself or the activities surrounding the game. We examine each in turn. In the final section we consider the contribution of team sports in the forging of community identity, or *communitas*, and the coalescence of community leadership around individual leaders.

THE BALLGAME AND MESOAMERICA'S FIRST GOVERNMENTS

By all accounts, the transition from egalitarian to complex societies in Mesoamerica was a torrid affair. After millennia of hunting, fishing, and gathering, by the second millennium B.C. people started to settle down and devote more time to horticulture and agriculture. Shortly thereafter, the first simple chiefdom societies arose (about 1600 B.C. in calibrated radiocarbon years) in the Pacific coastal lowlands of southern Mexico, and just three or four centuries later, there were state societies in the Gulf Coast lowlands (see Clark 1997 for summary). Fine points of the developmental sequence are arguable but not the overall sequence. Chiefdom and state societies first emerged in the lowland tropics of southern Mexico among cultures known as the Mokaya and the Olmec and later spread to the Mexican highlands and the Maya lowlands. Although there appears to be a clear link between early Mokaya and later Olmec developments, extant evidence is insufficient to trace its lineaments. For present purposes, however, it is sufficient to note that the Olmec developed the first state society in Mesoamerica (Cyphers 1996), and presumably in the Americas, and that the Mokaya were an earlier and less complex culture (Clark and Blake 1994). The Olmecs are best known for their monumental and dynamic stone sculptures of paramount chiefs and/or kings, a point that will become relevant below.

The emphasis of our joint research over the past decade has been on the development of what may have been the first simple chiefdom societies in Mesoamerica, and possibly America, first evident among the Mokaya of coastal Chiapas (Clark 1994). The archaeological record of this coastal zone brackets the transition from egalitarian to rank society and provides the best evidence of this critical process currently available for Mesoamerica. Clark and Blake (1994) argue that the emergence of hereditary social distinctions resulted from the favorable combination of special social circumstances in a productive environment that could sustain social competition. They argue that the natural abundance of the Mazatan region allowed some individuals, denoted as "aggrandizers," to accumulate social surpluses and to compete for local renown and followers, principally by sponsoring feasts, local exchanges, and craft activities, which set up a system of social debts between aggrandizers and their obligated clients (Clark and Blake 1994; see also Hayden and Gargett 1990 for a discussion of "accumulators"). This competitive social milieu promoted individual searches for innovations that could serve in outshining one's rivals in social displays. Some innovations included bringing in cultigens (corn and beans) from the highlands and ceramic technology from regions to the south (Clark and Blake 1994; Clark and Gosser 1995). The ballgame may have been another such borrowed innovation. The transition to hereditary inequality is thought to have occurred because several aggrandizers were able to sustain their prestige over the long run and to pass on benefits to heirs. The social circumstance of habitual privilege accorded to the same household or lineage heads was the basis for the institutionalization of hereditary rank distinctions.

Archaeologically, we place the transition to simple chiefdoms at about 1600 B.C. (see Blake et al. 1995 for details of chronology). The best evidence for its emergence is the coordinated construction history of special house platforms at the large village of Paso de la Amda. There is good evidence that prior to 1600 B.C. each ward of this extensive village had at least one big house, presumably of a lineage leader or headman (Clark 1994). But only one of these houses (Mound 6) was subsequently rebuilt and expanded over the course of many generations; the others were abandoned. This suggests that the lineage head of one household was successful in bringing the entire village under his leadership and that this centralizing leadership continued to be passed down within the same household and lineage afterwards. The chiefly residence at Mound 6 was rebuilt and elevated at least seven times over the next three centuries and appears to have been the principal residence in the community during all that time (Blake 1991; Clark 1994). The history of this household, and its supposed lineage of petty chiefs, is of particular interest because the fine chronology of its successive modifications allows us to narrow the time frame for the origins of hereditary village leadership to about 1600 B.C. As it turns out, the ballcourt discovered close by this chiefly residence was constructed just prior to the emergence of rank (Hill et al. 1998). These construction histories lead to our primary and strongest suspicion of a link between the ballcourt/ballgame and the emergence of hereditary leadership.

At the time of the construction of the ballcourt, the soon-to-be-chiefly residence at Mound 6 was still a pole and thatch structure built at ground level, and it appears to have been similar to other big houses in the village. Subsequently, the Mound 6 household built a broad basal platform and elevated their residence several feet. This is the first clear indication of social distinctions at Paso de la Amada. The proximity of the ballcourt to Mound 6 suggests to us that the residents there may have played a major role in constructing the ballcourt and in administrating its use. The ballcourt was built atop an elongated, compacted surface that may have served as an open playing field prior to construction of the formal playing court. Although rather modest by later standards, the Paso de la Amada ballcourt is the largest construction known for its time in Mesoamerica (Hill et al. 1998). It consists of two parallel, linear mounds bracketing a narrow playing alley. The alley is 80 m long, and the flanking mounds are each 1.5 m high, 30 m wide, and 80 m long. By our calculations, at least 1,375 person-days of labor went into making this earthen structure. Three significant questions arise from our reconstruction of the varied history of domestic and public structures at Paso de la Amada. Did the household at Mound 6 sponsor the construction and use of the ballcourt? If so, was this the critical difference in competition among lineage leaders that finally led to the emergence of hereditary leadership? If so, in what way might the construction or use of this ballcourt have been important? We explore these questions below.

The second piece of circumstantial evidence for connecting formal games and government comes from later developments in Mesoamerica. We consider it significant that the earliest representations of leaders among the Olmec about 1200 B.C. depict them in ballplaying gear. The famous multi-ton stone heads depict kings and/or high chiefs sporting leather helmets. Of equal significance, clay figurines of elites in other contemporaneous societies in the Mexican highlands depict them in ballplaying gear as well. The depicted helmets, heavy clothing, and padding were necessary protection from the solid rubber balls used in the game (see below). Why were early leaders portrayed as ballplayers? In later Mesoamerica, the ballgame had clear ritual and cosmological significance and was a key element in governance (see contributions in Scarborough and Wilcox 1991). It is of more than passing interest that the principal creation story of the Maya, recorded in the *Popul Vuh*, centers on the ballgame and sports contests between mortals and gods (Tedlock 1985). Civilization was believed, at least allegorically, to have derived from mortals playing ball and besting underworld gods in a contest to the death. The ballgame provided a means of unifying "the social and ideological fabric of a complex society" (Scarborough 1991:130). Although it is clear that the ballgame was important for governing within later societies, it does not follow that it was necessarily critical in the first emergence of complex society or government, but it may have been. For the past several years we have been investigating this possibility. Our investigation has required familiarity with the rules of the game and its associated activities.

THE MESOAMERICAN BALLGAME

At least five different games involving competitive play with a hard rubber ball are recorded for ancient Mesoamerica. Archaeological evidence traces some of these back at least to Late Archaic times (around 2000 B.C.). Variants of the game included versions of (1) handball, (2) stickball, (3) hipball, (4) kickball, and (5) "trick" games similar to the "keep-away" games played by children today (see Borhegyi 1980 and Stern 1950 for descriptions). As with today's sports, the different games were probably easily identified by the type of ball, bat or other equipment, and arena used. Some of the Mesoamerican games required different sized balls, with the hipgame requiring the largest and heaviest ones. We do not know whether all variants of the ballgame were played in ancient Mazatan, the region of our principal interest, but we are confident that hipball was played because it is the only one of the five requiring a formal court such as that constructed at Paso de la Amada. Ethnohistoric sources further suggest that the hipgame was the most important, frequent, and competitive of the five ballgames (Leyenaar 1978:42). We focus on this variant here because it qualifies as a true sport and not just as play. We follow Edwards (1973:55) in distinguishing sports from play; by sport we mean a competitive activity with formal rules where the outcome extends beyond the players to individuals and groups who do not participate directly in the activity.

The hipgame (hereafter the "ballgame") was played on a formal court consisting of a long, narrow playing alley that opened up at each end into an end zone. Anciently, ballcourts varied in length and width, but all possessed the same essential features: two lateral walls or platforms, gentle sloping "benches," and a central alley. The walls and benches figured prominently in keeping the ball in play and were used much like walls of a modern squash court. The game was played with two opposing teams, each of which defended an end zone. The number of players per team varied according to the game and its purpose. Much like modern soccer or football, the objective of the ballgame was to drive the ball past one's opponent into their end zone. This required great skill and physical conditioning because the players had to do this without using their hands or feet; the ball was kept in play by hitting it with one's hips, thus the designation for this game.

The ballgame was scored using different point systems. Early post-Spanish Conquest documents recount that the number of points needed to win a particular game was negotiated beforehand, and it is clear from these documents that the objective of the ballgame was to score points. In the case of the Aztec hipball game known as *ulama*, there were three ways to win a point: (1) by driving the ball past the opposing team's goal line, located at the beginning of their end zone, (2) by forcing an opponent to commit a body fault, or (3) by hitting the ball into one of the sidearms of the end zone so it could not be returned (Stem 1950:59).

As sporting arenas, Mesoamerican ballcourts varied widely. The largest of these was the great ballcourt at Chichén Itzá, Yucatan, measuring 150 by 50 m. The best measure of ballcourt variation is alley width, which ranged from 3.6 to 12.4 m for Aztec ballcourts of Central Mexico. Alley width and length determined the number of players that could be accommodated in the court. In ulama, teams of two to three players were common (Stern 1950:58). Occasionally, games of one-on-one also took place; nobles are the only ones recorded as having engaged in these special contests.

Ethnohistoric sources indicate that Mesoamerican ballcourts also doubled as stadiums, with spectators crowding together atop the lateral walls and outside of end zones to watch these contests. In some instances, special structures for elite patrons were constructed on top of the platforms. Sweat baths and other outbuildings were often built near ballcourts and were sometimes attached to the courts themselves. More frequently, ballcourts in large cities were centrally placed near palaces, temples, and central plazas, thereby underscoring their importance.

All lines of evidence indicate that ballgames were violent and dangerous affairs. Necessary protective gear included helmets, knee pads, thick gloves, arm-wraps, chest-protectors, and deerskin yokes for the hips. The solid-rubber balls weighed from 0.5 to 7.0 kg and could inflict serious injury; in fact, some athletes even died from heavy blows incurred (Durán 1971:316). During play, players aggressively jockeyed for position, sometimes knocking down teammates and opponents in the process.

As with all organized sports, winning was held in high regard, but little was gained merely by being victorious—contestants had to wager large stakes in order to profit from their triumphs. Players appear to have separated their wagers (wealth and income) from their standings as athletes (social prestige), but both were tied to winning. In one example, an Aztec noble, Xihuitlemoc, was taunted into competing in a ballgame by his rival, Axayacatl. Both players staked the rulership of their respective communities on the outcome of the match. Xihuitlemoc defeated his upstart rival and remarked that he was bothered "not so much [by] the income but the credit and standing as a player, on which he prided himself" (Torquemada 1975:250). In another contest, nominal stakes were used to emphasize the athletic prowess of an aging noble. He wagered his entire kingdom but only asked a counter bet of three turkeys from his challenger. This match was played to test the veracity of a prophesy, the outcome of which was validated by a victory (Torquemada 1975:291–292).

In terms of material gain, winning players were entitled to the cloaks and jewels of spectators, but only if they won outright by putting the ball through a vertically mounted hoop on the side of the court (Stern 1950:60). Opinions differ on this entitlement; one famous account states that winners were only due the capes of spectators who backed the losing team (Motolinia 1903:339). There is ample evidence to suggest that "professional" or full-time ballplayers were of noble rank but were not necessarily wealthy, and they often lost wealth gained in previous contests. In short, the consequences of winning were proportional to the stakes wagered, astute betting, and luck. The prestige value of winning was great but, unless parlayed into a larger fortune, was soon lost the same way it was gained. It is noteworthy that none of the ethnohistoric documents or pre-Columbian codices records any famous ballplayers.

More is known about losing than winning. As with winning, consequences of losing were tied to the stakes wagered. In extreme cases, losers forfeited their lives. The losers described in ethnohistoric accounts appear to be gamblers and not the players themselves. A passage from one of the first generation priests in the New World, Diego Durán (1971:318), illustrates how much was at stake in some wagers.

> These wretches played for stakes of little value or worth, and since the pauper loses quickly what he has, they were forced to gamble their homes, their fields, their corn granaries, their maguey plants. They sold their children in order to bet and even staked themselves and became slaves, to be sacrificed later if they were not ransomed in the manner which has been explained.
>
> —Their way of using themselves as stakes was this. Once they had lost their valuable articles such as pieces of cloth, beads, feathers, they would give their word saying that at home they had certain valuable articles. If this was believed, it was well, but if not, the winner would accompany [the loser] to his house and take the articles which [the loser] had offered upon his word. But if he did not possess them or find a way to make payment, he was sent to jail; and if his wife or children did not ransom him, he became a slave of the creditor. The laws of the republic permitted that he could be sold for the sum he owed and not for more. In case he wished to become free and if he discovered that he was unable to gather the sum for which he was enslaved, he lost [his liberty] if someone else could pay more. The same was applied to all the other games. This created fear and held back many who took warning in the example of others and did not bet that which they did not possess, in case the opponent took advantage of this and won [him]. As I have said, these were always people of the lower orders, because illustrious, noble people never lacked that with which to gamble. [The latter], however, played more for recreation and relief from their constant warfare and toil—not for profit.
>
> —This is an advantage of the rich: if they lose today, with what they have left they can win tomorrow. It is important that one who takes part in this sort of game have large wealth behind him.

Significantly, carved ballcourt panels and sculpture depict human sacrifice and decapitation, although it is not clear whether the losers were dispatched (but this is our presumption). Whichever the case, human sacrifice was integral to the ballgame in Classic times. While the antiquity of ballgame sacrifice remains unknown, such practices may well date back to the Early Formative Olmec about 1100 B.C. (see Taube 1996). Human sacrifice demonstrates some immediate, tangible benefits from winning ballgames and that stakes for some contests could not be higher.

Tangential to the ballgame, but equally important, was the gambling and feasting accompanying each match. These more informal competitions co-occurred alongside games and provided numerous opportunities for forcing one's competitors into debt. Sixteenth-century sources relate that fortunes were won and squandered at the ballcourt (Durán 1971; Torquemada 1975), the ancient equivalent to craps tables. The same accounts record that some individuals wagered on *credit*, offering their wives, children, property, or even personal servitude as collateral. The exploitation of such situations by self-aggrandizing individuals is not difficult to imagine.

Feasting was also an activity associated with ballgames, with the ballcourts doubling as feasting facilities (Fox 1994). Extant archaeological evidence for ballcourt feasts, however, remains equivocal because the messes generated during such events were cleaned up, thereby leaving behind few material traces. The combination of ballgames, ballcourts, gambling, and feasts provided an easy means for creating debtors by the dozen. Such a combination would have, in our estimation, permitted creditors and others to forge debt alliances and to promote their own greater renown. In Early Formative Mazatan, such debt creation and manipulation by aggrandizers may have been one of the principal means by which egalitarian social structures succumbed to a system of rank about 1600 B.C.

AGGRANDIZERS, BALLGAMES, AND HERITABLE PRIVILEGE

The origin of hereditary village leadership in southern Mexico is described by Clark and Blake (1994) as an accidental consequence of self-aggrandizing individuals pursuing personal fame through competitive acts designed to entice followers, clients, and other hangers-on to their groups. As framed, the aggrandizer model of competitive generosity is economic and political; it assumes that aggrandizers and their activities were focal points of social and political change and that material concerns were central to the process. Aggrandizers amassed and deployed resources in self-serving ways that obligated and indebted followers—that is, they marshaled resources to create liens on the future labor of those accepting their favors. Aggrandizers' stratagems privileged activities that might bring in the lion's share of resources, greater renown, or bind clients to them for future considerations.

As described, the ballgame would have provided numerous opportunities for winning and losing resources or for creating future social obligations among one's associates, either through gambling, gaming, feasting, or sponsorship of the event. Any explanations stressing material gains from the ballgame, however, merely extend the aggrandizer model and the field of activities that led to differential wealth and prestige. We believe the ballgame did play a critical role in the development of formal government, but one quite apart from any competitive materialism. We suspect that one totally unanticipated and salient effect of organizing team sports among a network of egalitarian Mesoamerican villages some 3,600 years ago was the emergence of community identities, or communitas, and of community representatives or leaders. Coupled with other aggrandizer activities, the emerging notion of "our community" and shared interests laid the basis for ascribed leadership among chiefdom societies.

We do not know, and cannot know for certain, of course, the details of the historic circumstances that led to the first formalized governments in early Mesoamerica. Discussion of these critical matters must necessarily be speculative. In the remainder of this essay we explore the possibility that the ballgame was integral to the origins of government in Mesoamerica, and we explore four possible ways in which it might have had a catalytic impact in the competitive egalitarian setting imagined. These include considerations of gambling, participation in the game, sponsorship of the game and its associated activities, and the effects of team sports on community identities.

Given the archaeological problem at hand, there are clear logical parameters for the activities and agents that may have made a difference. By definition, we are dealing with egalitarian society and a transition to hereditary inequality and government. Activities of primary interest, therefore, should meet at least three requirements that such a process implies. First, the activities in question must have the ability to confer some substantive benefits or advantage on a select segment of the population; differential hereditary privilege arises from prior achieved privileges of some sort. Second, the unequal distribution of benefits must not be socially divisive in the egalitarian setting; the ideal benefits would be those that could be shared with others of the community, at least in part, thereby fostering social beliefs of a win-win situation. Third, the benefits and privileges derived from such activities must have the potential to become chronic and, indeed, must become so over time, perhaps a generation or two. Social habituation of persistent differences in achieved statuses would be the first, and most important, step toward change in social perceptions about the nature of society and the inherent status of various persons (Clark 2000). Explanations of the origins of hereditary privilege must account for shifts in social beliefs as well as the distribution of privileges. Given the egalitarian tribal milieu imagined for early Mesoamerica, naked power and coercion would not have constituted viable paths to perdurable political power (see Clark and Blake 1994). But in an interesting way, the ballgame may have provided a formalized setting for acceptable intersocietal aggression that may have channeled aggression to productive ends.

In the following discussion we designate various possible paths to power and privilege with agentive labels such as "sponsor," "ballplayer," and "gambler." These are meant to highlight activities and social roles rather than provide stereotypes of past agents. Clearly, one individual could have engaged in all these activities. Also, the known role of "aggrandizer" is not exclusive to those proposed here. We suspect that aggrandizers were sponsors, players, and gamblers involved in ballgame events and associated activities. All these labels refer to competitive activities, albeit at differing social scales, as we describe in the following sections.

GAMBLING

For all its pageantry, blood, and bruises, the one aspect of the Aztec ballgame that captured the imagination of the early Spanish clerics was the side bets. As narrated by Durán, disproportionate resources were wagered on outcomes of games. Bettors were not confined to the elite class; commoners were allowed equal access to chances of easy wealth or personal ruin. In truth, debt was no respecter of persons in ancient Mesoamerica. Among the Aztecs, formal rules tantamount to laws provided for the payment of sums won or lost. Occasionally, wagers were made that exceeded the economic wherewithal of the bettor, and sempiternal servitude awaited him should he bet on the wrong colors.

As inherently titillating as these data for the Aztecs might be to clerics, they are of questionable relevance for the early Mesoamerican case of rank origins, coming as they do from a situation of traditional stratified societies. Of greater potential importance would be information from tribal societies. Fortunately, there is a wealth of such data on gaming for North and South American tribal societies that confirm the link between gambling and gaming seen in late Mesoamerica. We consider briefly a few select cases from this larger sample before turning to some of the implications of gambling for the origins of rank in early Mesoamerica.

Gambling was an integral component of nearly all tribal and rank societies, and it continues to form an important economic and social lifeline for many native communities (Gabriel 1996). As Kathryn Gabriel (1996:17) observes, "Native American traditions abound with myths and legends that reveal the sacred significance of gambling and the divine origin, power, and symbolism of these games." Information from Amerindian societies illustrates gambling's remarkable power to precipitate short-term social change. Anthropologists working in the Amazon Basin observed that gambling was commonplace, recording that "they played not merely for the fun of the game but to win substantial stakes," the wagers consisting of "baskets of maize, strings of glass beads, and, when necessary, everything the players had in their houses" (Cooper 1949:514). Players as well as spectators engaged in betting.

Ballgames enjoyed widespread popularity throughout North America but generally not within formal ballcourts as in Mesoamerica. In the latter part of the 19th century, George Catlin observed the Choctaw playing a ballgame at an astronomical scale. "It is no uncommon occurrence for *six or eight hundred or a thousand* of these young men to engage in a game of ball, with five or six times that number of spectators, of men, women, and children surrounding the ground, looking on" (Catlin 1953:290, emphasis added). Even compensating for exaggeration, the number of players is impressive and would have required an extremely large playing field. As in the South American examples, bets were placed prior to the game and held "in trust" by a third party until the game was completed. Although Catlin does not elaborate on outcomes of this gambling, the total goods wagered must have been substantial. The often violent determination of the players to score accentuates the nature of the stakes.

Stern (1950:84) reported that among the Acaxee of Nayarit, Mexico, large bets were integral to the ballgame. Stakes rose even higher for intercommunity games, though they still tended to be limited to personal property. A challenge by one village could not be refused by another. A messenger was sent to collect wagered articles, usually of equal value to those put up by the challengers. A "consolation prize" was awarded to the losing team unless they were the host team. If the host team won, everyone dined on a luxurious feast. However, if they lost, the hosts did not share their feast with the victors who had just made off with their possessions (Stern 1950:84).

Status could be greatly enhanced, or lowered, through gambling (Scarborough 1991:142). Among the Gros Ventre of Montana, for example, gambling was a means of social mobility (Flannery and Cooper 1946:398). Most gambling centered around a wheel game that required skill and dexterity. Supporters of competing players would often provide food for spectators and boast of their ability to cater the event. Reports show that social ambition could be snuffed out by a single bad day of gambling. White Owl, an older man of great standing among the Gros Ventre, was challenged to a wheel game by Lame Bull, an ambitious young upstart. So confident was Lame Bull of victory that he bet all his possessions and those of his wife and select relatives. The social stakes were even higher. A loss by White Owl would have meant his downfall; a win would make him even bigger in the eyes of his followers. Lame Bull lost the contest and all his possessions and became an object of ridicule to his family and former followers. Although White Owl gained numerous possessions in the contest, of greater importance was maintenance of his prestige.

Inevitably, gambling also led to serious conflicts. The Gros Ventre solved the most extreme conflicts by fissioning from the main group, which they were free to do at any time (Flannery and Cooper 1946:411). Gambling stakes seem to have been largest between rival bands. To prevent rivalries from destroying the social fabric, gambling was prohibited among ritual specialists and between certain kin relations (both fictive and sanguine). In Flannery and Cooper's (1946:415) list of gambling rules among Plains groups, the two overarching principles that emerge are (1) a prohibition of gambling between close relatives, and (2) its encouragement between rival groups. It is as if gambling were the quintessential means to effect Sahlins's (1972) version of negative reciprocity, the gaming version of "buying cheap and selling dear." Clearly, gambling provided an effective means of getting nearby villages or communities to interact with each other in competitive ways. Taboos against gambling with relatives channeled its power toward rivals, thus assuring that victorious gamblers would not accumulate wealth on the backs of their families. As one perspicacious informant put it, gambling within the family would be "like winning [property] from yourself" (Flannery and Cooper 1946:414).

Gambling power is a recurrent theme in tribal narratives. Some narratives attest to help from deceased ancestors (Flaskerd 1961:92) who brought success in gambling. In some societies, gambling is so powerful that it is thought to interfere with or threaten other powers and, therefore, must be controlled (Flannery and Cooper 1946:407). Few studies address the subject in any detail, however. A relatively unexplored component of this line of thought is the psychology of gambling and its effects on prehistoric societies. Did gambling and the associated debts incurred intensify existing inequalities and intercommunity rivalries?

Many more examples of gambling among tribal societies could be adduced; however, the few mentioned suffice to make several fundamental points. Gambling on ballgames and other games was widespread in the Americas and was engaged in for fun, profit, and prestige. Almost anything, and sometimes everything, could be wagered. Gambling of personal property was common and, among more complex societies, wagering of human labor for future considerations occurred. Gambling is widely acknowledged as a powerful activity, with an inherent power to elevate and debase those who engage in it. Moreover, its social divisive powers are well attested.

The conditions of possibility for gambling involve rules and protocols concerning bets, collections on bets, and challenges to games. Lady luck is also a pervasive theme, with some gambling successes attributed to one's supernatural connections. In many encounters, especially those with high stakes, wealth, prestige, and social good will were all on the line. Gambling was therefore an important means for a diverse range of societies to reconcile a divine plan with the random events of everyday life (Gabriel 1996).

Granting all of the above for sake of argument, is there a plausible link between the power of gambling, wealth accumulation, and the transformation of egalitarian society? On basic principles we suspect not. Given its pervasiveness in societies of all types, gambling may be a cultural universal and thus of dubious explanatory power. It is clearly a means of wealth redistribution and, secondarily, a means to gain greater prestige, both of which are probably important but not critical in social transformation. Gambling comes equipped with its own social-leveling mechanism, and unless one can rig the game, it would seem that in habitual gambling, wins and losses would eventually level out. So prospects of large material gains from betting over the long run appear few.

Perhaps of greater importance than gambling winnings are gambling debts. Those who bet and lose more than they possess must be re-possessed themselves. In some social circumstances, the ability to command the labor of such wretches for personal ends may have been important or even critical in the more general processes of debt management. A particularly apt way to obligate a follower would be to cover his gambling losses. The potential for gambling to create debts is obvious. Less clear are the long-term effects of such activity on the general social fabric and egalitarian ethos.

GAMING

The analytical distinction between the social effects of gaming and gambling is somewhat forced as the two appear to be sides of the same coin. In some of the personal and intercommunity rivalries mentioned above, playing a game was just the excuse to force a heavy wager on a rival that could not be refused without loss of face. Whereas gambling appears inherently to concern material gains and consequences of significant wins or losses, gaming relates more to social prestige. In the Aztec and Gros Ventre examples, challenge to a game appears to have carried the social force of a personal duel and involved the honor of one's name, as based in one's sports prowess. It is obvious that demonstrable high levels of sports skill and physical ability would carry prestige in most societies, but it is not clear how this could be parlayed into other long-term benefits.

In today's world, the association of sports prowess with success is synonymous with wealth, renown, and potential political power. Evidence from late Mesoamerica also indicates that some of these relationships between sports, renown, wealth, and power may be premodern. It is well to remember, however, that much of the linkage depends on the prior existence of societies based upon social stratification, monetary systems, and market economies. In the Aztec case, players were born to high privilege and do not appear to have won it through sporting victories. In fact, their privileged station was a necessary precondition for learning the sport in the first place because the ballgame was an elite activity. What benefits might derive from gaming and athletic skill in an egalitarian setting? The most obvious ones suggested by the Mesoamerican data are renown and wealth. But by themselves these seem rather unidimensional, and it is hard to imagine a scenario in which a sport's hero in an egalitarian milieu could leverage renown from sporting successes into hereditary benefits for his offspring. Also, the wealth actually won in playing the game would have been meager compared to potential gains from side-bets. Absent gambling winnings, the tangible remunerations from ballgame victories were rather insignificant.

The very nature of physical sports ties success on the field to biological parameters of strength, speed, coordination, and the like. The reality of sports is that the aging process eventually defeats all comers; one cannot forever prevail against younger rivals. In a sense, any prestige or wealth gained through successful sporting activity is likely to follow the life-cycle trajectory thought to apply to New Guinea Bigmen. No matter their fame, they cannot sustain their successes indefinitely because age and fatigue eventually catch up with them.

Several examples discussed above suggest that one benefit of gaming was the possibility of humiliating one's rivals on the field of play. This may have been an especially important benefit in the types of competitive egalitarian or bigman systems thought to be characteristic of early Mesoamerica. Competitive sports also occurred between rival communities. In this light, it is of interest that several scholars view ballgames as surrogates for costly warfare between competing polities (Fox 1991:227–228; Taladoire and Colsenet 1991). While true for late Mesoamerican societies, for our question it is more interesting to consider ballgames as a form of competition possibly analogous to warfare among New Guinea societies (see Wiessner and Tumu 1998). Although interpretations drawn from such analogies must be tentative, there was a strong link from the very beginning in Mesoamerican symbolism between militarism and the ballgame (Taladoire and Colsenet 1991:174). Competition between rival communities, in the form of ballgames, probably involved formal and informal rules of compensation.

Other interesting implications follow from possible consequences of the physical contest itself. If a player were killed or seriously injured in a ballgame, his death or injury may have required compensation to his close kin. Depending on compensation rules, such wealth transfers could have been of greater importance than any gambling winnings because they would have had longer term consequences. In New Guinea, compensation payments implicate formal systems of wealth valuables, and their payment is generally the first step in establishing long-term exchange relationships between parties (see Hayden 1995).

Perhaps the most important outcome of ballgames involved aspects of social knowledge, norms, and values. One of the clear outcomes of contests of physical prowess and skill could be, or would be, changes in social valuations of persons. The transition from egalitarian to rank systems essentially makes such disparate valuations permanent. So with all of their material gains, changes in social perceptions of individual worth would have been equally important. Information from the Maya area suggests one way in which the phenomenology of the ballgame may have been promoted in the emergence of ascribed leadership. Linda Schele (in Freidel et al. 1993) argued that ballgames in the Classic period (ca. A.D. 250–900) were contests of mortals against gods, with gods being represented by mortals. Such contests involved deceased ancestors who then "played" the game vicariously through living offspring. So perceived, victory in these matches signaled supernatural favor and, perhaps of greater importance, the efficacy of one's ancestors in mortal affairs compared to others' ancestors. By such simple means, players and/or their sponsors garnered greater prestige and higher status for themselves as well as their ancestors through successful play in the ballgame.

Links to apotheosized ancestors and sublime supernatural favor are widely sought these days as the most convincing way to have effected the transition from egalitarian to non-egalitarian social structures (see Friedman and Rowlands 1977; Marcus and Flannery 1996; McAnany 1995). Ballgame successes provide a compelling logic for such a link. However, it is worth pointing out in this regard that, given certain beliefs about connections between the living and the gods, success in any socially esteemed endeavor would do, including gambling, farming, weaving, hunting, fishing, and so forth As with the accumulation of material resources, the accumulation of symbolic capital (Bourdieu 1977, 1990) and social prestige appears to have been an important ingredient, but insufficient by itself. All paths to potential heritable power have the possibility of differential control of material goods, but these required investment and manipulation in particular ways to defeat the egalitarian system.

SPONSORING

Permanent architectural facilities such as ballcourts had multiple options for investment, first through their construction, which had their own managerial imperatives (Hill 1999), and subsequently through their maintenance and expansion. Ballcourt sponsorship could have taken several forms: coordination of initial construction and provision of labor, meals, building materials, ritual specialists, dedicatory feasts, and/or players. Underwriting construction of a ballcourt would have given aggrandizers a means of expanding their influence locally and regionally, while simultaneously debasing competitors who could not finance such endeavors.

Sponsorship may have conferred ownership in some instances. Ownership of the ballcourt and/or playing gear, or sponsorship of games and their associated activities, especially rituals, feasting, and gambling, would both have opened promising possibilities for long-term benefits. Depending on one's theoretical leanings, private ownership of the Paso de la Amada ballcourt or critical ballgame equipment provides a best or worst case scenario for the origins of rank based upon private property. There are many variants of such arguments going back to the Enlightenment, but they all involve control or monopoly of a critical resource that others want or need so badly that they willingly submit to the lucky soul who controls them. Ownership of the Paso de la Amada ballcourt, however, appears an unlikely candidate for such an explanation because it can hardly be construed as a necessity, and other ballcourts certainly could have been constructed just as easily as it was. All private property routes to rank involve some form of rent of material and social benefits that owners extract from users. We doubt that ownership of a sports arena in a tribal setting would have had such consequences.

The nagging question raised by discovery of the early earthen ballcourt at Paso de la Amada is whether or not the household at Mound 6 was responsible for its construction and use. We suspect so. Construction of the elevated Mound 6 house followed close on the heels of the construction of the ballcourt, so correlation in this instance is sufficient probable cause to consider individual sponsorship of this facility. Aggrandizers sought opportunities to demonstrate their magnificence, and sponsorship of a ballcourt would have been a grand way to do so. Sponsorship allowed aggrandizers to deploy resources, many of them perishable, and to put them into the hands of followers, with a promissory for later returns. Even excluding any material returns from extracting rents from use of the facility, management and control of the court would have brought important benefits in terms of wealth creation, debt management, and personal renown.

The presence of just one ballcourt in a region, of course, is as illogical as wearing only one shoe. Consequently, we expect that other large villages in the Mazatan region also had ballcourts and that village teams played "away-games" as they did in later times. If correct, the broader question concerns construction of several ballcourts and the organization and consequences of intervillage competition. If scheduling of ballgames were tied to maintenance of ballcourts, then aggrandizers who sponsored their construction and controlled use-rights could have bolstered personal prestige by successes in the ballcourt arena, qua players, gamblers, and/or sponsors.

As architectural facilities, ballcourts provided permanent loci for games and rituals connected with specific sponsors. Although there is no shortage of modern examples of sponsor aggrandizement, the one we imagine was small in scale, probably confined to the Mazatan region. The permanence of ballcourts created new opportunities for competitive interaction for subsequent generations by connecting players, sponsors, and participants in long-term relationships. Each time a ballgame was played, these connections would have been reinforced in the minds of participants and spectators. We suggest these connections were habitual in nature and eventually turned to the social advantage of those most closely associated with the ballcourt.

THE BALLGAME, COMMUNITAS, AND FIRST GOVERNMENT

The most consequential phenomenon resulting from the construction and use of the Paso de la Amada ballcourt may have been wholly unintended and had little to do with tangible material benefits, as great as these could have been; rather, it may have entailed new perceptions of community identity and related identities. In advancing this argument, we presume that ballplaying was inherently competitive and involved numerous teams within the Mazatan region. Further, we postulate that the formal construction of the ballcourt at Paso de la Amada coincided with construction of other courts at other villages, formation of village teams, and intervillage competition among teams, each sponsored by one or more aggrandizers. The village cluster at Paso de la Amada was large enough to have sponsored several teams; we suspect that, initially, competition among teams at Paso de la Amada may have been as intense and divisive as that among teams from different villages. Construction of a more formal facility at Paso de la Amada, however, appears to have changed matters significantly and to have promoted intravillage cooperation under the banner of a single village team.

We cannot resurrect the pageantry surrounding these early games, but what is known from later times indicates that games would have been highly charged affairs, ranging from sublimated warfare between villages to carnivals of fun, food, gambling, and hospitality. Indeed, ballgames were inherently social affairs and would have been obvious activities meriting aggrandizer sponsorship. Ballgames and their collateral activities provided numerous opportunities to deploy perishable resources and to be magnanimous to one's relatives, neighbors, and friends, and this would have been sufficient motivation for aggrandizers to stay involved.

Of special interest to us, however, is a probable consequence of league play among different villages. The emotions and excitement surrounding competitive matches would have promoted a mutual association of teams, sponsors, and villages that culminated over time in a shifting sense in the region of "we" versus "they" that had not been present before. Just as modern collegiate athletics easily fosters esprit de corps and polarizations of loyalties around school colors, we think that competitive team sports led to a polarization of team loyalties, village loyalties, and a heightened sense of belonging to a community. We call this sense of community identity *communitas*. We do not use this term to signal antistructure and intersubjective egalitarianism, as does Victor Turner (1969). Rather, it denotes a social perception among village coresidents of a common sense of belonging to the same community, a sense that crosscuts lineage loyalties.

Prior to construction of the formal ballcourt at Paso de la Amada, the internal evidence of the residence patterns for this site shows the presence of replicated residential units, or wards. Analytically, we see this as a village cluster of residences with no clear evidence of village-level integration. This changed soon after the construction of the ballcourt and the special residence at Mound 6. The entire Paso de la Amada village cluster appears to have become an integrated community. We suspect any growing sense of solidarity or communitas was largely an outgrowth of support for the village team and related activities. More importantly, this sense of community identity would logically have implicated a titular community head, a visible personification. In all the various activities involved with scheduling and sponsoring ballgame events, the team sponsor qua manager would have been seen by outsiders from other participating villages as the team and village representative. These external identities folded back into internal perceptions among one's coresidents, and the titular leader became viewed as such by foreigners and friends alike. These notions of village leader only strengthened the prestige of the aggrandizers in each village who sponsored the teams.

The emerging sense of community identity and embodiment of community leadership did not lead automatically from achieved to ascribed leadership, but we think it was an important piece of the puzzle that we have been slow to appreciate. In previous speculations on this matter, we began with a presumption of community solidarity and integration; this was inappropriate. Communitas arose from a complicated process of intervillage interaction; the obverse of this same process of emerging identities saw the association of sports teams with particular villages and of team sponsors as the embodiments of these same entities. With such perceptions in place, and with chronic disparities in responsibilities and perks, leadership roles created and filled by aggrandizers could have been amplified and passed on to heirs. If this were the case, formal government based upon hereditary rulership is one probable outcome of changing notions of communitas in Early Formative Mesoamerica.

CONCLUDING REMARKS

Throughout our discussion of the early Mesoamerican case we have been lax in separating anthropological concerns from traditional philosophical and political science ones. Our title alludes to traditional social contract theory for consensual government going back to Thomas Hobbes, John Locke, and the Mayflower Compact of the original Plymouth colony, but in our detailed arguments we considered the minimal level of government as that corresponding to simple chiefdoms (Service 1962), or the beginnings of hereditary rulership. Simple chiefdoms governed by hereditary chieftains probably fall short of the base level of *civitas* considered by early political thinkers. Therefore, possible disparities between categorical levels and disciplinary concerns here raise an important reservation about our proposal.

Our argument is historical and relies on getting right the absolute and relative sequence of events and practices. If we have misidentified the critical juncture for the crystallization of formal government, then our discussion of the critical events leading up to it is necessarily suspect. We argued that primitive government, or simple chiefdom societies, emerged in the Mazatan region of southern Mexico about 1600 B.C. To our knowledge, this currently would make it the oldest formal government in the Americas—but we anticipate older evidence will eventually be attested in coastal Ecuador and Peru. Given the vagaries of archaeological evidence and ground truthing, however, it is possible that we may have underestimated the Mesoamerican case. But it is unlikely that we would be off by more than a century. Even allowing such a margin of error, the ballcourt at Paso de la Amada was constructed very near the emergence of chiefdom societies in this region, either just before or just after. In either eventuality, this monumental construction activity, and the subsequent use of the facility, was tied to early government. It either aided in the initial emergence of government or in sustaining the new government through its first and most difficult years. The reality of the ballcourt and its timing are firmly established. Given the timing of the emergence of chiefdom societies, the presumption that the ballcourt/ballgame was integral to the development of fast government appears to be a reasonable one.

Based on information of the Mesoamerican ballgame from later periods, and of gaming among American tribal societies, we explored three possible paths to power and prestige that may have arisen through gambling, gaming, and ballgame sponsorship. Of course, the specific connections and their effects are unknowable, but manifold logical possibilities are entailed in such practices. Here we considered only the most plausible. The numerous ways in which individuals could gain some chronic material or social advantage over others are all compatible with the aggrandizer model proposed by Clark and Blake (1994). Our discussion suggests that this model is too materialist and political because it shortchanges the phenomenological side of cultural practices. We argue that nonmaterial outcomes from ballgame sponsorship may have been as important as material ones in the development of hereditary rulership.

As a new or modified cultural practice, the arrangement and promotion of intervillage ballgame competitions in early Mesoamerica may have been critical in changing perceptions of individual and group identity. Arising from basic fanatical spectator behavior, a sense of communitas may have emerged about the same time as the novel practice of recruiting village leaders from the descendants of previously successful tribal headmen. The transition from egalitarian lifeways to those based upon such hereditary distinctions was sustained by chronic disparities in privilege—both material and ideal—that led to habitual practices of inequality. We think the promotion of team sports had a significant impact on the accumulation of resources and debt management as well as on shifts in social valuations of various categories of persons. These possible connections certainly merit more research for the Mesoamerican case. The impact of competitive sports on early governments might also be worth investigating in other world areas.

In conclusion, we stress the need to consider sports and other social competition in terms of changing notions of personhood and community identity in tribal and transegalitarian societies. The large scale of investment in formal competitive games and gaming facilities in known tribal societies is sufficient grounds for suspecting that such activities are critical to social reproduction and, therefore, worthy of analytical attention. How were such endeavors financed in the past, and what kinds of tangible and intangible benefits were derived therefrom? In the Mesoamerican case, the unintended and unanticipated consequences of sports competitions may well have been more formal government and new perceptions of identity.

Little Brother of War

ADELE CONOVER

"Sticks" were the principal weapons used in a semi-sacred ball sport variously known as "They Bump Hips" or the "Little Brother of War" that American Indians believe was given to them by the Creator sometime in ages past.

More than three feet long and weighing a couple of pounds, they would seem unwieldy to modern lacrosse players, who pass the ball around and whack at each other with 12-ounce sticks of plastic, titanium and nylon. But they are symbols of triumph for a Native American culture that has otherwise been largely ignored, if not eradicated, by the modern white world. Year by year lacrosse grows more popular in North America (there are some 2,000 high school and more than 500 college teams in the United States alone) as well as in other parts of the globe from Japan to Germany and the Czech Republic. (When the Czechs first took up the game in the late 1970s, they reportedly used as a guide George Catlin's famous 1834 painting of Choctaws playing the game.) Yet lacrosse remains a uniquely Indian sport, requiring fierce competitiveness, speed and endurance, remarkable dexterity and tolerance of pain.

These days, of course, it is not lacrosse but professional football—with hockey as a close second—that people might reasonably describe as the "Little Brother of War." As played today, men's lacrosse involves ten players per team and lasts 60 minutes in a space roughly the size of a football field. It is still a game of hard knocks and bruises, played with fast-paced, passionate zeal by men and women. A remarkable witness to the demands and fascinations of the game is football's legendary running back Jim Brown. "Lacrosse is my favorite game," says Brown. "It takes tremendous endurance and skill."

According to Rick Hill, Sr., a lacrosse stalwart and a professor of Native American studies at the State University of New York at Buffalo, little is known about the two Smithsonian sticks. But studies by

Smithsonian researcher Thomas Vennum, Jr., author of *American Indian Lacrosse: Little Brother of War* (Smithsonian Press, 1994), suggest that in design lacrosse sticks are descendants of war clubs.

The butt of one elaborately carved stick at the University of Pennsylvania, crafted a century and a half ago, represents a hand holding a ball. Alongside it on the shaft is a carving of a handshake. The clasped hands, Vennum says, are not necessarily friendly. They may be symbolic of a dance in which warriors clasped hands to "strengthen themselves…as protective medicine" for battle. Some experts regard the carved ball in the hand as some kind of medicine ball, but Vennum thinks it is also linked to the ball end of war clubs, often carved as if held in the mouth of a snake or the claws of a bird of prey. The idea was that when such clubs were used in battle, the snake or hawk symbolically loosed its grip, sending the ball flying through the air to strike an enemy's head and kill him.

Sometimes the ball was carved as a human head that would fly off the club's handle and smack an enemy brave. One Iroquois legend tells of a flying head pursuing a whole family, bent on its annihilation. At the last second the ball is caught and thrown to its death in a vat of boiling bear grease.

As the game was played by its original inventors, from 30 to 50 players might take part on vast ball fields without sidelines whose variable length was determined by both teams prior to the match. Games lasted for days at times, and in some tribes players and nonplayers alike bet ponies, fortunes in fur and beadwork, even wives and children, on the outcome.

Early French and English settlers at first were both startled and horrified by the game. "Almost everything short of murder is allowable," one noted. "If one were not told beforehand that they were playing," another wrote, "one would certainly believe that they were fighting." Soon, however, they fell under the spell of the game, learning to watch (and place side bets) among themselves. So much so that lacrosse played a role during the period of Pontiac's Rebellion in which several Indian nations fought to reclaim lands from occupying British forces in what is now the Midwest. In 1763, during King George III's birthday celebration, Indians staged a game outside Fort Michilimackinac on Lake Michigan. While His Majesty's soldiers were caught up in the game's progress, warriors took the fort.

The later history of the "Little Brother of War" was sometimes as contentious as the relationship between Indians and Euro-Americans. According to U.S. Lacrosse, the Baltimore-based national governing body of the sport, white Canadians were playing as early as 1839. By 1856 in Montreal the first non-Indian team had been organized, and in 1860 a Canadian dentist, Dr. William George Beers, wrote the first Europeanized rules.

For a while lacrosse was promoted as the national game of Canada. Native American teams toured Europe playing exhibition games, including one for the benefit of Queen Victoria. Then, in 1880, the National Lacrosse Association of Canada banned Indians from championship play—officially on the grounds that the Indians were paid "professionals" not eligible for "amateur" sports. By that time the game was catching on in North American prep schools and colleges, with a scattering of Indian varsity players at such schools as Dartmouth and (later) Syracuse.

Today in Indian communities all over North America at the first sign of spring youngsters sally forth carrying lacrosse sticks. Many Indian players still request to be buried with their sticks beside them. The tradition of carved wooden lacrosse sticks still flourishes as well. In the Tuscarora Nation, near Sanborn, New York, Tuskewe Krafts, a firm owned by John Wesley Patterson, Jr., turns out 10,000 sticks a year at prices running from $60 to $90.

For many Indians in ancient days, and today as well, a lacrosse game was a ceremonial replay of the Creation story, and of the struggle between good and evil that followed it. The game could also be worldly practical—mock war used for diplomatic purposes or as a prudent step back from the threat of war. The story, retold by Vennum, of two lacrosse games played almost exactly 200 years ago between the Mohawk and the Seneca seems to offer a case in point.

Both belonged to the powerful league of Six Nations, the Iroquois confederacy that also included the Onondaga, Cayuga, Oneida and Tuscarora. The year was 1794. After the French and Indian Wars and the American Revolution, whites were again threatening Indian holdings in what is now Ohio and western New York. Chief Joseph Brant (Thayendanegea, in Mohawk), a powerful chief who had sided with the British during the Revolution, was negotiating with them for land in Canada, but the site offered was unacceptable. The Seneca agreed; if they took it the Mohawk would be isolated from the rest of the Six Nations. When Seneca intervention resulted in a better site for the Mohawk, Brant set up a ceremonial lacrosse match in part, Vennum speculates, to celebrate the Seneca help.

There was also bad blood between Brant and Red Jacket, an influential Seneca chief, going back to a time when Brant had called him a "cow killer," because it was said Red Jacket sent Seneca warriors off to battle while he stayed at home butchering their cows for himself. The match may have represented a fence-mending effort on Brant's part. If so, it apparently hit a snag. During the game, according to a report written at the time and cited in a biography of Brant published in 1838, a Mohawk lost his temper and "struck a sharp blow" to his opponent with his stick. All action stopped, the story goes; the Seneca team walked off the field. The Mohawk and the Seneca did not play each other again until 1797. But they kept on playing, and so did the other Iroquois nations. Lacrosse, in fact, was one of the things that helped hold the Six Nations together through the difficult years that followed.

In 1990 the Iroquois Nationals, an all-Iroquois lacrosse team, traveled to Australia for the world championship under their own flag and carrying Iroquois passports. "We stood tall," says Rick Hill. "For a few moments the lacrosse-playing nations (England, Japan, Australia, the Czech Republic, the United States, Canada, Wales, Scotland, Sweden, Germany) saluted our national flag. It was quite a change after 200 years."

Modern Survivals of Prowess

THORSTEIN VEBLEN

The leisure class lives by the industrial community rather than in it. Its relations to industry are of a pecuniary rather than an industrial kind. Admission to the class is gained by exercise of the pecuniary aptitudes—aptitudes for acquisition rather than for serviceability. There is, therefore, a continued selective sifting of the human material that makes up the leisure class, and this selection proceeds on the ground of fitness for pecuniary pursuits. But the scheme of life of the class is in large part a heritage from the past, and embodies much of the habits and ideals of the earlier barbarian period. This archaic, barbarian scheme of life imposes itself also on the lower orders, with more or less mitigation. In its turn the scheme of life, of conventions, acts selectively and by education to shape the human material, and its action runs chiefly in the direction of conserving traits, habits, and ideals that belong to the early barbarian age—the age of prowess and predatory life.

The most immediate and unequivocal expression of that archaic human nature which characterizes man in the predatory stage is the fighting propensity proper. In cases where the predatory activity is a collective one, this propensity is frequently called the martial spirit, or, latterly, patriotism. It needs no insistence to find assent to the proposition that in the countries of civilized Europe the hereditary leisure class is endowed with this martial spirit in a higher degree than the middle classes. Indeed, the leisure class claims the distinction as a matter of pride, and no doubt with some grounds. War is honorable, and warlike prowess is eminently honorific in the eyes of the generality of men; and this admiration of warlike prowess is itself the best voucher of a predatory temperament in the admirer of war. The enthusiasm for war, and the predatory temper of which it is the index, prevail in the largest measure among the upper classes, especially among the hereditary leisure class. Moreover, the ostensible serious occupation of the upper class is that of government, which, in point of origin and developmental content, is also a predatory occupation.

The only class which could at all dispute with the hereditary leisure class the honor of an habitual bellicose frame of mind is that of the lower-class delinquents. In ordinary times, the large body of the industrial classes is relatively apathetic touching warlike interests. When unexcited, this body of the common people, which makes up the effective force of the industrial community, is rather averse to any other than a defensive fight; indeed, it responds a little tardily even to a provocation which makes for an attitude of defense. In the more civilized communities, or rather in the communities which have reached an advanced industrial development, the spirit of warlike aggression may be said to be obsolescent among the common people. This does not say that there is not an appreciable number of individuals among the industrial classes in whom the martial spirit asserts itself obtrusively. Nor does it say that the body of the people may not be fired with martial ardor for a time under the stimulus of some special provocation, such as is seen in operation today in more than one of the countries of Europe, and for the time in America. But except for such seasons of temporary exaltation, and except for those individuals who are endowed with an archaic temperament of the predatory type, together with the similarly endowed body of individuals among the higher and the lowest classes, the inertness of the mass of any modern civilized community in this respect is probably so great as would make war impracticable, except against actual invasion. The habits and aptitudes of the common run of men make for an unfolding of activity in other, less picturesque directions than that of war.

This class difference in temperament may be due in part to a difference in the inheritance of acquired traits in the several classes, but it seems also, in some measure, to correspond with a difference in ethnic derivation. The class difference is in this respect visibly less in those countries whose population is relatively homogeneous, ethnically, than in the countries where there is a broader divergence between the ethnic elements that make up the several classes of the community. In the same connection it may be noted that the later accessions to the leisure class in the latter countries, in a general way, show less of the martial spirit than contemporary representatives of the aristocracy of the ancient line. These *nouveaux arrivés* have recently emerged from the commonplace body of the population and owe their emergence into the leisure class to the exercise of traits and propensities which are not to be classed as prowess in the ancient sense.

Apart from warlike activity proper, the institution of the duel is also an expression of the same superior readiness for combat; and the duel is a leisure-class institution. The duel is in substance a more or less deliberate resort to a fight as a final settlement of a difference of opinion. In civilized communities it prevails as a normal phenomenon only where there is an hereditary leisure class, and almost exclusively among that class. The exceptions are (1) military and naval officers—who are ordinarily members of the leisure class, and who are at the same time specially trained to predatory habits of mind—and (2) the lower-class delinquents—who are by inheritance, or training, or both, of a similarly predatory disposition and habit. It is only the high-bred gentleman and the rowdy that normally resort to blows as the universal solvent of differences of opinion. The plain man will ordinarily fight only when excessive momentary irritation or alcoholic exaltation act to inhibit the more complex habits of response to the stimuli that make for provocation. He is then thrown back upon the simpler, less differentiated forms of the instinct of self-assertion; that is to say, he reverts temporarily and without reflection to an archaic habit of mind.

This institution of the duel as a mode of finally settling disputes and serious questions of precedence shades off into the obligatory, unprovoked private fight, as a social obligation due to one's good repute. As a leisure-class usage of this kind we have, particularly, that bizarre survival of bellicose chivalry, the German student duel. In the lower or spurious leisure class of the delinquents there is in all countries a similar, though less formal, social obligation incumbent on the rowdy to assert his manhood in unprovoked combat with his fellows. And spreading through all grades of society, a similar usage prevails among the boys of the community. The boy usually knows to a nicety, from day to day, how he and his associates grade in respect of relative fighting capacity; and in the community of boys there is ordinarily no secure basis of reputability for any one who, by exception, will not or can not fight on invitation.

All this applies especially to boys above a certain somewhat vague limit of maturity. The child's temperament does not commonly answer to this description during infancy and the years of close tutelage, when the child still habitually seeks contact with its mother at every turn of its daily life. During this earlier period there is little aggression and little propensity for antagonism. The transition from this peaceable temper to the predaceous, and in extreme cases malignant, mischievousness of the boy is a gradual one, and it is accomplished with more completeness, covering a larger range of the individual's aptitudes, in some cases than in others. In the earlier stage of his growth, the child, whether boy or girl, shows less of initiative and aggressive self-assertion and less of an inclination to isolate himself and his interests from the domestic group in which he lives, and he shows more of sensitiveness to rebuke, bashfulness, timidity, and the need of friendly human contact. In the common run of cases this early temperament passes, by a gradual but somewhat rapid obsolescence of the infantile features, into the temperament of the boy proper; though there are also cases where the predaceous features of boy life do not emerge at all, or at the most emerge in but a slight and obscure degree.

In girls the transition to the predaceous stage is seldom accomplished with the same degree of completeness as in boys; and in a relatively large proportion of cases it is scarcely undergone at all. In such cases the transition from infancy to adolescence and maturity is a gradual and unbroken process of the shifting of interest from infantile purposes and aptitudes to the purposes, functions, and relations of adult life. In the girls there is a less general prevalence of a predaceous interval in the development; and in the cases where it occurs, the predaceous and isolating attitude during the interval is commonly less accentuated.

In the male child the predaceous interval is ordinarily fairly well marked and lasts for some time, but it is commonly terminated (if at all) with the attainment of maturity. This last statement may need very material qualification. The cases are by no means rare in which the transition from the boyish to the adult temperament is not made, or is made only partially—understanding by the "adult" temperament the average temperament of those adult individuals in modern industrial life who have some serviceability for the purposes of the collective life process, and who may therefore be said to make up the effective average of the industrial community.

The ethnic composition of the European populations varies. In some cases even the lower classes are in large measure made up of the peace-disturbing dolicho-blond; while in others this ethnic element is found chiefly among the hereditary leisure class. The fighting habit seems to prevail to a less extent among the working-class boys in the latter class of populations than among the boys of the upper classes or among those of the populations first named.

If this generalization as to the temperament of the boy among the working classes should be found true on a fuller and closer scrutiny of the field, it would add force to the view that the bellicose temperament is in some appreciable degree a race characteristic; it appears to enter more largely into the make-up of the dominant, upper-class ethnic type—the dolicho-blond—of the European countries than into the subservient, lower-class types of man which are conceived to constitute the body of the population of the same communities.

The case of the boy may seem not to bear seriously on the question of the relative endowment of prowess with which the several classes of society are gifted; but it is at least of some value as going to show that this fighting impulse belongs to a more archaic temperament than that possessed by the average adult man of the industrious classes. In this, as in many other features of child life, the child reproduces, temporarily and in miniature, some of the earlier phases of the development of adult man. Under this interpretation, the boy's predilection for exploit and for isolation of his own interest is to be taken as a transient reversion to the human nature that is normal to the early barbarian culture—the predatory culture proper. In this respect, as in much else, the leisure-class and the delinquent-class character shows a persistence into adult life of traits that are normal to childhood and youth, and that are likewise normal or habitual to the earlier stages of culture. Unless the difference is traceable entirely to a fundamental difference between persistent ethnic types, the traits that distinguish the swaggering delinquent and the punctilious gentleman of leisure from the common crowd are, in some measure, marks of an arrested spiritual development. They mark an immature phase, as compared with the stage of development attained by the average of the adults in the modern industrial community. And it will appear presently that the puerile spiritual make-up of these representatives of the upper and the lowest social strata shows itself also in the presence of other archaic traits than this proclivity to ferocious exploit and isolation.

As if to leave no doubt about the essential immaturity of the fighting temperament, we have, bridging the interval between legitimate boyhood and adult manhood, the aimless and playful, but more or less systematic and elaborate, disturbances of the peace in vogue among schoolboys of a slightly higher age. In the common run of cases, these disturbances are confined to the period of adolescence. They recur with decreasing frequency and acuteness as youth merges into adult life, and so they reproduce, in a general way, in the life of the individual, the sequence by which the group has passed from the predatory to a more settled habit of life. In an appreciable number of cases the spiritual growth of the individual comes to a close before he emerges from this puerile phase; in these cases the fighting temper persists through life. Those individuals who in spiritual development eventually reach man's estate, therefore, ordinarily pass through a temporary archaic phase corresponding to the permanent spiritual level of the fighting and sporting men. Different individuals will, of course, achieve spiritual maturity and sobriety in this respect in different degrees; and those who fail of the average remain as an undissolved residue of crude humanity in the modern industrial community and as a foil for that selective process of adaptation which makes for a heightened industrial efficiency and the fullness of life of the collectivity.

This arrested spiritual development may express itself not only in a direct participation by adults in youthful exploits of ferocity, but also indirectly in aiding and abetting disturbances of this kind on the part of younger persons. It thereby furthers the formation of habits of ferocity which may persist in the later life of the growing generation, and so retard any movement in the direction of a more peaceable effective temperament on the part of the community. If a person so endowed with a proclivity for exploits is in a position to guide the development of habits in the adolescent members of the community, the influence which he exerts in the direction of conservation and reversion to prowess may be very considerable. This is the significance, for instance, of the fostering care latterly bestowed by many clergymen and other pillars of society upon "boys' brigades" and similar pseudo-military organizations. The same is true of the encouragement given to the growth of "college spirit," college athletics, and the like, in the higher institutions of learning.

These manifestations of the predatory temperament are all to be classed under the head of exploit. They are partly simple and unreflected expressions of an attitude of emulative ferocity, partly activities deliberately entered upon with a view to gaining repute for prowess. Sports of all kinds are of the same general character, including prize-fights, bull-fights, athletics, shooting, angling, yachting, and games of skill, even where the element of destructive physical efficiency is not an obtrusive feature. Sports shade off from the basis of hostile combat, through skill, to cunning and chicanery, without its being possible to draw a line at any point. The ground of an addiction to sports is an archaic spiritual constitution—the possession of the predatory emulative propensity in a relatively high potency. A strong proclivity to adventuresome exploit and to the infliction of damage is especially pronounced in those employments which are in colloquial usage specifically called sportsmanship.

It is perhaps truer, or at least more evident, as regards sports than as regards the other expressions of predatory emulation already spoken of, that the temperament which inclines men to them is essentially a boyish temperament. The addiction to sports, therefore, in a peculiar degree marks an arrested development of the man's moral nature. This peculiar boyishness of temperament in sporting men immediately becomes apparent when attention is directed to the large element of make-believe that is present in all sporting activity. Sports share this character of make-believe with the games and exploits to which children, especially boys, are habitually inclined. Make-believe does not enter in the same proportion into all sports, but it is present in a very appreciable degree in all. It is apparently present in a larger measure in sportsmanship proper and in athletic contests than in set games of skill of a more sedentary character; although this rule may not be found to apply with any great uniformity. It is noticeable, for instance, that even very mild-mannered and matter-of-fact men who go out shooting are apt to carry an excess of arms and accoutrements in order to impress upon their own imagination the seriousness of their undertaking. These huntsmen are also prone to a histrionic, prancing gait and to an elaborate exaggeration of the motions, whether of stealth or of onslaught, involved in their deeds of exploit. Similarly in athletic sports there is almost invariably present a good share of rant and swagger and ostensible mystification—features which mark the histrionic nature of these employments. In all this, of course, the reminder of boyish make-believe is plain enough. The slang of athletics, by the way, is in great part made up of extremely sanguinary locutions borrowed from the terminology of warfare. Except where it is adopted as a necessary means of secret communication, the use of a special slang in any employment is probably to be accepted as evidence that the occupation in question is substantially make-believe.

A further feature in which sports differ from the duel and similar disturbances of the peace is the peculiarity that they admit of other motives being assigned for them besides the impulses of exploit and ferocity. There is probably little if any other motive present in any given case, but the fact that other reasons for indulging in sports are frequently assigned goes to say that other grounds are sometimes present to a subsidiary way. Sportsmen—hunters and anglers—are more or less in the habit of assigning a love of nature, the need of recreation, and the like, as the incentives to their favorite pastime. These motives are no doubt frequently present and make up a part of the attractiveness of the sportsman's life; but these can not be the chief incentives. These ostensible needs could be more readily and fully satisfied without the accompaniment of a systematic effort to take the life of those creatures that make up an essential feature of that "nature" that is beloved by the sportsman. It is, indeed, the most noticeable effect of the sportsman's activity to keep nature in a state of chronic desolation by killing off all living things whose destruction he can compass.

Still, there is ground for the sportsman's claim that under the existing conventionalities his need of recreation and of contact with nature can best be satisfied by the course which he takes. Certain canons of good breeding have been imposed by the prescriptive example of a predatory leisure class in the past and have been somewhat painstakingly conserved by the usage of the latter-day representatives of that class; and these canons will not permit him, without blame, to seek contact with nature on other terms. From being an honorable employment handed down from the predatory culture as the highest form of everyday leisure, sports have come to be the only form of outdoor activity that has the full sanction of decorum. Among the proximate incentives to shooting and angling, then, may be the need of recreation and outdoor life. The remoter cause which imposes the necessity of seeking these objects under the cover of systematic slaughter is a prescription that can not be violated except at the risk of disrepute and consequent lesion to one's self-respect.

The case of other kinds of sport is somewhat similar. Of these, athletic games are the best example. Prescriptive usage with respect to what forms of activity, exercise; and recreation are permissible under the code of reputable living is of course present here also. Those who are addicted to athletic sports, or who admire them, set up the claim that these afford the best available means of recreation and of "physical culture." And prescriptive usage gives countenance to the claim. The canons of reputable living exclude from the scheme of life of the leisure class all activity that can not be classed as conspicuous leisure. And consequently they tend by prescription to exclude it also from the scheme of life of the community generally. At the same time purposeless physical exertion is tedious and distasteful beyond tolerance. As has been noticed in another connection, recourse is in such a case had to some form of activity which shall at least afford a colorable pretense of purpose, even if the object assigned be only a make-believe. Sports satisfy these requirements of substantial futility together with a colorable make-believe of purpose. In addition to this they afford scope for emulation, and are attractive also on that account. In order to be decorous, an employment must conform to the leisure-class canon of reputable waste; at the same time all activity, in order to be persisted in as an habitual, even if only partial, expression of life, must conform to the generically human canon of efficiency for some serviceable objective end. The leisure-class canon demands strict and comprehensive futility; the instinct of workmanship demands purposeful action. The leisure-class canon of decorum acts slowly and pervasively, by a selective elimination of all substantially useful or purposeful modes of action from the accredited scheme of life; the instinct of workmanship acts impulsively and may be satisfied, provisionally, with a proximate purpose. It is only as the apprehended ulterior futility of a given line of action enters the reflective complex of consciousness as an element essentially alien to the normally purposeful trend of the life process that its disquieting and deterrent effect on the consciousness of the agent is wrought.

The individual's habits of thought make an organic complex, the trend of which is necessarily in the direction of serviceability to the life process. When it is attempted to assimilate systematic waste or futility, as an end in life, into this organic complex, there presently supervenes a revulsion. But this revulsion of the organism may be avoided if the attention can be confined to the proximate, unreflected purpose of dexterous or emulative exertion. Sports—hunting, angling, athletic games, and the like—afford an exercise for dexterity and for the emulative ferocity and astuteness characteristic of predatory life. So long as the individual is but slightly gifted with reflection or with a sense of the ulterior trend of his actions—so long as his life is substantially a life of naïve impulsive action—so long the immediate and unreflected purposefulness of sports, in the way of an expression of dominance, will measurably satisfy his instinct of workmanship. This is especially true if his dominant impulses are the unreflecting emulative propensities of the predaceous temperament. At the same time the canons of decorum will commend sports to him as expressions of a pecuniarily blameless life. It is by meeting these two requirements, of ulterior wastefulness and proximate purposefulness, that any given employment holds its place as a traditional and habitual mode of decorous recreation. In the sense that other forms of recreation and exercise are morally impossible to persons of good breeding and delicate sensibilities, then, sports are the best available means of recreation under existing circumstances.

But those members of respectable society who advocate athletic games commonly justify their attitude on this head to themselves and to their neighbors on the ground that these games serve as an invaluable means of development. They not only improve the contestant's physique, but it is commonly added that they also foster a manly spirit, both in the participants and in the spectators. Football is the particular game which will probably first occur to any one in this community when the question of the serviceability of athletic games is raised, as this form of athletic contest is at present uppermost in the mind of those who plead for or against games as a means of physical or moral salvation. This typical athletic sport may, therefore, serve to illustrate the bearing of athletics upon the development of the contestant's character and physique. It has been said, not inaptly, that the relation of football to physical culture is much the same as that of the bull-fight to agriculture. Serviceability for these lusory institutions requires sedulous training or breeding. The material used, whether brute or human, is subjected to careful selection and discipline, in order to secure and accentuate certain aptitudes and propensities which are characteristic of the ferine state, and which tend to obsolescence under domestication. This does not mean that the result in either case is an all-around and consistent rehabilitation of the ferine or barbarian habit of mind and body. The result is rather a one-sided return to barbarism or to the *feræ natura*—a rehabilitation and accentuation of those ferine traits which make for damage and desolation, without a corresponding development of the traits which would serve the individual's self-preservation and fullness of life in a ferine environment. The culture bestowed in football gives a product of exotic ferocity and cunning. It is a rehabilitation of the early barbarian temperament, together with a suppression of those details of temperament, which, as seen from the standpoint of the social and economic exigencies, are the redeeming features of the savage character.

The physical vigor acquired in the training for athletic games—so far as the training may be said to have this effect—is of advantage both to the individual and to the collectivity, in that, other things being equal, it conduces to economic serviceability. The spiritual traits which go with athletic sports are likewise economically advantageous to the individual, as contradistinguished from the interests of the collectivity. This holds true in any community where these traits are present in some degree in the population. Modern competition is in large part a process of self-assertion on the basis of these traits of predatory human nature. In the sophisticated form in which they enter into the modern, peaceable emulation, the possession of these traits in some measure is almost a necessary of life to the civilized man. But while they are indispensable to the competitive individual, they are not directly serviceable to the community. So far as regards the serviceability of the individual for the purposes of the collective life, emulative efficiency is of use only indirectly if at all. Ferocity and cunning are of no use to the community except in its hostile dealings with other communities; and they are useful to the individual only because there is so large a proportion of the same traits actively present in the human environment to which he is exposed. Any individual who enters the competitive struggle without the due endowment of these traits is at a disadvantage, somewhat as a hornless steer would find himself at a disadvantage in a drove of horned cattle.

The possession and the cultivation of the predatory traits of character may, of course, be desirable on other than economic grounds. There is a prevalent aesthetic or ethical predilection for the barbarian aptitudes, and the traits in question minister so effectively to this predilection that their serviceability in the aesthetic or ethical respect probably offsets any economic unserviceability which they may give. But for the present purpose that is beside the point. Therefore nothing is said here as to the desirability or advisability of sports on the whole, or as to their value on other than economic grounds.

In popular apprehension there is much that is admirable in the type of manhood which the life of sport fosters. There is self-reliance and good-fellowship, so termed in the somewhat loose colloquial use of the words. From a different point of view the qualities currently so characterized might be described as truculence and clannishness. The reason for the current approval and admiration of these manly qualities, as well as for their being called manly, is the same as the reason for their usefulness to the individual. The members of the community, and especially that class of the community which sets the pace in canons of taste, are endowed with this range of propensities in sufficient measure to make their absence in others felt as a shortcoming, and to make their possession in an exceptional degree appreciated as an attribute of superior merit. The traits of predatory man are by no means obsolete in the common run of modern populations. They are present and can be called out in bold relief at any time by any appeal to the sentiments in which they express themselves—unless this appeal should clash with the specific activities that make up our habitual occupations and comprise the general range of our everyday interests. The common run of the population of any industrial community is emancipated from these, economically considered, untoward propensities only in the sense that, through partial and temporary disuse, they have lapsed into the background of sub-conscious motives. With varying degrees of potency in different individuals, they remain available for the aggressive shaping of men's actions and sentiments whenever a stimulus of more than everyday intensity comes in to call them forth. And they assert themselves forcibly in any case where no occupation alien to the predatory culture has usurped the individual's everyday range of interest and sentiment. This is the case among the leisure class and among certain portions of the population which are ancillary to that class. Hence the facility with which any new accessions to the leisure class take to sports; and hence the rapid growth of sports and of the sporting sentiment in any industrial community where wealth has accumulated sufficiently to exempt a considerable part of the population from work.

A homely and familiar fact may serve to show that the predaceous impulse does not prevail in the same degree in all classes. Taken simply as a feature of modern life, the habit of carrying a walking-stick may seem at best a trivial detail; but the usage has a significance for the point in question. The classes among whom the habit most prevails—the classes with whom the walking-stick is associated in popular apprehension—are the men of the leisure class proper, sporting men, and the lower-class delinquents. To these might perhaps be added the men engaged in the pecuniary employments. The same is not true of the common run of men engaged in industry; and it may be noted by the way that women do not carry a stick except in case of infirmity, where it has a use of a different kind. The practice is of course in great measure a matter of polite usage; but the basis of polite usage is, in turn, the proclivities of the class which sets the pace in polite usage. The walking-stick serves the purpose of an advertisement that the bearer's hands are employed otherwise than in useful effort, and it therefore has utility as an evidence of leisure. But it is also a weapon, and it meets a felt need of barbarian man on that ground. The handling of so tangible and primitive a means of offense is very comforting to any one who is gifted with even a moderate share of ferocity.

The exigencies of the language make it impossible to avoid an apparent implication of disapproval of the aptitudes, propensities, and expressions of life here under discussion. It is, however, not intended to imply anything in the way of deprecation or commendation of any one of these phases of human character or of the life process. The various elements of the prevalent human nature are taken up from the point of view of economic theory, and the traits discussed are gauged and graded with regard to their immediate economic bearing on the facility of the collective life process. That is to say, these phenomena are here apprehended from the economic point of view and are valued with respect to their direct action in furtherance or hindrance of a more perfect adjustment of the human collectivity to the environment and to the institutional structure required by the economic situation of the collectivity for the present and for the immediate future. For these purposes the traits handed down from the predatory culture are less serviceable than might be. Although even in this connection it is not to be overlooked that the energetic aggressiveness and pertinacity of predatory man is a heritage of no mean value. The economic value—with some regard also to the social value in the narrower sense—of these aptitudes and propensities is attempted to be passed upon without reflecting on their value as seen from another point of view.

When contrasted with the prosy mediocrity of the latter-day industrial scheme of life, and judged by the accredited standards of morality, and more especially by the standards of aesthetics and of poetry, these survivals from a more primitive type of manhood may have a very different value from that here assigned them. But all this being foreign to the purpose in hand, no expression of opinion on this latter head would be in place here. All that is admissible is to enter the caution that these standards of excellence, which are alien to the present purpose, must not be allowed to influence our economic appreciation of these traits of human character or of the activities which foster their growth. This applies both as regards those persons who actively participate in sports and those whose sporting experience consists in contemplation only. What is here said of the sporting propensity is likewise pertinent to sundry reflections presently to be made in this connection on what would colloquially be known as the religious life.

The last paragraph incidentally touches upon the fact that everyday speech can scarcely be employed in discussing this class of aptitudes and activities without implying deprecation or apology. The fact is significant as showing the habitual attitude of the dispassionate common man toward the propensities which express themselves in sports and in exploit generally. And this is perhaps as convenient a place as any to discuss that undertone of deprecation which runs through all the voluminous discourse in defense or in laudation of athletic sports, as well as of other activities of a predominantly predatory character. The same apologetic frame of mind is at least beginning to be observable in the spokesmen of most other institutions handed down from the barbarian phase of life. Among these archaic institutions which are felt to need apology are comprised, with others, the entire existing system of the distribution of wealth, together with the resulting class distinction of status; all or nearly all forms of consumption that come under the head of conspicuous waste; the status of women under the patriarchal system; and many features of the traditional creeds and devout observances, especially the exoteric expressions of the creed and the naïve apprehension of received observances. What is to be said in this connection of the apologetic attitude taken in commending sports and the sporting character will therefore apply, with a suitable change in phraseology, to the apologies offered in behalf of these other, related elements of our social heritage.

There is a feeling—usually vague and not commonly avowed in so many words by the apologist himself, but ordinarily perceptible in the manner of his discourse—that these sports, as well as the general range of predaceous impulses and habits of thought which underlie the sporting character, do not altogether commend themselves to common sense. "As to the majority of murderers, they are very incorrect characters." This aphorism offers a valuation of the predaceous temperament, and of the disciplinary effects of its overt expression and exercise, as seen from the moralist's point of view. As such it affords an indication of what is the deliverance of the sober sense of mature men as to the degree of availability of the predatory habit of mind for the purposes of the collective life. It is felt that the presumption is against any activity which involves habituation to the predatory attitude, and that the burden of proof lies with those who speak for the rehabilitation of the predaceous temper and for the practices which strengthen it. There is a strong body of popular sentiment in favor of diversions and enterprises of the kind in question; but there is at the same time present in the community a pervading sense that this ground of sentiment wants legitimation. The required legitimation is ordinarily sought by showing that although sports are substantially of a predatory, socially disintegrating effect; although their proximate effect runs in the direction of reversion to propensities that are industrially disserviceable; yet indirectly and remotely—by some not readily comprehensible process of polar induction, or counter-irritation perhaps—sports are conceived to foster a habit of mind that is serviceable for the social or industrial purpose. That is to say, although sports are essentially of the nature of invidious exploit, it is presumed that by some remote and obscure effect they result in the growth of a temperament conducive to non-invidious work. It is commonly attempted to show all this empirically; or it is rather assumed that this is the empirical generalization which must be obvious to any one who cares to see it. In conducting the proof of this thesis the treacherous ground of inference from cause to effect is somewhat shrewdly avoided, except so far as to show that the "manly virtues" spoken of above are fostered by sports. But since it is these manly virtues that are (economically) in need of legitimation, the chain of proof breaks off where it should begin. In the most general economic terms, these apologies are an effort to show that, in spite of the logic of the thing, sports do in fact further what may broadly be called workmanship. So long as he has not succeeded in persuading himself or others that this is their effect the thoughtful apologist for sports will not rest content, and commonly, it is to be admitted, he does not rest content. His discontent with his own vindication of the practice in question is ordinarily shown by his truculent tone and by the eagerness with which he heaps up asseverations in support of his position.

But why are apologies needed? If there prevails a body of popular sentiment in favor of sports, why is not that fact a sufficient legitimation? The protracted discipline of prowess to which the race has been subjected under the predatory and quasi-peaceable culture has transmitted to the men of today a temperament that finds gratification in these expressions of ferocity and cunning. So, why not accept these sports as legitimate expressions of a normal and wholesome human nature? What other norm is there that is to be lived up to than that given in the aggregate range of propensities that express themselves in the sentiments of this generation, including the hereditary strain of prowess? The ulterior norm to which appeal is taken is the instinct of workmanship, which is an instinct more fundamental, of more ancient prescription, than the propensity to predatory emulation. The latter is but a special development of the instinct of workmanship, a variant, relatively late and ephemeral in spite of its great absolute antiquity.

Section II: History of Sport

The emulative predatory impulse—or the instinct of sportsmanship, as it might well be called—is essentially unstable in comparison with the primordial instinct of workmanship out of which it has been developed and differentiated. Tested by this ulterior norm of life, predatory emulation, and therefore the life of sports, falls short.

The manner and the measure in which the institution of a leisure class conduces to the conservation of sports and invidious exploit can of course not be succinctly stated. From the evidence already recited it appears that, in sentiment and inclinations, the leisure class is more favorable to a warlike attitude and animus than the industrial classes. Something similar seems to be true as regards sports. But it is chiefly in its indirect effects, through the canons of decorous living, that the institution has its influence on the prevalent sentiment with respect to the sporting life. This indirect effect goes almost unequivocally in the direction of furthering a survival of the predatory temperament and habits; and this is true even with respect to those variants of the spotting life which the higher leisure-class code of proprieties proscribes; as, *e.g.*, prize-fighting, cock-fighting, and other like vulgar expressions of the sporting temper. Whatever the latest authenticated schedule of detail proprieties may say, the accredited canons of decency sanctioned by the institution say without equivocation that emulation and waste are good and their opposites are disreputable. In the crepuscular light of the social nether spaces the details of the code are not apprehended with all the facility that might be desired, and these broad underlying canons of decency are therefore applied somewhat unreflectingly, with little question as to the scope of their competence or the exceptions that have been sanctioned in detail.

Addiction to athletic sports, not only in the way of direct participation, but also in the way of sentiment and moral support, is, in a more or less pronounced degree, a characteristic of the leisure class; and it is a trait which that class shares with the lower-class delinquents, and with such atavistic elements throughout the body of the community as are endowed with a dominant predaceous trend. Few individuals among the populations of Western civilized countries are so far devoid of the predaceous instinct as to find no diversion in contemplating athletic sports and games, but with the common run of individuals among the industrial classes the inclination to sports does not assert itself to the extent of constituting what may fairly be called a sporting habit. With these classes sports are an occasional diversion rather than a serious feature of life. This common body of the people can therefore not be said to cultivate the sporting propensity. Although it is not obsolete in the average of them, or even in any appreciable number of individuals, yet the predilection for sports in the commonplace industrial classes is of the nature of a reminiscence, more or less diverting as an occasional interest, rather than a vital and permanent interest that counts as a dominant factor in shaping the organic complex of habits of thought into which it enters.

As it manifests itself in the sporting life of today, this propensity may not appear to be an economic factor of grave consequence. Taken simply by itself it does not count for a great deal in its direct effects on the industrial efficiency or the consumption of any given individual; but the prevalence and the growth of the type of human nature of which this propensity is a characteristic feature is a matter of some consequence. It affects the economic life of the collectivity both as regards the rate of economic development and as regards the character of the results attained by the development. For better or worse, the fact that the popular habits of thought are in any degree dominated by this type of character can not but greatly affect the scope, direction, standards, and ideals of the collective economic life, as well as the degree of adjustment of the collective life to the environment.

Something to a like effect is to be said of other traits that go to make up the barbarian character. For the purposes of economic theory, these further barbarian traits may be taken as concomitant variations of that predaceous temper of which prowess is an expression. In great measure they are not primarily of an economic character, nor do they have much direct economic bearing. They serve to indicate the stage of economic evolution to which the individual possessed of them is adapted. They are of importance, therefore, as extraneous tests of the degree of adaptation of the character in which they are comprised to the economic exigencies of today; but they are also to some extent important as being aptitudes which themselves go to increase or diminish the economic serviceability of the individual.

As it finds expression in the life of the barbarian, prowess manifests itself in two main directions—force and fraud. In varying degrees these two forms of expression are similarly present in modern warfare, in the pecuniary occupations, and in sports and games. Both lines of aptitudes are cultivated and strengthened by the life of sport as well as by the more serious forms of emulative life. Strategy or cunning is an element invariably present in games, as also in warlike pursuits and in the chase. In all of these employments strategy tends to develop into finesse and chicanery. Chicanery, falsehood, browbeating, hold a well-secured place in the method of procedure of any athletic contest and in games generally. The habitual employment of an umpire, and the minute technical regulations governing the limits and details of permissible fraud and strategic advantage, sufficiently attest the fact that fraudulent practices and attempts to overreach one's opponents are not adventitious features of the game. In the nature of the case habituation to sports should conduce to a fuller development of the aptitude for fraud; and the prevalence in the community of that predatory temperament which inclines men to sports connotes a prevalence of sharp practice and callous disregard of the interests of others, individually and collectively. Resort to fraud, in any guise and under any legitimation of law or custom, is an expression of a narrowly self-regarding habit of mind. It is needless to dwell at any length on the economic value of this feature of the sporting character.

In this connection it is to be noted that the most obvious characteristic of the physiognomy affected by athletic and other sporting men is that of an extreme astuteness. The gifts and exploits of Ulysses are scarcely second to those of Achilles, either in their substantial furtherance of the game or in the éclat which they give the astute sporting man among his associates. The pantomime of astuteness is commonly the first step in that assimilation to the professional sporting man which a youth undergoes after matriculation in any reputable school, of the secondary or the higher education, as the case may be. And the physiognomy of astuteness, as a decorative feature, never ceases to receive the thoughtful attention of men whose serious interest lies in athletic games, races, or other contests of a similar emulative nature. As a further indication of their spiritual kinship, it may be pointed out that the members of the lower delinquent class usually show this physiognomy of astuteness in a marked degree, and that they very commonly show the same histrionic exaggeration of it that is often seen in the young candidate for athletic honors. This, by the way, is the most legible mark of what is vulgarly called "toughness" in youthful aspirants for a bad name.

The astute man, it may be remarked, is of no economic value to the community—unless it be for the purpose of sharp practice in dealings with other communities. His functioning is not a furtherance of the generic life process. At its best, in its direct economic bearing, it is a conversion of the economic substance of the collectivity to a growth alien to the collective life process—very much after the analogy of what in medicine would be called a benign tumor, with some tendency to transgress the uncertain line that divides the benign from the malign growths.

The two barbarian traits, ferocity and astuteness, go to make up the predaceous temper or spiritual attitude. They are the expressions of a narrowly self-regarding habit of mind. Both are highly serviceable for individual expediency in a life looking to invidious success. Both also have a high aesthetic value. Both are fostered by the pecuniary culture. But both alike are of no use for the purposes of the collective life.

Section III

Functions of Sport

Sport As Ritual:
Interpretations from Durkheim to Goffman

SUSAN BIRRELL

Sociologists concerned with understanding the social significance of sport have proposed many theses. These have included explanations based on sport as a significant socializing agent; as an agent of social control; as an agent of assimilation or, conversely, of minority group identification and resistance to assimilation (cf. Pooley); and as a provider of controlled excitement in relatively unexciting societies (Elias and Dunning). Numerous psychological theories have also been advanced by sport psychologists and social psychologists.

Logical and persuasive as these theses are, this paper focuses instead on the thesis that sport can be understood as a significant aspect of society because of the ritualistic overtones it possesses. The thesis of sport as ritual is satisfying for several reasons. First, some historians feel the roots of many modern day sports can be found in the ritualistic practices associated with fertility festivals and other religious ceremonies (Henderson; Simri). In some important way, then, sport is a legacy of ritual. Over time, the religious *meaning* of sporting activities may have been lost, yet the *form* of those activities remains, ready to take on new meanings. Thus it is possible that conceptualizing sport as a ritual may help to establish the historic continuity of the meaning of sport in society.

Second, emphasizing the ritual power of sport draws attention to an explanation of sport which takes into account both the personal gratification obtained by the individual through sport involvement and the social needs of the community. Specifically, when one utilizes a framework derived from Durkheim, as is suggested below, one can readily understand the encompassing power of sport to join together the individual and the community for the mutual benefit of both.

Section III: Functions of Sport

Finally, strong theoretical traditions dealing with the nature and significance of ritual exist in the sociological, anthropological, and social psychological literature. These can profitably be utilized to provide a respectable base from which to generate ideas about the social significance of sport as ritual.

Anthropologists and sociologists interested in play and sport certainly have not ignored the potential of using theories of ritual to understand these phenomena. Beginning with Huizinga, whose *Homo Ludens* contains the strong suggestion that play and ritual grow together as dual focuses of the same process, those who study play and sport have assumed a fundamental relationship between those activities and the ritual process. It is significant that a major thrust of research papers and theoretical discussions fostered by The Association for the Anthropological Study of Play concerns the relationship of play and ritual (see e.g., *TAASP Newsletter*). Moreover, several highly suggestive studies attest to the potential of using models of ritual to understand sport (e.g., Cheska; Deegan and Stein; Fiske). However, any convincing argument about the usefulness of understanding sport as a social phenomenon with ritualistic overtones is ultimately dependent on establishing logical connections to respectable theories of ritual, the persuasiveness of the theory of social ritual involved, and the ability of that theory to encompass the phenomenon of sport within its explanatory structure. Not all discussions of sport as ritual have fully developed the theoretical rationale that underlies their interpretation.

The argument developed in this paper is that sport is a significant modern day ritual which can most profitably be analyzed by joining together Émile Durkheim's social theory of religion with Erving Goffman's ideas of everyday life interaction rituals as significant social ceremonies. As the argument unfolds it will be discovered that Goffman is an important heir to the Durkheimian tradition whose specific contribution is the study of everyday life as a ritual: a highly significant theoretical extension of the function ritual behavior plays in the preservation of moral order. Furthermore, it will be suggested that sport as ritual can be examined from at least two vantage points: as a social situation during which individuals engaged in problematic and consequential action communicate to one another that they understand the ideal demands their roles place on them, agree with the values assumed by those ideals, and are capable of fulfilling role expectations; and as a social ceremony structurally capable of fulfilling social functions comparable to those of religious ceremonies, specifically by serving as an arena for the creation of symbolic leaders and the display of heroic action. Both aspects serve the same purpose: reaffirming the values of the social order.

RITUALS AND SYMBOLIC SYSTEMS

The Durkheimain Tradition

The conceptual definition of *ritual*, and the related concept *symbolic system*, on which this discussion of sport is based, are most familiar from Durkheim's *The Elementary Forms of the Religious Life* where he presented his thesis concerning religion as a social rather than psychological experience. While. Durkheim's treatment is perhaps the most integrated and complete, and certainly the best known, he was not the only scholar of his time to propound that thesis. Numa-Denys Fustel de Coulanges, an influential teacher of Durkheim, presented the thesis in less developed form in his work *The Ancient City*. Fustel argued that the social organization of Greek and Roman civilizations made little sense to the modern scholar unless they were understood as civic manifestations of religion. Using the *polis* as focal point, he delineated the nature of the intricate relationship between community and religion.

W. Robertson Smith, the Scottish anthropologist, presented a similar argument in his description of the Semite communities, and A. R. Radcliffe Brown's study of Andaaman Islanders led to the conclusion that: "…Rites can therefore be shown to have a specific social function when, and to the extent that, they have for their effect to regulate, maintain and transmit from one generation to another sentiments on which the constitution of the society depends" (66).

However, with the publication of *Elementary Forms*, the thesis was presented in its most complete form. Durkheim's strategy was to select "the most primitive and simple religion which is actually known" (13) as a model for understanding the nature of the religious in its most basic form. Deciding that totemism was the most elementary form extant, Durkheim made use of field studies of the totemic religions of the Australian Aborigines.

On the basis of his secondary analysis, Durkheim developed his ideas about religion. To Durkheim, the religious process is divided into two aspects: beliefs and rites. Beliefs are "states of opinion, and consist is representations" (51) while rites are "determined modes of action" (51).

According to Durkheim, all religious beliefs are founded on the fundamental classification of things as either *profane* or *sacred*. Profane things are the things of everyday existence. Sacred things are special things, protected, isolated, separated, prohibited, inaccessible, apart from the mundane world: they are invested with special properties.

Although Durkheim argues that the two categories exist *a priori*, the contents of the categories are culturally designated and are not the result of a priori characteristics of the things themselves. For example, in a non-Christian society, a cross is merely two crossed sticks and therefore. as profane as any two sticks. But in Christian communities, the cross carries a meaning beyond its own physical characteristics. It is encoded with meaning and treated as a sacred thing.

Thus the sacred may be more than the sacred idea itself (i.e., the belief in a Christian saviour) but usually includes symbols or representations of that special thing (i.e., the cross) which come to be treated as sacred. Symbols are, simply, things which stand for other abstractions. They are vehicles encoded with meanings, which serve as the basic units of meaning in rituals.

According to Durkheim, rituals are "rules of conduct which prescribe how a man should comport himself in the presence of…sacred objects" or their representations (56). Through ritual treatment of symbols of the sacred, the individual places self in respectful relationship to sacred things. Gradually, rituals become stylized patterns through which individuals express their respectful relationship to those objects or values designated as special or sacred.

Rituals are the *dynamics* of a process which joins together a system based on symbols. Durkheim conceives of this symbolic system as having three elements (see Figure 1). One element of the model is the individual member of a tribe or community. A second element is the moral order of the community, or the sacred: the values which are special to the community and worthy of respect and reverence. In other contexts this might be recognized as ideology. The third element is the symbol, a representation of the sacred which mediates between the individual and the moral order. Because it is difficult for the individual to pay homage to the abstract principle which constitutes the sacred, the symbol is a crucial element in the system. Through their treatment of the symbol, the individuals indicate affirmation for the abstract values for which it stands. Moreover, the symbol is a "collective representation" because it serves as a concrete reminder of the values of the community to which all individuals must subscribe and through which they maintain their community identity.

Transitions to Secular Rituals

Durkheim's conclusion about religion is that it is "an eminently collective thing" (63) and his definition of religion reflects that view: "A religion is a unified system of beliefs and practices relative to sacred things, that is to say, things set apart and forbidden—beliefs and practices which unites into one single moral community called a Church, all those who adhere to them" (62).

While Durkheim ostensibly focused attention on religious rituals, he fully realized that the principles he outlined were by no means confined to explaining phenomena labeled as religious. Clearly he viewed his thesis as a much more general one capable of explaining a class of phenomena of which religious phenomena were only one example. Thus, one of Durkheim's most significant contributions to social science is his thesis that religion must not be understood as a theological, philosophical, or psychological phenomenon, but as an experience which is eminently *social* in nature. The content of the symbolic system, the symbols venerated, the values and beliefs represented, all of these are relatively insignificant in relation to the fact that the ritual process itself serves to join the individual to a community of moral order. The *content* is not significant sociologically, but the *process* and the ceremonial effect are of profound significance.

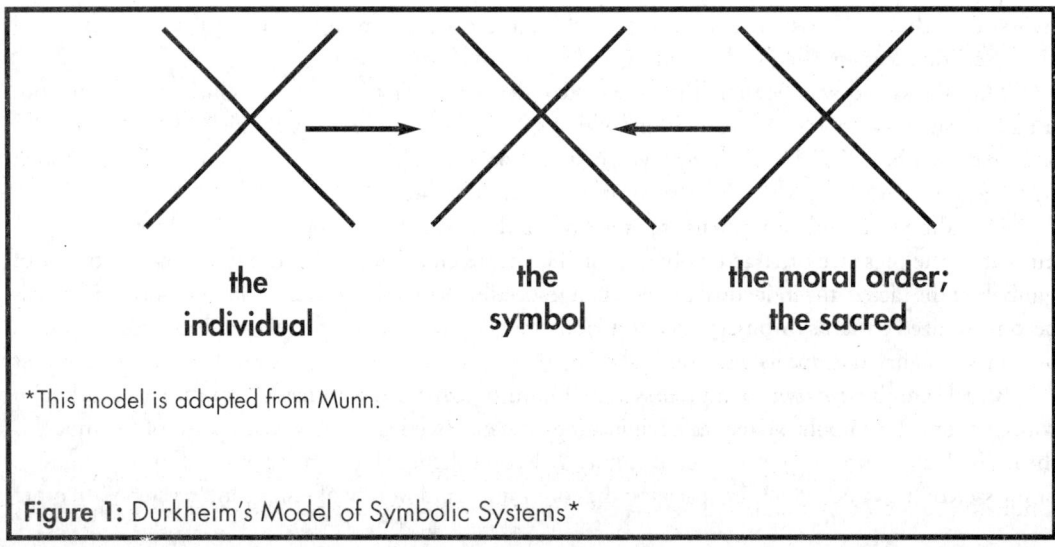

*This model is adapted from Munn.

Figure 1: Durkheim's Model of Symbolic Systems*

Several scholars have built on Durkheim's general theory of ritual, emphasizing the preeminence of secular rituals. As part of his study of Yankee City, W Lloyd Warner analyzed the Memorial Day celebration as An American Sacred Ceremony. Warner conceived of Memorial Day as both a sacred and a secular ceremony. His thesis was that:

> ...Memorial Day ceremonies and subsidiary rites (such as those of Armistice or Veterans' Day) of today, yesterday, and tomorrow are rituals of a sacred symbol system which functions periodically to unify the whole community, with its conflicting symbols and its opposing, autonomous churches and associations. It is contended here that in the Memorial Day ceremonies the anxieties which man has about death are confronted with a system of sacred beliefs about death which gives the individuals involved and the collectivity of individuals a feeling of well-being (8).

In the same year, Shils and Young's essay "The Meaning of the Coronation" appeared. Steeped in the Durkheimian tradition, Shils and Young argued

> ...the Coronation was the ceremonial occasion for the affirmation of the moral values by which the society lives. It was an act of national communion...

> The Coronation is exactly this kind of ceremonial in which the society reaffirms the moral values which constitute it as a society and renews its devotion to those values by an act of communion (67).

Both Warner and Shils and Young expand Durkheim's thesis to include secular aspects of ceremonies. However, it was left to Erving Goffman to take the thesis one step further and examine the interactions of everyday life as rituals of equal moral significance.

Goffman and Interaction Ritual

One of the most significant and overlooked theoretical contributions made by Erving Goffman is his extension of Durkheim's ideas as clues for understanding the maintenance of social order. In a number of places throughout his work, Goffman acknowledges his debts to Durkheim and even makes explicit his intention to apply Durkheim's ideas to the study of everyday life. For example, in "The Nature of Deference and Demeanor" he states:

> In this paper I want to explore some of the senses in which the person in our urban secular world is allotted a kind of sacredness that is displayed and confirmed by symbolic acts. An attempt will be made to build a conceptual scaffold by stretching and twisting some common anthropological terms. This will be used to support two concepts which I think are central to this area: deference and demeanor. Through these reformulations I will try to show that a version of Durkheim's social psychology can be effective in modern dress (c, 473).

In Durkheimian fashion, Goffman defines ritual as an activity which "represents a way in which the individual must guard and design the symbolic implications of his acts while in the immediate presence of an object that has special value for him" (b, 478; h, 62; k, 69). He also calls this, in true Goffman fashion, a "situated social fuss."

But unlike Durkheim, Goffman looks for ritual not in the eventful, exciting, or spectacular, but in the every minute, everyday-life interactions that comprise the bulk of social experience. To Goffman, those "objects that have special value" are not only crosses and waterholes and flags but simply—and profoundly—the self and the other in everyday interaction. Goffman calls the process of communicating respect for the self and other the rituals of *demeanor* and *deference* respectively. These are ritually important because interacting individuals continually take on the responsibility of embodying important social roles. They attempt to portray the ideal qualities demanded of them in these roles—the loyal friend, the faithful lover, the loving parent, the efficient secretary, the dedicated scholar, the tough athlete. Through the idealization of performance, Goffman says, individuals are not attempting in a deceitful way to claim values for themselves that they do not in fact possess. They are attempting to demonstrate through their selves the ideal role characteristics valued by society. Through their behavior, they are reaffirming significant values of the moral order.

This reaffirmation of values takes place within the context of several specific forms of ritual delineated by Goffman with an eye toward the Durkheimian tradition. Communicating respect for the self, through rituals of demeanor, includes such practices as showing self-respect (b, 215), maintaining poise (a, 275; b, 215; d, 103), and demonstrating skills of impression management or facework (b, 216; e, 208). Communicating respect for others, through rituals of deference, hinges on identificatory sympathy (h, 66), presentational deference (c, 485), the rule of considerateness (b, 215), and giving face when others inadvertently lose theirs (b, 215). Together, rituals of demeanor and deference comprise *positive rituals*, a term clearly adopted from Durkheim by Goffman (h) to indicate rituals which affirm the sacred qualities of objects.

These positive rituals are complemented by *negative rituals* which dictate behaviors required to avoid contaminating the sacred (h). These interdictions or avoidance behaviors occur when some threat to demeanor or deference is perceived. In Goffman's terms, these negative rituals can be *preventive practices* (e, 13) which occur in order to avoid such threats becoming reality and *remedial practices* (h, 64; g, 365) used to restore order when profanation has inadvertently taken place. Preventive practices include exploratory communication (a, 333), overplay gloss (i, 134–5), circumspection gloss (i, 132), referential avoidance (c, 482), and no contest signs (i, 124). Remedial practices include the rule of open laughter (j, 372) and a six move remedial process: challenge, offering, remedy, relief, appreciation, and minimization (b, 220; i, 140–3; l, 265).

In summary, in many essays Goffman concerns himself with the rituals of everyday interaction which celebrate the self and the other as significant moral beings. Clearly, Goffman's ideas of the significance of individuals in interaction build on Durkheim's model of religion. Figure 2 indicates that the concrete symbol within which societal values are encoded may very well take human form. In that special case, meanings are not encoded but embodied. Indeed, in Goffman's elaboration of Durkheim every individual is a symbol; every individual is a collective representation of moral values; every individual is sacred. Goffman is quite explicit about this in a number of places. For example, in his dissertation, he states:

> For the actor, others may come to be seen as sacred objects. The social attributes of recipients must be constantly honored; where these attributes have been dishonored, propitiation must follow. The actor must conduct himself with great ritual care....(a, 103).

> ...persons are ritually delicate objects which must be treated with care, with ceremonial offerings and propitiations (a, 175).

A few years later, in his essay on "The Nature of Deference and Demeanor," he reminds the reader of the Durkheimian heritage of his thesis by stating:

> In this paper I have suggested that Durkheimian notions about primitive religion can be translated into concepts of deference and demeanor and that these concepts help us to grasp some aspects of urban secular living. The implication is that in one sense this secular world is not so irreligious as we might think. Many gods have been done away with, but the individual himself stubbornly remains as a deity of considerable importance. He walks with some dignity and is the recipient of many little offerings. He is jealous of the worship due him, yet, approached in the right spirit, he is ready to forgive those who may have offended him. Because of their status relative to his, some persons will find him contaminating while others will find they contaminate him, in either case finding that they must treat him with ritual care. Perhaps the individual is so viable a god because he can actually understand the ceremonial significance of the way he is treated, and quite on his own can respond dramatically to what is proffered him. In contacts between such deities there is no need for middlemen; each of these gods is able to serve as his own priest (c, 499).

With such an undeniable moral current running throughout his work, it is difficult to understand the critiques of Goffman as a cynical purveyor of the alienation of man in society. Every encounter is conceived as a statement of moral reaffirmation.

Goffman's extension of the Durkheim tradition makes two major contributions. First, it extends the boundaries of ritual to include everyday life. Moreover, as Luckmann also contends, not only do interactions serve as the reaffirmation of societal values, they serve to recreate those values in negotiation. Thus encounters play a dynamic and not a passive part in the creation of the moral order.

The second contribution of Goffman is the emphasis on the individual as sacred. Interaction rituals in Goffman's work are interpersonal rituals, and the values reaffirmed are those related to the worth of individuals in the social order.

Section III: Functions of Sport

SPORT AS RITUAL

The Individual As Sacred: The Hero

Two ideas of ritual are at work here. One, the Durkheimian, focuses on the eventful, the exciting, the relatively infrequent homage paid to sacred values through ceremonial treatment. Such homage serves as a community act, i.e., an act which reaffirms the values which unite the community. The other, the Goffmanesque, focuses on the mundane, the trite, the commonplace everyday homage paid to idealized role performances presented in everyday interaction, i.e., the way actors perform their roles and react to others in theirs. This process represents a more private act, yet it is still an act of reaffirmation of values of significance to the community.

These two ideas are united in the concept of the individual in special situations, i.e., the hero as an exemplary interactant in social ceremonies. There are several developmental threads joined in this idea.

Weber's concept of *charisma* provides a link between Durkheim's concept of the sacred and Goffman's concept of character display. In its pure form, charisma is

> a certain quality of an individual personality by virtue of which he is set apart from ordinary men and treated as endowed with supernatural, superhuman, or at least specifically exceptional powers or qualities. These are such as are not accessible to the ordinary person, but are regarded as of divine origin or as exemplary, and on the basis of them the individual concerned is treated as a leader (358–9).

Clearly the individual with charisma approaches what Durkheim means by designation of sacred: "set apart" "exceptional" "not accessible to the ordinary person" "exemplary."

Bendix notes that charisma "depend(s) on a belief in concrete persons whose authority is regarded as sacred and to whom followers or subjects feel bound in religious reverence and duty" (quoted in Nisbet, 255). Nisbet continues that it is through its qualities as sacred that charisma "becomes a major part of social and political systems" (255).

From these comments, one can see that Weber's conceptualization of the charismatic leader as mediator between individual men and the moral order furnishes a direct line between Durkheim's notion of the symbol or emblem as mediator between the individual and the social order and Goffman's conceptualization of the individual as a symbol of the moral order. A further step is taken with the introduction of Klapp's concept of symbolic leaders and his thesis of the dialectic origin of heroism.

Klapp focuses on the modern day celebrity and the enigmatic process through which the celebrity emerges. Klapp conceives of the symbolic leader as "an emergent phenomenon" (32), born out of the process of interaction. He identifies seven steps in the process which generally seems to entail an almost serendipitous discovery of an image or attitude that strikes a responsive chord in the audience. From the first stage the leader and the audience embark on a dialectic in which the leader responds to the reactions to his presented self by altering his image to be congruent with the audience demands. Thus by a process of negotiation, a celebrity is born.

Particularly important for the creation of symbolic leaders is the dramatic encounter: "The very essence of drama—the high point of its most important scenes—is usually a confrontation in which parties are thrown on their mettle, reveal and expose themselves, drop their defenses, call on their personal resources to meet a crisis" (70). This concept is not only labeled in Goffman-like manner, but is conceptually similar to what Goffman discusses as action situations.

Luckmann's concern with "the fate of the individual in modern society" (12) follows in a direct line from Durkheim's like concerns, and like Durkheim, Luckmann looks for understanding in the sociology of religion. Luckmann sees his work as an extension of the Durkheimian tradition; it also has much in common with the central thesis offered by Goffman in his writings about interaction rituals.

Both Durkheim and Luckmann can be approached through their different interpretations of the basic model presented in Figure 1 for both are concerned with the interrelationships of the three aspects of the symbolic system: the individual, the social order, and the symbolic order, or religion. But where Durkheim conceptualizes the symbolic order as a mediating force between the individual and the moral order, Luckmann sees the moral order, or world view, as the ultimate construction of individuals.

There are several elaborations of Durkheim here. One is that the interaction itself is symbolic, in the sense that meanings are conveyed through symbolic communications. Thus the symbolic order is both the construction of the social order and the tool or method of that construction. A second idea is that the symbolic order expands to become the social order, for the social order is itself constructed through the manipulation of symbols and meanings by individuals. Important here is the notion of the history of the individual in the company of others. The expectations of his behavior are based on his history of interactions with others to which he is accountable. His behavior, his Self as Luckmann refers to it (Goffman would say "face"), has been created through a symbolic interchange which is religious in nature, and his behavior, restricted by historical expectations and the feedback of others, becomes a part of the moral order.

The final idea is that of the interchange of the social past with the constructed present. Luckmann states that, empirically, man is born into a social order (a culture) which restricts the meanings he can manufacture for his own actions and those of others. On this point, a basic difference between Luckmann and Durkheim emerges. Where Durkheim implies a mediation through symbols between the individual and the moral order, he has also implied a more static model than Luckmann proposes. Luckmann's model pays attention to the moderate state of flux which surrounds individuals by explicitly attending to the active part they play in reasserting or reconstructing the moral order.

This distinction is carried out to a lesser extent through their different conceptualizations of the sacred and the profane. Durkheim sees the categories (structurally) as existing *a priori* while the contents are culturally designated. The idea of separation is a significant one which is carried out through attitudes or actions which indicate deference and respect. But Luckmann speaks of the sacred and profane "uncategorically" by implying that within the hierarchy of meanings which individuals construct, the notions of sacred and profane are located. Thus the profane is a concrete and unproblematic level of understanding while the transcendent world order, or cosmos, is sacred or religious in nature.

Section III: Functions of Sport

Like Klapp's more popular analysis, Luckmann describes the dialectical nature of the creation of the self, but Luckmann emphasizes the process as a fundamentally religious process. Moreover, Luckmann's thesis clearly unifies what Hook perceived as two divergent forces: in Luckmann's thesis, man is both the symbol and the creator of his own history.

Another important variation on Durkheim's thesis expounded by Luckmann is closely related to Goffman's perspective. Here a purely functionalist interpretation of religion is supplemented by tenets of symbolic interactionism, specifically the creative potential of the individual as interactant in shaping the moral order. Goffman's ideas about the rituals of interaction provide further insight into the scope of the thesis.

Goffman's Concept of Character

Goffman's extension of these notions of the hero emanates from his concept of exaggerated rituals or special situations in which the moral statements generated through interaction take on a public, generalizable, and dramatic nature. Goffman believes that generally individuals try to minimize unpleasantness and the possibility of dysphoric, disruptive interaction (Birrell, b). Individuals try to avoid embarrassment and negative experience. But in some cases, some individuals approach these potential situations with relish. In "Where the Action Is" Goffman labels these situations *action situations*, and he defines them as fateful, that is, situations which are both problematic (the outcome is uncertain) and consequential (the outcome will have an impact on future events). Some individuals willingly and willfully seek out these risky situations. Moreover, only in such situations can *character* be demonstrated.

Character is an exaggerated portrayal of demeanor. It is an individual's response to action situations and entails "capacities for standing correct and steady in the face of sudden pressure" (f, 217). Goffman notes, "they do not specify the *activity* of the individual but how he will *manage* himself in this activity" (f, 217).

In action situations, when the interaction ritual is public, the actor generates character which reflects not only on self but has social significance because it reflects the values of the community. Such a situation exists in sporting contests witnessed by the public.

In many situations, as in sport, assessment of character focuses on characteristics highly prized in the particular setting. Goffman distinguishes four motifs around which character contests in North America might revolve: courage, gameness, integrity, and composure. From Goffman's definitions one can immediately perceive their ready applicability to sport.

> *courage*—the capacity to envisage immediate danger and yet proceed with the course of action that brings the danger on (218).
> *gameness*—the capacity to stick to a line of activity and to continue to pour all effort into it regardless of set-backs, pain, or fatigue (219).
> *integrity*—the propensity to resist temptation in situations where there would be much profit and some impunity in departing momentarily from moral standards (219).
> *composure*—self-control, self-possession, or poise (222).

The social significance of the demonstration of these and other valued qualities lies in society's understanding of them as inherently moral and worthy of deep respect. Goffman notes that

> Properties of character…are always judged from a moral perspective, simply because a capacity for mobilizing oneself for the moment is always subjected to social evaluation…character traits tend to be evaluated in the extremes, referring to failures in no way expected or successes out of the ordinary; mere conformance with usual standards is not at issue (218).

Moreover, the display of character not only makes a statement about the individual, but about the sanctity with which the abstract values he embodies should be treated. There is no question about the heritage of this idea in Goffman's work:

> To the degree that a performance highlights the common official values of the society in which it occurs, we may look upon it, in the manner of Durkheim and Radcliffe-Brown, as a ceremony—as an expressive rejuvenation and reaffirmation of the moral values of the community. Furthermore, insofar as the expressive bias of performances comes to be accepted as reality, then that which is accepted at the moment as reality will have some of the characteristics of a celebration (e, 35).

The following examples from the sport world are intended to substantiate the thesis that in sport, respectable qualities are demonstrated in dramatic and public situations, and that those demonstrations of character serve a dual purpose of establishing the character of the athlete and reaffirming the validity of the moral attributes the individual displays.

Courage

Because of the physical nature inherent in sport, it is not surprising that many sports have as their central feature the demonstration of physical courage. The most prominent examples are those sports in which death is a possible consequence. Bullfighting, if one considers it a sport, provides an excellent example, for the ethic of the bullfight demands that the matador take tremendous chances in order to prove his worth to the crowd. While generally the crowd is insatiable in its demands for danger (Zurcher and Meadow), some matadors display so much courage that the crowd begs them to be more careful. Such was the case with El Cordobes, the spectacular Spanish bullfighter, who demonstrated his courage by breaking into short pieces the barbed sticks (*banderillas*) the matador drives into the shoulders of the bull; by fighting in the center of the ring furthest from help, should he require it; by leaping over the back of the bull as it charged; and, on one fateful occasion, by refusing to cancel a fight although the sand in the stadium was soaked with rain, leaving him with poor footing.

Mountain and rock climbing and their kindred pursuits furnish another example. Along with the more traditional accounts (Hilary; Houston and Bates) of such daring, the public has recently been treated to a documentary relating one man's attempt to ski down Mt. Everest and a public drama in which a rock climber scaled the walls of the World Trade Center in New York City (Moses).

Auto racing is another world in which courage is prized. Drivers believe that someone who cannot demonstrate a minimal amount of courage, here synonymous with speed, does not have the character to compete with the other racers. Richard Petty illustrates this opinion when he acknowledges that

> I've drafted cars that slowed down on me, and I've had to shove them a spell to get going better. And a bunch of times I've come up behind somebody I've lapped maybe 10 or 15 times, and deliberately tapped him or maybe run him down off the track because he didn't belong out there racing (quoted in Libby, 62).

Much prestige or honor in football is related to how well one can demonstrate physical courage to the point of being macho, according to many (Meggysey; Shaw). Shaw claimed that at the University of Texas, a distinction was drawn between the hitters and the quitters. They even had a motto along this line: "if you're putting out you don't get hurt." Among hockey players, Faulkner (298) has noted a similar pattern: players use violence as a "presentational resource" for the display of honorable, respectable occupational behavior.

Hubert Green has shown that character based on courage can be demonstrated in the rather unlikely setting of a professional golf match. While leading by one stroke in the U.S. Open in 1977, Green was informed that the FBI had received word of a death threat against his life. Green decided to continue play. He finished the last three holes under police and FBI surveillance and won the Open title. As Dan Jenkins, writing for *Sports Illustrated*, put it "…now we know a bit more about his competitiveness as a golfer and an awful lot more about his nerve and his heart" (19).

Final examples might be drawn from the worlds of gambling. Scott states that bettors at a thoroughbred race track who bet the favorite are referred to with disrespect as "chalk-eaters" because they lack the courage to put their financial self on the line. Boyd notes that poker players classify one another as "tighties" or "loosies" according to the degree of chance they are willing to take; only the loosies are capable of displaying character, for only they are taking the big risks. Geertz discovered the same principle at work in the Balinesian cock fights. Geertz labeled the phenomenon "deep play," and described a sport setting in which it is customary to bet far more than one can afford to lose. According to Geertz's account, this system produces many poor but honorable Balinesians.

Gameness

Gameness is related to courage for it, too, represents overcoming physical odds in order to compete honorably. In sport, gameness means perseverance and spunk, and it is illustrated by cases in which the athlete has failed to live up to expectations of skill yet struggles valiantly to finish the task. To this athlete—the runner who has been hopelessly lapped by the competition or the gymnast who falls several times in one routine—the audience awards praise for gameness and applauds with sympathy and encouragement. The classic example concerns the marathon runner in the 1972 Olympics who struggled on to finish the race—but not until after the closing ceremonies had taken place.

No doubt because of the heavy physical punishment involved, boxing furnishes a setting for many examples of gameness related to perseverance (Weinberg and Arond).

It is the demonstration of this quality that turns the final, painful scene in *Rocky* to a heroic battle. "Ain't gonna be no rematch" says the bloodied defender Apollo Creed. "Don't want one," replies Rocky who has proved to himself that, at least once in his life, he was able "to go the distance." On a smaller scale, Rau reported a Golden Gloves welterweight fight in which the loser was a spunky boy whom Rau had pulled out of a car wreck ten hours before. The match was so tough that both boxers received standing ovations from the crowd. X-rays later showed that the boy had fractured a vertebra during the auto accident.

Collins and Lapierre cite another extraordinary example of gameness. When El Cordobes, the idol of the bullring, was almost fatally gored during a fight, the crowd responded "with a waving field of white handkerchiefs, beseeching (the bull's) ears for the matador who now lay unconscious on an operating table while a surgeon struggled to save his life" (313). Collins and Lapierre note: "It was an extraordinary gesture because tradition of the bullring demands that its trophies be awarded only to a matador who has completed his task by killing his bulls" (315). El Cordobes, who had proven his courage and composure time after time, was rewarded here for his gameness.

Other examples of perseverance include the crosscountry skier who finished his race in the 1976 Olympics on only one ski; Jim Ryun getting up to finish the 1,500 meters after being knocked off balance during the 1968 Olympics; and the legendary refusal of athletes like Dave Cowens and Pete Rose to give less than 100 percent in any contest, regardless of the score.

In many sports, as in other realms of life, the ability to come back after a serious injury can generate respect for an individual. Few could match the example set by Nicki Lauda during the 1976 Grand Prix season. Involved in a fiery accident in Nurhurgring, Germany, Lauda was given the last rites. Not only did he survive, but six weeks later he returned to the racing circuit wearing a flameproof mask to protect his scarred face and challenged James Hunt for the lead in the Grand Prix standings. There are some apparently who feel Janet Guthrie's quest for respect from other drivers will not be fulfilled until she has survived and bounced back from a serious accident like Lauda's.

> There are some men here who secretly may be hoping that Janet Guthrie does not return, that her car hits another machine and then the wall as Tom Sneva's car did two years ago, that it runs into a stalled racer on the track and explodes, as Mike Mosley's did in 1971, or that it loses a wheel and spins wildly out of control, as Al Unser's did in 1968. Then they will wait to see if Guthrie comes back, as Sneva and Mosley and Unser have many times since their brushes with instant immolation. Only then, the hard-liners say will she have proved that she belongs here with the big boys.(Abel, 49).

Integrity

Integrity is expected in sport, for without cooperative agreement to obey the rules and refrain from self-serving cheating, sport cannot continue; its nature is violated. Yet acts of integrity can be magnified in sport to provide a true test of character. The moral strength to follow the correct path when easier routes are available is constantly demanded of those who put themselves on the line in sport, for sport is an activity in which obstacles are purposely planted before one so that his or her reactions may be tested.

Goffman specifies two forms of integrity: self-discipline and gallantry. By *self-discipline* he means "the capacity to refrain from excessive involvement in the easy pleasures…" (f, 220). The self-discipline required try sport is such a catch word that it hardly needs to be documented. The most familiar examples center around the pain of training and the Spartan existence and self-denial necessary to shape a championship athlete. This form of physical self-discipline is such a commonplace in sport that it does not furnish as striking a basis for character display as do other aspects. Physical self-discipline is taken for granted in sport; it is expected of all top-calibre athletes; it is part of the bargain they make in their pursuit of physical excellence.

Moral self-discipline is another story. In some cases, this form of self-discipline can mean accepting one's defeat without excuses. Thus one writer was moved to commend Jimmy Connors for his restraint when, having lost two important tennis matches, he refrained from mentioning to the press that he was preoccupied with his father's serious illness ("A Man for A' That," 10).

Goffman defines *gallantry* as "the capacity to maintain the forms of courtesy when the forms are full of substance" (f, 220), i.e., when they really matter. In sport, this quality is often referred to as sportsmanship. Sportsmanship is a trait of moral character with a historical tie to social class and to sports whose clientele was drawn historically from the elite. In England during the middle of the nineteenth century, for instance, when football was the domain of the upper classes, umpires or referees were "unheard of and unnecessary (McIntosh). A gentlemanly code of conduct was the norm and a sportsman was quick to acknowledge whatever unintentional fouls or violations he had committed, apologize to his opponent, and make restitution.

In a more modern example, Kroll has suggested that sportsmanship, indeed any moral decision, matters only when the stakes are highest, i.e., when the decision could determine the outcome of the match. It is demonstrated whenever a player calls an undetectable but game-important foul on himself or when a player who has benefitted from an erroneous call restores the sporting balance, as in tennis when a player hits the next ball out of bounds after the lineman has wrongly called a point in her favor. More dramatic instances are exemplified by Lutz Long helping Jesse Owens qualify in the long jump in the 1936 Olympics, when Long knew that Owens was his toughest challenger (and indeed Owens went on to win the gold, Long the silver). (Another example is found in *Fair Play*, 4.)

Composure

Composure is a form of character emphasizing "self-control, self-possession, or poise." According to Goffman, composure has a "behavioral side, the capacity to execute physical tasks in a concerted, smooth, self-controlled fashion under fateful circumstances" (f, 222–3) and "an affective side, the emotional self-control required in dealing with others" (f, 224). Of all forms of character display, Goffman considers composure the most significant because the individual's capacity as a competent interactant is revealed in his or her ability to maintain proper demeanor, particularly in trying situations.

Goffman specifies three forms that composure may take: presence of mind, dignity, and stage confidence. Presence of mind, or mental calmness, is a prerequisite for many sports, particularly those self-paced tasks in which steadiness is necessary. Discussing this topic, the silver medalist in the 1976 Olympics small-bore, three-position rifle shooting competition Margaret Murdock stated:

> My emotional control is based on anticipation…I think out how I'm going to react, how I'm going to resist extraneous thoughts, how I'm going to deal with somebody coming up and telling me I'm behind or ahead, I prepare for all this, so the adrenalin doesn't go up and I stop thinking. One or two bad shots, and you're out of it (quoted in Fimrite).

Gymnasts, particularly those who compete on the balanced beam, experience the same thing (Birrell, a).

A second aspect of composure and one particularly important in sport is the demonstration of dignity. *Dignity* is a bodily form of composure which features "the capacity to sustain one's bodily decorum…" (f, 225). To exemplify this aspect of composure Goffman chooses surfing:

> Physical aplomb and dignity of upright posture must be maintained on a flat narrow board against rumbling forces that press to the limit the human capacity for this kind of bodily self-control. Here the maintenance of physical control is not merely a condition of effective performance but a central purpose of it (f, 226).

Of course all sports require some degree of dignity, or physical control; the term "natural athlete" seems to express the envy of those who must work hard at maintaining dignity. Goffman mentions skiers as a sport group particularly prone to displays of—or lack of—dignity.

Yet it is only in the fan-packed arena that the two aspects of composure discussed—presence of mind and dignity—are combined with and intensified by the final form of composure: *stage confidence*. Only when an individual puts self on the line in a situation of heightened emotional stress is character truly tested. Thus weekend skiing presents a challenge to one's physical control, but skiing for an Olympic gold medal intensifies the challenge, as this account of Franz Klammer's bid for the downhill title in 1976 demonstrates.

> Pressure defines the essential nature of athletic heroism. If an athlete cannot contend with it, neither strength nor skill will avail him, and few athletes have borne a greater burden of pressure than the 22-year-old Austrian skier Franz Klammer in the Winter Olympic Games….Klammer had drawn starting position No. 15, last among the top seeds in the downhill. All of his principal competitors had preceded him down the icy and irregular slope. The 27-year-old Swiss skier Bernhard Russi was the leader at 1:46.06.
>
> Klammer almost literally flew out of the start and careened down the hill like a bouncing ball. Still, he was .19 of a second behind Russi's pace after the first half of the run. He took even more chances in the next section but slipped farther behind the pace. In the last 1,000 meters he was confronted by the Compression, a jump followed by a dip that had proved breathtakingly dangerous to his predecessors. The Johannesweg turn lay behind that and it had already claimed

two skiers. As he ripped through this part of the course, Klammer nearly went out of control, but he regained his balance to execute the turn. Then he sailed over the last jump and sped to the finish. It was a daring run, but was it fast enough? Yes. The timer showed that Klammer had beaten Russi by .33 of a second. The mountain exploded in an avalanche of cheering (Fimrite).

Much of what is admired in sport can be summed up in one word: coolness. Scott illustrates this with some observations from the race track:

> The cool jockey can wait patiently with a horse in a pocket and get through on the inside, risking the possibility that there will be no opening. Coolness is waiting far back in the pack, risking the possibility that his horse will not 'get up' in time. Coolness is sparing the whip on a front-running horse when another animal has pressed into the lead, risking the possibility that once his horse is passed he will not get started again. All these activities are taken by observers as instances of a jockey's character. In short, moral character is coolness in risky situations (26).

Polsky observed the same coolness in the pool hall (45).

Another sport in which coolness is important is tennis, where Chris Evert plays with such presence of mind and dignity that she has been nicknamed "the ice maiden" and Bjorn Borg has been called "Ice Borg." Ironically, Evert's coolness is often held against her; she suffers particularly in comparison to the looser, less disciplined Evonne Goolagong, whose "walk-abouts" have earned her a contrasting reputation.

Coolness is important in most sports, but one would be hard put to find a group which exemplifies the demands of composure as well as gymnasts. For the gymnast, character hinges on poise, yet the gymnastics meet, by its very nature, seems designed to destroy one's composure. The irony of testing oneself to the very limit of one's ability while maintaining by face and posture the impression that one is coasting effortlessly and gracefully through a simple routine is not lost on the gymnasts. As more than one gymnast put it: "The object of gymnastics is to make something very difficult look very easy."

Cool competence is the trademark of the superior gymnast. The gymnast must give a solid performance, and her confidence in execution must be indicated by the absence of "major breaks" in the momentum of the routine as well as control over nervousness and unsteadiness. But sometimes poise is demonstrated by the gymnast's responses to problematic situations beyond her control. Bows can fall from her hair onto the mat where she must continue to perform as if its undesirable presence there is not an intrusion on her concentration; slippers can be lost during a balance beam routine leaving the gymnast with less purchase on the beam than she would desire; elaborate hairdos can become so disarranged that they hinder the sight or balance of the gymnast. Yet in all of these cases, the inconvenience must be totally ignored by the gymnast if she wishes to maintain her display of poise. In fact, kicking aside a bow or slipper or adjusting a falling hairdo are movements which the judges are likely to score as deductions from the "general impression" of the gymnast's performance.

An extreme example of character related to this sort of trying situation occurred to an injured gymnast during a meet. Because of her injury, she had an ace bandage wrapped around her knee. In the middle of her beam routine, the bandage became unwound and she finished the rest of the routine trailing the bandage. Even her dismount, which was a front somersault, she did with it flying through the air. To have touched the bandage would have permitted the judges the opportunity to deduct points under "general impression." Continuance of the routine, on the other hand, was actually quite dangerous, sparking an incredulous response from one observer "that the sport cannot make accommodations for things like that." But by continuing her performance, the gymnast demonstrated to all observing that she was a competent performer, able to maintain her composure in the face of the most unsettling challenges. Character thus has to do with keeping one's entire competitive self in order and under complete control at all times.

CONCLUSIONS

Sport has ritual significance when character based on valued social attributes is demonstrated. In such situations, the athlete is an exemplary figure who embodies the moral values of the community and thus serves as a symbol of those values. The salience of the incidents recounted here is evidenced by the very fact that they were reported by the mass media for the benefit of those who were not fortunate enough to witness the demonstrations in person. Publication of such deeds serves as institutionalized recognition that demonstration of character should be greeted with admiration, respect, and perhaps, worship.

An equally important indication of the strength of this thesis is the fact that individuals who fail to demonstrate character in sport after having made such exaggerated claims for themselves are regarded with disrespect and scorn. A dramatic example of the effects of losing character on the way in which others regard the individual can be found in this account of a young man's unsuccessful attempt to prove himself in the bullring:

> ...To Juan Horrillo, Little Almond's horns seemed wider than the branches of an almond tree....He felt he would never have the courage to confront the cow waiting for him in the ring. And yet he knew she was his to fight and kill, 'that filthy beast, before all those Palmenos with their dirty stares, looking like I would have to hang myself up on those horns before they would be happy.' Behind him, he could hear Manolo hissing, 'Go ahead, Juna, don't worry, I'll watch you.' Encouraged, he tried to go forward. But at each step, Horrillo felt his legs folding under him as though they were made of rubber. The arena began to spin around his eyes 'like a merry-go-round.' Many in the crowd sensing what they had come for, began to jeer. Still Horrillo couldn't move.
>
> 'I was paralyzed,' he could recall. 'I trembled all over. Those insults kept coming out and still I couldn't take a step. They began to throw stones and bottles at me. They started to yell *Fuera, fuera*—out, out. God, I hated it. And there was Almendrita in the middle of the ring staring at me with those murderous eyes of hers. Suddenly it happened. She came for me. I did a terrible thing then, an unforgivable thing. I dropped my muleta and ran. I ran as fast as I could for the *barrera*, as fast as I ever ran before from the Guardia Civil. When I got there, I jumped

the *barrera* and fell into the *callejon*. As I lay there, shaking, they spat on me. I could hear them all screaming, whistling. It was horrible, I don't know how long I lay there listening, but I knew one thing: for me, everything was finished. I could never put on the suit of lights again' (Collins and Lapierre, 272–3).

One can lose one's character if one loses courage. And one can also lose character by failing to display integrity or poise. Ilie Nastase, the tennis player, is an example of this form of character loss: his outrageous antics on the court have irreparably damaged his reputation. A more classic example can be found in the young boy's legendary plea to his former baseball hero, accused of throwing the 1919 World Series: "Say it isn't so, Joe." When character is so spectacularly lost, something else dies with it. If the moral order is to be preserved, those whose actions flagrantly violate the sanctity of systemic values must be regarded as villains or weaklings, just as those who spectacularly conform to moral values must be feted as heroes.

It may well be that an important aspect of the significance of sport as an arena for character lies in the fact that it is such a commonplace, everyday activity. It is true that in extraordinary cases an athlete comes to have enduring symbolic value; his or her deeds may become the basis of legends and his or her memory may be institutionally enshrined. However, an added significance of many of the examples offered above is the transient nature of the tales. The names may soon be forgotten, perhaps are never known, but the substance of the achievement has served its purpose by providing one of an endless number of reaffirmations of cultural values. Therefore it is the commonplace nature of sport that is one of the most significant attributes: on any given day people can approach the ballpark and witness not only an exciting, sport event, but also the display of attributes of character unseen in other areas of life.

Demonstration of character can be understood as something whose significance flows beyond the respect awarded to individuals by knowing peers—teammates and opponents. Character display has a more generalizable, public, and ceremonial significance. Thus the so-called "hero-worship" of athletes should not be regarded disparagingly as evidence of modern man's replacement of religious ideals with secular or even heathen images. The shift does not mark a fundamental change in social values but merely a substitution of the vessel in which they are contained.

Sport As Escape

Jeffrey O. Segrave

One of the sources of sport's enormous appeal is that it provides an escape, a brief and often intoxicating respite from the complexities and confusion of everyday life. The eminent social critic Christopher Lasch (1979), in fact, suggests, "Among the activities through which men seek release from everyday life, games offer in many ways the purest form of escape" (p. 100). To Murray Ross (1971), the great charm of sport is that it specifically "seeks to eliminate any reference to that bigger, more disturbing, more real world it has left behind" (p. 31). In other words, sport operates as an escape valve, a sort of symbolic refuge, one that takes us away from quotidian drudgery and boredom and allows us to forget the woes and turmoil of our daily existence: or as John Updike (1971) once put it, "Where any game is being played, a hedge exists against fury" (p. 115).

Americans embrace sport in much the same way as they embrace Disneyland, and I suspect for many of the same reasons. Like some of the rudimentary drama found in theater or even in the movies, sport and Disneyland offer familiar themes and plots, type characters, heroic and comic action, and a seemingly endless supply of new and unpredictable variations of each. No wonder the winning quarterback in the annual Super Bowl responds to the question, "What are you going to do now?" with the now highly predictable answer, "I'm going to Disneyland." The marriage of sport and Disneyland is perfect: Both offer a kind of theater of the fantastic.

Of course, different sports offer different fantasies. Baseball, as Ross (1971) has so eloquently argued, is a pastoral sport, a sentimental mirror of older America, a game played in the timeless world of spring, in a park. Football, on the other hand, is more sensational, heroic, and urbane; it is a winter game, played on a gridiron and characterized by mechanization and impersonality. Sports also evoke different symbolic echoes in different parts of the country. As Novak (1976) points out, football in western

Section III: Functions of Sport

Pennsylvania "is a celebration of local fighting spirit"; in the South, by contrast, it is "a statewide religion" (p. 234); in the Midwest, it is "businesslike," "hard, orderly, cleanly executed, disciplined and tight" (p. 236); in California, it is "more fun" (p. 238), the "exuberance of a healthy body delighting in its talents" (p. 239). Cross-cultural variations of any given sport are equally contrasting and equally appealing. Wimbledon, for example, stands in stark juxtaposition to the U.S. Open: the one a study in Victorian civility and charm, a monument to modernity, the other, the incarnation of postmodern pastiche, a spectacle well suited to the demands of a hyped-up super-consumerist society.

But despite regional and cultural distinctions, as well as the mythos attached to any specific sport, as a whole, sport offers us what Frank Deford (1985) once called "a cozy corner" (p. 44), a world far removed from the normal welter of our daily lives. This is the world I wish to explore here, and I wish to do so by drawing on a variety of sources from a variety of disciplines; although most especially, I will draw from the world of sport literature. In so doing, my intention is to uncover those features of sport that allow it to operate as such a powerful and seductive form of escape. My analysis, however, in the end also will serve as a cautionary tale, because buried not so far beneath my synopsis lies a warning, an admonition about our personal and collective obsession with the world of sport.

From the very beginning, however, let me offer two caveats. First, let me acknowledge that I tend toward a masculinist analysis of sport, partly no doubt because I cannot escape the construction of my own gender, but partly because the literature that deals with sport is written mostly by men, about men's experience in sport. Forced to face or flee from himself in an archetypal Jungian quest, the male sporting hero commonly chooses retreat. Recent literature by women, on the other hand, suggests a typically different scenario. For women, sport appears more likely to result in encounter rather than escape (see Bandy, 1997; Sandoz, 1997). So, from the outset, my approach is skewed toward a male perspective.

Second, let me also note that I tend to reify both "sport" and "life" in this article, suggesting that each exists as a sort of separate ontological category, which is clearly not the case. As a result, I tend to oversimplify a very complex set of relationships between sport and life, and between sport and a variety of other cultural activities, such as theater and commerce. But what separates sport from most other activities is its idealized form. In an interesting discourse on Ernest Hemingway's method of self-dramatization, Jackson Benson (1969) argues that the game stands in juxtaposition to life.

> The game creates a small, independent world, with its own sharply defined structure of physical consequences, its own laws, its own tribal customs and rituals, its own hierarchy of participants, its own set of conflicts and emotions, and its own set of rewards and punishments. (pp. 73–74)

At least in an idealized sense, sport can be appropriately and productively distinguished from ordinary life.

In what has become a classic depiction of play, the Dutch historian, Johan Hiuzinga (1970), describes his subject as follows:

> Summing up the formal characteristics of play we might call it a free activity standing quite consciously outside "ordinary" life as being "not serious," but at the same time absorbing the

player intensely and utterly. It is an activity connected with no material interest, and no profit can be gained by it. It proceeds within its own proper boundaries of time and space according to fixed rules and in an orderly manner. It promotes the formation of social groupings which tend to surround themselves with secrecy and to stress their difference from the common world by disguise and other means. (p. 13)

Contained within Huizinga's classic description of the play world are those very characteristics that constitute the world of modern sport as such an attractive and powerful form of escape, a fantasy world into which we are so readily and easily drawn. I am concerned primarily with the characteristics of space, time, community, order, purpose, and self: characteristics of fundamental ontological significance.

OF SPACE

Perhaps the most obvious way in which sport is detached from real life is that it is played in a place specifically set aside for such purposes. Not contiguous with normal space, space in sport is, as Heinegg (1976) notes, "an ideal space...a tidy microcosm, carefully lined and ordered, set off from its workaday environment" (p. 154). The sports arena or field serves as a sort of architectonic; the arbitrariness of natural space is tamed and configured according to the specifications of geometry (think of a tennis court) or the niceties of geography (such as a golf course). In short, sport offers us a distinct and easily identifiable locality for our escape; it offers us a place to escape to, and as with Disneyland, we are prepared to go to great lengths to get there.

There is something both coherent and reassuring about the simplicity and exactitude of space redesigned for our own devices, "nature humanized," to use Heinegg's (1976, p. 154) phrase. There is also something holy about it; after all, as Mircea Eliade (1959) once wrote, "To organize a space is to repeat the paradigmatic work of the Gods" (p. 32). Both sport and religion mark out a separate area for their activities; in other words, both celebrate the emergence of a finite world; and both, as Giamatti (1989) puts it, "aspire to Paradise." "Thus, whether in a real city or not," Giamatti writes,

> when we enter the simulacrum of a city, the arena or stadium or ballpark...and after we ascend the ramp or go through the tunnel and enter the inner core of the little city, we often are struck...by the suddenness and fullness of the vision there presented: a green expanse, complete and coherent, shimmering carefully tended, a garden. (p. 70)

Sports then do not just take place anywhere. The courts, courses, grounds, and pitches of sport are consecrated, culturally significant places that are eulogized and celebrated as repositories of history, folklore, and sentiment; as Novak (1976) puts it, they are "storied places. Universes of tales" (p.123). Like the athletes themselves, the arenas of sport take on powerful and profound persona; they encapsulate the hopes, dreams, and prejudices of any particular group. The Boston Garden of the Celtics embodies the heart of Boston as much as the Forum of the Lakers reflects the essence of Los Angeles. In places as diverse as Pawley Pavilion or Wrigley Field, Forest Hills or Candlestick Park, Yankee Stadium or Augusta, a culture validates and legitimizes itself. These "cathedrals" of sport, as Angell calls them, allow us to connect with a larger, more social sense of who we are as both individuals and as members of a culture. "Aimee Semple McPherson once saved sinners here," writes Leigh Montville (1986) about the Boston Garden.

> Billy Graham did the job for those sinners' children. Jimmy Swaggart took care of their grandchildren. Calvin Coolidge spoke here and so did Franklin Roosevelt and Winston Churchill. John F. Kennedy held his raucous rally on election eve in 1960 here. "Elvis," an announcer said on another memorable occasion, "has left the building." Elvis left by the same exit as Judy Garland, Rudy Vallee, Perry Como, James Brown, the Rolling Stones and Bruce Springsteen. Joe Louis fought here. Sugar Ray Robinson. Rocky Marciano. Marvelous Marvin Hagler. (p. 116)

In the arena of sport, we leave behind lives of private drudgery and the humdrum emotions that typify them: in the arena of sport, we find a moment of peace and pleasure, of aspiration and excellence. The stadium, as the poet Marianne Moore (1961) puts it, "is an adastrium" (p. 223).

OF TIME

Not only is space in sport not contiguous with normal space, so also is time in sport not contiguous with normal time—once again, the suspension of an ordinary reality in favor of an extraordinary one. Sport, as with Disneyland, is built on an agreed-on suspension of reality; or to put it another way, sport formally institutionalizes a world of unreality, a world in which "the clock" looms large, a world in which we can actually manipulate time.

In this sense, sport offers us control over that which of course can never be controlled—time. By stopping the clock, by calling time out, we embrace the ultimate illusion, the ultimate fantasy; we gain a fleeting glance of immortality, a moment of ecstasy. Because sport offers a temporary dam against the passage of time, it makes possible the momentary dissolution of angst, the obliteration of our normal everyday concerns, in the face of the game. As Boshoff (1985) notes, when Roy Hobbs's homer smashes the clock in *The Natural* (Malamud, 1952), time stands still and we are transported to a "world where Wall Street's fluctuations seem irrelevant, overdue credit cards cease, and nameless pains go away" (p. 61). But sport does not obliterate our sense of reality by diminishing our awareness of it; on the contrary, sport raises our awareness to a new level of intensity. As a result, the moment of the game becomes intoxicating. As he prepares to step on the ice at the beginning of a game, Felix Batterinski, the Polish-Canadian hockey player in MacGregors's *The Last Season* (1983), no doubt gives expression to the feelings of many an athlete when he declares,

> I love this moment, Christ, you can take all your orgasms and fine wine and fancy restaurants and movies and music and compliments and financial windfalls and you can shove them where…only the customs agent's flashlight ever shines. I love *this* moment, no matter what anthem or what arena or what country. (p. 162)

The moment is even more compelling because it emerges within the context of a finite operation. Because sport has a well-defined beginning and an end (an ersatz and contrived reflection of our own temporal existence), it offers the possibility of completeness, "a suggestion," as Hyland (1979) writes, "of a completed theme in a life characterized by the most radical and decisive partiality" (p. 94). It is also the finitude of sport, the carefully articulated and delimited manipulation of time, that gives sport its sense of urgency. The action is heightened even more because it offers what Heidegger calls a sense of Being-toward-death, a realization that there is a final whistle, or that time (like us) eventually expires. Consequently, although sport routinely offers us a rarefied sense of time, nowhere is the feeling more sublime than in the final seconds of a game, final seconds that as any fan knows, can last an eternity; time passes in slow motion, actions are magnified, emotions are held in abeyance, the athlete and the spectator live in suspended animation, in a silent vortex, as in Peter Stine's (1992) account of a last-minute penalty kick in soccer.

> "Penalty kick," said the ref.
>
> Everybody froze. There was silence....
>
> I thought to myself don't choke, don't choke, don't choke. I was so nervous. If I made this shot it meant the finals for the Detroit Jets because there was only one minute left in the game. I stood at the top of the penalty box. I looked down and saw my legs were shaking. I tried to stop them but couldn't, I have never been so nervous. I took a deep breath. The ref blew the whistle. I jogged up to the ball and struck it. I hit it nicely. Over toward the left-hand corner and about shoulder height. That was right where I was aiming. The goalie dove over to the side. It was close. Everyone stood staring from the sideline. It was completely silent. The ball was just out of reach of the goalie's hands. The ball hit the back of the net. It was a wonderful feeling. I jumped up in the air and pumped my fist. Suddenly the silence broke and from the sideline came a tremendous roar. I ran toward the sideline yelling with my fist clenched in the air. (pp. 194–195)

Hollywood, of course, thrives on such moments; it is their stock in trade, the marketing of dreams. And so in a seemingly endless supply of box office hits from *The Natural* to *Hoosiers*, from *The Big Green* to *The Mighty Ducks*, the essence of a game is distilled into the final pitch, the final shot, the final kick.

But there is something else, something beyond the hackneyed ending: Because the moment in sport is so intense, so powerful, so ecstatic, and because sport seems to delay the passage of time and so life, actions take on cosmic significance, and both performer and performance assume mythic proportions. Nowhere is the power of the moment more intense than in the classic confrontation between the batter and pitcher in baseball, as in John Updike's (1960a) celebrated account of Ted Williams's last at bat at Fenway ("Gods do not answer letters" [p. 16]; Updike writes of Williams's refusal to acknowledge the crowd after he hits a home run at his final appearance at the plate) or Malamud's (1952) account of the Whammer being struck out by the young Roy Hobbs.

> The ball appeared to the batter to be a slow spinning planet looming toward the earth. For a long light-year he waited for this globe to whirl into the orbit of his swing so he could bust It to smithereens that would settle with dust and dead leaves in some distant cosmos. At last the

unseeing eye, maybe a fortuneteller's lit crystal ball—anyway, a curious combination of circles—drifted within range of his weapon, or so he thought, because he lunged at it ferociously, twisting round like a top. He landed on both knees as the world floated by over his head and hit with a *whup* into the cave of Sam's glove. (p. 22)

Sport can give universal significance to a myriad of seemingly inconsequential actions, including those of our own.

OF COMMUNITY

Sport is also essentially social in nature: "It promotes the formation of social groupings," to reiterate Huizinga (1970, p. 13). In other words, sport affords the possibility of community, of Being-with, to borrow from Heidegger once again. Sport is a public activity that expects, in fact demands, both a performer and an audience: it is held in a public place for public pleasure, and for most of us today, the promise of togetherness is appealing and, in the case of sport, often electrifying. The social communion available in sport is compelling for both the athlete and spectator alike: for the athlete because of the joy of being part of a team, because being a part of a team offers deliverance from isolation, a brief interlude for many from an often desperate solitude; for the spectator because, as Heinegg (1976) notes, sport spectatorship delivers us "from the shackles of the self to union with the corporate ego of the Home Team" (p. 155). In either case, sport serves as a flight from loneliness, the end, as Nietzsche might say, of the principle of individuation.

Although the world of sport literature is replete with examples of men seeking to find in the bosom of sport the intimacy and belonging denied them in real life, nowhere is the point more poignantly made than in Miller's Pulitzer Prize winning play, *That Championship Season* (1972). Miller himself indicated that the play was about "men going into their middle age with a sense of terror and isolation" (p. i). The men in this case are five aging athletes—four players and their coach—whose emotional and personal salvation is dependent on one shining moment of victory on the basketball court. The play centers on the reunion of the players and their coach as they meet to commemorate their most memorable accomplishment to date: the Pennsylvania High School Basketball championship they won 20 years ago.

Although the professional lives of all the characters have paled into mediocrity and quiet despair, the central character, Coach Delaney, epitomizes the plight of all of them. Fired for striking one of his players, he finds himself "walking the streets at eight o'clock in the morning with nowhere to go." "I watch more TV than any man alive" (Miller, 1972, p.108), he laments. Bitter and disillusioned, his degeneration into loneliness and uselessness is virtually complete, mollified only by his infantile attachment to his four champions: "You, boys, are my real trophies" (Miller, 1972, p. 69), he mourns. The team is both sanctuary and salvation.

But as pitiful as the characters' professional lives are, their solitude and despair is best exemplified in their total inability to experience any genuine intimacy with the women in their lives. Rather than an occasion for exchanges about the vissitudes of family life, the reunion instead becomes a showcase for failed marriages, adulterous relationships, and illicit and degrading sexual encounters. "You know the only woman I ever loved," exclaims the aging power forward, Phil Romano, was "my mother, fuck the psychiatrists" (Miller, 1972, p. 103).

Ultimately, the reunion takes the form of a religious propitiation, as the team dutifully and desperately gathers around the trophy, the icon from which players and coach alike derive strength and community in lives and careers that have long since failed them. Forever members of their own juvenile peer group, their allegiance transcends personal betrayal, fraternal dissension, and power maneuvers. In the end, all is forgiven in the name of the team and in the memory of that championship season.

In every sense, the team offers the characters the community and camaraderie they simply do not have or cannot attain in real life. As the playwright, Victor Cahn (1973), so eloquently put it,

> In the outside world every man is alone. He lives and he dies alone. But not when he's with the team. On the field the players are never alone.... They are struggling to retain a few hours of ordered innocence in their lives and the great pleasure of this innocence is that they may share it with other human beings. (p. D 13)

Spectators, I suspect, are drawn to sport for many of the same reasons, which is hardly surprising because sport specifically sets out to institutionalize the bicameral roles of both actors and audience, athletes and spectators. At the most superficial level, sport spectatorship facilitates the formation of identity groups such as the "Copp" at Liverpool, or the "Bleacher Creatures" at Duke, or the "Dawg Pound" in Cleveland. But at the most profound level, sport spectatorship offers us what Victor Turner (1974) calls "communitas." In other words, being part of an audience allows us to feel and see "through and behind" the political, racial, ethnic, religious, and linguistic boundaries that separate us, not by eliminating them from consciousness but by invoking a deeper sense of commonality, one that transcends the normative order. Sport can be, and often is, specifically designed as a performance genre to provide predictable communitas experiences. Perhaps the most obvious example is the Olympic Games; after all, Olympism, with its emphasis on the idea of "world community," is the classic example of what Turner has also identified as ideological communitas in which the boundaries of the notion of humankind are "ideally coterminous with those of the human species" (p. 82). That people openly weep during the closing ceremonies of the Olympics as the flag is lowered and the flame slowly extinguished is in fact a remarkable instance of spontaneous communitas. Few spectators or athletes at the Olympics do in fact not find themselves touched by a profound sense of commonality, of belonging, of relatedness; and many talk in terms of feeling the beating pulse of a common humanity. Perhaps sport stands as one of the last true bastions in which each of us can find to some degree that sense of "feeling of kinship with the All" that Otto Rank (as cited in Becker, 1973) talks of and that we all yearn for, "the need to be delivered from isolation," the need to become "part of a greater and higher whole." "For only by living in close union with a god-ideal that has been erected outside one's own ego is one able to live at all," Rank once wrote (Becker, 1973, p. 152).

The hero of Nathaniel Hawthorne's *The House of the Seven Gables* (1981) is a lonely and isolated man. Born of high estate and accused of a crime he did not commit, Clifford Pyncheon seeks union with a world from which he feels completely estranged. To feel restored and connected, to become part of "the great center of humanity" (p. 166), Clifford contemplates a leap from his balcony into the midst of a passing political procession: He needed to take a "deep plunge into the ocean of human life" (p.166), as Hawthorne put it. But he might just have well sought the company of a sports crowd. The cheering multitude at any arena no doubt contains innumerable sufferers from a similar malaise, each sufferer seeking release from an overwhelming and debilitating sense of isolation, of aloneness; each seeking the warmth and security of human bonding, the sense of belonging and moral identification that sport spectatorship and fandom can offer. And let us not forget, as Balzac knew, "Man has a horror of aloneness. And of kinds of aloneness, moral aloneness is the most terrible" (as cited in Fromm, 1969, p. 35).

OF ORDER

The order and predictability of sport is another of its most appealing features: "Into an imperfect world," writes Huizinga (1970), "and into the confusion of life, it brings a temporary, limited perfection" (p. 12). Or to borrow from the poet. Wallace Stevens, we might describe sport as

> A new text for the world,
>
> A scribble of fat and fear and fate,
>
> From a bravura of the mind,
>
> A courage of the eye…
>
> A text of intelligent men
>
> At the center of the unintelligible. (As cited in Metheny, 1979, p.133)

In other words, whereas normal life muddles along in opaque confusion. the world of sport is both lucid and luminous; it is, as DiLillo (1972) wryly points out, "a form of society that is rat-free and without harm to the unborn" (p. 3).

The orderly nature of sport is predicated primarily on its strict adherence to the rulebook, that rationally clear legal code that ushers in the possibility of perfection—perfect justice (after all, NFL officials have been shown to be right 95% of the time) and perfect freedom, freedom from consequence and freedom from interference (cf. Hendricks, 1988). It is these freedoms that allow us so easily to lose track of reality within the world of sport: "In grim times," writes Neugeboren (1992),

> few things have cheered me as much as a few hours on the court, hours during which…I lose all sense of time and space ….And that while a missed shot or bad pass or miserable game may hurt, the consequences, in the world beyond basketball are, like those painful missed shots, mostly air. (p. 64)

As the eminent physical educator/philosopher, Eleanor Metheny (1979) once noted, the rules of sport are paradoxical: "They restrict in order to free" (p. 232). But within these restrictions, they offer a scenario whereby "every man might make full use of all the energies of his mortal being, unhampered and unhindered by the demands imposed by the realities of his existence" (p, 233). And herein lies the heart of the matter; herein lies one of sport's greatest appeal as an escape, namely, that it serves as a medium for achievement.

The world of accomplishment is a world to which many fictional heroes are drawn and to which many become addicted. "What will you hope to accomplish, Roy?" asks Harriet Bird, the *mater saeva cupidinum*, in Malamud's novel, *The Natural* (1952). "Sometimes," the natural replies, "when I walk down the street I bet people will say there goes Roy Hobbs, the best there ever was in the game." Roy's entire life in fact is circumscribed by his myopic adherence to the code of athletic performance: "I'll break every record in the book for throwing and hitting," he proclaims (p, 26). Roy of course does not retreat to the world of sport to escape his broader responsibilities (he is, in fact, blind to the communal and reproductive purposes of his vitality and potential); he remains in the world of sport in part because he cannot escape the lure of athletic accomplishment.

But even the most casual of players can be distracted and intoxicated by the sense of accomplishment embodied in the action of sport. As Jay Neugeboren (1992) reports,

> In the ordinary chaos that can mark any week, day, or hour of life, there is something wonderfully simple and clear about getting off a shot, seeing it rise in the air, dip, and slip cleanly through a net. Ah, I've often thought, if only the rest of my life were this clean and simple! (p. 64)

These same sentiments remind us of another athlete, perhaps the most celebrated example of a ball player for whom athletic achievement rescues life from the pall of mediocrity and despair. For Harry "Rabbit" Angstrom, the hero of John Updike's *Rabbit Run* (1960b), success on the basketball court becomes the teleological reference point for a life that after high school ball degenerates into dejection and disillusionment. In his quest to escape the unwelcome complexities of adult existence, Harry forever returns to the sport of his youth and the sense of accomplishment it once offered him. Recalling one of the finest moments on the court, he reminisces,

> I get this funny feeling I can do anything, just drifting around, passing the ball, and all of a sudden I know you see, I *know* I can do anything. The second half I take maybe just ten shots and every one goes right in, not just bounces in, but don't touch the rim, like I'm dropping stones down a well. (p. 65)

His success on the court stands in stark contrast to his failure off of it. On the court, Rabbit's skills endow him with confidence, self-assurance, and prescience; like many an athlete, he instinctively knows what to do and how to do it, and at times, he knows he will do it well. Off the court, Rabbit runs; he runs "out of a kind of sweet panic" (Updike, 1960b, p. 230) precisely because he does not know how to meet the social demands of a mature existence and because he cannot control the vagaries of his life. Living in an abortive present, he embraces his athletic skills with an almost religious reverence: Witness the great moment of epiphany he experiences on the golf course with the minister, Eccles.

> He looks at the ball, which sits high on the tee and already seems free of the ground. Very simply he brings the clubhead around his shoulder into it. The sound has a hollowness, a singleness he hasn't heard before. His arms force his head up and his ball is hung way out, lunarly pale against the beautiful black blue of storm clouds, his grandfather's color stretched dense across the east. It recedes along a line straight as a ruler-edge. Strikes; sphere, star, speck. It hesitates, and Rabbit thinks it will die, but he's fooled, for the ball makes his hesitation the ground of a final leap with a kind of visible sob takes a last bite of space before vanishing in falling. "That's it!" he cries and turning to Eccles with a smile of aggrandizement, repeats, "That's it." (Updike, 1960b, p. 126)

The sureness and security that Rabbit experiences in sport energizes him throughout his life. Even during his final moments, in one last pick-up game in *Rabbit at Rest* (1990), Rabbit experiences what his former coach, Tothero, once called "the *sacredness* of achievement" (p. 62):

> Harry takes the ball out and stops short a step inside the half-court line and, unguarded, lets fly an old-fashioned two-handed set shot, He knows as it leaves his hands it will drop; a groove in the shape of the day guides it in. (pp. 505–506)

Nowhere else and at no other time in life can Harry find such satisfaction and control.

OF PURPOSE

The rules of sport not only bring order and justice into the world, they also bring a sense of purpose and meaning. In a precise, clear-cut and definitive way, the rules of sport dictate the objectives of any given sport; there is no doubt about how a sport is to be played and how the outcome is to be determined. All too often, our day-to-day lives are shot through with aimlessness and ambivalence. The action of sport however is both purposeful and meaningful; the world of sport as Algozin (1976) puts it offers the possibility of "unalienated action," action that is neither trivial nor ambiguous but decisive and effective. In the midst of our normal existence, Algozin writes, "We sense that what we can effectively bring about in the world is utterly worthless"; sport on the other hand "carries to completion that mastery of our situation which we all glimpse in our daily lives but which often eludes us" (p. 193). The paralysis of doubt, indecision, and powerlessness that typifies life is replaced in sport with a kinesthetic of certainty, resolution, and authority. In other words, the relationship between action and purpose in sport is both immediately evident and practically obtainable. And here is another of sport's seductive charms; it can offer what life often cannot, a clear sense of purpose and meaning.

Sport becomes the most purposeful activity in life for many fictional characters, but it does so most especially for Felix Batterinski, the "big, dumb Polack" (p. 100) from Pomerania, Ontario, in MacGrègor's *The Last Season* (1983). Embarrassed and befuddled by his impoverished, superstitious. and unassimilated immigrant family (cf. Vanderwerken, 1993), Batterinski finds respect and peace on the ice: "I went to the half-shattered mirror but saw no pimples, just *Batterinski*, hulking in his pads, solid from blade to brushcut, a man oddly at ease while others about him panic" (MacGregor, 1983, p. 18). Guilt and anger fuel his aggressive style of play and his career; and although life off the ice muddles along in opaque confusion, life on the ice is both lucid and meaningful, the perfect check, the classic hit, "Batterinski doing what Batterinski does best" (MacGregor, 1983, p. 240): "All I know as I skate around is that there is nothing sweeter than the music of my own skates" (MacGregor, 1983, p. 83).

Imprisoned by his reputation as a goon, incapable of establishing a mature relationship in his life, and increasingly disturbed by the tragedies that surround his traditionally minded family in the outback of Canada, life on the ice becomes Felix's refuge, his raison d'etre if you will. From midget hockey to the NHL, from Philadelphia and Los Angeles to Tapiola, Finland, from player to player-coach, Felix Batterinski blunders through his existence, desperately seeking the sense of purpose in life that he only seems to be able to find in hockey. In the end, even though he senses the tragedy of his own circumstance, ice hockey becomes his life. As Freddie the Fog Shero, his Philadelphia Flyer coach writes, "We know that hockey is where we live . . . where we can best meet and overcome pain and wrong and death. Life is just a place where we spend time between games" (MacGregor, 1983, p.185). For Felix Batterinski, as it was for Karl Wallenda, "Life is on the wire: Everything else is just waiting" (as cited in Henricks, 1988, p. 143).

OF SELF

At its most profound and hence potentially most perilous and debilitating level, the world of sport also offers us the chance to escape ourselves. Where else can otherwise reserved and modest folk paint their faces or dress up like animals? Where else can grown men pat each other on the butt? Hug and kiss in public? Where else can mortals act like immortals?

When we enter the world of sport, we enter into an alternative universe, one in which we deploy certain actions and submit to our fate. It is also a world that allows us to forget, disguise, or shed our everyday personality in favor of another, a world in which the normal rules of etiquette and demeanor can be temporarily suspended, in which we can act to a certain degree with impunity, in which we can become an illusory character and behave accordingly. In fact, the opportunity to act as we will for one fleeting moment, rather than as we are or as we are expected to be, is both appealing and cathartic. To a certain extent, the arenas of sport offer us the possibility of a distinctly different ontology.

The danger of course arises when the illusory self of the playing field becomes the dominant self. When the young athlete embraces his playing identity beyond his normal self, when in fact his sobriquet looms larger than his real name, not only for the fans but for the athlete himself, then his very existentiale, his very security, is under threat. Such is the fate of Gavin Grey, the Grey Ghost, in Frank Deford's *Everybody's All-American* (1981). Gavin Grey is "famous, handsome, and heroic," and by his senior year at the University of North Carolina, "*everybody's* All-American" (p. 7) leading the Tarheels to a national championship on the gridiron. His feats both on and off the field are legendary: "He is Alexander, Robin Hood, General Washington…or even, if you prefer art to life, Gary Cooper" (pp. 14–15). His girlfriend (later to be his wife) is Babs Rogers, predictably "the most beautiful *creature* that God ever put on the face of the earth" (p. 10). Together Gavin and Babs model the perfect couple, "the great American athlete and the great American pretty girl" (p. 27). So successful is Gavin as a running back that he becomes known far and wide as the Grey Ghost, a sobriquet that appropriately conjures up images of the transcendent glory of the Old South and one that establishes him as a modern version of J.E.B. Stuart, the famous CSA cavalry general, whose biography Deford uses by way of an introduction.

Basking in his glory and success as an athlete, Gavin Grey becomes his sobriquet more than he becomes himself. "Do you know what you've been?" asks Judge Pace, Deford's (1981) wise old man of the novel; "you've been playing a role. The Grey Ghost is a role...Gavin Grey was a football player. But the Grey Ghost is a character" (p. 116). Presciently, the judge foresees the future and the real danger of living the fantasy life of an illusory self: "No man ever played Hamlet better" (p. 116), our sage Judge tells the Ghost.

Reflecting back years later after his retirement from professional football, the Ghost recognizes the nature of his existential plight: "It wasn't the Grey Ghost died," he intones, "it was Gavin Grey" (Deford, 1981, p. 167). He is right, of course. His real self, Gavin Grey as it were, has long since atrophied; only his illusory self, the Grey Ghost, lives on, a self that can never sustain itself in later life because it is a juvenile creation of an era long since past. Despite his complaints about those who refer to him as Ghost and not as Gavin Grey, in the end, even he himself imperially refers to himself as the Ghost, an indication that he in fact has surrendered all pretense to authenticity. His communion with an illusion is all but fully consummated.

Following his football career, the Ghost predictably fails at a variety of jobs—as a condominium salesman, as a corporate advertising spokesman, and as a regional manager for a food chain. His only success and satisfaction comes as an assistant golf pro at the Pine Lake Estates, a further indication of his infantile psyche and his adolescent preoccupation with games. The truth is that Gavin Grey's joy was only upon the field" (Deford. 1981, p.172).

Unlike the judge who quits his burgeoning Hollywood career as a singer because he recognized it for what it was, an "illusion" that "would be destructive" to his "entire life" (Deford, 1981, p. 91), the Ghost does not know when to quit. In a vain attempt to sustain his make-believe self, he searches for a job long after his talents have left him: "The Broncos are building" (Deford, 1981, p. 205), he wistfully explains. His pathetic effort to prolong his professional playing days is of course a clear manifestation of his degeneration. Imprisoned in a false self, and increasingly crippled by it, he seeks salvation by taking his own life.

According to J.E.B. Stuart, the "self is a better thing to cling to than life itself" (Deford, 1981, p.102). But for Gavin Grey, there is no real self and hence no need to cling to life. Gavin pays the supreme price for indulging an alternative ontology. In the end, he claims the fate of the failed warrior, the obliteration of whatever self there is, the ultimate escape.

Unlike daily life, the world of sport offers a world of functional simplicity and operational clarity—clarity of purpose, clarity of action, clarity of result, and to a great extent, ethical clarity. It is a world to which we readily turn, or return, when normal life becomes too onerous, or when reality becomes de trop. The sanctity and innocence, and hence charm of sport as an escape, is well expressed by Douglas Wallop's (1965) sports-writer hero when he remarks,

> Sports had meant a good deal to me. A game was a splendid thing, a clean, uncluttered clearing in the confusion of life. A game had precise bounds, precise limits, and was played according to precise rules. A game was life in miniature, life idealized. A man and a team were rewarded in direct proportion to their ability and how hard they tried and how well they cooperated. It was very satisfying. (p. 135)

For some, the idealized world of sport becomes more than satisfying; for some, such as Felix Batterinski, Gavin Grey, and Harry Angstrom, it becomes seductive and addictive, and so infantilizing and alienating.

Thorstein Veblen (1934) recognized the potentially regressive and injurious side of sports almost a century ago; "the addiction to sports," he wrote,

> in a particular degree make an arrested development in the man's moral nature. This peculiar boyishness of temperament in sporting men immediately becomes apparent when attention is directed to the large element of make-believe that is present in all sporting activity. (p. 170)

The theme of sport as regression has been reiterated many times in sports-centered novels and exposes. Tom House (1989), for example, called it "terminal adolescent syndrome," a syndrome whereby "the adult ballplayer is only a little more mature, advanced, or emotionally wise than he was when he was in Little League or high school ball" (p. 6). Seeking to explain Gavin Grey's intellectual and emotional juvenescence, Donnie "Cake" McClure rightly notices that "somewhere, sometime early on what is known as native intelligence was shadowed by what is known as natural ability, and only one was allowed to blossom" (p. 17).

Nor are such statements limited solely to fictional characters. Many athletes have portrayed their world as morally and emotionally regressive. George Sauer, the outstanding wide receiver for the New York Jets in the 1960s, for example, has said,

> The bad thing about football is that it keeps you in an adolescent stage, and you are kept there by the same people who are telling you that it is teaching you to be a self-disciplined, mature and responsible person. But if you were self-disciplined and responsible, they wouldn't need to treat you like a child. (As cited in Loy & Ingham, 1973, p. 302)

Similarly, 1983 French Open tennis champion Yanick Noah declared,

> It's a totally unreal world we live in.... I'm thirty years old, and when I quit I will have to make my first real decisions as a man. Up until now, everything in my life has taken care of for me. In one way it's nice to be thirty and still a kid. In another way, it's scary. (As cited in Feinstein, 1991, p. 232)

Section III: Functions of Sport

Expressing similar sentiments about her career as a tennis player, Chris Evert Mill says, "You know. I think it takes tennis players longer to grow up than other people. We're so pampered…so protected from the real world. I'm still trying to grow up, and, I believe I'm getting there" (as cited in Collins, 1984, p. 4).

However, I do not mean to totally deprecate sport here. The aesthetic of sport, the sheer thrill of performing, the celebration of physical excellence, the excitement, and the social camaraderie that sport offers are all profound experiences. Equally legitimate is the claim that participation in sport is truly recreative (in the proper sense of the word), an exhilarating and valuable interlude in life that promotes a healthy sense of physical and psychological well-being. Nor do I wish to paint a completely impoverished view of normal life. But self-realization for the sporting hero is typically realized through an identification with the simple and natural, within what Umphlett (1975) calls a state of "primal innocence" (p.11), and not through a mastery of an increasingly complex and urbanized existence.

The real danger lies not in a balanced approach to the world of sport but in an overexposure to it, an immersion that can easily lead to what Giamatti (1989) calls "the complete athleticization of life": "When we veer into the special world of sport in order to live there, rather than to visit, sport as a mediator dissolves and cult displaces convention" (p. 56). In other words, the inability to recognize the limited potential and value of sport can easily lead to what Huizinga (1936) once called a most pernicious form of "puerilism," one in which "the indispensable qualities of detachment, artlessness and gladness" (p.177) are easily lost. The reason so many fictional heroes choose to escape to the idealized world of sport is simply because they prefer it to their own lives: "The world of dreams is more desirable than reality" (p. 273), as Mosher (1991) puts it. Unable to define themselves or denied a meaningful existence in the actual world in which they live, they retreat to the world of sport and embrace immaturity.

At heart, sport is an illusion, an agreed-upon-fiction, to use Giamatti's (1989) phrase. The significant effect is not necessarily the relatively limited investment of fiction with reality but the derealization of life lived in largely fictitious terms. Art, even when dilettantish, can deepen our perception of life. But sport can conceal it, distract from it, and even become an obstacle to expressing it, to cherishing it, and most especially, to dealing with it. Sport cannot serve as an escape from life because it is a simplistic and artificial construction grounded in the themes of youth, and most adults must endure a life of moral ambiguity, emotional complexity, and troublesome involvements. At worst, sport is not so much an escape from life but an inversion of it first, and ultimately evasion altogether. Perhaps the greatest challenge for those of us who live in a culture seemingly besotted by sport is to learn how to escape from the world of sport as escape.

Baseball and the American Character

A. BARTLETT GIAMATTI

I thank the Massachusetts Historical Society, its speakers committee, and particularly, its gracious and learned director, Mr. Tucker, for the invitation to speak to you tonight. I sense keenly my unworthiness to address the topic set me—"Baseball and the American Character"—because while an enthusiast about both, I am no expert on baseball, or the American character. I could not, however, resist Mr. Tucker's invitation, which opened by asking "Can we lure you back to your native city this fall...." For what is baseball, and indeed so much of the American experience, about but looking for home? *Nostos*, the desire to return home, gives us a nation of immigrants always migrating in search of home; gives us the American desire to start over in the great green garden, Eden or Canaan, of the New World; gives us the concept of a settled home base and thus, the distance to frontiers; gives us a belief in individual assertion that finds its fulfillment in aggregation, a grouping with the like-minded and similarly driven; gives us our sentimental awe of old ways. The hunger for home makes the green geometry of the baseball field more than simply a metaphor for the American experience and character; the baseball field and the game that sanctifies boundaries, rules, and law and engages cunning, theft, and guile; that exalts energy, opportunism, and execution while paying lip service to management, strategy, and long-range planning, is closer to an embodiment of American life than to the mere sporting image of it.

In all its complementary contradictions, its play of antitheses, baseball captured a continent bounded to east and west by oceans, laced by mountains and rivers, dry, fertile, wet, wooded, and at its heart, or stomach, endlessly flat. America is a topography mythologized by its inhabitants as they crossed and re-crossed it into an image of themselves, diverse, demanding, unified by common acts of consent to a government of themselves, a government consciously checked and balanced, the formal antitheses of the state reflecting and shaping the inclusive ideals and isolationist tendencies of a people receptive and wary. It is a land simultaneously perceived as a field and a park, as a wilderness and a paradise, as raw material endlessly available and an enclosure infinitely significant. The inhabitants of such a land produce high principle easily and endlessly, as a form of native handicraft. We are capable of investing any principle with the systematic coherence, spiritual luminosity, and transcendent character of a religious belief as long as it seems to promise coherence, as long as it may bind us up so that we may go our separate ways.

In *Democracy in America*, de Tocqueville characterizes this capacity when he shrewdly says, "The Americans have combated [*sic*] by free institutions the tendency of equality to keep men asunder and they have subdued it" (I. 589). Here we are led to America's moral hunger for egalitarian collectivity, which impels us as individuals to aggregate and to invest the aggregation with numinous meaning, over and over again, as if for the first time every time. This American capacity for religious awe, especially applied to our social and political life, at first enchants and then appalls those from other cultures. They find it difficult to comprehend how so many different institutions can be laden with significance akin to religious value merely in order to expunge class and other distinctions and to promote and protect egalitarian diversity.

If such may be at least suggested by a quick look at a sympathetic French observer in the 1830s and 1840s, what can we learn of ourselves from an observer who did not visit and leave, but who left and visited? In 1877, Henry James published *The American*. The hero is Christopher Newman, and we meet him in the Louvre. The year is 1868. The confrontation between the new American man and the old world, urban and aesthetic in its values, is initially less striking than the contraries embodied in Newman himself. "His eye," says James, "was full of contradictory suggestions: and though it was by no means the glowing orb of romance, you could find in it almost anything you looked for. Frigid yet friendly, frank yet cautious, shrewd yet credulous, positive yet skeptical, confident yet shy, extremely intelligent and extremely good-humoured, there was something vaguely defiant in its concessions and something profoundly reassuring in its reserves" (Boston, 1907, p. 4).

James sees all the contradictions in his American, from frank oppositions yoked by "yet," to subtle blends of "defiant…concessions" and "reassuring…reserves." In this eye, this *Ego americanus*, there are contraries more complex and tensions more clear than in the generalizing characterizations of de Tocqueville. But the French visitor wrote in the glow of promise, in the 1830s and 1840s, when institutional coherence seemed to subdue the centripetal force of equality. James writes in the 1870s. By then the promise of a more perfect Union had been broken by a savage Civil War. Now America would, once again, be compelled to compose or re-compose herself in the aftermath of division and upheaval; once again, free institutions would have to play the role of subduing the tendency equals have to be asunder. Now there was no escaping the gap between America's promises and her execution of them. Post-Civil War America was complex in darker and subtler ways than de Tocqueville could have foreseen. The matter of race would now forever claim the American conscience, if not its consciousness, and that compound whose mix forms the American character—of moral energy and pragmatic efficiency, optimism and guile, respect for law, admiration for the maverick, and love of the underdog—would be forever changed.

But where in all this is baseball? It is amidst it all. Baseball spans the nineteenth century, its origins and first examples antebellum, its growth and first golden age coterminous with Reconstruction and the period through the First World War. Baseball grew in the surge to fraternalism, to fraternal societies, sodalities, associations, and aggregations that followed the fratricide. Baseball showed who had won the war and where the country was building, which was in the industrial cities of the North. It was a conservative game, remembering its origins or even making up origins (as in the myth of Abner Doubleday and the invention of the game in 1839 in Cooperstown, a legend created at a banquet at Delmonico's in New York City in 1889). In a fashion typically American, baseball carried a lore at variance with its behavior; it promoted its self-image as green game while it became a business. That gap in baseball between first promise and eventual execution is with us to this day, as it is with us in so many other ways.

Baseball was Janus, looking both ways by the 1860s. One face looked back at all the varied and original images of the country as a wilderness becoming a garden. This imagery, superbly elucidated by George Huntston Williams in *Paradise and Wilderness in Christian Thought*, runs through New England Puritanism, German Pietism, Quakerism, Mormonism, Black American spirituals, and the great debates on wilderness vs. conservation; it has been addressed in various contexts by such scholars as Henry Nash Smith, Leo Marx, and Roderick Nash, to mention a few. One cannot underestimate the power, whether derived from biblical images or classical, of the image of the enclosed green space (reified as well in such variety, from the same sources and with the same impact, on our campuses) on the American mind. Such imagery may be one reason why now almost forty-five million people a summer flow to baseball parks in the midst of urban wildernesses, flow in big cities to a place where perfection does not exist but which recalls in some distant way the place that promised perfection and whose name we derive from the enclosed park of the Persian king, paradise.

Do other American games, also played on green fields, have the same hold? In part, they do; in part, they cannot because they do not reach back to our origins the way baseball does. On April 17, 1778, George Ewing, a soldier in the Continental Army at Valley Forge, records in his diary that he played in a game of "base." In 1786, a Princeton student describes a game of "baste ball" on the campus. How could it be? Because in 1744 John Newberry published in London *A Little Pretty Pocket-Book* that contained a rhymed description of "base-ball" and a woodcut showing three boys standing at posts arranged in a diamond shape. Newberry's book was reprinted in America up to 1787. Americans played other ball games, Dutch "stool-ball," old cat, old-one cat, towne-ball, round-ball, and, derived from English rounders, what were called the "New York" and "Massachusetts" games. "By the early nineteenth century," says Harold Seymour in his excellent history of baseball, to which I am throughout indebted, "these simple, informal ball games were a common sight on village greens and college campuses, especially in the more settled areas of New York and New England, for it was only when communities became established and enjoyed a certain amount of leisure that ball games could flourish."

Section III: Functions of Sport

In 1834, Robin Carver published for children *The Book of Sports* (Boston) and called the game "Base, or Goal Ball"; in 1835, *The Boys and Girls Book of Sports* (Providence) established that a "feeder" tossed a ball underhand to a "striker"; if the striker missed three times with his hoe handle or stick, he was out; if he hit the ball behind him, he was out, if he hit the ball and it was caught, he was out; if he was hit by a thrown ball while running the bases, he was out. The striker ran the bases clockwise. In 1839, the rule became fixed that one runs counterclockwise. Time does not matter in baseball.

Thus, people were playing something called base-ball before the birth of the Republic. Within ten years of Jefferson's death, the early outlines of the game and some of its fearful symmetry (3 bases, 3 strikes) were in existence. Within fifty more years, the modern game in its essentials was set. But back there, before the Civil War, the new country experimented with the game.

On June 19, 1846, Alexander Cartwright led the Knickerbocker Base Ball Club of New York to play the New York Nine. We should regard this as the first modern baseball game. The Knickerbockers were a social club of young men in various professions and trades who were as interested in dining well as in playing well and who had even more elaborate rules for socializing than for baseball. They did, however, play according to a set of rules they had established, and thus the New York game became modern baseball. As Seymour sums up the Knickerbocker's contribution, they established: "The four-base diamond; ninety-foot basepaths; three out, all out; batting in rotation; throwing out runners or touching them; nine-man teams, with each player covering a defined position; the location of the pitcher's box in relation to the diamond as a whole," and they established the absolute authority of the umpire (1,18; 19–20). On June 19, 1846, the Knickerbockers lost 23–1; the contest lasted only four innings. But the game was permanently shaped. And, given my view of the congruence between America's deepest dreams and baseball, I never cease to marvel that by some splendid serendipity (or is it Providence?) the lovely, open tract fronting the Hudson and surrounded by woods, in Hoboken, where the Knickerbockers played on that June day, and always played, was called Elysian Field. The Biblical imagery of wilderness and garden from Genesis, the Canticles, Revelation 12 is caught up in the image of Elysium. It is meet and right that this place is the birthplace of our game.

After the Civil War, baseball exploded. Between 1876 and 1902, there were five, perhaps six, major league circuits—the National League (including from '92–'99 the consolidated 12-Club League); the American Association (1882–1892), Union Association (1884), Player's League (1890), and the American League. There was, therefore, at least one major league club in Altoona, Baltimore, Boston, Brooklyn, Buffalo, Chicago, Cincinnati, Cleveland, Columbus, Detroit, Hartford, Indianapolis, Kansas City, Louisville, Milwaukee, New York, Philadelphia, Pittsburgh, Providence, Richmond, Rochester, St. Louis, St. Paul, Syracuse, Troy, Washington, Wilmington, and Worcester. With few exceptions, to the victors of the war belonged the game.

Baseball became professional, gaudy, rowdy, and exciting. Skills developed, playing fields appeared everywhere, it swept the country and invaded the Caribbean and Central America. Cartwright took the game to Hawaii. The clergy approved, the president and Congress discovered they were fans, and the average person could not get enough. *Harper's Magazine*, 1886: "…the fascination of the game has seized upon the American people, irrespective of age, sex, or other condition." *Sporting News,* 1891: "No game has taken so strong a hold on Americans as baseball." Why? What accounts for this love affair between America and baseball that has matured and changed but never died?

Mark Twain hints at something when he says of baseball that it had become "the very symbol, the outward and visible expression of the drive and push and rush and struggle of the raging, tearing, booming nineteenth century" (Seymour, I. 345). Baseball became business as Business and wealth and population boomed across the country, as millions of immigrants poured in, as the tempo of life quickened and the country flexed its muscles. Baseball, increasingly played with increasing skill, caught the mood of America and rode it. But still one asks—why?

I think the answer lies in the convergence of many points we have touched upon. For those native to America, particularly in cities, the game, whether watched or played, recalled the earlier, rural America, a more youthful, less bitterly knowing country; for the immigrant, the game was a club to belong to, another fraternal organization, a common language in a strange land. For so much of expanding and expansive America, the game was a free institution with something for everyone.

To the working man, it was cheap to watch, cheap to play. One did not need to own property or a horse or a shell to participate. The players themselves tended to come from working America, and the game became rough, profane, strenuous, more exciting, and so did the crowds. But baseball had genteel origins, at least in its pre-Civil War version; the young gentlemen of the Knickerbocker Base Ball Club, the New York Nine, and their host of imitators did not often play professional ball, but they played in schools and colleges, with clubs and associations; and the educated or well-to-do never lost their taste for baseball.

Baseball was not dangerous, like prize-fighting or football. As we know from the early game books, girls and boys could play; indeed, anyone could, for you did not have to be extra big or extra strong or extra fast. Nor was it especially difficult. No arcane skill was required. In fact, to watch or play the only requirement was desire, desire to participate, to be part of the throng, the singing, the shouting, the swearing, the camaraderie, the noise, the sunshine. It was neither chic nor déclassé to care about baseball. It was simply part of being an American, for no one else had a game anything like it, any more than they had a country as raw, promising, and strong as America.

If you did not watch or play baseball, you could read about it. Newspapers grew with the sport, sports papers came into existence; sports writing flowered as baseball enriched the language and the language developed a vast subcontinent of circumlocutions, euphemisms, and new coinages for baseball. Vivid, opinionated, salty, redolent journalism matched the game. The reader found the box score; the box score provided the diamond in the mind, and, more importantly, gave statistics, data, arithmetic permutation, lore masquerading as quantifiable reality, history that the mind could encompass and retain. Baseball as scripture was born and developed. Then, as now, intellectuals could moralize about baseball; writers and poets could rhapsodize and mythologize; journalists could cover a story with a beginning, middle, and end, and a world of colorful characters, nicknames only matched by mobsters, and communal significance. No one who wanted to be in was left out. As America opened her arms to the foreign born and healed the wounds of the war, baseball embraced all classes, conditions, regions.

Never was a game better matched to its season, or better, never was a season—from spring to early autumn—better matched by a game. The game was outdoors, on grass, in the sun. It began at winter's end, and ended before frost. It made the most of high skies, clement weather, and the times of planting and growth. Until the advent of lights, then domed stadia and artificial turf, baseball was earthbound in the sense of using the earth and climate to advantage and the rhythms of light, shadow, and dusk and spring, summer, and early fall as part of itself. To be earthbound in such a fashion is, to me, pure heaven.

Baseball did not defy the elements. Excessive rain was respected; high wind was lamented; snow eschewed. Unlike football, whose industrial origins and organization force it to pretend to ignore nature, and unlike basketball, the urban game fitted best for small, indoor spaces, baseball in its true state respects natural occurrences and has adapted itself to nature's deep cycles of renewal. Baseball is at home in the natural world, mindful of its own fragility, respectful of the elements, almost civilized in its regard for the safety of its players, careful as it can be of the comfort of spectators.

Genteel in its American origins, proletarian in its development, egalitarian in its demands and appeal, effortless in its adaptation to nature, raucous, hard-nosed, and glamorous as a profession, expanding with the country like fingers unfolding from a fist, image of a lost past, evergreen reminder of America's best promises, baseball fits America. Above all, it fits so well because it embodies the antithetical, complementary interplay of individual and group that we so love, and because it conserves our longing for the rule of law while licensing our resentment of law givers.

Baseball, the opportunist's game, puts a tremendous premium on the individual, who must be able to react instantly on offense and defense and who must be able to hit, run, throw, field. Specialization obviously exists, but, in general, baseball players are meant to be skilled generalists. The "designated hitter" is so offensive because it violates this basic characteristic of the game. Players are also sufficiently physically separated on the field so that the individual cannot hide from clear responsibility in a crowd, as in football or Congress. The object, the ball, and what the individual must do are obvious to all, and each player's skill, initiative, zest, and poise are highlighted.

Individual merit and self-reliance are the bedrock of baseball, never more so than in the fundamental acts of delivering, and attempting to hit, the ball. Every game recommences every time a pitcher pitches and a batter swings. But before a swing or not-swing can trigger the vast grid of mental and physical adjustments that must proceed with every pitch, there is the basic confrontation between two lone individuals. It is primitive in its starkness. A man on a hill prepares to throw a rock at a man slightly below him, not far away, who holds a club. First, fear must be overcome; no one finally knows where the pitched ball, or hit ball, will go. Most of the time control, agility, timing, planning avert brutality and force sport. Occasionally, suddenly, usually unaccountably, the primitive act of throwing or of striking results in terrible injury. The fear is never absent, the fear that randomness will take over. If hitting a major league fastball is the most difficult act in organized sport, the difficulty derives in part from the need to overcome fear in a split second.

The batter is, they say, on offense yet batting is essentially a reactive and deeply defensive act. The pitcher is, they say, on defense, yet the pitcher initiates play and controls the game ("Pitching is 75 percent of the game"). It is not clear, at least to me, finally who is on offense and who is on defense in baseball. The individual at the plate takes on, alone, the entire team on the field, including the catcher, who may actually control the game. The catcher is the only defensive player in any sport I know of whose defined position requires him to adopt the perspective, if not the stance, of the player on offense. Part of what a batter must overcome, part of the secretive, ruthless dimension of baseball, is the batter's knowledge that an opposing player, crouching right behind him, signals wordlessly in order to exploit his weaknesses. Is it so clear who is the defense, who is the offense? I think it is clear that part of the appeal of baseball is that at the outset it focuses on the individual with such clarity in such ambiguous circumstances.

If the game flows from the constantly reiterated, primitive confrontation of an individual with the world, represented by another solitary individual, nothing that ensues, except a home run—the dispositive triumph of one over the other, the surrogate kill—fails to involve the team. A strikeout involves the catcher and anything else brings the community, either on the bench or in the field, into play. And while the premium on individual effort is never lost, eventually the marvelous communal choreography of a team almost always takes over. As soon as a batter becomes a runner, he begins to compensate for the privileged perspective of the catcher by participating from his vantage point in the perspective of the other team. Every assigned role on the field potentially can, and often does, change with every pitch and with each kind of pitch or each ball hit fair. The subsequent complexities and potential interactions among all the players on the field expand in incalculable ways. When in the thrall of its communal aspects, hitting, stealing, and individual initiative give way to combined play-making, acts of sacrifice or cooperation, and obedience to signs and orders. Whether on offense or defense, the virtuoso is then subsumed into the company. The anarchic ways of solo operators are subdued by a free institution.

The ambiguities surrounding being on offense or defense, surrounding what it means to stand where you stand, endlessly re-create the American pageant of individual and group, citizen, and country. In baseball and daily life, Americans do not take sides so much as they change sides in ways checked and balanced. Finally, in baseball and daily life, regardless of which side you are on and where you stand, shared principles are supposed to govern.

Law, defined as a complex of formal rules, agreed-upon boundaries, authoritative arbiters, custom, and a system of symmetrical opportunities and demands, is enshrined in baseball. Indeed, the layout of the field shows baseball's essential passion for and reliance on precise proportions and clearly defined limits, all the better to give shape to energy and an arena for expression. The pitcher's rubber, 24 inches by 6 inches, is on a 15-inch mound in the middle of an 18-foot circle; the rubber is 60 feet 6 inches from home plate; the four base paths are 90 feet long; the distance from first base to third, and home plate to second base, is 127 feet 3 3/8 inches; the pitcher's rubber is the center of a circle, described by the arc of the grass behind the infield from foul line to foul line, whose radius is 95 feet; from home plate to backstop, and swinging in an arc, is 60 feet. On this square tipped like a diamond containing circles and contained in circles, built on multiples of 3, 9 players play 9 innings, with 3 outs to a side, each out possibly composed of 3 strikes. Four balls, four bases break (or is it underscore?), the game's reliance on "threes" to distribute an odd equality, all the numerology and symmetry tending to configure a game unbounded by that which bounds most sports, and adjudicates in many, time.

The game comes from an America where the availability of sun defined the time for work or play—nothing else. Virtually all our other sports reflect the time clock, either in their formal structure or their definition of a winner. Baseball views time as if it were an endlessly available resource; it may put a premium on speed, of throw or foot, but it is unhurried. Time, like the water and forests, like the land itself, is supposedly ever available.

The point is, symmetrical surfaces, deep arithmetical patterns, and a vast, stable body of rules designed to ensure competitive balance in the game, show forth a country devoted to equality of treatment and opportunity; a country whose deepest dream is of a divinely proportioned and peopled (the "threes" come from somewhere) green garden enclosure; above all, a country whose basic assertion is that law, in all its agreed-upon forms and manifestations, shall govern—not nature inexorable, for all she is respected, and not humankind's whims, for all that the game belongs to the people. Baseball's essential rules for place and for play were established, by my reckoning, with almost no exceptions of consequence, by 1895. By today, the diamond and the rules for play have the character of *données*, of Platonic ideas, of preexistent inevitabilities that encourage activity, contain energy, and, like any set of transcendent ideals, do not change.

Symbolic of this sensibility, the umpire in baseball has unique stature among sport's arbiters. Spectator and fan alike may, perhaps at times must, object to his judgment, his interpretation, his grasp of precedent, procedure, and relevant doctrine. Such dissent is encouraged, is valuable, and rarely, if ever, is successful. As instant replay shows, very rarely should it be. The umpire is untouchable (there is a law protecting his person) and infallible. He is the much maligned, indispensable, faceless figure of judgment, in touch with all the codes, the lore, with nature's vagaries, for he decides when she has won. He is the Constitution and Court before your eyes, and he may be the most durable figure in the game for he, alone, never sits, never rests. He has no side, save the obligation to dispense justice speedily.

So much does our game tell us, about what we wanted to be, about what we are. Our character and our culture are reflected in this grand game. It would be foolish to think that all of our national experience is reflected in any single institution, even our loftiest, but it would not be wrong to claim for baseball a capacity to cherish individuality and inspire cohesion in a way that is a hallmark of our loftiest institutions. Nor would it be misguided to think that, however vestigial the remnants of our best hopes, we can still find, if we wish to, a moment called a game when those hopes have life, when each of us, those who are in and those out, has a chance to gather, in a green place around home.

Upward Mobility Through Sport?
The Myths and Realities

D. Stanley Eitzen

Typically, Americans believe that sport is a path to upward social mobility. This belief is based on the obvious examples we see as poor boys and men (rarely girls and women) from rural and urban areas, whether white or black, sometimes skyrocket to fame and fortune through success in sports. Sometimes the financial reward has been astounding, such as the high pay that some African American athletes received in recent years. In 1997 Tracy McGrady, an NBA-bound high school star, bypassed college, signed a $12 million deal over 6 years with Adidas. Golfer Tiger Woods in his first year as a professional made $6.82 million in winnings (U.S. and worldwide) and appearance fees plus signed a series of five-year deals with Nike, Titleist, American Express, and Rolex worth $95.2 million. In 1998 Woods's earnings from endorsements totaled $28 million. Boxer Mike Tyson made $75 million in 1996. It is estimated that Michael Jordan made over $100 million in 1998, including salary, endorsements, and income from merchandise and videos. The recent deals for baseball stars, some exceeding $15 million a year for multiyear contracts, further underscores the incredible money given to some individuals for their athletic talents.

But while the possibility of staggering wealth and status through sport is possible, the reality is that dramatic upward mobility through sport is highly improbable. A number of myths, however, combine to lead us to believe that sport is a social mobility escalator.

MYTH: SPORT PROVIDES A FREE EDUCATION

Good high school athletes get college scholarships. These athletic scholarships are especially helpful to poor youth who otherwise would not be able to attend college because of the high costs. The problem with this assumption is that while true for some, very few high school athletes actually receive full scholarships. Football provides the easiest route to a college scholarship because Division I-A colleges have 85 football scholarships, but even this avenue is exceedingly narrow. In Colorado there were 3,481 male high school seniors who played football during the 1994 season. Of these, 31 received full scholarships at Division I-A schools (0.0089 percent).

Second, of all the male varsity athletes at all college levels only about 15 percent to 20 percent have full scholarships. Another 15 percent to 25 percent have partial scholarships, leaving 55 percent to 70 percent of all intercollegiate athletes without any sport related financial assistance. Third, as low as the chances are for men, women athletes have even less chance to receive an athletic scholarship. While women comprise about 52 percent of all college students, they make up only 35 percent of intercollegiate athletes with a similar disproportionate distribution of scholarships. Another reality is that if you are a male athlete in a so-called minor sport (swimming, tennis, golf, gymnastics, cross-country, wrestling), the chances of a full scholarship are virtually nil. The best hope is a partial scholarship, if that, since these sports are under funded and in danger of elimination at many schools.

MYTH: SPORT LEADS TO A COLLEGE DEGREE

College graduates exceed high school graduates by hundreds of thousands of dollars in lifetime earnings. Since most high school and college athletes will never play at the professional level, the attainment of a college degree is a crucial determinant of upward mobility through sport. The problem is that relatively few male athletes in the big time revenue producing sports, compared to their non-athletic peers, actually receive college degrees. This is especially the case for African American men who are over represented in the revenue producing sports. In 1996, for example, looking at the athletes who entered Division I schools in 1990, only 45 percent of African American football players and 39 percent of African American basketball players had graduated (compared to 56 percent of the general student body).

There are a number of barriers to graduation for male athletes. The demands on their time and energy are enormous even in the off-season. Many athletes, because of these pressures, take easy courses to maintain eligibility but do not lead to graduation. The result is either to delay graduation or to make graduation an unrealistic goal.

Another barrier is that they are recruited for athletic prowess rather than academic ability. Recent data show that football players in big time programs are, on average, more than 200 points behind their non-athletic classmates on SAT test scores. Poorly prepared students are the most likely to take easy courses, cheat on exams, hire surrogate test takers, and otherwise do the minimum.

A third barrier to graduation for male college athletes is themselves, as they may not take advantage of their scholarships to obtain a quality education. This is especially the case for those who perceive their college experience only as preparation for their professional careers in sport. Study for them is necessary only to maintain their eligibility. The goal of a professional career is unrealistic for all but the superstars. The superstars who do make it at the professional level, more likely than not, will have not graduated from college; nor will they go back to finish their degrees when their professional careers are over. This is also because even a successful professional athletic career is limited to a few years, and not many professional athletes are able to translate their success in the pros to success in their post athletic careers. Such a problem is especially true for African Americans, who often face employment discrimination in the wider society.

MYTH: A SPORTS CAREER IS PROBABLE

A recent survey by the Center for the Study of Sport on Society found that two-thirds of African American males between the ages of 13 and 18 believe that they can earn a living playing professional sports (more than double the proportion of young white males who hold such beliefs). Moreover, African American parents were four times more likely than white parents to believe that their sons are destined for careers as professional athletes.

If these young athletes could play as professionals, the economic rewards are excellent, especially in basketball and baseball. In 1998 the average annual salary for professional basketball was $2.24 million. In baseball the average salary was $1.37 million with 280 of the 774 players on opening day rosters making $1 million or more (of them, 197 exceeded $2 million or more, while 32 of them made $6 million or more). The average salaries for the National Hockey League and National Football League were $892,000 and $795,000, respectively. In football, for example, 19 percent of the players (333 of 1,765) exceeded $1 million in salary. These numbers are inflated by the use of averages, which are skewed by the salaries of the superstars. Use of the median (in which half the players make more and half make less), reveals that the median salary in basketball was $1.4 million; baseball—$500,000; football—$400,000; and hockey—$500,000. Regardless of the measure, the financial allure of a professional sports career is great.

A career in professional sports is nearly impossible to attain because of the fierce competition for so few openings. In an average year there are approximately 1,900,000 American boys playing high school football, basketball, and baseball. Another 68,000 men are playing those sports in college, and 2,490 are participating at the major professional level. In short, one in 27 high school players in these sports will play at the college level, and only one in 736 high school players will play at the major professional level (0.14 percent). In baseball, each year about 120,000 players are eligible for the draft (high school seniors, college seniors, collegians over 21, junior college players, and foreign players). Only about 1,200 (1 percent) are actually drafted, and most of them will never make it to the major leagues. Indeed, only one in ten of those players who sign a professional baseball contract ever play in the major leagues for at least one day.

The same rigorous condensation process occurs in football. About 15,000 players are eligible for the NFL draft each year. Three hundred thirty-six are drafted and about 160 actually make the final roster. Similarly, in basketball and hockey, only about 40 new players are added to the rosters in the NBA and 60 rookies make the NHL each year. In tennis only about 100 men and 100 women make enough money to cover expenses. In golf, of the 165 men eligible for the PGA tour in 1997, their official winnings ranged from $2,066,833 (Tiger Woods) to $10,653 (Chip Beck). The competition among these golfers is fierce. On average, the top 100 golfers on the tour play within 2 strokes of each other for every

18 holes, yet Tiger Woods, the tops in winnings won over $2 million, and the 100th finisher won only $250,000. Below the PGA tour is the Nike Tour where the next best 125 golfers compete. Their winnings were a top of $225,201 to a low of $9,944.

MYTH: SPORT IS A WAY OUT OF POVERTY

Sport appears to be a major way for African Americans to escape the ghetto. African Americans dominate the major professional sports numerically. While only 12 percent of the population, African Americans comprise about 80 percent of the players in professional basketball, about 67 percent of professional football players, and 18 percent of professional baseball players (Latinos also comprise about 17 percent of professional baseball players). Moreover, African Americans dominate the list of the highest moneymakers in sport (salaries, commercial sponsorships). These facts, while true, are illusory.

While African Americans dominate professional basketball, football, and to a lesser extent baseball, they are rarely found in certain sports such as hockey, automobile racing, tennis, golf, bowling, and skiing. Moreover, African Americans are severely under-represented in positions of authority in sport—as head coaches, referees, athletic directors, scouts, general managers, and owners. In the NFL in 1997, for example, where more than two-thirds of the players were African American, only three head coaches and five offensive or defensive coordinators were African American. In that year there were 11 head coaching vacancies filled, none by African Americans. The reason for this racial imbalance in hiring, according to white sports columnist for the *Rocky Mountain News* Bob Kravitz is that: "something here stinks, and it stinks a lot like racism."

Second, while the odds of African American males making it as professional athletes are more favorable than is the case for whites (about 1 in 3,500 African American male high school athletes, compared to 1 in 10,000 white male high school athletes) these odds remain slim. Of the 40,000 or so African American boys who play high school basketball, only 35 will make the NBA and only 7 will be starters. Referring to the low odds for young African Americans, Harry Edwards, an African American sociologist specializing in the sociology of sport, said with a bit of hyperbole: "Statistically, you have a better chance of getting hit by a meteorite in the next ten years than getting work as an athlete."

Despite these discouraging facts, the myth is alive for poor youth. As noted earlier, two-thirds of African American boys believe they can be professional athletes. Their parents, too, accept this belief (African American parents are four times more likely than white parents to believe that their children will be professional athletes). The film *Hoop Dreams* and Darcey Frey's book *The Last Shot: City Street, Basketball Dreams* document the emphasis that young African American men place on sports as a way up and their ultimate disappointments from sport. For many of them, sport represents their only hope of escape from a life of crime, poverty, and despair. They latch on to the dream of athletic success partly because of the few opportunities for middle-class success. They spend many hours per day developing their speed, strength, jumping height, or "moves" to the virtual exclusion of those abilities that have a greater likelihood of paying off in upward mobility such as reading comprehension, mathematical reasoning, communication skills, and computer literacy.

Sociologist Jay Coakley puts it this way:

> My best guess is that less than 3,500 African Americans…are making their livings as professional athletes. At the same time (in 1996), there are about 30,015 black physicians and about 30,800 black lawyers currently employed in the US. Therefore, there are 20 times more blacks working in these two professions than playing top level professional sports. And physicians and lawyers usually have lifetime earnings far in excess of the earnings of professional athletes, whose playing careers, on average, last less than five years.

Harry Edwards posits that by spending their energies and talents on athletic skills, young African Americans are not pursuing occupations that would help them meet their political and material needs. Thus, because of belief in the "sports as a way up" myth, they remain dependent on whites and white institutions. Salim Muwakkil, an African American political analyst, argues that

> If African Americans are to exploit the socio-economic options opened by varied civil rights struggles more fully, blacks must reduce the disproportionate allure of sports in their communities. Black leadership must contextualize athletic success by promoting other avenues to social status, intensifying the struggle for access to those avenues and better educating youth about those potholes on the road to the stadium.

John Hoberman in his book *Darwin's Athletes* also challenges the assumption that sport has progressive consequences. The success of African Americans in the highly visible sports gives white America a false sense of black progress and interracial harmony. But the social progress of African Americans in general has little relationship to the apparent integration that they have achieved on the playing fields.

Hoberman also contends that the numerical superiority of African Americans in sport, coupled with their disproportionate under-representation in other professions reinforces the racist ideology that African Americans, while physically superior to whites are inferior to them intellectually.

I do not mean to say that African Americans should not seek a career in professional sport. What is harmful is that the odds of success are so slim, making the extraordinary efforts over many years futile and misguided for the vast majority.

MYTH: WOMEN HAVE SPORT AS A VEHICLE FOR UPWARD MOBILITY

Since the passage of Title IX in 1972 that required schools receiving federal funds to provide equal opportunities for women and men, sports participation by women in high school and college has increased dramatically. In 1973, for example, when 50,000 men received some form of college scholarship for their athletic abilities, women received only 50. Now, women receive about 35 percent of the money allotted for college athletic scholarships (while a dramatic improvement, this should not be equated with gender equality as many would have us believe). This allows many women athletes to attend college who otherwise could not afford it, thus receiving an indirect upward mobility boost.

Upward mobility as a result of being a professional athlete is another matter for women. Women have fewer opportunities than men in professional team sports. Beach volleyball is a possibility for a few but the rewards are minimal. Two professional women's basketball leagues began in 1997, but the pay was very low compared to men and the leagues were on shaky financial ground (the average salary in the American Basketball League was $80,000). The other option for women is to play in professional leagues in Europe, Australia, and Asia but the pay is relatively low.

Women have more opportunities as professionals in individual sports such as tennis, golf, ice-skating, skiing, bowling, cycling, and track. Ironically, the sports with the greatest monetary rewards for women are those of the middle and upper classes (tennis, golf, and ice skating). These sports are expensive and require considerable individual coaching and access to private facilities.

Ironically, with the passage of Title IX, which increased the participation rates of women so dramatically, there has been a decline in the number and proportion of women as coaches and athletic administrators. In addition to the glaring pay gap between what the coaches of men's teams receive compared to the coaches of women's teams, men who coach women's team tend to have higher salaries than women coaching women's teams. Women also have fewer opportunities than men as athletic trainers, officials, sports journalists, and other adjunct positions.

MYTH: SPORTS PROVIDES LIFELONG SECURITY

Even when a professional sport career is attained, the probabilities of fame and fortune are limited. Of course, some athletes make incomes from salaries and endorsements that if invested wisely, provide financial security for life. Many professional athletes make relatively low salaries. During the 1996 season, for example, 17 percent of major league baseball players made the minimum salary of $247,500 for veterans and $220,000 for rookies. This is a lot of money, but for these marginal players their careers may not last very long. Indeed, the average length of a professional career in a team sport is about five years. A marginal athlete in individual sports such as golf, tennis, boxing, and bowling, struggles financially. They must cover their travel expenses, health insurance, equipment, and the like with no guaranteed paycheck. The brief career diverts them during their youth from developing other career skills and experiences that would benefit them.

Ex-professional athletes leave sport, on average, when they are in their late 20s or early 30s, at a time when their non-athletic peers have begun to establish themselves in occupations leading toward retirement in 40 years or so. What are the ex-professional athletes to do with their remaining productive years?

Exiting a sports career can be relatively smooth or difficult. Some athletes have planned ahead, preparing for other careers either in sport (coaching, scouting, administering) or some non-sport occupation. Others have not prepared for this abrupt change. They did not graduate from college. They did not spend the off seasons apprenticing non-sport jobs. Exiting the athlete role is difficult for many because they lose: (1) What has been the focus of their being for most of their lives; (2) the primary source of their identities; (3) their physical prowess; (4) the adulation bordering on worship from others; (5) the money and the perquisites of fame; (6) the camaraderie with teammates; (7) the intense "highs" of competition; and (8) for most ex-athletes retirement means a loss of status. As a result of these "losses," many ex-professional athletes have trouble adjusting to life after sport. A study by the NFL Players

Association found that emotional difficulties, divorce, and financial strain were common problems for ex-professional football players. A majority had "permanent injuries" from football.

The allure of sport, however, remains strong and this has at least two negative consequences. First, ghetto youngsters who devote their lives to the pursuit of athletic stardom are, except for the fortunate few, doomed to failure in sport and in the real world where sports skills are essentially irrelevant to occupational placement and advancement. The second negative consequence is more subtle but very important. Sport contributes to the ideology that legitimizes social inequalities and promotes the myth that all it takes is extraordinary effort to succeed. Sport sociologist George H. Sage makes this point forcefully:

> Because sport is by nature meritocratic—that is, superior performance brings status and rewards—it provides convincing symbolic support for hegemonic [the dominant] ideology—that ambitious, dedicated, hard working individuals, regardless of social origin, can achieve success and ascend in the social hierarchy, obtaining high status and material rewards, while those who don't move upward simply didn't work hard enough. Because the rags-to-riches athletes are so visible, the social mobility theme is maintained. This reflects the opportunity structure of society in general—the success of a few reproduces the belief in social mobility among the many.

Section IV

Socialization and Sport

Parent and Sport Socialization: Views from the Achievement Literature

CHRISTI WOOLGER & THOMAS G. POWER

In spite of the rapidly growing literature on children's motivation and achievement in sport (e.g., Duda, 1987; Gould & Horn, 1984), the origins of individual differences in sport orientation are poorly understood. Although researchers have examined the influence of coaching style on children's experiences (e.g., Carron & Bennett, 1978; McPherson & Brown, 1988; Smith, Zane, Smoll, & Coppel, 1983), research on parental influences is limited. This is unfortunate, because, as has been documented in a variety of areas (e.g., academic achievement, intellectual competence, socio-moral development), parents play a major role in how their children come to view the world and respond to a wide range of situations and activities (e.g., Clarke-Stewart, 1977; Maccoby & Martin, 1983; Power & Manire, 1992).

Given the potentially important role of parents as sports socializers and the current lack of a conceptual framework for this area, the purpose of the present paper is to present a framework for understanding parental influences based upon the literature on academic achievement motivation.

Despite the obvious differences between the academic and sports contexts (e.g., nature of the skills requiring mastery, primary contexts in which the activities occur, role of the self and others), a striking number of similarities exist. For example, both contexts involve: a) learning, practicing, mastering, and hierarchically organizing basic skills in the development of expertise; b) developing, implementing, and evaluating short-term plans in the pursuit of long-term goals; c) learning to cope with and learn from failures and successes; d) learning to benefit from the evaluative feedback of others; and e) appreciating the value of motivation, drive, and persistence. Moreover, both contexts involve evaluation and social comparison, and often the results of one's efforts are made public to both peers and significant adults. In both the academic and sports contexts, parents often initially assume an instructive role, which is gradually taken over by peers and/or adult experts as the child improves. Parents may continue, however, to play an active role in motivating their children's performance throughout childhood.

Thus, independent of the specific skills or contexts in which learning and performance occur, the sports and academic contexts are similar regarding many of the basic psychological processes involved—goals, plans, skill acquisition, mastery, social comparison, evaluation, attributions, expectations, and so on. Because these are some of the same processes through which parental influences in the academic area are presumed to operate (see below), it is likely that the same aspects of parent behavior that affect academic performance and motivation may be important for the sports context as well.

Because parents undoubtedly influence their children's sports achievement and motivation in a variety of ways, our goal is to be broad. Specifically, after a brief review of the current literature on parental influences in sport, we will identify five specific aspects of parental behavior from the achievement literature that likely have an impact on children's motivation and achievement in sport: acceptance, modeling, expectations, rewards/punishments, and directiveness. We will review the existing sport and academic achievement literatures with these dimensions in mind, and outline some specific directions and methods for future inquiry and research.

PARENTAL INFLUENCES IN SPORTS:
A REVIEW OF THE CURRENT LITERATURE

Previous studies of sport socialization in the family context usually take one of two approaches: 1) college age or adult athletes provide retrospective reports of their parent's behavior during childhood (e.g., Greendorfer, 1977; Scanlan, Stein, & Ravizza, 1991; Synder & Spreitzer, 1973); or 2) primary or secondary school students provide reports about their parents' current childrearing practices (e.g., Greendorfer & Lewko, 1978; McElroy, 1982; Scanlan & Lewthwaite, 1984). Studies where parents provide self-reports of their own attitudes or behavior are rare (e.g., Averill, 1987; Melcher & Sage, 1978; Woolger & Power, 1988), and observational studies of parent-child interactions are apparently nonexistent. The reliance on self-reports from single sources is problematic, in that the associations identified may be due to shared method variance rather than to actual relationships between the constructs involved (Wiggins, 1973). This is especially problematic in retrospective self-reports where problems of forgetting, constructive memory, and social desirability response sets also come into play (e.g., Haggard, Brekstak, & Skard, 1960; Mednick & Shaffer, 1963).

Another problem with many of the studies in this area is that data from children who are engaged in a variety of sports activities are combined. This may work against finding patterns of parenting correlates, because the parenting styles that encourage competence in some sports may differ from those that are most beneficial for success in others. For example, a child may be removed from a basketball playing squad if his parents have stressed individual achievement so much that he is unable to work with his teammates and utilize their strengths on the court.

Despite these limitations, a review of the existing literature makes it possible to draw some tentative conclusions about parental influences. Specifically, adult athletes attribute many of their attitudes and behaviors in sport to the behavior of their parents (e.g., Snyder & Spreitzer, 1973). When discussing parental influences, adult athletes tend to report that parental behavior during their childhood (ages 5–12) was more influential than parental behavior during their adolescence (e.g., Greendorfer, 1977; Higginson, 1985; Weiss & Knoppers, 1982). Finally, studies show positive correlations between athletes' perceptions of the amount of parental encouragement, interest, or involvement and current levels of sport participation (e.g., Butcher, 1963; Higginson, 1985; Melcher & Sage, 1978). Parental encouragement or involvement appears to be particularly important for same-sexed children (e.g., Greendorfer & Ewing, 1981; McElroy & Kirkendall, 1980; Smith, 1979; Snyder & Spreitzer, 1973).

Although these studies point to the potential importance of parental influences, they do little to identify the specific parental behaviors that have an impact on children's sport experiences. Instead, in order to compare parental influences to those of peers, teachers, coaches, and others, researchers have generally obtained undifferentiated measures of the overall level of mother and father "encouragement" or "involvement" (e.g. Butcher, 1983; Greendorfer & Ewing, 1981; Higginson, 1985; Kenyon, 1970; Snyder & Spreitzer, 1973). This is unfortunate, because research on achievement in other contexts has demonstrated that the nature of parental involvement is much more important than undifferentiated measures of the overall amount (e.g., Clarke-Stewart, 1977). Though a few researchers have begun to explore specific parental behaviors (e.g., Averill, 1987; Brustad, 1988; Scanlan & Lewthwaite, 1986; Woolger & Power, 1988), it is probably most instructive to review these studies in the context of the organizational framework provided below.

SPECIFIC DIMENSIONS OF PARENTAL BEHAVIOR: CONTRIBUTIONS FROM THE ACADEMIC ACHIEVEMENT LITERATURE

In contrast to the rather small number of studies of parental influences in sport, the literature on parenting and achievement in the academic area is voluminous. Achievement researchers from a variety of perspectives including drive (e.g., McClelland, Atkinson, Clark, & Lowell, 1953), learning (e.g., Crandall, 1963), and attribution (e.g., Parsons, Adler, & Kaczala, 1982) theories have argued that parents play an important role in the socialization of achievement attitudes, motivation, and behavior. Research on parental influences helps identify five dimensions of parental behavior that appear to be important: acceptance, modeling, performance expectations, rewards/punishment, and directiveness. Given the similarities of the academic achievement and sports contexts discussed above, the utility of each of these dimensions for understanding children's sport motivation and behavior will be considered below.

ACCEPTANCE

In widely varying theoretical perspectives (e.g., Baldwin, 1948; Benjamin, 1974; Bowlby, 1958) parental acceptance of, or warmth towards, their children is believed to be one of the essential elements underlying the structure of the parent-child relationship. Empirical evidence showing the importance of acceptance/warmth as a general dimension in parenting is based upon early factor analytic studies (Becker, 1964; Schaefer, 1959). Within the literature, there has been extensive research relating parental acceptance/warmth to children's self-esteem (Coopersmith, 1967; Loeb, Horst, & Horton, 1980) and to their social (Baldwin, 1955; Baumrind, 1967) and cognitive competence (Baldwin, 1955; Hurley, 1965; Radin, 1973). Porter's (1954) definition of acceptance still captures its major qualities: "feelings and behavior on the part of the parents which are characterized by unconditional love for the child; a recognition of the child as a person with feelings who has a right and a need to express those feelings; a value for the unique make-up of the child; and a recognition of the child's need to differentiate and separate himself from the parents in order that he may become an autonomous individual."

Early studies demonstrated the relationship between parental acceptance and achievement (e.g., Morrow & Wilson, 1961; Rosen & D'Andrade, 1959; Winterbottom, 1958). Later studies (e.g., Bradley, Caldwell & Rock, 1988; Hess, Holloway, Dickson, & Price, 1984) have demonstrated that maternal acceptance and positive affective tone in the preschool years are strongly related to children's later achievement in school.

The importance of parental acceptance for children's sport experience was recently demonstrated in two studies at the University of Houston. In a study of 6- to 8-year-old boys in beginning soccer (Averill, 1987) and a study of advanced 8- to 14-year-old boys and girls in competitive swimming (Woolger & Power, 1988), parent ratings of support were positively correlated with parent ratings of child enjoyment and enthusiasm for the sport. In these studies, support was defined as: "(1) providing opportunities for practice and involvement in sport, and (2) providing unconditional emotional support for the child's performance" (Woolger & Power, 1988, Table 1). Example support items were: "After a meet, no matter how poorly my child performed, I try to point out something positive he/she did" and "I have been involved in supporting my child's swim team, either financially or as a volunteer."

In spite of the general consensus that parental acceptance is positively related to children's self-esteem, competence, and achievement, important distinctions relevant to the sport domain have yet to be investigated. Because the definition of acceptance is quite broad, covering a wide variety of parental behaviors and attitudes, it is not clear exactly which behaviors are most important or are the best indicators of acceptance. For example, some parents may express their acceptance through overt affection and praise, while others may be less overt, providing an environment where children know they can openly express themselves and communicate with a parent who will listen with empathy and understanding. Finally, supportive statements and behaviors need to be considered in the context of the individual parent-child relationship—what is supportive to one child (e.g., parent attending practices) may be aversive to another.

MODELING

Another dimension that has been argued to be associated with achievement behavior is identification with the parents, or modeling (e.g., Crandall, 1963). Although modeling is often cited theoretically as important for a child's acquisition of values, attitudes, and behavior (e.g., Bandura, 1965; Sears, Maccoby, & Levin, 1957), empirical studies relating parental modeling to achievement are rare. Although some achievement theorists have interpreted their results in terms of modeling theory (e.g., Solomon, Houlihan, Busse, & Parelius, 1971), direct investigations of modeling have usually focused on respondents' perceived identification with their parents, with high achievers tending to report greater identification with their parents than under-achievers (e.g., Bell, 1969; Crites, 1962; Morrow & Wilson, 1961; Shaw & White, 1965). Other studies have emphasized parents' occupation and education in relation to their children's aspirations. In general these studies have found that children often have educational and occupational aspirations that are similar to those of their parents (e.g., Hoffman, 1974; Viernstein & Hogan, 1975).

In one of the few direct investigations of the role of parents as achievement models, Parsons and associates (1982) compared two ways in which parents might influence child achievement in math: parents as role models and parents as expectancy socializers. They found that, as compared to parental expectations, parental role modeling of mathematical skills had very little relationship with children's math-related perceptions and performance.

Research in the sport area also shows inconsistent patterns. For example, Gregson and Colley (1986) examined the associations between parental sport involvement and sport participation of male and female adolescents, ages 15 to 16. Adolescents were questioned about their own, their mother's, and their father's sport participation and achievement in sport. Significant correlations were found between adolescent sport participation, mother and father participation, and maternal achievement in sport for females but not for males. These authors suggested that parents may serve as role models for the sport participation of females, and that parental role models may not be as relevant to the sport participation of adolescent males. Woolger and Power (1988), in the study of 8- to 14-year-olds cited earlier, defined modeling in terms of parental participation in competitive swimming. In contrast to Gregson and Colley (1986), they found that maternal modeling was positively related to both girls' and boys' ratings of enthusiasm for swimming, whereas father modeling was negatively correlated with child enthusiasm ratings, but only for boys.

Besides gender differences, several issues confuse the topic when exploring modeling in the sport context. Parents, as models, can engage in a variety of achievement behaviors which the child can imitate. Such behaviors include past and present achievement in school, work, home, recreational activities, and sports. This complicates the issue when one tries to specify the types of behaviors that are modeled. For example, a father may have been achievement-oriented in the classroom when he was in school, but lacks an achievement orientation in his current approach to occupation, recreational activities, and everyday issues. Confusion occurs when trying to assess whether modeling in this situation has occurred. That is, what child behaviors constitute modeling—achievement in the classroom, achievement in sports, both, or neither? Although modeling likely plays a role in the sports context, considerable additional research is needed before its role can be clarified.

EXPECTATIONS

Unlike the other parenting dimensions which apply to socialization in a wide variety of domains, parental expectations are the most specific to achievement settings. Most early achievement theorizing and research, however, focused on the individual's versus another's expectations. Almost all of the major achievement theorists (e.g., Atkinson, 1964; Crandall, 1967; Dweck, 1978; Nicholls, 1984; Weiner,

1974) have emphasized the important role of expectancies in predicting achievement behavior. Expectancies influence how individuals perform when faced with an achievement task and are partly based on attributions for past successes and failures. In making the link to adult expectations and their effects on children's behavior, research has shown that a teacher's expectations can have a powerful impact on student achievement (e.g., Jussim, 1990; Rosenthal & Jacobson, 1968). Research has also demonstrated the role that parents play in shaping their children's own expectancies and behaviors, with numerous studies showing parental expectations to be associated with children's achievement (Parsons et al., 1982; Phillips, 1987; Seginer, 1986). Findings suggest that parents exert a strong, and perhaps causal, influence on their children's achievement attitudes and behavior, often influencing children's achievement attitudes more than the child's own past history of successes and failures.

In the sports area, several studies find a positive relationship between parental expectations and children's success/enjoyment. Scanlan and Lewthwaite (1985, 1986) found that 9- to 14-year-old male wrestlers' expectations for success were positively correlated with their perceptions of significant adults' (including parents) satisfaction with their overall performance. Similarly, McElroy & Kirkendall (1980), in a study of 10- to 18-year-olds in a summer sports program, found that boys who reported their parents placed importance on their success in sports had more "professionalized" sport attitudes than boys whose parents had lower expectations. In the study of beginning soccer players cited earlier, Averill (1987), found a positive relationship between mothers' reported performance expectations and children's reported enjoyment.

Other studies, however, suggest that the relationship is more complex. In both the Scanlan & Lewthwaite (1986) study, and in a child-report study of 9- to 13-year-old basketball players (Brustad, 1988), children's reported enjoyment of sports was negatively associated with perceived parental pressure. Moreover, Woolger and Power (1988) found a curvilinear relationship between mothers' and fathers' reported performance expectations and child reports of enthusiasm for swimming. Parents with intermediate levels of performance expectations had children who reported the greatest enthusiasm; high and low expectations were associated with lower levels of enthusiasm.

Although the findings of these studies vary considerably, each is consistent with a curvilinear model. Clearly, however, the relationship between parent expectations and child attitudes/behavior is complex, and much more research is needed before any firm conclusions can be drawn.

REWARDS AND PUNISHMENTS

The next aspect of parenting to be discussed, rewards and punishments, differs from the previous dimensions in that it refers to some of the specific techniques that parents use to promote and encourage achievement in their children.

An activity that is valued for its own sake and does not require external prompts or rewards in order to continue is said to be intrinsically motivated (Shaffer, 1998). However, achievement behaviors are often not intrinsically motivating for some children. Rewards and punishments are techniques that parents use to intentionally increase or decrease the likelihood of the child engaging in a particular behavior through providing positive (reward) or negative (punishment) consequences contingent upon the child's behavior. Rewards include both social consequences (praise, affection) and nonsocial consequences (material goods, money, special privileges). Such consequences are not inherent in the activity they reinforce, and are called extrinsic rewards.

There has been much discussion over the years as to the various effects of rewards and punishments on performance. From the literature, the type of external motivators that parents use with a child fall into three categories: 1) punishments serving to discourage behavior, 2) rewards having a positive impact and thereby increasing future behavior, and 3) rewards having a negative impact and thereby decreasing behavior.

Punishments have routinely been shown to have a negative relationship with achievement behaviors in children (e.g., Clarke-Stewart, 1977). In addition to decreasing the likelihood of future behavior (e.g., Skinner, 1974), they can also negatively influence children's feelings of self-esteem and confidence. Parents' use of punitive techniques such as physical punishment, deprivation of material objects/privileges, or the overt nonphysical expression of disapproval or anger can lead a child to feel guilty and self-punishing (Benjamin, 1974); to lack belief in his/her own ability to control the environment (Clarke-Stewart, 1977); to feel resentment and fear (Mussen, Conger, Kagan, & Huston, 1984); and to feel anxious (Bandura, 1986) or frustrated (Hess & Shipman, 1967). Parents who use such techniques are likely to have children who make external attributions for their behavior (Dix & Grusec, 1983). In the study of wrestlers cited earlier (Scanlan & Lewthwaite, 1986), boys who reported that their mothers often responded negatively to their performance reported the lowest levels of sport enjoyment.

Rewards' effects on achievement behavior are more complex, having both a positive and negative impact. There is empirical evidence for rewards serving to increase achievement behavior (Crandall, Preston, & Rabson, 1960; Rosen & D'Andrade, 1959; Winterbottom, 1958). In this case, rewards would be serving an instrumental or incentive function (Lepper & Hodell, 1988). However, extrinsic incentives and sanctions may also have a detrimental effect, especially on the child's intrinsic motivation, task performance, and learning. Rewards can have a negative effect if they are perceived as controlling rather than providing information about the individual's performance (Deci, 1975; Lepper & Hodell, 1988). In a study of college students in both laboratory and naturalistic settings, Deci (1971) concluded that rewarding subjects with money and "closely related tangible rewards" for engaging in an intrinsically interesting task decreased subsequent interest when there were no rewards. Similarly, Lepper, Green, & Nisbett (1973) found that children lost interest in activities they originally enjoyed when they performed them in order to obtain a reward. Other studies (e.g., McLoyd, 1979; Loveland & Olley, 1979) however, showed that these effects only held true for activities with high initial interest—for activities of low interest, rewards tended to increase interest as measured by time engaging in the activity.

Pierce (1980, cited in Stratton & Pierce, 1980) evaluated the perceptions of youth sport participants, nonparticipants, and dropouts regarding the relative importance of rewards and the impact of rewards on levels of participation. A majority (greater than 53%) of the respondents reported that rewards from parents were either important or very important to them. Pierce also found that less than 13% of the respondents would quit or play less if there were no rewards. He concluded that rewards are important to children who participate in youth sport, but not important enough to drastically change patterns of participation.

Many issues remain unaddressed with regard to the effects of rewards. Because different types of parental "rewards" vary considerably in their salience (e.g., from a nod, a smile, or a pat on the back; to a swim pin for attending a meet; to $15 for every second shaved off a personal best), they are likely to have very different effects on children's motivation and behavior in sport. Based upon Lepper et al's (1973) theory of overjustification, the more salient the reward, the more likely it is to undermine intrinsic interest in an activity.

Rewards of equal salience may also vary considerably in their meaning. A trip to a favorite restaurant after a game may be interpreted by the child very differently than a talk about the possibility of obtaining a college scholarship. In addition to the salience of rewards and the degree to which they are seen as manipulative or controlling, rewards vary on other dimensions, such as: their value, whether they are short-term or long-term, their deservedness, their probability of attainment, and so on. Because all of these characteristics depend, at least partially, upon the meaning the child derives from the reward, the importance of child perceptions should not be overlooked.

DIRECTIVENESS

Directiveness refers to the degree to which parents actively instruct their child about what to do (or not do), with a particular emphasis on areas in need of improvement. Parents who are highly directive tend to tell their child directly what to do whether the child asks for it or not, versus making suggestions or only providing advice when the child requests it. Examples of directiveness items from the Woolger and Power (1988) study are: "Before a meet, I remind my child of what he/she needs to work on" (high directiveness) and "I give my child advice about how to improve in swimming only when he/she asks for it" (low directiveness).

Hess and associates (Hess et al., 1984; Hess & McDevitt, 1984) found that parental directiveness and criticism of children's errors were significantly negatively correlated with children's school readiness and later achievement. Bourg and Power (1986) assessed the strategies mothers used to keep their children working on an achievement task in the presence of distraction (television cartoons). Mothers who adopted a highly directive style when teaching/supervising their children (i.e., provided numerous directions and instructions, and responded often and immediately to off-task behavior) had children who later showed the least on-task behavior in the mother's absence.

In the Averill (1987) and Woolger & Power (1988) studies, mother and father directiveness showed either negative or curvilinear relationships with child or coach reports of enjoyment and enthusiasm for the sport. Apparently, too high (and sometimes too low) levels of directiveness are associated with low levels of sport enjoyment.

The existence of curvilinear effects suggests that there is a fine line between parental instruction that promotes children's achievement and enjoyment, and overdirectiveness that can hinder achievement.

Unfortunately, the literature has not established exactly what constitutes too much directiveness. If a parallel is drawn with research on the detrimental effects of rewards, it can be argued that the child's perception and interpretation of their parents' directiveness might affect the ways that achievement is impacted. If a parent's behavior is such that the child perceives it as controlling, and begins to attribute performance to external (e.g., parental training or feedback) rather than internal (e.g., effort, skill development) sources, then achievement is likely to be hindered. More research is needed to determine the levels and/or degrees of parental directiveness that positively and negatively affect children's achievement motivation and behavior.

SUMMARY

The achievement research reviewed above should provide numerous directions for future research in the sport area in terms of the types of parenting behaviors that should be studied. As indicated throughout the discussion, both perceptions and behaviors are important, so future studies should include measures of both. Moreover, the parenting dimensions should not be examined in isolation. It is very likely that the many dimensions described above interact in complex ways in influencing children's behavior. The effects of material rewards, for example, are likely to vary as a function of the amount of acceptance in the parent-child relationship. The same parental gift could be viewed as either appreciative or manipulative, depending upon the level of acceptance between parent and child.

Child age and gender differences should receive more study as well. In order to understand the possible gender differences in this area, future studies should assess mothers and fathers with their sons and daughters. Longitudinal data, where parental and child behaviors are assessed over time, would allow researchers to study some of the developmental changes that occur in the child and within the parent-child relationship. Another way to understand some of the developmental issues would be to study several age-groups in which within-group variability in ability level and experience exist. This would make it possible to examine the independent contributions of ability level, experience, and developmental level to the child's motivation and performance. Finally, studies of different types of sports: Individual versus team, contact versus noncontact, traditionally male versus traditionally female, should be conducted. Both within- and between-sport analyses should be conducted. Each approach has its advantages. For example, in an individual sport, variables such as effort, enjoyment, and performance can be more easily tested without the confound of other team members affecting the results.

If more specific parenting behaviors and attitudes can be identified as either enhancing or interfering with children's achievement motivation and behavior, researchers can make more specific predictions and suggestions regarding parental influences. In addition, parents can learn to understand their own behavior; and how they might impact their children. Although parents' main interest is to maximize the performance and benefits of their child in sport, they may be unaware that their involvement, expectations, or ways of motivating the child are actually hindering his/her enjoyment and ultimate achievement. If dysfunctional parental patterns are recognized, they can be changed before they prevent the athlete from realizing his or her potential, or before they inhibit the child's desire to compete in athletics altogether.

Coaches can help parents recognize such attitudes and behaviors, and replace them with more appropriate ways of interacting to promote the child's achievement.

From this review it appears that the effects of these five parenting dimensions can be applied to the interactions among parents, children, coaches, and professionals. Although coaches and other professionals play a significant role, different from that of the parent, in regards to the child's sport participation, the above information may help them direct their own attitudes and behaviors in ways that might enhance rather than hinder the child's achievement in sport. For example, a parent or coach who is totally accepting of a child regardless of his/her effort or performance, may fail to provide that child with the feedback necessary to improve and achieve. Adults, especially parents and coaches, are important role models for the child, and can help instill achievement-oriented attitudes, behavior, and values. It is also important for parents and coaches to have high expectations for children—in a sense telling them that the parents believe in them. Parents and coaches may want to focus on the social rewards such as a smile, handshake, hug, or praise for performances, rather than the monetary gifts such as money or trophies. These social rewards will help increase the child's intrinsic motivation and ultimate achievement. Most parents want to be involved, but some may become too involved out of concern for their child's success. This overinvolvement, which can take the form of directiveness, may ultimately hinder the child's enjoyment and achievement. However, once this behavior is identified, coaches can help parents to become less involved, by suggesting more appropriate ways to participate and be a part of the child's sport experience (e.g., volunteer positions associated with the sport activity).

Based on the literature reviewed above, it is clear that the aspects of parenting that influence children's achievement in academic settings are likely to be equally important when applied to sport. Given that most children get involved in sport at a time when their parents have a major influence on their developing attitudes and behaviors, it is unfortunate that more information on parental influences in the sport area is not available.

Factors in Withdrawal from Youth Sport: A Proposed Model

KOENRAAD J. LINDNER, DAVID P JOHNS, AND JANICE BUTCHER

With the increasing attention that the dropout phenomenon in youth sport is experiencing comes the need to summarize and evaluate the past research on this topic and to design strategies for future investigations. In this paper, two modifications for the research on sport withdrawal are proposed. First, we believe it is essential in future work that the type of dropout is clearly defined: either a study should focus on one specific type, or it should compare two or more well-defined types on the dependent variables of interest. We will propose a system for classifying dropouts below.

The second modification pertains to the consideration of a new model of factors influencing withdrawal that will guide future research. We believe that the search for dropout motives has concentrated on factors within sport, at the expense of milieu-related factors and factors of a developmental nature. In the second part of this paper we briefly review the theoretical literature and propose a revised model of potential factors that influence the decision by an athlete to withdraw from sport.

WITHDRAWAL REASONS PROVIDED BY DROPOUTS

It has been estimated that over one-third of all participants between ten and seventeen years of age withdraw from their sport every year (Sapp & Haubenstricker,1978, Gould & Horn, 1984). This large percentage represents many millions of youngsters in North America alone (Martens, 1978). In a substantial number of studies, dropouts have been questioned on their reasons for turning their backs on their previous sport. Some of these studies were sportspecific, e.g., soccer (Narciso, Otto & Mielke, 1984; Pooley, 1981), swimming (Brown, 1985; Gould, 1982; Gould, Feltz, Horn & Weiss, 1982; Sefton & Fry, 1981), hockey (Fry, McClements & Sefton, 1981), football (Robinson & Carron, 1982), gymnastics (Johns, Lindner & Wolko, 1990; Seye & Salmela, 1987; Klint & Weiss, 1986), and wrestling (Burton & Martens, 1986), while others were of an across sports nature (Seefeldt, 1989; Seefeldt et al., 1989; Ewing & Seefeldt, 1988; Petlichkoff, 1982; Sapp & Haubenstricker, 1978; Orlick, 1974).

While the frequency of the specific reasons given for withdrawal vary somewhat among these studies, a number of responses appear in some form or another in the majority of the reports. The most frequently encountered among these is: "Other things to do" which was the number one reason in seven investigations (Klint & Weiss, 1986; Narciso et al., 1984; Gould et al., 1982; Pooley, 1981, Frey et al., 1981, Sapp & Haubenstricker,1978; Orlick, 1974), and mentioned in many others. Closely related to and possibly largely overlapping the previous reason is the "It took too much time" response (Johns et al., 1990; Seefeldt, 1989; Roberts & McKelvain, 1987; LeBlanc & Salmela, 1987; Klint & Weiss, 1986; Tippin, van Hooft & Bratton, 1983; Sefton & Fry, 1981). Other important reasons frequently listed are: "No longer fun" (Seefeldt, 1989; Roberts & McKelvain, 1987, Klint & Weiss, 1986; Gould et al., 1982; Narciso et al., 1984), and, "I lost interest" (Johns et al., 1990; Seefeldt, 1989; Massimo, 1984; Sapp & Haubenstricker, 1978).

In team sports such as soccer, the reason "I did not get to play enough" is often heard (Seefeldt, 1989; Narciso et al., 1984; Sapp & Haubenstricker, 1978; Orlick, 1974), while negative aspects pertaining to the coach and the club were also reasons for dropping out (Seefeldt, 1989; Seye & Salmela, 1987; Klint & Weiss, 1986; Narciso et al., 1984; Gould et al., 1982; Sapp & Haubenstricker,1978). "Too much pressure" is frequently an additional reason for discontinuing (Johns et al., 1990; Seefeldt, 1989; Roberts & McKelvain, 1987; Gould et al., 1982; Pooley, 1981; Orlick & Botterill, 1975) and responses relating to the former athlete's competence and ability have been reported by Seye & Salmela (1987), Burton & Martens (1986), Gould et al., (1982) and Fry et al., (1981). Injury is rarely the main reason for withdrawal, but plays a role in the decision-making (Lindner & Caine, in press, 1988; Johns et al., 1990; Seye & Salmela, 1987; Klint & Weiss, 1986; Massimo, 1984). Finally, the financial aspects of the sport involvement and the costs-benefits assessment are infrequently found to play a role in sport withdrawal (Johns et al., 1990; Laberge & Segui, 1987; Massimo, 1984; Sapp & Haubenstricker, 1978).

LIMITATIONS OF DROPOUT STUDIES AND A PROPOSED CLASSIFICATION SYSTEM

The problem with asking dropouts why they quit is that usually intuitive, subjective and superficial reasons for withdrawal are elicited. Further probing about why interest was lost or why it was no longer fun, has generally not been attempted in these studies, but is necessary to arrive at the underlying factors. Conceivably, the reasons "It took too much time" and "Other things to do" may indicate the difficulties that the young athletes must contend with when they attempt to balance their efforts with perceived benefits. Additionally, such reasons may represent numerous other underlying factors which lay claim to their energy, interest and time. The point is that several theoretical viewpoints may claim support from the same superficial response, and that therefore this type of study is of limited use for the formulation of sport attrition theories.

Another important point is the consideration of the types of dropouts serving as subjects in the study (Weiss & Petlichkoff, 1989; Robinson & Carron, 1982). Most of the studies on attrition motives described above have involved unspecified mixtures of dropout types and the results are therefore difficult to interpret and generalize. Recently, Gordon (1990, 1989) has separated former participants into Sport-leavers (those discontinuing participation in one particular sport), Drop-outs (those withdrawing from sport altogether) and Sport-transfers (those taking up a new sport after leaving another sport). While this is a step in the right direction, such classification system still has some drawbacks, the main one being that no consideration is given to the extent and level of participation at the time of withdrawal. Dropouts from high-level sport participation may well have different motives for disassociation than participants withdrawing at beginners' levels. Figure 1 poses the viewpoint that dropping out is the natural conclusion of sport involvement and that anyone who enters a sport is a future dropout. The figure shows the various modes of attrition from sport and suggests that there are three main types of dropouts: the Sampler-Dropout, the Participant-Dropout, and the Transfer-Dropout.

The Sampler in sport (Burton, 1988; Burton & Martens, 1986) is a person who has a relatively brief involvement in a sport for the purpose of trying it out. He or she may flutter from sport to sport, become a Low- or High-Level Participant in one or more sports, or drop out of sport altogether without ever having been seriously involved. The Participant has made a commitment to one or more sports and sustains his/her participation over a number of years. He or she could compete at various levels and spend differing amounts of time on the sport or sports, and thus can be classified as a Low-, High- or Elite-Level competitor. The Elite participant competes at the highest levels (nationally and provincially) in his/her sport. When the sport no longer satisfies the Participants' needs, they drop out, but might transfer to another sport. Some will even return to the same sport later, but usually at a more recreational level (McCusker, 1989).

The Transfer participant (Weiss & Petlichkoff, 1989; Klint & Weiss, 1986) is a person who has previously left a sport after it no longer satisfied his/her needs and has become involved in another sport. Involvement in the transfer sport may be exploratory, or may become as serious and ambitious as that of the previous sport.

It is our contention that the patterns of participation, the withdrawal reasons reviewed above, and the withdrawal factors to be discussed later, are different for the three types of dropouts and that these types should be separated in sport withdrawal research.

The practical aspects of determining the dropout type of a given individual who has left a sport are rather complex. First, it would be necessary to establish the level of competition and the amount of time spent on that sport at the time of dropping out to classify the participant type the dropout was in that sport. Operational definitions for the Sampler and the three levels of Participants would be required. Second, it is of great importance to know the individual's involvement in other sports at the time of withdrawal. Dropping out of a single sport as a Low-Level Participant may well be associated with very different reasons from withdrawing from high-level participation with simultaneous involvements in one or more other sports. This implies that the participation category of the dropout in the simultaneous sports

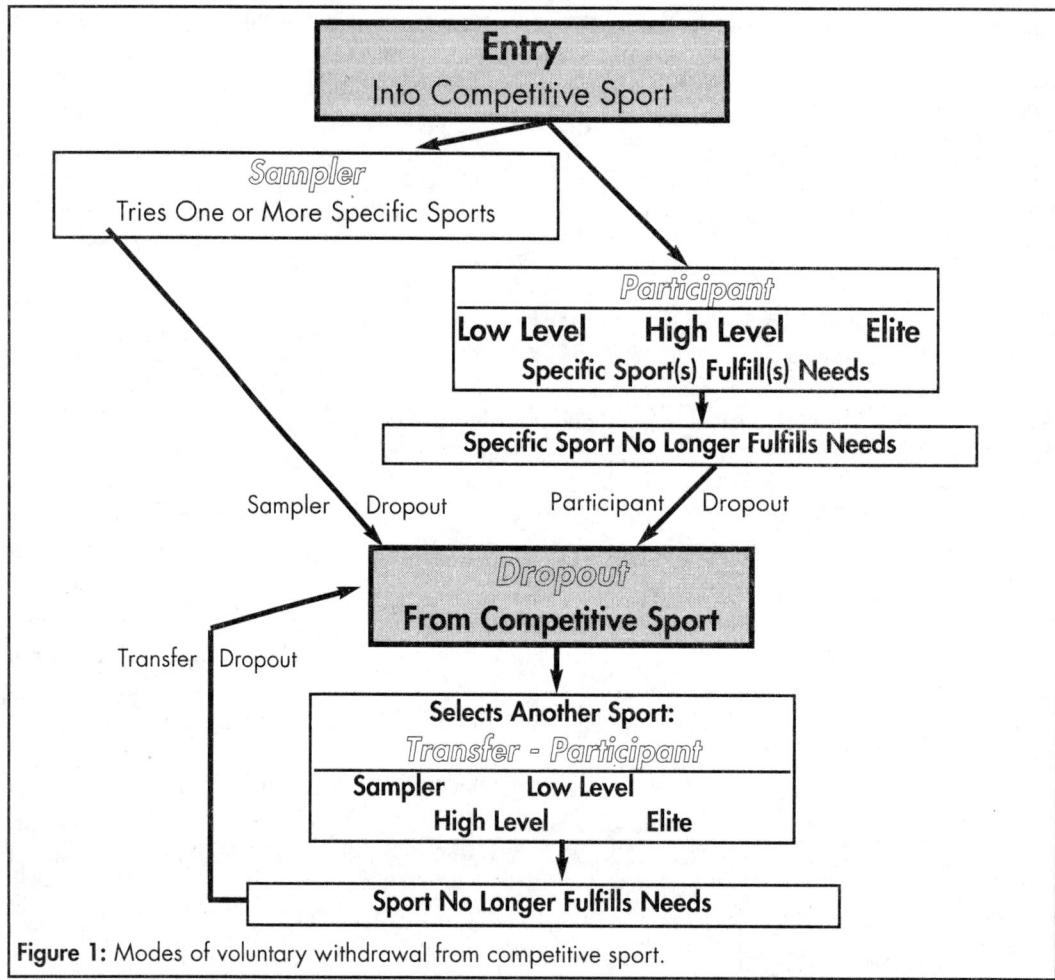

Figure 1: Modes of voluntary withdrawal from competitive sport.

must be determined as well and combined with that of the sport the athlete withdrew from. Such a system would become somewhat awkward with a multitude of categories, and simplification or delimitations may be necessary. Nevertheless, the general approach described here, cumbersome as it may appear, will provide more meaningful information about the dropout in sport than that which has been derived from previous studies where the classification of dropouts was avoided.

THEORIES OF SPORT WITHDRAWAL

The proposed factors underlying sport disassociation fall under six theoretical positions which are not mutually exclusive and in fact occasionally overlap considerably. These positions can be viewed as falling into three groups, i.e., (a) Perceived Ability Theories, (b) Burnout Theory, and (c) Developmental Theories.

Perceived Ability Theories

The perceived ability theories propose that adherence to sport is explained by the satisfaction derived from achievement and competence that the participant experiences in the sport, whereas dropping out is the result of such needs not being met by the sport. The first of the two theories pertaining to perceived ability is the Achievement Orientation Theory (Ewing, 1981; Roberts, 1984), which postulates that individuals may seek this satisfaction in three different ways: through competition ("ability orientation"), through performing to the best of one's ability ("task orientation"), or through the acknowledgment from significant others such as peers, coaches and parents ("social approval orientation"). Ewing (1981) found that dropouts tended to have ability orientations, whereas continuing athletes were more oriented to social approval. Since the objective of all three orientations is the positive perception of one's accomplishments or ability in sport, it is really a competence theory that has focused on the different modes through which this ability may be perceived.

The second theory, the Competence Motivation Theory was initially formulated by Harter (1978), who had operationalized White's (1959) theory. This theory in essence asserts that successful mastery attempts are sources of inherent pleasure and feelings of efficacy, and that these attempts increase or maintain the motivation to acquire further and higher competencies. In the sport domain, research has indeed found that participants have higher self-perceptions of competence than dropouts (Feltz & Petlichkoff, 1983; Feltz, Gould, Horn & Weiss, 1982; Roberts, Kleiber & Duda, 1981). The obvious threat to the theory by the "selection factor" (participants choose sport because of existing high competence feelings) was lessened by evidence in a study by Weiss, Bredemeier and Shewchuk (1986) which showed that perceived competence appears to indeed positively influence actual competence. Burton and Martens (1986) tested the Nicholas' (1984) Perceived Ability Model, which is similar to the Harter model, and found that continuing athletes scored higher on perceived ability than dropouts and actually were more successful and optimistic about future success. Dropping out, then, according to these theories, will occur when participants perceive themselves as lacking in competence (Weiss, 1986) and unable to satisfactorily demonstrate achievements. This point was emphasized as early as 1976 by Calkin, who warned of the dangers of bringing gymnasts to a level of incompetence by forcing too difficult moves too early.

However, the empirical evidence for the theory is not convincing: the selection factor has been insufficiently ruled out, and there are studies (e.g. Johns et al., 1990; Lindner, Caine & Johns, in press) that show that athletes who are successful, able and skillful, and who perceive themselves as highly competent, still drop out. In a recent paper, Petlichkoff (1990) reported that eventual dropouts from interscholastic sport did not score lower on perceived-ability self-rating at the beginning of the season than nonstarters, cuttees and survivors, while all of these rated themselves significantly lower than eventual starters. The Competence Motivation Theory may explain some instances of dropping out of sport, particularly for the sampler and the young participant, but many others require different or at least additional theoretical explanations.

Burnout Theory

An alternative explanation may be the burnout phenomenon which Smith (1986 a and b) suggests should be viewed as completely distinct from dropping out: it is the result of chronic stress which leads to the point where athletes feel that the demands on them exceed their capacities to meet those demands. Feigley (1987) described burnout as a psychological stress disorder with distinct symptomatic behaviors. Those most at risk are the athletes with the seemingly ideal characteristics (perfectionistic, highly energetic, lack of assertive personal skills, seekers of social approval), and who meet an accumulation of demotivators such as heavy training load, diminishing returns from practice, loss of confidence, injuries, judging or refereeing inconsistencies, awakening and increasing need for autonomy, etc. Fender (1989) considers feelings of mental exhaustion as an important aspect of burnout. Research on athletic burnout has hardly begun, as little is known about it and its role in attrition. Smith's (1986a) Cognitive-affective Model may guide future research in this area.

Undoubtedly, some competent and successful athletes drop out because the continuous demands wear them down, or the desire (not the capacity!) to maintain the high level of competence fades.

Developmental Theories

The preceding theories have assumed that reasons for withdrawal are to be found in sport-related factors such as the realization of lack of talent, the inability to deal with pressures, not liking the coach, or the emphasis on competition. However, the frequency of "Other things to do" as a reason for withdrawal should force researchers to look for factors outside the immediate sport milieu. Increasingly, the psychosocial as well as the physical changes that occur when the athlete reaches puberty are hypothesized to play roles in the decision to quit. With increasing age, for instance, the youngster develops a desire for autonomy (Feigley, 1987) and begins to resent the often strictly regimented lifestyle that accompanies sport involvement, especially at the high performance level. Feigley (1987) recognized that motivation generally drops in the teen years due to these cognitive developmental changes. In some sports, particularly gymnastics, bodily changes at puberty may decrease the suitability of the physique for the sport (Salmela, 1987), and may contribute to the dropping out decision. However, our own recent studies did not support this notion (Lindner et al., in press).

Another theory related to developmental change is the Social Exchange Theory, which Smith (1986a) borrowed from Thibaut and Kelley (1959) and applied to sport withdrawal. The theory proposes that the athlete begins to evaluate the benefits he or she is deriving from sport participation against the input that is required and the sacrifices that have to be made. Gould (1987), in his model of youth sport withdrawal, adopted this notion as part of the decision-making process, rather than an underlying factor. The fact, however, that such evaluation typically starts in the early teen years warrants the inclusion of this theory as a developmental one.

A final theory, that also is based on the social and psychological changes that come with increasing age, deals with the growing attractiveness of other leisure activities in which many of the athlete's peers are deeply involved. Hanging out with friends, spending time on hobbies and developing a relationship with boy or girlfriend are leisure pursuit activities which Johns (1980) has labeled "alternative status cultures" and which exert a strong magnetic force on the growing athlete. In addition, responsibilities related to school, work and the family tend to increase role conflicts as the athletes grow up and, unless they are specifically protected from these responsibilities, the economic and moral obligations they represent will influence the decision to discontinue sport participation. Evidence for this factor was found in a recent Western Australian youth survey (Gordon, 1989), where "conflicting interests" was the second most frequent dropout reason after "no longer fun."

A PROPOSED MODEL FOR VOLUNTARY YOUTH SPORT WITHDRAWAL

We submit that the reason why models explaining sport attrition, such as the one by Gould (1987), have received not more than modest empirical support, is that too much emphasis is placed on factors within the sports that are thought to drive the participant out. Rather, our own research and recent publications by others seem to suggest that there are many strong factors operating outside the sport sphere that draw the athlete away, and that those factors interact with the developmental changes that coincide with the typical age of withdrawal. Johns et al. (1990) found through questionnaire and interview techniques that dropout gymnasts were very positive about their previous sport involvement, including their perceived competence and the enjoyment they derived from participating. "Other interests" became more prominent in the gymnasts' lives and appeared to be the main reason for retiring. Gordon (1989) also reported that "other interests" and work, study and family commitments were more prominent than sport-related reasons given by dropouts from Western Australian sport associations. However, his survey of over 1300 participating youths indicated that "lack of fun" would rank first as the motive for eventually dropping out, with conflicting interests and injury as second and third.

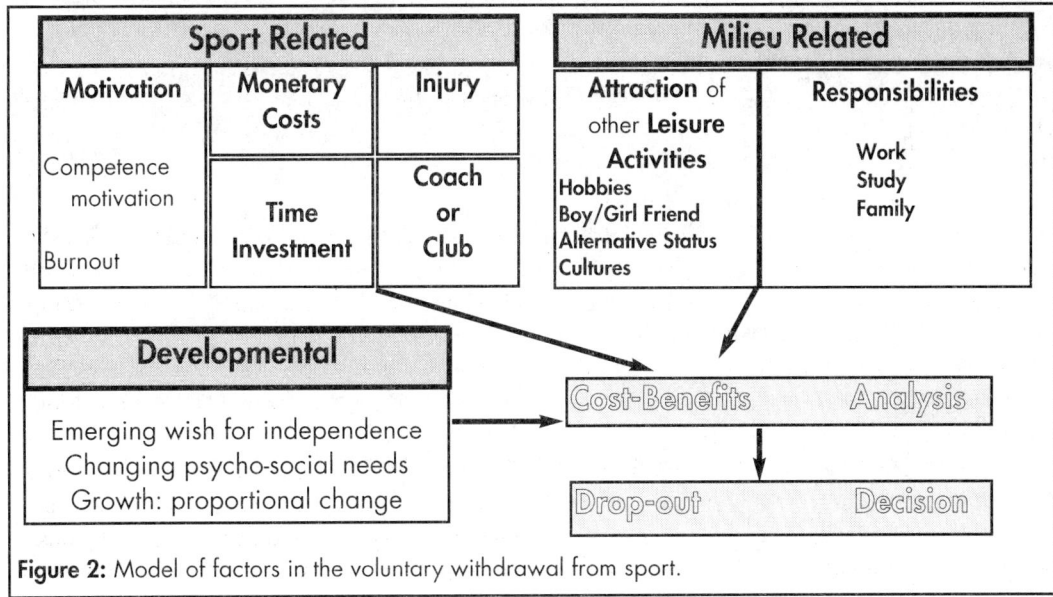

Figure 2: Model of factors in the voluntary withdrawal from sport.

Section IV: Socialization and Sport

Other evidence pointing to developmental and milieu factors in sport withdrawal comes from leisure-time behavior research which documents change in interests and activities with age. A recent Canadian Health and Welfare (1985) study reported that the activities that increased in amount of time spent from Grades 4 to 10 were: chores at home, listening to music, and part-time employment. Forty percent of these Grade 10 students held down part-time jobs. Butcher (in press) surveyed girls longitudinally from Grades 8 to 10, and determined the percentage of girls who participated in various activities outside of school and the number of hours per week they spent in those activities. Notable increases in time were seen for the activities of talking with friends/family, going out, being out with boyfriend, and working at a job. When younger, the girls had spent more time playing sports and watching television. A second Instrument in this study asked the girls to rank their level of interest in 11 leisure-time activities, and was completed every year from Grades 6 to 10. Interest in playing sports declined from being ranked first in Grade 6 to being ranked fifth in Grade 10. Activities that increased in preference were social activities such as dating, going out, and visiting with friends. Thus, it is evident that interests shift from sport to more social activities in adolescent girls.

The potential drawing power of other activities as reason for behavioral decisions has been recognized in related literature. For instance, Maehr and Braskamp (1986) speak of "Perceived Options," defined as behavioral alternatives or action possibilities that a person perceives to be available to him or her in any given situation (p.61), a facet of job motivation that in the opinion of the authors has remained largely unexplored. Applying this notion of perceived options to sport participation and withdrawal, it could be argued that alternatives become appealing when the sport no longer or insufficiently fulfills the needs of the participant. Such application would be congruent with the present models of sport withdrawal. However, an alternative viewpoint may be postulated, i.e., that with age changes in the perception of other alternatives, the sport scene loses in relative appeal. While the distinction between these two positions may at first glance seem trivial and in the realm of the chicken-or-the-egg question, it nevertheless is both of practical and theoretical importance. With the former we would be searching for "faults" within the sports, while with the latter we would focus on the strengths of the "options" as explanations for sport withdrawal.

We propose therefore an alternative model, which groups the factors into three categories: the sport-related, the milieu-related (these are the environmental factors lying outside the sport realm), and the developmental factors. The cost-benefits analysis, sometimes referred to as the "Social Exchange Theory," is presented here, as was suggested by Gould (1987), as a process rather than a factor. According to Gould's model, all voluntary attrition stems from three underlying motives: achievement orientation, competence motivation and burnout. We fail to see the benefit of the Achievement Orientation Theory as an explanation for sport disassociation, but rather, as discussed above, consider it a sub-theory of competence motivation. Gould's model also does not acknowledge the developmental factors, which in our opinion are very important for the understanding of youth sport disassociation.

Empirical testing of the proposed model in its totality will be nearly impossible because of the large number of factors, their interrelationship and the proposed variety of dropout types. However, parts of the model may be verified in specific research. We may, for instance, predict that the Sampler-Dropout will have mainly sport-related factors underlying his or her withdrawal reasons, particularly competence motivation, coach- or club-related negative factors and monetary costs. The Transfer Participant who dropped out of a previous sport may have done so also for sport-related reasons, notably injury, burnout or time investment, while the High-Level and Elite Participant-Dropouts more likely have a combination of developmental and milieu factors. Finally, the Transfer High-Level dropout may be predicted to have mainly milieu-related reasons for dropping out. The age variable will play a role as well. Future research must assess the merits of such predictions.

Student Council, Volunteering, Basketball, or Marching Band: What Kind of Extracurricular Involvement Matters?

JACQUELYNNE S. ECCLES AND BONNIE L. BARBER

The release of *A Matter of Time* by the Carnegie Corporation of New York (1992) put the spotlight on the role that productive use of time might play in successful adolescent development. It illustrated how much discretionary time adolescents have and how much of this time is spent on unstructured activities such as "hanging out" with friends, watching television, and listening to music. The authors argued that constructive, organized activities would be a better use of the adolescents' time for the following types of reasons: (a) idle time is the devil's playground—doing good things with one's time takes time away from opportunities to get involved in risky activities; (b) one can learn good things while engaged in constructive activities—for example, specific competencies and prosocial values and attitudes; and (c) involvement in organized activity settings increases the possibility of establishing positive social supports and networks. To date, however, there has been relatively little longitudinal, developmentally oriented research focused on either the benefits or costs of how adolescents spend their discretionary time. Most of the relevant research has been done in sociology and leisure studies, with some recent attention to the benefits of activity involvement growing out of concern with the potential importance of community-service activities for youth development. In this article, we investigate the longitudinal correlates of activity involvement during the high school years. Initially, we report on the patterns of involvement of high school sophomores to provide a richer picture of the social life of today's adolescents. Then, we report on both the short-term behavioral correlates and the long-term sequelae of engagement in different types of activities.

Section IV: Socialization and Sport

Most of the sociological research into the correlates of youth activity involvement has focused on extracurricular school activities. This research has documented a link between adolescents' extracurricular activities and adult educational attainment, occupation, and income, even after controlling for social class and ability (Landers & Landers, 1978; Otto, 1975, 1976; Otto & Alwin, 1977). Some of these studies also documented a protective association between extracurricular activity participation and involvement in delinquent and other risky behaviors (e.g., Landers & Landers, 1978).

Research within leisure studies has taken a slightly different path. In this area, there have been extensive discussions of the difference between relaxed leisure and constructive, organized activities. Relaxed leisure is characterized as enjoyable, but not demanding (watching TV). Constructive leisure requires effort and provides a forum in which to express one's identity or passion in sports, performing arts, and leadership activities (Agnew & Petersen, 1989; Csikszentmihalyi, 1990; Csikszentmihalyi & Kleiber, 1991; Fine, Mortimer, & Roberts, 1990; Grieves, 1989; Haggard & Williams, 1992; Kleiber, Larson, & Csikszentmihalyi, 1986; Larson & Kleiber, 1993; Larson & Richards, 1989). It is often assumed that there are more beneficial developmental outcomes for adolescents associated with constructive leisure than with relaxed leisure because constructive leisure provides the following opportunities: (a) to acquire and practice specific social, physical, and intellectual skills that may be useful in a wide variety of settings; (b) to contribute to the well-being of one's community and to develop a sense of agency as a member of one's community; (c) to belong to a socially recognized and valued group; (d) to establish supportive social networks of both peers and adults that can help one in both the present and the future; and (e) to experience and deal with challenges. We know little, however, about the instrumental role that relaxed and constructive leisure has on adolescent development.

Some recent research indicates positive consequences of participation in organized activities (e.g., Simmons & Blyth, 1987). For example, Mahoney and Cairns (1997) and McNeal (1995) found that extracurricular activities were related to a lower chance of school dropout, particularly during the early high school years and for high-risk youth. Mahoney (1997) has also shown a connection to reduced rates of criminal offending. In addition, adolescents involved in a broad range of adult-endorsed activities report lower rates of substance use than their noninvolved peers (Youniss, Yates, & Su, 1997). Sports, relative to other school-based activities such as student government and academic clubs, have been linked to lower likelihood of school dropout and higher rates of college attendance (Deeter,1990; Elliott & Voss, 1974; Hanks & Eckland, 1978; Holland & Andre, 1987; Howell & McKenzie, 1987; Kirshnit, Ham, & Richards, 1989; McNeal, 1995); this is especially true for low-achieving and blue-collar male athletes (see Gould & Weiss, 1987; Holland & Andre, 1987; Melnick, Vanfossen, & Sabo, 1988).

Participation in extracurricular activities has also been linked to increases on indicators of positive development such as self-concept, high school grade point average (GPA), school engagement, and educational aspirations (Lamborn, Brown, Mounts, & Steinberg, 1992; Newmann, Wehlage, & Lamborn, 1992; Winne & Walsh, 1980). This is particularly true if one is involved in a leadership role. Similarly, involvement in high school extracurricular activities is predictive of several indicators of healthy adult development, including active participation in the political process and other types of volunteer activities, continued sport engagement, and better mental health (DeMartini, 1983; Glancy, Willits, & Farrell, 1986; Youniss, McLellan, Yang, & Yates, in press; Youniss, McLellan, & Yates, 1997; Youniss, Yates et al., 1997). In contrast, sports have also been linked to increased rates of school deviance (Lamborn et al., 1992).

A third line of research involves studies that focus on the question of causal direction and selection. For example, Larson (1994) used longitudinal analyses to study the association between sport participation and delinquency. His results suggest that the apparent protective relation of sports to low rates of delinquency actually reflects the negative impact of delinquency on sports participation: that is, adolescents engaged in delinquent behaviors drop out of school athletic participation over time. He found no evidence that participation in sports led to a decline in engagement in delinquent activities. In contrast, participation in other youth organizations did predict a decline in engagement in delinquent activities.

In this article, we examine both the potential benefits (psychological attachment to school, better GPA, lower rates of school absences, and higher rates of college attendance) and the potential risks (engagement in risky behavior, including substance use) associated with participation in various forms of constructive leisure. Five types of involvement are considered: prosocial (church and volunteer activities), team sports (any school team), school involvement (pep club, student council), performing arts (drama, marching band), and academic clubs (science club, foreign language club). These organized extracurricular activities were selected because they require effort and are settings in which adolescents can express their identities and passions (Csikszentmihalyi & Kleiber, 1991). In the first section of the article, we explore the link between involvement in these types of activities and our indicators of positive and negative developmental trajectories. To both control for selection factors and better understand the causal direction of the relation, we use longitudinal analyses. In the second half of the article, we explore possible reasons for these associations. In this section, we focus on two possible mediators: peer associations and activity-based identity formation.

METHOD

Study Design and Sample

The data come from the Michigan Study of Adolescent Life Transitions (MSALT). This is a longitudinal study that began (in 1983) with a cohort of sixth graders drawn from 10 school districts in southeastern Michigan. The vast majority of the sample is white and comes from working- and middle-class families living in small industrial cities around Detroit. We have followed approximately 1,800 of these youth through eight waves of data beginning in the sixth grade (1983–1984), and continuing into 1996–1997, when most were 25 to 26. The analyses presented here include 1,259 respondents who both completed the survey items about activity involvement and had outcome data from the waves of data collected in 1990–1991 (Wave 6—when most were 12th graders) and in 1992–1993 (Wave 7).

Measures

The adolescents were administered an extensive interview with items tapping a wide range of constructs. The specific constructs used for the first part of this article are summarized below.

Section IV: Socialization and Sport

Activity Involvement
In the 10th grade, we collected detailed information on the adolescents' involvement in a wide variety of activities in and out of school. Adolescents were provided with a list of 16 sports and 30 school and community clubs and organizations. They were asked to check off all activities in which they participated. We clustered the extracurricular activities into five categories: *prosocial activities*—attending church and/or participating in volunteer and community service-type activities; *performance activities*—participating in school band, drama, and/or dance; *team sports*—participating in one or more school teams; *school involvement*—participating in student government, pep club, and/or cheerleading; and *academic clubs*—participating in debate, foreign language, math or chess clubs, science fair, or tutoring in academic subjects. These categorizations focus on the actual content or domain of the activity.

Risk Behavior
In addition to information on involvement in positive extracurricular activities, we also collected detailed information on the adolescents' involvement in risky/ problematic activities in 10th and 12th grades, such as drinking, getting drunk, skipping school, and using drugs. The risk behavior measures used the following categories to indicate frequency of engaging in the activity in the previous 6 months: $1 = none$, $2 = once$, $3 = 2$ *to 3 times*, $4 = 4$ *to 6 times*, $5 = 7$ *to 10 times*, $6 = 11$ *to 20 times*, and $7 = 21$ *or more times*. Drinking alcohol at Wave 6 had an extra category, with $7 = 21$ *to 30 times* and $8 = 31$ *times or more*.

Academic Outcomes
We also collected data on the students' attachment to school, using one 7-point item about how much they liked school in both 10th and 12th grades. In addition, information on academic performance and assessment test scores was obtained for every participant from their school files. For these analyses, we use school records of the participants' cumulative GPAs at the 11th and 12th grades, as well as verbal and numerical ability subscores on the Differential Aptitude Test (The Psychological Corporation, 1981) administered in the ninth grade. Finally, in our 1992–1993 wave, we collected college attendance information.

Family Characteristics
We included mother's education as a measure of family social economic status to use as a control variable in the multiple regression analyses. This variable was assessed based on the mothers' questionnaire collected at the first wave, when the adolescents were in the sixth grade. Mothers indicated on a 9-point ordinal scale their highest level of education with $1=$ *grade school*, $3 =$ *high school diploma*, $6 =$ *college degree*, and $9 = Ph.D. or other advanced professional degree such as an MD*. The modal responses for this sample were 3 (high school degree, 37.8%) and 4 (some college or technical school, 34.1%). We then collapsed this scale into a 3-point ordinal scale with $1=$ *no more than high school diploma* (46.2%), $2 =$ *some college* (38.3%), and $3 =$ *Bachelors' degree or more* (15.5%).

Procedure

The data were collected via self-administered questionnaires that were completed at school during regular school hours. For the 10th- and 12th-grade waves, the adolescents were released from their classrooms to fill out the questionnaire in a large common room—usually the lunchroom. In addition, complete school records from Grade 5 to Grade 12 were collected for all participants; these included grades, absences, courses taken, and any disciplinary measures taken by the schools. The young adult surveys were mailed to the participants' homes and returned via postage-paid envelopes. On completion of the survey, participants were sent $20.

RESULTS

Descriptive Patterns

First, we describe the patterns of males and females in activity involvement in the 10th grade. These results are presented in tables 10.1 and 10.2. Table 10.1 summarizes the distribution of in-school and out-of-school activities by gender, with team sports aggregated into a single category. Table 10.2 breaks down the team sports into individual school-based competitive sports teams.

Next, we computed a total number of activities by summing all the in-school and out-of-school clubs and activities that were checked. On average, these adolescents participated in between one and two activities and/or clubs. Females participated at higher rates than males, $F(1,1243) = 25.49, p < .001$; females' mean $=1.79$ ($SD =1.71$) and males' mean = 1.33 (SD = 1.44). However, 31% of the sample did not participate in any activities or clubs. Because sports were so common, we aggregated them separately by summing all of the different teams checked. Not surprisingly, males participated on more different teams than females. However, 45% of the sample had not competed on any school athletic team. Finally, we calculated the breadth of the adolescents' participation by summing the number of different types of activities for each adolescent (e.g., participation in several different sports, or several different types of clubs, only counted as one type of activity). Females also participated in a wider range of activities (mean = 1.54, SD = 1.19) than males (mean = 1.21, SD = .90; $F[1,1243] = 28.21, p < .001$).

Next, we aggregated the adolescents' responses into five broad categories of activities: prosocial, sports teams, performing arts, school involvement, and academic clubs. Participants were given a yes score if they had checked off at least one activity/ club within the broad category. A description of participation by gender is found in table 10.3. Consistent with results reported above, the males were more likely to engage in at least one sport activity than were females ($F[1, 1243] = 63.72, p < .001$). In contrast, the females were more likely to be involved in prosocial, performing arts, and school involvement activities ($F[1,1243] = 23.71, p < .001$; $F[1,1243] = 70.49, p < .001$; and $F[1, 1243] = 52.49, p < .001$, respectively).

We also assessed whether mother's education was related to participation in any of these five general categories. We divided mother's education into three categories and ran ANOVAs for each of the activity clusters. The only significant relation occurred for prosocial activity involvement ($F[2, 724] = 9.82, p < .01$): Adolescents with mothers having a college degree or higher were twice as likely (37%) to be involved in prosocial activities as adolescents with mothers having a high school degree or less education (18%); those with mothers having some college education fell in between (23%). Trends were evident for both team sports ($F[2, 724] = 2.82, p < .06$), and performing arts ($F[2, 724] = 2.60, p < .08$), with 53%, 63%, and 58% of adolescents in the three mother education categories participating in sports and 33%, 31%, and 42% of the adolescents in the three mother education categories participating in performing arts.

Table 10.1: Percentage of Females and Males Participating in Each Type of Activity

Activity	Females	Males
School team sports	45.6	66.7
Sports club	13.1	25.5
Dance classes	15.6	.7
Dance	14.4	5.2
Band/orchestra	19.1	14.3
Drama	13.0	6.1
Art	8.6	7.7
Student government	10.5	5.4
Pep club/cheerleading	12.4	3.1
Cheerleading as team sport	11.5	.2
Church	18.2	10.8
Service club	3.2	2.4
Tutoring/math, science, computers	2.3	2.3
Tutoring/other subjects	1.3	1.2
Science fair	1.0	.7
Math club	0.0	.5
Chess club	0.0	.7
Computer club	.6	2.3
Foreign language club	12.6	4.5
Debate club/forensics	1.2	1.4
Career-related clubs	2.9	2.4
Other school clubs	3.8	3.3
SADD	10.2	3.0
Peer counseling	3.5	1.2
ROTC	.4	3.3
Scouts/Girls' and Boys' Club	2.2	4.7
4H	3.5	1.9
Junior Achievement	.9	1.6

Reprinted from Eccles and Barber, 1999.

Concurrent and Long-Term Correlates

In this section, we report on the relation between 10th grade extracurricular activity involvement and other psychological and behavioral outcomes. We examine whether specific types of extracurricular activities are more beneficial or risky than others.

Prosocial Activity Involvement

Tables 10.4 and 10.5 illustrate the findings for involvement in prosocial activities. Adolescents involved in prosocial activities in 10th grade reported less involvement in problem behaviors; this difference is especially marked at Grade 12, 2 years after the activity data were collected. These results suggest that prosocial involvement is a protective factor with regard to the age-related increases in these risky behaviors.

Prosocial involvement is also linked to better academic performance and greater likelihood of being enrolled full-time in college at age 21.

Table 10.2: Percentage of Females and Males Participating in Each Type of Competitive School Sports Team

Type of Sport	Females	Males
Baseball	3.2	26.3
Basketball	10.7	25.3
Football	2.9	31.9
Golf	.6	8.9
Ice hockey	1.3	9.1
Soccer	3.5	8.4
Wrestling	1.3	15.9
Field hockey	.6	1.6
Swimming/diving	11.8	12.7
Tennis	9.2	8.0
Track/cross-country	12.0	16.2
Gymnastics	4.7	1.4
Softball	16.5	3.0
Volleyball	17.1	5.2

Reprinted from Eccles and Barber, 1999.

Table 10.3: Participation Rates of Female and Male Students in Extracurricular Activities (in Percentages)

	Females		Males	
	No	Yes	No	Yes
Prosocial activities	498	187	481	91
	(73)	(27)	(84)	(16)
Sports teams	372	313	191	383
	(54)	(46)	(33)	(67)
Performing arts	389	297	450	122
	(57)	(43)	(79)	(21)
School involvement	526	157	519	46
	(77)	(23)	(92)	(8)
Academic clubs	572	113	509	63
	(83)	(17)	(89)	(11)

Reprinted from Eccles and Barber, 1999.

We tested this hypothesis more directly using longitudinal regression analysis. The results are shown in table 10.6. In each equation, we entered the 10th-grade level of the risky behavior to get an estimate of the extent to which each of the other predictors explained change in frequency of engaging in the particular risky behaviors. We also entered gender, mother's educational level, and two intellectual aptitude variables (performance on the Differential Aptitude Tests for verbal and mathematical abilities) as controls because these constructs have emerged in other studies as predictors of both academic achievement and involvement in risky behaviors. Finally, we entered 10th-grade prosocial activity involvement. The standardized betas for each of these predictors are included in table 10.6 to allow for comparisons of the magnitude of the predictive relationship. As one would expect, the strongest predictor is the 10th-grade level of involvement in the risky behavior, suggesting considerable stability in the individual differences in these behaviors over the high school years. Nonetheless, involvement in prosocial activities is related to change in this engagement in a protective direction; that is, the students who are involved in activities such as attending church and doing volunteer work show less of an increase in these risky behaviors over the high school years than their noninvolved peers.

Involvement in prosocial activities at Grade 10 is also positively related to both liking school at that level and a higher GPA at the 12th-grade level. In addition, being involved in prosocial activities in the 10th grade is positively related to attending college full-time at age 21. Only the relation to 12th-grade GPA remained significant in the multiple regression analyses.

Team Sports

Tables 10.4, 10.5, and 10.7 show the relation of involvement in team sports to engagement in risky behaviors. Apparently, involvement in team sports at Grade 10 is a risk condition for engagement in one of these risky behaviors at Grade 12; namely, drinking alcohol. When one tests this hypothesis using the type of longitudinal regression analyses just described for prosocial activities, being involved with team sports does indeed contribute significantly to an increase in alcohol use and getting drunk over the high school years after controlling for mother's education, student gender, and intellectual aptitude (see table 10.7).

Involvement in team sports also serves as a protective condition for academic outcomes. Sports participants liked school better at both the 10th and 12th grades. They were also more likely to be attending college full-time at age 21 than nonparticipants. Finally, sports participation predicted an increase in liking school between the 10th and 12th grades, a higher than expected 12th-grade GPA, and a greater than expected likelihood of being enrolled full-time in college at age 21.

Performing Arts

Those adolescents who were involved in performing arts at Grade 10 were less frequently engaged in risky behaviors at both Grade 10 and 12 than those who were not. This is particularly true for alcohol-related behaviors (see tables 10.4 and 10.5). However, when one controls for prior levels of drinking in the longitudinal regression analyses (see table 10.8), we could find no evidence that 10th-grade involvement in performing arts affects the direction or magnitude of change in drinking behavior over the high school years.

Participation in performing arts was also related to greater liking of school at both the 10th and 12th grades (see tables 10.4 and 10.5) and to higher 12th-grade GPA and a greater likelihood of attending college full-time at age 21. The longitudinal regression analyses suggest that this protective role is only significant for 12th-grade GPA. The other two longitudinal relations become nonsignificant once the various control variables are included in the equation.

Table 10.4: Mean Levels (and Standard Deviations) of Risk Behaviors and Attachment to School in 10th Grade by Participation in Extracurricular Activities

	Prosocial activities		Sports teams		Performing arts		School involvement		Academic clubs	
	No	Yes	No	Yes	No	Yes	No	Yes	No	Yes
Drink alcohol	2.7	2.0**	2.5	2.6	2.6	2.4**	2.5	2.6	2.6	2.4
	(1.9)	(1.4)	(1.8)	(1.8)	(1.9)	(1.6)	(1.8)	(1.6)	(1.8)	(1.5)
Skip school	1.7	1.4**	1.7	1.6	1.7	1.5**	1.7	1.5+	1.7	1.5
	(1.0)	(.7)	(.9)	(.9)	(1.0)	(.7)	(1.0)	(.8)	(1.0)	(.9)
Use drugs	1.5	1.2**	1.5	1.4	1.5	1.4	1.5	1.4	1.5	1.3
	(1.4)	(1.0)	(1.3)	(1.2)	(1.3)	(1.2)	(1.3)	(1.2)	(1.3)	(1.1)
Like school	4.4	4.8**	4.3	4.7**	4.3	4.9**	4.4	5.0**	4.5	4.8**
	(1.7)	(1.6)	(1.8)	(1.6)	(1.7)	(1.6)	(1.7)	(1.6)	(1.7)	(1.5)

+$p<.10$. **$p<.01$.
Reprinted from Eccles and Barber, 1999.

Table 10.5: Mean Levels (and Standard Deviations) of Risk Behaviors and Academic Outcomes in 12th Grade and College Attendance in Young Adulthood by Participation in Extracurricular Activities

	Prosocial activities		Sports teams		Performing arts		School involvement		Academic clubs	
	No	Yes	No	Yes	No	Yes	No	Yes	No	Yes
Drink alcohol	4.5	2.8**	3.5	4.4**	4.3	3.6**	4.0	4.1	4.0	4.0
	(2.5)	(2.0)	(2.4)	(2.5)	(2.5)	(2.3)	(2.5)	(2.4)	(2.5)	(2.5)
Get drunk	3.9	2.4**	3.2	3.8**	3.7	3.2**	3.5	3.6	3.6	3.3
	(2.2)	(1.8)	(2.1)	(2.2)	(2.3)	(2.1)	(2.2)	(2.1)	(2.2)	(2.1)
Skip school	3.2	2.6**	3.1	3.0	3.0	3.1	3.0	3.1	3.1	2.8
	(1.6)	(1.5)	(1.7)	(1.5)	(1.5)	(1.7)	(1.6)	(1.5)	(1.6)	(1.6)
Use marijuana	2.0	1.3**	1.7	1.9	1.9	1.6+	1.8	1.6+	1.8	1.7
	(1.8)	(.9)	(1.5)	(1.6)	(1.7)	(1.4)	(1.7)	(1.1)	(1.6)	(1.5)
Use hard drugs	1.4	1.2*	1.3	1.4	1.4	1.3	1.4	1.1*	1.4	1.3
	(1.2)	(.8)	(1.0)	(1.2)	(1.2)	(1.0)	(1.2)	(.5)	(1.1)	(1.1)
Like school	4.6	4.8	4.5	4.8**	4.7	4.7	4.6	4.8	4.6	4.8
	(1.8)	(1.8)	(1.8)	(1.6)	(1.8)	(1.9)	(1.8)	(1.8)	(1.8)	(1.8)
High school grade point average	2.5	2.9**	2.6	2.6	2.5	2.8**	2.6	2.9**	2.5	3.0**
	(.7)	(.6)	(.7)	(.7)	(.7)	(.7)	(.7)	(.7)	(.7)	(.7)
Percentage in full-time college	.48	.65**	.47	.56*	.49	.58**	.49	.68**	.48	.72**
	(.50)	(.48)	(.50)	(.50)	(.50)	(.49)	(.50)	(.47)	(.50)	(.45)

+$p<.10$. *$p<.05$. **$p<.01$.
Reprinted from Eccles and Barber, 1999.

Section IV: Socialization and Sport

Table 10.6: Standardized Regression Coefficients for Risk Behaviors and Academic Outcomes in 12th Grade and College Attendance in Young Adulthood Predicted From 10th-Grade Participation in Prosocial Activities

Predictor Variable	Drink alcohol	Get drunk	Skip school	Use marijuana	Use hard drugs	Like school	High school grade point average	Full-time college
10th-grade level of dependent variable	.48**	.46**	.22**	.45**	.27**	.31**		
Gender	.07	.10*	-.03	.06	-.03	.01	-.14**	.00
Maternal education	.00	.00	-.05	.04	-.03	-.04	.07*	.13**
Verbal ability	-.05	.03	.05	.03	-.04	.00	.16**	.16**
Math ability	.05	.02	-.19**	.05	-.05	-.10	.47**	.16**
Prosocial activities	-.20**	-.20**	-.10+	-.14*	-.11*	.02	.13**	.04
Adjusted R^2	.31**	.30**	.10**	.23**	.10*	.09**	.42**	.12**

+$p<.10$. *$p<.05$. **$p<.01$.
Reprinted from Eccles and Barber, 1999.

Table 10.7: Standardized Regression Coefficients for Risk Behaviors and Academic Outcomes in 12th Grade and College Attendance in Young Adulthood Predicted From 10th-Grade Participation in Sports

Predictor Variable	Drink alcohol	Get drunk	Skip school	Use marijuana	Use hard drugs	Like school	High school grade point average	Full-time college
10th-grade level of dependent variable	.51**	.50**	.23**	.47**	.29**	.29**		
Gender	.07	.11*	-.02	.07	-.02	-.01	-.18**	-.03
Maternal education	-.03	-.04	-.06	.01	.02	-.04	.08*	.13**
Verbal ability	-.04	.04	.06	.04	-.04	.01	.17**	.17**
Math ability	.03	-.02	-.21	.04	-.07	-.10+	.49**	.16**
Sports participation	.15**	.09*	.01	.04	.02	.12*	.07*	.10*
Adjusted R^2	.30**	.27**	.09**	.21**	.09**	.10**	.41**	.13**

+$p<.10$. *$p<.05$. **$p<.01$.
Reprinted from Eccles and Barber, 1999.

Finally, this was the only activity domain in which we found consistent evidence of a gender-by-activity involvement interaction: Males, but not females, engaged in performing arts were less likely than their peers to drink alcohol and skip school in Grade 10 and to drink alcohol in Grade 12 ($p < .01$ in each case).

School-Involvement Activities

As can be seen in tables 10.4 and 10.5, participation in school-related clubs and nonathletic activities was not related consistently to engagement in risky behaviors. In contrast, it was positively related to liking school at Grade 10 and to both 12th-grade GPA and the likelihood of attending college full-time at age

21. By and large, these patterns were confirmed in the longitudinal regression analyses (see table 10.9). Participating in these kinds of school-related activities predicted better than expected 12th-grade GPA and greater than expected likelihood of attending college full-time at age 21.

Table 10.8: Standardized Regression Coefficients for Risk Behaviors and Academic Outcomes in 12th Grade and College Attendance in Young Adulthood Predicted From 10th-Grade Participation in Performing Arts

Predictor Variable	Drink alcohol	Get drunk	Skip school	Use marijuana	Use hard drugs	Like school	High school grade point average	Full-time college
10th-grade level of dependent variable	.52**	.51**	.23**	.47**	.29**	.31**		
Gender	.08	.12*	.01	.08	-.01	.01	-.12*	.02
Maternal education	-.02	-.03	-.06	.01	.02	-.04	.09*	.13**
Verbal ability	-.04	.03	.05	.03	-.04	.00	.14**	.15**
Math ability	.03	-.01	-.21	.04	-.07	-.09	.49**	.17**
Performing arts	-.10⁺	-.05	.10*	.01	.02	-.01	.13**	.07
Adjusted R^2	.28**	.27**	.10**	.21**	.09**	.09**	.42**	.12**

⁺$p<.10$. *$p<.05$. **$p<.01$.
Reprinted from Eccles and Barber, 1999.

Table 10.9: Standardized Regression Coefficients for Risk Behaviors and Academic Outcomes in 12th Grade and College Attendance in Young Adulthood Predicted From 10th-Grade Involvement in School Leadership or School Spirit Activities

Predictor Variable	Drink alcohol	Get drunk	Skip school	Use marijuana	Use hard drugs	Like school	High school grade point average	Full-time college
10th-grade level of dependent variable	.53**	.51**	.22**	.46**	.28**	.30**		
Gender	.11*	.14**	.01	.07	-.02	.02	-.14**	.02
Maternal education	-.02	-.02	-.04	.01	.01	-.03	.10**	.14**
Verbal ability	-.05	.01	.03	.04	-.03	-.01	.15**	.14**
Math ability	.03	-.01	-.21**	.04	-.07	-.09	.48**	.16**
School involvement	.03	.06	.10⁺	-.03	-.07	.04	.10**	.10*
Adjusted R^2	.27**	.27**	.10**	.21**	.09**	.09**	.41**	.12**

⁺$p<.10$. *$p<.05$. **$p<.01$.
Reprinted from Eccles and Barber, 1999.

Academic Clubs

Participation in academic clubs was primarily related to academic outcomes (see tables 10.4, 10.6, and 10.10). This was true at both the bivariate and longitudinal multivariate level. Adolescents who participated in academic clubs had higher than expected high school GPAs and were more likely to be enrolled in college at 21 than their noninvolved peers.

DISCUSSION

Consistent with the majority of studies, we found clear evidence that participation in extracurricular activities during the high school years provides a protective context in terms of both academic performance and involvement in risky behaviors. Participation in all five types of extracurricular involvement predicted better than expected high school GPAs. Participation in sports, school-based leadership, school-spirit activities, and academic clubs predicted increased likelihood of being enrolled full-time in college at age 21. Involvement in sports also predicted increases in school attachment. Participation in prosocial activities was related to lower increases in alcohol and drug use, as well as to lower levels at both Grades 10 and 12, and participation in performing arts served this same function for males. Furthermore, each of these results holds true when social class, gender, and academic aptitude are controlled.

Table 10.10: Standardized Regression Coefficients for Risk Behaviors and Academic Outcomes in 12th Grade and College Attendance in Young Adulthood Predicted From 10th-Grade Involvement in Academic Clubs

Predictor Variable	Drink alcohol	Get drunk	Skip school	Use marijuana	Use hard drugs	Like school	High school grade point average	Full-time college
10th-grade level of dependent variable	.53**	.51**	.22**	.47**	.29**	.31**		
Gender	.11*	.13**	-.02	.08	-.01	.02	-.15**	.02
Maternal education	.03	-.03	-.05	.01	.02	-.04	.07*	.12**
Verbal ability	-.05	.03	.06	.03	-.05	-.01	.14**	.14*
Math ability	.03	-.01	-.20**	.04	-.07	-.10	.49**	.16**
Academic clubs	.02	-.02	-.06	.02	.02	.03	.11**	.13**
Adjusted R^2	.27**	.27**	.09**	.21**	.09**	.09**	.41**	.13**

*$p<.05$. **$p<.01$.
Reprinted from Eccles and Barber, 1999.

In contrast, participation in sports is also linked to increases in use of alcohol. Contrary to the results reported by Larson (1994), our results provide good evidence that participation in sports does lead to increases in some behaviors that might be considered problematic. In addition, our results clearly support the conclusion that participation in sports has positive academic consequences. It is likely that the difference in our outcome measures explains this discrepancy. Larson (1994) used a very global indicator of delinquency, in which alcohol and drug use was only a small component. His measure also included no indicators of academic success. In contrast, we used quite specific outcome measures, and our results indicate that participation in sports has both positive and potentially negative consequences.

What can we conclude? The evidence presented thus far is mostly consistent with the conclusion reached in the Carnegie Corporation (1992) report, *A Matter of Time*. However, the pattern is not as simple as one might expect. Both the magnitude and the direction of the relations depend on the outcome being considered and, to some extent, on the gender of the adolescent. For example, although participation in team sports is related to increased GPA and increased probability of attending college full-time, it is also related among males to such risky behaviors as drinking alcohol. Similarly, although being involved in school spirit and leadership clubs does not appear to reduce the frequency with which one does risky things such as use drugs, drink alcohol, and skip school, it is related in a positive direction to our indicators of academic success. Only involvement in prosocial activities (in this case, primarily church attendance) appears to be protective against increases in alcohol and drug use and increases in skipping school.

Several investigators have offered explanations for these effects. For example, in 1969, Rehberg suggested five possible mediators for the effects of sports participation: association with college-oriented peers, exposure to academic values, enhanced self-esteem, generalization of a high sense of personal efficacy, and superior career guidance and encouragement. In 1961, Coleman stressed the values and norms associated with the different peer clusters engaged in various types of extra-curricular activities. Spady (1970) stressed the benefits in self-esteem one attains from the increases in peer status associated with successful participation in extracurricular activities. Otto and Alwin (1977) added skill and attitude acquisition (both interpersonal and personal) and increased membership in important social networks (more recently relabeled social capital by Coleman and Hoffer, 1987).

More recently, investigators have focused on the links between peer group formation, identity formation, and activity involvement. For example, Fine (1987) has explored the relation of participating in Little League to both peer group and identity formation. He has stressed how participation in something like Little League shapes both children's self-definition as a "jock" and their most salient peer group (see also Eccles, 1993; Hantover, 1978; Kirshnit et al., 1989; Kleiber & Kirshnit, 1990). In turn, these characteristics (one's identity and one's peer group) influence subsequent activity choices—creating a synergistic system that marks out a clear pathway into a particular kind of adolescence. Similarly, Eckert (1989) has explored the link between peer-group identity formation and activity involvement. As one moves into and through adolescence, individuals become identified with particular groups of friends or crowds (see also Brown, 1990). Being a member of one of these crowds helps structure both what one does with one's time and the kinds of values and norms one is exposed to. Once again, over time, the coalescence of one's personal identity, one's peer group, and the kinds of activities one participates in as a consequence of both one's identity and one's peer group can shape the nature of one's pathway through adolescence. Consistent with these perspectives, we are interested in how activity participation is linked to both peer group and identity formation. We assume that activity choices are a part of a larger system of psychological and social forces that influence development—forces linked to peer group affiliation and identity formation. Knowing what an adolescent is doing often tells us a lot about who the adolescent is with. Many of the activities we study take up considerable amounts of the adolescents' time and are done with other adolescents and adults. Thus, it is likely that participation in some of these activities directly affects adolescents' peer groups precisely because such participation structures a substantial amount of peer group interaction. One's coparticipants become one's peer crowd, and such peer crowds often develop an activity-based culture, providing adolescents with the opportunity to identify with a group having a shared sense of style. Similarly, leisure may help to clarify personal identity while maintaining relationships with peers. Involvement in a school organization or sport links an adolescent to a set of similar peers, provides shared experiences and goals, and can reinforce friendships between peers (see also Larson, 1994). Thus, extracurricular activities can facilitate adolescents' developmental need for social relatedness and can contribute to one's identity as an important and valued member of the school community.

SYNERGISTIC FORCES WITH PEER GROUP CULTURES AND IDENTITY FORMATION

The ideas outlined above are consistent with the work of Erikson (1968), and more recently, Adams and Marshall (1996) and Youniss, Yates, and Su (1997). These scholars suggest that adolescents seek out an identity that allows them to be actors in their social world and that allows them to feel effective, successful, and connected in their everyday activities (see also Williams & McGee, 1991). Extra-curricular activities of the kinds we are studying provide youth with the opportunity to form just such identities. In addition, because participation also influences peer group formation, participation feeds into the type of synergistic system described above and depicted in figure 10.1.

We explore these ideas in this section. This work represents the beginning of our efforts to explore these issues. In this section, we focus first on the link between activity participation and peer group characteristics and then on the link between activity participation and peer-group and activity-based identities.

METHOD

Additional Measures

Friend Characteristics

Composition of the peer network was measured in 10th grade with a series of questions asking "what proportion of your friends are each of the following?" The items included in these analyses were "planning to go to college," "doing very well in school," "regularly drink alcohol," "irregularly use drugs," and "likely to skip class." The response scale ranged from 1 = *none* to 5 = *all*, with 3 = *half.*

Identity Group

At the 10th grade, we asked the participants to make a prototype judgment regarding their identity. Because the movie *The Breakfast Club* (Hughes, 1985) was quite popular at the time, we decided to use it as the basis of our measure of identity. There are five main characters in this movie—each one representing a stereotypic adolescent type. We asked the participants to indicate which of five characters (the princess, the jock, the brain, the basket case, and the criminal) was most like them. We told them to ignore the sex of the character and base their selection on the type of person each character was. The adolescents had no difficulty with their selection—less than 5% left the question blank. About 9% selected the criminal, 11% selected the basket case, 12% selected the brain, 28% selected the jock, and 40% selected the princess. Although the gender distribution was sex-typed, there were substantial numbers of each sex in each of the given identity groups to allow for analyses.

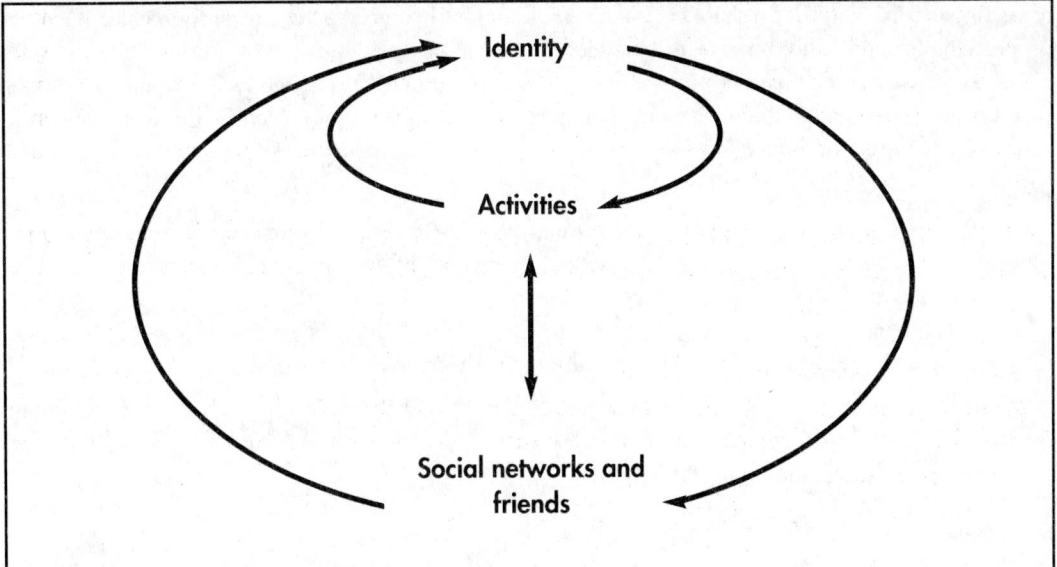

Figure 10.1: Synergistic influences among identity, friendship networks, and activity involvement. Reprinted from Eccles and Barber, 1999.

RESULTS AND DISCUSSION

Peer Groups

As noted above, activity settings provide a peer group as well as a set of tasks. To the extent that one spends a lot of time in these activity settings with the other participants, it is likely that one's friends will be drawn from among the other participants. It is also likely that the collective behaviors of this peer group will influence the behaviors of each member. To the extent that this is true, some of the behavioral differences associated with activity participation may be a consequence of the behavioral differences of the peer groups associated with these different activity clusters.

The relevant results are summarized in tables 10.11 and 10.12. At both 10th and 12th grades, the peer group characteristics were consistent with the outcomes reported in the first section of this article. This is particularly true at Grade 12. Consistent with the positive association of activity group membership with academic outcomes, the peer groups for participants are characterized by a higher proportion of friends who plan on attending college and are doing well in school (with the exception of the sports participants). Concordant with the protective association of prosocial participation with drug and alcohol use, adolescents involved in prosocial activities, compared to their peers, have fewer friends who use alcohol and drugs; they also have few friends who skip school. Finally, congruent with the association of sports participation with increased drinking, adolescents who participate in team sports have a higher proportion of friends who drink than their peers.

These results are compatible with the analysis outlined above. Consequently, it is certainly possible that peer group association is one of the mediators of the association between activity group membership and adolescent outcomes.

Identity Categories

Table 10.13 summarizes the distributions of identity types for each of our five activity groups. The significance levels for these one-way ANOVAs are indicated with stars after the activity group. The significant contrasts are summarized in the last column.

One of our activity groups is clearly related to the identity characters: sports. As one might expect, the jocks stand out in the team sports group. This is clearly an activity-based identity. The evidence for activity-based identities is less clear for the other four identities, primarily due to the high proportion of adolescents in all identity groups who participated in at least one team sport during their 10th grade school year. Ignoring team sports, the princesses are overrepresented in both the performing arts and school-involved activity groups, and the brains are overrepresented in the prosocial activity group. The criminals are characterized by either very low or relatively low participation in all activity groups except team sports, and the basket cases are characterized by relatively low participation in all groups except the performing arts.

Table 10.11: Mean Levels (and Standard Deviations) of Friend Characteristics in 10th Grade by Participation in Extracurricular Activities

	Prosocial activities		Sports teams		Performing arts		School involvement		Academic clubs	
	No	Yes	No	Yes	No	Yes	No	Yes	No	Yes
College plans	3.7	4.0**	3.6	3.9**	3.7	3.9**	3.7	4.1	3.7	4.0**
	(1.1)	(.9)	(1.1)	(1.0)	(1.1)	(1.0)	(1.1)	(.9)	(1.1)	(1.0)
Do well in school	3.3	3.6**	3.3	3.5**	3.3	3.5**	3.4	3.6	3.4	3.6**
	(1.0)	(.9)	(1.0)	(.9)	(1.0)	(.9)	(1.0)	(.9)	(1.0)	(.9)
Drink regularly	2.8	2.4**	2.6	2.7	2.7	2.6*	2.7	2.8	2.7	2.6
	(1.3)	(1.1)	(1.2)	(1.3)	(1.2)	(1.2)	(1.3)	(1.2)	(1.2)	(1.2)
Use drugs	1.8	1.5**	1.9	1.7*	1.8	1.7**	1.8	1.6	1.8	1.6*
	(1.1)	(1.0)	(1.1)	(1.1)	(1.1)	(1.0)	(1.1)	(1.0)	(1.1)	(1.0)
Skip class	2.7	2.4**	2.8	2.6**	2.7	2.5**	2.7	2.6	2.7	2.5+
	(1.2)	(1.1)	(1.2)	(1.1)	(1.2)	(1.2)	(1.2)	(1.2)	(1.2)	(1.2)

+p<.10. *p<.05. **p<.01.
Reprinted from Eccles and Barber, 1999.

Student Council, Volunteering, Basketball, or Marching Band

Table 10.12: Mean Levels (and Standard Deviations) of Friend Characteristics in 12th Grade by Participation in Extracurricular Activities

	Prosocial activities		Sports teams		Performing arts		School involvement		Academic clubs	
	No	Yes	No	Yes	No	Yes	No	Yes	No	Yes
College plans	4.0	4.2**	3.9	4.1**	3.9	4.2**	4.0	4.4**	4.0	4.3**
	(1.0)	(.9)	(1.0)	(.9)	(1.0)	(.9)	(1.0)	(.7)	(1.0)	(.7)
Do well in school	3.4	3.6**	3.4	3.5	3.4	3.6**	3.4	3.7**	3.4	3.7**
	(.8)	(.8)	(.9)	(.8)	(.8)	(.8)	(.8)	(.8)	(.8)	(.8)
Drink regularly	3.2	2.6**	2.9	3.2**	3.2	2.9*	3.1	3.1	3.1	2.9
	(1.3)	(1.2)	(1.3)	(1.3)	(1.3)	(1.2)	(1.3)	(1.1)	(1.3)	(1.2)
Use drugs	2.0	1.6**	1.8	1.9	2.0	1.8*	1.9	1.8	1.9	1.8
	(1.1)	(.9)	(1.0)	(1.1)	(1.1)	(.9)	(1.1)	(.9)	(1.0)	(1.0)
Skip class	3.1	2.7**	3.0	3.0	3.0	3.0	3.0	3.1	3.1	2.9
	(1.2)	(1.2)	(1.3)	(1.2)	(1.2)	(1.3)	(1.2)	(1.3)	(1.2)	(1.2)

†p<.10. *p<.05. **p<.01. Reprinted from Eccles and Barber, 1999.

It is possible that some of the activity group differences on the outcomes identified in the first part of this article reflect behavioral differences associated with these different peer-group identity categories.

Tables 10.14 and 10.15 summarize the differences between these identity groups on both the risky behaviors and academic outcomes discussed earlier at both Grades 10 and 12. As one would expect, the criminal was highest on most of the risky behaviors, and the brain was the lowest at both grade levels. But consistent with the results reported earlier on the association of activity involvement with drinking behavior, the jocks reported relatively high levels of alcohol use at Grade 12. This finding is especially interesting given the stability of group differences across the 2-year gap between the self-identification as a criminal or jock and the rating of the risk behaviors. Interestingly, the princesses also report rather high levels of alcohol use in Grade 12.

Table 10.13: Mean Levels (and Standard Deviations) of Activity Participation in 10th Grade by *Breakfast Club* Identity

	Princess	Jock	Brain	Basket case	Criminal	Contrasts
Prosocial activities**	.26	.16	.35	.26	.12	Br > P, J, C;
	(.44)	(.37)	(.48)	(.44)	(.32)	Ba, P > J, C
Sports teams**	.45	.87	.49	.28	.47	J > P, Br, Ba, C;
	(.50)	(.34)	(.50)	(.45)	(.50)	P, Br, C > Ba
Performing arts**	.50	.19	.39	.44	.24	P > J, Br, C;
	(.50)	(.40)	(.49)	(.50)	(.43)	Br, Ba > J, C
School involvement**	.28	.15	.12	.15	.05	P > J, Br, Ba, C;
	(.45)	(.36)	(.32)	(.36)	(.22)	J > C
Academic clubs**	.19	.08	.21	.18	.12	P, Br, Ba > J
	(.39)	(.27)	(.41)	(.39)	(.32)	

**p < .01. Reprinted from Eccles and Barber, 1999.

Section IV: Socialization and Sport

Table 10.14: Mean Levels (and Standard Deviations) of Risk Behavior in 10th Grade by *Breakfast Club* Identity

	Princess	Jock	Brain	Basket case	Criminal	Contrasts
Drink alcohol**	2.7	2.6	1.8	2.5	3.6	C > P, J, Br, Ba;
	(1.8)	(1.8)	(1.1)	(1.7)	(2.4)	P, J, Ba > Br
Skip school**	1.6	1.6	1.3	1.7	2.5	C > P, J, Br, Ba;
	(.8)	(.9)	(.8)	(.9)	(1.5)	P, J, Ba > Br
Use drugs**	1.4	1.3	1.1	1.5	2.9	C > P, J, Br, Ba;
	(1.1)	(1.0)	(.5)	(1.4)	(2.5)	P, Ba > Br
Like school**	4.8	4.8	4.8	4.0	3.6	P, J, Br > Ba, C
	(1.6)	(1.5)	(1.5)	(1.8)	(2.0)	

†$p<.10$. *$p<.05$. **$p<.01$.   Reprinted from Eccles and Barber, 1999.

Tables 10.14 and 10.15 also show the results for the positive academic outcomes. The expected pattern of results occurred for each of these measures as well: The brains had the highest rates of college attendance, followed closely, however, by the princesses and the jocks; the criminals had the lowest. Princesses, jocks, and brains also reported enjoying school the most at both grade levels. The results for college attendance are especially interesting, given that this outcome was measured 4 to 5 years after the self-categorization as a *Breakfast Club* stereotype.

These preliminary results suggest that there is a link between identity, patterns of activity involvement, and other indicators of successful and risky adolescent development. This is most evident in the contrast between the jock and the criminal. These two groups are doing equally well in school in terms of their GPAs, and both are equally involved in alcohol consumption at Grade 12. What distinguishes them? The jock has a school-based activity identity whereas the criminal does not. It is not that the criminal is not involved in sports; although less likely to be involved in sports than the jocks, 47% of the criminals were participating in school-based team sports in the 10th grade. Unfortunately, this changed between 10th and 12th grades. Consistent with the findings of Larson (1994), 70% of these sports-participating criminals had dropped out of sports by Grade 12. This represents the largest dropout rate for all five identity types. Eckert (1989) suggested that one of the key distinguishing characteristics of the burnouts in her study (a group much like the groups who labeled themselves the criminal and the basket case in this study) was the lack of a school-based identity. Over time, this group became increasingly detached from school, leading in many cases to dropping out of high school prior to graduation. A similar process may be going on for our criminal group. They also appear to be disconnecting from school and school-based activities over their high school years and are least likely to graduate from high school and least likely to be attending college at age 21. Although not quite so extreme, a similar process may also be going on in our basket case group.

As noted earlier, it is also likely that the nature of the peers one hangs out with as the result of one's identity and of one's activity patterns is a primary mediator of this link. Table 10.16 summarizes the identity group differences in peer network characteristics. Both the criminals and the brains had consistent profiles of friends. On one hand, the criminals stood out as having the fewest proportion of friends who were doing well academically and planning to attend college and the highest proportion of friends engaged in risky behaviors. Consequently, it should not be surprising then that this group had the worst outcomes on both of these sets of outcomes despite the fact that they were actually doing all right in terms of their own GPAs.

On the other hand, the brains had the highest proportion of friends rated high on academic outcomes and low on risky behaviors. Consequently, it is not surprising that these youth themselves had the most consistent set of outcomes.

In contrast, the jocks and princesses had a more mixed pattern in terms of risks and protective factors. On one hand, the proportion of their friends with good academic outcomes was about the same as the brains' peer network. On the other hand, the proportion of their friends who drank and skipped school was also quite high. This pattern is consistent with the jocks' own behavior patterns.

Table 10.15: Mean Levels (and Standard Deviations) of Risk Behavior in 12th Grade by *Breakfast Club* Identity

	Princess	Jock	Brain	Basket case	Criminal	Contrasts
Drink alcohol**	4.4	4.8	2.9	3.5	5.2	P, J, C > Br, Ba
	(2.4)	(2.7)	(2.1)	(2.1)	(2.5)	
Get drunk**	3.8	4.1	2.6	3.3	4.5	J, C > Br, Ba
	(2.1)	(2.4)	(1.8)	(2.1)	(2.3)	P > Br
Skip school**	3.1	3.1	2.5	3.2	4.1	C > P, J, Br, Ba
	(1.5)	(1.5)	(1.7)	(1.7)	(1.6)	P, J, Ba > Br
Use marijuana**	1.6	2.0	1.4	1.9	3.2	C > P, J, Br, Ba
	(1.4)	(1.8)	(1.2)	(1.5)	(2.4)	J > Br
Use hard drugs**	1.3	1.4	1.2	1.4	2.0	C > P, J, Br, Ba
	(1.0)	(1.2)	(.9)	(.9)	(1.6)	
Like school	4.7	4.8	4.8	4.6	4.8	
	(1.8)	(1.8)	(1.7)	(1.8)	(1.9)	
High school GPA**	2.6	2.5	3.0	2.6	2.2	Br > P, J, Ba, C
	(.7)	(.7)	(.7)	(.7)	(.7)	P, J, Ba > C; P > J
Percentage in full-time college**	.55	.56	.62	.39	.31	P, J, Br > Ba, C
	(.50)	(.50)	(.49)	(.49)	(.46)	

†$p<.10$. *$p<.05$. **$p<.01$.
Reprinted from Eccles and Barber, 1999.

Section IV: Socialization and Sport

Table 10.16: Mean Levels (and Standard Deviations) of Friend Characteristics in 10th Grade by *Breakfast Club* Identity

	Princess	Jock	Brain	Basket case	Criminal	Contrasts
College plans**	3.9	4.0	4.0	3.5	3.1	P, J, Br > Ba, C;
	(1.0)	(1.0)	(.9)	(1.2)	(1.2)	Ba > C
Do well in school**	3.5	3.5	3.6	3.2	2.9	P, J, Br > Ba, C;
	(.9)	(.8)	(.8)	(1.1)	(1.1)	Ba > C
Drink regularly**	2.7	2.8	2.2	2.6	3.4	C > P, J, Br, Ba;
	(1.2)	(1.2)	(1.1)	(1.1)	(1.2)	P, J, Ba > Br
Use drugs**	1.7	1.6	1.4	1.9	2.8	C > P, J Br, Ba;
	(1.0)	(.9)	(.9)	(1.1)	(1.5)	Ba > P, J, Br; P > Br
Skip class**	2.8	2.6	2.1	2.8	3.5	C > P, J, Br, Ba;
	(1.2)	(1.1)	(1.0)	(1.1)	(1.2)	P, J, Ba > Br

⁺$p<.10$. *$p<.05$. **$p<.01$.
Reprinted from Eccles and Barber, 1999.

CONCLUSIONS

The analyses reported in the second section represent the beginnings of our exploration of possible ways that participation in various types of activities might influence other indicators of adolescent development. In the first section, we documented a predictive link between activity participation and increases in both academic outcomes and engagement in risky behaviors. In the second part, we documented relations among activity participation, peer-group identity formation, and friendship networks. What can we conclude as we look across these three aspects of adolescents' lives? Adolescents who participated in prosocial activities had the most consistently positive outcomes—high academic achievement and low rates of involvement in risky behaviors. They were also the group most likely to identify themselves as brains and the group who had the most friends who were academic-oriented and the fewest friends engaged in risky behaviors. These identity and peer group patterns could help explain why it was only participation in prosocial activities that served as a protective influence for both sets of outcomes. It is among this group of adolescents that the three spheres of influence converge on both positive academic outcomes and low involvement in risky behaviors.

A different pattern of convergence characterized those youth involved in team sports. For this group, both identity group and peer group were associated with positive academic outcomes and relatively high levels of alcohol consumption. This pattern of convergence could help explain why being involved in team sports is associated with increases in both drinking and academic achievement.

A less extreme example of this type of convergence was also evident for those adolescents involved in school-related and school spirit-related clubs/organizations. This group also exhibited positive academic trajectories; in addition, however, they were just as likely to drink alcohol as their nonparticipating peers and showed a trend toward increasing rates of skipping school from the 10th to the 12th grade. They were also the group most likely to label themselves as princesses, who, in turn, were especially likely to have a high GPA, to be attending college at age 21, to drink alcohol and skip school on a fairly regular basis, and to have a substantial proportion of friends who evidenced the same profile.

Consequently, it should not be surprising that involvement in sports and school-based/school spirit-related activities was related to a different pattern of change over the high school years than participating in prosocial activities. The results for all three of these groups are consistent with the perspective on synergistic relations among these three domains of adolescent development outlined earlier and illustrated in figure 10.1. Activity choice is likely to both grow out of and reinforce emerging identities—particularly those aspects of identity linked to instrumental success and finding one's place in the social milieu. Activity choice also channels friendship networks due to propinquity and to shared interests. Friendship networks further reinforce the value of various types of activities and identities. Friendship networks also develop cultures of their own, which set the norms for a wide range of behaviors and long-term expectations and aspirations, thus influencing adolescents' behaviors across several domains (see Brown, 1990; Eckert, 1989; Sherif & Sherif, 1964). Consequently, the patterns of associations of activity participation with other indicators of adolescent development should depend on the nature of the peer culture and shared values associated with the groups of adolescents who dominate each activity setting.

Although our results are consistent with this analysis, the results reported here are basically correlational. In the future, we plan to do the detailed longitudinal causal modeling to verify the directional relations implied in this analysis. In addition, we will investigate the influences on activity participation. Given our interest in identity, we will pay particular attention to those characteristics of the self-system that are likely to influence activity choice, such as ability self-concept, expectations for success, subjective values, and perceived norms (see also Ajzen & Driver, 1991; Eccles, 1983; Fishbein & Ajzen, 1975). We also have data on the role of family, school, and elementary school participation patterns as influences on activity choices during adolescence.

We had a second goal in this article. Information regarding the patterns of involvement of adolescents in a variety of out-of-school and extracurricular activities provides us with a more complete picture of the social context of development during this period. What do adolescents do when they are not in formal educational or family settings? About 40% of adolescent waking hours are discretionary (no school, homework, employment, or chores), yet we know almost nothing about what teenagers do with their leisure time (for an exception, see Carnegie Corporation, 1992; Larson & Kleiber, 1993). We need to know more about a wider range of social settings, including athletics, school clubs and activities, and community service. Consequently, we also presented the patterns of activity involvement of this sample of adolescents as important descriptive information about the lives of today's youth.

The majority of the youth (69%) in this study were involved in some type of organized activity during their discretionary time. On average, most of the females were involved with more than one such activity, and most of the males were involved in less than two such activities. The range of activities was quite broad, with females exhibiting a more diverse pattern than males. For both males and females, the three most common activities were team sports, bands or orchestras, and church, with participation on sports teams being the most common by a substantial margin. Within sports, males and females exhibit sex role-

Section IV: Socialization and Sport

stereotyped patterns. It is noteworthy, however, that the 10th-grade males and females in this sample were equally likely to be participating on swimming/diving teams and tennis teams, and females were more likely than males to be participating on softball and volleyball teams.

In conclusion, we have documented the types of activities U.S. adolescents were participating in during the early 1990s. We also documented the relation of activity participation to indicators of other positive and risky developmental outcomes. Involvement in prosocial activities was linked to positive educational trajectories and low rates of involvement in risky behaviors. In contrast, participation in team sports was linked to positive educational trajectories and to high rates of involvement in one type of risky behavior: drinking alcohol. The fact that this activity was associated with both good educational outcomes and drinking is consistent with other studies reporting that some involvement in risky activities such as drinking and cutting school is not necessarily problematic in terms of the consequences for long-term educational success (Schulenberg, Maggs, & Hurrelmann, 1997). One must take into account the meaning of the particular behavior in the broader context of the adolescent's life and development. If the risky behavior takes place in the context of a group of highly motivated and otherwise mentally healthy adolescents, it is unlikely that the risky behavior will, in and of itself, have extremely negative consequences (e.g., drinking among athletes and princesses). In contrast, if the risky behavior is part of a broader syndrome of behaviors and disaffection from socially accepted institutional settings such as schools, then the risky behavior is likely to be prognostic of poor subsequent developmental outcomes (Eckert, 1989; Jessor & Jessor, 1977).

Section V

Academic Achievement and Involvement in Sports

Participation in High School Competitive Sports: A Subversion of School Mission or Contribution to Academic Goals?

Naomi Fejgin

This study examines the relationship between participation in high school competitive sport and student outcomes such as grades, self-concept, locus of control, discipline problems, and educational aspirations. Then, assuming that participating in sports may have certain effects, this study also analyzes background factors that relate to participation, such as family and school attributes.

EFFECTS: IS SCHOOL SPORT A CHARACTER BUILDER?

Functional theorists have long viewed school sport as an integration mechanism for individual students, for school as an organization, and for society at large (Coleman, 1985). It has been argued (Evans & Davies, 1986; Frey, 1986) that team sports, especially interscholastic competitions, offer an opportunity for all students—active athletes, cheerleaders, and spectators—to congregate and fight for a common goal. These events are viewed as social rituals that socialize youth into some of the basic values of American life: competition, determination, fair play, and achievement.

At the individual level, in light of the developmental model, participation in school teams is viewed as affecting outcomes and building character. Character aspects and outcomes said to be affected include honesty, courage, cooperation, acceptance of authority, social prestige, and opportunities for educational and occupational advancement (Frey, 1986). Various studies have examined different psychological, attitudinal, and behavioral aspects of school and work performance in relation to sport participation. Several reviews of empirical studies of the effects of sport participation (Holland & Andre, 1987; Marsh,

Section V: Academic Achievement and Involvement in Sports

1993; Otto, 1982; Stevenson, 1975) reported that the most commonly studied outcomes were academic achievement, educational and occupational aspirations, educational and occupational attainments, self-concept, and popularity. These outcomes tend to be positively related to participation in sport. For example, Otto and Alwin (1977) found that sport participation of male students in the senior year of high school was positively related to educational and occupational aspirations, after controlling for socioeconomic status (SES), IQ, and school grades. In a subsequent study Otto (1982) reported that sport participation in high school positively affected educational attainment, occupational status, and income 15 years later.

Howell, Miracle, and Rees (1989) found that sport participation in high school was related to educational attainment 5 years later, but not to income of those who did not attend college. Later, using the same sample, they reported that some forms of sport participation affected several measures of educational/occupational motivation, such as valuing of academic achievement, self-esteem, college plans, occupational plans, and positive attitudes toward the high school experience, but also some antisocial outcomes, such as irritability and reduced belief in "being honest" and in "social responsibilities" (Rees et al., 1990).

In more recent studies Melnick, Vanfossen, and Sabo (1988), using the nationally representative High School and Beyond data, found that girls' athletic participation was positively related to extra-curricular involvement, educational aspirations, and perceived popularity. They also found differential effects of sport participation on perceived popularity, extracurricular involvement, school grades, standardized achievement scores, dropout rates, educational aspirations, college attendance, degree sought, and advancement in college—for Hispanic boys and girls from urban, suburban, and rural areas (Melnick, Sabo, & Vanfossen, 1992a). In a subsequent study (Sabo, Melnick, & Vanfossen, 1993) they reported other differential effects on educational and occupational attainment of black, white, and Hispanic boys and girls from different areas; sport participation positively affected mostly suburban white male students and, to a lesser degree, white female students and Hispanic females from rural areas.

Marsh (1993), using the same sample, found that sport participation during the last 2 years of high school favorably affected 14 of 22 outcomes, including social and academic self-concept, educational aspirations, course work selection, homework, reduced absenteeism, and college attendance.

Other studies have suggested a zero-sum model in which more time spent on nonacademic goals—for example, sports (Coleman, 1961) or part-time employment (Marsh, 1991)—diverts attention from school, leading to less time spent on homework and less investment in school. Greenberger and Steinberg (1986) found that student part-time employment was related to lower GPA, and Marsh (1991) found that total hours of work during high school "unfavorably affected going to college, high school attendance, academic track, parental involvement, educational aspirations, standardized test scores, staying out of trouble,…and academic self-concept" (p.179). Coleman's argument about sport participation relied on his findings that athletic participation was the main determinant of social status of male high school students (1961). Therefore, he argued, students may prefer to invest time and energy in sport activities and neglect academic work that is not as valued by their peers. Later studies, however, found that athletic participation ranked only fifth among six status criteria for female high school students (Felz, 1978), and fourth for boys (Thirer & Wright, 1985). None of the studies actually found that sport participation negatively affected academic outcomes.

Most of the studies, however, especially those taking the developmental approach, had serious methodological problems. Nearly all of them used small, nonrepresentative samples (Hauser & Lueptow, 1978; Otto & Alwin, 1977; Snyder & Spreitzer, 1977; Spady, 1970). Many employed cross-sectional comparisons, without longitudinal perspectives (Braddock, 1981; Edwards, 1967; Hanks, 1979; Johnson, 1972; Malumphy, 1968; Pyecha, 1970; Snyder & Spreitzer, 1977). These cross-sectional studies may have found different attitudes and behaviors between athletes and nonathletes, but could not determine causality and direction of effect. They could not conclude, for example, whether sports participation builds self-discipline, or whether self-disciplined students choose to participate in sport teams and are able to endure the strenuous training regime.

Several studies employing longitudinal perspectives and using nationally representative samples (Hanks & Eckland, 1976; Howell et al., 1989; Rees et al., 1990) also used data from the 1960s and 1970s, and thus lack current relevance. The most recent studies employing a longitudinal perspective used data from the nationally representative sample of the High School and Beyond survey collected in the early to mid-1980s. Three of the four studies published by Melnick, Sabo, and Vanfossen examined subsamples of girls (Melnick et al., 1988), Hispanic students (Melnick et al., 1992a), or Hispanic and African-American youths (Melnick, Sabo, & Vanfossen, 1992b). One study considered educational and occupational mobility after high school, finding differential effects for various subgroups of students (Sabo et al., 1993).

Only one study examined some character-building effects (i.e., behaviors, attitudes, and concepts relevant to schoolwork), together with post-secondary achievement for the whole sample (Marsh, 1993). Marsh's conclusions, however, are different from those of Melnick et al. (1992a), although both agree that sport participation has no negative effects. While Melnick et al. concluded that "the 17 statistically or marginally significant, positive findings do not represent an overwhelming endorsement of the competitive high school sport experience" (p. 65), Marsh concluded that "participation in sport has many positive effects with no apparent negative effects and these positive effects are very robust," and "participation in sport leads to an increased commitment to, involvement with, or identification with school and school values" (p. 35). He also suggested that future studies take into account the type of sport the student is involved in and the degree of commitment to sport participation, variables not available in the High School and Beyond data set. The present study uses a more recent data set, which enables a more detailed measure of athletic participation.

Juxtaposing the predictions of the developmental and the zero-sum theories, this study addresses the effects of participation in school competitive sport on several student outcomes. Not all student outcomes examined in previous studies are analyzed in the present study, only those central to the predictions of these theories and to the key school missions. They are academic achievement and educational aspirations (for which the theories have opposing predictions). Also examined are self-concept, locus of control, and discipline problems, which have long been related in social-psychological theory to the first two outcomes. These behaviors and attitudes are seen here as important characteristics that contribute to individual advancement in school. Other characteristics such as moral or prosocial behaviors, which some scholars argue are positively affected by school sport (Arnold, 1984) (although others hold a contrary view; Eitzen, 1992), are not examined here.

The effect of athletic participation is also compared to that of participation in other extracurricular activities, such as academic clubs, music/drama, student government, and other hobby clubs. These activities have been positively related to several school-related behaviors (Finn, 1989; Spady, 1970), and to the total development of the individual (Holland & Andre, 1987).

BACKGROUND FACTORS: SCHOOL SPORT AND CONFLICT THEORY

In contrast to those who espouse the functional arguments, conflict theorists argue that while participation in school teams may result in a variety of positive outcomes, school sport is often detrimental to those individuals who do not participate and to the school organization, since it has the potential of increasing tension and antagonism between groups within the school. Hendry (1978) found underinvolvement of lower class students in sports teams in Britain, which resulted in an antisport, antischool subculture. Other studies speculate on the harmful effects that unequal opportunity in sports and physical education may have for girls (Carrington & Leaman, 1986; Schafer, 1981; Scraton, 1986), enhancing their passivity, lack of competitiveness, and low self-esteem. Hargreaves (1986) put sport in a larger, macrosocial perspective, suggesting that it is used by more powerful groups in society for their benefit. Sage (1990) added that college and professional sport opportunities in America are unequally distributed across race, gender, and social class, and that the few cases of "rags to riches" athletes are made so visible in order to maintain belief in social mobility and equal opportunity, and to preserve the existing social structure. These beliefs trickle down to lower grades and encourage minority youth to invest in sport instead of academic work, believing it will offer them opportunities for social mobility.

Following these suggestions, this study addresses a second issue, whether sports in American high schools in the 1990s are unequally distributed across race, gender, and socioeconomic levels, and whether these variations are associated with certain school attributes.

METHODOLOGY

Sample

This study draws on data from the National Educational Longitudinal Study (NELS) of 1988 Base Year and First Follow-Up (Ingels, Scott, Lindmark, Frankel, & Myers, 1992). The base-year study (NELS 88) was carried out on a clustered, stratified national probability sample of 1,052 schools and 26,432 students (8th graders), while the first follow-up studied the same students in 10th grade (22,696) as well as a freshened sample to replace dropouts. The analyses in the present study use the panel sample of sophomores in 1990, who were in 8th grade in 1988, in order to present a longitudinal perspective. The sample was adjusted and weighted according to the formula suggested by the study's designers (Ingels et al., 1992, p. 58), to correct for sample design effects and ensure representativeness. The data for each student were collected by four questionnaires administered to students, parents, teachers, and schools. The present study uses mainly information available through the student questionnaire, some parent information, and school reports, together with standardized test scores from tests administered specifically for this study.

Measures

Most of the variables used for the examination of this study's questions are clearly defined in the NELS 88 data set—either as simple measures or as composites, compiled by the NCES (National Center for Education Statistics). Some are new measures composed for this study from the available data. The variables are described in detail in the appendix. Following are the variables, as used in the model. The main independent variable, athletic participation, is described in detail.

Independent Variables

The independent variable used in the main model, athletic participation (Athletic), is a continuous measure, composed of student self-reports on nine questionnaire items regarding participation in one or more sports, such as baseball/softball, basketball, football, soccer, swim team, other team sport, individual sport, cheerleading, or pom-pom. Participation in each sport was ranked on a scale of 0 to 3 (*did not participate* = 0, *participated in intramural sport* =1, *participated on a junior varsity/freshmen team* = 2, *participated on a varsity team, or as a captain* = 3). Scores for each sport were summed so that the composite score (0 to 27) reflects athletic involvement as a combined measure of number of sports played, and the level of participation.

Also an alternative model considers the following independent variables: participation in music/drama (Music/Play), academic clubs (Academic Cl), student government (Student Cl), and other hobby clubs (Other Cl). In the model where athletic participation is the dependent variable, additional independent variables were introduced: school size, school affiliation (Private Scl), and 8th-grade participation in varsity sport (8th Varsity), intramural sport (8th Intramur), and private sport lessons after school (8th Private Sports AS).

Dependent Variables

Dependent variables were student 10th-grade measures of grades, self-concept (Self Cpt), locus of control (Locus), discipline problems (Discip), and educational aspirations (Ed Asp).

Background and Control Variables

These variables included gender (Female), race (Black, Asian, Hispanic), standardized composite test score (Std Achv), family income (Fam Inc), parent education (Par Ed), and 8th-grade measures of student grades (8th Grade), self-concept (8th Self), locus of control (8th Locus), discipline problems (8th Discip), and educational aspirations (8th Asp).

Section V: Academic Achievement and Involvement in Sports

Statistical Analysis

Multiple regression analysis was used to examine the relationship between background, independent variables, and dependent variables. Multiple regression explains the extent to which variance in the dependent variable can be accounted for by the variance in a set of independent variables. Standardized beta coefficients indicate the weight of each variable in explaining the variance in the dependent variable (Norusis,1993).

In order to estimate the effects of athletic participation on student grades, self-concept, locus of control, discipline problems, and educational aspirations, a set of independent multiple regressions were performed, where the background variables and athletic participation were regressed with each dependent variable separately. For each dependent variable, the 8th-grade measure was added to the equation in order to control for prior level and to show the net effect of athletic participation. Such a strategy allows interpretation of the relations between sport participation and outcome variables as effects of sport participation, since not only student background was controlled for but also prior measures of the outcome variables.

In order to examine relationships between background variables and sport participation, some cross-tabulations were presented first to demonstrate rates of participation of various groups in various sports. Then, another regression analysis examined in four steps the relative effect of each background variable on athletic participation, and the additional contribution of some school properties and prior athletic experience to the explained variance in 10th-grade athletic participation.

FINDINGS

Effects of Athletic Participation

After controlling for the background variables and for prior measures of each dependent variable, I show additional significant effects of athletic participation on grades ($\beta = .041$), self-concept ($\beta = .053$), locus of control ($\beta = .057$), educational aspirations ($\beta = .068$), and discipline problems ($\beta = -.057$).

Evidently, each dependent variable is mostly related to its measure in 8th grade (e.g., student grades in 10th grade are highly related to grades in 8th grade; student self-concept in 10th grade is highly related to self-concept in 8th grade, and so on), However, additional direct effects of athletic participation on each of these variables are observed, meaning that athletic participation appears to contribute to increased levels of grades, self-concept, locus of control, and educational aspirations, and to decreased levels of discipline problems. In fact, in each of these models except for educational aspirations, the effect of athletic participation is greater than that of family income, parent education, gender, and Asian or Hispanic origin. These variables explain about 38% of the variance in educational aspirations, 27% of the variance in self-concept, 21% of the variance in locus of control, 19% of the variance in student grades, and 15% of the variance in discipline problems.

In order to look for differential effects of being involved with sports at higher levels of intensity and exposure, varsity team players and intramural players were entered into the model and computed against nonplayers (in place of the Athletic variable). In these models, playing on intramural teams has diminishing or insignificant effects on the dependent variables, while playing on varsity teams has increasing effects ($\beta = .053$ for grades, $\beta = .063$ for self-concept, $\beta = .102$ for educational aspirations, and $\beta = -.064$ for discipline problems).

This analysis shows that students who are more involved in school sports have higher grades, higher self-concept, more internal locus of control, higher educational aspirations, and less discipline problems in school. The longitudinal approach, which enabled me to control for these behaviors prior to students' participation in high school sports teams, permits a cautious causal interpretation of the relationship between the intervening and the dependent variables. That is, regardless of whether students with higher grades, self-concept, locus of control, and educational aspirations and fewer discipline problems choose to participate in sport teams in high school, participation seems to affect in turn the same outcomes.

When participation in specific sports such as baseball/ softball, basketball, football, and so on replaces athletic participation in these models, no significant effects are shown on any of the dependent variables (table not shown). This does not necessarily mean that different sports do not have distinct effects, but rather that these effects cannot be sorted out in the analysis, since all sports categories are not mutually exclusive and some students participate in more than one sport.

Other Extracurricular Activities

The contribution of participation in high school athletic competitions may also be assessed in comparison to other extracurricular activities. Each activity has a different nature and is expected to draw different students and to have distinct effects on development. Some activities are more competitive than others, some are more creative, and some demand high intellectual ability, specific physical skills, or social skills. It is logical to assume that participation in any extracurricular activity has some effects on student behavior. When such participation is entered into the model along with athletic participation, the relative effects may be compared.

The partial regression coefficients for participation in athletic teams are compared to those of participation in other clubs, when all are regressed with each of the dependent variables separately. Participation in nonathletic clubs was grouped into four categories, according to the nature of the activities: academic clubs (math, science, debate), creative clubs (music, drama), student self-management clubs (student council, school paper), and other activities, usually labeled as hobbies. When the relative effects within each regression are compared, it appears that the effects of athletic participation resemble more the effects of participation in academic clubs than those of other clubs. The effect of athletic participation is similar to the effect of participation in academic clubs for educational aspirations ($\beta = .082$ and .080, respectively) and locus of control ($\beta = .043$ and .055); smaller than the effect of participation in academic clubs and similar to the effect of participation in music/ drama ($\beta = -.045$ and -.075 and -.050) for discipline problems and for grades ($\beta = .032$ and .092); and larger than the effect of participation in academic clubs for self-concept ($\beta = .061$ and .034). All the other effects are insignificant.

The interesting point here is the consistency of effects of participation in these two types of extracurricular activities on all the dependent variables, while participation in other activities is mostly insignificant (except music/ drama on educational aspirations and discipline, student clubs on educational aspirations, and other clubs on grades). While the effects of participation in academic clubs on these variables, especially on educational aspirations and grades, would be more readily anticipated, the effects of athletic participation are more surprising, since no clear link has been established between such physical and mental activities. Furthermore, participation in school sport teams is sometimes considered an alternative activity and an energy release outlet for low-performing students, which may have positive effects on self-esteem and conformity to school rules but not on academic values. It seems, however, that contrary to the zero-sum theory assumptions, there is no negative academic price for the positive effects that athletic participation has on self-concept and locus of control.

Athletic Participation and Student Background

Since the apparent contribution of athletic involvement to the development of certain student qualities has been established, the question that follows is what factors determine the degree of participation. Available data do not permit control for physical ability, which is probably related to participation in school sport. However, it is important to examine whether such participation is equally distributed across certain social groups. It is not. The percent of athletes (in any sport, on both intramural or varsity teams) is presented for each sex, SES quartile, school type, urban status (within the public sector only), and school size. Cross-tabulations were subjected to chi-square tests, and significance levels are reported.

They show total participation of 53.4% in high school sports and significant differences in rates of participation between all categories except race. Male students participate more than female; students from higher SES quartiles participate more than their counterparts in lower SES quartiles; students who attend private (non-Catholic) schools participate more than those who attend Catholic schools; and those attending Catholic schools participate more than students who attend public schools. In the public sector, students attending suburban schools participate more than urban students. And finally, athletic participation increases as school size decreases.

In order to examine the relative contribution of background variables and school attributes to athletic participation, a set of regressions were performed, where background variables were regressed with athletic participation first. School size, school type, and previous engagement in school or private sports teams were then entered as additiontal steps.

Participation is affected first by gender ($\beta = -.119$ for females), and then by parent education ($\beta = .075$) and family income ($\beta = .050$). Standardized achievement score and race/ethnicity have no additional significant effects. It seems then, contrary to common myth, that youths from lower SES families do not engage in sports activities more than do those from higher SES families, at least when it comes to school-organized activities. Except for the traditional relationship of gender and sport, the single most powerful explanation for individual athletic involvement is parent education. When the model is estimated for males and females separately, it shows an even more powerful influence of parent education on female sport participation. Gender differences are even more extreme when participation in varsity teams is considered. And when such participation is used as the dependent variable instead of Athletic, the effect of being female increases ($\beta = .133$), but that of race/ ethnicity stays insignificant.

School Attributes

Another explanation for student participation in school sport may be derived from the opportunity structure within the school. Some schools offer many different sports, while others offer only a few. Some schools focus mainly on interscholastic teams, which can involve only a small number of athletes, and only the best, while other schools offer more opportunities to participate via intramural teams. Some schools offer various kinds of sports, but do not encourage students to participate, while others do everything to promote school sport involvement. The position of sport is an important aspect of the school's culture and probably depends on community norms and values as well as the relative power of the principal, coaches, and teachers, who strive to promote certain ideas (Coleman, 1985). The sport culture of a school undoubtedly affects student participation.

Available data in this set do not allow detailed analysis of actual sport opportunities in each school. Although the students were asked whether the school offered each sport, their answers did not reflect enough variance to enable any meaningful statistical analysis. Only about 1 to 5% of the students stated that their schools did not offer baseball/softball, football, basketball, cheerleading, or any individual sport, and 13 to 27% said that their schools did not offer pompom, soccer, or swimming. Still, in some schools there was a higher participation rate than in others. The question is whether rate of participation is related only to individual student inclination or to some school properties that may be indirect measures of an opportunity structure within the school. Therefore, four different proxies for such opportunity structure were entered into the model separately: school affiliation, size, region, and urban status, all of which are known to affect certain school outcomes. Region and urban status had insignificant effects on athletic participation.

A small additional effect of private school attendance ($\beta = .038$) is shown, and a larger effect of school size is reported ($\beta = -.154$). When both school type and school size are introduced into the same equation, school type loses significance, probably due to the high correlation between the two, and possibly to the small cell number, after controlling for all other variables. It seems, then, that school type and school size are related to some type of opportunity structure that encourages or discourages athletic participation. Note that these are net school effects, after individual socioeconomic measures have been controlled, so that school size is not another proxy for family income, or educational level, but a school property.

Since school attributes together with background variables explain a small percent of the variance in athletic participation (about 5% with school size), another group of variables were introduced, previous involvement in sports in 8th grade. The coefficients here suggest that students who played on varsity teams in 8th grade are much more likely to play in high school ($\beta = .255$). So are students who played on intramural teams ($\beta = .071$) and those who played in private nonschool clubs ($\beta = .127$). One may argue that these effects conceal the contribution of natural physical skills to participation in high school sports. While this is probably partially true, it may also point to earlier effects of parent education and income, which are correlated with each of these variables.

Section V: Academic Achievement and Involvement in Sports

SUMMARY AND CONCLUSIONS

The information from students in this nationally representative sample about their involvement in school-organized sports seems to support the predictions of developmental theory on the one hand and those of conflict theory on the other. The main goal of this study was to examine whether sport participation in high school was positively related to some school-related behaviors that enhance individual academic success, as several researchers maintain (Grove & Dodder, 1979; Marsh, 1993; Otto & Alwin, 1977), or whether the "sport builds character" belief is just a myth supported by conventional wisdom, as Rees et al. (1990) argued, and may even impede investment in academic work, as Coleman (1961) suggested.

As predicted by developmental theory, students who are more involved in high school competitive sports have higher grades, a higher self-concept, higher educational aspirations, a more internal locus of control, and fewer discipline problems. Although the effects are small, they are statistically significant and very consistent across all the analyses.

It appears that the repetitive experiences associated with competitive athletic activities may have some character-building qualities. The mechanisms through which these qualities are developed are not entirely clear. Possible explanations are offered here; some are supported by previous research while others are mere speculations.

First, I will consider the relationship between competitive sport activities and the development of locus of control. These activities offer experiences of both success and failure, which are highly visible to the individual and to the peer group. The clear and direct link between performance and achievement, as measured in a game score or a swimming time, may very well help to establish a more internal locus of control. The individual realizes that it is up to him or her to perform better or worse, and that it is difficult to blame other people or circumstances for failure.

Although sport competitions offer both success and failure experiences, being admitted to any sports team is a recognition of some kind of physical (and sometimes social) capability or skill. This recognition is associated with some social rewards, which probably help to develop a more positive self-concept. The higher social status of high school athletes (Coleman, 1961), together with physical skill itself, may very well feed the ego and enhance self-esteem (Snyder & Spreitzer, 1990).

Participation in sports teams requires adjustment to rigid rules, regulations, and practice times, as well as to the coach's authority (Whitson, 1986). Ongoing training of individuals to comply with these rules and to endure long hours of practice, while delaying the fulfillment of other physical and social needs, teaches the importance of and the rewards associated with such compliance, possibly making it easier to accept other school rules and formal authority. Furthermore, being on a school team means being recognized by the system as a "good citizen" who participates in community life beyond basic requirements. This may in turn create deeper commitment by the student, not only to the school's rules but also to its basic values and to the academic work that is its main mission. Thus, conforming to school rules and values may result in more disciplined behavior and higher grades. Higher grades could reflect either student self-discipline and willingness to put forth effort, learned partially through sport training, or teacher inclination to prefer these students and mark their work more favorably (Snyder & Spreitzer, 1990). Other studies have suggested that sport participation positively affects academic performance and acceptance of school rules through identification with the school (Finn, 1989; Marsh, 1993).

The effect of athletic participation on educational aspirations may be attributed to students' plans to use athletic prowess as "human capital" in gaining access to college, as Snyder and Spreitzer (1990) posited. Or, as Spady (1970) suggested, athletic participation may enhance educational aspirations through increased perceived social status. Or, it may be that athletic involvement affects educational aspirations not only directly, but also through self-concept, locus of control, discipline, and grades. The positive effects of these variables on educational aspirations are well-known although not always clear-cut, as in the case of female students, who have lower self-concept but higher educational aspirations.

Whatever the explanations, it appears that participation in high school competitive sports provides some kinds of positive experiences that enhance student adjustment to school rules, schoolwork, and the basic values of an achievement-oriented society.

Lately several sport sociologists have embraced a more critical approach to school sports, pointing out the possible negative aspects of high school and college competitive sport. Eitzen (1992), for example, claimed that school sports as they are organized now are nondemocratic, opportunistic, and oppressive; they legitimate income inequalities between players, coaches, and managers; and they leave no room for freedom of choice, privacy, and individualism. Fernandez-Balboa (1993) argued that through the hidden curriculum in physical education and sport in school, students are socialized into "accepting particular modes of thinking and acting that support and legitimize power structures and social inequalities. These modes are characterized by apathy, indifference, apolitical attitudes, dependence on institutional control, compliance with authority, anxiety and powerlessness" (p. 248). Thus, he added, physical education lacks some fundamental human values, such as equity, freedom, cooperation, and self-actualization. Sage (1993) called on physical educators to rethink their roles and to challenge "the values that are unjust, insensitive, sexist, racist, and limiting" (p.162), so that they would not automatically reproduce the power system that supports the interests of the dominant elites.

That critique is mostly theoretical, but one aspect central to the idea of social reproduction is reflected in the present findings. The statistical analysis supports the basic arguments of conflict theory and reaffirms the established knowledge that the school curriculum is unequally distributed across gender and socioeconomic groups. In this case, it is school extracurricular activities that are disproportionately used by different groups. As might be expected, gender is the strongest determinant of participation in school sport, and a great deal of work in the sociology and history of sport has been devoted to explaining such findings. Some advocates of equal rights for women, particularly those adopting a liberal feminist perspective, argue that since sports are an important aspect of modern American life, women should participate not just as spectators but as players. And, the exclusion of any social group from any form of social activity, whether by law, force, or negative socialization, is coercion used by the dominant group for its benefit. In fact, there is growing evidence that schools contribute to the observed disproportionality

(Scraton, 1990; Wright, 1993). Accordingly, an appropriate part of the school mission could be to change this situation.

The other major bias in sports participation is that of social class. The model shows that once again, and against common myth, youths from lower socioeconomic groups have less opportunities to use this "social good" in order to better their educational and cultural adjustment. There are several theoretical explanations for this finding, and two clues are evident in the data presented here. First, the model shows that after gender, parents' educational level is the strongest determinant of athletic participation in school; thus, parental attitudes may be involved. Parents with more education may value the benefits of sport participation and possibly may encourage their children to participate. They also probably give them a head start in participation at a younger age, via private or community classes and summer camps. Second, the negative effects of public school affiliation and school size, which are related to student socioeconomic background, offer another explanation: Students from lower socio-economic groups have fewer opportunities to participate in school sports because the schools they attend offer fewer such activities or do not encourage active participation. This finding is in line with other findings about unequal opportunities for students in public versus private and Catholic schools (Coleman, Hoffer, & Kilgore, 1982). One may argue, at least against the first explanation, that extra-curricular sport activities are voluntary and that it is up to the student to use them. The same is true, however, regarding regular academic work. School is mandatory but studying is not. Still, we look for ways to reduce dropout rates and achievement gaps between social groups, and research in the sociology of education is primarily concerned with finding the factors that make a difference and suggesting ways of using them to increase all students' opportunities for better social adjustment.

Some policy implications of this study are that school sports have some positive effects, but their social distribution is unequal, and we should increase opportunities to participate. More teams for each type of sport would enable students to participate at different levels. Transportation home after practices and competitions would ease burdens of after-school participation. Incorporating sports in the schedule as elective classes, for credit, would facilitate during-school participation. Accommodating the needs of special populations may help make school sport less elitist and more humane. More research about methods that schools use to encourage sport participation, and about criteria that they use to allocate time and money and to select athletes, would assist policy makers in such decisions.

Another possible implication of this study is that educational research, and schools, should look into ways of organizing academic schoolwork following the sport pattern. It seems that school sport has some characteristics that may enhance student and coach self-worth and achievement orientation: It is voluntary, it is competitive, it is established on both intra- and inter-school comparisons, and it rewards all participants—students (and indirectly their parents), coaches, principals, and schools as a whole. This structure has a built-in incentive system for each participant and for the group to put forth effort, as well as cooperation, in order to achieve a clear, measurable, externally established goal (Coleman, 1993).

In some ways school sports, normally perceived as leisure activities, are more like work (Fine, 1987) or like the business world, since performance is judged not only against one's colleagues but also against the competition—the team of another school, another district, or another state. From this point of view, school sport is the only activity that may help students to internalize the universalistic norms that Dreeben (1968) argued to be an important latent function of school, while carrying achievement orientation to its limits. In most schools, universalistic criteria are not employed regarding academic work, since different teachers and different schools set different criteria. Therefore, the "universe" against which the student is judged is very small—his or her specific class, or the wider age group in the school. Following Coleman's suggestions for output-driven schools (1993), if schools could reorganize academic work to operate more like sports teams, where universalistic criteria are employed and a reward system is built in, they could inject into the system what is missing in so many schools today—a real achievement orientation.

Linking Extracurricular Programming to Academic Achievement: Who Benefits and Why?

BECKETT A. BROH

American schools are under increasing public pressure to improve students' achievement. Extracurricular programming, particularly school sports, is one of the most widespread and costly practices in our educational system, yet there is relatively little scientific information on the potential academic benefits of the extracurriculum. Does participating in sports or other activities promote higher achievement? Longitudinal studies on school sports have suggested that such participation raises students' grades and test scores (Fejgin 1994; Hanson and Kraus 1998, 1999). However, the literature has overwhelmingly focused on sports, largely ignoring participation in other types of activities (Holland and Andre 1987; Marsh 1992). Furthermore, surprisingly little effort has been made to incorporate sociological theory into research on extracurricular activities to help explain why participation may help students achieve. Consequently, two key questions remain unanswered: (1) how participating in sports promotes achievement or (2) whether the benefits of participation are unique to sports or if participating in nonsports activities also improves achievement. In this article, I address these two questions so that we may better understand the role of the extracurriculum in students' achievement.

EXTRACURRICULAR ACTIVITIES

High School Sports
School sports have been the focal point of research on extracurricular activities. Early analyses of the effect of participation in sports on academic achievement produced inconsistent evidence. Whereas some studies supported the "dumb jock" stereotype (Coleman 1961; Landers et al. 1978), others suggested that athletes outperform nonathletes in school (Rehberg 1969; Schafer and Armer 1968). Regardless of their

findings, none of these studies analyzed nationally representative samples, and many failed to control for background differences (e.g., race, family income, and parents' educational attainment) between athletes and nonathletes. Furthermore, as cross-sectional designs, none of them was able to provide evidence that the relationship between sports and achievement is causal, not simply a function of the selection of better students into sports participation. Indeed, more recent studies have indicated that there is a large selection bias of higher-achieving, "good" students into participation in extracurricular activities, including sports (Fejgin 1994; Quiroz, Gonzalez, and Frank 1996).

Recent research on sports and achievement has addressed this selection bias by using longitudinal data that provide outcome measures at two points in time and estimate changes in academic performance. Longitudinal studies are more powerful than cross-sectional studies for limiting the effects of selection bias and establishing a better case for causal order between independent and dependent variables.

Melnick and his associates (Melnick, Sabo, and VanFossen (1992a, 1992b; Melnick VanFossen, and Sabo 1988; Sabo, VanFossen, and Melnick 1993) completed numerous longitudinal studies on sports and education. Utilizing the High School and Beyond (HSB) study (U.S. Department of Education), their analyses tested the effect of sports participation on various educational outcomes (e.g., grades, test scores, educational aspirations, expectations and attainment, and college attendance) for racial and gender subgroups. Their results indicated that with the exception of a few subgroups and outcomes, participation in sports is generally unrelated to educational achievement. Additional findings from Marsh's (1993) longitudinal study of the HSB data supported Melnick et al.'s results. Marsh found that playing sports in high school has no significant effect on grades or standardized test scores in the general student population.

However, other studies that have drawn on more recent longitudinal data have offered evidence that participation in sports improves academic performance. Fejgin (1994) and Hanson and Kraus (1998, 1999), analyzing the National Educational Longitudinal Study of 1988 (NELS:88), both found support for the contention that participation in sports improves students' grades. Fejgin found that participation in sports in the 10th grade has a significant, positive effect on students' grades in the same year, controlling for performance in the 8th grade, and Hanson and Kraus found that for high school girls, participation in sports is related to higher achievement in science.

The disparate results of these studies are of some concern in efforts to understand the educational consequences of participation in school sports. However, there are many possible methodological explanations for the variability in the results. One is that measures of "sports participation" differ across studies, including various combinations of inter-scholastic sports, intramural sports, non-school sports, and cheerleading. It is possible that participation in these different types of sports does not affect students' achievement equally. To address this concern, I isolated these specific types of participation in the study presented here.

Other Extracurricular Activities

Research on other extracurricular activities has been limited by the use of small, nonrepresentative samples and cross-sectional data (Holland and Andre 1987). However, Marsh (1992) and McNeal

(1995) both used nationally representative, longitudinal data to examine the effects of participating in various extracurricular activities. Marsh examined the effect of total extracurricular activity participation (TEAP) on various educational outcomes by summing dichotomous scores for 16 categories of participation (e.g., sports, drama, music) to create a TEAP score. Controlling for background variables and prior measures of outcome variables, he found that TEAP is associated with an improved grade point average, higher educational aspirations, increased college attendance, and reduced absenteeism. McNeal studied the effect of different types of participation on the risk of dropping out of high school (see also Davalos, Chavez, and Guardiola 1999). He separated participation in extracurricular activities into four categories (i.e., sports clubs, fine arts, academic clubs, and vocational clubs) and examined the effect of each type of participation simultaneously. The results of logistic regression analyses indicated that once all forms of activity participation are controlled, only participation in sports clubs is significantly related to a reduced risk of dropping out of high school. This effect persists even after critical dropout forces, such as race, socioeconomic status, and employment, are taken into account.

These studies suggest that not all students who participate in the extracurriculum gain the same advantages from participation. Still, the literature has not yet explored how different types of participation affect academic achievement. Is mere participation enough to promote higher achievement, or do certain activities benefit students more than do others? To answer this question, I also tested how participating in music, drama, student council, yearbook, and vocational clubs affects students' achievement.

LINKING THE EXTRACURRICULUM TO STUDENTS' OUTCOMES

Why may participating in school sports or other school activities boost achievement? What do student-athletes gain through sports that help them academically? Researchers have speculated for decades about the potential benefits of participation, but little empirical evidence exists. Furthermore, the evidence that does exist is largely indirect and inconclusive. The following sections present three explanations (the developmental model, the leading-crowd hypothesis, and the social capital model) linking participation in sports to educational achievement. The developmental model and leading-crowd hypothesis represent long-held beliefs on the benefits of sports participation that have yet to be thoroughly tested. The social capital model is a newer perspective, refined in this article, which synthesizes various sources of social capital theory as it applies to school achievement. Because our knowledge, to date, has derived almost solely from research on school sports, I center my review and discussion on the effects of participation in sports and address the generalizability to participation in other forms of extracurricular activities.

Developmental Model
It has long been believed that participating in sports socializes adolescents in ways that promote educational success. Conventional wisdom holds that by teaching characteristics, such as a strong work ethic, respect for authority, and perseverance, sports participation develops skills that are consistent with educational values and thus helps students achieve (Coleman 1961; Miracle and Rees 1994). Furthermore, repeated successful experiences in sports, such as learning a new skill or winning a competition, are thought to develop self-confidence and maturity, which also carry over into educational pursuits (Fejgin 1994;

Section V: Academic Achievement and Involvement in Sports

Marsh 1993; Snyder and Spreitzer 1990). Therefore, playing sports develops "character" in athletes that increases their desire and ability to achieve academically (Rehberg 1969).

Miracle and Rees (1994) called these beliefs the "myth" of school sports because they arose and prospered for decades without scientific grounding. However, a few recent studies have offered some evidence that these beliefs are not without merit. Results from nationally representative, longitudinal studies have indicated that sports participation increases students' academic self-concept, locus of control, and work ethic (i.e., school attendance and time on homework) (Fejgin 1994; Marsh 1993). However, the research has not directly tested whether these developmental benefits significantly explain how participation in sports influences achievement. My study fills this void by testing the explanatory power of individual development in mediating the effect of participation on achievement.

The Leading-Crowd Hypothesis
The commonly held belief that playing sports develops "character" has dominated discussions on school sports and achievement to such an extent that there have been only modest attempts to explore alternative explanations. The prevailing alternative explanation, the leading-crowd hypothesis, suggests that sports participation offers student-athletes higher peer status that facilitates membership in "the leading crowd." Comprised of the most popular high school students, the leading crowd disproportionately consists of college-oriented, high achievers (Rehberg 1969). Thus, it is argued that by increasing social status, sports participation provides the student-athlete with membership in an academically oriented peer group that, in turn, facilitates higher academic performance.

Although indirect, there is enough evidence in support of this argument to warrant further investigation. For example, classic works by Coleman (1961), Eitzen (1975), and Thirer and Wright (1985) all indicated that male athletes hold the highest status in American high schools. Furthermore, Wells and Picou (1980) found that athletes are more likely to be associated with a college-oriented peer group than are nonathletes. This evidence, coupled with Lueptow and Kayser's (1973) finding that only high school athletes with status (e.g., "the athletic stars") have higher grade point averages relative to nonathletes, offers indirect support for the leading-crowd hypothesis. Unfortunately, these studies were unable to disentangle the causal ordering of sports participation, peer status, peer-group orientation, and academic performance. I directly tested the explanatory power of peer-group orientation in mediating the relationship between participation and achievement.

An extension of the leading-crowd hypothesis posits that sports participation is beneficial to the educational process by connecting student-athletes not only to academically oriented peers, but to adults, specifically parents and teachers (Wells and Picou 1980; Snyder and Spreitzer 1990). Building on this tenet, I argue that the academic benefits for athletes that operate through social networks are more fully conceptualized by applying social capital theory.

Social Capital Model
Social capital is generally recognized as the ability to accrue benefits through membership in social networks (Portes 1998). Coleman (1988), among others, argued that the family is a primary site of

social capital. Indeed, research has indicated that both human and social capital in the family play vital roles in a child's educational success (Coleman 1990; Parcel and Dufur 1998). Specifically, children whose parents are well educated (human capital) and actively involved in their children's lives (social capital) have greater success in school (Coleman 1988; Downey 1995; Hagan, MacMillan, and Wheaton 1996; Teachman, Paasch, and Carver 1996). In this light, participation in sports and other extracurricular activities may serve to create social capital within the family by providing opportunities for increased social interaction between the parents and the child.

As powerful as familial ties may be, extrafamilial networks are thought to be an additional and important source of social capital (Portes 1998). In this respect, social capital can exist among students, parents of students, and the school. Thus, it is possible that sports or other activities, by offering opportunities for the formation and intensification of social ties among students, parents, and the school, also create social capital outside the family.

Exactly how does social capital, within or outside the family, operate to provide educational benefits? A review of the literature suggests that these familial and nonfamilial social ties affect educational success primarily by providing a source of social control and a source of the dissemination of information and resources (Bourdieu 1985; Coleman 1988; Portes 1998). Thus, whereas previous investigations of sports have merely emphasized the benefits of having access to "adult culture," social capital theory introduces a network-analytic approach, illuminating specific mechanisms through which the social ties developed in school activities may benefit educational outcomes. I briefly review these mechanisms next.

Social capital, operating through strong social ties between parents and students, students and other students, and teachers and students, can act as a social control mechanism by promoting compliance and trust among group members (Hirschi 1969). As a means of social control, social capital is useful to parents and school personnel who seek to maintain discipline and adherence to school norms and values. It is possible that school activities, especially sports, which offer increased opportunities for familial and extrafamilial social interaction, create and strengthen social ties among students, their parents, and their teachers. These relations act as a source of social control that encourages students to comply with school norms and expectations and, in turn, have greater success in school.

Social ties are also beneficial in the cognitive and social development of adolescents by creating channels for disseminating information and resources (Coleman 1990). Social ties may act as conduits for human capital, educational resources, and/or the transmission of information that directly benefit students' achievement. For my purpose here, it is possible, for instance, that as parents congregate to observe their children participating in sports activities, they exchange information about standards of behavior, school norms, and educational resources. Furthermore, the relations among students, parents, and teachers that act as a source of social control may also provide conduits for the transmission of important educational information and resources that would otherwise be unavailable to the students.

Some caution is necessary in assuming the uninhibited flow of information and resources through social ties. There are four conditions that are essential for successful transmission to occur and for benefit to be gained. The actors involved in the interaction must (1) have human capital or an educational resource to transmit, (2) be willing to share these resources (see Portes 1998), (3) engage in an education-related interaction (e.g., parents talk to each other about educational issues at a sports event), and (4) use any resource obtained. Although I was not able to measure each of these conditions, I tested whether students who participate in extracurricular activities are more likely than nonparticipants to talk to their teachers and whether their parents are more likely to engage in education-related interactions with other parents and the school.

In sum, the literature leaves us with several unanswered questions regarding the relationship between participation in extracurricular activities and educational achievement:

- Why does sports participation boost students' achievement? Does sports participation benefit students' development and social networks, and are these the mechanisms that link participation to educational outcomes?
- Are the educational benefits of sports participation unique to sports, or do nonsports extracurricular activities also promote achievement?
- Do nonsports extracurricular activities benefit students' development and social networks?

METHODS

Sample

In my analysis, I used NELS:88, a nationally representative, longitudinal study sponsored by the National Center for Education Statistics (NCES), U.S. Department of Education. NELS is an excellent database for studying changes in educational achievement during the high school years. It is particularly suited for this study because of its abundance of specific measures of students' participation in extracurricular activities across waves of data. Thus, it is the most recent nationally representative, longitudinal data appropriate for this study.

The base-year study of NELS:88 used a stratified, clustered national probability sample of 24,599 eighth graders from 1,052 public, private, and parochial schools in the United States. The students were asked to complete survey questionnaires about schoolwork, relationships, family, attitudes, and behaviors. Follow-ups were conducted two and four years after the base year when most respondents were in the 10th and 12th grades, respectively. Curriculum-based achievement tests in math, science, reading, and history were also administered to students in each year of the survey. All my analyses were weighted using appropriate sample weights in the data.

I used data from the first (1990) and second (1992) follow-ups, when students were in their high school years (the 10th and 12th grades, respectively). To be included in the analysis, students must have participated in the base-year (8th-grade) survey, remained in school through the 12th grade, and had valid measures on each of the four educational outcome measures (math grades, English grades, math test scores, and reading test scores) ($n = 12,578$).

In this sample, interscholastic sports claimed the highest portion of consistent student participation during both the 10th and 12th grades (32 percent). Whereas 42 percent of the boys participated in interscholastic sports during these two years, only half as many girls (21 percent) did so. The next most popular participation was musical groups, which claimed only half as many participants as interscholastic sports (15 percent). These types of participation were followed by vocational clubs (7 percent); drama clubs (6 percent); intramural sports (5 percent); and cheerleading, student council, and yearbook/journalism clubs (each at 4 percent). The disproportionate number of students who participated in interscholastic sports is consistent with earlier work indicating the relative importance of high school sports in adolescent culture (see Coleman 1961; Thirer and Wright 1985).

Dependent Variables

The central focus of my study was to address the relationship between participation in extracurricular activities and academic achievement. Given the evidence in support of a positive relationship between sports participation and grades and tests scores (Fejgin 1994; Hanson and Kraus 1998, 1999), I also measured academic performance with both grades and standardized test scores (in the 12th grade). NELS provided official math and English grades from students' 12th-grade (1992) transcripts. I further measured achievement with the item-response theory math and reading standardized achievement tests administered by NCES specifically for NELS. These tests are designed to guard against ceiling and floor effects that may occur in repeated testing, making them particularly suited for longitudinal analysis.

I included 10th-grade (1990) measures of each dependent variable as controls to measure changes in grades and test scores as a function of participation in activities. Because the scales of some measures differ across waves of the NELS, many measures are standardized.

Independent Variable

I created a measure of sports participation from multiple indicators in the 10th and 12th grades. Measures of sports participation differ in each wave of the NELS data. However, it is possible in each wave to distinguish interscholastic sports participation from other types of sports participation (e.g., intramural or nonschool sports). I separated interscholastic sports from intramural sports and cheerleading to test the similarity of these types of participation. Thus, my main participation measure reflects whether a student participated in interscholastic sports during both the 10th and 12th grades (1 = participated in both years, 0 = did not participate in both years). I also created and used two additional dichotomous variables as participation controls that reflect whether students participated in the 10th grade but not in the 12th grade and in the 12th grade but not in the 10th grade. In all the analyses, participation in interscholastic sports during both the 10th and 12th grades was the main independent variable, and participation in the 10th grade only and participation in the 12th grade only were included in the models as controls. Participation in neither year was omitted from the analyses. Thus, all analyses represent the effect of continued participation in high school ("athletes") compared to not having participated at all ("nonathletes"). Using this method, I constructed and used the same three dichotomous variables for participation in each type of extracurricular activity, including intramural sports, cheerleading, music, drama, student council, yearbook and vocational clubs, to test whether continued participation in these activities affects academic achievement.

Section V: Academic Achievement and Involvement in Sports

Mediating Variables

Developmental Model—Following Marsh (1993) and Fejgin (1994), I included three measures of students' development: self-esteem, locus of control, and time on homework. Self-esteem and locus of control are both composite measures in the NELS data, each comprised of multiple measures of students' global self-esteem and sense of control, respectively. Previous research has suggested that realm-specific self-esteem (e.g., feeling toward oneself as a student) is more highly correlated with academic achievement than is global self-esteem (Rosenberg et al. 1995). However, in this analysis, I used global self-esteem for two reasons. First, the "myth" of school sports, as described by Miracle and Rees (1994), argues that sports participation increases students' general self-esteem, which, in turn, has benefits for students' educational outcomes. Second, there is little evidence to suggest that sports participation has a direct effect on realm-specific (i.e., academic) self-esteem. Thus, using general self-esteem as a mediating link between participation and educational outcomes is more theoretically and empirically warranted.

Following the literature, I measured work ethic as the self-reported time that the students spent on homework each week. I used measures of self-esteem, locus of control, and time on homework from 1990 (the 10th grade) and 1992 (the 12th grade) and examined changes in each measure across this two-year period as a function of participation in an activity. Because measurement scales for these three variables differ across waves, all three measures are standardized.

Leading-Crowd Hypothesis—To test the leading-crowd hypothesis, I created a composite measure representing the academic orientation of students' peer groups. This measure ranged from 0 to 8 and was created by summing scores on four variables: (1) the importance among friends to attend class, (2) the importance among friends to study, (3) the importance among friends to get good grades, and (4) the importance among friends to get an education beyond high school. Students could respond to each of these four variables with "not important," "somewhat important," or "very important."

Social Capital Model—It would be ideal to have direct measures of the two forms of social capital outlined in this article. However, NELS does not provide adequate data on the content of relationships among students, parents, and the school to enable a clear distinction between social capital as a source of social control or as a source of the transmission of resources. For example, as measured in NELS, indicators of student-teacher and student-parent relations may reflect either a source of social control or a source of resource transmission since the data do not indicate the subject matter of these interactions. Thus, I measured social capital more broadly with available indicators in the NELS.

Specifically, I measured social capital between (1) students and the school, (2) students and parents, (3) parents and the school, and (4) parents and other parents. The best measures available in NELS to measure social capital between students and the school is whether students talk to their teachers outside class (teachers' report; 0 = no, 1 = yes).

Social capital between students and parents is best measured by the frequency with which students talk to their parents about school courses, activities, and studies. Again, these variables may measure social control and/or the transmission of resources as conceptualized in this study. Possible responses included "never," "sometimes," or "often." Responses on the three questions were summed to create a single measure of "student-parent talk," which ranged from 0 to 6.

Social capital between parents and the school, as an indirect measure of the transmission of resources, was measured by the frequency of contact a parent has initiated with the school in the previous year regarding (1) the student's plans after leaving high school, (2) the student's selection of courses, and (3) volunteering for or at the school. Possible responses from the parent were "never," "once or twice," "three or four times," or "four or more times." Responses on the three questions were summed to create a single measure of parent-school contact (ranging from 0 to 9).

Finally, I measured how much parents networked with each other from three indicators in the data. These measures asked parents how often they talked to parents of their children's friends about (1) things that were going on at their children's school, (2) their children's educational plans after high school, and (3) their children's career plans. Possible responses from the parents were "seldom or never," "once or twice a month," "once or twice a week," or "almost daily." These scores were summed to create a single measure of parent-parent contact (ranging from 0 to 9).

Background Characteristics

I included measures for known predictors of educational outcomes to control for potential omitted variable bias when estimating the effect of sports participation on outcomes. These measures included gender, race-ethnicity, family income, parents' educational attainment, parent structure, school classification, school geographic location, and school size. Gender is dichotomous (1 = female). For race-ethnicity, I constructed four dichotomous categories: black, Asian American, Hispanic, and American Indian; white was the omitted category. Parent's educational attainment was taken directly from the NELS data and reflects the highest educational level achieved by either parent. Family income is total household income and was measured in $10,000s. Parent structure was taken from a single measure in the NELS and collapsed into a dichotomous variable (1 = dual, biological parents; 0 = other). School classification is a dichotomous variable reflecting the distinction between public and private institutions (1 = public). I constructed three dichotomous variables to represent the geographic location of a student's school (urban, suburban, and rural). Finally, school size was also taken from a single measure in NELS and collapsed into a categorical variable ranging from 1 to 5 (1 = 0–399, 5 = over 2,000). The 10th-grade (1990) measures of each dependent variable were also included in the analyses, when available, as baseline controls for prior achievement to create change models. I performed mean substitution for missing values on measures of parent's educational attainment and family income.

Analytic Strategy

I centered my analysis on interscholastic sports and performed additional analyses for participation in other types of activities. I performed ordinary least squares (OLS) regression analysis on three models. The first model tests whether participation in interscholastic sports affects changes in students' grades and test scores between the 10th and 12th grades. The second model tests whether sports participation

Section V: Academic Achievement and Involvement in Sports

affects changes in indicators of the developmental model, the leading-crowd hypothesis, and the social capital model. The final model directly tests the explanatory power of these three theories in mediating the relationship between sports participation and academic achievement. I then performed additional analyses on other extracurricular activities to test the generalizability of the interscholastic sports findings to other school activities.

RESULTS

Does playing high school interscholastic sports benefit students' academic performance? Participation in interscholastic sports during both the 10th and 12th grades has small but consistent benefits for students' grades. The zero-order relationship between sports participation and grades suggests that participation is positively associated with students' math grades ($b = .230$, $p < .001$) and English grades ($b = .219$, $p < .001$). A substantial portion of this effect is attributed to the selection of higher-performing students into sports; however, a significant, positive effect persists even after these background characteristics are taken into account. Net of controls, participating in interscholastic sports throughout high school is related to improved math ($b = .044$, $p < .01$) and English grades ($b = .073$, $p < .001$).

The benefit of participating in sports also generalizes to scores on math tests but not to scores on reading tests. The scores on math tests are significantly higher for students who participate in sports during the 10th and 12th grades, net of background characteristics ($b = .034$, $p < .001$), but scores on reading tests are lower ($b = -.042$, $p < .01$).

Does participation in interscholastic sports have personal and social benefits? Participating in sports during the 10th and 12th grades significantly improves self-esteem, locus of control, and time on homework (the developmental model). Even after individual background is controlled, school characteristics and the baseline measure of the dependent variable (Model 2), playing sports is associated with significant increases in self-esteem ($b = .085$, $p < .001$) and time on homework ($b = .162$, $p < .001$) and a more internalized locus of control ($b = .076$, $p < .001$) between the 10th and 12th grades. Playing sports is positively associated with increasing athletes' number of academically oriented friends ($b = .215$, $p < .001$) (the leading-crowd hypothesis).

Furthermore, participating in sports in the 10th and 12th grades significantly increases social ties between students and parents, students and the school, parents and the school, and parents and parents, net of individual and school controls (the social capital model). In addition, playing sports significantly increases how often students talk with their parents about school-related issues ($b = .195$, $p < .001$) and increases students' contact with teachers outside class ($b = .070$, $p < .001$). Participation is also positively associated with social ties between parents and the school. Specifically, playing interscholastic sports is positively related to how much parents have contact with the school ($b = .644$, $p < .001$), as well as parents' contact with other parents ($b = .615$, $p < .001$).

Contrary to previous research, this study supports "the myth" of high school sports. Participating in interscholastic sports has multiple benefits for students, including all the measures tested in this analysis.

Do the personal and social benefits explain athletes' improvements in grades and test scores? The results demonstrate that participation in sports has both educational and personal benefits for student-athletes. However, one can only speculate from these results whether the personal benefits (developmental outcomes, peer-group orientation, and social capital) actually explain how sports participation boosts students' achievement.

The Developmental Model

The benefits of sports participation on students' self-esteem, locus of control, and time on homework explain, on average, one-third of the effect of sports on grades and test scores. Comparing Models 1 and 2 for each educational outcome, one sees that measures of the developmental model modestly reduce the effect of sports participation on achievement. Of note, however, the developmental model reduces the effect of sports participation on math grades to insignificance (Model 2). These results offer empirical evidence that sports participation does help "build character," which, in turn, directly aids students' academic achievement.

The Leading-Crowd Hypothesis

It is clear from this analysis that playing sports offers students membership in an academically oriented peer group. But, does membership in an academically oriented peer group promote improved academic performance? Only a small part of the positive effect of sports participation on grades and test scores is attributed to the academic orientation of athletes' peer groups. Peer group orientation mediates less than 10 percent of the effect of sports participation on grades and 23 percent of the effect on math test scores. Having more academically oriented peers does not explain away the significant effect of sports participation on any of these educational outcome measures. In all, while peer group orientation seems to provide some academic benefit for student-athletes, this link is weak relative to other mechanisms.

Social Capital Model

Increases in social capital attributed to sports participation help students improve their grades more than their test scores. The data indicate that measures of social capital explain almost half the effect of sports participation on math grades and over a third of the effect on English grades, but only about one-fifth of the effect on scores on math tests. Like the developmental model, measures of social capital reduce the size of the effect of sports on math grades to insignificance and only slightly reduce the magnitude of the effect on English grades and scores on math tests. Thus, social capital appears similarly effective to developmental characteristics in explaining the academic benefits of participation in sports.

It appears that participation in interscholastic sports in high school has developmental and social benefits that at least partially explain the educational advantages of participating. None of the three explanations though, as measured here, is independently able to link sports participation to all educational outcomes. Collectively, however, measures of the developmental model, the leading-crowd hypothesis, and the social capital model significantly reduce the effect of sports participation on all the educational outcomes in this analysis, particularly in math.

Section V: *Academic Achievement and Involvement in Sports*

Do the academic benefits of interscholastic sports participation generalize to other extracurricular activities? Interscholastic sports differ from intramural sports and other athletic activities, such as cheerleading, in many ways. For instance, compared to intramural sports, interscholastic sports are more selective, typically require a greater commitment by the participants, have more formalized rules for participation and behavior, and offer competition between schools. As a result, interscholastic sports typically offer greater structure and routinization, much larger and more intense social networks, higher social status for student-athletes, and a stronger identity with one's school (Coleman 1965; Cusick 1973; Eder and Parker 1987; Finn 1989; Morgan and Alwin 1980; Quiroz et al. 1996). But do the differences between these two types of sports activities alter the effects of participation on students' lives? Do intramural athletes gain the same benefits from participation as do interscholastic athletes? Moreover, are the benefits accrued by interscholastic athletes specific to sports participation, or are they generalizable to participation in any type of school activity?

When all types of activities are included in the model simultaneously, the results suggest that not all forms of participation are equally beneficial for students' achievement. Most notably, intramural athletes do not reap the same benefits from participation as do interscholastic athletes. In fact, students who participate in intramural sports actually lose academic ground relative to their nonparticipating peers. Their math grades ($b = -.194$, $p < .001$), English grades ($b = -.193$, $p < .001$), scores on math tests ($b = -.067$, $p < .001$), and scores on reading tests ($b = -.096$, $p < .001$) all significantly decline over the two-year period. Notably, these effects are almost three times as large as the positive effects of participating in interscholastic sports. The only other type of participation to have a consistently negative effect on achievement is vocational clubs, which, in fact, is not as harmful for grades and test scores as is playing intramural sports.

The educational benefit of participating in interscholastic sports, once multiple forms of participation are controlled, becomes more convincing. All positive coefficients increase in magnitude, and particularly notable is the disappearance of the negative effect on scores on reading tests. Once all forms of participation are controlled, sports participation is no longer associated with a decline in students' performance on reading tests.

Participation in music groups is the only other activity to yield such consistent benefits for achievement. Similar to interscholastic sports, music participation improves math and English grades and scores on math tests but not on reading tests. Participating in the student council does help students improve their grades but not their test scores. Besides interscholastic sports and music, no other form of participation renders consistent benefits for grades and test scores. Also of note, scores on reading tests seem to be fairly insensitive to participation in activities. The only participation that generates improved scores on reading tests is participation in a drama club ($b = .064$, $p < .05$).

Overall, interscholastic sports appear to be the most beneficial form of participation for students' achievement. Participation in music groups has a similar, but less impressive, impact on achievement, whereas participation in the student council, the drama club, and the yearbook/journalism club have limited academic benefits. Finally, cheerleading is unremarkable, and intramural sports and vocational clubs consistently impair achievement.

Do the personal and social benefits of participation in interscholastic sports generalize to other extracurricular activities? Ranking the different types of activities in terms of their effects on achievement places the two different types of sports participation on polar ends of the hierarchy. Interscholastic athletes gain the most from participation, while intramural athletes lose the most. What may explain why these two seemingly similar forms of activity have such vastly different effects on students' achievement?

The analyses show that when prior achievement and participation in all types of activities are controlled simultaneously, intramural athletes do not gain any of the developmental or social capital benefits enjoyed by interscholastic athletes. Their self-esteem, time on homework, friendship groups, and relationships with parents and teachers are no different from those of their nonparticipating peers. Moreover, intramural athletes' sense of personal control significantly diminishes over the two-year period. Thus, intramural athletes do not gain any of the tested individual or social benefits that mediate the positive relationship between interscholastic participation and achievement, and what is more important, they lose ground on a critical link to academic achievement: locus of control.

Students who participate in music groups have similar gains in development and social networks as interscholastic athletes. With the exception of self-esteem and locus of control, music participants gain on all the tested mediators. And while participation in cheerleading, school drama, student council, and the yearbook seem to be beneficial for some developmental characteristics and social relationships, none proves as consistently beneficial as music participation or, more so, interscholastic sport participation. All these results are consistent with the findings presented earlier demonstrating the relative explanatory power of the developmental and social capital models.

DISCUSSION

Consistent with conventional wisdom, participating in school sports does seem to have real benefits for students. In line with the findings of Fejgin (1994) and Hanson and Kraus (1998, 1999), the results of my study further support the tenet that playing school sports boosts students' achievement in the classroom and on standardized math tests. However, this study has demonstrated that not all sports activities are equal in consequence. Participation in interscholastic sports has different consequences for students' achievement than has participation in intramural sports or cheerleading. In the same light, although I focused the analysis on sports participation, another contribution of the study is the inclusion of participation in other types of extracurricular activities. Nonsports activities have been largely overlooked in the literature, and according to Quiroz et al. (1996), students become "hyper-networked" in the extracurriculum, meaning that many students participate in multiple activities during the school year. Thus, it is imperative to test participation in different types of activities simultaneously to isolate the effects of participation in specific activities. Doing so identifies interscholastic sports, intramural sports, and music as unique forms of participation, all having consequences for students' achievement. Hence, not all forms of participation in extracurricular activities are similar in consequence, which strongly implicates the need to distinguish the types of activities in subsequent research as well as in policy and funding decisions regarding extracurricular programming in schools.

The distinctive contribution of this study is the incorporation of sociological theory to explain how participating in nonacademic activities translates into improved achievement. The results primarily support the developmental and social capital explanations linking sports to achievement. Indeed, students who participate in interscholastic sports have a stronger sense of control over their lives and a value system that is concordant with the American educational system. I also found that participation in interscholastic sports creates and intensifies students' social ties, which can be advantageous to students' educational pursuits. The results further suggest that the link that participation in extracurricular activities can forge between parents and schools is equally important.

Although social capital theory conceptually delineates the multiple ways that these social networks may enhance students' achievement (i.e., social control, the dissemination of resources, and attachment to the school), limitations in the NELS data prevented me from making such empirical distinctions in the present study. Measures of social capital in this analysis do not render a clear understanding of this link between sports and achievement. For example, the results indicate that student-athletes are more likely to talk with their teachers outside class than are nonathletes, but given that the contents of these discussions are not known, relations between students and teachers may act as sources of social control; the dissemination of resources; or other, unmeasured advantages, such as teachers' bias. The more students talk to their teachers, the more opportunities they have to gain information that could be used to improve their grades or test scores. Yet, these interactions may also act to (1) encourage behavior that conforms to school expectations and norms, which, in turn, helps students succeed in school, and (2) create social bonds that motivate students to perform better for teachers with whom they have personal relationships. Furthermore, others have suggested that athletes' visibility and popularity with teachers may lead to leniency in grading and result in inflated grades (see Hanks and Eckland 1976).

Relationships with teachers, or simply increased visibility within the school, may lead to bias in grade assignments. There is some evidence of bias toward particular students in the classroom (see Farkas 1996). Unfortunately, no one has tested the possibility of teachers' bias toward athletes or students participating in other particular extracurricular activities. Given that my findings suggest that participation in extracurricular activities boosts grades more than test scores for athletes and participants in other high-status activities (e.g., the student council), there is reason to investigate this possibility in explaining the added benefit of participation for grades. Further research on participation in extracurricular activities should empirically distinguish different forms of social capital and the possibility of leniency in grading for particular students.

While my study offers an understanding of the consequences of participation in different types of activities, it did not address some other important considerations. For example, does the effect of sports participation on academic performance differ by type of sports? Or do the benefits of sports participation vary by students' characteristics? The findings provide room for some speculation.

Participation in different types of sports may differentially affect academic performance. For example, while team sports may lead to stronger social ties with peers (social capital), individual sports may build a stronger individual work ethic and locus of control. Moreover, higher-status sports (e.g., basketball and football) may make students more well known in the school and thus create more opportunities for relations with school personnel relative to athletes in lower-status sports. Analyses of different sports may help to illuminate other processes that are important in linking involvement in extracurricular activities to academic success.

The literature on sports has also overwhelmingly failed to consider whether the consequences of participating in sports vary by students' characteristics. There is great theoretical debate over whether sports participation improves the upward mobility of disadvantaged groups. A small body of literature has explored the differential effects of sports participation by socioeconomic status. It has found that participation in sports provides a greater boost to educational aspirations and expectations for students from low-income families than those from high-income families (Rehberg and Schafer 1968; Schafer and Armer 1968; Snyder 1969; Spreitzer and Pugh 1973). Unfortunately, analyses of the interaction between sports participation and socioeconomic status have not examined the effects on academic performance. However, my finding that participation in specific types of extracurricular activities forges relationships among students, parents, and schools suggests the possibility that participating in these programs may significantly boost disadvantaged students' achievement relative to their more advantaged peers.

Because human capital and other educational resources are highly circumscribed in low-income families, creating social capital through social ties with school personnel is vital for these students. Yet, research has indicated that social capital between students and the school is lacking for the majority of disadvantaged, inner-city students (Heath and McLaughlin 1993; Natriello, McDill, and Pallas 1986). Disadvantaged students are less attached to school, and their parents are less apt to take an active role in their schooling (Lareau 1987; MacLeod 1987). The results of this study suggest that specific extracurricular programming could be a vehicle for generating social capital among disadvantaged students, their parents, and schools that may, in turn, help improve their achievement. In light of this finding, the fact that extracurricular programming is largely restricted in inner-city schools may work to reproduce the disadvantage of inner-city students relative to their suburban peers by further limiting opportunities to build social capital.

Unlike socioeconomic status, the roles of race and gender in moderating the relationship between sports participation and educational outcomes has received some attention. For example, Melnick et al.'s (1992a, 1992b) and Sabo et al.'s (1993) series of longitudinal studies on African American and Hispanic high school students found no evidence that sports participation improved the grades or test scores of these students. And the results of Hanson and Kraus's (1999) study suggest that while girls seem to benefit in math and science from their participation in sports, boys do not. Overall, however, there have been few strong theoretical and empirical examinations of participation and its educational consequences for students from different economic, racial, and gender groups, thus warranting further examination of how students' characteristics moderate the experiences of participating in sports and other high school activities.

Finally, the results suggest that indicators of the three theoretical perspectives (or something highly correlated with them) capture the key mechanisms linking participation in extracurricular activities to grades and test scores. Although there may be other benefits of participation, the developmental and social capital benefits represent the central means by which particular extracurricular activities enhance students' achievement. It appears that structure, adult supervision, and parental involvement are all characteristic of the activities that promote development and social capital. The lack of these attributes in activities that are negatively related to achievement, such as intramural sports and vocational clubs, may explain their relationship to achievement. Thus, increasing these attributes in other school activities may serve to enhance the educational effectiveness of extracurricular programming.

The findings in this study generate the need for future research on the long-term educational effects of participation in extracurricular activities. While participating in some activities helps students improve their high school grades and test scores, does the experience of participating continue to benefit students beyond high school? Past research has not provided a clear understanding of the effect of high school sports or other extracurricular activities on long-term educational attainment, such as college graduation (see Braddock 1981; Hanks and Eckland 1976; Landers et al. 1978; Otto 1975; Purdy 1980; Spady 1970). The results of these studies have been inconsistent, yet seem to suggest that participating in high school sports is beneficial for long-term attainment only if it is coupled with participating in other, service-related (e.g., student council) activities. Still, by illuminating some of the processes by which participation in activities is beneficial to achievement, my findings suggest that sports participation alone (or other activities that promote individual development or social ties related to educational pursuits) may promote achievement beyond the high school years, a question that begs further attention.

Are Athletes Also Students? The Educational Attainment of College Athletes

DEAN A. PURDY, D. STANLEY EITZEN, AND RICK HUFNAGEL

The foundations of college sports in the United States have been shaken by revelations of academic compromises made in the interests of intercollegiate athletics (Axthelm, 1980; Sanoff, 1980; Underwood, 1980). Among the unethical practices that have been uncovered are falsified transcripts by colleges, athletes receiving credit for courses not taken, and the financial and academic exploitation of athletes. Implicit in the criticisms leveled at college sports is the fundamental issue of their relationship to the educational process (Hanford, 1979:363).

The public is aware of the potential problems regarding the quality of education that college athletes receive through the efforts of muck-raking journalists (Axthelm, 1980; Underwood, 1980) and ex-athletes (Meggysey, 1970; Scott, 1971; Shaw, 1972). The anecdotal evidence they provide suggests that while coaches publicly espouse that their athletes are students first and athletes second, their primary interest is to keep players eligible by whatever means, including credit for phantom courses, surrogates for tests, and counseling on which easy courses do not lead to graduation. These practices are widespread enough to lead some to conclude that the corruption of academic ideals is endemic in universities with major sports programs (Eitzen and Sage, 1982). The organization responsible for policing the athletic programs of major U.S. universities, the National Collegiate Athletic Association (NCAA), has focused on violations of amateurism, such as athletes receiving financial inducements to play, and neglected the investigation of charges that athletes may be receiving inferior educations.

Although educational ethics have been violated by college coaches for some time, they have been exacerbated by the financial climate of contemporary intercollegiate sports programs. Winning programs attract lucrative television money, "bowl" contracts, alumni donations, and high attendance figures

(Atwell, 1979; Davis, 1979; Grant, 1979; Lopino, 1979; Nyquist, 1979). Society has created "an educational dilemma concerning the place and mission of athletics within our intellectual estates by mixing 'dollar values with eduational ones'" (Hanford, 1978:232). Studies by universities and social scientists of the educational attainment of college athletes have been few and contradictory. Two variables are commonly used in these studies: graduation rate and grade-point average.

Graduation rate: Several studies indicate that athletes stand a better chance of graduating than non-athletes. Billick (1973) found that 93 percent of the 1963 University of Pittsburgh football team had graduated and 46 percent had received graduate degrees. Pilapil *et al.* (1970) found that 50 percent of the athletes from the University of Minnesota's class of 1967 had graduated, compared to 41 percent of non-athletes. Michener (1976:237) studied Stanford university male athletes from the baseball, basketball, football, swimming, and track squads during the academic year 1969–70; he found that 88 percent of the athletes graduated compared to 82.5 percent of the total student body.

Other studies yield a different conclusion. Webb's (1968) study of all Michigan State University athletes over a five-year period revealed that 49 percent of team sport and 60 percent of individual sport athletes had graduated. Harrison (1976) found that less than 20 percent of football players who entered North Texas State University from 1966 to 1971 went on to attain degrees from the university. A study by the University of New Mexico (1980) revealed that only 21 percent of its football players had graduated since 1970. Other graduation rates cited in this study were track (24 percent), wrestling (24 percent), and basketball (28 percent). Studies conducted by the Southeast and Southwest Conferences have shown similar results (Benagh, 1976:127).

Grade point average (GPA): Results using this variable are also mixed. Stecklein and Dameron (1965) found no significant difference between the grade-point averages of athletes and non-athletes at the University of Minnesota. A later study at the same institution demonstrated that athletes had GPA's of 2.42, compared with 2.40 for non-athletes (Pilapil *et al.*, 1970). However, Harrison (1976) found that football players at North Texas State University had a mean GPA of 2.00.

THE PROBLEM

Nyquist (1979), in his critique of the exploitation of college athletes, suggested that unethical conduct will continue to embarrass educational institutions until they realize the magnitude of the problem and correct the situation. However, research on the relationship between college sport participation, educational attainment, and the possible negative effects on athletes is meager and generally limited to a single indicator of educational success (Hanford, 1974; Hanks and Eckland, 1976; Harris, 1980; Harrison, 1976; Litchfield and Cope, 1962; Moran, 1980; Pilapil et al., 1970; Roper and Snow, 1976; Sage, 1967; Stecklein and Dameron, 1965; Webb, 1961). Moreover, the literature lacks empirical studies assessing the general academic preparation and achievement level of college athletes. This is unfortunate in view of Spady's (1970) research which indicated that participation in high school sport may lead to increased educational aspirations but does not necessarily enhance or develop those academic characteristics necessary for success in college.

Our research assesses the degree to which college athletes are disadvantaged educationally by their sports participation. Unlike previous studies, we consider a number of dimensions—academic preparation for college, college grade-point average, and graduation rate. Moreover, we compare athletes with non-athletes, and various categories among the athletes—males and females, whites and non-whites, scholarship and non-scholarship holders, and participants by sport.

METHOD

We studied the academic achievements of athletes at Colorado State University from the fall of 1970 through to the spring of 1980. This university is classified as Division 1-A by the NCAA, which means that it is one of the nation's "big-time" sports programs.

The time frame for our study was determined by the fact that computerized educational data from the university's admissions and records department were only available from 1970. This period of 10 years is long enough to determine and include the percentage of athletes who take more than the normal four to five years to complete their undergraduate education. In 1975, the institution changed from the quarter system, but this had no effect on our analysis.

We identified athletes by the eligibility reports supplied by the athletic department to the Western Athletic Conference. Athletes had to complete one academic term to be included in our sample. These criteria yielded a sample of 2,091 athletes, both men and women.

We obtained grant-in-aid information from the athletic department and transformed it into the percentage of financial aid extended to each of the athletes. The expected cost of an academic term, obtained from the university bulletin, was divided into the amount of financial aid received by an athlete to obtain a percentage. We used the largest percentage of financial aid by athletes during their residence at the university in our analysis.

We used athletic department records to determine the number of years that an individual played on an athletic team at the university. In cases where the individual participated in several sports, we used the largest number of years of participation to any one sport. Athletic department records also identified students who received an athletic letter and those who participated while classified as a senior.

We obtained educational records from official university records in the department of admissions and records. Variables used in the analysis consisted of cumulative university grade-point averages, American College Test (ACT) and Scholastic Aptitude Test (SAT) scores, high school grade-point average, high school class rank, and the number of years spent at the university to achieve graduation. The official university records also provided information on the demographic variables of sex and race.

RESULTS

This study examines two sets of data: (1) the comparison of athletes to the general student population (GSP) on several variables that measure educational ability and achievement; and (2) an analysis of the same variables within various sub-categories of athletes, including sport, letter-winner, and participation as a senior. Both sets of data helped determine whether athletes were substantially different from the GSP and if any significant differences in educational preparation and attainment existed among the athletes by social characteristics.

Section V: Academic Achievement and Involvement in Sports

TABLE 1: Demographic and Academic Information for Athletes and the General Student Population

	Athletes [a]	General Student Population (GSP)[b,c]
Sex:		
Male	79.7%	45.5%
Female [d]	20.3%	54.5%
Race:		
Caucasian	88.1%	94.3%
Black	7.9%	1.0%
Other	4.0%	4.4%
College of Last Declared Major:		
Agriculture	5.3%	7.2%
Business	16.1%	12.0%
Engineering	5.1%	7.1%
Natural Resources	7.2%	10.7%
Home Economics	3.3%	10.2%
Natural Sciences	11.6%	13.5%
Professional Studies [e]	17.5%	6.3%
Arts, Humanities & Social Science	30.7%	29.4%
Biological Sciences	3.2%	6.8%
High School GPA [f]	2.99 (743)	3.31 (6,402)[j]
Average Percentile High School Class Standing [g]	69 (1,550)	71
Average SAT Combined Score [h]	949 (1,389)	997 (19,944)
Average ACT Composite Score	20.8 (451)	22.1 (25,529)
Average College GPA	2.56 (2,075)	2.74
Graduate Rate [i]	34.2% (1,457)	46.8% (4,188)

Notes:

[a] Entire population for the 10-year period: fall 1970 to 1980. N = 2091.

[b] GSP statistics are from a study completed by the university for the period fall 1973 to 1979. Exceptions to this are the high school class standing (fall 1971 to 1979) and the graduation rate, which is from a study following the freshman class of 1975.

[c] N for sex and race = 25,519. N for college of last declared major = 14,201.

[d] Women do not appear as varsity athletes until 1975.

[e] Professional studies was created in 1975. Before that it was part of the college of arts, humanities and social sciences. Physical education is included in the college of professional studies.

[f] High school grade-point average was not recorded before 1975.

[g] Class standing is a percentile ranking, calculated as:

$$100 - \frac{\text{Class Rank} \times 100}{\text{Class Size}}$$

[h] Scholastic Aptitude Test (SAT) combined score computed by adding the scores of the verbal and math components.

[i] Since students were given at least five years to graduate, the students entering since 1976 were not included in the computation of the graduation rate.

[j] Ns (in parenthesis) vary because of occasional incomplete data.

Athletes and Non-Athletes.

Table 1 shows the demographic characteristics and mean educational attainment scores for both athletes and the GSP. These data show that athletes in the aggregate differ from the GSP on every dimension. Most significant for our purposes is that the athletes were consistently less prepared than the GSP for college, as shown by lower high school grade-point average, high school class rank (percentile), SAT score, and ACT score. Similarly, the college performance of athletes was lower than the GSP as measured by college grade-point average and the graduation rate. Concerning the latter, we made no attempt to determine whether athletes or members of the GSP had transferred to another institution of higher education and proceeded to graduate, because the academic records of the GSP did not contain this information.

Table 2 examines more closely the conclusion of Table 1 that athletes score lower than non-athletes on the various measures of educational attainment. Male athletes scored lower on all indicators of academic achievement than their male counterparts from the GSP. Similar, though somewhat smaller, differences were discovered between female athletes and females from the GSP on most indices of educational success. However, female athletes had a slightly higher GPA. Graduation rates factored out by sex were not available for the GSP. Among the athletes, women scored significantly higher than men on all measures of educational achievement except for the ACT score, where men scored one-tenth of a point higher.

TABLE 2: Indicators of Educational Attainment by Sex for Athletes and the General Student Population

	Athletes [a]		General Student Population (GSP)[b]	
	Male	Female	Male	Female
SAT Combined Score	940 (1,077)	977 (312)**	1024 (8,943)	979 (10,996)
ACT Composite Score	20.8 (290)	20.7 (161)	22.8 (11,614)	21.3 (13,915)
High School Class Standing	66 (1,181)	79 (369)***	—	—
High School GPA	2.85 (455)	3.21 (288)***	3.23 (2,987)	3.38 (3,415)
College GPA	2.48 (1,651)	2.88 (424)**	2.65	2.84
Graduation Rate	33% (1,270)	41% (189)	—	—

Notes:
$**p<.01$, $***p<.001$
[a] Significant differences (t-test) refer only to mean differences between male and female athletes.
[b] GSP averages were taken from a university administration study covering the period from fall 1973 to fall, 1979. College GPA was computed from yearly averages for the period from fall 1970 to spring 1980.

Variations Among Athletes

Female athletes differ from male athletes in preparation for college and in college achievement. There are additional characteristics of athletes which indicate that this is not a monolithic category. We consider: race, participation as a senior, letterwinner, number of years of athletic participation, and extent of grant-in-aid. Of the athletes studied, 11.9 percent were non-white, 38.9 percent of those whose entering class had graduated participated as a senior, over half (54.9 percent) participated for only one year, and 39.4 percent received an athletic letter. Full athletic grants were given to 28.7 percent of the athletes, while 48.4 percent received no financial aid.

Table 3 shows black athletes had significantly lower scores on the entire range of educational achievement measures. These results are similar to those found by Spivey and Jones (1975). Comparison data by race were not available for the GSP. However, a study conducted by the university's administration that followed the freshman class of 1975 revealed graduation rates of 40.5 percent (N=42) for blacks and 48.6 percent (N=3,986) for Caucasians.

TABLE 3: Indicators of Educational Attainment By Race For Athletes

	Athletes	
	Black	Caucasian
SAT Combined Score	753 (86)	965 (1,247)***
ACT Composite Score	14.9 (22)	21.2 (405)***
High School Class Standing	62 (99)	70 (1,390)***
High School GPA	2.48 (43)	3.04 (658)***
College GPA	2.11 (163)	2.61 (1,830)***
Graduation Rate	21% (118)	35% (1,290)***

Note:
***p <.001

Table 4 shows the results of the mean scores for the educational achievement measures for various athletic sub-groups. The first comparison investigates the differences between those athletes who participated as seniors and those who had not yet attained senior status. We included this comparison because some coaches and universities have used only athletes who were seniors to compute graduation rates. This is useful if one wishes to distort the findings by a inflating the graduation rates, since the more education received, the more likely a student is to graduate. We found that almost twice as many athletes who had achieved senior status graduated compared to those who were not yet seniors. However almost half (48.9 percent) of those athletes who played as seniors did not graduate. This is an important indicator of the potential for athlete exploitation, since these athletes had given four years to the school yet had not received a diploma.

Table 4 also shows that athletes receiving full grants-in-aid had the lowest mean scores on each of the measures of educational attainment. Scholarship athletes, compared to non-scholarship or partial scholarship athletes, were the least prepared for the academic rigors of college and were the least successful in college, as measured by GPA and graduation rate.

Table 5 presents the educational achievement measures by sport. Athletes in football, basketball, and wrestling had relatively lower mean scores for the educational achievement measures used for university admission. However, those athletes who participated in basketball and wrestling while attaining GPAs similar to those of football players graduated at a higher rate. The data also show that athletes involved in individual sports secured better college grades and were more likely to graduate than those who participated in team sports.

TABLE 4: Indicators of Educational Attainment by Various Criteria of Athletic Participation

	SAT Combined Scores	ACT Composite Scores	High School GPA	High School Class Standing	College GPA	Graduation Rate
Underclass Participation	949 (1,072)	20.8 (397)	2.99 (661)	69 (1,231)	2.51 (1,521)	26.2% (991)
Senior Participation	948 (317)	21.0 (54)	3.02 (82)	70 (319)	2.69 (554)***	51.1% (468)***
Non-letter Winner	958 (891)	20.8 (339)	3.05 (553)	70 (1025)	2.54 (1,253)	28.2% (816)
Letter Winner	932 (498)**	20.7 (112)	2.82 (190)***	67 (525)**	2.59 (822)	41.8% (643)***
Years of Participation						
1 Year	956 (769)	20.7 (283)	3.01 (463)	69 (897)	2.48 (1,134)	25.5% (774)
2 Years	927 (231)	20.8 (93)	2.95 (134)	67 (274)	2.55 (401)	35.0% (274)
3 Years	915 (190)	20.6 (42)	2.92 (92)	68 (184)	2.67 (234)	41.9% (148)
4 Years or More	981 (199)***	21.8 (33)	3.04 (54)	73 (195)*	2.78 (306)*	54.8% (263)***
Grant-in-Aid:						
No Aid	979 (722)	21.5 (295)	3.10 (489)	73 (820)	2.69 (1,005)	37.0% (622)
1–33%	949 (134)	20.3 (58)	2.92 (83)	70 (151)	2.72 (182)	44.6% (112)
34–66%	942 (119)	19.2 (31)	2.92 (54)	66 (133)	2.54 (205)	37.8% (156)
67–99%	943 (53)	19.3 (9)	2.76 (14)	64 (54)	2.54 (88)	39.5% (76)
100%	892 (361)***	18.3 (58)***	2.59 (103)***	62 (392)***	2.30 (595)*	26.4% (493)***
Non-graduate	920 (655)	19.7 (116)	2.84 (223)	63 (682)	2.32 (945)	
Graduate	988 (343)***	21.4 (73)*	3.25 (28)***	72 (350)***	2.86 (498)*	

Notes:
  *p<.05, **p<.01, ***p<.001

Only three percent of the athletes admitted with a high school GPA under 2.50 graduated. Only 18 percent of those who scored under 700 on the SAT graduated, as did 24 percent of those admitted with ACT scores of less than 15. The admission of academically marginal students is primarily a problem of the "revenue" sports of football and basketball. While these two sports accounted for only 29 percent of the athletes who had taken the SAT exam, they accounted for 47 percent of those who had scores of under 700. Results for the ACT test are similar. Of the athletes admitted with a high school GPA of under 2.50, basketball and football accounted for 36 percent, while representing only 18 percent of the athletes for whom high school GPA records were available. Basketball and football athletes accounted for 33 percent of the athletes in the sample, while simultaneously accounting for 50 percent of those athletes whose cumulative college GPA was less than 2.00 and 44 percent of those under 2.50. The case is even stronger if just football is considered since basketball includes female as well as male athletes and the women inflate the academic results. Football players were the least prepared of all the athletes for the educational experience of college. They had the lowest college GPA (2.30) and the lowest graduation rate (26.8 percent) of all athletes by sport.

TABLE 5: Indicators of Educational Attainment by Sport

	SAT Combined Scores	ACT Composite Scores	High School GPA	High School Class Standing	College GPA	Graduation Rate
Baseball	926 (113)	21.3 (43)	2.90 (62)	68 (123)	2.52 (184)	41.4% (128)
Basketball	893 (100)	19.3 (40)	2.89 (50)	68 (117)	2.49 (165)	39.4% (115)
Field Hockey	992 (34)	20.4 (11)	3.10 (26)	72 (33)	2.81 (44)	47.6% (21)
Football	899 (310)	18.6 (41)	2.60 (81)	61 (336)	2.30 (518)	26.8% (441)
Golf	1,008 (61)	22.0 (23)	3.08 (33)	74 (71)	2.67 (90)	52.2% (67)
Gymnastics	955 (97)	20.4 (45)	3.10 (51)	74 (105)	2.76 (123)	34.1% (88)
Softball	938 (36)	20.6 (20)	3.23 (32)	83 (42)	2.73 (48)	47.6% (21)
Swimming	998 (138)	22.0 (47)	3.04 (86)	69 (153)	2.70 (193)	32.0% (128)
Tennis	993 (63)	22.0 (20)	3.18 (38)	78 (66)	2.77 (89)	33.9% (59)
Track	966 (299)	21.5 (109)	3.08 (201)	71 (341)	2.67 (416)	34.5% (249)
Volleyball	1,001 (30)	21.6 (12)	3.29 (28)	81 (35)	2.95 (40)	36.8% (19)
Wrestling	945 (106)	20.1 (40)	2.79 (53)	65 (126)	2.52 (162)	36.4% (121)

DISCUSSION

This study demonstrates that college athletes over a 10-year period in one major university scored lower than non-athletes on the measures most commonly used to assess educational attainment. They entered with poorer academic backgrounds, they received lower grades than their non-athletic peers, and fewer of them graduated.

Two findings in particular challenge those who espouse the educational value of college sports:

1) Scholarship athletes fared worse than non-scholarship or partial-scholarship athletes in academic achievement. There are at least two possible explanations for this. Full scholarship athletes have in a sense become employees of the university. They "owe" their coaches their undivided attention because these coaches are paying the bills. This creates a role conflict for student-athletes, with the student role often being neglected or de-emphasized. Second, full-scholarship athletes are likely to be the best athletes. They derive their social status from their athletic endeavors and they may believe that, ultimately, they will have a lucrative professional career in sports (Oates, 1979). Thus, they may overemphasize their sport at the expense of academic pursuits.

2) There is evidence that athletes in the male revenue sports of football and basketball have a relatively low probability of receiving an education compared to non-athletes or athletes in the other sports. Because of the revenue producing potential of football and basketball, the pressures

are intense to win (Odenkirk, 1981; Underwood, 1980). This means that coaches in these sports are likely to be excessive in their demands on the time of their athletes during and between sessions. The serious and far-ranging financial consequences of "big-time" sports also increase the likelihood that coaches will recruit exceptional athletes who are unqualified for the academic demands of college. To the degree that this occurs, coaches are then faced with keeping these marginal students eligible. At some schools this has meant obtaining bogus credits for them out of difficult courses leading to graduation, and other tactics. When these practices occur, the goal of higher education has been subverted and the athletes have been exploited (Eitzen and Sage, 1982; Frey, 1979; Moran, 1980; Santomier *et al.*, 1980; Underwood, 1980; White, 1980).

However, all colleges are not guilty of impeding the educational attainment of athletes. Academic achievement by athletes in the "minor" (non-revenue) sports is similar to that of the general student population. Female athletes, too, resemble their non-athlete peers in academic accomplishments. There is some evidence, however, that women's college sports programs nationally are moving in the direction of men's programs with scandals, unethical practices, and overemphasis on winning (Eitzen and Sage, 1982:342). If this trend continues, women's sports programs will increasingly interfere with the educational achievement of their athletes.

There appears to be a positive relationship between athletic participation and academic performance at the interscholastic level (Coakley, 1982; Eitzen and Sage, 1982; Loy *et al.*, 1978; Snyder and Spreitzer, 1978), although the research has methodological problems (Stevenson, 1975). Why is the relationship positive in high school and negative at the college level? Loy *et al.* (1978) have suggested studies at the college level to evaluate whether sport aids or hinders the attainment of the professed goals of the educational system. An explanation of the process dynamics at both levels is urgently needed.

The ideal study would compare several measures of educational attainment for both athletes and non-athletes at all levels of intercollegiate sport—from major universities with huge budgets, national schedules, and full scholarships for athletes to colleges without scholarships playing regional teams and non-scholarship athletes. As Snyder and Spreitzer (1978:76) have suggested: "Valid comparisons between collegiate athletes are difficult because of the variations in institutional quality, degree programs, type of sport and other potentially contaminating factors." These "obstacles" must not deter future efforts to understand the relationship between participation in college sports and educational attainment.

A Reexamination of How Athletic Success Impacts Graduation Rates: Comparing Student Athletes to All Other Undergraduates

PATRICK JAMES RISHE

McCormick and Tinsley (1987) found that athletic success served as an important marketing tool for universities, in that it attracted students with higher incoming SAT scores. Shughart, Tollison, and Goff (1986) found that athletic success hurt the academic productivity of economics professors in terms of fewer journal pages per faculty member. Tucker (1992) found a similar result, in that undergraduate graduation rates were inversely correlated to the success of football, though Tucker and Amato (1993) found that changes in incoming freshman SAT scores over time was positively correlated to football success.

This paper also focuses on how athletic success impacts college graduation rates. The departure from the papers mentioned above is that this paper separates the student-athlete graduation rate from the graduation rate of all other undergraduates, and it looks at a more complete sample of Division I schools. Separating the graduation rate of student-athletes from all other undergraduates allows us to address three questions: Is the academic success of the consumers of college athletics (undergraduates) impacted by the success of their school's athletic program? Do pressures to produce athletically impact the academic success of the producers of college athletics (student-athletes)? Is the relative academic success of student-athletes compared to all other undergraduates sensitive to the success of the school's athletic program and/or the school's perceived status as a major Division I athletic power?

Section V: Academic Achievement and Involvement in Sports

LITERATURE REVIEW

McCormick and Tinsley (1987) measured athletic success with a dummy variable distinguishing the 63 universities in 1984 that belonged to either major athletic conferences or were a major independent (e.g., Notre Dame) in Division I. In their dynamic model of explaining changes in SAT scores over time, they reduced their sample to just the 63 "big-time" universities and measured athletic success as a 14-year trend in football winning percentages.

Tucker (1992) and Tucker and Amato (1993) introduced a new method of measuring athletic success that involved aggregate football and basketball rankings by the Associated Press. They were uncomfortable with classifying athletic success with a dummy variable because the disparity in athletic success of teams from the same conference could not be distinguished (such as the quality of Florida's athletic program versus Vanderbilt's program). The "rankings" measurement of athletic success allowed a more accurate, quantitative measure of athletic success than did past studies.

But Tucker and Amato only considered the 63 "big-time" schools examined in earlier papers, thereby not allowing for a more comprehensive cross-sectional comparison across Division I schools. Perhaps more important is that Tucker (1992) did not distinguish the athlete graduation rate from the graduation rate of all other students. If the student-athlete graduation rate differs significantly from that of all other students, one obtains a muddied picture concerning whose academic performance is impacted by athletic success when the graduation rate variable is defined to encompass all students.

The graduation rate for student-athletes for the entire sample is 58.15 percent, whereas the graduation rate for all other undergraduates is 54.62 percent. A paired t-test confirms that this difference is statistically significant. This graduation gap in favor of athletes would be greater if not for the increasing phenomenon of college athletes in football and basketball leaving school early to play professionally. Hence, it seems important to separate the two graduation rates from each other in order to obtain a clearer picture of which students are influenced the most by athletic success.

EMPIRICAL ANALYSIS

Three dependent variables are used to address the three separate questions posed in the introduction: the graduation rate of all non-athlete undergraduates, the graduation rate of student-athletes only, and the difference between the graduation rate of student-athletes and the graduation rate of all other undergraduates.

The graduation rate used is the average graduation rate of the four freshman cohorts from 1988 to 1991, and means that a student earned his or her diploma within six years of his or her freshman year. Using a four-year average graduation rate makes this variable more resistant to an unusual cohort's graduation rates. All transfer students are omitted from consideration. The data is from the 1998 NCAA Division I Graduation-Rates Report.

Several variables are used to proxy athletic success. ALLSPT measures the number of Sears' Director's Cup points a school accumulated between 1993 and 1997, the years in which the freshman cohorts in question were competing in NCAA competition. The top 64 teams in a given sport are awarded points.

The top team receives 64 points, the runner-up receives 63 points, and so on through the top 16 teams. Teams 17 through 25 receive 40 points, teams 26 through 44 receive 20 points, and teams 45 through 64 receive 10 points. All sports are weighted equally so that, for example, a national champion in men's basketball is awarded the same number of points as the women's field hockey champion.

MPTS is a subset of ALLSPT, and measures the Sears' Director's Cup points accumulated by men's sports only. This distinction is made because women's college sports have a lower profile financially and less media exposure, and arguably, less impact on graduation rates. MPTS allows us to determine if the success of men's sports specifically impacts graduation rates. All data on Sears' points is obtained from their tournament's headquarters in Louisville, Kentucky.

SAGBB and SAGFB are specified in much the same way Tucker and Amato (1993) measured basketball and football success. *USA Today* started publishing the Sagarin college football and basketball rankings in the early 1990s. Jeff Sagarin has developed complicated statistical models ranking all Division I teams that compete in a particular sport. The Sagarin rankings have two benefits over the AP polls used by Tucker and Amato. First, the rankings are based on a widely accepted statistical model rather than the votes of sportswriters. Second, one can compare all Division I schools, not just the schools designated as being major powers simply because of their conference affiliation. SAGBB and SAGFB are the aggregate ranking achieved by a school in that sport between 1993 and 1997. For example, there are 308 schools with Division I basketball teams. If Duke finishes on top of the Sagarin rankings, they receive 308 points for that year. This data was collected from past issues of *USA Today*.

TPROFIT is a measure of the financial success of a school's athletic program. It is assumed that there should be a positive correlation between financial success and success in terms of the collective athletic success of the school's athletic teams. TPROFIT is calculated as the average total profit reported by a given school from the 1995–1996 and 1996–1997 academic years and is measured in thousands of dollars. This information is available from past copies of *The Chronicle of Higher Education*, and their source was the NCAA's *Revenues and Expenses Report* prepared by Daniel Fuchs of Transylvania University.

MAJOR is a qualitative measure of a school's athletic prowess. MAJOR has a value of 1 for all 63 schools designated as having "big-time" athletic programs in past studies and includes an additional 18 schools that, in the author's opinion, have approached this status in the time since these past studies. Many of these additional 18 schools are member schools of the Western Athletic Conference and Conference USA. It may be that some of the quantitative measures used to measure athletic success do not capture the aura of a school's history of being athletically successful, and so this generic division of the "majors" from the "have-nots" is an attempt to capture this effect.

The other non-academic variable included in the model is a dummy variable designating whether a school is located in a city. The argument provided in Tucker (1992) suggests that students in city environments face more distractions, thereby raising the opportunity cost of academics. The expectation is for a negative sign on the CITY coefficient.

The data for the various academic variables to be defined below (unless noted otherwise) were obtained from *Peterson's Guide to Colleges and Universities* for the 1996–1997 academic year. STDTEST

Section V: Academic Achievement and Involvement in Sports

measures the percentage of students that scored above 1000 on the SAT or above 21 on the ACT. The higher the percentage of entering freshman achieving these test scores, the higher the supposed academic quality of the student body, and the more likely the school is to have a higher graduation rate.

SALARY measures the average salary of full professors at a given school. Higher salaries are considered to imply higher quality instruction, which in turn should yield higher graduation rates. Salary data was obtained from an Internet search engine provided through Arizona State University. SFR measures the student-faculty ratio at a particular school. The lower the student-faculty ratio, the more individualized attention students receive, which should increase graduation rates. STATE is a dummy variable with a value of 1 if the school is a state-supported school and 0 if it is a private school. It is assumed that private schools have a greater incentive to graduate students, so the expected sign on STATE is negative.

TUITION measures the tuition and fees associated with attending a particular school. Higher tuition and fees are generally considered to mean that the school has a greater quantity of resources, which should more effectively supplement a student's academic endeavors. VOLUMES refers to volumes in the library, and is perhaps a more specific measurement of the quantity of academic resources available to students. The expected sign on both VOLUMES and TUITION is positive.

AGE and ENROLL require slightly more explanation. Older universities generally are steeped in academic heritage, thereby offering that added signal of quality to prospective students and faculty alike. Hence, it is hypothesized that older schools have higher graduation rates. There is no *a priori* prediction on the sign of the ENROLL coefficient. Though smaller universities may hire more "teaching-oriented" faculty, large universities may offer more courses and degree options that facilitate graduation.

RESULTS

The sample includes all 308 Division I schools. We have omitted 56 schools (including all 18 historically African-American schools) from the sample because of incomplete data, which leaves 252 schools remaining in the sample. There are 104, 64, and 84 schools, respectively, that can be classified as I-A, I-AA, and I-AAA schools. I-A and I-AA schools both have football programs, whereas I-AAA schools do not. The football programs at I-A schools are much larger in terms of stature and exposure than are the football teams at the I-AA schools.

Table 1 compares the graduation rate of student-athletes to all other undergraduates. Comparisons are reported for the entire sample and across each divisional level. Results from paired t-tests (available upon request from the author) show that student-athlete graduation rates are statistically greater than undergraduate graduation rates in all cases. There seems to be no statistical difference in graduation rates between undergraduates and athletes at I-A schools (especially when focusing the comparison on white men), and there is no statistical difference between male athletes and undergraduates in the full sample.

Table 1 Graduation Rates of Undergraduates and Student-Athletes

	Full Sample (N = 252)	I-A (N = 104)	I-AA (N = 64)	I-AAA (N = 84)
(U)ndergraduates	54.62	57.25	51.48	53.77
(A)thletes	58.15	57.34	55.85	60.91
(M)aleU	51.46	54.64	47.75	50.36
(F)emaleU	57.21	59.82	54.40	56.10
MA	52.46	52.19	50.59	54.25
FA	67.51	67.69	66.92	67.74
(W)hiteMU	52.98	56.30	49.10	51.86
WFU	58.89	61.54	55.68	58.08
WMA	55.56	56.45	53.75	55.86
WFA	68.52	69.26	67.90	68.06
(B)lackMU	37.39	38.12	36.06	37.52
BFU	44.92	45.87	43.28	45.02
BMA	43.32	42.72	40.45	46.28
BFA	58.86	61.85	55.27	57.64

The graduation gap is defined as the student-athlete graduation rate minus the graduation rate for all other undergraduates. Graduation gaps are extremely sensitive to gender. The graduation gap is over 10 percentage points for women (67.51% compared to 57.21%) and roughly only 1 percentage point for men (52.46% compared to 51.46%). This is not surprising. Male athletes in general face greater present and long-term pressures to succeed athletically than do female athletes. This burden to succeed most likely impacts the intensity and time dedicated to athletic training and preparation, leaving much less time to focus on academics. Additionally, male athletes have far more opportunities to leave college early to play professional sports than do women athletes.

Graduation gaps for white men, white women, black men, and black women are 3, 10, 6, and 14 percentage points, respectively. That the female graduation gaps are more than twice the size of the male graduation gaps, irrespective of ethnicity, is consistent with the notion that male athletes face greater pressures to succeed and have greater opportunities to compete professionally.

A more interesting result is that, for both men and women, athletics has a *relatively* stronger *positive* impact on black athletes. Though black athletes have lower graduation rates than white athletes in absolute terms, black athletes realize a greater improvement compared to black undergraduates than white athletes realize in comparison to white undergraduates. The graduation rate for black male athletes is 15% higher than for all other black male undergraduates, yet the graduation rate for white male athletes is only 6% higher than for all other white male undergraduates. Similarly, the graduation rate for black female athletes is 30% higher than for all other black female undergraduates, yet the graduation rate for white female athletes is only 18% higher than for all other white female undergraduates.

Section V: Academic Achievement and Involvement in Sports

Table 2 compares the graduation rates and average SAT scores across football players, men's and women's basketball players, and all other men's and women's athletes. Data on SAT scores comes from the 1996 freshman cohort of student-athletes. Though different than the graduation rate cohorts, it is assumed that these relative differences across sport with respect to SAT scores would not change dramatically over the course of five years.

The results in Table 2 show a strong correlation between high school preparation for college (as proxied by the SAT scores) and graduation rates. The athletes that participate in football and men's basketball come to college less prepared to succeed in their academic pursuits, and this partially explains why their graduation rates are so much lower. With respect to either gender, the non-revenue athletes come to college with better academic preparation and, coupled with less financial pressures to turn professional in their sport of choice, are able to graduate with greater frequency. Female athletes have higher graduation rates, which in part is due to superior high school preparation and in part because they do not have the same opportunities to sign a lucrative professional athletic contract.

Table 2 Graduation Rates and SAT Scores for Revenue and Non-Revenue Athletes

	Full Sample (N = 252)	I-A (N = 104)	I-AA (N = 64)	I-AAA (N = 84)
Football Graduation Rate	52.46	53.05	52.17	—
SAT Football	956	950	964	—
Male Basketball Graduation Rate	42.36	40.22	40.87	46.15
SAT Male Basketball	950	949	957	946
Male "Others" Graduation Rate	58.45	58.93	58.74	57.65
SAT Male "Others"	1044	1054	1039	1037
Female Basketball Graduation Rate	67.14	68.05	66.82	66.22
SAT Women's Basketball	991	984	993	998
Female "Others" Graduation Rate	68.88	69.75	67.65	68.73
SAT Female "Others"	1046	1059	1040	1034

None of the proxies of athletic success have a statistically significant impact on the graduation rate of undergraduates. None of the proxies of athletic success have a statistically significant impact on the graduation rate of student-athletes.

The various proxies for athletic success are significant when explaining differences in the graduation rates of these two groups of students. We find that 1000 additional ALLSPORT points would decrease the graduation gap by 2.7 percentage points. The coefficient on MAJOR suggests that the graduation gap is 2.55 percentage points lower at schools characterized by major athletic programs. An additional 1000 MPTS points would decrease the graduation gap by 5.3 percentage points. An additional 1000 SAGFB points would decrease the graduation gap by 7.1 percentage points. An additional $10,000 in the total profits of the athletic program would decrease the graduation gap by roughly 4 percentage points. In short, the graduation gap is sensitive to the various measures of a school's athletic success.

Though undergraduates and student-athletes have higher graduation rates at schools with major athletic programs (most likely because these schools have superior academic resources), the difference between the two groups of students statistically differs when comparing schools with major athletic programs to all other schools. Undergraduates outperform student-athletes in terms of graduation rates at schools with major athletic programs, yet the reverse is true at all other schools.

A comparison of WBADIF and WBDIF across the two groups of schools is employed to determine if black male athletes disproportionately suffer academically from their involvement in major collegiate sports. WBADIF, the difference in graduation rates between white male and black male athletes, is greater at schools with major athletic programs, but the difference is statistically insignificant. WBDIF, the difference in the ethnic graduation gap of athletes minus the ethnic graduation gap of undergraduates, is lower at schools with major athletic programs, but again this difference is statistically insignificant.

A comparison of FMADIF and FMDIF across the two groups of schools is employed to determine if male athletes disproportionately suffer (or that female athletes disproportionately benefit) academically from their involvement in major collegiate sports. FMADIF, the difference in graduation rates between female and male athletes, is significantly larger at schools with major athletic programs. FMDIF, the difference in the gender graduation gap of athletes minus the gender graduation gap of undergraduates, is also significantly larger at schools with major athletic programs.

The most plausible explanation for these results is that male athletes face higher opportunity costs of investing in academics at schools with major athletics. Male athletes (especially in football and basketball) generally face greater pressures to succeed because they face more media exposure and because their performance can have major financial implications for their athletic departments. Furthermore, male athletes have more opportunities to pursue professional careers, raising their current opportunity costs of investing in academics. This conclusion is identical to the conclusion reached by DeBrock, Hendricks, and Koenker (1996). They find that male athletes in football and basketball have lower graduation rates because they realize a higher expected financial return from a professional sports career than from whatever career a college degree would afford them.

Section V: Academic Achievement and Involvement in Sports

SUMMARY

There is no evidence that suggests that the consumers of athletics (i.e., the undergraduates) are negatively impacted by a higher degree of success of their school's athletic program. There is actually evidence that undergraduates have higher graduation rates at schools with major athletic programs, though this is most likely due to the fact that these same schools have more academic resources compared to other schools. There is also a lack of evidence to support the idea that the graduation rate of student-athletes suffers from higher levels of athletic achievement. In fact, descriptive statistics for the entire sample reveal that the average graduation rate for student-athletes exceeds that for all other undergraduates.

The relative difference in academic success between athletes and undergraduates, however, seems to be quite sensitive to athletic success. Higher levels of athletic success create a larger disparity between student-athlete and undergraduate graduation rates in all cases but one (the success of men's basketball). Furthermore, results from paired t-tests suggest that gender differences in academic success are more acute at schools with major athletic programs, while the same cannot be said for ethnic differences in academic success.

The conclusion is that the only thing that the degree of athletic success truly influences is the relative difference in the graduation rates of undergraduates and student-athletes. Although athletes have higher graduation rates than all other undergraduates for the entire sample, pressures to succeed athletically compromise their relative academic standing compared to other students. With respect to gender comparisons, women have higher graduation rates than men for the entire population of students, and this difference is exacerbated the more prominent a school's athletic program. Men have historically had greater opportunities to pursue an athletic career beyond college and face greater financial and media pressure while attending college, thereby raising their opportunity costs relative to female athletes of investing in academics.

While many observers may be shocked to find that athletes have higher graduation rates than all other students, it is not very surprising. Student-athletes face institutional controls (e.g., minimum academic standards to maintain athletic eligibility, mandatory study halls, and specialized academic advising) that other students do not. These controls produce the general result that student-athletes have higher graduation rates than all other undergraduates. This paper shows that this general rule depends upon which groups of schools and/or students are being compared. Both the comparison of schools with major athletic programs to those without and the male/female comparison show that the success of athletics hurts the relative academic success of the group that faces the greatest expectations to succeed athletically and/or stands the most to gain from athletic success. The myth of the "dumb jock" exists primarily because the most visible college sports of football and men's basketball consistently yield lower graduation rates than any other sports teams.

The biggest shortcoming of the present paper is that there is not enough data available that would directly test how athletic success impacts academic performance as measured by a student's grade point average (GPA). It seems plausible to suggest that athletes' college GPA will be lower during their season of athletic participation. Maloney and McCormick (1993), using a four-year sample of Clemson

University students, found evidence that supports the idea that the athletes of the big-money sports suffer adversely in the classroom during their semester of athletic participation.

The only drawback of Maloney and McCormick's approach is that they focus on a single school. If Clemson happens to be an outlier, then the results they found could not be generalized. It would be interesting to see whether the academic experiences of Clemson's athletes are similar to other Division I schools in Clemson's conference (the Atlantic Coast Conference) or to other schools in the South. Rishe (1999) found that gender biases in athletics were more pervasive in the South than at all other schools. A larger sample of schools using the Maloney and McCormick approach to data selection would be a great extension for future research on sources of graduation rate differentials.

Section VI

Gender Issues in Sport

Sports, Sex, and Title IX

STEVEN E. RHOADS

This past July, the Department of Education reaffirmed existing Title IX regulatory policy, rejecting several changes proposed earlier in the year. Title IX supporters were surprised, delighted, and triumphant; would-be conservative reformers were bitterly disappointed.

Contentious from its inception, the 1972 law to end sex discrimination in publicly funded schools had become the subject of intense controversy when the Department of Education's Commission on Opportunity in Athletics announced proposed modifications to it earlier this year. Women's sports groups and feminists argued that several of the commission's recommendations threatened to undermine Title IX's central guarantee that "no person in the United States shall, on the basis of sex, be excluded from participation in, be denied the benefits of, or be subjected to discrimination under any education program or activity receiving Federal financial assistance." Those in favor of reform, meanwhile, argued that the way in which Title IX has been interpreted by federal regulatory agencies and the courts has resulted in significantly decreased athletic opportunities for men. Reformers were cautiously optimistic that at least some changes were forthcoming. Title IX reform was on the 2000 Republican agenda, and many prominent women on the commission supported reform measures, including a female coach, an athletic director, and a WNBA All-Star.

In the end, the Department of Education adopted none of the recommended changes, promising instead to aggressively enforce the existing regulations. Why did the Department of Education back away from reform, rejecting the recommendations of its own commission? Many political observers believe the decision was a matter of politics, in light of the upcoming presidential election year. There is clearly broad public support for equal opportunities for women in sports. The question is whether Title IX as currently interpreted is the right vehicle for achieving this goal.

Section VI: Gender Issues in Sport

THE QUOTA FACTOR

Under the current law, institutions can meet Title IX requirements in one of three ways. The first (and safest) is essentially a quota system in which schools orchestrate their ratio of athletes in proportion to the male-female ratio on campus. The second does not involve a quota system as long as the school is moving toward quotas through a "history and continuing practice" of expanding opportunities for female athletes. The third way is to ensure that the interests and abilities of female athletes have been "fully and effectively accommodated." As interpreted, this means in effect that a school cannot deny a female student the opportunity to play the sport of her choice simply because the school does not offer the sport.

Not surprisingly, most universities have chosen the first option, aiming for an athlete sex ratio as close as possible to the male-female student ratio on campus. Given tight budgets, they have attempted to reach this goal by cutting or trimming male teams and adding new teams for women. The effects on athletic departments have been substantial. From 1985 to 1997, more than 21,000 spots for male athletes have been cut, and more than 359 male teams have disappeared since 1992. Christine Stolba of the Independent Women's Forum reported to the Title IX commission that "between 1993 and 1999 alone 53 men's golf teams, 39 men's track teams, 43 wrestling teams, and 16 baseball teams have been eliminated. The University of Miami's diving team, which has produced 15 Olympic athletes, is gone."

Wrestling teams have been particularly devastated. Intercollegiate wrestling has been a sport for nearly 100 years and ranks fourth in revenue production of all NCAA Championships. Wrestling is also growing at the high school level and attracts nearly a quarter-million boys—numbers that make it the sixth most popular high school male sport. Yet, as Stolba testified, scores of collegiate wrestling teams have been discontinued to satisfy Title IX strictures. With athletes represented in numerous weight classes, eliminating the wrestling team, or the number of slots on the team, can make sports-participation proportions much closer to student-enrollment proportions with respect to sex.

Brown University's sports program offers another example of Title IX's effects on male sports. In 1995, Brown had 17 women's teams and 16 men's teams, yet the number of male and female participants was nowhere near equal, and not just because the football team was large. Almost all of the women's teams had room for additional athletes (93 slots in total) whereas the men's teams had an overabundance of players competing for available positions. To increase the number of women athletes, Brown began creating new women's teams and cutting the benchwarmers on male teams. Male students interested in minor sports were told they could try out only if they could recruit two women who would try out for other teams. The Brown athletic director found turning away the male walk-ons the hardest part of complying with Title IX. "Eager, willing athletes" who would not travel and who cost the university little or nothing were told to "stay in [your] dorms so [you] won't screw up the numbers."

As a result of Title IX, teams and slots on teams are being cut for male athletes, some of whom have been committed to a sport since early childhood, while new teams are created for women who have never played the sport. In some cases, full scholarships are awarded to women with no experience.

PLAYING POLITICS

The objective of the Title IX reformers was not to eliminate the law or to return to an era when girls and women rarely participated in athletics. Rather, the reforms sought to provide athletic opportunities for both sexes based on actual interest. Because men are on average more interested in playing intercollegiate sports than women, a policy that creates an equal number of places on sports teams on the basis of sex means that men will have fewer athletic opportunities than women. Equal opportunity, reformers assert, requires that colleges provide athletic opportunities based on interest, not on the male-female proportion of its enrollment.

This general concept was endorsed by a majority of the Title IX commission which recommended that schools be permitted to engage in "interest testing" to help satisfy Title IX compliance regulations. These recommendations suggested that institutions "conduct continuous interest surveys on a regular basis as a way of ... allowing schools to accurately predict and reflect men's and women's interest in athletics over time." Furthermore, they would have allowed schools to compare the ratio of male-to-female athletic participation with "the demonstrated interests and abilities shown by regional, state, or national youth or high school participation rates."

Such recommendations did not sit well with traditional Title IX advocates. Defenders of the current law note that statistical equality has yet to be achieved—women represent 56 percent of the national collegiate student body but only 42 percent of intercollegiate athletes. Many advocates also view the shrinking disparity in rates of sports involvement as proof that women will participate in intercollegiate sports if opportunities are created.

But there is also a less frequently articulated reason why so many feminists resist changes to Title IX, especially when those changes would not necessarily decrease sports opportunities for women. Advocates of the law argue that "interest surveys may prevent future progress in providing opportunities for women because offering opportunities regardless of interest may encourage participation even where none currently exists." Thus Title IX, originally an antidiscrimination law, is transformed into a federal endeavor to adjust women's interests in ways favored by their feminist betters. A *Village Voice* essayist recently explained some other reasons to reject the commission's recommendation for interest testing:

> [Reformers] insist that universities conduct surveys to determine student interest in sports and use those numbers as the basis for determining proportional spending, but that misses the substantive work of Title IX, which aims, among other things, to redress a culture that consistently applauds boys for athletic achievement and pours resources in their direction. Is it any wonder that they would express more interest?

Title IX, by this interpretation, is one part of a sociological campaign to aid the broad feminist endeavor to "redress a culture"—American society—that is seen as sexist and that discourages females from playing sports. Actress and amateur archer Geena Davis told the commission: "I am here to take you on a short ride in Thelma and Louise's car if you think it's fair and just to limit a girl's opportunity to play sports based on her response to an interest survey."

That feminists and women's sports groups have so vociferously opposed even mild reforms to Title IX makes a dispassionate public discussion of the issues difficult. This is unfortunate. For the law in fact raises two very important questions—namely, are men more interested than women in competitive sports, and if they are, is this interest rooted in natural differences or is it the result of societal discrimination?

THE SPORTS FAN

There are two primary ways that interest in sports can be measured: One is to look at rates of participation in athletics and the other is to measure how often sports competitions are viewed or followed. One would expect that college students who like to play competitive sports would be more interested in watching them than those who prefer non-sport activities. Not surprisingly, in psychological tests administered to establish areas of interest, one of the greatest differences between the sexes concerns sports. Young men are much greater sports fans than young women; in one study, Loyola Marymount professor Lawrence Wenner found that 20 percent of men but only 4 to 5 percent of women are avid sports fans.

There is further differentiation when it comes to what types of sporting events the sexes prefer to watch and to the details they focus on. Many women find an emotional connection to sports through watching personal profiles of the athletes, whereas men tend to find the emotion in the competition itself. It is no accident that the Olympics are one of the few major sporting events that attract almost as many female viewers as male. Television executives carefully structure broadcasts to emphasize the personal lives of the athletes, to attract more female viewers. The president of NBC Sports once said:

> Men will sit through the Olympics for almost anything, as long as they get to see some winners and losers....Women tend to approach this differently. They want to know who the athletes are, how they got there, what sacrifices they've made. They want an attachment, a rooting interest.

A study by Stephanie Sargent and colleagues, published in the *Journal of Sport and Social Issues*, found that college men prefer to watch combative sports in which there is "direct physical contact between performers," and in which one individual or team wins at the expense of another. Men's favorite sports emphasize strength, stamina, power, domination, agility, and speed, whereas women prefer stylistic sports that "emphasize beauty and elegance of body position and movement but also stress speed, agility and strength." Women's favorite sports do not involve "physical contact between competitors," and competitions are judged by comparative rankings "rather than in [a] one winner/one loser fashion."

One of the sports most popular among women is female ice-skating, which emphasizes grace and artistry as much as strength and speed. Ice-skating is one of the few sports where female interest dwarfs that of males. According to the 2002 *By The Numbers*, edited by John Genzale, more than 70 percent of girls follow figure skating while less than 20 percent of boys do.

WHO PLAYS?

The patterns researchers have found in sports-viewing preferences consistently predict male and female preferences for playing sports. Surveys of college students invariably show that young men are more interested in intercollegiate athletics than are young women. At California State University, for example, a survey found that 61 percent of enrolled students interested in intercollegiate athletic competition were male.

Examining patterns of interest and participation in the school setting is a generally reliable method, but suffers because there are reasons other than interest that explain why an individual chooses to participate: Doing so might help win or maintain a scholarship, earn prestige among a student's peer group, or please the student's parents. The best way to judge interest in playing competitive sports may be to compare how the sexes participate at the recreational level, where participation is based on nothing more than the love of competitive sport itself. Here the differences are even more significant. A 1992 National Educational Longitudinal Study of high school seniors probed for participation in a wide range of activities: sports, music, art, dance, religion, spending time with parents or friends, and volunteering, among others. Far and away the largest sex difference was participation in "nonschool sports," with male participation three times greater than that of females. At the collegiate level, anyone may play intramural sports, but an article published in the *Chronicle of Higher Education* reported that typically there are three or four times more men than women who do so.

THE BIOLOGY OF SPORTS

Why are males more interested in sports? Title IX defenders insist that societal discrimination is the culprit. A typical view is articulated by Valerie Bonnette, head of Good Sports Inc., a Title IX consulting firm, who says that "women aren't born less interested in sports. Society conditions them." Those who advance this position rarely if ever have evidence to buttress their views, and it is no wonder, because there are no data to support their position. If the cumulative impact of social conditioning explained the different interest levels of the sexes, one would expect that the youngest boys and girls would show a rough equality of interest in sports and that they would display similar levels of competitiveness. The reality, however, is that very young girls and boys show marked differences in their interests and levels of competitiveness.

Differences in athletic interest between the sexes begin early. According to Thomas Power's comprehensive book, *Play and Exploration in Children and Animals*, studies show that in the preschool years girls are more interested in dance and boys are more interested in balls and rough play, and that these differences begin to appear before the age of two. By grade school the boys' games are more competitive, longer in duration, with more rules and interdependence between players, and with clear winners and losers. By contrast, psychologist Anne Campbell, in her book *A Mind of Her Own*, reports that girls prefer turn-taking games such as skipping or hopscotch where the form of competition is more indirect. In fact, girls seem to dislike situations where winning means that another person must lose.

Psychologist Eleanor Maccoby, a leading expert on sex differences in children, cites a study which shows that, during the free play of fourth and sixth graders, boys competed with other boys 50 percent of the time, whereas girls competed only 1 percent of the time. Both Campbell and Maccoby present numerous other findings of sex differences. Boys often compete as part of a group, and their groups are larger than girls' groups. There are frequently arguments among the boys, but the disputes are not taken personally and tend to be resolved by rules. Boys enjoy these adversarial situations and prefer to have the best players, and not necessarily their friends, on their team. Girls, in contrast, want their friends on their team and don't want to compete against them. They usually prefer to play in smaller groups and, as Campbell notes, will "abandon a game if it causes arguments." These differing preferences obviously make team sports more attractive to boys.

But observations of early childhood behavior are only part of the considerable evidence that explains why males are more interested in sports than females. The most important evidence is hormonal rather than developmental. Experiments with nonhuman primates and the study of girls exposed to high levels of androgens—the male hormones testosterone and androsterone, which control the development and maintenance of masculine characteristics—compellingly demonstrate the importance of hormones, from early fetal development through puberty, in directing boys' and girls' interests.

In-utero exposure to male hormones is crucial in understanding sex differences. Girls exposed to anomalously high in-utero doses of androgens show more interest in rough play and are more interested in sports, including more violent ones like football. These results are consistent whether one looks at girls whose excess hormonal exposure comes from congenital adrenal hyperplasia (CAH) or because their mothers were given hormones to sustain at-risk pregnancies. For example, Sheri Berenbaum and Elizabeth Snyder report in their 1995 study in the journal *Developmental Psychology* that 70 to 80 percent of girls affected by CAH engaged in competitive athletics more often than most girls.

TWO CHEERS FOR CHEERLEADING

Cheerleading and competitive dance are two sports that appeal broadly to young women and attract some of the best female athletes in school. These sports emphasize beauty and elegance but also require speed, agility, and strength; their athletes make use of the weight room and athletic trainers; and their coaches are on salary. Cheerleaders often earn varsity letters and receive scholarships.

If officially recognized as sports, cheerleading and competitive dance could enable many colleges to meet the Title IX proportionality standards. Yet the Department of Education and the NCAA do not recognize competitive dance or cheerleading as sports, and members of these teams do not count for Title IX compliance purposes. The Department of Education's principal objection is that cheerleading and dance teams usually perform to raise spirit at contests between other athletes, and Title IX guidelines stipulate that at least half of all outings must be in a competitive setting or the activity will not be considered a sport. In response, the University of Maryland recently divided its cheerleading team into a "spirit squad" and a competitive squad. The latter group will attend only cheerleading competitions and will be eligible for scholarship money, a move the school made "to keep Maryland in compliance with Title IX while returning some scholarships to the school's eight underfunded men's programs." Senior team member Erin Valenti opted to stay with the spirit squad, which must fundraise to cover its costs. "They're splitting us only so they can convince whoever the head of Title IX is that cheerleading can be considered a sport," she said. "To make it a sport, you're taking out the whole reason to do cheering to begin with." That is, the cheering part.

One suspects that an important but unarticulated source of indifference to the dancers and cheerleaders is simply that dance and cheerleading have traditionally attended male sports performances and as such are monuments to the pre-feminist cultural norms that women's sports advocates struggle so intensely to discard. Jessica Gavora, author of *Tilting the Playing Field: Schools, Sports, Sex, and Title IX*, comments, "It is a measure of the scorn Title IX activists have for what they regard as traditionally female pursuits—and the perverse reverence they have for traditionally male activities—that they refuse to recognize these talented and dedicated young women as athletes."

Instead of encouraging competitive dance and cheerleading, women's sports advocates concentrate on promoting sports that many young women find uninteresting. The majority of the NCAA's "emerging" sports are not, in fact, growing fast at the grass-roots level. For example, collegiate crew for women is expanding only because colleges see it as a way of accommodating a large number of female athletes in first, second, third, and fourth boats at very little expense. Collegiate women are also attracted because, as a recent "60 Minutes" program explained, it is sometimes possible for a woman to get a full scholarship for crew even though she has never rowed before. In 2002, there were a grand total of 88 high school crew teams in the country. Compare this with the 64,000 girls on competitive cheerleading squads who have received little or no help from women's sports organizations.

BEYOND LOVE OF THE GAME

At the same time that Title IX has marginalized two sports that many young women are genuinely interested in, it has caused much-publicized trauma to men's athletics. Yet the damage caused by Title IX cannot be measured simply in terms of lost recreational opportunities for men. If Title IX advocates were not so intoxicated by ideology, they would acknowledge that men and boys need sports more than women do. Eleanor Maccoby believes that sports can be necessary to cement male friendships in a way that they are not for most women. In her book *The Two Sexes*, she explains that "boys' friendships tend to be less intimate than those of girls" because they are activity-dependent. Men bond with other men through activity, especially competition and sports, and uniquely value the nonverbal friendship that develops with a male teammate or even with a competitor.

Consider what Title IX advocates call the "hapless tackle dummies" who ride the bench on football teams and the other male walk-on athletes who rush to join teams they know they will most likely never play for. It is widely acknowledged that women are different in this regard. The female softball coach at

California State University, Northridge says that "most [women] tend to quit the team" once they "realize that they will not be able to play in games." As Norma Cantu, enforcer of Title IX regulations in the Clinton administration, explains: "They decide that, with no scholarship and no playing time, they are better off doing other things." In other words, women offered the same type of opportunity as their male counterparts will often choose to pursue other interests.

Why are men more willing to ride the bench? Men will do so because it helps them connect with other men, which is much harder for them to do absent an activity such as sport. The bench warmer who plays in practice and cheers on game day is a member of a team on a mission. Women, on the other hand, dislike hierarchy on teams and they often need encouragement from coaches to maintain enthusiasm. Bench warmers in college rarely get encouragement, and their parents don't come to the games to see them ride the bench. Moreover, the emotional connection with peers that many men can get only with competitive activity women are able to get from close friends outside of sports.

Another benefit young men derive from participation in sports is that it reduces displays of aggression and violent behavior. One effect of testosterone is its tendency in some young males to stimulate pointless violence, and sports—especially rough ones such as wrestling and football—can channel male violence into a rule-bound activity, providing a healthy outlet for aggression.

REFORM TITLE IX

The obsessive attention that many Title IX defenders pay to ratios of male and female athletes is even more surprising when one considers that in high schools and colleges, girls outnumber boys in almost every extracurricular activity—student government, honor societies, school newspapers, debating clubs, and choir, among others. Girls outperform boys in virtually every academic category as well. Nationally, men currently represent only 44 percent of all college students, and the federal government predicts that by 2010 the percentage will have fallen to 41 percent. Women are more likely to finish college and currently earn 25 percent more bachelor's degrees than do men.

It is time to think seriously about how to reverse these trends. If more young men had a chance to play sports, more would likely stay in school, especially at those colleges where men's teams have been harshly treated to conform to Title IX requirements. The Department of Education would do well to revisit this issue, and identify competitive dance and cheerleading as sports to be included in Title IX calculations. Also, schools should be allowed to engage in testing to determine student interest in sports. It is to the benefit of neither young men nor young women to persist in a policy that reduces opportunities for dedicated athletes by creating unwanted sports opportunities for others.

Female Gymnasts and Ice Skaters: The Dark Side

Joan Ryan

Unlike women's tennis, a sport in which teenage girls rise to the highest echelon year after year in highly televised championships, gymnastics and figure skating flutter across our screens as ephemerally as butterflies. We know about tennis burnouts Tracy Austin, Andrea Jaeger, Mary Pierce and, more recently, about Jennifer Capriati, who turned pro with $5 million in endorsement contracts at age thirteen and ended up four years later in a Florida motel room, blank-eyed and disheveled, sharing drugs with runaways. But we hear precious little about the young female gymnasts and figure skaters who perform magnificent feats of physical strength and agility, and even less about their casualties. How do the extraordinary demands of their training shape these young girls? What price do their bodies and psyches pay?

I set out to answer some of these questions during three months of research for an article that ran in the *San Francisco Examiner*, but when I finished I couldn't close my notebook. I took a year's leave to continue my research, focusing this time on the girls who never made it, not just on the champions.

What I found was a story about legal, even celebrated, child abuse. In the dark troughs along the road to the Olympics lay the bodies of the girls who stumbled on the way, broken by the work, pressure, and humiliation. I found a girl whose father left the family when she quit gymnastics at age thirteen, who scraped her arms and legs with razors to dull her emotional pain, and who needed a two-hour pass from a psychiatric hospital to attend her high school graduation. Girls who broke their necks and backs. One who so desperately sought the perfect, weightless gymnastics body that she starved herself to death. Others—many—who became so obsessive about controlling their weight that they lost control of themselves instead, falling into the potentially fatal cycle of bingeing on food, then purging by vomiting or taking laxatives. One who was sexually abused by her coach and one who was sodomized for four years by the father of a teammate. I found a girl who felt such shame at not making the Olympic team that she slit her wrists. A skater who underwent plastic surgery when a judge said her nose was distracting. A father who handed custody of his daughter over to her coach so she could keep skating. A coach who fed his gymnasts so little that federation officials had to smuggle food into their hotel rooms. A mother who hid her child's chicken pox with makeup so she could compete. Coaches who motivated their athletes by calling them imbeciles, idiots, pigs, cows.

I am not suggesting that gymnastics and figure skating in and of themselves are destructive. On the contrary, both sports are potentially wonderful and enriching, providing an arena of competition in which the average child can develop a sense of mastery, self-esteem, and healthy athleticism. But this book isn't about recreational sports or the average child. It's about the elite child athlete and the American obsession with winning that has produced a training environment wherein results are bought at any cost, no matter how devastating. It's about how our cultural fixation on beauty and weight and youth has shaped both sports and driven the athletes into a sphere beyond the quest for physical performance.

The well-known story of Tonya Harding and Nancy Kerrigan did not happen in a vacuum; it symbolizes perfectly the stakes now involved in elite competition—itself a reflection of our national character. We created Tonya and Nancy not only by our hunger for winning but by our criterion for winning, an exaggeration of the code that applies to ambitious young women everywhere: Talent counts, but so do beauty, class, weight, clothes, and politics. The anachronistic lack of ambivalence about femininity in both sports is part of their attraction, hearkening back to a simpler time when girls were girls, when women were girls for that matter: coquettish, malleable, eager to please. In figure skating especially, we want our athletes thin, graceful, deferential, and cover-girl pretty. We want eyeliner, lipstick, and hair ribbons. Makeup artists are fixtures backstage at figure skating competitions, primping and polishing. In figure skating, costumes can actually affect a score. They are so important that skaters spend $1500 and up on one dress—more than they spend on their skates. Nancy Kerrigan's dresses by designer Vera Wang cost upward of $5000 each.

Indeed, the costumes fueled the national fairy tale of Tonya and Nancy. Nancy wore virginal white. She was the perfect heroine, a good girl with perfect white teeth, a 24-inch waist and a smile that suggested both pluck and vulnerability. She remained safely within skating's pristine circle of grace and femininity. Tonya, on the other hand, crossed all the lines. She wore bordello red-and-gold. She was the perfect villainess, a bad girl with truck-stop manners, a racy past, and chunky thighs. When she became convinced Nancy's grace would always win out over her own explosive strength, Tonya crossed the final line, helping to eliminate Nancy from competition. The media frenzy tapped into our own inner wranglings about the good girl/bad girl paradox, about how women should behave, about how they should look and what they should say. The story touched a cultural nerve about women crossing societal boundaries—of power, achievement, violence, taste, appearance—and being ensnared by them. In the end, both skaters were trapped, Tonya by her ambition and Nancy by the good-girl image she created for the ice—an image she couldn't live up to. The public turned on Nancy when foolish comments and graceless interviews made it clear she wasn't Snow White after all.

Both sports embody the contradiction of modern womenhood. Society has allowed women to aspire higher, but to do so a woman must often reject that which makes her female, including motherhood. Similarly, gymnastics and figure skating remove the limits of a girl's body, teaching it to soar beyond what seems possible. Yet they also imprison it, binding it like the tiny Victorian waist or the Chinese woman's foot. The girls aren't allowed passage into adulthood. To survive in the sports, they beat back puberty, desperate to stay small and thin, refusing to let their bodies grow up. In this way the sports pervert the very femininity they hold so dear. The physical skills have become so demanding that only a body shaped like a missile—in other words, a body shaped like a boy's—can excel. Breasts and hips slow the spins, lower the leaps and disrupt the clean, lean body lines that judges reward. "Women's gymnastics" and "ladies' figure skating" are misnomers today. Once the athletes become women, their elite careers wither.

In the meantime, their childhoods are gone. But they trade more than their childhoods for a shot at glory. They risk serious physical and psychological problems that can linger long after the public has turned its attention to the next phenom in pigtails. The intensive training and pressure heaped on by coaches, parents, and federation officials—the very people who should be protecting the children—often result in eating disorders, weakened bones, stunted growth, debilitating injuries, and damaged psyches. In the last six years two U.S. Olympic hopefuls have died as a result of their participation in elite gymnastics.

Because they excel at such a young age, girls in these sports are unlike other elite athletes. They are world champions before they can drive. They are the Michael Jordans and Joe Montanas of their sports before they learn algebra. Unlike male athletes their age, who are playing quarterback in high school or running track for the local club, these girls are competing on a worldwide stage. If an elite gymnast or figure skater fails, she fails globally. She sees her mistake replayed in slow motion on TV and captured in bold headlines in the newspaper. Adult reporters crowd around, asking what she has to say to a country that had hung its hopes on her thin shoulders. Tiffany Chin was seventeen when she entered the 1985 U.S. Figure Skating Championships as the favorite. She was asked at the time how she would feel if she didn't win. She paused, as if trying not to consider the possibility. "Devastated," she said quietly. "I don't know. I'd probably die."

Chin recalled recently that when she did win, "I didn't feel happiness. I felt relief. Which was disappointing." Three months before the 1988 Olympics, Chin retired when her legs began to break down. Some, however, say she left because she could no longer tolerate the pressure and unrelenting drive of her stern mother. "I feel I'm lucky to have gotten through it," she said of skating. "I don't think many people are that lucky. There's a tremendous strain on people who don't make it. The money, the sacrifices, the time. I know people emotionally damaged by it. I've seen nervous breakdowns, psychological imbalances."

An elite gymnast or figure skater knows she takes more than her own ambitions into a competition. Her parents have invested tens of thousands of dollars in her training, sometimes hundreds of thousands.

Her coach's reputation rides on her performance. And she knows she might have only one shot. By the next Olympics she might be too old. By the next year she might be too old. Girls in these sports are under pressure not only to win but to win quickly. They're running against a clock that eventually marks the lives of all women, warning them they'd better hurry up and get married and have children before it's too late. These girls hear the clock early. They're racing against puberty.

Boys, on the other hand, welcome the changes that puberty brings. They reach their athletic peak after puberty when their bodies grow and their muscles strengthen. In recent years Michael Chang and Boris Becker won the French Open and Wimbledon tennis titles, respectively, before age eighteen, but in virtually every male sport the top athletes are men, not boys. Male gymnastics and figure skating champions are usually in their early to mid twenties; female champions are usually fourteen to seventeen years old in gymnastics and sixteen to early twenties in figure skating.

In staving off puberty to maintain the "ideal" body shape, girls risk their health in ways their male counterparts never do. They starve themselves, for one, often in response to their coaches' belittling insults about their bodies. Starving shuts down the menstrual cycle—the starving body knows it cannot support a fetus—and thus blocks the onset of puberty. It's a dangerous strategy to save a career. If a girl isn't menstruating, she isn't producing estrogen. Without estrogen, her bones weaken. She risks stunting her growth. She risks premature osteoporosis. She risks fractures in all bones, including her vertebrae, and she risks curvature of the spine. In several studies over the last decade, young female athletes who didn't menstruate were found to have the bone densities of postmenopausal women in their fifties, sixties and seventies. Most elite gymnasts don't begin to menstruate until they retire. Kathy Johnson, a medalist in the 1984 Olympics, didn't begin until she quit the sport at age twenty-five.

Our national obsession with weight, our glorification of thinness, have gone completely unchecked in gymnastics and figure skating. The cultural forces that have produced extravagantly bony fashion models have taken their toll on gymnasts and skaters already insecure about their bodies. Not surprisingly, eating disorders are common in both sports, and in gymnastics they're rampant. Studies of female college gymnasts show that most practice some kind of disordered eating. In a 1994 University of Utah study of elite gymnasts—those training for the Olympics—59 percent admitted to some form of disordered eating. And in interviewing elites for this book, I found only a handful who had not tried starving, throwing up or taking laxatives or diuretics to control their weight. Several left the sport because of eating disorders. One died. Eating disorders among male athletes, as in the general male population, are virtually unknown.

"Everyone goes through it, but nobody talks about it, because they're embarrassed," gymnast Kristie Phillips told me. "But I don't put the fault on us. It's the pressures that are put on us to be so skinny. It's mental cruelty. It's not fair that all these pressures are put on us at such a young age and we don't realize it until we get older and we suffer from it."

Phillips took laxatives, thyroid pills, and diuretics to lose weight. She had been the hottest gymnast in the mid-1980s, the heir apparent to 1984 Olympic superstar Mary Lou Retton. But she not only didn't win a medal at the 1988 Summer Games, she didn't even make the U.S. team. She left the sport feeling like a failure. She gained weight, then became bulimic, caught in a cycle of bingeing and vomiting. Distraught, she took scissors to her wrists in a botched attempt to kill herself. "I weighed ninety-eight pounds and I was being called [by her coach] an overstuffed Christmas turkey," Phillips said in our interview. "I was told I was never going to make it in life because I was going to be fat. I mean, in *life*. Things I'll never forget."

Much of the direct blame for the young athletes' problems falls on the coaches and parents. Obviously, no parent wakes up in the morning and plots how to ruin his or her child's life. But the money, the fame, and the promise of great achievement can turn a parent's head. Ambition gets perverted. The boundaries of parents and coaches bloat and mutate, with the parent becoming the ruthless coach and coach becoming the controlling parent. One father put gymnastics equipment in his living room and for every mistake his daughter made at the gym she had to repeat the skill hundreds of times at home. He moved the girl to three gyms around the country, pushing her in the sport she came to loathe. He said he did it because he wanted the best for her.

Coaches push because they are paid to produce great gymnasts. They are relentless about weight because physically round gymnasts and skaters don't win. Coaches are intolerant of injuries because in the race against puberty, time off is death. Their job is not to turn out happy, well-adjusted young women; it is to turn out champions. If they scream, belittle, or ignore, if they prod an injured girl to forget her pain, if they push her to drop out of school, they are only doing what the parents have paid them to do. So, sorting out the blame when a girl falls apart is a messy proposition; everyone claims he was just doing his job.

The sports' national governing bodies, for their part, are mostly impotent. They try to do well by the athletes, but they, too, often lose their way in a tangle of ambition and politics. They're like small-town governments: personal, despotic, paternalistic, and absolutely without teeth. The federations do not have the power that the commissioners' offices in professional baseball, football, and basketball do. They cannot revoke a coach's or an athlete's membership for anything less than criminal activity. (Tonya Harding was charged and sentenced by the courts before the United States Figure Skating Association expelled her.) They cannot fine or suspend a coach whose athletes regularly leave the sport on stretchers.

There simply is no safety net protecting these children. Not the parents, the coaches, or the federations.

Child labor laws prohibit a thirteen-year-old from punching a cash register for forty hours a week, but that same child can labor for forty hours or more inside a gym or an ice skating rink without drawing the slightest glance from the government. The U.S. government requires the licensing of plumbers. It demands that even the tiniest coffee shop adhere to a fastidious health code. It scrutinizes the advertising claims on packages of low-fat snack food. But it never asks a coach, who holds the lives of his young pupils in his hands, to pass a minimum safety and skills test. Coaches in this country need no license to train children, even in a high-injury sport like elite gymnastics. The government that forbids a child from buying a pack of cigarettes because of health concerns never checks on the child athlete who trains until her hands bleed or her knees buckle, who stops eating to achieve the perfect body, who takes eight Advils a day and offers herself up for another shot of cortisone to dull the pain, who drinks a bottle of Ex-Lax because her coach is going to weigh her in the morning. The government never takes a look inside the gym or the rink to make sure these children are not being exploited or abused or worked too hard. Even college athletes—virtually all of whom are adults—are restricted by the NCAA to just twenty hours per week of formal training. But no laws, no agencies, put limits on the number of hours a child can train or the methods a coach can use.

Some argue that extraordinary children should be allowed to follow extraordinary paths to realize their potential. They argue that a child's wants are no less important than an adult's and thus she should not be denied her dreams just because she is still a child. If pursuing her dream means training eight hours a day in a gym, withstanding abusive language, and tolerating great pain, and if the child wants to do it and the parents believe it will build character, why not let her? Who are we to tell a child what she can and cannot do with her life?

In fact, we tell children all the time what they can and cannot do with their lives. Restricting children from certain activities is hardly a revolutionary concept. Laws prohibit children from driving before sixteen and drinking before twenty-one. They prohibit children from dropping out of school before fifteen and working full-time before sixteen. In our society we put great value on protecting our children from physical harm and exploitation, and sometimes that means protecting them from their own poor judgment and their parents' poor judgment. No one questions the wisdom of the government in forbidding a child to work full-time, so why is it all right for her to train full-time with no rules to ensure her well-being? Child labor laws should address all labor, even that which is technically nonpaid, though top gymnasts and figure skaters *do* labor for money.

In recent years the federations have begun to pay their top athletes a stipend based on their competition results. The girls can earn bonuses by representing the United States in certain designated events. Skaters who compete in the World Figure Skating Championships and the Olympic Games, for example, receive $15,000. They earn lesser amounts for international competitions such as Skate America. They also earn money from corporate sponsors and exhibitions. The money might not cover much more than their training expenses, which can run $75,000 for a top skater and $20,000 to $30,000 per year for a top gymnast, but it's money—money that is paid specifically for the work the athletes do in the gym and the skating rink.

The real payoff for their hard work, however, waits at the end of the road. That's what the parents and athletes hope anyway. When Mary Lou Retton made millions on Madison Avenue after winning the gold medal at the 1984 Olympics, she changed gymnastics forever. "Kids have agents now before they even make it into their teens," Retton says. Now the dream is no longer just about medals but about Wheaties boxes and appearance fees, about paying off mom and dad's home equity loans and trading in the Toyota for a Mercedes. It doesn't seem to matter that only six girls every four years reach the Olympics and that winning the gold once they get there is the longest of long shots. Even world champion Shannon Miller didn't win the all-around Olympic gold in 1992.

Figure skating, even more than gymnastics, blinds parents and athletes with the glittering possibilities, and for good reason. Peggy Fleming and Dorothy Hamill are still living off gold medals won decades ago. Nancy Kerrigan landed endorsements with Reebok, Evian, Seiko, and Campbell's soup with only a bronze medal in 1992. With glamorous and feminine stars like Kerrigan and Kristi Yamaguchi to lead the way, the United States Figure Skating Association has seen the influx of corporate sponsorship climb 2000 percent in just five years. Money that used to go to tennis is now being shifted to figure skating and gymnastics as their popularity grows. The payoff in money and fame now looms large enough to be seen from a distance, sparkling like the Emerald City, driving parents and children to extremes to reach its doors.

I'm not suggesting that all elite gymnasts and figure skaters emerge from their sports unhealthy and poorly adjusted. Many prove that they can thrive under intense pressure and physical demands and thus are stronger for the experience. But too many can't. There are no studies that establish what percentage of elite gymnasts and figure skaters are damaged by their sports and in what ways. So the evidence I've gathered for this book is anecdotal, the result of nearly a hundred interviews and more than a decade of covering both sports as a journalist.

The bottom line is clear. There have been enough suicide attempts, enough eating disorders, enough broken bodies, enough regretful parents and enough bitter young women to warrant a serious reevaluation of what we're doing in this country to produce Olympic champions. Those who work in these sports know this. They know the tragedies all too well. If the federations and coaches truly care about the athletes and not simply about the fame and prestige that come from trotting tough little champions up to the medal stand, they know it is past time to lay the problems on the table, examine them, and figure out a way to keep their sports from damaging so many young lives. But since those charged with protecting young athletes so often fail in their responsibility, it is time the government drops the fantasy that certain sports are merely games and takes a hard look at legislation aimed at protecting elite child athletes.

It is also my hope that by dramatizing the particularly intense subculture of female gymnastics and figure skating, we can better understand something of our own nature as a country bent on adulating, and in some cases sacrificing, girls and young women in a quest to fit them into our pretty little boxes.

Section VII

Race and Sport

Racial Inequality and Sport

George H. Sage

It is said that the history of sport is one that reveals all that has been bad as well as good throughout the history of the United States. This is true for African Americans in sport: sport has simultaneously been a powerful reinforcer of racist ideology and an instrument of opportunity for African Americans.

Unlike the patriarchal ideology that historically barred most women from sport, the ideology underlying racism has not been incompatible with African American sport participation, but it has dictated that African American athletes be subordinate and in certain times and places totally segregated from playing with whites. Still, despite pervasive and systematic discrimination against African Americans, they have played a continuing and significant role in every era of American history. Their involvement can be roughly divided into three stages: (1) largely exclusion before the Civil War, (2) breakthroughs immediately after the Civil War but segregation beginning in the last two decades of the 19th century continuing to the mid-20th century, and (3) integration during the latter 20th century.

THE ERA OF SLAVERY

Social relations among African Americans during the more than 200 years of slavery involved a wide variety of games and sports played among themselves. Many plantation owners actually encouraged such use of leisure time because it was seen as preferable to other options such as drinking, fighting, and general mischief. They may have also encouraged games and sports to dissuade slaves from plotting acts of insurgency against plantation owners. Sporting social relations between whites and blacks during the slavery era (1619 to 1865) centered on two activities: boxing and horse racing. Holidays and special occasions in the colonial (1607–1789) and antebellum periods were often enlivened with sports and games, especially those on which people could wager. Many plantation owners selected—and even trained—one or more male slaves to enter in boxing matches held in conjunction with festive occasions.

The black boxers under such conditions were merely used to entertain their white "masters" and their friends.

Horse racing was another popular sporting event that allowed spectators to bet on the outcome. Horses were, of course, owned by whites, and training was done usually by whites, but African Americans were used as jockeys. There was little status and no significant material reward for jockeying because slave labor of any kind was unpaid; jockeying was viewed as basically mechanical, so slaves were trusted with a task that whites did not care to do anyway. Social relations, then, were seen as distant, with whites in control and African Americans in subordinate roles, pleasing the dominant white groups.

LATTER 19TH CENTURY TO MID-20TH CENTURY

Emancipation had little effect on the social relations between African Americans and whites in sports. Although a number of African Americans played on professional baseball teams in the early years of the National League, Jim Crowism (segregation) gradually raised its ugly head. White players threatened to quit rather than share the diamond with black men. White opponents tried to spike African American players at every opportunity; pitchers aimed at their heads. Finally, in 1888 major league club owners made a gentlemen's agreement not to sign any more African American players. This unwritten law against hiring black players was not violated until 1945 when Branch Rickey, general manager of the Brooklyn Dodgers, signed Jackie Robinson to a contract.

As other professional sports developed, African Americans were likewise barred from participation. This exclusion maintained the segregation of the wider society as well as the segregation of Major League Baseball. One of the many consequences of excluding African Americans from professional sports was to perpetuate privileges for white athletes, who did not have to compete with an entire segment of the population for sport jobs.

Excluding African Americans from white-only professional leagues did not stop them from forming their own teams and leagues. These so-called Negro baseball leagues (that is the term that was used) flourished for more than 40 years; they staged their own versions of the World Series and All-Star Games and produced their own heroes who were idolized in African American communities. All-black basketball teams and leagues succeeded in many cities of the Northeast and Midwest.

African Americans were active in boxing throughout the time of slavery, but they found their aspirations for top prizes blocked when they tried to compete as free men after the Civil War. For example, when John L. Sullivan became the first American heavyweight boxing champion in 1882, he announced that he would fight any contender: "In this challenge, I include all fighters—first come, first served—who are white. I will not fight a Negro. I never have, and never shall." And he never did. One of the greatest heavyweight boxing champions of all time, Jack Dempsey, in his first public statement after he won the championship in 1919, said that he would not under any circumstances "pay any attention to Negro challengers." Despite barriers like these, two African Americans—Jack Johnson and Joe Louis—managed to win the heavyweight championship during the first half of the 20th century.

During the late 19th and early 20th centuries, education in the South was totally segregated, so African American high school and intercollegiate athletes competed only against other African American athletes. Although not segregated, schools and colleges in other parts of the country managed to bar most African Americans from high school and college sports teams. Until the 1960s, most African American college athletes played at black colleges in black leagues (known as Negro colleges and Negro leagues), which existed because of institutionalized racial prejudice and discrimination.

Black colleges fielded teams in all the popular sports and played a leading role in promoting women's sports, especially in track and field—Tuskegee Institute (now Tuskegee University) and Tennessee State are prominent examples. They provided opportunities for women before such opportunities were available on predominantly white campuses. Although the educational system was segregated, the so-called Negro colleges provided an avenue of opportunity for many African American athletes—both men and women—though few were ever recognized outside the African American community.'

LATTER 20TH CENTURY

The past 50 years has been a time of remarkable change for African Americans in sports. They have become a significant presence at every level of organized sports. From a condition of exclusion from "white" sports, they have passed through periods of tokenism, during which they were admitted in small numbers, to a period of "stacking," during which only specific positions on teams were thought appropriate for them (because racist ideology stereotyped them as having speed, quickness, and jumping ability, but not intellectual and complex thinking ability), to a period of open acceptance in many sports.

Professional Sports

African Americans have gradually assumed a remarkably prominent role in several professional sports. When Jackie Robinson took the field for the Brooklyn Dodgers in 1947, he broke the all-white exclusion barrier of Major League Baseball that had been in place for more than 50 years. The next 10 years was a period of tokenism by which most teams integrated by signing one or two African American players. By 1959, when the Boston Red Sox finally signed an African American player, every major league team was integrated, but even in the mid-1960s, less than 10 percent of all Major League Baseball players were African American. Most African American players were "stacked" at the outfield and infield corner positions of first and third base. Currently about 18 percent of Major League Baseball players are African American, and they are more widely distributed in the various playing positions.

Other popular professional team sports have passed through essentially the same phases as Major League Baseball. Exclusion was largely the situation in professional football before World War II. Then from the 1950s to well into the 1980s, periods of tokenism and "stacking" players into running back, wide receiver, and defensive back positions followed. African Americans have become dominant in the National Football League (NFL) in the 1990s; in 1998 68 percent of NFL players were African American, and they are distributed in all the playing positions (though very few are quarterbacks).

The most striking increase of African Americans in professional sports has taken place in basketball; in the late 1950s, only about 10 percent of National Basketball Association (NBA) players were black.

Tokenism and stacking, while present for periods in basketball, were not as conspicuous as in baseball and football. At present, more than 80 percent of NBA players are African American; they dominate at all the positions.

When the two women's professional basketball leagues, the American Basketball League and the Women's National Basketball Association, began their inaugural seasons in 1996 and 1997, more than 75 percent of the players were African American. This reflects the prominent place that African American women have played during the past decade on intercollegiate and U.S. Olympic basketball teams, for it was from these teams that the professional leagues recruited their players.

Intercollegiate Sports

Intercollegiate sports at predominantly white institutions remained segregated, with isolated exceptions, until after World War II. At the University of Michigan, for example, from 1882 to 1945 there were only four black lettermen in football and none in basketball. The impact of World War II in opening up social and economic opportunities for African Americans, the 1954 Supreme Court decision forbidding racially separate educational facilities, and the growing commercialization of collegiate sports led more and more formerly white colleges and universities to recruit talented African American athletes to bolster their teams. Consequently, black colleges lost their monopoly on African American athletic talent. The best athletes found it advantageous to play at predominantly white schools because of greater visibility, especially on television, which boosted their chances for signing professional contracts at the conclusion of their eligibility. Athletic programs at black colleges were rapidly depleted, forcing several schools to drastically modify their athletic programs and some black leagues to disband.

In 1948 only 10 percent of predominately white college basketball teams had one or more African Americans on their rosters. This proportion increased to 45 percent of the teams in 1962 and 92 percent by 1975. Universities in the southern states maintained white-only teams until the latter 1960s. The conversion from segregated to integrated programs in the South is well illustrated by the University of Alabama: in 1968 there were no African Americans on any of its teams, but by 1975 its basketball team fielded an all-black starting lineup.

The percentage of African American athletes has exceeded the percentage of African American nonathletes in higher education for many years. In the late 1990s, less than 6 percent of all students at Division I universities are African American, while overall, 27.5 percent of the scholarship athletes in Division I institutions are African American; 60 percent of the men's basketball players, 37 percent of the women's basketball players, and 42 percent of the football players are African American.

Remaining Barriers to Access

Despite the many opportunities now available in sport for African Americans that did not exist a generation ago, racial inequality in sport has not been eliminated. Many professional and college sports still have very few African American participants. Those sports most closely linked to upper-class patronage and with less spectator interest, and thus less economic impact, have been slow to provide access to African Americans. Both men's and women's professional tennis and golf have conspicuously few African

Americans. But socially elite sports are not the only ones still lacking significant African American presence. Auto racing, ice hockey, and soccer are others. Laws that prevent African Americans from being kept out do not assure that they will get in. Ample evidence shows that those who control certain sports have created barriers to black participation, thus reproducing some of the more odious features of racial injustice.

It is important to understand that where barriers to access have been eliminated for African Americans in sports, these changes have not taken place purely from humanitarian concerns. Political, legal, and economic factors have played interlocking roles. The civil rights legislation of the 1960s opened up many sectors of life for African Americans, including sport. Sport opportunities for African Americans in professional sport grew only as discrimination became incompatible with good capitalist financial policy. It was in those team sports in which spectator appeal was strong and growing, and in which the profit motive was foremost, that African Americans were given a chance, and the valuable contributions of outstanding African American athletes in winning championships opened up further opportunities.

It is also important to understand that racism has not been eliminated in sport even though more sports opportunities are available and even though there is more equitable distribution of African Americans in professional and intercollegiate sports. Racial attitudes are not necessarily changed by laws or political and economic pressures. Prejudice, discrimination, and injustice remain, albeit in more subtle, even unconscious, forms. African American athletes, coaches, and sport administrators report that rarely a day goes by that they do not experience racial prejudice or discrimination of some kind. Their accounts have been corroborated by empirical research as well as by testimonials by their white teammates and friends.

LEADERSHIP AND MANAGEMENT OPPORTUNITIES

Employment patterns in sports leadership for African Americans have been similar to that of female sport coaches and administrators. Access for black athletes has expanded greatly in recent years, but very few African Americans—men or women—have been hired for positions high in the sport hierarchy. At the present time, blacks account for less than 5 percent of the key management positions in professional and intercollegiate sports. Racist ideology, stereotypes, and caricatures have portrayed African Americans as lacking the requisite intelligence and rational thinking capabilities for leadership. The same racist ideology claims that whites will not follow black leaders.

Another barrier to leadership positions in sport for African Americans is the dominance of the entrenched white "ol' boys" network. Those who control access to those higher levels can subtly insulate themselves against those with whom they do not wish to associate. Of course, the extent to which any of these factors account for the hiring for any given sport leadership position is hard to determine, but the perpetuation of racial stereotypes and the dominant social network certainly are powerful forces.

In both professional and intercollegiate sports, coaching and administration jobs are under the control of those who have the power for determining who gets selected for the upper-level positions. Statements made by powerful persons in sport organizations suggest racist beliefs play a role in excluding

African Americans from administrative positions. In 1987 Al Campanis, an executive for the Los Angeles Dodgers, appeared on the television program *Nightline* and was asked by host Ted Koppel why there are no black managers and general managers in Major League Baseball. Campanis replied that blacks "may not have some of the necessities to be…a field manager or perhaps a general manager." In 1992 Marge Schott, owner of the Cincinnati Reds, reportedly said she would rather "hire a trained monkey than a nigger" to work in her front office. These statements, and the hiring practices of those who make hiring decisions for sports organizations, clearly suggest that race has been a factor in those decisions.

As of 1998 there were only three black head coaches in the NFL, and conditions are not promising for improvement. During the 1997 season and before the 1998 season began, the NFL had 11 head coaching openings and none of the jobs were filled by an African American. Twenty-six percent of NFL assistant coaches in 1997 were black, and only four were offensive or defensive coordinators—the most responsible and prestigious coaching positions below head coaching. This in a league in which about 68 percent of the players are black. Major League Baseball has had only a handful of black managers to date, and currently only about 18 percent of the coaches and one of the general managers are African American. In fall 1996, six Major League Baseball manager positions were open; no one was hired from the list of minority candidates. Professional basketball has had the most African American head coaches. In recent years, as many as seven blacks have held these positions at once, but this is in a league with more than 80 percent African American players.

African American coaches are equally scarce in intercollegiate athletics. The first African American to be hired as a head football coach at a major college was Ron Cooper at Eastern Michigan University in 1992. As of spring 1998, less than 8 of 112 head football coaches in NCAA Division IA are African American. Nearly all African American college coaches are assistants, and most coaching staffs have only one black. Of about 1,220 head coaching positions in NCAA Division I sports, not including the predominantly black colleges, in which African American athletes have a significant presence (football, basketball, track, baseball), less than 5 percent are held by African Americans.

Executive positions in professional and intercollegiate sports continue to elude African Americans. In the commissioner's offices of pro sports, in the front offices of professional clubs, among the top-level NCAA administrators, and among university athletic directors, there are scandalously few African Americans. As of 1998, the NFL has had fewer than six black general managers, and about 10 NBA general managers have been African American. Of more than 20 new general managers hired by Major League Baseball from 1990 to 1998, one was African American. The one bright spot in this otherwise dim picture for baseball was the choice in February 1989 of Bill White, an African American, as the president of the National League.

In 1994 the NCAA's Minority Opportunity and Interests Committee reported that the proportion of black sport administrators at member institutions of the NCAA had changed little over the past four years. Two years later, the situation was much the same. In 1998 only about 5 percent of the athletic directors at NCAA Division I institutions were African American.

African American women who aspire to leadership positions in professional and intercollegiate sports are faced with two obstacles. First, they are victims of racist ideology that militates against their employment. Second, there are fewer women's sports than men's; the opportunities simply do not exist for females—white or black—to coach or manage in professional or intercollegiate sports. But where positions exist for which African American women might be employed, they are not being hired. Only one sport—women's intercollegiate basketball—has a significant number of black female coaches. In 1998 there were about a dozen NCAA Division I basketball teams coached by an African American woman.

The sports leadership situation for African Americans had become so disgraceful in the early 1990s that some of the sport governing bodies and civil rights groups formed committees and task forces to help seek out minorities for management and executive positions and to monitor team hiring. In 1993 the Rainbow Commission for Fairness in Athletics was created by the Reverend Jesse Jackson to reduce racism and gender barriers in the hiring practices of professional and collegiate sport. Substantial and meaningful results have been slow; the ranks of managers, head coaches, and front-office personnel continue to be filled by whites, sometimes using thinly disguised ploys that eliminate African Americans from serious consideration.

SOCIAL MOBILITY THROUGH SPORT FOR AFRICAN AMERICANS

It has often been contended that sport is one of the most responsive social practices for serving as an avenue of upward social mobility for African Americans; indeed, it has been argued that sport has done more in this regard than any other social practice or institution. Although it is certainly true that sport has provided some African American athletes with opportunities for social mobility denied them in other sectors of American life, and a few have become prominent figures in American life—Jackie Robinson, Muhammad Ali, Wilma Rudolph, "Magic" Johnson, Jackie Joyner-Kersee, and others—sport has not moved large numbers of African Americans into higher social-class standing. The rags-to-riches stories of individual, high-profile African American athletes disguise the actual reality of how little social mobility results from sports participation.

There are fewer than 3,400 male professional team sport athletes. There are about 50.2 million American males age 15 to 39 (the age range of most professional athletes), 6.2 million of whom are African Americans. So that makes the odds of an African American male becoming a professional athlete about one in 5,000. Meanwhile, there are 12 times more black lawyers and 15 times more black doctors than there are black professional athletes.

Sociologist Harry Edwards once remarked about an African American's chances of becoming a professional athlete: "You have a better chance of getting hit by a meteorite in the next 10 years than getting work as an athlete." Henry Louis Gates Jr., professor of humanities at Harvard University and an African American, made a similar point: "An African American youngster has about as much chance of becoming a professional athlete as he or she does of winning the lottery. The tragedy for our people, however, is that few of us accept the truth.... The blind pursuit of attainment in sports is having a devastating effect on our people." Still, many young African American athletes have bought into the myth that sport is the highway to financial success and upward social mobility. According to a national survey, 51 percent of African American high school athletes believe they can become professional athletes.

African Americans have received an increasing number of athletic scholarships at predominantly white schools since the early 1970s, but this has been a mixed blessing. On one hand, a few athletically talented African Americans have been able to attend and graduate from colleges otherwise inaccessible to them, and this has allowed them to achieve upward social mobility. On the other hand, the evidence is clear and abundant that the athletic talent of many African American college athletes has been exploited by their schools. They have been recruited even though they lacked the academic background to succeed in higher education, and they have been advised into courses that keep them eligible but are dead-end choices for acquiring a college diploma. When their eligibility is used up or they become academically ineligible to compete for the team, they are discarded and ignored by the coaches who recruited them. From 55 percent to 75 percent of African American NCAA Division I football, basketball, and track athletes do not graduate. This represents a much lower rate of graduation than the overall graduation averages in those universities.

The evidence is overwhelming that professional sport cannot provide much in the way of upward social mobility for large numbers of African Americans. Yes, the very few who become professional athletes make a lot of money and become wealthy for a time. But even for those who do become professional athletes, the average professional sports career is very short—less than five years. That's right. The average professional athlete remains at the top level of competition for less than five years.

An athletic scholarship has the potential to help an African American college student from a poor family earn a college diploma, which can then lead to a high-paying position in a professional field or business. But every year thousands of African American college athletes leave college without the diploma. For them, their future occupation will be determined by their educational achievement and by chance, just as it is for other men and women without a college degree.

The Stacking of Latinos in Major League Baseball: A Forgotten Minority?

G. Letitia González

The theory of stacking, or the disproportionate relegation of athletes to specific sport positions on the basis of ascribed characteristics such as race or ethnicity, was first developed by Loy and McElvogue (1970). Their classic study, which combines Blalock's (1962) proposition that "there will be less discrimination where performance of independent tasks is largely involved" (Loy and McElvogue, 1970, p. 7) with Grusky's (1963) concept of spatial location within the formal structure of organizations, hypothesizes that "racial segregation in professional team sports is positively related to centrality" (Loy and McElvogue, 1970, p. 7). The theory implies that minorities are assigned to playing positions on the basis of what they are, not what they have achieved. Whereas Loy and McElvogue's stacking theory is still being used today as the foundation for many studies, the validity and usefulness of Grusky's theory of "centrality" has been questioned when applied to the players on the field. This is due to the fact that it does not take the role of coaches and managers into account. As they make decisions regarding position alignments and responsibilities, the centrality of positions on the field may become irrelevant. Nevertheless, stacking plays an important role in the assignment of players to designated playing positions.

As a result, stacking is usually seen as a negative phenomenon because it is a discriminatory process. For example, according to existing research, stacking moves minority players to a supporting rather than a leading role. In addition, stacking causes minorities to compete with each other for specific or limited playing positions, which reduces the number of minorities on the playing field (e.g., Dubois, 1980; Eitzen and Yetman, 1977; Jiobu, 1988; Pattnayak and Leonard, 1991; Phillips, 1983).

Section VII: Race and Sport

For about 25 years, sociologists and other scholars have worked to find explanations for the occurrence of stacking in sports organizations (see Curtis and Loy, 1978, for an excellent overview of early studies). Most stacking theories are based on one of several alternative perspectives that may be labeled as biological, psychological, or sociological. Empirical evidence for each of these perspectives varies. The biological explanations focus on the genetic differences between whites and blacks but appear to have the weakest scientific foundation of the three perspectives (Jordan, 1969; Malina, 1965). The psychological justifications for stacking are based on two theories: the idea that blacks are better at reactive tasks whereas whites excel at self-paced tasks (Worthy and Markle, 1970) and the idea that blacks and whites have different personalities (Jones and Hochner, 1973). Finally, the majority of proposed explanations for stacking fall under the sociological perspective. Under this perspective, there are two groups of three interpretations each. In the first group of interpretations, discriminatory processes consist of stereotyping (Eitzen and Furst, 1989), interaction and discrimination (Loy and McElvogue, 1970),. and outcome control dynamics (Edwards, 1973). The second group of interpretations can be labeled as "levels of socialization" and includes hypotheses dealing with prohibitive cost (Medoff, 1976, 1986), differential attractiveness of positions (Eitzen and Yetman, 1977; Scully, 1974), and role modeling (McPherson, 1974). Sociological explanations are the predominant focus of contemporary scholars.

As a result, there is a substantial amount of stacking literature available covering a wide variety of sports such as baseball (e.g., Eitzen and Yetman, 1977; Guppy, 1983; Jiobu, 1988; Leonard, Pine, and Rice, 1988; Medoff, 1976, 1977, 1986; Pattnayak and Leonard, 1991; Scully, 1974), football (e.g., Brower, 1972; Eitzen and Sanford, 1975; Eitzen and Yetman, 1977,1982; Madison and Landers, 1976), basketball (e.g., Berghorn, Yetman, and Hanna, 1988; Eitzen and Yetman, 1977; Leonard, 1987), ice hockey (e.g., Lavoie, 1989; Marple, 1975; Marple and Pirie, 1978; Roy, 1974), volleyball (e.g., Eitzen and Furst, 1989), and soccer (e.g., Maguire, 1988).

The vast majority of the stacking studies explore the stacking phenomenon as a black and white issue. However, an issue that must not be overlooked in today's multicultural society is the absence of studies that analyze the situation with regard to races and ethnic groups other than black and white (see, e.g., Leonard, 1977; Leonard et al., 1988; Pattnayak and Leonard, 1991). The lack of available research concerning the positional occupancy patterns of Latinos is especially noteworthy because Latinos have played (and still play) a prominent role in professional baseball. What makes an indepth analysis of this ethnic group important is the impression that Latinos are overrepresented in central positions, thereby defying the traditional stacking theory that minorities are found mostly in noncentral playing positions. Phillips indicated in 1983 that Latinos are stacked just like blacks and whites, but there was insufficient evidence to support this idea at the time. However, Phillips's argument did point out that the stacking of baseball players involves more than a simple division between black and white.

Finally, stacking is more than a mere cross-tabulation of specific player positions by race. Consequences of stacking are often felt outside the domain of sport itself, both during and after an athlete's career. Examples of these consequences are differences in leadership recruitment (e.g., Fabianic, 1984; Grusky, 1963; Kjeldsen, 1981; Klonsky, 1977; Loy, Curtis, and Hillen, 1987; Loy, Sage, and

Ingham, 1972; Roy, 1974), endorsements (e.g., Eitzen and Yetman, 1977), career length (e.g., Berghorn et al., 1988; Curry and Jiobu, 1984), and retirement benefits (e.g., Curry and Jiobu, 1984; Eitzen and Sage, 1978).

DATA AND METHODS

Within this theoretical framework, positional occupancy patterns as a function of ethnicity were analyzed and evaluated for Latinos in major league baseball for the years 1950–1992.

Sample

In 1947, baseball was "integrated" by Jackie Robinson, and racial and ethnic minorities began to enter the major leagues with some regularity. Because of this, the time period sampled for this study was set at 1950–1992. The justification for this time frame is the argument that only after integration had been achieved did minorities (including Latinos) enter professional baseball in large enough numbers to expect the sample to be reliable.

The time frame was then broken down by year. This assisted in identifying any trends such as underrepresentation or overrepresentation and increases or decreases in the positional distribution of Latino athletes in major league baseball during the 43 years studied. Whereas previous studies have limited their samples to one playing season (e.g., Maguire, 1988) or different years at regular intervals (e.g., Leonard et al., 1988), the present study covers a continuous time period spanning more than four decades.

Stacking research has relied mainly on data that are readily available in printed form. Sources that have been used include press brochures and media guides (Berghorn et al., 1988; Eitzen and Yetman, 1977), record book data (Dubois, 1980), and even team photographs (Fabianic, 1984). This study followed in the footsteps of earlier studies in that it used *The Baseball Encyclopedia* (Wolff, 1993) as its main reference source.

Procedures

The subjects of the sample are all major league baseball players who could be identified as Latino or non-Latino and were active in the major leagues between 1950 and 1992. A database was created, using Microsoft Works and Claris Works databases and spreadsheets, in which each player was entered as a separately coded case and categorized according to country of birth, position, number of games played, years played, and ethnicity. The second step was to separate the eligible players from the ineligible players in this database. This was done according to the criteria that are listed in this subsection. The database was cross-checked with another reference guide, *Total Baseball* (both in book form [Thorn and Palmer, 1993] and on CD-ROM), to verify numbers and correct any possible mistakes.

The third step was to cross-check the list of eligible players with various other sources to determine the ethnicity of all players. This was done by using lists of Latino players such as those published in *Hispanics in the Major Leagues* (Evans, 1992, 1993), *The International Pastime* (Bjarkman, 1992), various lists and articles from *Nuestro* magazine, and the help of Mario Longoria, an independent historian from

San Antonio, Texas, whose field of study is the presence of Latinos in professional sports. Thus ethnicity was the last variable coded.

To make valid comparisons and draw valid conclusions with regard to existing stacking studies, criteria were set that follow patterns and trends found in existing studies as much as possible. However, as a result of the inconsistencies and limited availability of stacking literature on Latino baseball players, some criteria that are unique to the present study had to be set.

The following criteria were used to set the parameters of the data sample and increase reliability:

1. A player was considered a Latino if he is "from North and Central America (such as Mexico, Guatemala, Nicaragua, El Salvador), South America (such as Argentina, Brazil, Uruguay), and the Spanish-speaking Caribbean (such as Puerto Rico, Dominican Republic, Cuba). The term also includes Chicanos (Mexican Americans). The term LATINO refers to a shared cultural heritage (Black, Native American, and Spanish), a history of colonization by Spain, and a common language (Spanish)" (Lapchick and Benedict, 1993, p. 23). Therefore, persons originating from Spain are also included in this term.
2. For a player to be counted in a season, he needs to have played at least 50 games in that particular season (see Jiobu, 1988; Loy and McElvogue, 1970).
3. If a player played more than one position, he was assigned to the position in which he played the most games.
4. When categorizing positions as core, peripheral, and noncentral, the core positions are catcher, second base, and shortstop; peripheral positions are first base and third base; noncentral positions are in the outfield.
5. Pitchers and designated /pinch hitters were considered separately and were not included in this study.

Descriptive Analysis

The research problem consisted of the questions where Latinos tend to be stacked and whether this stacking increases as the number of Latinos in major league baseball rises. To answer these questions satisfactorily, the analysis was broken down into several steps. The first step was to determine the ethnic composition (Latino, non-Latino) by playing positions in major league baseball for the years mentioned under study as well as the distribution by ethnicity across the various playing positions. The second step was to analyze and interpret the data according to the stacking model and centrality concept for the following:

1. The total sample, by year (positions were divided by position and as core /peripheral/ noncentral)
2. The Latino segment of the data sample, by year (positions were categorized by position and as core /peripheral/noncentral)
3. Answers to the question whether Latinos are stacked by position as a function of ethnicity
4. Answers to the question that if Latinos are stacked by position as a function of ethnicity, in what positions do they appear most?

The final step was to determine whether any substantial changes in the ethnic composition of playing positions have taken place between 1950 and 1992. If this was the case, the changes were analyzed and interpreted.

The following procedures were followed:

1. For every year, every player was identified by position and ethnicity.
2. The totals and percentages of Latino and non-Latino players were calculated by year, both by position and for the overall population of players.
3. The totals and percentages of Latino and non-Latino players were calculated, comparing the core, peripheral, and noncentral categories.
4. Finally, the information was used to make analyses, interpret possible patterns, and draw conclusions.

RESULTS

According to the existing stacking literature, the results of this study are expected to show that Latino baseball players are stacked in noncentral positions and that this trend becomes more pronounced as increasing numbers of Latinos enter the major leagues every year. These expectations are based on the fact that another minority group in professional sports (i.e., blacks) has shown a similar pattern.

First, the total number of Latinos was calculated for each year from 1950 to 1992. Next, it was determined what percentage of the total number of players these numbers constituted.

Even though there was a slump during the 1970s and early 1980s, there has been a steady increase in the percentage of Latinos who play professional baseball. This increase was almost sevenfold over the 43-year period, from 3.0% in 1950 to 19.9% in 1992.

Distribution of Latino Players by Position As a Percentage of All Players

The data show that Latino players tend to be stacked in the infield (especially at the core positions of shortstop and second base), not in the outfield as was predicted. This argument is strengthened by the fact that the category of outfield encompasses three positions (left field, center field, and right field), unlike all other categories. This is a finding that is diametrically opposed to the prevailing stacking theories.

Distribution of Latino Players by Position As a Percentage of All Latinos

To verify the finding that Latinos tend to be stacked in the infield when they are studied as a percentage of all players, the distribution of Latino players by position as a percentage of all Latinos was studied. When looking at all positions by year, it becomes apparent that the positions of second base and shortstop have the highest percentages overall, that is, proportionately more Latinos have been playing these positions than have been playing other positions. This is a pattern that can be detected throughout the period studied.

Based on these results, a rank order of the stacking of Latinos in major league baseball would be as follows (high to low): shortstop, second base, outfield, first base, catcher, third base. The same conclusion remains: Latino baseball players are over-represented in the core positions, especially at second base and shortstop.

Distribution of Latino Players by Centrality As a Percentage of All Players

Although there is no significant pattern in the percentages of Latino players for each of the three categories until about 1960, during the period from 1960 to 1992 there was a gradual but nonlinear growth of Latinos in the core positions, from 15.7% in 1961 to 25.9% in 1992, with a low of 11.0% in 1964 and a peak of 27.9% in 1990. The peripheral and noncentral positions show a similar pattern of growth, but the percentages lag behind those for the core positions. Both categories started from a lower percentage in 1950 (2.2% for peripheral and 1.3% for noncentral positions, as compared to 5.4% for core positions) and ended with a lower percentage in 1992 (14.6% for peripheral and 14.4% for noncentral positions, as compared to 27.9% for core positions).

In conclusion, the following overall picture of the distribution of Latinos in core, peripheral, and noncentral positions is evident. All three categories show signs of increased Latino representation. However, whereas the core positions show the strongest signs of growth, the peripheral positions are more varied, and the noncentral positions indicate a steady but slower increase in the percentage of Latinos. The most recent decades seem to show the most dramatic changes.

Distribution of Latino Players by Centrality As a Percentage of All Latinos

From table 14.1, the conclusion can be drawn that, of the total number of Latinos in major league baseball, there is a large representation in the core positions. For most years, the percentages are in the 40%–60% range, and this surpasses the percentages for the other two categories for most years studied. When compared to the expected percentages (in the ideal situation in which no stacking exists, each of the eight positions being given an equal share of 12.5%), the importance of these percentages surfaces. Whereas 37.5% of Latinos are expected to occupy the core positions, the observed percentages are generally substantially higher. On the average, the percentage of Latinos playing core positions between 1950 and 1992 was 47.2%. This is 9.7% higher than expected, thus indicating the possibility of stacking.

The percentages for first and third base (peripheral positions) are substantially lower. For most years, the percentage of Latinos in these two positions varies from 10% to 20% with a few minor exceptions. The expected percentage is 25.0%, but on average only 15.0% of all Latino players are in peripheral positions, a finding that expresses under-representation.

For the noncentral positions, Latinos follow the expectations. Whereas 37.5% of all Latinos are expected to play in the outfield, the real percentage is 37.8%, or only 0.3% above what is expected. However, whereas the percentage of all Latinos in the core positions continues to increase and the percentage of peripheral players appears to be fairly stable, there seems to be a slow decline in the percentage of Latinos playing in the outfield.

Positions in Which Latinos Are Stacked

The data have established that Latino players tend to be stacked in the core positions. To determine in what particular position(s) they are stacked within this category, the positions of catcher, second base, and shortstop were studied separately. The data reveal that shortstop is the most heavily populated by Latinos in core positions, followed by second base and catcher. Even though the sample is relatively

Table 14.1: Latinos in Core, Peripheral, and Noncentral Positions As a Percentage of All Latinos (1950–1992), by Year
Note: Pitchers and designated hitters are excluded.

Year	Core	Peripheral	Noncentral	Total n
Expected [a]	37.5	25.0	37.5	
1950	66.7	16.7	16.7	6
1951	66.7	0.0	33.3	9
1952	42.9	14.3	42.9	7
1953	50.0	0.0	50.0	6
1954	33.3	11.1	55.6	9
1955	28.6	21.4	50.0	14
1956	41.7	16.7	41.7	12
1957	37.5	25.0	37.5	16
1958	44.4	16.7	38.9	18
1959	40.0	26.7	33.3	15
1960	42.8	19.1	38.1	21
1961	48.2	18.5	39.1	27
1962	53.6	14.3	32.1	28
1963	42.3	10.3	41.4	29
1964	31.4	20.0	48.6	35
1965	48.6	11.4	40.0	35
1966	37.1	22.9	40.0	35
1967	43.2	16.2	40.5	37
1968	47.6	16.7	35.7	42
1969	48.2	18.5	33.3	54
1970	51.9	13.5	34.6	52
1971	46.2	13.5	40.4	52
1972	52.1	10.4	37.5	48
1973	55.1	10.2	34.7	49
1974	58.7	8.7	32.6	46
1975	56.3	12.5	31.3	48
1976	46.7	13.3	40.0	45
1977	41.2	17.7	41.2	51
1978	39.2	15.7	45.1	51
1979	45.7	19.6	34.8	46
1980	50.0	10.4	39.6	48
1981	38.5	18.0	43.6	39
1982	46.7	17.8	35.6	45
1983	55.1	24.5	20.4	49
1984	49.0	23.5	27.5	51
1985	53.7	13.0	33.3	54
1986	54.6	9.1	36.4	55
1987	53.5	10.3	36.2	58
1988	50.9	15.3	33.9	59
1989	47.8	16.4	35.8	67
1990	52.2	18.8	29.0	69
1991	50.0	21.1	29.0	76
1992	49.3	18.8	31.9	69

a. The expected percentages were calculated as follows. There are eight positions, and if the distribution is equal for all positions, they account for 12.5% each. The core positions are catcher, second base, and shortstop (3 x 12.5% = 37.5%); the peripheral positions are first base and third base (2 x 12.5% = 25%); and the noncentral positions are left field, center field, and right field (3 x 12.5% = 37.5%).

small during the early years of the period studied here, this need not be a barrier in a longitudinal analysis of the stacking phenomenon. Thus it can be concluded that the more recent the years, the more balanced and pronounced the stacking of Latinos in core positions becomes.

This observation helps to substantiate the theory that states that the increasing number of Latinos in the major leagues results in an increase in the stacking of Latinos by position as a function of ethnicity. To test this, a comparison of the growth patterns of each of the stacked positions was made (see table 14.2).

The position of shortstop is the most stacked position; even during the years in which the total percentage of Latinos dropped (mid-1970), the percentage of Latinos playing shortstop increased. The position also showed strong growth during periods of increasing Latino participation in major league baseball (e.g., 1958–1961, 1980–1986). The positions of second base and, to a lesser extent, catcher show a similar pattern, although the percentages are lower. Overall, then, overrepresentation does increase at certain positions when the percentage of Latinos in the major leagues grows.

DISCUSSION AND CONCLUSION

Racial and ethnic discrimination is deeply embedded in American society. In the realm of professional sports, this phenomenon is often described as stacking and is usually measured in terms of centrality, or relative distance to the center of the action on the playing field. In this case, minorities are often seen as being stacked in noncentral positions, that is, those positions that require the smallest amounts of leadership qualities, interaction, and decision making.

Over time, historical data have shown a distinctive pattern of distribution of professional baseball players by position and by race. Black players have tended to occupy positions in the outfield, whereas white players have been concentrated in the infield. This distribution pattern has been accounted for by various stacking theories. Such theories purport to account for the segregation by position that is evident in the empirical data.

In addition, Latino stacking patterns tend to be different from traditional stacking patterns for blacks, as developed in the landmark study of Loy and McElvogue (1970). According to the existing stacking literature, minorities should be under-represented in central positions and over-represented in noncentral positions. Generally speaking, data for Latino baseball players for the 1950–1992 period reveal that Latinos are stacked in central positions, especially the core positions of second base and shortstop.

Thus the traditional stacking theories do not explain the positional occupancy patterns of Latino players. As Phillips (1983) argued,

> It would seem unlikely that prejudiced white coaches and managers would place foreign, colored players who do not speak English well in positions requiring interaction and control. But they do, and the "stereotyping" version of the centrality theory does not explain this. (pp. 13–14)

The data show that "blackness" or color does not necessarily put Latinos in the outfield. Why this is the case is uncertain, and when considering the overall stereotypes, which may play a role in positional

Table 14.2: Totals and Percentages of All Latino Players in Catcher, Second Base, and Shortstop Positions (1950–1992), by Year

Year	Catcher n (percentage)	Second base n (percentage)	Shortstop n (percentage)	Total n
1950	2 (50.0)	1 (25.0)	1 (25.0)	4
1951	3 (50.0)	2 (33.3)	1 (16.7)	6
1952	0 (0.0)	1 (33.3)	2 (66.7)	3
1953	0 (0.0)	1 (33.3)	2 (66.7)	3
1954	0 (0.0)	1 (33.3)	2 (66.7)	3
1955	0 (0.0)	1 (25.0)	3 (75.0)	4
1956	0 (0.0)	1 (20.0)	4 (80.0)	5
1957	0 (0.0)	1 (16.7)	5 (83.3)	6
1958	0 (0.0)	3 (37.5)	5 (63.5)	8
1959	0 (0.0)	3 (50.0)	3 (50.0)	6
1960	0 (0.0)	4 (44.4)	5 (55.6)	9
1961	1 (7.7)	4 (30.8)	8 (61.5)	13
1962	3 (20.0)	2 (13.3)	10 (66.7)	15
1963	2 (14.3)	4 (28.6)	8 (57.1)	14
1964	1 (9.1)	2 (18.2)	8 (72.7)	11
1965	2 (11.8)	5 (29.4)	10 (58.8)	17
1966	2 (15.4)	5 (38.5)	6 (46.2)	13
1967	2 (12.5)	9 (56.3)	5 (31.3)	16
1968	4 (20.0)	8 (40.0)	8 (40.0)	20
1969	7 (26.9)	12 (46.2)	7 (26.9)	26
1970	5 (18.5)	11 (40.7)	11 (40.7)	27
1971	5 (20.8)	10 (41.7)	9 (37.5)	24
1972	3 (12.0)	13 (52.0)	9 (36.0)	25
1973	4 (14.8)	14 (51.9)	9 (33.3)	27
1974	3 (11.1)	14 (51.9)	10 (37.0)	27
1975	4 (14.8)	12 (44.4)	11 (40.7)	27
1976	3 (14.3)	9 (42.9)	9 (42.9)	21
1977	2 (9.5)	11 (52.4)	8 (38.1)	21
1978	3 (15.0)	7 (35.0)	10 (50.0)	20
1979	4 (19.1)	7 (33.3)	10 (47.6)	21
1980	4 (16.7)	6 (25.0)	14 (58.3)	24
1981	3 (20.0)	6 (40.0)	6 (40.0)	15
1982	5 (23.8)	6 (28.6)	10 (47.6)	21
1983	7 (25.9)	9 (33.3)	11 (40.7)	27
1984	5 (20.0)	6 (24.0)	14 (66.0)	25
1985	6 (20.7)	7 (24.1)	16 (55.2)	29
1986	5 (16.7)	7 (23.3)	18 (60.0)	30
1987	6 (19.4)	9 (29.0)	16 (51.6)	31
1988	5 (16.7)	12 (40.0)	13 (43.3)	30
1989	5 (15.6)	10 (31.3)	17 (53.1)	36
1990	9 (25.0)	14 (38.9)	13 (36.1)	36
1991	8 (21.1)	14 (36.8)	16 (42.1)	38
1992	8 (23.5)	10 (29.4)	16 (47.1)	34

Reprinted from González, 1996.

distribution of different racial and ethnic groups, this is not a satisfactory explanation for the stacking of Latinos in the infield. Latinos range from black to white; they represent an ethnic group, not a racial group, and so far only one study has been done that uses a five-level classification of the color of black faces, ranging from light to dark (Scully, 1974). Obviously, classifying Latinos by the color of their skin to determine whether darker Latinos tend to be positioned in the noncentral positions is tricky because pictures of players do not always show their true color due to age and differences in printing procedures. However, skin color remains an important issue in stacking.

The traditional stacking theory is premised on the biological view that blacks are strong athletes whose speed and strength make them good outfielders, whereas Latino players are considered to be better infielders because they are relatively short, are more agile, and have better hands. Latinos are not seen as having the power or the speed to be outfielders. This is illustrated by a statement made by Pittsburgh Pirates scout Angel Figueroa, who argued in an interview for *USA Today* that it is very rare to find Mexican players with speed or power. But, he added, because of their Indian blood, Mexicans could run to the city of New York without stopping; they just could not do it very fast (Beaton and Myers, 1993, p. C1).

In addition, the psychological explanations for stacking are based on the idea that blacks and whites are different. According to supporters of these explanations, whites possess an orientation toward the team, success, and competition—qualities that are needed to play in the central positions. By contrast, blacks supposedly express the characteristics of the noncentral positions, which include a focus on the individual, style, and play. In short, blacks and whites are seen as having different sports personalities and motivational systems, which account for racial stacking (Jones and Hochner, 1973).

Both the biological and the psychological explanations for stacking have been heavily criticized, and rightly so. In addition, for the purposes of this study, they do not apply given that Latinos are classified as an ethnic group, not a racial group. Therefore, another explanation for the stacking of Latinos needs to be developed.

The sociological explanations, which have come to the foreground as a third source of explanation for stacking, seem to hold their ground a little bit better when applied to Latino players. Even though this third group of explanations is based primarily on race, most of them can be applied to an ethnic group such as Latinos. However, the category of "discriminatory processes" seems to be stronger than the explanations falling under the header "levels of socialization."

A possible explanation for this could be the fact that the focus of the two categories is completely different. Whereas the discriminatory processes tend to focus on the perspective of management and the players of the majority group in a sports organization, the levels of socialization theories are centered around self-selection of members of the minority group.

Although there is something to say for the latter category, an explanation for the stacking of Latinos will probably be based on the decisions of the management of major league organizations. Managers, and especially scouts, seem to have preconceived notions that are based on their knowledge and beliefs regarding biology, culture, experience, and, above all, organizational needs. These beliefs then play a role in the decision-making process as to what type of players the scouts will seek.

The levels of socialization theories may play a minor role, but they are definitely overshadowed by the theories mentioned previously. Role modeling, cost, and opportunities to play in a certain position may have some effect, but in the end it is the major league organization that decides who will be signed and what position they will play. In the case of baseball, a unique feature that plays an important role in this respect is the existence of major league baseball academies in the Dominican Republic. These academies train prospects to play certain positions, a decision that is based on the preconceived notions mentioned earlier.

The fact that minorities are stacked in certain positions has profound implications. The most important of these is that minority players have to face heightened competition with one another for a limited number of positions, that is, the positions in which they tend to be stacked (see, e.g., Eitzen and Yetman, 1977, p. 4). For Latino players, this means that they will mostly compete for the positions of second base and shortstop. As a result, talented Latino players may not be drafted as second basemen or shortstops due to an overabundance of Latinos for those two positions. Further, often they are not considered for any other infield positions even though they are quite adept in these positions. Research has shown that white bench (reserve) players tend to be chosen over minority bench players (see, e.g., Phillips, 1983, p. 3). In short, competition among Latinos, or for that matter all minorities, is fiercer than it is among whites because minorities are competing among themselves and for fewer positions as a result of stacking. Whites, by contrast, compete more equally for all positions.

Finally, even though Latinos tend to be stacked in the positions from which coaches and managers are recruited most often, there is an obvious lack of Latinos in these nonplaying positions. Thus, parallel to the argument that traditional stacking patterns do not apply to Latino baseball players, neither does the present mobility theory, which holds that career advancement is related to former playing positions. It seems that for Latinos, holding an infield position may not be sufficient to lead to advancement from a player to a managerial position.

If the current research on managerial recruitment cannot explain the gross under-representation of Latino managers, what might be the necessary conditions leading to a managerial position? What accounts for the virtual absence of Latinos from managing positions? One possible explanation is that upward movement from player to manager is an infrequent occurrence (a 1 in 15 chance) even for whites. Between 1980 and 1992, there were 115 different managers, 22 of whom never played in the major leagues. The remaining 93 are but a small fraction of the total number of players who populated the major leagues during the same time period. If Latinos were to advance at the same rate as whites, they would do so in smaller numbers than those of whites (63% of all players excluding pitchers) given the much smaller base of Latino players (16.6% of all players excluding pitchers). Consequently, the lack of Latino managers might be alleviated only by drastically increasing the number of Latino players.

Another possible explanation is that Latinos may not be part of the relevant networks of social contacts. Latino players tend to bond together (because of a common language or cultural background) and associate primarily within a Latino community of players. As a result, they may lack the social connections (i.e., mostly with whites) that could be a necessary factor in the hiring of managers. This is an especially convincing argument for those who believe that managers are hired by a so-called "old boys" network in which the right connections, in addition to qualifications, are crucial.

Moreover, Latinos who are foreign born may return to their countries of origin, families, and friends after their playing days are over. Consequently, they would not be available to be considered for managing positions. This would lead to a diminishing basis of Latino players available for postplaying careers. However, it remains to be determined whether denial of a postplaying career as a manager leads to a return to the country of origin or vice versa.

Along the same lines, networking might be a factor as well. A large percentage of Latinos are foreign nationals, which is not the case for whites. As a result, Latino players may not be able to make the same important career contacts that are afforded to whites early in their careers, through influential coaches in high school and college or even in the minor leagues. These coaches may be highly networked within the professional baseball world and may act as mentors or role models for the native white players. A counterargument could be that foreign-born Latinos have the option of entering baseball academics (e.g., in the Dominican Republic), but several things need to be kept in mind. First, baseball academies do not exist in every Latin American country. Second, prospects are picked by the academies, not vice versa. Networking is irrelevant in this situation.

One can also speculate that Latinos are not hired as managers because of the color of their skin. If this is the case for Latinos, then Afro-Latinos should have a smaller chance of getting hired than non-Afro-Latinos, and all Latinos should have a smaller chance of getting hired than whites.

Finally, it is possible that Latinos are held to a higher standard of play than are others (consider the firing of Tony Perez as manager of the Cincinnati Reds in 1993 after only a few months on the job). Maybe they are expected to perform better simply because they are Latinos. This appears to be similar to the argument that Latino players have been held to a higher standard ever since they entered the major leagues, which would explain the theory that good (not superior) white players are considered for playing positions before good Latino players are. Both skin color and higher standards imply that discriminatory hiring practices are at work.

In sum, even though the data in this study show that Latinos are overrepresented in core positions, there are virtually no Latino managers. So far, no plausible explanation for this phenomenon has been proposed. Even though there is a wide range of possible explanations, the necessary research has yet to be conducted to support one or another of these explanations.

Crimes Against Humanity

WARD CHURCHILL

During the past couple of seasons, there has been an increasing wave of controversy regarding the names of professional sports teams like the Atlanta "Braves," Cleveland "Indians," Washington "Redskins," and Kansas City "Chiefs." The issue extends to the names of college teams like Florida State University "Seminoles," University of Illinois "Fighting Illini" and so on, right on down to high school outfits like the Lamar (Colorado) "Savages." Also involved have been team adoption of "mascots," replete with feathers, buckskins, beads, spears, and "warpaint" (some fans have opted to adorn themselves in the same fashion), and nifty little "pep" gestures like the "Indian Chant" and "Tomahawk Chop."

A substantial number of American Indians have protested that use of native names, images, and symbols as sports team mascots and the like is, by definition, a virulently racist practice. Given the historical relationship between Indians and non-Indians during what has been called the "Conquest of America," American Indian Movement leader (and American Indian Anti-Defamation Council founder) Russell Means has compared the practice to contemporary Germans naming their soccer teams the "Jews," "Hebrews," and "Yids," while adorning their uniforms with grotesque caricatures of Jewish faces taken from the Nazis' anti-Semitic propaganda of the 1930s. Numerous demonstrations have occurred in conjunction with games—most notably during the November 15, 1992 match-up between the Chiefs and Redskins in Kansas City—by angry Indians and their supporters.

In response, a number of players—especially African Americans and other minority athletes—have been trotted out by professional team owners like Ted Turner, as well as university and public school officials, to announce that they mean not to insult but to honor native people. They have been joined by the television networks and most major newspapers, all of which have editorialized that Indian discomfort with the situation is "no big deal," insisting that the whole thing is just "good, clean fun." The country needs more such fun, they've argued, and "a few disgruntled Native Americans" have no right to undermine the nation's enjoyment of its leisure time by complaining. This is especially the case, some have argued, "in hard times like these." It has even been contended that Indian outage at being systematically degraded—rather than the degradation itself—creates "a serious barrier to the sort of intergroup communication so necessary in a multicultural society such as ours."

Okay, let's communicate. We are frankly dubious that those advancing such positions really believe their own rhetoric, but, just for the sake of argument, let's accept the premise that they are sincere. If what they say is true, then isn't it time we spread such "inoffensiveness" and "good cheer" around among *all* groups so that *everybody* can participate *equally* in fostering the round of national laughs they call for? Sure it is—the country can't have too much fun or "intergroup involvement"—so the more, the merrier. Simple consistency demands that anyone who thinks the Tomahawk Chop is a swell pastime must be just as hearty in their endorsement of the following ideas,. Which—by the logic used to define the defamation of American Indians—should help us all really start yukking it up.

First, as a counterpart to the Redskins, we need an NFL team called "Niggers" to honor Afro-Americans. Halftime festivities for fans might include a simulated stewing of the opposing coach in a large pot while players and cheerleaders dance around it, garbed in leopard skins and wearing fake bones in their noses. This concept obviously goes along with the kind of gaiety attending the Chop, but also with the actions of the Kansas City Chiefs, whose team members—prominently including black team members—lately appeared on a poster looking "fierce" and "savage" by way of wearing Indian regalia. Just a bit of harmless "morale boosting," says the Chiefs' front office. You bet.

So that the newly formed Niggers sports club won't end up too out of sync while expressing the "spirit" and "identity" of Afro-Americans in the above fashion, a baseball franchise—let's call this one the "Sambos"—should be formed. How about a basketball team called the "Spearchuckers"? A hockey team called the "Jungle Bunnies"? Maybe the "essence" of these teams could be depicted by images of tiny black faces adorned with huge pairs of lips. The players could appear on TV every week or so gnawing on chicken legs and spitting watermelon seeds at one another. Catchy, eh? Well, there's "nothing to be upset about," according to those who love wearing "war bonnets" to the Super Bowl or having "Chief Illiniwek" dance around the sports arenas of Urbana, Illinois.

And why stop there? There are plenty of other groups to include. "Hispanics"? They can be "represented" by the Galveston "Greasers" and San Diego "Spics," at least until the Wisconsin "Wetbacks" and Baltimore "Beaners" get off the ground. Asian Americans? How about the "Slopes," "Dinks," "Gooks," and "Zipperheads"? Owners of the latter teams might get their logo ideas from editorial page cartoons printed in the nation's newspapers during World War II: slant-eyes, buck teeth, big glasses, but nothing racially insulting or derogatory, according to the editors and artists involved at the time. Indeed, this Second World War—vintage stuff can be seen as just another barrel of laughs, at least by what current editors say are their "local standards" concerning American Indians.

Let's see. Who's been left out? Teams like the Kansas City "Kikes," Hanover "Honkies," San Leandro "Shylocks," Daytona "Dagos," and Pittsburgh "Polacks" will fill a certain social void among white folk. Have a religious belief? Let's all go for the gusto and gear up the Milwaukee "Mackerel Snappers" and Hollywood "Holy Rollers." The Fighting Irish of Notre Dame can be rechristened the "Drunken Irish" or "Papist Pigs." Issues of gender and sexual preference can be addressed through creation of teams like the St. Louis "Sluts," Boston "Bimbos," Detroit "Dykes," and the Fresno "Fags." How about the Gainesville "Gimps" and Richmond "Retards," so the physically and mentally impaired won't be excluded from our fun and games?

Now, don't go getting "overly sensitive" out there. None of this is demeaning or insulting, at least not when it's being done to Indians. Just ask the folks who are doing it, or their apologists like Andy Rooney in the national media. They'll tell you—as in fact they *have* been telling you—that there's been no harm done, regardless of what their victims think, feel, or say. The situation is exactly the same as when those with precisely the same mentality used to insist that Stepin Fetchit was okay, or Rochester on the Jack Benny Show, or Amos and Andy, Charlie Chan, the Frito Bandito, or any of the other cutesy symbols making up the lexicon of American racism. Have we communicated yet?

Let's get just a little bit real here. The notion of "fun" embodied in rituals like the Tomahawk Chop must be understood for what it is. There's not a single non-Indian example used above which can be considered socially acceptable in even the most marginal sense. The reasons are obvious enough. So why is it different where American Indians are concerned? One can only conclude that, in contrast to the other groups at issue, Indians are (falsely) perceived as being too few, and therefore too weak, to defend themselves effectively against racist and otherwise offensive behavior.

Fortunately, there are some glimmers of hope. A few teams and their fans have gotten the message and have responded appropriately. Stanford University, which opted to drop the name "Indians" from Stanford, has experienced no resulting drop-off in attendance. Meanwhile, the local newspaper in Portland, Oregon recently decided its long-standing editorial policy prohibiting use of racial epithets should include derogatory team names. The Redskins, for instance, are now referred to as "the Washington team," and will continue to be described in this way until the franchise adopts an inoffensive moniker (newspaper sales in Portland have suffered no decline as a result).

Such examples are to be applauded and encouraged. They stand as figurative beacons in the night, proving beyond all doubt that it is quite possible to indulge in the pleasure of athletics without accepting blatant racism into the bargain.

NUREMBERG PRECEDENTS

On October 16, 1946, a man named Julius Streicher mounted the steps of a gallows. Moments later he was dead, the sentence of an international tribunal composed of representatives of the United States, France, Great Britain, and the Soviet Union having been imposed. Streicher's body was then cremated and—so horrendous were his crimes thought to have been—his ashes dumped into an unspecified German river so that "no one should ever know a particular place to go for reasons of mourning his memory."

Section VII: Race and Sport

Julius Streicher had been convicted at Nuremberg, Germany of what were termed "Crimes Against Humanity." The lead prosecutor in his case—Justice Robert Jackson of the United States Supreme Court—had not argued that the defendant had killed anyone, nor that he had personally committed any especially violent act. Nor was it contended that Streicher had held any particularly important position in the German government during the period in which the so-called Third Reich had exterminated some 6,000,000 Jews, as well as several million Gypsies, Poles, Slavs, homosexuals, and other untermenschen (subhumans).

The sole offense for which the accused was ordered put to death was in having served as publisher/editor of a Bavarian tabloid entitled *Der Sturmer* during the early-to-mid 1930s, years before the Nazi genocide actually began. In this capacity, he had penned a long series of virulently anti-Semitic editorials and "news" stories, usually accompanied by cartoons and other images graphically depicting Jews in extraordinarily derogatory fashion. This, the prosecution asserted, had done much to "dehumanize" the targets of his distortion in the mind of the German public. In turn, such dehumanization had made it possible—or at least easier—for average Germans to later indulge in the outright liquidation of Jewish "vermin." The tribunal agreed, holding that Streicher was therefore complicit in genocide and deserving of death by hanging.

During his remarks to the Nuremberg tribunal, Justice Jackson observed that, in implementing its sentences, the participating powers were morally and legally binding themselves to adhere forever after to the same standards of conduct that were being applied to Streicher and the other Nazi leaders. In the alternative, he said, the victorious allies would have committed "pure murder" at Nuremberg—no different in substance from that carried out by those they presumed to judge—rather than establishing the "permanent benchmark for justice" which was intended.

Yet in the United States of Robert Jackson, the indigenous American Indian population had already been reduced, in a process which is ongoing to this day, from perhaps 12.5 million in the year 1500 to fewer than 250,000 by the beginning of the 20th century. This was accomplished, according to official sources, "largely through the cruelty of [Euro-American] settlers," and an informal but clear governmental policy which had made it an articulated goal to "exterminate these red vermin," or at least whole segments of them.

Bounties has been placed on the scalps of Indians—any Indians—in places as diverse as Georgia, Kentucky, Texas, the Dakotas, Oregon, and California, and had been maintained until resident Indian populations were decimated or disappeared altogether. Entire peoples such as the Cherokee had been reduced to half their size through a policy of forced removal from their homelands east of the Mississippi River to what were then considered less preferable areas in the West.

Others, such as the Navajo, suffered the same fate while under military guard for years on end. The United States Army had also perpetrated a long series of wholesale massacres of Indians at places like Horseshoe Bend, Bear River, Sand Creek, the Washita River, the Marias River, Camp Robinson, and Wounded Knee.

Through it all, hundreds of popular novels—each competing with the next to make Indians appear more grotesque, menacing, and inhuman—were sold in the tens of millions of copies in the U.S. Plainly, the Euro-American public was being conditioned to see Indians in such a way as to allow their eradication to continue. And continue it did until the Manifest Destiny of the U.S —a direct precursor to what Hitler would subsequently call Lebensraumpolitik (the politics of living space)—was consummated.

By 1900, the national project of "clearing" Native Americans from their land and replacing them with "superior" Anglo-American settlers was complete; the indigenous population had been reduced by as much as 98 percent while approximately 97.5 percent of their original territory had "passed" to the invaders. The survivors had been concentrated, out of sight and mind of the public, on scattered "reservations," all of them under the self-assigned "plenary" (full) power of the federal government. There was, of course, no Nuremberg-style tribunal passing judgment on those who had fostered such circumstances in North America. No U.S. official or private citizen was ever imprisoned—never mind hanged—for implementing or propagandizing what had been done. Nor had the process of genocide afflicting Indians been completed. Instead, it merely changed form.

Between the 1880s and the 1980s, nearly half of all Native American children were coercively transferred from their own families, communities, and cultures to those of the conquering society. This was done through compulsory attendance at remote boarding schools, often hundreds of miles from their homes, where native children were kept for years on end while being systematically "deculturated" (indoctrinated to think and act in the manner of Euro-Americans rather than as Indians). It was also accomplished through a pervasive foster home and adoption program—including "blind" adoptions, where children would be permanently denied information as to who they were/are and where they'd come from—placing native youths in non-Indian homes.

The express purpose of all this was to facilitate a U.S. governmental policy to bring about the "assimilation" (dissolution) of indigenous societies. In other words, Indian cultures as such were to be caused to disappear. Such policy objectives are directly contrary to the United Nations 1948 Convention on Punishment and Prevention of the Crime of Genocide, an element of international law arising from the Nuremberg proceedings. The forced "transfer of the children" of a targeted "racial, ethnical, or religious group" is explicitly prohibited as a genocidal activity under the Convention's second article.

Article II of the Genocide Convention also expressly prohibits involuntary sterilization as a means of "preventing births among" a targeted population. Yet, in 1975, it was conceded by the U.S. government that its Indian Health Service (IHS), then a subpart of the Bureau of Indian Affairs (BIA), was even then conducting a secret program of involuntary sterilization that had affected approximately 40 percent of all Indian women. The program was allegedly discontinued, and the IHS was transferred to the Public Health Service, but no one was punished. In 1990, it came out that the IHS was inoculating Inuit children in Alaska with Hepatitis-B vaccine. The vaccine had already been banned by the World Health Organization as having a demonstrated correlation with the HIV syndrome, which is itself correlated to AIDS. As this is written, a "field test" of Hepatitis-A vaccine, also HIV-correlated, is being conducted on Indian reservations in the northern plains region.

Section VII: Race and Sport

The Genocide Convention makes it a "crime against humanity" to create conditions leading to the destruction of an identifiable human group, as such. Yet the BIA has utilized the government's plenary prerogatives to negotiate mineral leases "on behalf of" Indian peoples paying a fraction of standard royalty rates. The result has been "super profits" for a number of preferred U.S. corporations. Meanwhile, Indians, whose reservations ironically turned out to be in some of the most mineral-rich areas of North America, which makes us the nominally wealthiest segment of the continent's population, live in dire poverty.

By the government's own data in the mid-1980s, Indians received the lowest annual and lifetime per capita incomes of any aggregate population group in the United States. Concomitantly, we suffer the highest rate of infant mortality, death by exposure and malnutrition, disease, and the like. Under such circumstances, alcoholism and other escapist forms of substance abuse are endemic in the Indian community, a situation which leads both to a general physical debilitation of the population and a catastrophic accident rate. Teen suicide among Indians is several times the national average.

The average life expectancy of a reservation-based Native American man is barely 45 years; women can expect to live less than three years longer.

Such itemizations could be continued at great length, including matters like the radioactive contamination of large portions of contemporary Indian country, the forced relocation of traditional Navajos, and so on. But the point should be made: Genocide, as defined in international law, is a continuing fact of day-to-day life (and death) for North America's native peoples. Yet there has been—and is—only the barest flicker of public concern about, or even consciousness of, this reality. Absent any serious expression of public outrage, no one is punished and the process continues.

A salient reason for public acquiescence before the ongoing holocaust in Native North America has been a continuation of the popular legacy, often through more effective media. Since 1925, Hollywood has released more than 2,000 films, many of them rerun frequently on television, portraying Indians as strange, perverted, ridiculous, and often dangerous things of the past. Moreover, we are habitually presented to mass audiences one-dimensionally, devoid of recognizable human motivations and emotions; Indians thus serve as props, little more. We have thus been thoroughly and systematically dehumanized.

Nor is this the extent of it. Everywhere, we are used as logos, as mascots, as jokes: "Big Chief" writing tablets, "Red Man" chewing tobacco, "Winnebago" campers, "Navajo" and "Cherokee" and "Pontiac" and "Cadillac" pickups and automobiles. There are the Cleveland "Indians," The Kansas City "Chiefs," the Atlanta "Braves," and the Washington "Redskins" professional sports teams—not to mention those in thousands of colleges, high schools, and elementary schools across the country—each with their own degrading caricatures and parodies of Indians and/or things Indian. Pop fiction continues in the same vein, including an unending stream of New Age manuals purporting to expose the inner works of indigenous spirituality in everything from pseudo-philosophical to do-it-yourself styles. Blonde yuppies from Beverly Hills amble about the country claiming to be reincarnated 17th-century Cheyenne Ushamans ready to perform previously secret ceremonies.

In effect, a concerted, sustained, and in some ways accelerating effort has gone into making Indians unreal. It is thus of obvious importance that the American public begin to think about the implications of such things the next time they witness a gaggle of face-painted and war-bonneted buffoons doing the "Tomahawk Chop" at a baseball or football game. It is necessary that they think about the implications of the grade-school teacher adorning their child in turkey feathers to commemorate Thanksgiving. Think about the significance of John Wayne or Charlton Heston killing a dozen "savages" with a single bullet the next time a western comes on TV. Think about why Land-o-Lakes finds it appropriate to market its butter with the stereotyped image of an "Indian princess" on the wrapper. Think about what it means when non-Indian academics profess—as they often do—to "know more about Indians than Indians do themselves." Think about the significance of charlatans like Carlos Castaneda and Jamake Highwater and Mary Summer Rain and Lynn Andrews churning out "Indian" bestsellers, one after the other, while Indians typically can't get into print.

Think about the real situation of American Indians. Think about Julius Streicher. Remember Justice Jackson's admonition. Understand that the treatment of Indians in American popular culture is not "cute" or "amusing" or just "good, clean fun."

Know that it causes real pain and real suffering to real people. Know that it threatens our very survival. And know that this is just as much a crime against humanity as anything the Nazis ever did. It is likely that the indigenous people of the United States will never demand that those guilty of such criminal activity be punished for their deeds. But the least we have the right to expect—indeed, to demand—is that such practices finally be brought to a halt.

"There's No Race on the Playing Field"
Perceptions of Racial Discrimination Among White and Black Athletes

Tony N. Brown, James S. Jackson, Kendrick T. Brown,
Robert M. Sellers, Shelley Keiper, & Warde J. Manuel

Entrenched beliefs about the meaning and significance of race negatively influence interactions between individuals of different racial backgrounds. There are few arenas that remain untouched by race-related conflict and tension and in which desegregated relations are commonplace (Bell, 1992; Cose, 1993; DuBois, 1969; Hacker, 1992; Kinder & Sanders, 1996; Myrdal, 1944; Sigelman & Welch, 1991; Wachtel, 1999). It is interesting that the contemporary sports arena or "playing field" is perceived by many to be a sociological space where athletes of different races are freed from the constraints of racial conflict and division (Hoberman, 1984, 1997; Jefferson, 1998). This perception may be linked to the observation that some athletes—specifically, those deeply identified with sports—appear to be "raceless" (Fordham, 1988). This select group of athletes appears to be unaware of race on the playing field and racial problems affecting the larger society.

When individuals representing different races participate in integrated, organized team sports and feel committed to the role of athlete (i.e., possess a central athletic identity), some of them may become oblivious to racial division. We argue that this can occur because the playing field is a context in which athletes are typically socialized to believe race does not matter. In addition, athletes might become oblivious to racial conflict because their sense of connectedness to their racial group (i.e., racial identity centrality) may diminish when they participate in integrated, organized team sports or when they develop an engrossed sense of identity linked to sports. We argue that the augmenting of athletic identity and diminution of racial identity, both a function of participation in integrated, organized team sports, can influence whether some athletes perceive that racial and ethnic discrimination is no longer a problem in the United States.

This study reviews race differences in public opinion regarding perceptions of racial discrimination, suggests how athletic and racial identity centrality might be linked, and predicts why high levels of athletic identity centrality might be correlated with the perception that racial discrimination is no longer a problem. Finally, we empirically examine whether White and Black athletes differ in their perceptions of discrimination, whether athletic identity and racial identity are negatively associated, and whether athletes who identify strongly with sports tend to perceive that discrimination is no longer a problem.

RACE DIFFERENCES IN PERCEPTIONS OF DISCRIMINATION

White and Black people rarely agree about racial issues, particularly the prevalence and consequences of racial and ethnic discrimination (Cose, 1993; Kinder & Sanders, 1996; Klugel, 1985; Klugel & Smith, 1982; Schuman & Hatchett, 1974; Schuman, Steeh, & Bobo, 1985; Schuman, Steeh, Bobo, & Krysan, 1997; Sigelman & Welch, 1991; Smith & Seltzer, 2000). In their review of national trend data collected by ABC News and the *Washington Post*, Sigelman and Welch (1991) reported that in comparison to 11% of White respondents, 37% of Black respondents perceived that racial discrimination prevented Blacks from getting a good education. In terms of getting decent housing, 52% of Blacks perceived that racial discrimination was a barrier and only 20% of Whites agreed with them. In terms of getting skilled labor jobs and being promoted into managerial positions, 53% and 61% of Blacks, respectively, felt that Blacks experienced discrimination; the percentages for Whites were 15% and 23%, respectively. When asked about income, 57% of Black respondents believed racial discrimination influenced the wages they were paid; only 14% of White respondents agreed.

Schuman et al. (1985, 1997) reviewed national trend data on racial attitudes from several sources (e.g., Gallup, National Opinion Research Center, General Social Survey). One set of questions asked why White people seem to get more of the good things in life. One reason given was that "generations of slavery and discrimination have created conditions that make it difficult for Blacks to work their way out of the lower class." The average proportion of Whites agreeing with this reason in the years 1988, 1990, 1992, and 1994 was approximately 48%. In contrast, the average proportion of Blacks agreeing with this reason during the same time period was approximately 72%.

In a recent, comprehensive review of White and Black public opinion, Smith and Seltzer (2000) investigated a range of issues including discrimination, alienation, attitudes toward government spending, affirmative action, belief in conspiracy theories, attitudes toward foreign policy, and attitudes toward the criminal justice system. They reported either racial gaps (10% to 19% disparity), gulfs (20% to 39% disparity), or chasms (40% or more disparity) in nearly all perceptions of these issues. In terms of the consequences of discrimination, 64% of Blacks compared with 35% of Whites agreed that the main cause of contemporary inequality is past discrimination.

As reviewed here, the gulf in public opinion between Whites and Blacks in the general population concerning the existence of racial and ethnic discrimination in the United States has been well documented. Many Whites tend to perceive that discrimination is no longer a problem, whereas many Blacks tend to perceive that discrimination has consistent and adverse consequences in their lives. Divergence in perceptions of racialized issues is important because it contributes to conflict and interracial estrangement and inhibits development of prescriptive programs and policies that might promote racial equality (Kinder & Sanders, 1996; Wachtel, 1999).

Racialized issues are rarely openly discussed within sports except in discourse about the elimination of the color barrier (e.g., Jackie Robinson in major league baseball) or in reference to outlandish statements (e.g., John Rocker's comments about New Yorkers). To date, no studies have examined whether White and Black athletes agree about the prevalence of racial and ethnic discrimination in the United States. For reasons we hypothesize related to athletic and racial identity centrality (discussed in the following sections), White and Black athletes' perceptions of discrimination may not correspond to patterns found in the general population.

ATHLETIC AND RACIAL IDENTITY CENTRALITY

Self-concept is a function of commitment to norms and expectations and the centrality of role and status identities (e.g., student, athlete, woman, lawyer, doctor, Black, son, and so forth). In the current study, we focus on the centrality of athletic and racial identity. Centrality refers to the extent to which a person defines a core part of their self-concept with respect to a particular role or status (Stryker & Serpe, 1994). Some roles and statuses as well as identities that derive from them can be more or less discordant depending on the social context. For example, Adler and Adler (1987) and Adler and Adler (1991) and others (Coakley, 1990; Edwards, 1973; C. K Harrison, 1998; Lapchick, 1996) have investigated the potentially discordant nature of athletic and academic identities and roles among high school and college athletes. There are, however, few investigations of the potentially discordant relationship between athletic and racial identity centrality (see the discussion in Jefferson, 1998).

Among athletes playing on integrated, organized sports teams, athletic identity centrality may supersede or be discordant with racial identity centrality for at least two reasons. First, racially and ethnically diverse athletic teams train, travel, compete, and win or lose together. That is, goal-oriented interracial interaction on sport teams can lead to reduction of racial distinctiveness and downplaying of racial division for some athletes (Brown, Brown, Jackson, Sellers, & Manuel, in press; Jefferson, 1998). Second, diminution of racial group attachment can occur because athletes are socialized to see only opponents and teammates (Carron, 1982; Murrell & Gaertner, 1992; Widmeyer, Carron, & Brawley, 1993; Williams & Widmeyer, 1991), not individuals representing distinct racial and ethnic groups. The team essentially becomes the "ultimate in-group" (Canon, 1982; Murrell & Gaertner, 1992; Widmeyer et al., 1993; Williams & Widmeyer, 1991), trumping other social group memberships, which in the case of racial group membership, is unusual given its master status (Bell, 1992; Cose, 1993; DuBois, 1969; Hacker, 1992; L. Harrison, Lee, & Belcher, 1999; Myrdal, 1944; Wachtel, 1999).

THERE'S "NO RACE" ON THE PLAYING FIELD

Athletes are a unique population because they are endowed with physical talents that distinguish them from the average person. They are often faster, taller, and stronger than comparable others in their age group. Some athletes are especially unique because they do not seem to be constrained by racial politics. These athletes appear, at least superficially, to have little regard for their own, their team members', or the opposing team members' racial and ethnic distinctiveness; they are consumed by sports, defining themselves first and foremost as athletes. Such athletes are raceless (Fordham, 1988) and may be subjectively freed from ideological constraints of race that are operative in other social contexts and institutions (Bell, 1992; Cose, 1993; DuBois, 1969; Hacker, 1992; Myrdal, 1944; Sigelman & Welch, 1991; Wachtel, 1999). Raceless athletes envision and subjectively experience the sports arena and maybe even the larger society as milieus where race does not matter.

Athletes that strongly identify with athletics and therefore define a core part of their self-concepts through athletics can be "colorblinded" by participation in sports because they are socialized to competition-related norms (Jefferson, 1998; McPherson, 1984; Stevenson, 1975) such as fair play (i.e., no discrimination), meritocracy, teamwork, and cooperation (Coakley, 1990, 1993; Lapchick, 1996; MacClancy, 1996). In addition, coaches, advisors, and other persons in power over athletes encourage homogenization of team members and work to minimize racial and other social group distinctiveness (Jefferson, 1998; Lapchick, 1996; Widmeyer et al., 1993). Furthermore, athletes pay heavy prices when they speak out about the prevalence and consequences of racial or ethnic discrimination (Lapchick, 1996; Rowe, 1998). They are often ostracized from the team and labeled problem players. Finally, White spectators often cleave to contrived expectations of "acceptable" athletes—athletes who do not express racial pride or speak about inequality. Thus, identification with sports and competition-related norms along with the pressures exerted by coaches and spectators are predicted to influence how some athletes view racial and ethnic discrimination in the larger society.

HYPOTHESES

This study examined whether race differences in perceptions of racial discrimination found in the general population are also found among athletes. We expected that White and Black athletes would not differ in the degree to which they perceived that discrimination is no longer a problem in the United States. This study also addressed whether athletes with high athletic identity would report low levels of racial identity and whether athletic identity was positively related to perceiving that racial and ethnic discrimination is no longer a problem. We expected athletes who identify strongly with sports to report low levels of racial identity centrality and to report high levels of agreement with the perception that discrimination is no longer a problem.

METHOD

Sample

Data to test these hypotheses were collected from freshman intercollegiate student athletes at 24 predominantly White, Division 1 institutions across the United States. With support from the NCAA, we attempted to survey all incoming student athletes on full athletic scholarship. Student athletes completed the Progress in College/Social and Group Experiences questionnaire along with an instrument that assessed basic academic skills in the fall of 1996. Athletic counselors at each university and college administered the questionnaires to groups of student athletes during a mandatory skills assessment session; thus, the response rate was nearly 100%.

The sample size for the 1996 Progress in College/Social and Group Experiences data set was 533:1.0% were Asian American, 4.0% were Latino or Hispanic Americans, 75.3% were White, 18.3% were Black or African American, and 2% self-identified as other. The remaining 6.6% of student athletes had missing data on racial status. We were centrally interested in those student athletes who self-identified as White or Black and/or African American. Men constituted 54.1% of this subsample of 466 student athletes. There was little variation in age or education because respondents were incoming college freshmen. A total of nine sports for both women and men were represented, and 50.1% of respondents classified themselves as first-team members (i.e., starters).

Our sample does not include individuals who might represent a control group (e.g., nonathlete college students in extracurricular activities) for comparison with student athletes. Without an appropriate control group, we cannot make definitive statements regarding athletic identity and the impact of participation in athletics on the centrality of racial identity or its impact on perceptions of racial discrimination because it may be the same among nonathletes.

MEASURES

Perceptions of discrimination. The dependent variable was a single-item indicator that gauged the degree to which student athletes agreed with the following statement: "Discrimination against people of different racial/ ethnic groups is no longer a problem in the United States." Student athletes could choose 1 (*strongly disagree*) to 6 (*strongly agree*) or any number in between to represent their opinions. We did not have other measures that captured perceptions of discrimination, and therefore our dependent variable may have more measurement error than constructs measured by multiple items. In addition, discrimination was framed in broad terms—the question did not refer to a specific group.

Athletic identity centrality. Athletic identity centrality was measured using items from the Athletic Identity Measurement Scale developed by Brewer, Van Raalte, and Linder (1993). We selected the following five items based on psychometric properties and substantive content: (a) My main sport is the most important thing in my life, (b) I spend more time thinking about my sport than anything else, (c) other people mainly see me as an athlete, (d) I need to participate in sports to feel good about myself, and (e) I would be very depressed if I was injured and could not compete in my sport. The response format ranged from 1(*strongly disagree*) to 6 (*strongly agree*). In maximum likelihood common factor analyses (not shown), these items represented one underlying factor. Cronbach's alpha for the athletic identity centrality items was .74. We used the arithmetic mean of the five items in our analyses.

There is sparse research that examines correlates of athletic identity centrality. C. K. Harrison (1998), for instance, predicted that a select group of Black men from low socioeconomic backgrounds were likely to report extremely high levels of athletic identity. In addition, we know little about the properties of athletic identity centrality. For instance, researchers should explore whether athletic identity is psychometrically similar and operates in the same way among athletes playing "individualistic" sports (e.g., boxing, swimming, or table tennis) compared with those playing "cooperative" sports (e.g., football, volleyball, or lacrosse).

Racial identity centrality. Racial identity centrality was assessed by a single item: "In general, belonging to my ethnic/racial group is an important part of my self-image." Student athletes were allowed to choose 1 (*strongly disagree*) to 6 (*strongly agree*) to represent their opinion. An important measurement limitation was that we did not have multiple indicators of racial identity centrality.

Background variables. The following control variables that might confound relationships among racial identity, athletic identity, and perceptions of discrimination were included in the multivariate models: gender, parental education, experience of a racial conflict, first-team classification, and importance of religious beliefs. Gender was self-reported and coded as a dummy variable; men were 1 and women were 0. Parental education was an ordinal measure that combined respondents' years of schooling for fathers and mothers. If information for one parent was missing, the educational attainment of the other parent was used. Parental education ranged from 1 (equivalent to parental education of junior high school or less) to 8 (equivalent to having both parents earn a doctoral degree).

Experiencing a racial conflict was assessed by a single item that asked respondents, "Have you ever been involved in any conflicts involving someone of a different race or ethnic group?" Racial conflict was coded as a dummy variable; not having a conflict was the excluded group (0). Student-athletes were asked about their playing status in their main sport with the following question: "In terms of your playing time or position on the roster, how are you classified in your main sport?" Using a dummy variable, student athletes on the first team were contrasted against those responding second team, third team, red shirt, and not eligible. The importance of religious beliefs was a single item indicator that asked, "In general, how important are religious or spiritual beliefs in your day-to-day life?" This item ranged from 1 (*not at all important*) to 6 (*of the greatest importance*). The importance of religious beliefs was included in the model because there are large racial differences in religiosity and religious beliefs may be linked to perceptions of racial and ethnic discrimination. Zero-order correlations among perceptions of discrimination, athletic and racial identity centrality, and background variables are shown in the Appendix.

Table 1 Race Differences in Perceptions of Discrimination, Racial Identity, Athletic Identity, and Background Variables in 1996 Progress in College/Social and Group Experiences Study

	Range	White Student Athletes M	White Student Athletes SD	Black Student Athletes M	Black Student Athletes SD	Difference
Discrimination no longer a problem in the United States	1–6	2.01	1.18	1.87	1.26	0.14
Racial group important	1–6	3.02	1.58	4.31	1.62	1.29***
Athletic identity	1–6	3.83	1.04	3.54	1.09	0.30**
Gender (% men)	0–1	48.80	0.50	75.82	0.43	27.02***
Parental education	1–8	4.94	1.38	4.54	1.56	0.40**
Racial conflict (% yes)	0–1	26.84	0.44	58.23	0.50	31.39***
First team (% yes)	0–1	53.53	0.50	35.29	0.48	18.24***
Religious beliefs	1–6	4.04	1.53	4.89	1.39	0.83***
N		375		91		

**$p < .05$. ***$p < .01$.

ANALYTIC STRATEGIES

Hypotheses were tested using independent sample t tests, one-way ANOVA models with Student-Newman-Keuls post hoc tests, and multivariate ordinary least squares regression analysis. These techniques were chosen because the dependent variable was treated as an interval scale, whereas the independent variables were a combination of dichotomous and interval measures. Independent sample t tests and ANOVAs were used to explore differences in perceptions of discrimination, racial and athletic identity centrality, and background variables among subgroups of student athletes. Ordinary least squares regression was used to examine whether relationships found at the bivariate level remained statistically significant after controlling for background variables.

RESULTS:
RACE DIFFERENCES IN PERCEPTIONS OF DISCRIMINATION

Table 1 presents statistics describing univariate distributions of perceptions of discrimination, racial identity centrality, athletic identity centrality, and background variables by race. The first column presents the ranges of the variables. The second column presents means and standard deviations for White student athletes, the third presents means and standard deviations for Black student athletes, and the fourth presents the absolute racial difference. Contrary to patterns found in the general population, we expected that White and Black respondents would report similar levels of agreement with the statement that racial and ethnic discrimination is no longer a problem. As expected, we found no significant racial differences in perceptions of discrimination. The mean for both groups was near 2 on a scale where 1 was *strongly disagree*.

When asked about the importance of their racial group in relation to their personal self-images, Black athletes rated its importance more than one response scale point higher than did White athletes. In contrast, White student athletes tended to define their self-concepts in terms of participation in athletics more than did their Black counterparts.

Table 1 shows that Black men were disproportionately represented in the sample. It also shows that parents of White student athletes had average education that was roughly equivalent to a college degree, whereas Black athletes' parents had average educational attainment equidistant between some college and receipt of a college degree. About 27% of White intercollegiate student athletes contrasted with 58% of Black student athletes experienced racial conflict. In descriptive analysis (not shown), we found that 66% of White respondents experiencing racial conflict reported it was not related to sports. Roughly 80% of Black student athletes reported that it was not related to sports. In our sample, 54% of White student athletes compared with 35% of Black student athletes were starters. Also consistent with the literature on religious participation, Black student athletes tended to indicate that religious beliefs were more important in their daily lives than did White student athletes.

PERCEPTIONS OF DISCRIMINATION AND RACIAL IDENTITY BY LOW AND HIGH ATHLETIC IDENTITY

We predicted that similarity in perceptions regarding racial and ethnic discrimination, which is not generally found among Whites and Blacks, was related to the intersection of athletic and racial identity centrality. Table 2 presents summary statistics by race and the level of athletic identity centrality. Athletic centrality was split by the median into low and high subgroups. Subgroup means were presented in the first four columns, and the overall F statistic and post hoc test results were shown in the last two columns, indicating subgroups that were statistically different from each other. We found evidence that race and athletic identity centrality interact to influence how student athletes view racial group membership and how they perceive discrimination.

We found that White student athletes with low and high athletic identity centrality did not differ from each other in their perceptions of racial and ethnic discrimination. On the other hand, Black student athletes with low athletic identity reported lower levels of agreement that discrimination is no longer a problem than did their counterparts with high athletic identity. Black student athletes with low athletic identity were also less likely than White student athletes with either low or high athletic identity to agree at high levels that discrimination is no longer a problem.

Table 2 Race and Athletic Identity Differences in Perceptions of Discrimination, Racial Identity, and Background Variables in 1996 Progress in College/Social and Group Experiences Study

	White Student Athletes' Athletic Identity		Black Student Athletes' Athletic Identity			
	Low 1	High 2	Low 3	High 4	F Statistic	Post Hoc Tests[a]
Discrimination no longer a problem in the United States	1.95	2.07	1.56	2.34	3.66**	1 & 3, 2 & 3, 3 & 4
Racial group important	2.79	3.26	4.51	4.06	19.13***	1 & 2, 1 & 3, 1 & 4, 2 & 3, 2 & 4
Gender (% men)	48.15	49.73	73.08	80.00	7.31***	1 & 3, 1 & 4, 2 & 3, 2 & 4
Parental education	5.00	4.88	4.70	4.41	1.97	
Racial conflict (% yes)	26.37	27.49	61.70	53.57	10.28***	1 & 3, 1 & 4, 2 & 3, 2 & 4
First team (% yes)	51.09	55.74	36.17	35.29	3.04**	2 & 3
Religious beliefs	4.06	4.01	4.78	4.91	6.62***	1 & 3, 1 & 4, 2 & 3, 2 & 4
N	189	185	52	35		

a. Indicates columns that are significantly different at the $p < .05$ level. **$p<.05$. ***$p<.01$.

Table 3 Standardized Coefficients From Ordinary Least Squares Regression of Discrimination on Background Variables, Racial Identity, and Athletic Identity

	Discrimination Is No Longer a Problem	
	Model 1	Model 2
Race (1 = Black)	−.098*	−.083
Gender (1 = men)	.198***	.192***,
Parental education	−.050	−.043
Racial conflict (1 = yes)	−.033	−.034
First team (1 = yes)	.081	.075
Religious beliefs	.081	.086*
Racial group is important	.033	.020
Athletic identity		.106**
N	407	
R^2	5.20%	6.30%
Change in R^2		1.10%**

*$p<.10$. **$p<.05$. ***$p<.01$.

Overall, Black student athletes reported higher levels of agreement than did White student athletes with the statement that racial group membership is an important part of their self-images. It is interesting that White student athletes tended to view racial group membership as an important part of their self-images when their athletic identity was high. In contrast, Black student athletes tended to agree that belonging to their racial group was an important part of their self-images when their athletic centrality was low. The mean difference, however, in racial centrality between Black student athletes with low and high athletic identity centrality was not statistically significant.

Table 2 also shows that compared with sample estimates (see Table 1), Black men were slightly overrepresented in the high athletic identity centrality subgroup. No significant differences in average parental education by race were found controlling for athletic identity. White student athletes were significantly less likely than were Black student athletes to report experiencing racial conflict. The proportion of Blacks with low athletic identity centrality on the first team differed significantly from the proportion of Whites with high athletic identity centrality on the first team. Regardless of athletic identity, Black student athletes tended to report that religious beliefs were more important in their day-to-day lives than did Whites.

PREDICTING PERCEPTIONS OF DISCRIMINATION

In Table 3, the perception that racial and ethnic discrimination is no longer a problem was regressed on racial and athletic identity centrality controlling for background variables; standardized coefficients are shown.

Table 4 Standardized Coefficients From Ordinary Least Squares Regression of Discrimination on Background Variables, Racial Identity, and Athletic Identity by Race

| | Discrimination Is No Longer a Problem | | | |
| | White Student Athletes | | Black Student Athletes | |
	Model 1	Model 2	Model 1	Model 2
Gender (1= men)	.178***	.176***	.288*	.244*
Parental education	−.013	−.009	−.167	−.160
Racial conflict (1= yes)	−.027	−.027	−.143	−.132
First team (1 = yes)	.080	.076	.092	.070
Religious beliefs	.070	.071	.239*	.249*
Racial group is important	.085	.074	−.236*	−.199
Athletic identity		.058		.240*
N	340		67	
R^2	4.80%	5.10%	17.20%	22.70%
Change in R^2		0.30%		5.40%*

*$p<.10$. **$p<.05$. ***$p<.01$.

In Model 1, White student athletes tended to report marginally higher levels of agreement than did Black student athletes that discrimination is no longer a problem in the United States, controlling for other variables. Men were significantly more likely than were women to report high levels of agreement with the statement that discrimination is no longer a problem in the United States. Parental education, racial conflict, first-team classification, importance of religious beliefs, and racial identity centrality were not significantly associated with the perception that discrimination is no longer a problem.

Athletic identity was added to the equation in Model 2. Athletic identity significantly increased the proportion of explained variance and was directly related to the perception that discrimination is no longer a problem. Consistent with our predictions, intercollegiate student athletes with high levels of athletic identity centrality reported high levels of agreement with the perception that discrimination is no longer a problem. With the addition of athletic identity, the marginal race difference in perceptions of discrimination was attenuated and the importance of religious beliefs became marginally significant. Those student athletes reporting that spiritual beliefs were important in their day-to-day lives tended to perceive that discrimination is no longer a problem.

PREDICTING PERCEPTIONS OF DISCRIMINATION BY RACE

Controlling for background variables, perceptions of discrimination were regressed on racial identity and athletic identity separately for White student athletes and Black student athletes (see Table 4). Across race, Model 1 shows associations between racial identity and perceptions of discrimination; Model 2 adds athletic identity centrality to the equation.

In Model 1 (left panel), compared with White women, White men reported significantly higher levels of agreement with the perception that discrimination is no longer a problem. Gender was the only statistically significant predictor of perceiving racial and ethnic discrimination among White student athletes. Athletic identity was added to the equation in Model 2 (left panel) but was not statistically related to discrimination; gender remained a significant predictor.

In Model 1(right panel), compared with Black women and similar to the pattern found for White respondents, Black men reported marginally higher levels of agreement with the perception that discrimination is no longer a problem. Although the coefficients were large, neither parental education nor having a racial conflict were statistically significant. The more important religious beliefs were to Black student athletes, the more they tended to perceive that racial and ethnic discrimination is no longer a problem. When racial group membership was an important part of Black student athletes' self-images, they tended to disagree with the statement that racial and ethnic discrimination is no longer a problem. This marginal relationship suggests that Black athletes who identify with their racial group tend to express perceptions about discrimination that are similar to those held by Blacks in the general population.

In Model 2 (right panel), we found that Black student athletes with high levels of athletic identity centrality tended to perceive that discrimination is no longer a problem in the United States, controlling for other variables. When athletic identity was added to the model, gender and importance of religious beliefs remained marginally related to perceiving discrimination, but the marginally significant association between racial identity centrality and perceiving discrimination was reduced to statistical nonsignificance. Consistent with our propositions, this suggests that athletic identity might influence the relationship between racial identity and perceptions of racial discrimination.

Comparing the full regression models for White and Black respondents in Table 4 suggests a statistical interaction (i.e., moderating effect) between race and athletic identity centrality predicting the perception that discrimination is no longer a problem. In ordinary least squares regression analysis (not shown), we found an interaction between race and athletic identity such that athletic identity was a marginally significant ($p < .08$), positive predictor of high levels of agreement that discrimination is no longer a problem but only among Black student athletes.

DISCUSSION

We expected that White and Black athletes would report similar levels of agreement with the statement that racial and ethnic discrimination is no longer a problem in the United States. Results indicate that overall, White and Black intercollegiate student athletes held similar perceptions regarding racial and ethnic discrimination (see Table 1). This is a pattern rarely observed in the public opinion literature.

We predicted that athletic and racial identity centrality would be negatively related such that when one type of centrality was high, the other would tend to be low. Athletic identity and racial identity were negatively correlated among Black student athletes but, surprisingly, were positively related among White student athletes (see Table 2). This unexpected finding for White athletes might be a function of stereotypes about the superiority of Black athletes or may emanate from psychological and normative expectations about race and sports. White intercollegiate student athletes with high athletic identity may experience dissonance because Blacks are often stereotyped as superior (i.e., natural) athletes (Edwards, 1973; Hoberman, 1997; Jefferson, 1998; Sailes, 1996). Thus, the centrality of White student athletes' racial identity may be heightened if they feel they are prejudged to be inferior athletes because of their race. Or, the centrality of White student athletes' racial identity may be heightened if they feel they are participating in a sport that is the purview of their racial group (e.g., hockey is a White sport) (L. Harrison et al., 1999).

Finally, we expected that athletes with high levels of athletic identity would tend to perceive that discrimination is no longer a problem in the United States. Support for this hypothesis was found but only among Black student athletes (see Table 3 and 4).

RACE, SPORTS, AND SPORT INDUCED RACELESSNESS

Participation in sports may have different sociological meaning and importance for White and Black athletes. We found, for example, that athletic identity centrality was linked to racial identity centrality and perceptions of discrimination in divergent ways by race. More research is needed that characterizes how participation in sports may be differentially experienced or interpreted by White and Black athletes. For instance, Anshel and Sailes (1990) examined the extent to which 64 White and Black male intercollegiate student athletes differed in their psychological needs and perceptions of their sport environments. The authors found significant racial differences in several domains, indicating that race may be operative in subtle ways on the playing field. Black respondents were less receptive than were White student athletes to negative feedback from the coach, more likely than Whites to believe that coaches should earn the respect of their players, felt that coaches exerted too much control prior to the game, were more prone to making internal attributions for winning and losing compared with White student athletes, and were more focused on scouting reports of opposing teams and less on game films than were their White counterparts.

As for more blatant ways, some scholars believe that racial conflict and entrenched beliefs about the meaning and significance of race are evident in every social context (Bell, 1992; Cose, 1993; DuBois, 1969; Hacker, 1992; Kinder & Sanders, 1996; Myrdal, 1944; Sigelman & Welch, 1991; Wachtel, 1999), including sports (Eitzen, 1993; C. K Harrison, 1998; Hoberman, 1984, 1997; Jefferson, 1998; MacClancy, 1996; Shropshire, 1996). For example, to support that racial division, discrimination, and entrenched beliefs about race are evident in sports, researchers (Anshel & Sailes, 1990; Edwards, 1973; Eitzen,1993; C. K Harrison, 1998; L. Harrison et al., 1999; Jefferson, 1998; Lapchick, 1996; Sailes, 1996) highlight racial differentials in professional team ownership, coaching and managerial positions, leadership positions on teams, endorsements, commentators' descriptions of players, and fines and/or penalties for rule violations. Similarly, egregious statements made by prominent men and women in contemporary sports suggest that racial division and primitive beliefs about race are operative on the playing field (e.g., the comments and assertions of Fuzzy Zoeller, Al Campanis, Marge Schott, Chris Simon, Jimmy "the Greek" Snyder, and John Rocker). We believe that some athletes are keenly aware of these dynamics and would quickly acknowledge racial conflict and tension on the playing field as well as in the larger society.

Nonetheless, team-sporting activities create an atmosphere in which the political and ideological constraints of race are subjectively loosened for a select group of athletes (and spectators). An intervention that involves the use of integrated, organized team sports could be one way to help alleviate interracial tension by urging individuals to shift the relative weight attached to being White or Black to the identity of teammate. But before we advocate mass participation in sports as a means of reducing interracial estrangement and challenging race as a master status, attention should be focused on the reproduction of inequality in sports (C. K. Harrison, 1998; Hoberman, 1984, 1997; Jefferson, 1998; MacClancy, 1996; Rowe, 1998). Of particular relevance for this study, we must investigate how racialized constraints are purportedly loosened and examine the sociological consequences of racelessness (Fordham, 1988).

Fordham (1988) suggested that racelessness is an ineffective strategy invoked by Blacks when they are in contexts that historically have been off-limits to members of their racial group or in which they are tendentiously separated from other Blacks (e.g., academic high achievers in Fordham's research). Black student athletes at predominantly White, Division 1 schools satisfy these criteria to some extent. They are in a situation that has historically been off-limits to members of their racial group, and they are often separated from the few Black students on campus who are not athletes. Black athletes at Division 1 schools may engage racelessness as a response to dislocation from racially homogeneous situations (e.g., schools, neighborhoods, or peer groups) to which they and the majority of Blacks in the United States are accustomed. In this case, some Black athletes might develop a sense of athletic identity that makes it comfortable for them to be estranged from their communities. Results in this study may portend processes of racial disconnection among Black intercollegiate student athletes who are strongly identified with sports on predominantly White campuses.

There are other important consequences to racelessness. Black athletes with high levels of athletic identity, for instance, in visible positions on prominent college and professional teams are in a position to publicize structural impediments facing the average Black person. Black athletes, however, who seldom acknowledge racial discrimination, are proof that hard work really does result in success and economic gain regardless of race. That is, racelessness is intertwined with the propagation of beliefs about meritocracy and fair play (Edwards, 1973; Hoberman, 1984, 1997; Jefferson, 1998; Kinder & Sanders, 1996; Klugel & Smith, 1982; Shropshire, 1996). In heated debates about affirmative action and similar policies designed to reduce discrimination faced by Blacks and other groups, visible Black athletes strongly identified with sports can be induced, perhaps unwittingly, by those opposed to equalized opportunity to support a position that no assistance is needed. Such athletes are icons that can be "pedestaled" because they may feel less attached to their racial group and may be less likely to perceive discrimination.

Another consequence of racelessness is economic. Many professional Black athletes strongly identified with sports have achieved great wealth, but their reduced sense of racial identity centrality and blunted awareness of discrimination might hinder investments that strengthen their communities. Jefferson (1998), for example, suggested that Black professional athletes rarely provide business opportunities for members of their racial group because they are brainwashed and whitewashed by participation in sports. She reported that although 80% of the players in the NBA and 67% of the players in the NFL are Black, less than 2% of them use Black agents, attorneys, financial planners, doctors, or business consultants.

Is there no race on the playing field? The answer depends on the characteristics of the athletes or individuals asked the question. Some athletes may not see race. Some avid spectators may not see race. Some coaches may not need or want to see race. In contrast, other individuals in the sports institution, including some athletes, cannot free themselves from the dynamics of racial division and conflict or the ideological constraints of race when they are on or off the playing field.

Section VIII

Deviance in Sport

Sports in School:
Source of Amity or Antipathy?

LAURA LANGBEIN & ROSEANA BESS

If children do not feel safe in their school surroundings it may be difficult for them to learn and achieve. Previous research suggests that safer schools are conducive to academic learning (Mackenzie, 1983; Bryk and Thum, 1989). If there is a relationship between school safety and increasing students' chances of learning, then it is important to examine sources of school safety—and its absence. One possible determinant of school safety is a school's sports programs, but the effect is not clear. Proponents argue that school sports programs foster teamwork and cooperative norms, thereby enhancing social capital and sociable behaviors (McNeal, 1999). If this expectation is true, we should expect school sports to contribute to school safety. However, detractors argue that school sports are competitive, involve conflict that is often physical, and, especially when sports teams are regarded as an exclusive high school elite, may even inspire hostility among those who are left out. In this case, sports programs may reduce cooperative norms and social capital, alienating those who do not participate. The consequence may be less school safety. With these conflicting expectations in mind, we have attempted to place athletic participation within the conceptual framework of social capital, which may increase safety in schools when it is present, or decrease safety when it is not.

Most studies reveal a beneficial effect of extracurricular activities, including, but not limited to, sports, on the social and human capital of the participants themselves (McNeal, 1999; Fejgin, 1994; Landers and Landers, 1978). But previous research has not systematically examined the effect of prominent extracurricular activities, such as varsity sports, on nonparticipants. Nor has previous research on the relation between sports participation and cooperative behavior systematically controlled for school size, even though school size affects both these variables (McNeal, 1999; Schoggen and Schoggen, 1988;

Morgan and Alwin, 1980; Gottfredson, 1985). Thus it is critical to hold school size constant when examining the impact of extracurricular participation on behavior. The possible interaction between participation and school context, especially school size, has not been studied either. Our research begins to fill these gaps by looking at school-level outcomes of sports programs and by controlling for both observed and unobserved factors, including school size and its possible interaction with sports programs, which may affect the estimation of the impact of sports programs on these outcomes.

In light of the recent tragedy in Littleton, Colorado and similar incidents that occurred during recent school years, Americans' attention has been increasingly focused on violence in schools. It is not clear what factors are influencing children and youth to commit these acts, but everyone is placing blame somewhere, whether that be music, television, family, peers, or drug and gun laws. While adolescents are still more likely to be injured while away from school than while at school (Kaufman et al., 1998), this study is important because it attempts to shed some empirical light on two potential sources of antisocial incidents in high schools, namely, varsity sports, big schools, and their possible interaction. The evidence presented below suggests that to reduce disturbances, opportunities for participation in varsity sports should be expanded in the large high schools that comprise most of those in this study. At the present time, however, those opportunities are scarcest in the large schools where they may be the most useful.

THEORETICAL CONTEXT AND LITERATURE REVIEW

According to James Coleman (1988), social capital is defined as "social structures...which facilitate certain actions of actors within the structure" (Coleman, 1988:S98). Schools provide many opportunities for the development of adolescents' social capital. In this context, interscholastic athletic participation may provide a structure within which interactions with other students are frequent and repeated. Such a framework makes it possible to build supportive and cooperative networks with peers and with adults who work with sports teams (Bryk and Driscoll, 1988; Lee and Croninger, 1996).

In fact, most, but not all, prior evidence suggests that participating in school sports increases prosocial behavior. For example, a study by Segrave and Hastad (1984) concluded that athletes (male and female) reported on average 10.5 percent less involvement in delinquent behavior than nonathletes, supporting the expectation that athletic participation will have a positive effect on school safety. Fejgin (1994) shows similar results in a study of 10th graders. Also, Shields (1995) found that athletic directors observed and/or perceived drug use among the general student body to be more of a problem than drug use among student athletes. Similar results appear in Purdy and Richard (1983), Segrave and Hastad (1982), Hastad et al. (1984), Melnick, Sabo, and Vanfossen (1992), and Landers and Landers (1978). An exception to these results finds no difference in drug use between athletes and nonathletes (Pope et al., 1990).

There are conflicting results about the effect of sports participation on academic achievement; however, there is a relationship between poor academic achievement and delinquent behavior (Segrave and Hastad, 1984). The authors concluded that athletic participation and higher academic achievement decrease the likelihood of a male participating in delinquent activities. Melnick, Sabo, and Vanfossen (1992) found that high sports participation was a social resource for students of color; however, it did not have any effect on their academic achievement. It did have a positive impact on their school retention. Silliker and Quirk (1997) found that athletes tended to have higher grade point averages in season than out of season. Academic performance appears to have been enhanced by their athletic participation.

While these results suggest that students who participate in organized school sports programs may themselves be more likely to exhibit "pro-social" behavior, one cannot infer from this evidence that *schools* with larger sports programs will necessarily have fewer "antisocial" incidents overall. Proponents of school sports often make the explicit argument that there is a positive spillover from sports programs. They argue that sports programs not only foster cooperative behavior among participants, but also build school spirit and social cohesion among nonparticipants in the school.

Although cooperative behavior within a subgroup may spill over to those not in the subgroup, the opposite effect could be equally or even more likely. Specifically, as the in-group (the varsity sports "community") grows in relative prestige and in numerical proportion to the total group (but only up to the point where it still remains an exclusive, but still identifiable, subgroup), those not in the subgroup may feel increasingly insecure, threatened, and left out. One possible consequence is greater open hostility and antisocial behavior. Thus, while sports participation may increase cooperative behavior among those who participate, as the sports in-group grows (especially if it grows more rapidly in relative prestige than in relative size), hostile incidents in the threatened out-group may also increase. Such a story is possibly consistent with reports characterizing the alleged assailants at Columbine, who were said to resent the popularity of the sports "clique" and reacted in a dramatically antisocial manner.

It follows that one set of hypotheses stemming from the possible connection between sports and social capital is that schools with proportionately larger (and even more prestigious) sports programs could well have more "violence"—not because those who participate in the sports programs are more disruptive, but because those who do not participate are more likely to misbehave. For three reasons, the opposite expectation is also plausible.. First, if the hypothetically positive effects of sports programs on the participants outweigh the hypothetically adverse effects on the nonparticipants, then one would expect schools with larger sports programs to exhibit fewer, rather than more, disruptive, "antisocial" incidents. Second, if the hypothetically beneficial effect of sports programs on participants spills over to nonparticipants, one would also expect that schools with larger sports programs will have less social disruption. Third, as sports programs grow proportionately larger, they become relatively more inclusive than exclusive and consequently less likely to foster antisocial behavior among nonparticipants.

A second set of hypotheses follows from the theory of social capital and related theories about the origins of cooperative behavior in groups. Specifically, small groups are theoretically, if not empirically, more likely to foster cooperative behavior (and hence more trust and greater social capital) than larger groups (Ostrom, 1998). In smaller groups, it is harder to free ride. Repeated contacts are more likely, which means that cooperation rather than defection or conflict yields a higher payoff for each individual in the group, and shirking or fighting is easier to detect and sanction. This is one reason that students in organized sports programs are themselves more likely to cooperate than those not in sports or other organized small-group activity. Those within the small group work together, have repeated contacts, monitor one another, and build informal networks and norms of reciprocity, creating the foundations for social capital.

However, another implication is that, apart from subgroups, increasing the size of the total group has an independent, deleterious effect on cooperative behavior. In particular, large schools, independent of subgroups, will have a harder time fostering cooperative behavior than small schools (Cotton, 1996; Lee and Croninger, 1996; Gottfredson, 1985; Bryk and Driscoll, 1988). Students in a large school, especially if they are not a part of a subgroup or many subgroups, are less likely to know one another. If the students do know one another, they are acquaintances, not friends; repeated contacts become less likely as school size increases. In a large school, it is harder to foster cooperative norms and informally sanction antisocial behavior: the lack of likely frequent interactions makes it easier to get away with misbehavior at a large school that would be sanctioned within a smaller group. For example, trying to establish dominance by picking a fight with someone who bumps you in a crowded hallway would not be rational if it is targeted at someone the potential aggressor needs to get along with in the future, but if it is aimed at someone the aggressor does not know directly or even indirectly then such misbehavior might not seem so irrational. Thus, holding sports participation (and other variables) constant, bigger schools will be expected to have more antisocial incidents than smaller schools.

A third implication of social capital theory is that organized sports programs will mitigate the antisocial consequences of larger school size. One way to counter the disruptive behavior that is expected in larger schools is to foster the growth of organized subgroups within larger schools (Cotton, 1996; National Association of Secondary School Principals, 1996). If large schools provide organized extracurricular small-group activities (including sports, cheerleaders, marching band, theater, art, chess, and other structured "in-groups"), then antisocial incidents will be reduced. The empirical expectation is that there is a likely interaction between in-groups (like sports) and the size of the total group. Significant, organized in-groups within larger groups will reduce antisocial behavior more than an equivalent in-group within a smaller overall group. In the context of school sports programs, the implication is that even if sports programs generate antisocial behavior by those not in the group, they will be less likely to do this as school enrollment increases. The pro-social effects of being in an in-group as school size increases will counter the antisocial, anomic effects of increasing school size itself.

In addition to the three social capital hypotheses that frame this research, this study separates these factors from the socioeconomic context of the school. This is particularly important because sports participation is not independent of demographic characteristics. Youth who participate in high school sports "tend to be from more advantaged social backgrounds in terms of parental social class, level of cognitive ability, academic achievement, and level of self-esteem" (Spreitzer, 1994). In attempting to determine the social capital effect of athletic participation, this study accounts for. the effect of higher socioeconomic status as a variable affecting both the likelihood of participating in sports and the likelihood of antisocial behavior by controlling for it statistically.

Antisocial behavior in this study is regarded as an indicator of school safety, or, rather, the lack thereof. School safety is measured by the relative absence of crimes or other harmful incidents occurring within the school building and on school grounds. It is unrealistic to expect any school to have no record of crimes or violence occurring within one school year, and we do not define a minimum number, or a standard, by which to label a school as being safe. Rather, we measure relative safety, assuming that schools with fewer disturbances are safer than those with more disturbances.

Safer schools are important: they appear conducive to academic learning. One possible way to create safer schools is to increase athletic participation, but, based on the theories presented above, the reverse is also possible. Therefore, depending on whether sports programs add more to the social capital of participants or to the resentment of nonparticipants, increases in the percent of students participating in sports will be associated either with decreases or increases in suspensions and serious incidents. Further, the effect is expected to be different in different size schools. Knowing the site-specific effect is important before sports programs are universally viewed as one remedy for reducing disturbances in school: the reform could sometimes make the problem worse.

RESEARCH DESIGN AND MEASUREMENT

This study uses detailed data on suspensions and other reported incidents in a single countywide school system in Maryland. Montgomery County public high schools have the largest enrollment in Maryland. More importantly, the county includes urban, suburban, and rural areas. Over the school years ending 1996, 1997, and 1998, the number of students enrolled in the 180 public schools increased from just over 120,000 to just over 125,000 (Montgomery County Public Schools, 1996–1998). Over the same school years, the per-pupil expenditure was $7,697, $7,887, and $8,035, respectively (Montgomery County Public Schools, 1996–1998). This study focused on the 20 high schools and one middle/high school that were open during the school years ending 1996–1998 for a total sample size of 63. Each of the 21 high schools participated in the interscholastic sports program that is coordinated by the Montgomery County Public Schools Athletic Department.

The research design is a pooled cross-section of 21 schools with three years of data for each school. Interscholastic athletic participation is the main independent variable. Serious incidents and suspensions comprise the dependent variable. Total school enrollment, indicators of sociodemographic characteristics, and the interaction of school enrollment and sports participation are also used both as control variables and as theoretically relevant independent variables. Fixed effects dummy variables for each school and year (relative to a reference school and year, respectively) serve to control the portion of our theoretical ignorance that is specific to each unit and year (Stimson, 1985:923).

There are many reasons to use a pooled rather than a single cross-section (Stimson, 1985). Having multiple observations for each unit of analysis increases the efficiency of parameter estimates. Further, the design significantly improves the chance that parameter estimates are unbiased. Along with the control variables, the design potentially captures unmeasured characteristics of each school and year by including a fixed effect dummy variable corresponding to each school and year (relative to a reference school and year). The constant is then different for each school and year, effectively removing events unique to one school (e.g., a new principal) or to the entire system in a particular year (e.g., a budget crunch) that could otherwise be plausible rival explanations for parameter estimates.

The dependent variable, called "disturbances," is the sum of two components—serious incidents and suspensions. Serious incidents refer to the number of incidents perpetrated by students involving guns, knives, bats, or any other weapons, drugs or drug paraphernalia, altercations, thefts, and vandalism. This number was collected directly from the stack of paper files of the Montgomery County Public Schools Office of Information, and ranged from a minimum of three incidents to a maximum of 52 incidents with a mean of 16. Relative to the school population, the proportion of incidents ranged from just over 1 in 1,000 students (0.0014) to just over 2 per 100 students (0.025). The mean proportion is 1 in 100. Only those incidents perpetrated by students were considered because the relationship to the school of other perpetrators is unknown. Other perpetrators could be neighborhood residents, students from other schools or jurisdictions, or any other individual who is not a student in the school. Incidents of bomb threats and fire alarms were included only when they could be clearly linked to a student in the school.

The other component of the dependent variable is suspensions. Many incidents result in a recommendation for suspension, but not all recommendations for suspension wind up as an actual suspension. Further, not all suspensions originate as a serious incident; in fact, suspensions are far more common than incident reports. The number of suspensions ranged from 27 to 284, with a mean of 101. Relative to school enrollment, the proportion of students who were suspended ranged from a low of 17 out of 1,000 (0.017) to a high of 11 out of 100 (0.112).

In the analysis reported below, suspensions and incidents are added together to measure "disturbances," and then examined as a percentage of the total school enrollment. Adding these variables together effectively creates a self-weighting scale by double counting the serious incidents that wind up as suspensions. Since the underlying concept is to be a measure of public disturbances, such double counting is justifiable. Serious incidents that wind up as suspensions are very likely more serious than those that do not wind up as suspensions. Further, suspensions that began as serious incidents are likely to be more important for measuring public disturbances than other suspensions that did not begin as a serious incident. Thus, in this case, the two variables summed are likely both a more reliable and more valid measure of public disturbances than either measure alone. For the schools in this study, the mean percentage of disturbances is 7 percent; the range is from 2 to 13 percent. More importantly, over the three years of the study, the mean percent of disturbances increased slightly but consistently from 6.76 percent in 1995–1996 to 7.06 percent in 1996–1997 and 8.00 percent in 1997–1998.

Even though the summed measure of disturbances is probably superior to each measure alone, regression parameters were estimated for incidents and suspensions separately; the results were the same as those reported below. Total incidents and suspensions are highly correlated ($r = 0.63$), and the proportions are also positively correlated ($r = 0.38$).

The percent of students receiving free/reduced priced lunch, the percent minority, and the percent of students having English as a second language (ESL) were indicators of socioeconomic characteristics. Together they reflect the challenges that schools face due to the diversity and needs of students that place varying but relatively great demands on the use of limited school resources. They are control variables in the regression equation. The percent minority was measured as the percentage of the enrollment who were classified as African American, Latino, and Asian American. In the Montgomery County high schools, this percentage ranges from 3.6 to 74.2 percent, with a mean of 44 percent. The percent receiving free/reduced price lunch ranged from 1.8 to 38 percent; the mean is 14 percent. The percentage. having ESL ranged from none to 11.8 percent; the mean is 5.8 percent during the three years of the study. The three pairwise correlations among these variables ranged from 0.54 to 0.83; when they were separately included in a regression, one or two were always significant, but the significant pair varied from regression to regression.

These signs of collinearity, together with the intent to use these variables as a measure of the relative diversity and degree of demands placed on school resources, led to the decision to create a "school challenges" factor scale. Principal components, as well as other factoring methods, showed one dominant vector, accounting for 77 percent of the three-dimensional space. The school challenge scale is the sum of the standardized scores of the percent minority, percent in ESL, and percent with free/reduced price lunch, weighted by the factor score of each percentage on the dominant component. None of the results with respect to the main theoretical variables change if the components of the school challenges scale had been used separately rather than added together.

The treatment variables, boys and girls participating in junior varsity and varsity sports, were measured as a percentage of the total school population. Admission to these interscholastic sports teams is competitive, and participation in junior varsity sports is a route to varsity competition. The scarcity of slots on interscholastic sports teams is expected to contribute to its prestige. From the perspective of social capital, it follows that interscholastic sports teams (or other similarly prestigious teams) may foster cooperation among the participants but envy and consequent antisocial behavior among nonparticipants. The net impact on disturbances, measured in this study, could be positive or negative.

There were a total of 15 sports with varsity and junior varsity teams available for boys and girls to join. They were: boys' varsity and junior varsity baseball, girls' varsity and junior varsity softball, boys' and girls' varsity tennis, boys' and girls' varsity and junior varsity soccer, boys' varsity volleyball, girls' varsity and junior varsity volleyball, coed varsity volleyball, boys' and girls' varsity lacrosse, girls' gymnastics, boys' and girls' outdoor track, boys' varsity and junior varsity football, girls' varsity and junior varsity field hockey, boys' and girls' golf, boys' and girls' cross-country track, boys' and girls' varsity and junior varsity basketball, boys' varsity and junior varsity wrestling, boys' and girls' swimming, and boys' and girls' varsity indoor track.

The number of boys participating in varsity or junior varsity sports ranged from 236 to 527 with a mean of 369. As a percentage of the school population, these numbers correspond to a minimum of 13.6 percent and a maximum of 44.5 percent, with a mean of 24 percent. Somewhat fewer girls are active in varsity and junior varsity sports. The numbers ranged from 183 to 445 with a mean of 291. Relative to school enrollment, these numbers correspond to 11 percent and 33 percent, respectively, with a mean of 19 percent. Preliminary analysis showed the same results for boys and girls and for contact sports (football and wrestling) versus other sports. The results reported add the boys' and girls' sports participation, and do not distinguish between contact and noncontact sports. As a proportion of high school enrollment, total junior varsity and varsity sports participation ranges from 25 to 77 percent, with a mean of 44 percent. (The median is 42 percent.) At the county level, there is no upward or downward trend, nor much variation, in this statistic during the three years of the study.

Most of this participation reflects varsity (and not junior varsity) sports. The mean (and median) percent who participate in boys and girls varsity sports is 31 percent. But participation in the varsity sports likely to draw the biggest crowds of spectators (boys football and boys and girls basketball) is considerably smaller, with a mean and median of 5 percent.

Total enrollment in Montgomery County high schools ranges from 609 to 2,529; the mean is 1,573. The median is 1,592. Over the duration of the study, enrollment increased steadily from a mean of 1,525 in 1995–1996 to a mean of 1,617 in 1997–1998.

This secondary data was gathered from reports completed by the Montgomery County Public Schools. The *Montgomery County Public Schools School Performance Program Report* and the *Annual Report on the Systemwide Outcome Measures* for 1996–1998 provided the data on suspensions, minority enrollment, number of students receiving free/reduced price lunch, number having English as a second language, and total enrollment. Athletic participation numbers were provided by the Montgomery County Public Schools Athletic Department.

Finally, sports programs in larger schools are expected to have more ameliorative effects than those in smaller schools. Consequently, the model includes an interactive term that multiplies school size by the sports participation rate.

The parameter estimates in Table 1 are generalized equation estimates, with a fixed effects term for each school and year (relative to a reference). The reported estimates allow for first-order autocorrelation within each panel, and for heteroscedasticity among the panels (i.e., schools). The results do not change if they are generated by the same theoretical model using different statistical estimators, including, but not limited to: simple and robust OLS regression; logistic OLS regression with robust standard errors, where the dependent variable is the log of the likelihood ratio; a log-log model with robust standard errors; a Poisson model of the count of disturbances, conditioned on school enrollment; and OLS and GLS estimates where the dependent variable is also a count of disturbances. While the use of fixed effects makes the estimates more likely to be unbiased, the use of estimators that deal with probable heteroscedasticity and autocorrelation in the stochastic terms makes the variance estimates reported in Table 1 more robust, and the results of the hypothesis tests more reliable.

Table 1 Estimates of Effect of Disturbance Rate on Sports Participation, Challenges, School Enrollment, and Interaction of Sports Participation Rate and School Enrollment

Independent Variable	Panel 1 Participation in Junior Varsity and Varsity Teams		Panel 2 Participation in Top 3 Varsity Teams	
	Unstd. Coefficient	Prob. |z| = 0	Unstd. Coefficient	Prob. |z| = 0
Constant	−18.64	0.38	−18.13	0.28
Percent in junior varsity & varsity	0.313	0.012	—	—
Percent in top 3 varsity	—	—	1.86	0.004
School challenges scale	−3.94	0.051	−3.68	0.08
Enrollment	0.019	0.027	0.017	0.018
Percent in (jv + v) * enrollment	−0.000271	0.001	—	—
Percent in top3 * enrollment	—	—	−0.0014	0.017
Year dummies	(included)		(included)	
School dummies	(included)		(included)	
Goodness of fit:				
Dispersion	1.52		1.51	
Pearson chi2 (36)	54.84		54.38	
Chi2 prob.	< 0.005		< 0.005	
R2 (implied)	0.86		0.86	
Number observations	63		63	

Note: Generalized equation estimates, corrected for first-order autocorrelation within panels and between-panel heteroscedasticity.

Finally, it is possible that school administrators expand sports programs in response to high levels of school disturbances. The consequence would be biased estimates because of reverse causation or simultaneity between independent and dependent variables. However, the Hausman test for simultaneity consistently returned an insignificant coefficient, meaning that the null hypothesis of no simultaneity cannot be rejected (Gujarati, 1995:670–72).

FINDINGS

At the bivariate level, schools with greater sports participation have fewer disturbances: the simple correlation between the proportion of students participating in sports and disturbances as a percent of enrollment is negative (−0.39). But this simple association is likely to reflect many common underlying causes. For example, school enrollment could confound this bivariate relation: larger schools have more disturbances (r = 0.27) and a lower sports participation rate (r = –0.73). Further, larger schools have more challenges (r = 0.21), where challenges are measured as the factor scale discussed above. Schools that face more challenges also have more disturbances (r = 0.43) and a lower sports participation rate (r = –0.51).

Table 1 reports the results from two full, theoretical fixed effects models. One model reports results for the impact of participation in junior varsity and varsity sports; the other reports results for participation in the most popular varsity sports—boys' football and basketball, and girls' basketball. The models' goodness of fit is quite high, with implied R^2s of 0.86.

The results in the first panel of Table 1 show that both junior varsity/varsity sports and school enrollment have a significant effect on the disturbance rate in schools, as does their interaction. Further, the level of challenges also has a significant impact. While the simple correlation between the challenge scale and disturbances was positive, once other school variables are held constant, the level of challenges is associated with fewer disturbances: for every unit increase on the standardized challenge factor scale, which varies from –2.7 to +3.3, the percent of disturbances drops by almost 4 percent.

Ex post, this result may be consistent with the theory of social capital and cooperation used to explain the results for sports participation. School challenges, as measured in this study, indicate the relative presence of demographic, ethno-racial, and language subgroups within a school. Theoretically, being part of a subgroup fosters cooperative, pro-social behavior among those within the subgroup. As long as the subgroup is not given any special, socially protected status, such as that usually accorded to those who participate in varsity sports but not accorded to minority groups, the overall effect of subgroups will be to reduce disturbances in school rather than increase them (Miller and Brewer, 1985).

The significant interaction between sports participation and school size makes the individual coefficients associated with sports participation, school size, and their interaction difficult to interpret in a straightforward manner. However, the fact that the sign on the interaction term is negative while the sign on the sports term is positive means that the impact of sports participation increases disturbances in small schools but, at some point of inflection, as schools grow larger, sports participation decreases disturbances. Given the numerical estimates in the first panel of Table 1, that point of inflection is a school of size 1,155. This is not an exact point, since the coefficients are estimated with error. In fact, only two schools in the sample have enrollments that average less than 1,200. Thus, most of the impact of sports participation reflects its effect in larger schools, where it decreases disturbances as enrollment increases.

For example, in schools with enrollment in the first quartile of 1,289 or less, a 10 percent increase in the sports participation rate reduces disturbances by 0.4 percent on a scale ranging from 2–13%. For schools at the 75th percentile (enrollment = 1,800), the same 10 percent increase in sports participation reduces disturbances by nearly 2 percent, which is not small on a scale with a range of 11 percent.

The first panel of Table 1 also reveals that school size affects the disturbance rate; of course, its effect also depends on the sports participation rate. The results in Table 1 imply that when the sports participation rate is below a certain threshold, the effect of greater school size is to increase the disturbance rate; however, the coefficient becomes negative when the sports participation rate exceeds 70.1 percent. Since there is only one observation in the data set with this high a participation rate, the overall impact of school size on disturbances in the sample is to increase them. For a school with the average sports participation rate of 44 percent, the impact of increased enrollment on disturbances is 0.019–0.000271 (44%) = 0.007. That is, for a school with the average sports participation rate, each additional 100 students increases the disturbance rate by nearly 1 percent. Given that the disturbance rate in the sample ranges from 2 to 13 percent with an average of 7 percent, a nearly 1 percent increase is not small.

So far, the results in the first panel of Table 1 show that the impact of participation in junior varsity and varsity sports depends on school size. In Montgomery County, where the high schools are mostly over 1,500 in enrollment, the impact of increased sports participation is to reduce disturbances from what they would be otherwise.

The next panel replicates the same estimating equation, but examines only the impact of the subset of varsity sports likely to be the most glamorous because of their presence on TV as professional sports—boys' football and boys' and (arguably) girls' basketball. With the exception of the two key coefficients for the sports variables (the "direct" and interactive terms), the estimates are similar to those in the first panel of Table 1. But the coefficient for sports participation increases from 0.313 for those in overall junior varsity and varsity sports (Panel 1) to 1.86 for those on the top three varsity teams (Panel 2), and from –0.000271 for the interaction term between interscholastic sports and enrollment in Panel 1 to –0.0014 for the corresponding term for the interaction of top varsity sports with enrollment in Panel 2. However, since the ratio of these terms determines the sign of the overall impact of sports on disturbances in schools of different sizes, the substantive implication is no different. Participation in the top three sports reduces disturbances in schools with enrollments exceeding 1,329, which includes most of the schools in the sample. Thus, even participation in the allegedly prestige sports appears to mitigate disturbances, at least in the large high schools typical of those in Montgomery County.

CONCLUSIONS AND LIMITATIONS

This study provides evidence to suggest that Montgomery County Public Schools (MCPS) may want to foster more interscholastic athletic participation, especially as its schools grow larger. For most schools in the sample, widespread varsity and junior varsity athletic programs reduce the rate (and number) of disturbances. Moreover, the rate of reduction increases as the schools get larger. The results further show that participation in the interscholastic sports likely to be the most glamorous, and hence the most elite, also mitigates disturbances as schools get larger.

This study does not explain why expanding interscholastic sports programs apparently reduces disturbances in larger schools. It is possible that expanding opportunities for between-school sports in large schools may have two effects—one on the out-group, and one on the in-group. For the nonparticipants (the out-group), expanding junior varsity and varsity sports programs may make participation less scarce and therefore less valuable, less prestigious and less an affront to the nonparticipants. For the participants (the in-group), increasing the availability of different varsity sports programs in big schools may create a structure for the repeated interactions within each team (i.e., subgroup) that foster cooperative behavior. Expanding the seemingly most glamorous interscholastic sports programs appears to have similar effects, possibly because expansion may make participation less exclusive and therefore less of a snub to outsiders, even as it may create cooperative behavior among the insiders.

Further research is clearly needed to examine the reasons for disturbances in high schools and to verify the findings from this study in other settings. However, the findings, if they are upheld, have a clear implication for current policy. Within MCPS, and in high schools more generally (McNeal, 1999; Cotton, 1996), the largest schools have the fewest opportunities for sports and other extracurricular activities; they also have the highest rate of disturbances. The findings in this study suggest that, in respect to fostering pro-social behavior in high schools, the status quo of big schools with relatively small extracurricular programs is less than optimal: either the schools should be smaller, or opportunities for numerous and diverse interactive smaller groups within the larger group should be expanded (NASSP, 1996; Cooper, 1999).

However, there are several limitations to this study and further study is needed to provide more knowledge on the subject before any recommendations, especially costly ones, should be implemented. Selection is always a threat in nonexperimental studies such as this one because omitted confounding variables, left out because they are either unmeasureable or unknown, could result in biased estimates. Dummy variables for each school and year are a partial control for these omitted variables, but they are not a complete remedy for theoretical ignorance or measurement problems. For example, it would be useful to measure whether it is sports participants themselves, or nonparticipants, who are more involved in disturbances. This study posits that sports participation binds participants and, under certain conditions, such as those in large schools with small and apparently exclusive sports programs, alienates nonparticipants, but, without data on individual students, this explanation cannot be tested.

If, as this study conjectures, football and basketball (the principal "TV sports") are more glamorous than the others, then the results suggest that the expectation that high-prestige sports are more likely than "ordinary sports to alienate nonparticipants is incorrect. In fact, the study finds that the effect of between-school sports participation on disturbances does not depend on the apparent social status of the sport. However, this research, with no direct measure of the prestige of individual sports, cannot settle this issue at all. If the sports programs in this study are equally prestigious, then there is no test of the social status hypothesis in this study.

Although the findings of this study are based on data from only one suburban school system, there is little reason to believe that they are not generalizable to similar school districts. While the county is wealthier and spends more per pupil than most jurisdictions, the county is increasingly diverse in its race/ethnicity, income, and the percent who need English as a second language. Thus, in many respects, the county is representative of many other large suburban jurisdictions in the nation as a whole.

IMPLICATIONS

As violence in the schools and crimes committed by juveniles has shocked the nation on the nightly news, one possible method of decreasing the occurrence of these incidents might be to encourage involvement in diverse interscholastic sports as a method of building social capital, especially in large high schools.

It is not clear from this study alone what initiatives school officials in Montgomery County can take to provide a safer environment conducive to learning for their students. In a time when school violence is popularly viewed as being on the rise (Kaufman et al., 1998), viable solutions other than increased school security, which may violate students' rights, and longer suspensions need to be proposed. Yet, as school systems and individual schools grow, maintaining pro-social behavior in high schools is likely to become increasingly difficult. This study raises questions about the ability of small and presumably highly exclusive sports programs to generate social cooperation in all high school settings. It also suggests that enlarging and diversifying varsity sports programs in large high schools, by having lots of students on lots of different teams, or reducing the size of high schools, might be practical options for fostering social capital in high schools.

Positive Deviance Among Athletes: The Implications of Overconformity to the Sport Ethic

ROBERT HUGHES AND JAY COAKLEY

Since the mid-1970s the media have frequently reported cases of deviance among those connected with sports. Exposés on sport often infer that deviance is pervasive and that it is grounded in widespread disregard or rejection of norms by coaches and athletes, especially black athletes in highly visible or revenue producing sports, who underconform to commonly held rules of conduct. Since popular beliefs have traditionally emphasized the positive consequences of sport participation, the seemingly unending litany of publicized cases of deviance in sport has shocked and disappointed many people. In their disappointment, some have concluded that deviance in sport is simply proof that the moral basis of society is eroding. Many have called for new selection standards to keep "troublemakers" out of sport, tougher methods of rule enforcement, and stronger sanctions.

Often overlooked in these calls for more rigid external systems of social control is the fact that deviant behavior among athletes is a complex, diversified phenomenon, and that athletes' lives are already controlled through often repressive systems of social control. We argue that a significant portion of deviance among athletes does not involve disregarding or rejecting commonly accepted cultural goals or means to those goals, nor does it result from alienation from society. Instead, it is grounded in athletes' uncritical acceptance of and commitment to what they have been told by important people in their lives ever since they began participating in competitive programs; in a real sense, it is the result of being too committed to the goals and norms of sport.

Throughout their lives, athletes have heard again and again of the need to be dedicated, to set goals, to persevere until goals are achieved, to define adversity as a challenge, and to be willing to make sacrifices and subjugate other experiences generally associated with "growing up" all for the sake of their quest to become all they can be in sport. Coaches have emphasized the need to "pay the price," to "play with pain," and to "shoot for the top." These messages have been and continue to be repeated in the words of sport commentators who praise those who play with injuries as "courageous" and those who return to play after serious injuries as being "dedicated to the game" (Gifford & Mangel, 1977). Locker room slogans and sport publicity reinforce these norms (Snyder, 1972; Snyder & Spreitzer, 1989).

Most people in sport, including journalists, fans, owners, sponsors, commentators, coaches, trainers, *and athletes*, accept these norms. Indeed they often internalize them and use them as standards for evaluating themselves and others as "real athletes." In many cases, strict conformity to these norms becomes the basis for acceptance onto a team and a measure of status among athletes themselves. This encourages some athletes to overconform to these norms in ways seen as deviant within society as a whole and even within the governing bodies of sport itself.

This type of deviance is dangerous and certainly a case for concern. However, it is important to recognize that it is grounded in a different set of social dynamics than the deviance of young people who reject commonly accepted rules and expectations and engage in underconforming behavior. It is our contention that this difference between what might be called positive deviance and negative deviance must be taken into account when studying behavior in sport, and when recommending ways of controlling deviance in sport. This is *not* to say that all deviance in sport or all deviance among athletes is positive deviance; nor is it to say that overconformity to commonly accepted norms within sport is characteristic among the majority of athletes. But positive deviance does exist in sport, and that constitutes an especially serious challenge for those interested in reforming sport.

POSITIVE DEVIANCE AND THE SPORT ETHIC

This is intended as a working paper in which we outline a conceptual framework for explaining a special type of behavior within sport. Our intention is not to explain all behavior among athletes or all deviance in sport. Our hypothesis is simply that many forms of deviance in sport are not caused by a disregard or rejection of social values or norms; instead, they are caused by an unqualified acceptance of and an unquestioned commitment to a value system framed by what we refer to as the sport ethic.

The sport ethic refers to what many participants in sport have come to use as the criteria for defining what it means to be a real athlete. The criteria described below are not intended to be exhaustive, but informal reports from athletes and from coaches in coaching education programs, combined with information from autobiographies of numerous sport figures, strongly suggest that the following four beliefs are commonly accepted as factors defining what it means to identify oneself as an athlete and to be treated as an athlete by others in sport:

1. *Being an athlete involves making sacrifices for The Game.* The idea underlying this dimension of the sport ethic is that real athletes must love The Game above all else and prove it by

subordinating other interests for the sake of an exclusive commitment to their sport. To prove they care about their sport, participants must have "the proper attitude" (a term commonly used by coaches), make a commitment, meet the demands of fellow athletes, and sacrifice to stay involved. In this sense, being an athlete means that a person will consistently do what is necessary to meet the demands of a team or the demands of competition. This is the spirit underlying the notion that athletes must make sacrifices, that they must be willing to pay the price to stay involved in sport. Pep talks and locker room slogans are full of references to this guideline (Snyder, 1972; Snyder & Spreitzer, 1989).

2. *Being an athlete involves striving for distinction.* The Olympic motto of *"Citius, Altius, Fortius"* (swifter, higher, stronger) captures the meaning of this normative dimension of the sport ethic. True athletes seek to improve, to get better, to come closer to perfection. Winning symbolizes improvement and establishes distinction; losing is tolerated only to the extent that it is part of the experience of learning how to win. Breaking records is the ultimate standard of achievement in sport. This is because real athletes are a special group dedicated to climbing the pyramid, reaching for the top, pushing limits, excelling, and exceeding or dominating others. Of course external rewards may be associated with involvement, but the validation of one's identity as an athlete is primarily tied to one's immersion in the quest for distinction rather than gaining external rewards. It is worth noting here that sport scientists have intervened in sport in ways that certainly reinforce this guideline and promote overconformity to it; their development of and occasional unquestioned application of many new performance enhancing technologies has become an important part of this process of striving for distinction among athletes at elite levels.

3. *Being an athlete involves accepting risks and playing through pain.* According to the sport ethic, an athlete does not give in to pressure, pain, or fear. Many sport activities pose inherent risks of injury, but voluntarily accepting the possibility of injury is a sign of courage and dedication among athletes (Donnelly, 1980, 1981; Williams & Donnelly, 1985). In addition to courage in the face of physical challenges, moral courage is also implied in this normative guideline. This is reflected even in golf and tennis, for example, wherein athletes are expected to sustain high levels of physical performance under extreme psychological and social pressure. The idea is that athletes never back down from challenges in the form of either physical risk or pressure, and that standing up to challenges involves moral courage.

Furthermore, athletes are expected to display "coolness" (as conceptualized by Lyman & Scott, 1970, p.145) and "composure" (as conceptualized by Goffman, 1967, pp. 222–223) as they willingly confront and overcome the fears and challenges associated with competition and accept the increasing risk of failure and injury that comes with higher levels of competition. As American athletes prepare for the 1992 Olympic Games in Barcelona, one of the most popular T-shirts at the U.S. Olympic Training Center carries the slogan, "No pain, no Spain." If the willingness to conform to this aspect of the sport ethic wanes, then sport physicians, sport psychologists, and other sport scientists will help athletes overcome and deal with risks, pain, and fears.

4. *Being an athlete involves refusing to accept limits in the pursuit of possibilities.* People in sport generally stress the possibilities for achievement and the imperative to wholeheartedly pursue them. An athlete does not accept a situation without trying to change it, overcome it, turn the scales. It is believed that sport is a sphere of life in which anything is possible, *if* a person lives by the sport ethic. An athlete is a person obligated to pursue dreams without reservation. External limits are not recognized as valid. True athletes are obligated to believe in *the attempt* to achieve success. And when the perception of limits threatens to impede achievement, there are many sport experts who will provide pep talks, therapy, or technology to alter those perceptions.

How is the sport ethic related to deviance in sport? Deviance is usually assumed to involve a rejection of norms (or at least allegiance to norms that conflict with other, more well-established norms), and it is also defined by most social scientists as negative in the sense that it is behavior that is morally condemned and punished. However, a portion of the deviance (i.e., behavior that is morally condemned and dangerous) among athletes does not involve a rejection of norms, or conformity to a set of norms not endorsed in the rest of society. Instead, many problem behaviors are created when athletes care too much for, accept too completely, and overconform to what has become the value system of sport itself, including both goals and means (cf. Merton's terminology from his 1957 discussion of anomie and deviance). This is especially true for high performance athletes, although it is certainly not limited to them; the phenomenon even occurs at youth league levels.

Although there is a need to empirically investigate this phenomenon, some studies have identified the existence of normative overconformity among athletes. Ewald and Jiobu (1985) found that serious athletes often zealously pursued and overconformed to the norms within their sport groups to such an extent that their sport participation was disruptive to everything from their family relationships and work responsibilities to their physical health and personal comfort. Other people saw these athletes as deviant, but the behavior of the athletes themselves actually reflected commonly held values and norms, although involving an unrestrained commitment and overconformity to these norms. Hilliard and Hilliard (1990) identified not only an awareness of and commitment to the guidelines of the sport ethic as it is explained in this paper, but also overconformity to the sport ethic among triathletes and weightlifters. Another study, developed along very different lines, found strong similarities between compulsive long-distance runners and anorectic patients in a treatment program (Nash, 1987). Both behaviors were classified as "addictive-like" overconforming responses to commonly accepted norms. In other words, the runners and anorectics went too far in conforming with the expectations that people should exercise and control their diets; they overconformed to the point that they engaged in positive deviance.

Similarly, 32% of the women athletes surveyed at a major university in the U.S. admitted to using various forms of pathogenic weight control behaviors in conjunction with their sport participation

(Rosen, McKeag, Hough, & Curley, 1986). As with athletes in the other studies, the behavior of these women was deviant in the sense that they had gone too far in their efforts to live up to widely accepted expectations for physical appearance and for what it means to be an athlete.

We hypothesize that rates of positive deviance in sport are related to the special characteristics of sport experiences and systems of sponsorship in sport organizations. Overconformity to the sport ethic is prompted by the following factors:

1. Athletes find the action (Ball, 1972) and their experiences in sport so exhilarating and thrilling that they want to continue participating as long as possible.
2. The likelihood of being chosen or sponsored for continued participation is increased if athletes overconform to the sport ethic (i.e., coaches praise overconformers and often make them models for other athletes; furthermore, coaches often accuse athletes of lacking hustle, effort, and caring, and athletes can only prove hustle and effort through unquestioned conformity to the sport ethic).

Thus many athletes do not see their overconformity to the sport ethic as deviant; they see it as confirming and reconfirming their identity as athletes and as members of select sport groups. Following the guidelines of the sport ethic to an extreme is just what you do as an athlete, especially when continued participation and success in sport take on significant personal and social meaning.

Although developed here primarily in relation to sport, the concept of positive deviance has applications in many other contexts. However, our major point (to be developed below in the section on theoretical support) is that it identifies a type of behavior not easily explained by general theories of deviance. Through positive deviance people do harmful things to themselves and perhaps others while motivated by a sense of duty and honor. Those who engage in such behavior do not claim or accept a deviant identity, nor do they see their deviant behavior as a basis for a master status (Wasielewski, 1991). They are not members of low status groups whose behavior threatens those with higher status; therefore, they are not generally labeled as deviant. *But* they clearly engage in extreme behaviors at a rate and in a manner that distinguishes them from others in society.

Despite its social implications, this kind of problematic behavior is often ignored by sociologists and left to be explained by psychologists, who refer to it in terms of individual differences. Yet we know that good people acting for good reasons have clearly done great harm to themselves and others. Milgram (1974), Zimbardo, Haney, Banks, & Jaffe (1982), and Arendt (1963) have shown that following the prescriptions for "being the best one can be" is an accurate albeit frightening explanation of the behaviors of Nazi prison guards. Furthermore, evidence to be summarized below shows that test pilots, mountain climbers, and scores of others consistently take unnecessary risks, exposing themselves and others to danger in order to prove they are good and worthy persons who have earned the right to claim a restricted (achieved) social identity.

Important to note is that attempting to change the behavior of such persons by helping them learn to conform to social rules and live up to social expectations would only increase their deviance. Although this paper deals with overconformity and positive deviance in the context of sport, the conceptual framework offered has implications for how sociology might define and explain a wide range of deviance outside the context of sport as well.

Conditions Leading to Overconformity

Not all athletes are equally likely to engage in overconformity to the sport ethic. We hypothesize that positive deviance is most common among the following:

1. Those athletes who have low self-esteem or who, for other reasons, are vulnerable to group demands and less able to withstand pressures to sacrifice themselves for the group;
2. Those athletes who see sport as an exclusive mobility route, and for whom mobility demands an extreme commitment to achievement and a willingness to make great personal sacrifices as they strive for achievement.

In other words, athletes whose identity or future chances for material success are exclusively tied to sport are most likely to engage in overconforming behavior. This too needs to be explored through research, but it is expected that overconformity to the sport ethic would be more characteristic among men than women (since men are more likely to use sport as an exclusive identity and/or mobility source), among low income minority athletes in revenue producing sports (for similar reasons), and among those whose relationships with significant others have been based exclusively on continued involvement and success in sport.

As self-identification becomes lodged within sport, a person is increasingly susceptible to control that is grounded in the demands of the sport and sport groups. Therefore, what we might refer to as the corruption of sport at least partially involves a process by which common restraints on behavior give way to encouragement to engage in potentially self-destructive behaviors in an effort to demonstrate worthiness for continued group membership and status within a specific sport group. It is the athlete's vulnerability to group demands, combined with the desire to gain or reaffirm group membership through overconforming to these demands, that is a critical factor in the incidence of positive deviance.

Along these lines, it has been suggested that one of the qualities of great coaches is their ability to create an environment that keeps athletes in a perpetual state of adolescence. This leads athletes to continually strive to confirm their identity and eliminate self-doubts by engaging in behaviors that please their coaches and teammates. When this dependency based commitment occurs, overconformity to the sport ethic becomes increasingly common and many young people willingly sacrifice their body and play with reckless abandon in the pursuit of affirmation and approval as athletes. Coaches often encourage this, intentionally or naively. For example, Jerry Kramer, a former Green Bay Packer football player, alluded to this when he made the following observation about his coach, Vince Lombardi:

> I suppose I shouldn't have been, but I was amazed by how Vince Lombardi, the high school coach, paralleled Vince Lombardi, the professional coach, down to his insistence…that every player show up for every meeting and every practice not on schedule, but ahead of schedule. (Kramer, 1971, pp. 14–15)

Kempton (1971) also attributed Lombardi's success to his ability to keep groups of grown men at the maturity level of the average high school sophomore. A coach who can do this encourages, intentionally or naively, positive deviance in the form of overconformity to the sport ethic.

Overconformity and Bonds Between Athletes

Collective commitment to the sport ethic, especially under conditions of extreme stress, may also lead to the creation of special bonds between athletes in certain sport groups. To the extent that this occurs, these bonds not only reaffirm their unqualified acceptance of and commitment to the sport ethic on a day-to-day basis but also generate special feelings of fraternity, especially in groups of athletes in the same sports, and especially in sports wherein athletes are perceived to be unique because they endure extreme challenges and risks. These special feelings separate athletes from other people when it comes to what athletes see as a true understanding of the sport experience. Most athletes do not think outsiders know what it is really like to be an athlete; nonathletes just do not understand. This is illustrated by former professional football player Dave Meggyesy:

> Being a professional athlete was so strange. The real beauty of the experience is the actual play, the exhilaration of it, physically and emotionally. But because you have fans...who get so crazy about the game and feel so deeply about it, you have...people dissecting your every move and thought. [After the game] there are microphones all over the place, and everyone wants you to explain things: "Why did you screw up?" "Why did you hit that hole instead of the other one?" "How does it feel?" And you have to respond to all these people who never knew the first thing about what it feels like....It's like making love and having to explain it to someone every time. (quoted in Remnick, 1987, p. 46).

When this sense of separateness and uniqueness is combined with the fact that athletes are often held in awe by outsiders and attract more media attention than heads of state, athletes may develop a feeling of superiority. Although there is a need to study the existence, origins, and correlates of these feelings of superiority, we suggest that they do exist among some athletes and that they are often accompanied by a sense of disdain for those "normal" members of the community who live their lives without sacrificing for sport, seeking distinction, taking risks, or pushing limits, and who therefore do not have an experiential basis for understanding the pure exhilaration of living life in this way.

Tom Wolfe (1979), in his analysis of test pilot/ astronauts, identified very similar feelings of fraternity, superiority, and disdain for outsiders. These feelings were so evident that he captured them in the title of his book, *The Right Stuff*. Wolfe's description could easily be applied to athletes in many sport settings:

> in this fraternity, men were not rated by their outward rank....No, herein the world was divided into those who had it and those who did not.

> A career in flying was like climbing one of those ancient Babylonian pyramids made up of a dizzy progression of steps and ledges...and the idea was to prove at every foot of the way up that pyramid that you were one of the elected and anointed ones who had *the right stuff* and

could move higher and higher and even...that you might be able to join that special few at the very top. (Wolfe, 1979, p. 24)

Wolfe further imagined how these feelings of separateness and uniqueness might affect a test pilot/astronaut's perception of "normal outsiders"; his words clearly infer the existence of disdain:

From up here at dawn the pilot looked down upon the poor hopeless [city below]...and began to wonder:...how could they live like that...if they had the faintest idea of what it was like up here in this righteous zone? Danger, excitement, special standing, a way of life more significant than possible for all but a very few, a small slice indeed of mankind who can obtain it—facing danger, overcoming fear, shooting dice with death, a small price to pay for such extraordinary living, for the opportunity to be among the very best. (Wolfe, 1979, p. 39)

In the case of athletes in highly visible sports, this process of developing fraternity, superiority, and disdain for outsiders might also lead some of them to naively assume they are somehow beyond the law, and that people outside the athletic fraternity do not deserve their respect. This could lead to serious cases of negative deviance including, for example, assault, sexual assault, and rape (including gang rape), the destruction of property, reckless driving, and alcohol abuse.

Another possibility is that this disdain can become such a part of an athlete's view of the nonsport world that it may even be turned inward and transformed into self-disdain or panic when athletes fail to overconform to the guidelines of the sport ethic in their own behavior, or when they must retire from active participation. This may be one of the reasons why athletes try so hard to extend their playing careers and why some even mourn its passing. Losing membership in the special and elite athletic fraternity presents difficulties in itself, but the threat of entering the disdained category of nonathlete or outsider is especially upsetting. Becoming separated from those few others who truly understand what it means to be an athlete can be a frightening experience, especially for those whose identity and feelings of significance and superiority are exclusively tied to sport. This is probably one reason why the retirement of highly competitive athletes has been conceptualized as a form of "social death" in some research (Brandmeyer & Alexander, 1982; Lerch, 1984; Rosenberg, 1984).

This may also be one reason why some athletes have knee surgery after knee surgery so they can play for "just one more year," and why others inject unbelievable amounts of hormones into their bodies on a regular basis without even thinking twice. The motivation is *not* just to win, or to make money, or to please a TV audience; more important, it is simply *to play, to be an athlete*, and *to maintain their membership in the special and elite athletic fraternity*. This is why a mediocre athlete on a second rate team may also engage in positive deviance such as taking performance enhancing substances, whether they be megadoses of vitamin B-12 or anabolic steroids: The athlete knows there are no championships to be won or money to be made, but there is an identity and moral worth to be established and reaffirmed, and a connection to a coach and a group of teammates to be honored. These are powerful motives.

This emphasis on the connection between positive deviance and identity and social relationships clearly grounds our model in a sociological framework. Our explanation of deviance cannot be reduced to a psychological model in which deviance is tied to an individual pursuit of self-interest in the form of external rewards.

Positive Deviance and Social Control Problems

Deviance grounded in overconformity to the sport ethic presents special control problems in sport. Owners, managers, sponsors, and coaches—all of whom exercise control within sport—often benefit when athletes overaccept and overconform to the sport ethic (Young, 1991). Having athletes who overzealously pursue the ideals framed by the ethic is seen by most of these people as a blessing. The fact that athletes have learned to use overconformity to the sport ethic as a gauge of personal commitment and courage for themselves and fellow athletes works to the advantage of those concerned with victories or entertainment. The issue of social control is even further complicated by the tendency to promote extreme overconformers into positions of power and influence in sport—after all, they have already proven they are willing to pay the price and live the sport ethic to the fullest.

This guarantees that athletes receive continued strong encouragement to overconform to the guidelines of the sport ethic. This also means that a powerful source of deviance and ethical problems among athletes lies in sport itself, in athletes' relationships with one another, and in their relationships with coaches and managers. Paradoxically, the sport ethic when taken to an extreme actually promotes the corruption of sport (see below).

THEORETICAL SUPPORT FOR THE CONCEPT OF POSITIVE DEVIANCE

Sagarin (1985) and Goode (1990) have argued that positive deviance is an oxymoron—unless behavior is defined as different in kind and unless it is despised and punished, it does not qualify as deviant. However, even though a strong case can be made for the concept of positive deviance (e.g., Buffalo & Rodgers, 1971; Dodge, 1987; Ewald & Jiobu, 1985; Heckert, 1989), the debate is confusing because the sociology of deviance as a whole is characterized by theoretical chaos and by the tendency to ignore the relationship between deviance and social dynamics within total social structures (Ben-Yehuda, 1990).

Our purpose is not to enter this debate. In this working paper we follow the lead of Ewald and Jiobu (1985) and Dodge (1987), and suggest that many aspects of the problem behaviors engaged in by athletes cannot be explained simply as violations of sport norms or as conformity to a set of norms that are not endorsed within society at large. We argue that these problem behaviors, including such things as the use of performance enhancing substances (both legal and illegal) in excessive amounts, engaging in excessive on-the-field violence (both legal and illegal), and violating certain game or association rules (such as those restricting eligibility, limiting practice times, prohibiting participation in unsanctioned competitive events) are best explained as the result of overconformity to the norms of sport itself. In other words, they are the result of caring too much for or accepting too completely the goals and values of sport.

We are not arguing that athletes engage in what Merton (1957) has identified as "innovation" grounded in the acceptance of cultural goals and the concomitant rejection of accepted means to those goals. Merton's framework renders athletes as mere opportunists. This is inappropriate since athletes who engage in positive deviance accept goals as well as means to an extreme degree and without critical examination of either. Both goals and means are "overdetermined" and extended to an excessive degree. Instead of innovation, positive deviance in sport reflects more the notion of the hero's quest, or the extraordinary, rather than mere utilitarianism. Therefore if Merton's framework is applicable in any way, the behavior we are describing would best fit into an extension of the conformity category, but this misses the point.

Our approach is also slightly different from that proposed by Dodge (1987), and very different from that criticized by Sagarin since much of the publicized positive deviance athletes engage in is indeed negatively evaluated and sanctioned by those outside of sport, and often by administrators within the governing bodies of the sports themselves. However, these behaviors, even though defined as deviant, are different *only in degree, not in kind*, from behaviors valued positively in the rest of society. Again, it is emphasized that the norms of the sport ethic are positive norms; it is under the condition of uncritical acceptance and extreme overconformity that they are associated with dangerous and destructive behaviors. We are referring to deviance that would ultimately lead to fascism, not anarchy.

Our conceptualization of positive deviance is also somewhat different from "semi-deviance" as described by Etzioni-Halevy (1975). Semi-deviance refers to behaviors generally perceived as too extreme or bizarre to be normal, yet not negative enough to be defined as morally bad. In other words, Etzioni-Halevy infers that deviance can be conceptualized in terms of a continuum of behaviors varying from normal, to slightly deviant, to semi-deviant, to very deviant; semi-deviance "falls in to a no-one's land between behavior that is normatively fully condoned and that which is flatly condemned by a given group or society" (p. 356). However, describing deviance in this way infers that extremely conforming behavior is the ideal and that digressions from the ideal represent varying degrees of deviance. We would argue that this approach miscasts empirical reality.

Our intent is to abandon the traditional assumption that extreme conformity to an ideal pattern of good behavior should be considered the norm for evaluating human action across all social situations. When this assumption is made, there is the implication that the appropriate response to any deviant or problem behavior is to introduce additional programs of social control intended to increase conformity to the ideal. But if efforts to generate extreme conformity actually produced ideal moral behavior, there would be little or no deviance among the police, in the military, or among athletes for that matter. However, these groups are often the settings for serious problems of deviance.

Although abstinence from just about everything (the "just say no" approach) is the ideal proposed by numerous moral entrepreneurs and those in the clutches of moral panics of one form or another, we would argue that it is dangerous to accept such a definition of prosocial or desirable behavior. When conformity is conceptualized in terms of total abstinence, the analysis of deviance misrepresents what is normal, often necessary, and usually desirable in social life. After all, behaviors such as drinking, sexual expression, fighting, and questioning authority are not only socially acceptable and moral across a wide range of social situations but they are sometimes even necessary or morally prescribed.

Similar to our conceptualization of positive deviance, Wasielewski (1991) uses the notion of *defiance* to capture the idea that some kinds of deviance are created by groups who take good and acceptable behaviors, such as working for peace or physical fitness, to the extreme. She notes that the "deviance of the athlete and the [peace] activist resides not only in the acts in which they engage, but more precisely in the degree to which they carry these activities" (p. 85). For example, ultramarathon athletes thrive "on pushing the limits of physical and mental endurance" (p. 85). Wasielewski argues that although people who engage in extreme activities are deviant, their status as such is highly transitory. She points out that deviance is not always or only a status created by others who label a person as deviant; sometimes deviance is grounded in self-initiated efforts to establish social uniqueness through a pursuit of specific goals. In this way, deviance is tied to "a process of self- and social discovery" (p. 89).

In addition to Wasielewski's discussion, there are several other discussions of deviance that are closely aligned with our conceptualization of positive deviance. For example, Cavan and Ferdinand (1981) and Dodge (1987) use the notion of a normal statistical distribution and conceptualize deviance as behaviors falling outside the middle range of the distribution. According to their conceptualization, most behaviors fall within a normally accepted range and the rest involve deviance in terms of either underconformity or overconformity to norms. Unfortunately, those using this model often infer that overconformity is associated with excessive virtue, or that it is the source of virtue, and that persons who deviate through overconformity tend to be rewarded positively for their extreme excellence.

This association between positive deviance and virtuosity has been seriously challenged by studies of alcohol use among adults (Valliant, 1983) and drug use among adolescents (Shedler & Block, 1990). For example, Valliant's study of drinking behaviors among adult males in the United States found that abstinence, as achieved by overconformers and the self-righteous, was *not* associated with psychological well-being or social adjustment. Adults who engaged in moderate social drinking exhibited the highest levels of overall mental health.

A similar pattern was found by Shedler and Block in their study of adolescent drug use: both substance abusers *and abstainers* seem to be psychologically impaired in serious ways and have social histories characterized by family relationships that created anxiety, inhibitions, and a lack of social responsiveness. Within the context of the 1980s peer subculture, it was the adolescents who had used alcohol and experimented with marijuana (without developing abuse patterns) who exhibited the highest level of psychological health, and whose social histories led them to score high on measures of social adjustment. In other words, in both these studies, overconformity was not found to always be a virtue or the source of virtue, and moderate amounts of social drinking or experimentation with drugs are not indicative of varying degrees of deviance (as some prohibitionists are now arguing).

The serious problems often associated with extreme conformity to cultural ideals have also been identified by Westkott (1986). She notes that many so-called personality disorders among women are the result of their tendency to overconform to traditional gender role expectations. According to Westkott's analysis, many distraught women are most accurately described as "supranormal" rather than abnormal. These women experience difficulties because their sense of self is not strong enough to overcome the demands for conformity to a set of expectations defined for them by others. As they conscientiously or desperately attempt to conform to these expectations, their selves are diminished and weakened and psychological problems arise.

The importance of distinguishing deviance (either positive or negative) that results from excessive compliance with norms from deviance originating in outright norm violations or conformity to alternative norms has been outlined in Tinto's (1987) discussion of Durkheim s original typology of the sources of deviance. Tinto views the relationship between the individual and the social order in terms of two dimensions: control and integration. A person may be overcontrolled (fatalistic) or undercontrolled (anomic), overintegrated (altruistic) or underintegrated (egoistic, i.e., alienated from an otherwise satisfactorily organized group). This typology indicates that inducements to deviance exist on the positive side of each dimension, that is, among those who are overcontrolled or overintegrated. Deviance in these cases results from external demands encouraging a person to act in the best interests of others rather than self (overcontrolled, fatalistic; e.g., gladiators or slaves, respectively), or to act out of a sense of membership in a group wherein one's status as a member calls for sacrificing self-interest and personal preferences (overintegrated, altruistic).

This conception of deviance differs from traditional conceptions in which negative deviance is seen as the result of (a) confusion about norms or rules, (b) being caught between conflicting norms or rules, and/or (c) feelings of alienation from established groups.

Finally, we suggest that excessive commitment to the sport ethic tends to be defined among many athletes as supranormal, in the sense of the Neitzschean "superman," and in the sense of the hubris that can emerge among those who feel or believe they are above the ordinary and live a life at the edge. This hubris, coming in the form of arrogance grounded in excessive pride, may include a disdain for those ordinary persons who only live by the rules to the extent that they never push limits. This disdain for others, as exhibited by many athletes, may also be an important motivational source for their off-the-field deviance.

Positive Deviance and Identity Issues

Overconforming to the normative demands of sport involves a process in which the role of athlete (player, climber, skier, runner, etc.) becomes extremely salient to a person's identity. Since identity is social in nature, the acceptance and confirmation of one's status as an athlete is crucial (Donnelly & Young, 1988). The process of being defined and gaining acceptance in society as a real athlete is interactive, progressive, and voluntary.

By *interactive* we mean that the qualities used to define a person as able and acceptable as an athlete in a certain group must be demonstrated to others in a way that proves worthiness. As was pointed out in the discussion of the sport ethic, this usually takes the form of paying the price in one way or another.

By *progressive* we mean to call attention to the notion that continued participation in any sport generally demands increasing levels of commitment and the sacrificing of outside interests in order to keep moving up the hierarchy or the pyramid to the next competitive level. In baseball for example, this move would be from sandlot to Little League, to high school, to semi-pro or college, to minor league, to major league. If individuals drop out of this sequence at some point, they can continue participating in a recreational sense but will be denied status and identity as a real athlete. Since defining athlete as a status gives significance to obtaining social recognition of that which a person claims to be, this notion of the progressive demonstration of competence is as true for climbing and tennis as it is for football and volleyball.

By *voluntary* we mean to imply that a person can choose not to participate and suffer no general negative sanction (other than being called a quitter by some people), or the diminishment of life chances (as would be the case if the person dropped out of school or a job). Indeed, it is the voluntary nature of sport involvement that is key to its moral significance. When a person makes sacrifices for the sake of achievement and winning in sport, it is because a choice and personal commitment has been made. An excellent description of the process of taking on a voluntary and highly salient identity is provided by Dornbush (1955) in his analysis of the military academy.

Donnelly and Young (1988) also outline a similar process of establishing a sport identity in informal, self-controlled sport situations associated with climbing and North American rugby. The process they identify is characterized by a four-step sequence: presocialization, selection and recruitment, socialization, and acceptance/ostracism. They note that the process of identity construction and confirmation that occurs during socialization into a subcultural career "involves ceasing to consider outsiders [i.e., not athletes] as a valued audience" (1988, p. 224). Their findings certainly imply that rules created by persons external to the group are of limited importance. Similarly, Ewald and Jiobu outline a slightly different series of four steps leading to positive addiction for runners and bodybuilders. They point out that "What the outsider perceives as self-torture, the insider redefines as enjoyable and worthy of pursuing for its intrinsic rewards" (1985, p. 147).

Positive Deviance and the Commitment to Action

The process by which norms that encourage deviant and dangerous behavior actually emerge through the interaction of peers has been outlined by Sato (1989) in his "play theory of delinquency." Sato focuses on a more general, informal context than sport but uses concepts very similar to those describing the development of a sport identity. Sato argues that youth are naturally drawn to action, typically during their leisure time with peers outside the purview of adults. This action may involve some illegal activity but is most accurately characterized by comparing it to its opposite, which is sitting around the house doing nothing, being bored, or doing whatever parents want you to do all the time. Sato builds on this point and explains that this focus on action among young people is inherently volatile and subject to corruption. This process of corruption is conceptualized in the same way we are conceptualizing positive deviance as a form of overconformity. His words are informative:

> While the playlike definition of the situation can provide youngsters with a sense of meaning and purpose, *excessive commitment* to the definition sometimes leads to fatal and irrevocable consequences, because "action" has an inherent tendency towards "corruption"...There are at least three elements in "action" which lead to such consequences: collective encouragement, intense involvement, and a challenge to reach the limit. (1989, p. 203, emphasis added)

In other words, interaction among peers can lead to an excessive commitment to action. This action, used as proof of group membership or attachment to peers, often pushes limits and comes in extreme forms; the more extreme the behavior, the more one is able to demonstrate commitment to group norms. Initiation rites are institutionalized demands for excessive commitment to group norms.

This process is very similar to the process identified by Donnelly and Young (1988) and Ewald and Jiobu (1985) in their analyses of the behavioral implications of the development of sport identities. Seeking and participating in action is the norm; negative deviance occurs when a person avoids action altogether, and positive deviance occurs when a person becomes overcommitted to maintaining and extending action. Intensive involvement in a group in which there is collective encouragement to push limits and pay the price produces an excessive commitment to action that is destructive, not necessarily desired, and deviant. The "corruption of action" and the promotion of deviance, therefore, lie in the processes of group interaction among athletes themselves. This creates a situation in which what might be called the sport ethic is a crystallization of norms that tend to corrupt sport. It is *"citius, altius, fortius"* taken seriously, and to the extreme. This happens in the same way that norms among young peers in informal play situations tend to corrupt action.

The notion of being overcommitted to action in play, or to pushing the limits in sport, has been clearly explained in the account of Daedalus and Icarus:

> When Daedalus, who can be thought of as the master technician of most ancient Greece, put the wings he had made on his son Icarus, so that he might fly out of and escape the Cretan labyrinth which he himself had invented, he said to him: "Fly the middle way. Don't fly too high, or the sun will melt the wax on your wings, and you will fall. Don't fly too low, or the tides of the sea will catch you." Daedalus himself flew the middle way, but he watched his son become ecstatic and fly too high. The wax melted, and the boy fell into the sea…but Daedalus, who flew the middle way, succeeded in getting to the other shore. (Campbell, 1988, pp. 131–132)

Campbell follows this story with an interpretation of the tragic fates often endured by heroes and a word of advice to those who take the hero's journey:

> When you are doing something that is a brand new adventure, [such as living in a way] that is not what the community can help you with, there's always the danger of too much enthusiasm, of neglecting certain…details. Then you fall off. When you follow the path of your desire and enthusiasm and emotion, keep your mind in control, and don't let it pull you compulsively into disaster. (Campbell, 1988, p. 132)

Unfortunately, many athletes never bear these words of caution; they are not encouraged to seek excellence by "flying the middle way," by following the example of Daedalus. Instead they are encouraged to fly too high—into the sun. Not surprisingly, they get caught up in the adventure and, when they do, they frequently meet the same fate as Icarus. With this in mind, it is appropriate to use the positive deviance model to explain a specific form of deviance in sport.

APPLICATION OF THE POSITIVE DEVIANCE MODEL

The positive deviance model provides a useful explanation of athletes' use of performance enhancing substances, especially the potentially dangerous ones. For most athletes the use of these substances is not the result of defective socialization or lack of moral character. After all, users are often the most dedicated and committed athletes in sport! Nor are the users helpless victims of coaches and trainers who lack moral character, although when coaches and trainers get carried away in their endorsement of the sport ethic, they may directly or indirectly encourage the use of performance enhancing substances. But most substance use and abuse is clearly tied to an overcommitment to the sport ethic itself; it is grounded in overconformity—the same type of overconformity that leads injured distance runners to continue training even when training may cause serious physical problems, and American football players to risk their bodies through excessively violent physical contact week after painful week in the NFL.

Those sport critics who argue that an emphasis on winning or human greed is *the* cause of deviance in sport are creating a smokescreen, subverting efforts to deal with some serious problems. Ironically, these critics conclude that the only way to deal with problems in sport is to institute even more controls over athletes who are overcontrolled already! In this way, "humanistic" critics unwittingly offer recommendations that could have come from the pages of *Beyond Freedom and Dignity* (Skinner, 1971). At the same time, these critics ignore the fact that many athletes who clearly realize they will never win championships or make money from their athletic accomplishments still engage in deviance, including on-the-field violence and taking performance enhancing drugs. This is not to say that a desire to win or make money is irrelevant to athletes; both are important parts of the overall context in which many forms of deviance occur. But much deviance among athletes clearly rests in overconforming to the positive values promoted through the sport ethic itself.

The implications of this model become especially clear when programs to control the use of performance enhancing substances and other forms of deviance are considered. Making recommendations to try to control deviance grounded in overconformity to accepted values is a challenge, because one must realize that athletes themselves assume a good deal of complicity in perpetuating substance use. More rules and tougher rule enforcement are only of limited value when trying to control this type of deviance. For example, Terry Todd's own history of abuse of performance enhancing drugs as a power lifter (Todd, 1983) clearly shows how athletes continually seek to defeat rather than comply with drug testing programs.

As long as athletes are committed to the sport ethic without qualification, they will think it honorable to try anything to stay involved in sport. This is not only the spirit in which Ben Johnson took steroids but also the spirit in which a substitute football player on an American football team with a mediocre record takes steroids. Of course they want to win, but the main reason for their deviance is to live up to the ideal of being an athlete and to maintain membership in the athletic fraternity. Their goal is to show through their deeds that they belong in a special group, a group comprised of people willing to pay the price, strive for distinction, accept risks, and exceed limits.

Section VIII: Deviance in Sport

This sense of membership and superiority is so important and powerful that it may be the reason why no other athletes blew the whistle on Ben Johnson's steroid use until he rejected his connection with them by naming so many others. Athletes know that the real measure of one's membership in the athletic fraternity is the response of fellow athletes; coaches and the rules of eligibility are only important in that they determine who competes in certain events.

Effectively controlling forms of overconforming deviance ultimately rests in getting athletes and others who are directly involved in sport to strike a balance between accepting and questioning the norms comprising the sport ethic, to fly the middle way. As in other settings, limits on commitment and conformity must be made more explicit so that athletes who engage in overconforming deviance will not be defined as heroes by those within sport or in the media. In appointing Arnold Schwarzenegger, a steroid user for 14 years, director of the President's Council of Physical Fitness, George Bush has certainly subverted efforts to discourage pushing limits in potentially self-destructive ways.

The questioning and qualification of the sport ethic also need to be combined with a process of creating new norms related to the use of medical science and technology in sports. This challenge of using new forms of technology in constructive ways is not unique; it is faced in many spheres of life apart from sport, although the pervasiveness of the sport ethic guarantees that it will create serious problems for athletes.

Specific changes suggested by the positive deviance model include the following:

- Lest we be hypocritical in our efforts to make changes, we need to eliminate the distinction between the so-called legal performance enhancing drugs or procedures that may harm the health of athletes and the illegal ones. Pain killers, massive injections of vitamin B-12, blood boosting, the use of erythropoietin to stimulate red blood cell production, playing with pins in broken bones or with high tech casts to hold broken bones in place during competition, and playing with special harnesses to restrict the movement of injured joints can be as harmful to health as taking anabolic steroids, and they must be regulated and controlled before the use of performance enhancing drugs can be effectively limited.
- Rules are needed to clearly indicate that risks to health are undesirable and unnecessary in sport.
- Athletes who are injured should not be allowed to play until certified as well, not simply "able to compete," by a physician outside the athletic program; team physicians may be vulnerable to collective overconformity to the sport ethic within sport organizations.
- There is a need for new norms emphasizing an awareness of one's limits so that courage can be defined as being able to accept the discipline necessary to become well instead of disregarding the consequences of injuries.
- The goals of sport science must be reframed to emphasize the growth and development of athletes through the expansion of the sport experience at all levels of involvement. Concerns about the enhancement of performance must be informed by these goals, or sport scientists become high tech pimps. For example, sport psychologists should help athletes understand

the consequences of their choice to participate in sport and to reduce the extent to which guilt or pathology influence their participation and training decisions. This is the alternative to the increasingly popular technique of "psycho-doping" which encourages positive deviance by making athletes more likely to give their all to sport without ever questioning why they are doing what they are doing.

The process of questioning and qualifying the sport ethic should be formalized and it should involve all sport participants. Unless this happens, deviance grounded in overconformity will continue to be commonplace and expected among athletes. Therefore athletes and coaches are the ones who need to develop new guidelines that discourage overconformity to the sport ethic, guidelines that emphasize health and development as well as performance. This is the major reason why dealing with most drug issues in sport requires the education of coaches, not just athletes.

At present we face a future without any clearly defined ideas about what achievement in sport means in light of the escalated rewards associated with participation, the increased importance assigned to sport participation in the lives of many young athletes, and the new technologies available to enhance performance. There is a need for new guidelines to replace the old ones. There is a need for new models of excellence shaped by a commitment to flying the middle way. Continuing to emphasize unquestioned acceptance of the sport ethic, and instituting increasingly invasive and repressive systems of social control, will not eliminate the self-destructive and dangerous behaviors characteristic in much of sport today.

The Underground Economy of College Football

ALLEN L. SACK

There is considerable anecdotal evidence to indicate that professionalism has always played a role in college sport in America. According to Samuel Eliot Morison (1936, p. 110) a number of Harvard baseball players during the 1880s were actually "professionals" whose tuition fees as law students were paid by generous alumni. Before the turn of the century it was not uncommon to find players involved in intercollegiate competition who were not even students. These "ringers," or "tramp athletes" as they were called, were paid per game and sometimes played for a number of different universities during the same season (Savage, 1929, p. 28). One reason the National Collegiate Athletic Association (NCAA) was founded in 1906 was to help to control professionalism.

It is an oversimplification to blame these deviations from amateur rules on morally flawed individuals or on isolated character defects. There were also social and cultural factors that made American universities less than hospitable environments for the British model of amateur sport. In British universities sport was an exclusive preserve for the sons of aristocrats. As Smith (1989, p. 162) points out, amateurism "was an elitist attitude contrived to keep the lower classes froth mixing with their social superiors on the athletic field." In American universities, on the other hand, sport often served as a bridge between the high culture of the university and the highly competitive mass society on which it depended for students and resources. To capture the attention of these broader constituencies, teams had to win. Furthermore, the American emphasis on winning meant that high quality athletes had to be recruited without regard for their social class backgrounds.

Although the recruitment of skilled athletes by meritocratic criteria made winning more likely, it also presented American universities with a dilemma. How would skilled athletes from working and lower class backgrounds be able to pay tuition and living expenses? Openly paying athletes for their services was out of the question because professionalism, even in American universities, was ideologically inconsistent with the elite culture and intellectual values of academic life. The solution that finally evolved was to retain the amateur label while at the same time relying on an under-the-table payment system to compensate athletes for their services. The following letter, written in 1902 by Henry P. Wright, Dean of the Yale College faculty, to Walter Camp, Yale's famous football coach, suggests that an underground payment system began to evolve very early and that it was a response to very real financial needs:

> Dear Mr. Camp,
>
> Has anything been done for Daly? I understand that some grad could be found from whom he might borrow $100 occasionally, giving his note, to be paid after graduation. He is pretty hard up and is getting rather restless. I do not see how he can come back after this term unless he is able to raise something somewhere. (Wright, 1902)

In the early 20th century the NCAA developed fairly rigorous definitions of amateurism which prohibited any form of direct or indirect inducements to college athletes based on their athletic ability. At the same time, the growth of college sport as a mass commercial spectacle placed an even greater emphasis on winning. The results were predictable. *The Carnegie Foundation Report* (Savage, 1929) concluded that NCAA rules regarding recruiting and subsidizing athletes had largely been ignored. Violations of amateur rules continued unabated for the next several decades. In 1952 the NCAA changed its rules to allow athletes to receive financial compensation based on their athletic ability. By approving athletic scholarships, the NCAA actually instituted the first formal payment system for college athletes.

But even this radical alteration of NCAA rules did not eliminate what Hart-Nibbrig and Cottingham (1986) have called the "underground economy" of college sport. Between 1952 and 1985 the NCAA put 150 universities on probation for illegal recruiting or for offering athletes improper benefits (Farrell, 1989). And of the 45 universities placed on NCAA probation between January of 1988 and November of 1989, the cause for action in 34 cases was improper benefits to athletes. Nine others were sanctioned for recruiting violations. In recent years the media have been filled with reports of athletes receiving illegal benefits such as low interest loans, money for travel, profits from the sale of game tickets, jobs for parents and relatives, the use of expensive cars and motel rooms, and in some instances enough money from boosters and agents to be considered salaried employees (Brown, 1990; Hartley, 1989; Lederman, 1989, 1990).

Few people would dispute the facts presented in this brief historical account of the evolution of the underground economy of college sport. However, there is considerable disagreement as to the scope and causes of this *sub rosa* payment system. The NCAA, for instance, tends to argue that the problem is limited to a few renegade institutions and to a handful of maverick athletes, coaches, and overzealous alumni (Schultz, 1989). The NCAA position is an example of what Eitzen and Zinn (1989) call a person-blame approach to deviance. From this perspective, deviance is the result of personal defects, character flaws, or maladjustment. "The flaw is a function of the deviant, not of societal arrangements"

(Eitzen & Zinn, 1989, p. 12). Person-blame approaches to social problems, according to Eitzen, are most likely to be embraced by those who benefit from existing social arrangements and see deviant acts as a threat to their interests.

A system-blame approach to under-the-table payments, on the other hand, would argue that violations of amateur rules are widespread and result from fundamental contradictions in the way college sport is organized. Labeling theory, one variant of the system-blame approach, argues that "deviance is not a quality of the act the person commits, but rather the consequence of the application by others of rules and sanctions to the offender" (Becker, 1963, p. 9). According to labeling theory, definitions of deviance reflect the ability of certain groups to legitimize and enforce their interests over those of other groups (Schrag, 1971, pp. 1–2), and groups with the greatest financial resources and internal organization are more likely than others to be able to impose their moral definitions (Spector & Kitsuse, 1987). From this perspective, athletes who accept money in excess of that allowed by NCAA rules are no more morally culpable than coaches who make millions of dollars by endorsing basketball sneakers. The only difference is that the former lack power and can therefore be labeled as deviant by those who make the rules (Coakley, 1990, p. 117; Sage, 1990, p. 186).

The policy implications of adopting either the system-blame or the person-blame approach to the problem of under-the-table payments are radically different. The person-blame solution would be to aggressively pursue those who violate NCAA rules and to impose severe sanctions. The focus would be on deviant universities and individuals. The NCAA's current policy of imposing "the death penalty" on universities that violate its rules is consistent with the approach. Labeling theorists and others who favor a systemic approach to deviance are likely to view athletes as highly exploited employees and to argue that it is the NCAA and its amateur code that is defective and in need of reform. From this perspective the solution would be to eliminate the amateur label from college sport altogether and to pay athletes openly for their services. Supporters of this position range from those who favor monthly stipends for athletes to those who insist that college athletes should have all of the rights and benefits of other American employees.

Given the important theoretical and public policy questions related to under-the-table payments, it is surprising that no systematic empirical study has been undertaken to examine this example of sports deviance. As Coakley suggests, "systematic studies of deviance among athletes are rare. Instead of doing systematic studies, people often take lists of alleged cases of athletes' misconduct from newspaper accounts, pick the behaviors they dislike most and then try to come up with some explanation for those behaviors" (1990, p. 121). The purpose of this study was twofold. First, an attempt was made to assess the scope of college football's underground economy. Are rule violations limited to a handful of universities or, as the common stereotype would have it, is everyone taking money? The second purpose was to examine the data for theoretical insights as to the causes of this phenomenon.

METHODS

Gathering data on under-the-table payments is no easy task. The NCAA keeps data on rule violations, but as Leonard (1984, p. 122) points out, the rule violations detected by the NCAA's modest enforcement staff probably represent only the tip of an iceberg. Another approach would be to interview a representative sample of current college athletes. The problem with this is that current players are unlikely to speak candidly about behavior that could result in severe NCAA sanctions for themselves and their universities. Athletes might also be reluctant to admit deviant acts because of embarrassment or lingering feelings of guilt. There may also be problems in obtaining cooperation from universities and athletic departments to carry out a study whose findings might damage the image of collegiate sport. For all of these reasons, it was decided to focus on a population of former college football players from a wide variety of universities and conferences.

Not only are these former collegiate athletes more free to talk about rule violations but their added years of maturity permit them to provide insights not likely to be obtained from athletes still in college. A very practical consideration that led to the decision to use current and retired National Football League (NFL) players as a population for this survey was the availability of a mailing list provided by the National Football League Players Association (NFLPA). Although such a sample is limited in that NFL players may not be representative of all college athletes, a data base of several thousand former collegiate football players provides a unique opportunity to at least begin to examine this area of sports deviance.

The method of data collection was a mailed questionnaire. The sampling frame provided by the NFLPA included two types of athletes. Some 1,700 surveys were mailed to current members of NFL teams. Another 1,800 were sent to a list of retired players with whom the NFLPA continues to be in contact. The overall return rate was 1,182, or 34%. Technically speaking, the 3,500 athletes selected for this study constitute the population to whom the findings can legitimately be generalized. The 1,182 athletes who responded are not a random sample, but even a nonrandom sample that contains one in three elements from a larger population suggests considerable internal validity. It is impossible to know whether this population of athletes is representative of a universe of all collegiate and professional football players who have ever played the game, but athletes from a wide variety of teams, conferences, age groups, racial and socioeconomic backgrounds, and levels of perceived athletic ability as high school recruits comprised the sample.

Included in the survey were questions to determine whether the NFL players had ever accepted financial benefits not allowed by the NCAA. Athletes were asked about their involvement with agents and with college recruiters. They were also asked if they saw anything wrong with accepting under-the-table payments. Questions were included on background variables—age, conference, race, family income when the respondent was in college, number of universities recruiting the athlete; whether the respondent could have afforded to attend college without an athletic scholarship, and whether financial aid was adequate to cover the athlete's living expenses while in college. The survey was anonymous, but athletes who wished to discuss issues raised in the survey in greater detail were asked to include their name and phone number where they could be reached. Several hundred respondents took this opportunity.

Most of the variables in the survey were categorical in nature. Therefore the findings were presented in a series of bivariate and multivariate contingency tables. Throughout the analysis, use was made of what Rosenberg (1968), Lazarsfeld (1959), and Bobbie (1989) refer to as the elaboration model. In this approach, the nature of the relationship between an independent and a dependent variable is clarified by introducing other variables as controls. Mechanically this is accomplished by examining the relationship between an independent and a dependent variable within a single category of the variable to be controlled. The statistical significance of bivariate relationships in this study was determined by use of the chi-square statistic. No test was performed to determine the statistical significance of interactions in multivariate tables, but percentage differences suggested patterns in the data.

FINDINGS

The Scope of the Underground Economy

Table 1 reveals that under-the-table payments are fairly common in the major football conferences. For instance, 83% of Southeast Conference athletes whose classes graduated between 1970 and 1988 said they knew players on their teams who were taking money. This was true of only 27% of the athletes who played in universities in Divisions II and III and in Division IAA. In some conferences, the period in which the athletes played college football was also related to the athletes' knowledge of under-the-table payments. Knowledge of such payments has increased over the years in the Southeast, Southwest, Big Eight, and Western Athletic conferences. In the Pac Ten, Big Ten, and among the major independents there has not been much change.

Table 2 indicates that 31% of the NFL players in the sample admitted to accepting improper benefits while they were in college. However, there were again substantial differences by conference. The Southeast Conference tops the list with 67% of the younger (post 1970) athletes admitting that they took payments. Just as in Table 1, there seems to be substantial growth in the underground economy in the late 1960s in the Southeast, Southwest, Big Eight, and Western Athletic conferences. In the Big Ten and the Pac Ten, the trend is actually in the other direction. Although Tables 1 and 2 suggest changes through time in the frequency of illegal payments, small cell values make these findings rather tentative. In Table 3, conferences are combined so that changes can be seen over several decades. It is clear from this table that the biggest increases in illegal payments have occurred in the Southwest, Southeast, Big Eight, and Western Athletic conferences, and that the turning point was in the 1960s and 1970s. In other conferences the frequency of reported payments has been fairly constant.

Respondents who admitted accepting improper benefits were asked to give examples. Although only 41% of athletes completed this section of the questionnaire, their responses were very informative. The best paid athlete in the sample made $80,000 while in college in addition to room, board, tuition, and fees. Another was offered part interest in an oil well by a recruiter, but stated that he turned it down. However, these were clearly exceptions. Most of the payments involved small amounts of money that seldom amounted to more than $1,000 over a 4-year period. Some commonly mentioned benefits were clothing, meals, money for travel, the use of cars, and small amounts of spending money.

Section VIII: Deviance in Sport

Table 1: Percentage of NFL Players Who Knew Athletes at Their Colleges Who Took Under-the-Table Payments, by Graduating Class and Conference

	Graduating class					
	1970 and after		Before 1970		Total	
Conference	%	N	%	N	%	N
Southeast	83	57	53	58	67	115
Big Eight	66	44	53	32	60	76
Southwest	65	48	47	32	58	78
Pac Ten	60	80	57	51	59	131
Big Ten	50	90	58	70	48	160
Maj. ind.	49	129	40	93	45	222
West. Ath.	49	33	33	18	43	51
ACC	35	40	29	19	32	59
Other*	27	137	22	60	25	197
Total**	50	656	45	433	48	1089

*The "other" category Includes Division IAA, II, III, and NAIA.
**The major conferences (Mid Atlantic and Big West) were dropped because of low frequencies.

Table 2: Percentage of NFL Players Taking Illegal Payments by Graduating Class and Conference

	Graduating class					
	1970 and after		Before 1970		Total	
Conference	%	N	%	N	%	N
Southeast	67	57	38	58	52	115
Southwest	48	46	28	32	40	78
Big Eight	41	44	26	31	35	75
West. Ath.	40	33	17	18	31	51
Pac Ten	35	79	45	51	39	130
Big Ten	32	90	41	69	36	159
Maj. ind.	30	129	24	93	27	222
ACC	20	40	18	17	19	57
Other	13	138	12	59	13	195
Total	33	654	27	428	31	1082

Of the 479 athletes who identified the benefits they received, 150 mentioned cash payments from alumni and other sources. These cash payments took a number of forms. Several athletes referred to "money handshakes" whereby alumni would shake hands with them after a game and pass them a small amount of money. There were also what were referred to as "big play" awards whereby athletes would receive a certain amount of money for tackles, touchdowns, or other big plays made during a game. One athlete said he would receive a certain amount of money in his helmet every Monday morning from an unknown source. Another mentioned money slipped under his door in an envelope. Still others said they received monthly stipends of several hundred dollars.

The Underground Economy of College Football

Table 3: Percentage of NFL Players Taking Illegal Payments by Conference and Decade of Graduation

Decade	Conference							
	Sunbelt*		Other Div I**		Small time		Total	
	%	N	%	N	%	N	%	N
1980s	50	96	34	203	16	70	35	369
1970s	51	84	26	135	11	66	30	285
1960s	35	87	37	114	15	33	33	234
1950s	23	52	30	128	8	26	26	204
Total	42	319	31	578	13	195	31	1082

*Sunbelt conferences include the Southeast, Southwest, Big Eight, and Western Athletic.
**Other Div. I includes the Big Ten, Pac Ten, ACC, and major independents.

Only 17 athletes said they had been given cars. Another 23 said they had the use of cars while in college and were given expense money for gasoline. By far the biggest and most lucrative source of under-the-table income reported in this study came from the sale of complimentary game tickets. Some 25% (115) of those responding to this question reported that they had sold complimentary game tickets at well above face value. One respondent said he often received as much as $1,000 a ticket, and a sizable minority of athletes were able to make several thousand dollars over a 4-year period through ticket sales.

With few exceptions, the typical payments to college athletes appeared to be intended to meet living expenses or emergencies. In some instances coaches paid travel expenses for athletes to attend the funeral of relatives. This was mentioned several times. A number of married athletes were helped with housing and moving expenses. Sometimes an athlete arrived at college without a suit, and a coach or alumnus bought him one. Athletes received small amounts of money for giving talks, were given loans by local banks, or were given jobs at which very little if any real work was expected. In all of these cases the dollar amounts were modest compared to what some of these athletes could have received if their market value had not been restricted by NCAA rules.

Another growing source of payments to college athletes involves agents. Because few respondents reported being contacted by agents before the mid-1960s, Table 4 includes only athletes whose classes graduated after 1969. Of these athletes, only 17% reported being offered money by agents while still in college. However, there were fairly large differences by race and by the number of universities that had recruited the athletes in high school. Highly recruited athletes were twice as likely to have been offered benefits as those who were not highly sought after. And black athletes were much more likely to have been offered money than whites. It may be that black athletes, given their lower-class backgrounds and limited career options, are more likely than whites to begin serious discussions about their professional sports career while still in college.

Variables Related to Accepting Payments

In this section a number of independent variables are examined which, on logical grounds, might be expected to influence whether an athlete would accept payments that violate NCAA rules. Table 5 examines the relationships among race, the number of schools that recruited the athlete in high school, and whether an athlete accepted improper benefits. It would appear that both race and number of schools recruiting the athlete were related to accepting benefits. Chi-square values for both relationships were significant at the .0001 level. Regardless of recruitment rate, black athletes were somewhat more likely than whites to have accepted money. At the same time, accepting benefits increased with recruitment level within each race. It should be noted that the vast majority of athletes in this sample were recruited by fewer than 20 colleges to play football. This suggests that even though the athletes in this sample all played professional football, they were not much more heavily recruited in high school than many other athletes going to big-time football universities.

Table 4: Percentage of NFL Players Who Were Offered Improper Benefits by Agents, by Race and Number of Colleges That Recruited Them*

No. of colleges	Black %	Black N	White %	White N	Total %	Total N
50+	63	43	17	94	31	137
20–49	39	39	17	108	22	147
0–19	32	133	8	265	16	398
Total	40	215	12	467	17	682

*This table includes only those athletes who played in college after 1965, because of the limited number of agents before 1969.

Table 5: Percentage of NFL Players Taking Illegal Payments by Race and Number of Colleges That Recruited Them

No. of colleges	Black %	Black N	White %	White N	Total %	Total N
50+	55	53	43	150	48	203
20–49	47	57	32	188	36	245
0–19	36	181	21	530	25	711
Total	42	291	27	868	31	1159

One question that emerges at this point is whether the race differences in Table 5 are actually the result of socioeconomic differences. Table 6 indicates that there is a relationship between race and income of the athletes' families but that this relationship only holds for younger athletes. Black and white athletes whose college classes graduated before 1970 were fairly similar in that they both tended to come from lower income families. In recent decades, however, white athletes were recruited from somewhat more privileged economic backgrounds while blacks continued to be recruited from lower income levels. It seems reasonable to argue that among younger athletes, at least, it may be the lower income of black families that explains why black athletes were more likely than whites to accept payments. To test this hypothesis, Table 7 shows the relationship between race and accepting payments controlling income level. Because of the greater difference in background after that date, this table includes only players who graduated in 1970 or later.

Table 6: Percentage Distribution of Income by Race and Graduating Class

Income*	1970 and after				Before 1970				Total	
	Black		White		Black		White			
	%	N	%	N	%	N	%	N	%	N
1–40	48	87	21	88	48	28	43	155	35	358
41–80	32	60	47	206	37	22	38	137	41	425
81+	20	36	32	136	15	9	19	68	24	249
Total	100	183	100	430	100	59	100	360	100	1032

*Family income while the athlete was in college was adjusted to 1987 dollars using the consumer price index. Incomes were rounded to the nearest thousand.

Table 7: Percentage of NFL Players Taking Illegal Payments by Race and Income*

Income**	Black		White		Total	
	%	N	%	N	%	N
1–40	46	85	39	88	42	173
41–80	42	60	23	206	27	266
81+	42	36	27	136	31	172
Total	44	181	28	430	32	611

*This table includes players whose classes graduated in 1970 and after.
**Family income while the athlete was in college was adjusted to 1987 dollars using the consumer price index. Incomes were rounded to the nearest thousand.

Table 7 shows that race differences in accepting under-the-table benefits persist even when income level is held constant. The overall effect of race on under-the-table payments is statistically significant at the .0001 level. The main effect of income is statistically significant at the .01 level. It should be noted that there is almost no relationship between income and accepting benefits among blacks. Table 8, which examines the joint impact of race, income, and level of recruitment on accepting payments, reveals that regardless of income background and recruitment level, blacks were more likely than whites to have accepted payments. Highly recruited athletes were also more likely to have accepted payments than those who were not highly sought after. It is important to note that although the difference between blacks and whites in accepting payments is fairly minimal under some conditions, in no instance is the relationship reversed. Among highly recruited athletes from low income backgrounds, blacks are 20% more likely to have taken payments than are whites.

Are Improper Benefits Really Improper?

One final question addressed in this study is whether athletes viewed it as wrong to accept money under the table for such things as travel and living expenses. This question is important because it sheds light on the degree to which athletes actually accept the legitimacy of the NCAA's amateur code. According to Table 9, 53% of the athletes in the total sample saw nothing wrong with accepting money under the table. There were large differences in responses to this question by race and by age. Whereas 72% of the black athletes saw nothing wrong with accepting benefits, this was true of only 47% of the white athletes.

And the younger the athletes, the less likely they were to see anything wrong. The chi-square values for both age and race as they influence attitudes toward payments were statistically significant at the .0001 level.

Table 8: Percentage of NFL Players Taking Illegal Payments by Race, Income, and Number of Colleges Recruiting Them

| | Not highly recruited | | | | Highly recruited | | | | Total | |
| | Black | | White | | Black | | White | | | |
Income*	%	N	%	N	%	N	%	N	%	N
1–40	30	69	27	150	64	44	42	92	36	355
41–80	42	55	16	209	50	26	31	132	26	422
81+	41	22	24	121	39	23	37	83	33	249
Total	36	146	23	480	24	93	36	307	31	1026

*Family income while the athlete was in college was adjusted to 1987 dollars using the consumer price index. Incomes were rounded to the nearest thousand.

Table 9: Percentage of NFL Players Who See Nothing Wrong With Accepting Money Under the Table, by Race and Age

| | Black | | White | | Total | |
Age	%	N	%	N	%	N
20–30	77	145	55	233	64	378
31–50	69	120	45	418	51	538
51+	55	20	41	181	42	201
Total	72	285	47	832	53	1117

In Table 10 it is clear that the race differences in response to this question hold up regardless of the athlete's income background. Regardless of income level, blacks were far less likely to see anything wrong with violating NCAA rules regarding payments to athletes than were whites. Income had no effect on how athletes responded. This finding is consistent with those of a national survey of college basketball players (Sack, 1989) which also asked players if they felt it was wrong to accept benefits under the table. In that survey, however, race differences were reduced when social class was controlled. The survey also found that black athletes had a much more instrumental view of sports than whites, regardless of class.

Table 10: Percentage of NFL Players Who See Nothing Wrong With Accepting Money Under the Table, by Race and Income

| | Black | | White | | Total | |
Income	%	N	%	N	%	N
1–40	73	113	52	232	56	345
41–80	70	81	45	333	50	414
81+	71	45	46	196	51	241
Total	72	239	46	761	52	1000

SUMMARY AND CONCLUSIONS

One of the major conclusions of this study is that the underground economy is extensive in the major football conferences. Among athletes who played in the Southeast, Southwest, Big Eight, and Western Athletic conferences during the past two decades, about half reported that they accepted under-the-table payments. About 35% of the football players in the other major conferences during this period took money. Much larger percentages of players said they knew of others on their teams who took illegal benefits, even if they themselves did not. These findings, plus the fact that illegal payments were found to be related to a number of structural variables, suggest that the causes of this form of athletic deviance are systemic in nature. Illegal payments are simply too pervasive to be caused by a few "rotten apples."

It is not surprising that accepting illegal payments was related to the number of colleges that recruited an athlete while he was in high school. Athletes who are highly recruited are obviously in great demand and are more likely than other athletes to be offered a variety of legal as well as illegal benefits. Eitzen and Sage (1986), Hart-Nibbrig and Cottingham (1986), and Rader (1990) have pointed out that the growing influence of television on college sport in the late 1960s and early 1970s has greatly increased the competition among big-time football universities for athletic talent. In their quest for television revenue and exposure, universities have intensified their recruiting efforts and one would expect this to be reflected in an increase in under-the-table payments.

The findings in part support this argument. There was definitely a sharp increase in illegal payments in the Southwest, Southeast, Big Eight, and Western Athletic conferences starting in the 1960s. This increase in under-the-table payments seemed to parallel the improving athletic fortunes of conferences in the Sunbelt. In the 1930s, 44% of the teams in the Top 10, according to seasonending polls, were from the Sunbelt. The figure rose to 63% in the 1980s (Rader, 1990). In 1988, 14 of the Top 20 teams were from the Sunbelt. These universities also had the highest rates of under-the-table payments. The intense regional interest in college football in the South, the recent population growth and business expansion in the area, the willingness of wealthy boosters to give financial support to college football programs, and the growing influence of television are all factors that have fueled the underground economy in the Sunbelt.

Although a variety of factors may help to explain why some universities and conferences are more likely than others to offer athletes benefits in excess of those allowed by NCAA rules, the question still remains as to why some athletes accept such payments and others do not. One variable that was found to influence whether athletes had accepted illegal payments was race. A commonsense explanation for this racial difference is that blacks come from lower socioeconomic backgrounds than whites do and are therefore more in need of financial assistance. The evidence does not support this position. One of the most significant findings of this study is that even when the income of athletes' families of origin was held constant, black athletes were more likely than whites to have accepted payments. Black athletes were also much less likely than whites to see anything wrong with taking under-the-table payments. Labeling theory provides a possible explanation for this difference.

Few groups have greater firsthand experience than blacks do with legal codes designed by one group to exploit another (Burns, 1973, pp. 156–166). The laws of slavery defined blacks as property. Jim Crow laws excluded blacks from broad areas of American life and supported a system of discrimination from which they have yet to fully recover. It was the legal system that denied blacks the right to vote and forced them to sit in the back of buses. Black Americans who challenged these laws were labeled as deviant and faced severe sanctions. Blacks have been in the vanguard of efforts to fight discrimination and exploitation in sport (Edwards, 1970, 1983; Tygiel, 1983). From the perspective of labeling theory, it is not surprising to find black athletes to be the least likely to accept an amateur code that limits financial compensation to young athletes but encourages profit seeking by those who make the rules.

According to labeling theory, the fact that large numbers of former college athletes, both black and white, saw nothing wrong with accepting under-the-table payments has more to do with the perceived injustice of NCAA rules than with immorality on the part of athletes. Over 50% of the athletes in this study saw nothing wrong with violating the NCAA's amateur code. Table 11 reveals that 78% of NFL athletes think that college athletes deserve greater compensation than NCAA rules allow. Among the younger athletes, the percentage was 85%. What these findings may indicate is that from the perspective of college athletes, it is NCAA rules that are ethically flawed. This is a perfect example of how a well-organized group with financial resources can impose moral definitions that suit its interests. Athletes who accept money in excess of what NCAA rules allow are deviants because the NCAA has chosen to label them as such, not because there is something inherently wrong with sport professionalism.

Because this study was largely exploratory in nature and not a direct test of labeling theory, no conclusions can be drawn with regard to the best interpretation for the empirical reality of the underground economy. But questions raised in this study should provide useful starting points for future research. A number of studies (Gilligan, 1982; Sack, 1989) have found that males and females often take differing positions on a variety of moral questions. Systematic empirical studies of athletes' responses to ethical issues in sport, with emphasis on gender as well as race and class differences, could reveal a great deal about how social and political factors influence moral judgments.

Table 11: Percentage of NFL Players Who Think College Athletes Deserve Greater Compensation Than NCAA Rules Allow, by Age

Deserve more	Age 22–30	Age 31–50	Age 51–99	Total	
Agree	85%	78%	66%	78%	911
Disagree	12%	20%	30%	17%	224
Don't know	3%	2%	4%	3%	28
Total	**386**	**568**	**209**	**1163**	

Another ethical issue that deserves attention is how NCAA rules concerning amateurism have been able to maintain moral legitimacy even though critics have been attacking the seeming hypocrisy of those rules for over a century. Sack (1985), Sage (1989), Smith (1989), Sperber (1990), Telander (1989), and many other writers have presented thoughtful arguments and empirical data to debunk what they view as the myth of amateurism. Yet the NCAA, the courts, and the public in general have held on tenaciously to the notion that college sport differs significantly from the games of paid professionals in leagues such as the NFL. We need an adequate sociological analysis of the NCAA's continuing hegemony despite growing resistance and evidence that amateurism is no longer a relevant concept.

Gender, Sport, and Aggressive Behavior Outside Sport

HOWARD L. NIXON II

Sexual assault on college campuses has received increasing public and scholarly attention in recent years. Among the factors thought to explain such assaultive behavior is membership on an athletic team (Boeringer, 1994; Crosset, Benedict, & McDonald, 1995; Ellin, 1995; Frintner & Rubinson, 1993; Jackson, 1991; Koss & Gaines, 1993; Koss, Gidycz, & Wisniewski, 1987; Malamuth, Sockloskie, Koss, & Tanaka, 1991; Melnick, 1992; Neimark, 1991). Several surveys have found that a disproportionate number of admitted acquaintance rapes on campus were committed by male athletes or fraternity members. Members of football, lacrosse, hockey, and basketball teams have been among those college men most likely to be accused of participating in gang rape. According to one authoritative source (Bohmer & Parrot, 1993), the most important characteristics of college men who engage in acquaintance rape are exaggerated masculine or "macho" attitudes, a pattern of antisocial behavior, and regular or binge alcohol abuse (p. 23). Criminal justice professor Michael Clay Smith of the University of Southern Mississippi argued that athletes are more involved in violent behavior than are their peers because they are physical people who are expected by others to be physically aggressive (cited in Lederman, 1990).

Mary Koss did pioneering work on sexual assault on campus in the 1980s. She and her colleagues explained the disproportionate representation of college athletes in cases of gang rape in terms of male bonding occurring on sports teams (Curry, 1991), which have subcultures of sexism, insensitivity, and aggression (Koss & Gaines, 1993; Koss et al., 1987; see also Messner, 1990). Curry (1991) found in his study of the locker room talk of two male intercollegiate sports teams that the competitive sports environment put male egos and self-esteem at risk. In this setting, peer group pressures and insecurities fostered antisocial talk and behavior as well as the affirmation of traditional masculinity. More specifically, talk often focused on sex and aggression and expressed sexist attitudes toward women, who were viewed in depersonalized and insensitive terms as objects to be used for a man's pleasure. Although it is important not to make unfounded causal leaps, one could assume that where the main focus of male locker room talk is sex and aggression, male athletes may become more inclined to engage in sexual aggression against women.

Questions have been raised about whether such prevalence rates of sexual assault among male athletes have been exaggerated and whether higher rates of gang rape among members of male gender-segregated groups such as athletic teams necessarily imply that athletes are more likely to engage in sexual assault as individuals (Crosset et al., 1995). Studies of male college athletes and sexual assault raise broader questions about the relationship between athletic participation and violent or aggressive behavior of various types outside sport. Not long ago, Melnick (1992) proposed that "little is known about whether there is a correlation between on-the-field and off-the-field violence; yet one has to wonder about the interpersonal consequences of sports which teach participants to use their bodies as instruments of force and domination" (p. 33). The current research is an exploratory effort to begin addressing this issue.

A distinctive aspect of the research reported here is the focus on females as well as males. This article reports new evidence indicating how various aspects of college athletic participation are related to male and female physical aggression outside sport. It looks at sports variables given little direct attention in prior research, and it examines female aggressive behavior as well as male aggression. It also focuses on a more broadly defined concept of physical aggression than sexual assault.

Although physically aggressive behavior is generally associated with sport, the traditional exclusion of females from sport has resulted in little attention to the aggressiveness of female athletes. Although we talk about the macho male locker room and the aggressive and antisocial attitudes it might spawn, sport sociologists have had little to say about the possibility of comparable attitudes and subcultures in the female locker room. However, no evidence exists that shows whether female athletic participation is related to physical aggression outside sport. We may tend not to ask the question because we presume that aggression or violence and associated attitudes are unique products of the interaction, bonding, identity building, and beliefs that characterize male socialization and involvement in sport, especially when they are members of segregated all-male groups in sport. Evidence from a recent study of members of an elite women's ice hockey team in Canada (Theberge, 1993) indicates that there are female athletes who value physicality and aggression. Even though the women in Theberge's research did not act in the antisocial or aggressive ways in which male athletes sometimes have been found to act, this research nevertheless gives a reason to look at the connection between sport and aggression for females as well as males.

The elements of aggression, pain, and injury in sport suggest the need for athletes to be "tough" to succeed or endure in athletic competition (Nixon, 1993). Those who are tough are not supposed to be afraid to face aggression or be aggressive toward others. Indeed, in sport and other environments where aggression is valued, being tough often involves being aggressive, which can be proof of one's manhood for male athletes. There is no clear stereotype of what female athletes learn about toughness and aggression when they are socialized into sport. But logically, if male or female athletes frequently engage in behavior that intentionally or unintentionally hurts their opponents, then we might expect a pattern to develop that carries over to roles outside sport. That is, we would expect athletes who learn to express tough attitudes and engage in aggressive or violent behavior as part of their sports role to be more physically aggressive or violent outside sport. These assumptions loosely follow findings in the sexual assault literature indicating that campus sexual assault is associated with macho attitudes and patterns of antisocial behavior.

The possibility that both males and females become generally more aggressive as a result of their sports involvement suggests that sport socialization reinforces stereotypical gender role learning for males and teaches females to act in nonstereotypical ways. Thus, the patterns of physical aggression may be stronger for males than for females, but a general socializing influence of sport is demonstrated if both learn aggression in sport and carry it over into interactions and relationships outside sport.

Among the aspects of sport thought to contribute to male aggressive behavior outside sport are involvement on a team and, especially, participation in a contact sport. Stereotypical male bonding and learning how to hit one's opponent are assumed to reinforce aggression as a normal or valued part of role-playing for males, which may be difficult to restrain in roles outside sport. In this article, I question the implicit notion that the culture and socialization of team and contact sports teach males alone to be more aggressive by considering whether females act more aggressively outside sport when they participate in these types of sports.

The arguments that have been presented suggest a number of hypotheses concerning gender, attitudes about toughness, aspects of sports involvement, and physical aggression outside sport. The purpose of the remainder of this article is to present evidence providing an initial test of hypothesized relationships among these factors. The results should point future research in this area in fruitful directions. For the ensuing hypotheses, the proposed relationship between variables is assumed to exist for both males and females, but these hypotheses also assume that the relationship will be stronger for males. This gender assumption follows stereotypical thinking about male and female aggressiveness. The hypotheses tested by this exploratory research are as follows:

Hypothesis 1: *Athletic participation and aggression outside sport.* Especially among males but also among females, athletes are more likely than non-athletes to engage in physically aggressive acts in everyday life outside sport.

Hypothesis 2: *Gender, attitudes about toughness in sport, and aggression outside sport.* Male athletes are more likely than female athletes (a) to express stronger beliefs in the value of toughness in sport and (b) to engage in physically aggressive acts in everyday life outside sport.

Hypothesis 3: *Attitudes about toughness in sport and aggression outside sport.* Especially among male athletes but also among female athletes, having stronger beliefs in the value of toughness in sport is associated with being more likely to engage in physically aggressive acts in everyday life outside sport.

Section VIII: Deviance in Sport

Hypothesis 4: *Hurting people in sport and aggression outside sport.* Especially among male athletes but also among female athletes, hurting people in sport, either accidentally or intentionally, is associated with engaging in physically aggressive acts in everyday life outside sport.

Hypothesis 5: *Team and contact sport participation and aggression outside sport.* Especially among male athletes but also among female athletes, (a) team sport participants and (b) contact sport participants are more likely than their counterparts in individual sports and non-contact sports, respectively, to engage in physically aggressive acts in everyday life outside sport.

METHODS, MEASURES, AND PROCEDURES

This research concentrated on college students and student-athletes. In the spring of 1992, students were surveyed at a medium-sized (11,500-student) southern comprehensive university that competes at the NCAA Division I level. Questionnaires were distributed by instructors to several introductory sociology classes, and students were asked to return their completed questionnaires by mail within two weeks. Questionnaires were distributed by student athletic trainers to the entire population of approximately 425 varsity athletes and cheerleaders, and these questionnaires were returned to a box in the athletic training room. Participation in this study was voluntary for both students and student-athletes. The convenience sample of introductory sociology students yielded 218 responses. A response rate of 45.9% yielded a sample size of 195 student-athletes, who represented the full range of 8 women's and 10 men's varsity sports teams and the coed competitive cheerleading squad.

The total sample size of 413 was a broad cross section of the student population. For the student-athlete population, females were overrepresented (37.9% of the sample versus an estimated 25.4% of the student-athlete population). However, females were underrepresented in the total sample (approximately 46% of the total sample versus 52% of the overall student population of this university). It was not possible to calculate the composition of the student-athlete population by race or class standing, but non-whites and freshmen were overrepresented in the overall student sample. The percentage of non-white respondents was nearly 14% (versus approximately 6% of the total student population), and the percentage of freshmen respondents was more than 41% (versus about 24% of the total student population). The overrepresentation of non-whites may be partially explained by the relatively high proportion of student-athlete respondents who were non-white (16.4%). The overrepresentation of freshmen is largely explained by the use of a convenience sample of lower level sociology classes to generate respondents from a cross section of students not involved in varsity athletics.

The main dependent variable of engaging in physically aggressive acts in everyday life outside sport was measured by one item that asked, "Have you ever physically harmed or injured another person *outside sport* in a fight or disagreement of some sort?" This item, admittedly, is a simple and gross measure of a potentially complex variable that could incorporate a variety of types of physical aggression in different contexts of everyday life. It is useful, however, in providing a first general indication of possible connections between sports participation and physical aggression outside sport for both males and females.

The toughness variable, concerning strength of belief in the value of toughness in sport, was measured by an attitudinal scale that was constructed for this research. The scale was derived from 11 items generally reflecting beliefs about toughness in dealing with pain and injury in sport that were highly loaded (from .46 to .66) on a factor analysis. The factor analysis included 31 statements about risk, pain, and injury in sport that were created on the basis of the results of a content analysis of approximately one decade of *Sports Illustrated* magazine articles (Nixon, 1993). Respondents indicated their agreement or disagreement with these statements on a 4-point scale ranging from *strongly agree* to *strongly disagree*. Three categories of belief in toughness—low, medium, and high—were created by reversing and combining the values of responses to the 11 component items. The response values of this scale were combined so that approximately one-third of the responses were in each of the three categories. Other measures used in this data analysis were items indicating gender, whether or not the respondent had participated or was participating in college athletics, whether or not he or she had accidentally or intentionally hurt another athlete in competition, and whether he or she had participated in a team or individual sport or in a contact or noncontact sport.

RESULTS

Hypothesis 1: *Athletic participation and aggression outside sport.* Especially among males but also among females, athletes are more likely than nonathletes to engage in physically aggressive acts in everyday life outside sport.

Results. Among both males and females, there was no difference between college athletes and nonathletes in their likelihood of being aggressors outside sport.

Hypothesis 2: *Gender, attitudes about toughness in sport, and aggression outside sport.* Male athletes are more likely than female athletes (a) to express stronger beliefs in the value of toughness in sport and (b) to engage in physically aggressive acts in everyday life outside sport.

Results. A higher percentage of male than female athletes held the strongest belief (37.4% versus 21.1%) and a moderately strong belief (39.1% versus 33.8%) in the value of toughness in sport. Male athletes were more likely than female athletes (32.2% versus 10.8%) to have engaged in physically aggressive acts in everyday life outside sport. Both results agree with Hypothesis 2.

Hypothesis 3: *Attitudes about toughness in sport and aggression outside sport.* Especially among male athletes but also among female athletes, having stronger beliefs in the value of toughness in sport is associated with being more likely to engage in physically aggressive acts in everyday life outside sport.

Results. A statistically significant relationship between belief in toughness and being an aggressor was found for male athletes. 51.2% of male athletes with the strongest belief in toughness had been aggressors, 22.2% of male athletes with a moderately strong belief in toughness had been aggressors, and 22.2% of male athletes with the weakest belief in toughness had been aggressors. The distinction, therefore, is between those with the strongest belief in toughness and all others with weaker beliefs.

Hypothesis 4: *Hurting people in sport and aggression outside sport.* Especially among male athletes but also among female athletes, hurting people in sport, either accidentally or intentionally, is associated with engaging in physically aggressive acts in everyday life outside sport.

Results. The relationships of accidentally hurting someone in sport and trying to hurt someone in sport to aggression outside sport were statistically significant only for male athletes. Male athletes who accidentally hurt other athletes were much more likely than those who did not (42.2% versus 3.2%) to have been aggressors outside sport, and male athletes who intentionally hurt other athletes were much more likely than those who did not (55.6% versus 25.5%) to have been aggressors outside sport.

Hypothesis 5: *Team and contact sport participation and aggression outside sport.* Especially among male athletes but also among female athletes, (a) team sport participants and (b) contact sport participants are more likely than their counterparts in individual sports and noncontact sports, respectively, to engage in physically aggressive acts in everyday life outside sport.

Results. A statistically significant relationship between team sport participation and aggression outside sport was found only for male athletes. Male participants in team sports were substantially more likely than their counterparts in individual sports (43.4% versus 9.4%) to have engaged in physically aggressive acts in everyday life outside sport. A relationship between contact sport participation and aggression outside sport was found for both male and female athletes. Male contact sport athletes were much more likely than male participants in noncontact sports (49.0% versus 22.7%) to have engaged in physical aggression outside sport. A similar pattern was found among female athletes, with female contact sport participants significantly more likely than females in noncontact sports (22.7% versus 6.0%) to have engaged in physically aggressive acts in everyday life outside sport.

CONCLUSION

Because the results are based on self-reporting by students at a single campus, and because the measure of the main dependent variable is a single item, caution must be exercised in generalizing. Yet, in breaking new ground in research on athletic participation and physical assault, these results bear serious consideration. In addressing a number of important hypotheses about sport and male and female physical aggression outside sport, this study points the way for future research with potentially important implications for college administrators and policymakers concerned about the occurrence of physical assault of various types on their campuses.

Several relationships among gender, sport, and physical aggression outside sport are suggested by this research. It appears that a belief in the value of toughness in sport is related to physically aggressive acts in everyday life for male athletes but not for female athletes. Similarly, accidentally or intentionally hurting other athletes in sport and participating in a team sport are related to physical aggression outside sport for male but not for female athletes. These results are consistent with the findings that male athletes were more likely than female athletes to have engaged in physical aggression outside sport and to hold highly or moderately strong beliefs in the value of toughness in sport. These finding also are consistent with stereotypical ideas in society about gender differences.

The chain of reasoning suggested by this research is that athletic participation by itself does not make people more likely to be physically aggressive in everyday life. The likelihood of such aggressive behavior seems to be increased for males by certain aspects or types of sports participation. A prominent factor increasing the likelihood of aggression outside sport for females as well as males is participation in a contact sport, but a higher proportion of male athletes than female athletes tend to be affected by this factor. It may be that more aggressive females are attracted to contact sports or that recurrent contact in a sport leads to an internalization of aggressive patterns of behavior for females, which carries over to roles and relationships outside sport for a number of them. In view of the general pattern of findings in this study, we can reasonably speculate that contact sports have to reinforce or induce aggressive nonsports behaviors among females that attitudes about toughness, accidentally and intentionally hurting opponents in sports competition, and team sport participation do not possess. Among male athletes, all of these sports-related factors are related to a heightened tendency to engage in aggressive acts in everyday life outside sport.

It is important to move beyond speculation, correlations, and an undifferentiated conception of physical aggression outside sport to evidence from a variety of sports settings at different levels of sport showing the causal linkages between aspects of sports participation and different types and patterns of aggressive behavior outside sport. Although exploratory, this research clearly conveys the need to examine more extensively the factors that make female athletes more likely to engage in physical aggression outside sport. Even though a number of aspects of sports participation may increase or reinforce the tendency among males but not among females to engage in physical aggression outside sport, there are other aspects of sport, such as contact, that seem related to physical aggression outside sport for female athletes as well.

The competitiveness of women's intercollegiate athletics arguably has intensified over the past 15 years of governance by the NCAA. If female athletes seek to emulate male physical aggression and male macho values in team and contact sports as their sports become more competitive under male governance, we could see a closer approximation of male and female results concerning the relationship between aggression and related values in sport and physical aggression outside sport. This research has produced evidence that contact sport participation may induce, or at least reinforce, aggressive behaviors outside sport among females as well as males in intercollegiate athletics. By contrast, Theberge's (1993, 1995) recent study of an elite women's ice hockey team suggests that emphases on physicality and aggressiveness in highly competitive contact sports do not necessarily translate into the types of antisocial or aggressive behaviors in or out of sport that have been associated with male team and contact sports. Therefore, future research must address these apparent contradictions. More generally, what we must understand better are how particular types of norms, roles, identities, attitudes, relationships, and social influence processes associated with physicality and aggression in sport are linked to various types and contexts of aggressive acts in everyday life for both males and females. These understandings will enable us to address more effectively, through interventions ranging from education of coaches and athletes to a restructuring of sport, the risk factors in sport that make athletes more likely to engage in violence outside the sports arena.

Section IX

Sport Subcultures

The Construction and Confirmation of Identity in Sport Subcultures

Peter Donnelly and Kevin Young

Since the earliest well-known ethnographies of sport / leisure subcultures (Polsky, 1967; Scott, 1968), three principal themes have been apparent. The first and most prominent of these involves the description of characteristics of the subculture and behavior of the members—the presentation of "insider" information that is only accessible to the participant observer. While this theme is apparent in all subcultural ethnographies, the second and third themes—descriptions of typical subcultural careers and career contingencies, and descriptions of appropriate subcultural identity or demeanor—are presented less frequently, and even more rarely found in combination. For example, Faulkner (1975) and Pearson (1979) primarily emphasize the subcultural careers of hockey players and surfers, while Birrell and Turowetz (1979) and Klein (1986) am more concerned with the identities of gymnasts, wrestlers, and bodybuilders.

However, there are a few studies that implicitly or explicitly combine the concepts of career and identity with the implication that the act of becoming a member of a particular subculture is also the act of taking on an appropriate subcultural identity. For example, Rosenberg and Turowetz note that, "Ordinarily there is a sequence in role performance and its concomitant internalization of the role, its experience as part of one's identity. This sequence involves qualifying for the role performance, training, certification, and performance" (1975, p. 567). This study also employs the concept of career to examine the processes of identity *construction* and *confirmation* in two specific sport subcultures.

More specifically, we propose that previous references to identity formation provide a far too passive characterization of this process, and even the notion of identity "work up" (Rosenberg & Turowetz, 1975) does not fully capture what is often a far more deliberate act of identity construction. That is, through a variety of means, the most significant of which is modeling, new members of subcultures begin to deliberately adopt mannerisms and attitudes, and styles of dress, speech, and behavior that they perceive to be characteristic of established members of the "achieved" subculture (Donnelly, 1981a).

Such perceptions among neophytes are usually far from being completely accurate and are frequently stereotypical. Thus, it is necessary to examine also the complementary process of identity confirmation in order to conduct a more complete examination of socialization into a subcultural career. As if to symbolize the neophyte's position on the borderline between the larger culture and a specific subculture, identity construction is intended for two distinct audiences—members of the larger society and members of the subculture.

Because of stereotypes held by the neophyte, the initial attempts at identity construction are often inaccurate but are frequently confirmed by outsiders because they do conform to the stereotype. That is, the neophyte has achieved the first stage of distancing from nonmembers through their acceptance of his or her membership in the subculture. The second stage, having the identity confirmed by actual members of the subculture, is more difficult and, in the final analysis, involves ceasing to consider outsiders as a valued audience.

In addition, we propose a career model that is derived from several earlier models (e.g., Miller & Form, 1980; Prus, 1984; Rosenberg & Turowetz, 1975; Super, 1957) but that is more parsimonious and more appropriate to the particular subcultural careers under examination. A four-stage contingency model is suggested, with each stage playing a significant part in the development of actors' subcultural identities and in ensuring their (career) membership within the group: presocialization, selection and recruitment, socialization, and acceptance/ostracism.

CAREER STAGES

Presocialization

Presocialization refers to all of the information an individual acquires about a specific subculture prior to initial participation in the subculture. Uninitiated knowledge and understanding of specific subcultures may be gained through a number of sources, including family and peer group awareness, direct or indirect contact with established members of the subculture and, most significantly, the media (Young, 1983). Media coverage may range from straight reportage and documentary accounts of the activities of a particular subculture to fictional and artistic accounts, and even joking references to the particular proclivities of a subcultural group (e.g., cartoons showing groups of roped mountaineers all falling together, or references to and samples of rugby songs). This knowledge may be absorbed to facilitate a process of anticipatory socialization whereby characteristics and roles of the subculture may be enacted before the actor's current audience. Presocialization represents the first phase of identity construction and, as noted previously, such tenuous knowledge of a specific subculture frequently results in a caricatured and stereotypical image of the group, and certain misconceptions regarding members' behaviors may be developed. Presocialization is an ephemeral stage that ends when an actor makes direct contact with the subculture and is recruited and/or received as a member.

Selection and Recruitment

Before more accurate identity construction can occur, an individual must actually become a member of a specific subculture. Donnelly (1980) has characterized the prerequisites for membership as opportunity, motivation, and interest. Thus, whether an individual selects and seeks out membership or is actually recruited by an established member, it is necessary to consider issues such as proximity, life circumstances, and even chance in the initiation of subcultural membership. Unlike presocialization, selection and recruitment is a flexible stage that may be renewed if the actor is geographically mobile and desires to maintain membership in a specific subculture.

Socialization

Socialization is an initially active but ongoing stage wherein members undergo training in the characteristics of the subculture. They soon discover whether early conceptions of the subculture developed during the presocialization stage are accurate or misplaced. Members learn to adopt the values and perspectives of the group, taking on new roles and modifying others, and thus establishing valuable new identifications with the politics and symbols of the group as a whole. In turn, these mechanisms function to cement in the actor a new concept of self, one that will continue to develop and guide the actor in his or her new subcultural career.

Acceptance / Ostracism

Acceptance in subcultures is directly related to demonstrations of appropriate job and/or skill requirements, appropriate roles and identities under specific circumstances, successful socialization procedures, and general value homophyly between the actor and the larger group. Acceptance may also necessitate the actor's flexibility toward activities he or she usually considers negatively but which are condoned in the larger context of the subculture. Whereas the first three stages in the model are concerned with identity construction, the crucial element of this final stage is the confirmation of that identity by established members of the subculture. As Stone suggested,

> When one has identity, he is situated—that is, cast in the shape of a social object by the acknowledgment of his participation or membership in social relations. One's identity is established when others place him as a social object by assigning to him the same words of identity that he appropriates for himself or announces. (Stone, 1970, p. 399)

However, when identities are not confirmed and role conflicts do arise, members of subcultures who are unable to meet role requirements (we say unable because it is unlikely that those unwilling to satisfy expectations would have been attracted to a subculture initially) may face ostracism and/or banishment from the group. While some subcultures will be less rigorous in their internal policing procedures and allow such role conflicts to persist, others will require unconditionally that they be resolved.

This combination of identity construction and confirmation with the concept of subcultural career is examined with respect to previously conducted ethnographies of rock climbers and rugby players (Donnelly, 1980; Young, 1983), together with supporting material from studies of other sport subcultures.

Section IX: Sport Subcultures

THE CONSTRUCTION OF IDENTITY

After the preconceptions, and frequent misconceptions, of presocialization, accurate identity construction begins during the socialization stage. Following selection/recruitment, early interactive exchanges and events such as initiation ceremonies represent the apprenticeships that novices in sport subcultures must serve before they may fully begin their subcultural career. This is a time when the construction of a subcultural identity already inaugurated during the presocialization stage comes to the fore for established members to view and perhaps confirm. However, we have also suggested that initial attempts at identity construction are often inaccurate, and thus it is common in subcultures for certain misidentifications, misrepresentations, and inappropriate comments to be made during early apprenticeship.

Of course, the number of gaffes made by rookies will depend on the accuracy of information received during presocialization. If an individual's preconceptions are accurate they will likely facilitate a good base from which a career in a subculture may commence. One rugby player, for example, gaining prior knowledge from an established player, was attracted to the sport's reputation for a boisterous social life, and found few surprises once he was on the inside:

> I had heard from a friend some of the things that had happened after games but had never really bothered to find out for myself. Then this guy told me a story about the players at his club playing a trick on a stripper that made her run off-stage. Apparently one guy made out that he was really interested in her while his friend knelt down behind her and bit her ass so bad that it bled. Now I've started hanging around with those guys I've never seen so much butt-biting in all my life!

On the other hand, one ex-football player, entirely misconstruing the essentially nonprofessional approach of rugby and fully expecting rugby behavior to be far less rowdy than tales predicted, found certain aspects of the sport rather alarming, and his preliminary attempts at identity construction grossly inaccurate:

> It was my first night and people had warned me that Rookie Night was a bit of an ordeal, but I'd just shrugged it off. Well we [the rookies] were forced to chug three full beers right at the start. After that things slowed down for a while and I thought it wasn't going to be so bad. Then they [veterans] lined us up and brought out the goldfish. Live goldfish! We had to bite each fish in half with our teeth, chew them, and pass them mouth to mouth amongst each other. I couldn't believe it. And it got worse!

> I didn't expect anything like it. We'd train real hard for two hours a day and then go down to the bar and get hammered; and [post-game] beer-ups…well, they're twice as bad. I was surprised because I thought the coach would be angry if we didn't try to keep in shape. In actual fact he condones it as much as the rest of us. If we were on the football or hockey team we'd have been benched by now.

Similarly, Thomson cites a far more serious example of rookie misconceptions:

> I was really mad at being cut from the football team because I was sure I had the ability to make the team. So when I first went out for rugby I started with the attitude that I was going to show them how tough I was. I was going to break people apart. Like in football, that's my attitude, that's the only way to win. All the guys have got helmets and pads on, and they think they are hot crap. Anyway I decided to go out at rugby and try to hurt as many people as I could. In one of the first practices I jumped on J's foot and broke two of his toes. In my first game I back off about ten yards and ran at this loose ruck. I hit one of the guys on our own team and broke two of his ribs. Then, in this game in Portland I dislocated a guy's shoulder, and I was really proud of myself for doing it. Then all of a sudden, you know, after all those games and going to parties afterwards and meeting all of the other players, I lost this attitude completely. I was starting to feel really ashamed of myself because this just isn't the rugby spirit. If you're playing football that's something else. But in rugby as long as it's a good game you don't really mind if you win or not. I don't hold any animosity to anybody now. (Thomson, 1976, p. 113)

Because of such misconceptions, often made early in the presocialization stage, novices are frequently faced with some traumatic role-transitions that are vital to constructing an accurate subcultural identity. Implicit in the socialization of neophytes is a controlling function. That is, because individuals treed to acquire new role definitions and behaviors that are appropriate to constructing a new career identity, they are in a sense being controlled extraneously. As Stryker (1980) has suggested, two mechanisms prevail here: first, actors will seek to validate their identity "by behaving in ways that elicit validating responses from others" (p. 64); second, because subcultural identity is important for all actors, they will play their roles in a manner that shows deference for the governing values of the group. Thus, in the interaction that occurs between actors in the subculture, impression management plays a significant role.

Whenever role conflict occurs, members may "role-take" or manage impressions to appear as though they identify with the values of the groups more than is actually the case. For example, novice climbers learn quite quickly about hiding obvious symptoms of fear and about never avoiding an opportunity to climb. While it is perfectly acceptable for an established climber to waste a day by being off-form, hungover, or just too lazy to do any climbing, a rookie can never appear unenthusiastic for fear of being thought of as a camp-follower / groupie type, or even a pseudo—an individual who seeks the glory without the risk:

> One of the wardens told me that there are people at the 'Gunks who go down to Rock and Snow [the climbing equipment store in New Paltz], outfit themselves completely with all the latest climbing gear, and then just parade up and down the Carriage Road [along the foot of the main cliff] and hang around at the Uberfall [a central meeting and gathering place at the foot of the main cliff] without ever doing any climbs. I never believed this until I saw two of them doing that very thing. It was quite obvious that they weren't climbers because they had a complete rack each and all of the nuts were threaded upside down! I watched them for a while and they just walked up and down, stopped and had a drink, and every now and again they would put the

rope down and chalk up [their hands] as if they were going to do a climb. Then they would pick up their gear and move on. Unbelievable!

Rookies must also take all opportunities to climb because to decline may lead to the offer not being repeated, the establishment of a negative reputation, and consequent difficulties with status advancement in the subculture.

It is also under these circumstances that novices may be tested by being taken on climbs that are well beyond their ability. While there is little actual danger to those not leading a climb, the experience can create a great deal of subjective terror. Novices, especially those who appear to be precocious or boastful, are sometimes given the "treatment" ("Let's take on_____a route and scare the shit out of him!"). In order to pass this test, and in order for all novices to begin constructing an appropriate subcultural identity, it is necessary to manifest qualities of coolness and gameness to establish a reputation for reliability. A frequent sign of tension in novices is the shakes, or "sewing machine legs," the result of strain on the calf muscles from standing on small holds and the inability to relax on those holds. The ankles jump up and down spasmodically and uncontrollably, thereby increasing the novice's tension and fear that he or she will be shaken off the holds. The ability to control this phenomenon is a sure sign that one is beginning to relax in the stressful environment.

Overt displays of fear can destroy an individual's potential career (presuming that the individual would wish to continue) because it would be difficult to rely on such a person in genuinely dangerous circumstances. Donnelly (1980) describes an experience in which he had to effect the rescue of a novice partner who "froze" on a climb. The individual burst into tears upon reaching safety, but neither Donnelly nor the third member of the team could bring themselves to comfort him. By freezing, losing composure, he had jeopardized the safety of the party, and in the harsh and somewhat unfeeling social world of climbers he could not be forgiven. The incident was never discussed, the individual never climbed again, and the resulting awkward interaction led him to drop out of the circle of friends. A similar incident is described in Cherry's (1974, pp. 86–93) book on ironworkers and has similar consequences, indicating that in all avocations or occupations where risk and mutual dependence are involved, composure is perhaps the most important character trait.

Under less extreme circumstances, novices develop a variety of techniques to express composure when fear is actually felt. One method, often modeled for them by more experienced climbers, is to purposely overstate the degree of one's fear. An individual may state that he or she was "scared shitless," "gripped," or "sweating bullets," in each case employing the humor of exaggeration in order to diminish the degree of fear that is actually felt, or to indicate that no real fear existed in a situation where it should exist. In one sense it is a confessional act, but in another sense the message is, "If I really felt that scared would I be telling you?"

Similar forms of impression management may be apparent in rugby. As one player commented,

> Sometimes I just don't feel like partying or singing and drinking my brains out at all but I feel I should. It's like, I don't want to be seen as not being one of the guys. So I go with the flow

usually....I do feel like there's an element of pressure to do all these things sometimes that, to be honest with you, really aren't my style. But when all the other guys are watching you, its really hard to avoid joining in, you know.

There is an important distinction to be drawn between roles played up front or on stage in a subculture and those played in the everyday course of events. The player in question, for example, was settled in a respectable professional career, participating in the rugby subculture on game days only. Thus, a peripheral member and a weekend deviant of sorts, he did not experience the same degree of role-identification as more central members, the latter being content to act out their disaffiliation (Goffman, 1963) on a more permanent basis, and deriving from it a significant sense of belonging.

As we have noted, in order to pay homage to the subculture's focal concerns (Miller, 1958), some novices will undergo anticipatory socialization procedures. That is, they will vicariously perform roles in various situations that they assume are expected of them. For example, a typical trait of novice climbers is to want to display to both climbers and nonclimbers that they are now climbers. This is part of the first stage of identity construction. Display involves wearing climbing clothes and boots in nonclimbing settings, carrying equipment, books, and magazines about climbing as conspicuously as possible, and turning the conversation to climbing as often as possible. Novices have even been seen wearing the extremely uncomfortable boots designed specifically for rock climbing (removed immediately upon completion of a climb by veterans) in a number of nonclimbing situations such as attending class or in a bar. While they may claim to be breaking in the boots, such novices are invariably pleased that one has recognized their boots, thereby recognizing them as a fellow climber. In fact, the purpose of the display is to indicate to nonclimbers that one is now different, and to signal to other climbers that one is now a fellow member and may be approached as such.

Of course, what such display actually does is indicate to climbers that one is a novice. Experienced climbers have been known to take advantage of the novice's tendency to display by allowing them to carry all of the equipment, particularly if the approach to the cliff involves a long, uphill walk. While such an act may appear to be parasitic, it is actually symbiotic because the novice is allowed to indulge his or her tendency to display and may even fantasize (quite accurately, in fact) that nonclimbers who see the group may think that the novice is actually the leader because he or she is carrying the equipment. As novices become more experienced and more secure in their identity as climbers, their need for display will decrease, and they will gradually become conscious that such behavior is not "cool."

Overt display is a rookie error that highlights the subcultural values of coolness and understatement. While display is expected from novices, it may be ridiculed as the individual becomes more experienced. Normally, the more obvious signs of display are removed—ropes are removed from the outside to the inside of a backpack, climbing boots are removed and more comfortable shoes worn when not climbing, and conversations with other climbers turn to the subject more naturally. Recognition of other climbers becomes more subtle. Without quite realizing it, the individual begins to notice the rolled-up magazine, the guidebook in the hip pocket, and the cuts and scars on an individual's hands that could only have come from climbing rock. One climber, who worked in an equipment store, described a method of identifying the skill of climbers by their dress and demeanor:

> Those in beat-up looking clothes were either good or doing a lot. The ones in new clothes were usually beginners but they would talk as if they were good. The good climbers had an aura about them. They didn't talk about climbing all the time but they were very aware of equipment and knew their stuff. They did not come in the store during the day—only late at night and early morning.

As a novice becomes more confident in the construction of identity during the very active stages of socialization, he or she also becomes more certain and accurate in the reading of others' identities.

Anticipatory socialization may take other forms in rugby. Initiates in the rugby subculture frequently pick up on symbolic cues (Stryker, 1980) and act out anticipated roles. One neophyte in particular performed the requisite "Zulu" (or striptease) on rookie night without any of the usual coercion from veterans: "I knew I was going to have to strip but I didn't know when or how. I was feeling pretty hammered and I wanted to show the rest of the team that I could party as well as anyone, so away I went. I guess I was a little over-eager in retrospect!" Approximately 3 weeks in to the Canadian university rugby season, another neophyte, endowed with as much skill and talent as any of his teammates, found himself cut to the second team after a series of disappointing performances. The problem actually lay in the fact that he had, observing veteran members' behavior and modeling himself upon it, developed a habit of staying up all night drinking before games, rendering him tired and lethargic during games:

> I don't understand it. All those guys get away with it but I don't seem to be able to. Maybe its because they've been doing it for so long they're used to it and I'm not. All I know is that when I stay up with those guys I play real lousy the next day....I think I'm playing "seconds" rugby right now. So I'm going to have to make a choice here.

It seems that rugby players are aware from the presocialization and recruitment stages that certain forms of behavior are expected of them, and their subsequent behavior often shows something of a cyclical orientation. Conscious of bolstering their career identities by conforming to a set of subcultural role expectations, rookies and more established players make deliberate efforts to demonstrate modes of "typical" rugby behavior to other members of the group, and to undergo rituals, often before they are expected of them. Again, the construction of identity is an initially active, but essentially ongoing, process.

Perhaps the final and most important stage of identity construction involves the actor resolving, or at least learning to live with, the contradictions that characterize most sport and career subcultures. These contradictions are between the "front" and "back" regions of the subculture, or between the organizational and informal charters of the group (cf. Ingham, 1975; Vaz, 1972). Contradictions are readily apparent in both the rugby and climbing subcultures, and it is the novice's ability to deal with them that determines the final outcome of the process of identity construction. The true values of the subculture are acted out constantly for the novices by experienced members, and novices are expected to model the appropriate attitudes and behaviors. But the values are also continually emphasized in the gossip and in the repeated stories that become the myth and legend of a subculture.

The core values of rugby are truly mystifying for the average North American male who has grown up believing in success at all costs, ascetic training regimens, and high levels of fitness. The amateuristic aspects of rugby are demonstrated in a variety of ways, including the mandatory heavy drinking, but also in the stories of players who leave their cigarettes and matches next to the goal-post to be retrieved at halftime, in the legends of players who started the game in drunken stupors, and in gossip about who played with a massive hangover. In his ethnography of college and city rugby teams in North America, for example, Young (1983) discovered that a normative behavior, particularly of core members of rugby teams, was to pull all-nighters and to arrive at games hungover, unprepared, and generally devoid of energy following a night without sleep.

Other stories concern aspects of sportsmanship, in which players are lent to an opposing team in order to equalize the numbers, actions are taken to assist referees and officials, and players have great times fraternizing with opponents following hard-fought games. This is amply illustrated by one of Orloff's respondents in her study of the San Diego State rugby team:

> Rugby is the only sport I know of in the world where you can go out drinking with your opponents before the game, try to kill them during the game and then have a party afterwards. If you play any team anywhere, then the host team provides a party for the opposing team. This is a tradition. We also provide two kegs of beer for our opponents after every single game, and we would expect them to do the same. (1974, p. 45)

Such subcultural values of sportsmanship and generosity are also evident among British and Canadian ruggers. The general approach is epitomized in statements made, first, by a young college player in Canada: "Whether we win or lose it's important to us all that we enjoy the game and that both teams get together afterwards and party"; and second, by an English club veteran: "For me, the rugby club has always symbolized a type of second home and I think most of the lads feel that way. Over the years we've established some happy and lasting bonds with other clubs and we intend to keep it that way. Come to the clubhouse after any game…and you'll see what camaraderie really means."

As we can see from recent literature distributed by a provincial Rugby Union board in Canada, at the present time the administrators of North American rugby are clearly concerned with officially promoting the game as one that is rich in the ethos of sportsmanship: "Many…teams are providing athletes the facilities to enjoy the sense of loyalty and friendship…only the Rugby team spirit can provide." Noticeable here is an explicit attempt to elevate rugby above other North American sports because of this subcultural emphasis on sportsmanship and player fraternization.

A further set of rugby stories emphasizes playing with abandon, and mythologizes players who were found, upon completion of a game, to have suffered a broken leg, arm, or neck. But, the major set of stories concerns the rowdiness of postgame social behavior, and includes feats of drinking, damage to property and reputation, nights in prison, and who can outdo whom in terms of outrageous and obscene behavior. Young's (1983) cross-cultural ethnography of the rugby subculture is replete with cases of ruggers urinating in public and on tour buses, and bus drivers refusing to travel with them; conducting player stripteases and "mooning" in bars and other public places; being ejected from restaurants for having massive food fights; conducting souvenir-hunting escapades in bars, on road trips and in opponents' club houses; participating in public vandalism; objectifying and vilifying women and homosexuals in scatological songs and chants; staging "elephant walks"—a line of naked players marching one behind the other, to the tune "The Baby Elephant Walk," with one hand on the shoulder of the player in front and the other hand grasping the penis of the player behind—on campuses and through women's dormitories.

Examples are legion: After being requested to leave the premises of a popular restaurant following a mass food fight, a Canadian university rugby team drew away from the parking lot to a crescendo of breaking glass when players hurled empty beer bottles out of windows; one Canadian subject was arrested and jailed for attempting to steal an enormous mirror from behind a crowded bar while on tour in the U.S.; a Canadian university secretary revealed that on her way home from work during the rugby season she had never driven past the playing fields without team members dropping their shorts and "mooning" her and other passers-by; one subject acquired legendary status at his English club for his pièce de résistance, which involved excreting down his pant leg while standing on top of the club piano and displaying the results to the audience at special events.

It becomes clear to rookies that these are the standards they will be expected to live up to, although some variation is clearly possible. The paradoxes lie in playing a vigorous game wherein victory is important but how one plays the game is even more important, in tackling opponents with abandon while knowing that one will be drinking with those same individuals after the game, and in practicing social habits that render one almost incapable of meeting the physical requirements of the game. (Donnelly & Young, 1985, have noted some additional paradoxes in rugby.) The construction of an identity as a rugby player proves to be an interesting balancing act for most individuals.

The contradictions in climbing are primarily between the public and private voices of climbers. The sport is subject to public criticism on occasion (as are most high-risk sports), particularly after accidents or expensive rescues. As a consequence, climbers and participants in other high-risk sports have tended to develop an entire mythology that is primarily for public consumption. This organizational charter emphasizes safety (it's not really dangerous if you know what you are doing), character-building, noncompetitiveness, and comradeship (the kinship of the rope) (Donnelly, 1981b, 1981c, 1981d, 1982a). Even novice climbers are presented with this view of the sport, but as Donnelly (above) and Vanreusel and Renson (1982) have shown, the reality presented to the novices both as models and in myth and legend is quite different.

It soon becomes apparent to many novices that real risks are frequently taken, character and friendship are by no means an automatic consequence of participation, and competition between climbers is rampant. Again, these values are modeled for the neophytes by established climbers and are represented in the gossip and lore of the subculture. For example, competition is evident in gossip concerning who may be working secretly on a new cliff in order to make first ascents before anyone else, who has cheated by not following the informal rule structure of the sport, and in legendary accounts of first ascents that were snatched from the grasp of unsuspecting opponents. The kinship of the rope is disputed in clique formations, in rivalries that are sometimes tense between adherents of different climbing areas, and in numerous stories of fistfights on the heights and tantrums during expeditions. And, the idea of character-building does not appear to be in complete accord with social behavior that is only rivaled, on occasion, by that of rugby players, by gossip about who was seen smoking what on a ledge several thousand feet up a cliff face, and by stories about how a whole valley full of climbers were able to achieve temporary wealth after a dope smuggler's plane crashed in a location that was inaccessible to police but not to climbers.

The major theme of climbing lore concerns risk and accidents, the significance of which may be determined from the number of terms used to describe these conditions. If climbing were actually safe for those who are knowledgeable, climbers would not be constantly talking about who was "gripped" on a particular climb, or about their latest epic. Recent accidents are analyzed; dissected, dwelled upon, joked about, and the victims mourned or vilified. Some accidents slip into the lore of climbing, and climbers will occasionally point out the site of accidents. Narrow escapes become even more famous because they indicate that there is always hope of survival, even in the most impossible circumstances. Individuals who fell the whole length of a cliff and then got up and walked away become folk heroes, even though the circumstances are often exaggerated with repeated telling.

Another class of story that provides additional reassurance regarding survival and a continued normal existence, and also carries with it the moral implication that it is all worth it, involves the remarkable or rapid recovery. In these stories, climbers dismiss themselves from hospitals, confound doctors' opinions by climbing again, and return to climbing while wearing their casts, or after losing fingers and toes, or even with artificial limbs. An example of this type of story concerns the climber who was badly hurt in an accident, and who was informed that he would be in the hospital for at least 6 months and that he would never climb again. The doctors also told him that alcohol would kill him during recovery, but his friends, feeling that his life was over anyway if he could not climb again, decided that he should part happily, and they continually smuggled beer and scotch into his hospital room. The climber dismissed himself from the hospital after 2 months and returned to climbing while still wearing a leg cast. The story clearly suffers from exaggeration and embellishment, but the point is that the exaggeration and constant retelling are precisely what make it revealing as a source of subcultural values. Similar stories are found in most high-risk sport subcultures and rarely become public knowledge, although Nicki Lauda's miraculously rapid return to Grand Prix auto racing after suffering nearly fatal burns in an accident has precisely the same point in its often exaggerated retelling.

Klein (1986) has recently shown how bodybuilders must learn to resolve, or at least cope with, yet another set of contradictions in order to develop an appropriate subcultural identity. In this case the contradictions are between the public image of rugged individualism and the reality of submitting to a feudal organizational structure, the public image of health and fitness and the reality of steroid abuse and extraordinary dietary practices, and the public image of heterosexual masculinity and the reality of homosexual hustling. The construction of normal identities as rugby players, climbers, or bodybuilders therefore frequently involves a complete turnaround from the preconceptions that may have been acquired during the presocialization stage—from courses, instructional books, television documentaries, and so on. While many subcultures are able to accommodate a wide range of internal differentiation, some individuals are unable to adjust during the active stage of socialization to a set of values that may be diametrically opposed to the public image of the sport.

THE CONFIRMATION OF IDENTITY

Under normal circumstances, identity confirmation is a relatively straightforward process. A novice begins to accept the actual values of the subculture and to leave behind any misconceptions. Confirmation may occur gradually, in rugby for example, in the process of making the team, undergoing the rigors of rookie night, and becoming more and more involved with established players both on and off the field. It is the process of establishing a reputation as a reliable individual whose values and behavior apparently conform to subcultural expectations. It is not necessary to do something crazy either on or off the field, but in the rugby subculture, crazy acts can certainly speed up and enhance the development of a reputation. In climbing, confirmation may be more immediate, for example, being asked to take the lead by an established member of the subculture.

In each case one's reputation is made, and one's membership has been confirmed. But reputations are such that they must constantly be remade, and it is this aspect of identity confirmation that is most interesting. The fragility of reputations has been an ongoing theme in interactionist sociology, and credentialing or verification procedures are a part of the norms of social conduct. New members of subcultures, geographically mobile members, and members who are attempting to have claimed achievements accepted each place their reputations, their constructed identities, at risk.

Based on Goffman's premise that all interactants desire smoothly flowing or euphoric exchanges, the rules of deference (particularly the rule of acceptance— "An individual's claims about himself must be accepted as valid unless proved otherwise" [Birrell, 1978, p. 267]); and demeanor (particularly the rule of sincerity— "The individual must be the person he has claimed to be" [Birrell, 1978, p. 265]) are most appropriate to the process of identity confirmation. If one or more parties to an interaction are suspected of not complying with the rules, then verification becomes an issue. A related concern here is the concept of trust. Garfinkel's (1963) definition, in which he refers to trust as taking for granted the constitutive expectancies or basic rules of the game, is clearly related to Birrell's derived rules of deference and demeanor. Henslin further suggests that, "Where the actor has offered a definition of himself and the audience is willing to interact with the actor on the basis of that definition, we are saying that trust exists" (1968, p. 140).

The actor's definition of self, or the front that is offered to an audience, may be seen as a coherence between the various parts of the front—the setting in which an actor appears, the appearance of the actor, and the manner of the actor (Goffman, 1959). If an actor is attempting to have a previous achievement accepted, we may add to these the appropriateness of the claim being made, and what is known by the audience of the actor's previous (verified) achievements. A coherence between these various parts of the actor's identity will usually result in trust, in the confirmation of the actor's claims.

Under normal circumstances, because record keeping is so much a part of sport and because of the requirements for third-party verification for claimed achievements, verification is not an issue in sport. Most individuals joining a team, for example, are either complete novices who need to establish a reputation or they arrive with a documented reputation. It is the exceptions to these conditions that are of interest. Donnelly (1978, 1982b) has examined verification procedures in climbing and birding, two activities that have no formal requirement for third-party verification, and a recent study has examined verification as applied to geographical mobility in Canadian rugby clubs. (Parnoja, 1985).

On the rare occasions in climbing when an individual is unknown to a particular group either personally or by reputation, or when an unobserved solo ascent is being claimed for which there is no photographic evidence, it is necessary for the safety of the members and the integrity of the subculture to determine the legitimacy of the individual. This is done by examining the coherence between the various parts of an actor's front, and possibly by engaging in the type of strategic interaction or information games outlined by Goffman (1969) and Scott (1968). For example, the pseudo-climbers mentioned previously were certainly making unspoken claim about their identity, but were easily revealed by experienced climbers because of an equipment error. However, it is apparent that poor climbers, or climbers who may have a tendency to panic, can be a very real hazard to climbers who accept exaggerated claims from them and who climb with them. Similarly, in cycling and particularly cycle racing, knowledge of and ability to use equipment (as in climbing) serves a gatekeeping function, because if one is unable to ride in a straight line at 60–70 kph one is a hazard to other riders (Albert, 1984).

In keeping with the old exploratory and geographical aspects of climbing, it is not customary to doubt the claims made by an individual, particularly if it is possible for the climber to have done what is being claimed (given such variables as the weather, ice and snow conditions, time available, and the climber's ability, equipment, and physical condition) and if the claimed achievement is in keeping with the individual's known ability, past experience, and previous reliability. If there are apparent reasons to dispute the claims, judgment is withheld, and an individual may suffer a loss of reputation (what might, in this context, be termed a disconfirmation of identity).

The problem of confirmation in rugby concerns players from other countries with a long tradition and reputation in the game (e.g., United Kingdom, New Zealand, South Africa) joining North American clubs. Such players arrive in North America with an aura of excellence that is sometimes undeserved. But because North American players, most of whom are new to the game, are primed to accept claims of excellence from these players, it is not unusual for the players from outside North America to take advantage of the situation by exaggerating their ability. As a result, sometimes a foreign player will make the team over some more deserving North American players. The Canadian players interviewed (Parnoja, 1985) were all aware of such a possibility and suggested that it would be resolved in the long term purely on playing ability, particularly if there are no other ways to confirm the claimed identity.

In all of these cases, when there are genuine suspicions, or when an individual is being particularly tiresome by making obviously invalid claims, a number of sanctions are available to legitimate members of the subculture. Climbers have been known to take such a person on particularly terrifying routes, or to demonstrate his or her lack of ability in obvious and public ways. Cyclists have caused those who are unable to handle their bikes in an appropriately safe manner to crash. And rugby players note that tongues can be loosened and indiscretions revealed with the liberal application of beer (although, they also note, culprits can be punished in practice games).

Entrapment may be employed as a form of strategic interaction in order to reveal cheats (e.g., asking "How did you find the final overhang?" when it is known that there are no overhangs on the climb), the results of which are not necessarily shared with the culprit but certainly spread to all other members. Birders employ similar strategies against those members of the subculture who develop a reputation for being the only person in a region to see a particular species—often a sign of exaggeration or citing. However, outright accusations are rare because of the tendency to avoid confrontation and the preference for euphoric exchanges; but when deliberate embarrassment does occur it is entirely appropriate in the manner outlined by Gross and Stone:

> embarrassment is deliberately perpetrated as a negative sanction as in "calling" one who is giving an undesirable (role) performance. Since embarrassment does incapacitate the person from performing his role, it can clearly be used to stop someone from playing a role that might discredit a collectivity. Empirical categories include public reprimands, exposure of false fronts, open gossip or cattiness, or embarrassment perpetrated as a retaliation for an earlier embarrassment. In some of these cases, a person is exposed as having no right to play the role he has laid claim to, because the identity in which his role is anchored is invalid. In others, the person is punished by terminating his role performance so that he can no longer enjoy its perquisites. (1964. pp. 14–15)

In the more format sport subcultures, it is entirely possible to construct an identity that will convince nonmembers and even novice members that one has a reputation and a valid claim to membership. But the ongoing process of identity confirmation ensures that such individuals cannot do too much damage to the subculture itself, or to individual members.

CONCLUSIONS

The roles and identities of members of subcultures should not be thought of as static positions and entities. They are constantly undergoing revision and change due to a variety of processes both within and outside the subculture. We have argued that a career contingency model represents a useful means of characterizing subcultural membership, and that the active processes of cultural production in sport subcultures ensure that socialization is an ongoing stage, while acceptance / ostracism is likely to be a repeated stage. The key contingencies within this model, then, are the construction / reconstruction of an appropriate subcultural identity, and the confirmation / reconfirmation of that identity by other members of the subculture.

Although many subcultures are able to tolerate a great deal of diversity, there are frequently some critical aspects for which little tolerance is allowed. These typically concern circumstances wherein it is necessary to trust that a partner or opponent will play his or her part, that is, will have constructed and be prepared to display an appropriate aspect of subcultural identity. For example, professional wrestlers must be able to trust that their opponents will have learned and will play their parts appropriately, both for reasons of safety and to generate "heat" (Birrell & Turowetz, 1979); racing cyclists must trust that their opponents will have enough skill and composure to ride in a straight line at speed (Albert, 1984); hockey players need to trust that their teammates will come to their defense in the case of cheap shots or mismatched fights (Faulkner, 1974); birders most be able to rely on the integrity of the reports of fellow birders before embarking on long and expensive journeys to observe particularly rare species (Donnelly, 1982b); climbers must trust that partners will retain composure and not endanger anyone through panic or freezing (Donnelly, 1980); and rugby players need to maintain their sportsmanship in a particularly rough game, and not spoil the celebrations afterward by moderation or temperate behavior (Young, 1983).

In addition, resolving the contradictions of many subcultures exposes members to insider knowledge that must often be retained in order to maintain the integrity of the subculture. For example, much of the work as instructors, now available to many climbers, would disappear if insider conversations about risk reached a much wider audience; and bodybuilders need to retain insider knowledge about steroid abuse and homosexual hustling. Although some information inevitably leaks out through sociologists and ex-members, as long as the majority deny such information a level of plausible deniability is maintained.

The model developed here, concerning identity construction and confirmation in a subcultural career, is by no means limited to sport subcultures. Similar patterns of identity construction and confirmation, contingencies, and aspects of cultural production may be found in all achieved subcultures. Thus, whether reference is made to a greater range of avocational subcultures (leisure, hobbyist, and collector groups), to occupational and military subcultures, or to youth and deviant subcultures, the construction / reconstruction of an appropriate subculture identity and the confirmation / reconfirmation of that identity by other members are key processes.

This analysis of sport subcultures is grounded in interactionist approaches to the topic (cf. Fine & Kleinman, 1979). However, such focused views of specific processes within subcultures should not lead researchers to consider subcultures in isolation from their structural, historical, and geographical contexts, or to neglect the fact that "the dominant values of wider society are transmitted, resisted or negotiated" (Bishop & Hoggett, 1987, p. 32) through subcultures in general, but perhaps particularly through avocational subcultures. Without such contextualization, subcultural research will remain an interesting appendage to more mainstream consideration of changing patterns of social development.

What Is So Punk About Snowboarding?

Rebecca Heino

It is not a surprise to most that snowboarders and skiers have animosity toward each other. This has been well documented in the public press. When someone asks, "Do you ski or snowboard?" it is often not merely an innocent question of inquiry. Either you are a skier and practice those cultural norms or you are a snowboarder and participate in that culture. To many who practice the sports, one cannot be both. What causes people to insist that you must participate in one at the expense of the other? What causes this dichotomy between two sports that share the same playing fields and in practice are more similar than different?

The intersection between snowboarding and skiing, or more specifically between snowboarders and skiers, exposes important issues surrounding the cultural significance of the practice of sports and the commodification of sport in contemporary times. Sport is an active battleground for cultural significance and is not immune to issues of social class, domination and resistance, legitimation, and race/gender. When a new sport develops or is adopted, such as snowboarding, it is another site in which these issues must be renegotiated. Bourdieu (1991) explains, "The appearance of a new sport…causes a restructuring of the space of sporting practices and a more or less redefinition of the meaning attached to various practices" (p. 367). The rise of snowboarding offered resistance to the dominant culture of skiing and sports as a whole; it made transparent the meaning and capital involved in skiing as well the commodification and legitimation of sports in general. This is where the animosity began.

RESISTANCE IS BORN IN A BOARD

The still contestable history of snowboarding seems to have its roots somewhere in the 1960s with kids riding Snurfers. Jake Burton, known to many as the father of snowboarding, reported in an interview that it was his experience with snurfing on grass that first led him to imagine snowboarding as a new sport.

In the late 1970s, he began to make, ride, and sell snowboards (Cohen, 1996). From the beginning of this new practice, there was considerable resistance to its presence on the tamed and orderly ski slopes. Burton recalls attempting to convince many ski resorts into allowing him to ride his snowboard. Others document their own removal from various resorts because of their board. This new equipment, and also style, was not accepted at the ski resorts. Although this battle is well documented in the popular media, and lived out by many snowboarders, the reasons behind it need to be fleshed out.

At first glance, the practice of snowboarding does not seem that different from skiing. Both activities require their participants to bind their feet on to Plexiglas technologies, ride a lift up the mountain together, and then proceed down the same snow-covered slopes while turning to control speed. One person has two boards attached to their feet and the other has one, with slightly different turning techniques because of that. So, why wasn't snowboarding seen as merely an extension of skiing? What was so different about it that people resisted its integration on the slopes? The difference is not so much that of technique but that of culture: the threat of not-so-subtle resistance to the dominant ski culture.

When snowboarding began to establish its presence in the 1980s, the once unwieldy sport of skiing had become fairly orderly and disciplined. Skiing required spare time, significant economic capital, and cultural capital, three of the determining factors of the distribution of sport across class (Bourdieu, 1991). Cultural capital includes how to dress, language to use, and how to interact on and off the slopes. This expensive and bourgeois sport developed a strong set of rules of conduct that most followed. Those that participated were mostly middle- to upper-class Whites. The rationalization of the sport and development of governing bodies ensured its predictability beyond local differences. In other words, similar rules and practices were established at many ski resorts. In understanding "distinctive" sports, such as skiing, golf, and gymnastics, the hidden entry requirements such as family tradition, obligatory clothing, and techniques of sociability also work to keep those sports closed to working classes (Bourdieu, 1991). These entry requirements developed over time. In the 1960s, skiing was less expensive, and clothing consisted of the warmest items in your closet. Reflecting the prosperity and materialism of the United States in the 1980s, the equipment and dress of skiing became expensive, flamboyant, bright, and technologically advanced. Even beginners often seemed to be clothed in the latest fashion and innovation. Ski hills developed into ski resorts, charging $30 to $40 a day for a ski lift ticket and often attracting the rich and famous on their holidays. Skiing was also a popular competitive sport and gained legitimacy in its importance to the Winter Olympics as well as to other established competitive events.

Snowboarding began for different reasons than did skiing. "Every other snow sport was born out of a need for transportation—except one, snowboarding. There's nothing practical about it" (Hodgson, 1998, p. 93). It was not developed for practical or competitive reasons. Youth were immediately attracted to the snowboard. It was new and different, a way for youths to differentiate themselves from their parents' practices. Instead of the snowboarders aligning themselves with the dominant ski culture, they presented their cultural roots in surfing, skateboarding, and the "gangsta" (Anderson, 1999). Often, the similarities in technique of surfing, skateboarding, and snowboarding (they all use one board and a sideways stance) is the argument used to align the groups; yet, the stronger connection is not in technique but in the resistance of their predominantly youth cultures to the dominant culture. This subculture "represent [s] symbolic challenges to the symbolic order" (Hebdige, 1979, p. 92).

The differences are manifest not only in style, "the area in which opposing definitions clash with most dramatic force" (Hebdige, 1979, p. 3), but also in the meaning of the activity itself. Style incorporates the symbolic representations of the subculture. As the beginning quote noted, "Separated by age, fashion, etiquette, lingo and per capita income, the skier and snowboarder rode up the mountain together in chilly silence" (Wulf, 1996, p. 69), although difference in income might have been more due to age than social class.

Snowboarders clashed with skiers in style of dress and body presentation, equipment, and language. Whereas skiers, especially in the 1980s, favored tight, aerodynamic clothing in bright and flashy colors, snowboarders appropriated styles popular in the skateboarding culture. In sharp contrast to the skier's costume, these outfits were usually very baggy in drab colors such as olive green and brown. They crossed a grunge and hip-hop style to appear nondescript with an "I don't-care-about-my-appearance attitude." How does urban style reach the snow slopes? The popularity of the hip-hop look, and its appropriation by suburban youth from its urban origins, allowed for an easy jump from skateboard and surfing style to snowboard style. Anderson (1999) takes this argument further to say that these styles are ways to establish masculinity in snowboarding. The codes enmeshed in this dress resisted the wealth, show of skill, and personal attention demanded by the neon tight ski outfit.

After the early days, in which many probably did just grab an old flannel out of the closet, snowboard companies began to produce winter clothing with the same out-of-the closet look. The irony became that snowboarders paid just as much for the grunge/hip-hop/gangsta look as the skiers paid for their outfits. The snowboarders expended just as much economic capital to change the cultural capital necessary for participation; they expended economic capital to express the "I don't care" attitude, to fit in with the antimaterialism style, and to gain acceptance into the subculture. So because of their White, middle-class status, they can appropriate these styles with little fear of discrimination that Black gangsta youth might experience from the same style (Anderson, 1999). The right clothing is essential in the snowboarding subculture. There is no easier way to spot a new crossover snowboarder than one who is still wearing a ski jacket while riding.

Presentation of the body simultaneously expressed resistance through the means of shock and undifferentiation. Snowboarders often were cited, or at least remembered, as wearing hair that was wild, fro-like, sticking up and dyed a variety of colors. It was a familiar form of resistance recalled from the punks and mods, and more recently in Dennis Rodman and other NBA stars. Earrings, nose rings, and eyebrow rings were other forms of bodily resistance. Whereas these presented resistance in a shocking, very visible manner, the baggy clothing covered the rest of the body in a resistance based on invisibility.

The body plays an important role in sport. It is not just the discipline or rationalization of the body when engaged in sport but the presentation of the body for others. The gaze of others on the body is accepted, if not encouraged, in sports (Aycock, 1992; Miller, 1998). It is no surprise that women have different standards placed on them for the body than men. For example, in female body building, they are judged on femininity, which implies muscles that are not too big, because female bodies are socially constructed to be seductive (Guthrie & Castelnuovo, 1992).

Obviously, in winter sports, the body is not exposed in the same way that most other sports allow. Yet, skiers still tended to wear clothing that was tight and accentuated the body, especially women. The tight polyester/lycra snowpants allowed for women to still be seductive and feminine, while the total body suits tended to emphasize the figure. Snowboarder's style was loose and baggy. Distinctions between male and female clothing were minimal. Although clothing specifically for females was produced, it was still just as baggy as male's clothing. It covers and hangs rather than accentuates. Except for the hair, it could be difficult to distinguish between male and female snowboarders. It diverts the gaze from the body and resists the dominant social constructions of gendered bodies. This is true for those actually on the mountain, but in snowboard advertising, sexualized images of women were still more prevalent than images of women as talented riders (Anderson, 1999).

Another site of resistance was the equipment itself. A snowboard is a very expressive and personalized piece of equipment in contrast to the distant and professional skis. Skis represented professionalism, competitive skill, and uniformity; they tended to be bright colors with some limited design and little variation between the style of one ski to another. In contrast, snowboards were often very unique. The space available on the top of the snowboard allowed for individual expression. Many snowboards had pictures, cartoons, or abstract designs on them. These range from pictures of enlarged kernels of corn to impressionistic snowflakes to animation bordering on obscene. They favor personalization over professionalism. Snowboarders often cover their boards with stickers of their favorite snowboard, skateboard, and surfing companies, showing a certain disdain for the equipment itself. It becomes a highly expressive piece of equipment representing the individual's personality as well as the resistance to the uniformity and sterility of skis.

Skis also were used in acts of bricolage, which is the relocation of a sign within the discourse to change its meaning. Lib Tech, a snowboarding company, first made skis called the Acme Opal as a trophy for the Mt. Baker Legendary Banked Slalom, one of the oldest and most cultish snowboarding competitions. They would give the winner a single ski, obviously one that never could (or should) be used. The ski represented a small token for doing well in the challenging world of snowboarding. Lib Tech then made 10 pairs of Acme Opals and priced them at $1,000 a pair. A spokesperson for the company explained, "We want to discourage people from buying them" (White, 1994). This was the production of skis not for the sport of skiing but to prove that snowboarding companies could produce skis and still have no need for them—to render them physically capable but culturally disposable.

Three years later, Santa Cruz Snowboards mockingly developed all-mountain skis as a "patch" to help skiers wean themselves off of skis and onto snowboards. It began as a sort of prank but turned lucrative when they surprisingly sold more than 1,000 pairs. The CEO, Richard Novak, mused "Sometimes gags backfire" (Metzler, 1998, p.18). This "gag" received considerable outrage from the ski companies because it upset the established order of power and production: Ski companies produced snowboards, but snowboard companies should not be allowed to produce skis.

Another act of bricolage revolved around the Golden Duct Tape trophy. Duct tape was first appropriated from its typical use, in manual labor jobs, to patch and waterproof aging gloves and pants of snowboarders. The duct-tape look coincided with the seeming ambivalence or hostility to fashion and was perceived as a symbol of a well-seasoned rider. The popularity of duct tape, and its symbolism to the snowboard community, was furthered when it was "goldenized" and presented as the trophy, again, at Mt. Baker. The symbolically, but not monetarily, rich rewards represented the ironic tension between snowboarders' general disdain for competition while participating in it. The worth of the trophy was in its symbolism that established snowboarding as its own sport.

As symbolic power was manifested in clothing and equipment, language itself became a point of differentiation and resistance. The first most important word to develop was what to call the practice of snowboarding (besides its obvious term). Snowboarders quickly were known to "shred" the mountain. This word was appropriated from surfers who "shredded" the waves. Snowboarders were called "shredders," and female snowboarders were called "shred bunnies." This word has since become passe and was replaced by *ride* (e.g., Are you going to ride today?).

Snowboarding appropriated other words from skateboarding and surfing such as *goofy footed* (riding with your right foot in front) and *sick* (excellent, as in "That was sick air") but also has developed its own lingo. Snow can either be *freshie* (as in fresh snow) or *pow pow* (powder). As you ride, you could *bonk* (bang off a nonsnow object), *fakie* (ride in reverse stance), *hit* (jump), or *switchstance* (a fakie while doing a trick). They constructed a language that not only was expressive of new forms and practices of snowboarders but also was distinct from the language of skiing (i.e., hit vs. jump) and was aligned with the skateboard and surfing culture. The resistance to the established ski culture was obvious in the clothing, equipment, and language of the growing youth culture of snowboarding.

CONTESTED MEANING OF SPORT

This subversive style reflected and constituted the redefinition of meaning attached to sport in general through the practice of snowboarding. It was not only a subculture resistant to skiing but resistant to the meaning and symbolism of sport itself, which skiing had come to represent. Rinehart (1994) marked the move from expressive sport (driven by the participant) to spectacle sport (driven by rewards). Expressive sport is practiced by individuals for their personal expression and fulfillment. Spectacle sport is sport performed for others, often highly mediated, with the promise of economic or cultural returns. It is packaged for consumer entertainment rather than for sport for its own sake (Smith, 1996). The term *marginal sport* defined sports on the fringe of bureaucratized and rationalized sport. Yet, these marginal sports (i.e., American Gladiators) were still linked more strongly to spectatorship than to self-expression, often because they were mediated through television.

The commodification, professionalization, and bureaucratization of sport, as well as the move from expressive to spectatorship, had led to the ethic of winning at all costs. Many have mourned this turn in sports. "Indeed there is something perverse when sport becomes a zero-sum game where winning means all, and competition, improvement, and camaraderie are inconsequential" (Smith, 1996, p. 516).

Section IX: Sport Subcultures

Bourdieu (1991) attributed this "must win" mentality to the mass spectacle transmitted by media beyond the circle of past and present participants themselves. This creates an audience that is one step removed from the sport because they never participated in it. The spectators, then, have a more superficial perception that enjoys the sensationalism of the sport. This has encouraged sports participants and organizers to pursue victory at all costs. Perhaps this is why soccer (football to most of the world) is not as popular in the United States as in South America and Europe. Soccer is a game of subtlety; enjoyment is in the beauty of a well-placed pass or the complex strategy that orchestrates the players rather than in high-scoring games. Often, the better team loses because very few points are ever scored, especially relative to basketball, football, or baseball. United States' audiences, who in general play less soccer than the "big 3," perhaps do not have as much patience for subtlety over sensationalism.

The political purposes of sports have also been historically established. It often is used as a vehicle to promote nationalism. For example, the Argentinian government, host of the 1978 World Cup, blatantly used it as a platform to counteract the negative press about the torture of citizens by the totalitarian government (Arbena, 1992; Pye, 1994). The East versus West drama was played out in the US boycott of the 1980 Olympics in Moscow and the Soviet Union's boycott of the 1984 Olympics in Los Angeles.

Miller (1997), in his introduction to the journal *Social Text* dedicated to sport, recognizes the negative aspects of sport but also its positive aspects. He notes that since the 1970s, there has been a "generation of new, noncompetitive sport alternatives that connect to environmental awareness and [personal] experience" (p. 8). The meaning of snowboarding, or at least how it is articulated by its participants, is situated somewhere between embracing Miller's definition and resisting sport's dominant culture and values.

Snowboarders view themselves as individuals who participate for their own "rush." It is the personal experience between the rider and the mountain. This is an experience that claims not to be practiced for the spectator or external rewards but for the individual enjoyment between the participant and nature. Many describe snowboarding as more fluid than skiing, a motion that works with the mountain rather than against it. In this way, snowboarding is aligned closely with surfing culture (Farmer, 1992). Both blend the creativity of movement with the beauty of nature and the thrill of vertigo, a flirting with danger. Neither was founded in a competitive practice (versus team sports, where competition was inherent).

> Snowboarding is about fresh tracks and carving powder and being yourself and not being judged by others. It's not about nationalism and politics and big money. (Terje Haakonsen, the best freestyle rider in the world, as cited in Lidz, 1997, p. 114)

> Those big toe turns at the bottom of the pitch where I feel like I'm surfing Waimea Bay, hauling ass at 60 miles an hour, making turns that would scare the hell out of me if I were driving a car... that's what keeps me racing. (Jeremy Jones, Alpine snowboarder in the 1998 Nagano Olympics, as cited in Berkley, 1998, p. 100)

It's always been an individual thing. But that gives you freedom to express your own style. What drew me to the sport is that I didn't need anyone to be with me. The perks that come along with the sport, such as friends and travel, are the bonus. (Athena, a professional snowboarder, as cited in Coulter-Parker, 1997, p.57)

As these quotes epitomize the attitude toward snowboarding, it is ironic that they were all spoken by professional snowboarders. Even though they received their money from the competition and commodification of snowboarding; they still established their personal motivations as the individual experience in the sport. The meaning of snowboarding is rarely symbolized in money, winning, or personal glorification. Traditional symbols of this, such as trophies, are reappropriated to show the disdain for competition while engaging in it (e.g., the Golden Duct Tape trophy).

Another example of the perception of snowboarders as resistant to the dominant culture was the bestseller, *Snowboarding to Nirvana* by Frederick Lenz (1997), a popular manifestation of snowboarding culture. It was second in a series that began with *Surfing the Himalayas: A Spiritual Adventure* (Lenz, 1995). How did a book about snowboarding, which a small percentage of the total population has practiced, make the bestseller lists? Albeit, the book also deals with Eastern religion and philosophy, which is currently popular, but it is not without significance that snowboarding was chosen as the vehicle. Snowboarding represented a resistance to materialism and separation of mind and body, while embracing a holistic view of nature that was similar to Zen and Buddhism. The story begins with a Californian snowboarding the Himalayas, who meets Master Fwap, a Buddhist monk. Master Fwap teaches lessons of oneness in snowboarding, that the board, rider, and mountain are all part of one force, and in life. When he achieves this level of meditation, he will be more enlightened and gain a better understanding of the universe. The Zen of snowboarding is far removed from the competitive nature and bureaucratization of contemporary sport. The book reified snowboarding's roots in resistance to the dominant sport culture.

It is style that conveys the meaning given to the sport by its participants. The importance of style, in being accepted as a snowboarder, cannot be overemphasized. This relationship was exemplified in the attitude toward Alpine snowboarders. Alpine snowboarders compete in slalom and giant slalom races, carving sharply around flags, and are judged on time, similar to the ski slalom races. They inhabit an ambiguous space between skiers and snowboarders, even though they ride a board. Skiers consider them snowboarders, while other snowboarders are not sure how to classify them. In a *Skiing* article titled "The Outsiders," snowboard racers are described as wearing "skintight speed suits and helmets, and ride boards that hardly resemble anything you'd find on the racks at your local snowboard shop. They wear ski boots for crying out loud" (Berkley, 1998).

The media-driven industry knows how to categorize them—they belong to a nonmarketable category. Magazines never use racers in their advertising, and TV gives very little coverage to these events, because racers do not represent the resistant style that their freestyle counterparts embody. Because of this, the snowboarders that choose to race do not enjoy the same "cake" (sponsorship and prize money), that their freestyle and half-pipe counterparts eat. Often, racers do some freestyle riding to support themselves. The media's power in deciding what is considered snowboarding, and what will be lucrative, significantly affects the popular digestion of the sport, its commodification, and its practice.

MARKETING THE REBELLIOUS YOUTH: REPERCUSSIONS FOR SUBCULTURE

With the development of new sports in this mediated age, there is often only a short period of time before the sport is marketed and commodified and turned into sports entertainment. This has a significant impact on its symbolic potency as well as the development of the sport itself.

Hebdige (1979) argues that the use of media situates subcultural resistance within the dominant framework of meaning. The youth in the subculture are "simultaneously returned, as they are represented on TV and in the newspapers, to the place where common sense would have them fit" (p. 94). This incorporation of the subculture as a "diverting spectacle" within the dominant framework happens through the "conversion of subcultural signs into mass-produced objects" and by "labeling and redefinition of deviant behavior by dominant groups—the media, the police" (p. 94).

Although snowboarding is the fastest growing winter sport, the total number of participants in North America was about 3.7 million in 1996. This is significantly less participation than games such as badminton or table tennis. Yet, the amount of advertising for snowboarding products, and the amount that uses freestyle snowboarding to sell other products, is much greater than even skiing or other popular sports. Although the spectators far outnumber the participants, they play an important consumer role. Magazines and television have commodified the subcultural signs of style of snowboarding. The stylistic resistance of the subculture is what makes it valuable to the advertiser. According to Brad Steward, president of Bonfire Snowboarding, a clothing manufacturer, "Snowboarding has always been about youth confronting adult society. That's why it has dramatically affected sports, fashion, and music" (Galbraith, 1998, p. 79).

The advertisers themselves are highly conscious of the image they are trying to market. Brett Smith of Fuse Integrated Sports Marketing said, "Snowboarding has become more than a sport. It symbolizes youth culture" (Kafka, 1998). In advertising, it is not the individual attitude that is important but the symbolic representation of resistance. Hence, they never use Alpine snowboarders in their advertisements because their symbolic style does not represent the resistant youth that is represented in the freestyle snowboarders. *American Demographics* printed an article aimed at "shredding myths" of snowboarding participation. "Advertisers may spin snowboarding as the winter equivalent to rebel sports like skateboarding, but it's bloated with healthy, wealthy, not-so-rebellious people. Like sailing" (Spiegler, 1998).

"The creation and diffusion of new styles is inextricably bound up with the process of production, publicity, and packaging which must inevitably lead to the diffusion of the subculture's subversive power…[They feed] back into high fashion and mainstream fashion" (Hebdige, 1979, p. 95). Snowboarding "techno" style has fed directly back into mainstream fashion. Bright silver jackets and baggy pants adorn the store's shelves. Tag Heuer, a very expensive brand of watch (more than $1,000 each) recently replaced Coca-Cola as the sponsor of the snowboard park in Vail. The ultimate marriage of subcultural signs commodified for dominant paradigms is Jake Burton, the "father" and "soul" of snowboarding, appearing in an American Express ad, a credit card company usually marketed to the middle to upper classes for their vacations to Europe. His voice-over of shots of him jumping off a cliff and riding down the powdered hill explained that American Express was always there for him, even when others did not support snowboarding. American Express was expanding its image into a company that supports youth and innovation, a card that will back anyone anywhere. This packaging of snowboarding has led to its diffusion of the symbolic potency of its style.

A small backlash has occurred because of the commodification of snowboarding. A growing number of snowboarders are turning back to skiing to once again subvert the symbolic order. Although this is a small number, it is done with reflexive consciousness. According to Jamie Meiselman, managing editor of *Trans World Snowboarding* magazine,

> Skiing is punk again. The opposite of what convention is. A lot of it has to do with how hyped-up snowboarding is. Now people who are anti-establishment are going to what they once considered mainstream. In this case, it's skiing. (White, 1994, p. 44)

Although this was proclaimed in 1994, the numbers of participants have not reflected this trend completely. Meiselman used the word punk to signify anti-establishment. The subcultural resistance of the punks, as made apparent by Hebdige, now represents a very conscious and mindful effort to subvert the dominant culture. Snowboarders are also giving up their funky-colored hairstyles to go clean cut. Those who once sported dreadlocks, colored spikes, or long manes are now buzzing their hair off. The potential for shock value has worn off, so they reinvent their resistance in a clean-cut look (St. John, 1996).

SPORTS ENTERTAINMENT:
REPERCUSSIONS FOR THE PRACTICE OF SNOWBOARDING

The use of television for more than just advertising, as the mediation of the practice of snowboarding itself, significantly affects the sport. Radar (1984) in *In Its Own Image: How Television Has Transformed Sports*, methodically examines how "one sport after another packaged or repackaged itself for the media" (p. 140). Mediated sports had to compete with other forms of entertainment, especially for those spectators who were not devoted to the sport itself. This manifested itself in the introduction of cheerleaders and time-outs for commercial breaks. As a new sport in the 1980s, snowboarding was introduced to television as the sport was still developing. There is not a clear "before and after" the media line, as in baseball or football. The mediation itself has always been a part of the sport, so that its rise in popularity is not only from a roots-up growth in the popularity of its practice but also from a popularity in the sport as consumed through media. This creates a large consumer/spectator arena compared to those who have ever actually practiced the sport.

Bourdieu (1991) claims that this divorce between practice and consumption is often masked, so that the commodification or the entertainment of sport is not consciously acknowledged.

Section IX: Sport Subcultures

> We may consider that sport as a spectacle would appear more clearly as a mass commodity, and the organization of sporting entertainments as one branch among others of show business (there is a difference of degree rather than kind between the spectacle of professional boxing, or Holiday on Ice shows, and a number of sporting events that are perceived as legitimate, such as the various European football championships or ski competitions), if the value collectively bestowed on practicing sports (especially now that sports contests have become a measure of relative national strength and hence apolitical objective) did not help to mask the divorce between practice and consumption and consequently the functions of simple passive consumption. (p. 363)

There is a high value placed on practicing sports that helps to hide the difference between practice and consumption. This is almost to the point that passive consumption could be considered participation.

Bourdieu (1991) also delineates social class difference between participation and spectatorship. As place on the social hierarchy increases, the chance of participating in sports when older increases, while the chance of being a spectator decreases. This can be seen in the participation practices of a "working-class" sport such as football and a bourgeois sport such as golf. Those who play football are much less likely to continue playing into old age than those who play golf.

The increase in spectators who have not practiced a sport also equals an increase in the superficiality of their consumption. Spectators have a need for sensationalism over subtlety, and the television producers know this. In 1997, ESPN hosted its first Winter X Games (X is for eXtreme). They invented a new snowboarding competition for these games titled "Boarder X." Instead of just one snowboarder racing down the mountain or being judged on his or her tricks in the halfpipe, ESPN put six snowboarders on a course at once.

The snowboarders raced up 20-foot side embankments, over bumps, and around sharp curves, and launched off a 40-foot jump at the end. The simultaneous action of six snowboarders getting air, doing tricks, and pushing off each other as they race down the course was quite sensational. It was spontaneous and unpredictable rather than rigid and controlled. The moment everyone recalls from that competition was the act of one snowboarder passing another one in the air while doing a back flip off the 40-foot jump. The fairly noncompetitive sport of snowboarding, with just the rider, his board, and the mountain, was transformed into high-drama entertainment.

The use of television to promote and change the practice of the sport is not as openly challenged by many snowboarders. Many of the professionals correlate a relationship between the amount of media exposure and their ability to earn money to continue what they love to do—snowboarding. It is its marketability as entertainment, not the broadcast of the sport for its own sake, that allows the professionals to earn a living from it. Yet, the values of television seem to directly contradict some of the meaning that snowboarders find in their riding: the noncompetitive atmosphere, the fluidity with nature, and the focus on individual expression.

Many counteract this tension by appealing to a notion of their personal "pure" motivation in the sport. In an interview with Michelle Taggart, a competitive snowboarder, she answers the question of the effect of commercialism on snowboarding.

> A lot of people think it's taking away from the soul of the sport, but I think you can control that within yourself. I want to keep a love of sports and at the same time make a living at it, so there needs to be a balance. The big companies are not going to ruin snowboarding if you don't let them. (Williams, 1997, p. 25)

This justification comes from the need to make money and stay within the system while trying to stay pure in their motivations. The paradox is that they are riding for money but attempting to keep their initial motivation to ride for their personal experience and enjoyment.

Media's power to shape the sport has not been questioned often. Snowboarders have raised concern over decisions regarding the future of the sport from the governing bodies of snowboarding and its entry into the Olympics, but many see media as a necessary means to make the sport popular. The media affects and controls the development of the new sport but in a more subtle way and for different purposes. For media, the purpose of control is for consumerism, to drive the market. Therefore, decisions about snowboarding are made to make its mediated presentation more entertaining. For the Olympics, and other bureaucratizations of sport, control is about disciplining a sport. Decisions are made to conform the sport to a certain standard or level. Both significantly control the development and acceptance of new sports.

MAINSTREAMING, INCORPORATION, AND DISCIPLINE: SNOWRIDERS

Simultaneously, the development of a new sport tracks with the subcultural cycle of resistance and incorporation. As new sports, born in resistance, become more popular and accepted, the subcultural resistance is incorporated. Now there is an increased integration between skiers and snowboarders at a physical and symbolic level. Physically, there are very few resorts left that do not allow snowboarding. Many now cater to snowboarders with snowboard parks and half pipes, especially because the number of skiers has decreased in the past couple of years. The symbolic power of snowboarders has been mainstreamed and incorporated in advertising and media. In 1997, Warren Miller, the main producer of ski films for 30 years, produced a film called *Snowriders*, highlighting both skiers and snowboarders, in an attempt to bridge the animosity between the two groups. Also, the fastest growing group of new snowboarders are adults, and many of the first snowboarders are now adults themselves, making its youthful edge less relevant.

Snowboarders are marketed as the rebellious youth, but the demographics of those who participate are those who have enough economic capital to continue in an expensive, middle- to upper-class sport. There is not an easy relationship between subcultural resistance to the dominant culture and social class in the case of snowboarding. Subcultures express "a fundamental tension between those in power and those condemned to subordinate positions and second-class lives" (Hebdige, 1979, p. 132). Snowboarders, as youth, might be at a power disadvantage but are not necessarily condemned to second-class lives. Part of the resistance from snowboarders pulls heavily from the skateboarding subculture, which is an urban, middle-class sport that is cheap and widespread. The move of this subculture from the streets to the slopes represents a sharing of cultural capital but not necessarily economic capital.

The gender differences in participation in skateboarding and snowboarding also delineate the social class lines. There are very few females who skateboard. It is a tough, street sport whose membership is limited to males and not to their lower- to middle-class female counterparts. Although snowboarders try to masculinize the sport (Anderson, 1999), snowboarding began to close the gender gap in sport faster than other sports. It is a more bourgeois sport in which female participation is welcomed and celebrated. Almost 30% of snowboarders are women, and the competitive females are beginning to receive considerable media time. There has also been focus on the development of women's snowboarding equipment and clothing.

Another place of difference between skateboarding and snowboarding is that of race. Skateboarding is accessible to those with lower incomes and has been embraced by more people of color than snowboarding. The snow slope is still often strikingly White, whether skiing or snowboarding.

Snowboarding has perhaps fragmented its class across lines of age and challenged the values and assumptions of that class. These values include materialism, the need to always win or be on top, and gender stereotypes. It is still not a sport for the masses; it offers spectatorship but not participation. But now as its resistance is subverted in commodification, snowboarding has been allowed to enter the international ring of legitimation for sport, the Olympics.

Discourse around the acceptance of snowboarding into the Olympics was a dialectic between the positive aspects of mainstreaming and legitimation, and the negative aspects of control and discipline. The entry of snowboarding into the 1998 Winter Olympics made it closer to the status that skiing enjoys in the world, as well as offering much more exposure to the sport worldwide. "The Olympics will definitely make snowboarding a mainstream sport. Obviously, the better we do, the more interest there will be in snowboarding," said Mark Fawcett, one of Canada's top contenders (Davies, 1998, p. 54). Analyzing the effects after the Olympics, the most powerful force was not its acceptance into the Olympics (several other sports were also accepted) but the amount of TV time it received. The majority of people only know that snowboarding is in the Olympics through mediation. In the future, the amount of television time will do much more to legitimate a sport than its acceptance into the Olympics itself.

There were many points of opposition in the journey to the Olympics. To begin with, many snowboarders questioned if they were merely allowed in to draw a younger audience. A real outcry, as well as a lawsuit, came when the International Olympic Committee (IOC) appointed the Federation Internationale du Ski (FIS), skiing's regulatory body, as the governing organization over snowboarding rather than the International Snowboard Federation. This was an obvious exercise of power over snowboarding. There was considerable concern that the FIS was only interested in the network money and that it did not understand the practice or culture of snowboarding.

The loudest voice of resistance came from Terje Haakonsen, the world's best halfpipe snowboarder. His refusal to enter the Olympics significantly weakened the level of competition. His reason for not participating was his belief that the IOC was Mafia-like and that going to the Olympics was like going to the army. He did not want to be turned into a uniform-wearing, flag-bearing, walking logo. He was also suspicious of the IOC's ability to deal with the evolving sport. Many are worried that snowboarding's inclusion into the Olympics at such a young age in its development might inhibit growth in the sport.

This discourse against the inclusion in the Olympics is basically a resistance to the discipline of bureaucracy and power. Foucault (1975) writes that discipline is essentially corrective. The IOC began to discipline its new rebellious sport so that it could be included in the high-brow event. The clearest example of this is the stripping of Ross Regliabati's gold medal because he tested positive for marijuana, hardly a performance-enhancing drug. Marijuana is usually identified as a youth drug. It was an attempt to control the snowboarder and snowboarding as youthful resistance.

This attempt was one of discipline and not punishment. Compared with punishment,

> disciplinary power, on the other hand, is exercised through its invisibility; at the same time it imposes on those whom it subjects a principle of compulsory visibility. In discipline, it is the subjects who have to be seen. Their visibility assures the hold of the power that is exercised over them. (Foucault, 1975, p. 25)

The focus of the story was on the supposed wrongdoing of Regliabati, while the almost completely hidden IOC continued on with their business. This changed when the nature of the discipline itself caused people to question the governing body's power. Why discipline an athlete who has traces of a drug that would more likely hurt than enhance his performance? Regliabati's defense was that the traces were left over from breathing marijuana smoke-filled air before he left Canada. The decision then went to a review board. They found that the IOC does not have a right to take away a medal based on a positive marijuana test. Marijuana is only banned if the sport's governing body, the FIS, has banned it. Because they had not banned it specifically for giant slalom snowboarding, then it cannot be sanctioned. Regliabati's gold medal was returned but not without tarnish to himself and the sport, a symbolic slap on the hand.

The life cycle of a new sport, and its cultural implications, is apparent in the sport of snowboarding. Snowboarding was born in youthful resistance to the popular sport of skiing. Its symbolic style is commodified as one of resistance to the dominant paradigm of skiing and the values of sport it represents. This is apparent in clothing, language, and motivation. Although snowboarding has been deemed as the snow sport for the lower classes, its expense and accessibility still limit it to mostly middle- and upper-class participants. Snowboarding is now going through the process of becoming more mainstream, suffering from pains of growth and discipline. The media has appropriated the image of youthful rebellion in snowboarding and has commodified it. The growth and discipline is evident not only in the acceptance in the 1998 Winter Olympics but also by the controversy that surrounded it. So, as snowboarding becomes more mainstream and is more accepted, it might continue to be commodified as the resistant sport to skiing, but there will be much less animosity between the two.

Buckle Bunnies:
Groupies of the Rodeo Circuit

DeAnn K. Gauthier & Craig J. Forsyth

The rodeo attracts many people who want to see the epitome of the Old West when roping calves and taming wild horses was part of everyday life on the ranch. Fans play an important part in the rodeo cowboy's life on the road. Among these fans are women that those around the rodeo circuit call "buckle bunnies." They are essentially cowboy groupies, who purposefully seek encounters with contestants who have proven successful in their particular rodeo event(s) (Carroll 1985; Morris 1993; Stern and Stern 1992). An easy identification system exists whereby bunnies can quickly locate their "winners" via his wearing of the winning belt buckle—hence the term "buckle bunny." These women come into contact with the cowboys at the rodeo, or in the hotels and bars where the cowboys stay. Once identified, bunnies offer the cowboys many different things, such as a ride to a rodeo, a place to sleep, a shower, or many times, just sex. There is little research on buckle bunnies, but literature does exist on rock star groupies and high profile sports groupies.

METHODOLOGY
Data for this study were gathered through interviews and observation. Subjects were identified by a key informant. Additional subjects were identified via snowball sampling, in which each subject suggests other subjects (Babble 1998). The Internet also provided data about the rodeo. Interviews were conducted at the homes of rodeo cowboys, rodeos, and bars and hotels. Thirty-eight interviews were conducted with individuals who currently compete on the rodeo circuit at the college, amateur, or professional levels. Seven interviews were conducted with former professional cowboys. Eight wives of rodeo cowboys were also interviewed. Twelve single women who follow the rodeo and one rodeo promoter were also interviewed.

Section IX: Sport Subcultures

The data presented here are part of a larger occupational study of the rodeo cowboy. The intent of this article is to describe the interaction between buckle bunnies and rodeo cowboys.

GROUPIES

"Groupie" is a term usually used to refer to a young woman who follows rock groups around on tours. The popular San Francisco-based group of the 1960s, The Grateful Dead, attracted a large contingent of traveling fans numbering in the thousands from all over the world. These fans were given the name "Deadheads." Being a Deadhead was a master status in the eyes of the Grateful Dead. Deadheads traveled at their own expense to see the band and they invested a great deal of time and money into their traveling. There was a shared sense of commitment that is reflected by the hardships Deadheads encounter while traveling to see the band. These experiences gave rise to a subculture that was startling in the depth of its commitment. There were information hotlines set up by the Grateful Dead organization to keep fans informed of the latest ticket sales and concert information, such as dates and venues of upcoming shows, as well as miscellaneous information about the band and its activities. The most common experience was to see the Deadheads at the large yearly Grateful Dead shows (Pearson 1982). In her autobiography, Pamela DesBarres tells of her days of chasing stars and living life in the fast lane. Many of her encounters with these stars ended in sexual exploits (DesBarres 1988). DesBarres was the epitome of a groupie.

The groupie subculture also surrounds professional athletics, with each sport having specific names for these women (Elson 1991). Baseball players refer to these girls as "Annies" and hockey players call them "puck bunnies." The girls who follow athletes around and wait for them at bars or hotels all want to become an "acquaintance" of the athlete. Many athletes find these women very appealing because "it is easy sex" with no expectations following the encounter. These women make themselves readily available to the athletes. Some say that baseball attracts more groupies than the other sports because baseball has such a long season and the teams stay in one place for a longer time than in other sports. Others suggest that basketball players are just as attractive to groupies because of the amount of free time the players have on road trips as well as their visibility in a crowd (Elson 1991; Wahl and Wertheim 1998).

Groupies who follow athletes can be innocent teenagers who just want to catch a glimpse of their favorite star (Oller 1998), but most are between the ages of 18 and 25. They are seeking money, attention, and status from being associated with high-profile athletes. These women rarely approach the athletes on the court or field. They often become acquainted with the hotels where the teams are staying or the popular after-game hang-outs. Many of the same people are seen from town to town and they are very straightforward about their intentions (Elson 1991; Oller 1998).

BUCKLE BUNNIES

As the wife of one cowboy commented:

> There's a lot of them [buckle bunnies]...at the bigger rodeos. If you were in one certain area for a while...you'd see a lot of the same groupies. It's just like in any sport. You have it in

> professional football. Girls who like athletes. [in] hockey (they) call them puck bunnies. I guess it is the ruggedness of a cowboy that they like.

Bunnies come from a variety of backgrounds, but the majority have some family association with the rodeo. In the past, bunnies wore a distinct style of revealing Western attire. This is still true in some cases, depending on the location of the rodeo.

> It all depends on where you go. The ones down in the circuit I was in…wore the tightest pants they could get in, the latest style Western shirts…Roper boots and a buckle. Most of the time it was a buckle from some cowboy.

Several cowboys stated that these girls are getting away from the Western attire. As one steer wrestler stated:

> Not a lot of people dress the rodeo part unless they're at the rodeo. A lot of the girls are doing the same thing. They're wearing Levi's, Girbaud's, Guess, something like that. They don't look the part they used to, but you can still pick them out pretty easy.

Today, "picking them out" seems to depend in large part on the bunnies' lack of attire: "real skimpy shirts," "tank tops;" "slutty," or as one interviewee put it, "They wear clothes so you can see their boobs."

Motivations behind bunny behavior seem multifaceted. One primary motivation is the atmosphere of excitement surrounding the rodeo and the cowboys. Bunnies admit to being physically attracted to cowboys in general, although looks are not the main motivation. One interviewee said:

> I'm attracted to them, but they have to be successful in their event.

Another explanation is offered by the wife of a cowboy

> I don't understand why girls like cowboys. Most of them are a piece of shit. I guess it's that different…free lifestyle. I guess everybody's got to try it. You're so different from society when you're a cowboy.

Carroll (1985:134) offered a simple, yet telling, explanation: "Cowboys are great in bed. Cowboys make the girth move under you."

One cowboy had its own idea about why the buckle bunnies attend rodeos.

> I think maybe sometimes they go to these rodeos to find a cowboy, but professional cowboys don't want to be found. They don't want to be tied down. They're in this town today, tomorrow they may be in another town or state. These girls…think they might date or get married to one of the cowboys and travel with them; go to rodeos with them and everything. But at the end of the night the cowboy is going to tell her he has to leave. Maybe they might try to do it again, maybe they can't stop. Then I guess they become buckle bunnies.

Buckle bunnies are visible at various places around the rodeo.

> About the time the rodeo ends, they're usually the first ones gone…headed to the bar waiting on the guys to get there. If you see them at the rodeo early and you see them at the bar, you

pretty much know. Some guys had regulars every year at that same rodeo. Go back and it was the same girls waiting on them. I'm sure that girl went there expecting to see that same guy.

Many of the buckle bunnies hang out behind the bucking chutes or around the alley way at the rodeo waiting for the cowboys to come through.

> This is what they live for. This is like their weekend pass…they're gonna have fun. They are always behind the chutes somewhere where they can see the cowboys and talk to them.

Buckle bunnies also wait at the gates of the sponsor tents that only the participants can enter. They wait for the cowboys to get their drinks and make their way out of the tents so that the bunnies can be seen by the cowboys and perhaps talk to them.

> Always walking around with a cold one in their hand or a mixed drink having a good time. They were always behind the chutes somewhere where they could see the cowboys and talk to them, or at the beer stand where we would go after we rode.

Buckle bunnies are likely to frequent the host hotel of the major rodeos. The host hotels usually send out papers so the contestants will know where to stay for these rodeos, including the Cheyenne Frontier Days, Denver, Houston, Fort Worth, and the National Finals Rodeo. The buckle bunnies usually find out the host hotel and try to get rooms there so they can be near the cowboys.

The most common place for the cowboys to encounter buckle bunnies is in a night club after the rodeo. This is where the majority of the buckle bunnies seek out the participants. Buckle bunnies surround the participants, waiting for them to sign an autograph, take a picture with them or to see if they can get the attention of a cowboy, each hoping she might be the favored girl of the night. As one cowboy wife notes:

> If they have a beer garden, they're there…a hospitality room at the hotel…they're there. They're everywhere the guys are socializing at.

Many times the buckle bunnies flirt with cowboys to let them know that they are interested. One cowboy told us:

> The girls kind of flirt with you, buy you a drink and they talk about rodeo. All of a sudden they pop the question on you. Who you here with? Are you going home with anybody? Do you mind if I come home with you?

Some buckle bunnies are overt and direct about their intentions

> I've seen them ask guys if they've got a motel, or should they get one, or would they like to go back to their motel room. Some of them get off on doing guys in their campers…truck…horse trailers.

Buckle bunnies usually do not expect anything more than sex from the rodeo participants and vice versa. The majority of cowboys on the circuit are married, therefore it is even more understood by the buckle bunnies that nothing is to be expected.

> A lot of guys are married out there that they chase after…being with somebody who's married or just being with somebody who's going to be there for one night. They don't expect nothing from them.

A wife of a cowboy described the code of secrecy that surrounds sex with buckle bunnies on the road.

> (There is) a lot of infidelity on the road. Most of the time the guys would never let on about it. That was between them. You hope somebody would tell you if it were your husband, [but] what happens on the road stays on the road. It doesn't come back home.

Even though the cowboys enjoy the company of the buckle bunnies, many of them stated that there are negative connotations associated with them. For instance, several cowboys called these girls "whores" or "sluts." Some cowboys labeled buckle bunnies, "cut queens."

> It's the girls we actually know for sure that are gonna put out or be with somebody. You can tell your friends to go talk to them…they can get a home run.

Buckle bunnies go to several rodeos a year. Many of them take their vacations around the time of the larger rodeos, such as Cheyenne and Houston. Others attend as many small rodeos as big ones.

> The first time we ever went somewhere was to meet somebody that rodeoed that called my girlfriend. He would call her from gas stations from all over the place. He said to come and meet him in Jasper, Texas at this certain time [and] we did.

Some of the girls tend to frequent the rodeos that are near their hometowns or stay in a particular circuit. It is difficult to generalize how many rodeos these women attend. For many girls, it varies from year to year. Contestants stated that most of the time they will see the same buckle bunnies present at the larger rodeos. At the smaller rodeos, which last one or two days, the groups of buckle bunnies will be different. This is likely because these are hometown girls there for the once a year event.

> At the small rodeos, they come out of the woods. We go to rodeos that there will be a population of 700 people, [but] there will be 1,000 people at the rodeo. They come from every little town around. Them are the fun ones. They get wild. They party. When the rodeo starts until the rodeo ends [it's] like the Super Bowl for a lot of them, because they don't never get out of town. It's cheap entertainment for them.…There's a lot of hometown girls who break up with their boyfriends for the week.

As far as the sexual encounters go, these range from relatively mild flirtations to open exhibitionism. One bunny illustrates the mild form of pursuit:

> I meet cowboys at the local country bar. If I see a new bird in town I make it my business to find out who they are, buy them a drink and make them feel welcome. If they don't show an interest, I don't bother with them.

On the other hand, pursuit may be more intense, as these cowboys state:

> In Calgary, everything was different. Sex was out in the open, so to speak. The girls love cowboys and they aren't afraid to walk up to you and just ask you if you wanted to go to their hotel room or yours. They just cut to the chase and said what they wanted.

And finally, bunnies may be so enthralled with the chase that they become exhibitionists. One typical cowboy story goes as follows

> In Fort Worth, (a bunny wanted) oral sex in the bar. She asked, I obliged her. She told everybody to turn around and put their backs to us. She dropped to her knees. They had two girls on the dance floor who watched. She did it and then went on about her business. I went home with her that night later on. Somebody do that at the bar, you think I'm gonna let her go home by herself? What you think she gonna do by herself? The guys cheered me on. They were high-fiving me.

Another cowboy commented similarly:

> [I've] seen people have sex outside the car in the parking lot of the bar. I've seen other guys walk out the bar and hop in the camper, have sex, and then go back in the bar looking for someone else.

The casual treatment the women receive was not begrudged by the bunnies themselves. They have little to no expectations of the cowboys, beyond that night or the next morning. In fact, it was a common observation that:

> They could be with you one weekend and then be with your best friend the next…or the same weekend, the same night, it doesn't matter.

The typical cowboy perception of the buckle bunny and who she is and what she represents is stated as follows:

> A buckle bunny…she's been…rode hard and put up wet a couple times.

The cowboys recognize that bunnies want to be able to say that they had sex with a real cowboy and, as a consequence, they expect the cowboys are the nontraditional gatekeepers of sex. Traditionally, women have been recognized as sexual game players (Ronai and Ellis 2000), but the situation seems to be somewhat reversed on the rodeo circuits. Women are seeking to acquire the "best" cowboy, whose sexual "conquest" will be viewed as a form of status attainment. One cowboy points this out by saying:

> It's a status thing for the girls…like being with a movie star. They brag about it.

THE RATING SYSTEM

To determine the "best" among cowboys, there are many ways that buckle bunnies are able to rate the rodeo participants in terms of desirability. The most obvious way is through the type of event in which the cowboy participates. Several cowboys felt that many of the buckle bunnies rated them in terms of their events.

> Some of them, all they like are bull riders, some of them, all they like are steer wrestlers.

Most of the buckle bunnies stated that they prefer rough stock riders to timed event participants. The popularity of bull riders may be because of the publicity given to this particular event. This is the only rodeo event that has its own professional rodeos set aside from the Professional Rodeo Cowboys Association (PRCA). The Professional Bullriders Association (PBR) sanctions their own bull riding events. Bull riding is considered by spectators and cowboys to be the most exciting and challenging rodeo event. Bull riders are usually the rodeo contestants who are seen on television and glamorized in the movies (Hochman 1998). Repeatedly, we were informed of this perception:

> During the National Finals Rodeo (NFR), the guys who do different events stay at different hotels. You see lots of girls at each hotel. More women go to the rough stock riders' hotels. Not that there aren't a lot of women hanging out at all of them, [but] most go to the bull riders' hotel.

Other cowboys respond

> [Bunnies] seem to be more interested in the bull riders than anything else. I think because it's the most glamorous event.

> I have a friend, he's a champion steer wrestler. All he has to do is walk into a bar. He can go home with anybody. The winner basically has it made, especially if you're a bullrider. Steer wrestlers have it good, [but] bullriders have it better. That's the two big events that girls like. It's like the big, tough guy. You got to be a tough guy to ride bulls, got to be a tough guy to steer wrestle. It's the image.

Image and recognizability play important roles in the ranking of cowboy desirability.

> [Bull riding's] the most challenging event. That's who (bunnies) see on TV. They know them by face and name. That's what they want. It's always been like that.

Another way the buckle bunnies rate cowboys is using the various rodeo rankings. Buckle bunnies find rodeo participants who have excelled in their events more desirable than those who have not. As one wife stated:

> Rank and standing has something to do with who the buckle bunnies choose to be with. The ones that make more money are obviously better known because they're at the top of the rankings and they're more popular. To be with a world champion or the guy who won the Salinas Rodeo or Cheyenne is a prestigious thing.

Section IX: Sport Subcultures

Cowboys are aware of this use of ranking by the bunnies

> The girls inquire about your ranking or how much money you've made, but they know. They probably get the *Pro Rodeo Sports News* and get on the Internet to check out what's going on. Most of them keep up with the standings. They're interested in the status of a cowboy.

Another cowboy stated:

> They want to know what you're ranked in the standings. How much you've won this year. How much you won last year. If you go to a rodeo and you're staying there and you win…it's easy.

Many buckle bunnies said they would not consider being with a contestant unless he was successful in his event.

> I inquire about a cowboy's ranking or how much money they've made, but I never ask them. I keep up with who's doing what by subscribing to the *Pro Rodeo Sports News*.

> I keep up with their ranking or how much money they make and I always have ever since I can remember.

> Ranking has attraction.

Winners of the rodeo are most sought after by the buckle bunnies. The majority of the contestants stated that if they won an event in the rodeo, they could count on buckle bunnies seeking them out after the rodeo. They said that it made the encounter with the buckle bunnies much easier than if they were just an ordinary competitor.

Some groups of buckle bunnies have created point systems to keep track of the cowboys with whom they have been intimate. In one such system, points were given in order of prestige of the cowboy's achievements.

> [One] group of girls had a point system. Sex had to be involved to get the points. If you had your PRCA card it was one point. If you made it to the finals it was two points. Won the world, it was three points. At the end of the year, whoever had the most points accumulated out of the group, it's like eight or 10 of them, the losers had to pay the one with the most points trip to the finals, plus their own way out there.

Although success in the event is important to the buckle bunnies, it seems to be more an issue of status than an issue of money. It was the mid-1980s before a rodeo cowboy earned a million dollars in a lifetime (Sine 1996). Very few cowboys have a great deal of money, simply because they spend most of their winnings on expenses while traveling. Cowboys, unlike many high profile athletes, are different because they do not have a set salary. They only get paid if they are successful in the rodeo. Consequently, ranking (status) is more important than income/ salary. Status markers, or symbols, are readily identifiable in cowboy attire. For example, buckle bunnies can pick out contestants who have achieved in their event by viewing the cowboy's buckle. Cowboys know this:

> If you had a nice buckle on, they were coming for you. If you had that belt buckle that said you were a champion…

Jackets are also marks of status. Rodeo participants who have been to the national finals usually wear their NFR jackets wherever they go.

> They give each contestant a jacket and it has their number and their name and everything on it in Las Vegas at the national finals. The night I got there, (my husband) had won the round and they gave him a buckle, so that night afterward we were sitting down at the bar. Several girls came up to him, even while I was there and they propositioned him. They see that jacket.

> I don't care who you are, if you show up at the NFR and you're not a contestant, you don't have a shot [with the bunnies]. If they can't get the jacket, they'll go after somebody else.

> …they want the jacket.

Snowden (1995) commented on the visibility of the contestants at the local hot spot after the rodeo:

> It's easy to spot the competitors at the press rodeo parties, since they wear their National Finals Rodeo competitor jackets like a pack of varsity cheerleaders and never take them off, even if it's so hot in the ballroom that a woman in a buckskin halter top has beads of sweat running down her back. The jackets make it easier on the buckle bunnies…if it's too dark or they're too nearsighted to read belt buckles accurately. The jacket tells you more than the buckle, anyway, since it bears the cowboy's event, his full name, and the number he wears in competition (1995:3).

The PRCA has made it extremely easy for any individual interested in the sport of rodeo to find out who is ranked at the top of each event. The official magazine of the PRCA is the *Pro Rodeo Sports News*. In this publication, individuals can discover various information on upcoming events, as well as the latest standings in particular series, such as the Dodge Truck Series, Resistol Hats Rookie of the Year, and Copenhagen Skoal championship awards. There are numerous web sites to keep interested rodeo fans up-to-date with their favorite events and contestants. Buckle bunnies also have a web site: "A Taste of the Old West (R U a Buckle Bunny?)" (1998). This site has pictures of cowboys on each page, and as you click on each picture, a nude picture of a cowboy appears with the phrase: "Is this what you were looking for?"

THE SOCIAL TRANSACTION

Many times, the buckle bunnies allow the cowboys to stay in their hotel rooms or at their homes so the cowboys do not have to spend another night in the truck or on the road. Cowboys often do not rent rooms of their own because they don't have enough money or because the hotel doesn't accommodate a horse trailer. Some cowboys offer to buy the women dinner if they allow them to sleep in their room and take a hot shower. If one of the guys in a group would find a woman to go home with, all of the cowboys traveling with him would follow to partake of a shower and place to sleep.

Section IX: Sport Subcultures

Many of the participants travel constantly and rarely go home. When they do get to stay in the same place for four or five days, they want to have fun. Buckle bunnies assist greatly in this goal.

> I was at a rodeo in Oklahoma. We didn't have any place to stay, so any time one of the guys in the car would get a girl and no one else would, we would follow them to their house and that's a shower, maybe breakfast and we'd sleep. We were real young, just pro and we weren't winning hardly any money. Five days without a shower. We were scrungy. And, we went to their home and we were all sitting in the living room. I was kind of getting scared, there were three of us sitting down, and my buddy was with that other girl and there was two of them and she said, "Well, there's a couch right there," and I said, "I'll sleep on the floor;" and she said, "No, you have a place to sleep in here with me." I ended up sleeping in the bed with her. The daughter was in the other room with my friend. The mother and daughter, she raised to be a buckle bunny. The next morning we got up and had pancakes and eggs. She handed me a paper with her number on it.

Most of the cowboys stated that they like the attention given to them by these girls. One cowboy said that the girls who followed his circuit were extremely supportive and reliable and some consider them friends. He recalled a time when he got much needed help from one of the buckle bunnies.

> The first time I called, I didn't even know this girl. A buddy of mine told me to call this girl, gave me the number and he said she'll pick you up at the airport. I called her and said this is so-and-so, and I'm flying in to Orlando airport and I need a ride to Kissimmeie to the rodeo. She said, "What time you getting in?" Didn't know what she looked like and she didn't know what I looked like. She had a sign with my name on it.

Buckle bunnies gave similar comments regarding this exchange.

> We let people sleep in our room and take showers and stuff without question because they're tired and sick of traveling. There is not always sex. It's like…we're tired, can we sleep in your room?

> A contestant will go home with a girl and all of his friends follow him back to the girl's hotel room. We've had our share of them sleep. They're cheap. Some of them will offer to help pay for the room, but most don't. Some of them will stay in their trailers and come take a shower in our room.

Buckle bunnies act as surrogate spouses for the rodeo participants when they are on the road traveling. In Carroll's book (1985), a buckle bunny interviewed at the finals stated:

> We pick the cowboys up at the airports, we give them a bed, we buy them a beer, we make them a meal, we mend their shirts, and for their birthdays, I design their brands in needlepoint (1985:131).

Buckle bunnies are groupies; they are dedicated fans who are enthralled by the rodeo subculture and its participants.

DISCUSSION AND CONCLUSIONS

Several factors make the behavior of buckle bunnies deviant: having sex with married men, having sex in public, women initiating the sexual encounters, having sex with too many people, and the overt and utilitarian rating of sexual partners. None of these are crimes, but all fall under the heading of sins or poor taste (Smith and Pollack 2000).

The rating of sex partners, which may be the most perverse of these roles, seems to be an extension of Waller's (1937) concept of rating and dating. Waller focused on the desirability of dating partners on college campuses in 1937. Each prospective date was discussed and criticized by the members of the group. Thrill-seeking developed exploitative relationships on campus. When a woman exploits, it is usually for gifts and expensive amusements whereas males usually exploit to seek thrills from the body of the woman. However, if the relationship was founded on frank and admitted barter in thrills, nothing that could be considered exploitative arises. For example, during the off-season of school, women teachers would flock to the school and would treat their male students with special care. They would lend the men their cars, take them out to dinner, treat them to drinks, and buy expensive presents for them. Many of these male recipients were available for sexual relations in terms that require no sort of commitment. Waller also identified what he called the principle of least interest. This principle stated that the person who controls the relationship is the one who is least interested in the continuation of the affair (Waller 1937). In the rodeo scene, there is a frank understanding that what is being bartered is thrills and status, and that the cowboy is the person with the least interest, and therefore, in most control of the exchange.

Several other conclusions can be drawn about buckle bunnies and their behavior. These women share a preference for macho men. In their study of women in biker gangs, Hopper and Moore found that macho men also ranked high in terms of attractiveness.

> I'm attracted to strong men who know what they want. Bikers are authentic. With them, what you see is what you get. I've always liked my men rough. I don't mean I like to be beat up, but a real man. Bikers are like cowboys; I classify them together. Freedom and strength I guess are what it takes for me (199;377).

A further similarity is that women in the biker gangs of the 1960s initiated sex as much as the men. In our research, women were the sexual aggressors the majority of the time, although men also initiated the encounters on occasion. Yet the purpose of the sex for bunnies most resembles that of the male bikers in the biker gangs of the 1980s. Hopper and Moore found biker sex in the 1980s to be more concerned with achieving status and brotherhood than with physical gratification. The behavior of buckle bunnies, like the behavior of men in biker gangs, reflects a similar concern with status and group solidarity, rather than physical or relationship satisfaction. These concerns are formed by their membership in a specific subculture during a specific era. Subcultures are, indeed, difficult for outsiders to understand. Norms of a subculture can be an antithesis to the conventional, but it is the material from which identities are constructured. The identities of the buckle bunnies emphasize a relation of unattachment, a dislocation from the confinements of work and committed relationships, and a genuine experiment with free time. It delineates the buckle bunny from others, and assists her with finding companionship with like-minded peers, enabling her to construct an identity from the symbols found in the rodeo subculture. Subculture reinforces meaningful statements about one's position relative to others. The subculture is composed of a variety of purists, those who do not quite fit in, and rebels. The attraction of the rodeo subculture is its hedonistic escape from the conventional. It offers a place to have fun and explore and expand both the traditional concepts of masculinity and femininity, but also modern roles regarding sexual pursuit. Traditional ideology maintains hegemony; it is a male-dominated culture. But what has been negotiated is a fetished image that is a twist on traditional sex roles. The new images consist of males, still dominant in a subculture that glorifies males and masculinity, but also now in possession of a role traditionally reserved for women as a group—the gatekeepers of sex. Alternatively, women are free to pursue sexually, a role traditionally denied them as adult women in mainstream U.S. culture. If one feels like a maverick, the scripts composed in this subculture are highly attractive.

Section X

Sport Economics and Business

Unpaid Professionals: The Student As Athlete

ANDREW ZIMBALIST

Thus, a youngster gambling his future on a pro contract is like a worker buying a single Irish Sweepstakes ticket and then quitting his job in anticipation of his winnings.
—*Tom McMillen, a former basketball star at the University of Maryland and the NBA, former member of the U.S. Congress, and co-chair of the President's Council on Physical Fitness*

Resolved: That as ministers of the Kansas conference, being more fully convinced than ever that intercollegiate games are dangerous physically, useless intellectually, and detrimental morally and spiritually, we respectfully request, with renewed emphasis, the trustees and faculties of our institutions of learning to do all in their power to abolish such games.
—*Kansas Annual Conference of the Methodist Episcopal Church, March 1899*

In 1996 the Wildcats of Northwestern University went to the Rose Bowl for the first time since 1949. The Wildcats had not had a winning record since 1971. In September 1995 their odds of making it to the Championship Game of the Big Ten and Pacific Ten Conferences could not have been much better than Ross Perot's chances of being elected president. There were good reasons for Northwestern's 47-year Rose Bowl drought. Northwestern spent $363,000 on recruiting (just three-fifths what their competitors in the conference spent) and graduated a Big Ten high 93 percent of their student-athletes (compared to an average of 66 percent for the rest of the conference). Overall, the graduation rate of scholarship athletes for the entering classes of 1987, 1988, 1989, and 1990 at Northwestern was an impressive 85 percent, compared to the NCAA Division I average athlete graduation rate of 58 percent.

Section X: Sport Economics and Business

The star running back on Northwestern's Cinderella team, Darnell Autry, was majoring in drama and attempting seriously to pursue a career in acting. He was offered a part in a movie being filmed in Rome during the summer of 1996. Since the NCAA had a rule that one cannot be an amateur qualified to play in intercollegiate competition and still receive remuneration in any activity connected to one's sport, Autry thought it best to ask for the Association's permission to accept the role.

The Association reasoned that former football stars, such as Jim Brown, O. J. Simpson, and Alex Karras, used their football careers to launch acting careers and that Autry would not have been offered the role had it not been for his football accomplishments; thus, if Autry went to Rome he would have to abandon his status as an amateur football player and forfeit his remaining two years of eligibility. After several months of unsuccessfully trying to persuade the NCAA, Autry took his case to court and obtained a temporary restraining order which permitted him to undertake his unpaid part (only his expenses were covered) and retain his eligibility. Since Brooke Shields was able to earn a million dollars in a movie while enrolled at Princeton and countless other undergraduates were allowed to pursue remuneratively their careers during the summer months, the NCAA, ever flexible, modified the rule at their 1997 Convention. Future Darnell Autrys will be able to go to Rome—on the condition that they are not compensated for their services.

Unhappily, Autry's experience is just the tip of the iceberg for Division I athletes. In March 1985, Kenny Blakeney was a starting senior basketball guard for the Duke Blue Devils. Blakeney had a "full ride" grant-in-aid (the NCAA has used this felicitous phrase since 1956 for financial support to athletes, rather than the more common "scholarship," for reasons which should be, or will shortly become, obvious) for his four years at Duke, nominally covering his tuition and fees, room and board, and books. Blakeney received a $725 monthly scholarship stipend; of which, $337.50 paid the rent at his off-campus apartment, $143 went for utilities and phone, $20 for cable television (apparently *de rigueur* for college students in the 1990s), $181.50 for food (training table did not cover all his meals), $32 for dry cleaning (team dress code required a jacket and tie on the road), and so on. Blakeney did not come from an affluent family. His mother, a clerk at a grocery store in Washington, D.C., sent him $60 a month so he could meet his bills. It was not uncommon for Blakeney to have a Snickers bar and Gatorade for breakfast and to call a $2 rental movie a "date."

Yet Blakeney followed a six-day-a-week practice schedule, including team workouts, film sessions, conditioning, and weightlifting. He suffered injuries and he played hurt. During his years at Duke the team won two national championships and appeared in three Final Fours. Duke's Associate Athletic Director said that the team averaged $750,000 a year in revenue sharing from the Atlantic Coast Conference during Blakeney's years at the school. Duke's basketball coach, Mike Krzyzewski, is reputed to receive compensation in excess of $1 million yearly. Blakeney said he and his teammates talked about these financial contrasts all the time: "End of the month, we all talk about it. We're hanging together—broke. A scholarship just isn't enough."

But Blakeney at least received his full ride for four years. Chad Wright was recruited in 1993 to play football at the University of Washington. At the time, he remembers being promised a full scholarship until he graduated. Wright suffered a spinal cord injury while participating in the team's weight-training program, ending his football career. Unfortunately, it also ended his grant-in-aid. Since 1973 the NCAA has only allowed athletic scholarships on a year-to-year basis. Thus, when a student's services as an athlete are no longer required, his hopes for a degree are frequently shattered.

Autry, Blakeney, and Wright are just three of thousands who are yearly caught in the web of contradictions that is intercollegiate athletics. The NCAA maintains a myriad of restrictions, all in the virtuous name of preserving athletics' subservience to the educational mission and amateurism in intercollegiate sports:

- pay for play is prohibited;
- athletes are not allowed to hold a job during the school year (modified beginning 1998–99 academic year);
- the number of grants-in-aid per sport is restricted;
- the size of the maximum grant is limited;
- athletes cannot sign with an agent and still retain their eligibility;
- first year students must have attained a certain SAT score and high school grade point average (GPA) to be eligible to compete;
- athletes who sign a letter of intent to attend a college must go to that school or they are forced to sit out a year before competing for another school (even if the coach who signed them departs for another school or the NBA);
- athletes who transfer from one college to another must sit out a year;

and so on. There are hundreds more such rules. Trying to keep together an association of 900-odd colleges, to get them all to follow a similar code of behavior, and to reconcile a multibillion-dollar industry with the alleged principles of amateurism is complicated.

Most economists look at the NCAA's rules and see a cartel, endeavoring to maintain a player reserve system and contain its costs. The NCAA, in contrast, maintains that it is upholding the ethical standards of amateurism, as is proclaimed, for instance, in Rule 2.15 of the Manual: "The conditions under which postseason competition occurs shall be controlled to…protect student-athletes from exploitation by professional and commercial enterprises." *Sports Illustrated*'s Steve Rushin adds: "With the exception, one presumes, of the Thrifty Car Rental Federal Express Poulan Weedeater Tough-Actin Tinactin Ty-D-bol bowls at the end of the season."

Walter Byers was Executive Director of the NCAA from 1951 to 1987. Indiana University basketball coach Bob Knight says of Byers: "[He] has done more to shape intercollegiate athletics than any single person in history. He brought a combination of leadership, insight and integrity to intercollegiate athletics that we will never again see equaled." Byers oversaw the introduction of academic rules, the Association's enforcement system, the development of grants-in-aid and he signed more than fifty television contracts with ABC, CBS, NBC, ESPN, and Turner Broadcasting. Byers has an unequivocal view on exactly what values the NCAA is upholding: "Collegiate amateurism is not a moral issue. It is an economic camouflage for monopoly practice."

Whatever the motives, it is clear that disallowing over-the-table compensation for college athletes has fostered a perverse system of incentives as well as some bizarre behavior. Like the airlines which, unable to compete over prices prior to deregulation, lavished resources on travel amenities and advertising, college coaches, unable to compete over top high school prospects with salary offers, lavish millions of dollars on recruitment and special services for athletes once in college. Then they arrange for "boosters" (usually sports-crazed local businessmen) to make payments on the side to the athletes, while salivating sports agents and their lackeys dangle dollars before the immature, impecunious athletes attempting to induce them to sign over 5 percent of their future earnings should they become pros.

When star athletes who generate $1 million or more in revenue for a school receive compensation worth only $10–40,000, there is a lot of surplus left over. The beneficiaries of this surplus are the football and basketball coaches, the athletic directors, the conference commissioners, the "non-revenue sports" (in the NCAA lingo, all sports other than men's basketball and football), and Divisions II and III. In effect, college sports is an elaborate system of cross-subsidies.

Testifying before Congress in 1992, Charles Farrell expressed the transfer pattern in stark terms: "The majority of football and basketball players in Division I, the NCAA's top competitive division, are black, yet blacks receive only 10 percent of the athletic scholarships awarded in the division. In essence, it is the black athlete who provides the blood, sweat and tears that support college sports." LSU basketball coach Dale Brown is equally strident: "This one-billion dollar TV contract is the paramount example of the injustices in the game. Look at the money we make off predominantly poor black kids. We're the whoremasters."

Byers writes that colleges have appropriated the right to "financially exploit their young players and designate others (such as athletics conferences and the NCAA) to exploit them." When college sports entered the second half of the twentieth century, the NCAA coexisted with other prominent sports organizations in the United States, such as the U.S. Lawn Tennis Association, the U.S. Golf Association, and the U.S. Olympic Committee. The latter three associations have since overseen the professionalization of their industries. Today, golf and tennis stars make millions, and the U.S. Olympic Committee provides grants of up to $15,000 a year to athletes in training, in addition to covering various expenses, allowing the athlete to pursue commercial opportunities, and offering bonus payments for winning Olympic medals. Mike Moran, the U.S. Olympic Committee's Director of Public Information, explains why his organization no longer claims to embody the principles of amateurism: "We wanted to rid ourselves of the hypocrisy." Gulp.

But the NCAA continues to defend the principles of amateurism and nominally maintain the subservience of athletics to the educational mission of academia. Many in the university wonder whether the hypocrisy hasn't gone far enough. Gary Becker, Nobel Prize-winning economist from the University of Chicago, for instance, writes:

An association of companies that limits payments to employees and punishes violators would usually be considered a labor cartel. Why should the restrictions on competition for athletes among...the members of the NCAA be any different? And especially since these restrictions primarily affect the low-income athletes—most of whom are black or from other minorities—who dominate big-time college football and basketball.

To see what can be done about the present state of affairs, it is important to inquire into the details of collegiate amateurism and how it has come to be what it is today.

The Impact of Stadiums and Professional Sports on Metropolitan Area Development

ROBERT A. BAADE AND RICHARD F. DYE

Stadium mania is sweeping the United States. City officials from Tampa Bay to San Francisco have embraced the idea that stadiums and commercial sport are essential in projecting a "world-class" image. Furthermore, it is widely held that the image of respectability imparted by sport is fortified by economic substance. Simply put, the argument is that stadiums and sports provide tangible economic benefits for the local economy and the resulting prosperity further enhances the city's reputation. Does the image of what stadiums and sports contribute to a municipality's economy conform to reality? The purpose of this paper is to examine two questions bearing on this issue. First, does the construction or renovation of a stadium or the adoption of a professional sports franchise correlate with an increase in a city's economic activity? Second; does a new or refurbished stadium or a professional football or baseball team increase the municipality's share of regional economic activity?

Before describing the empirical approach and evidence appropriate for addressing these two questions, it is logical to describe first the economic benefits claimed by stadium proponents, and the municipal response to that economic promise. As more cities build stadiums in response to the economic promise described by advocates, it becomes less likely that stadiums will deliver the economic goods to the individual cities that build them. These issues are the subject of the first section of the paper. Since the argument for public subsidization of stadiums ultimately depends on their ability to spawn positive economic externalities in excess of external costs, the next section of the paper discusses and critiques the theory underlying public stadium financial support. In the third section, a model for considering the economic contribution of a stadium is presented and explained. Next, the empirical results are presented and discussed. Then conclusions are drawn and the work is summarized.

Section X: Sport Economics and Business

THE CASE FOR PUBLIC SUBSIDIZATION OF STADIUMS, THE MUNICIPAL RESPONSE, AND THE IMPLICATIONS OF THAT RESPONSE

Proponents of public subsidization of stadiums have argued that it is a fiscally responsible strategy. In other words, stadium advocates propose that stadium economic benefits exceed costs. Economic benefits generated by stadiums are broadly identified as direct and indirect. Currently, direct economic benefit or stadium revenue is derived primarily from rent, concessions, parking, advertising, suite rental, and other preferred seating rental. Direct expenses generally include wages and related expenses, utilities, repairs and maintenance, insurance, and debt amortization. Independent research has not supported the notion that direct economic benefit exceeds cost. Benjamin Okner (1974) concluded that while revenues are sufficient to cover stadium operating expenses, the first four costs identified above, they are insufficient to cover operating costs plus debt amortization. Of course, Okner's work in some sense is dated. Stadium advocates argue that the sale or rental of premium seating promises to revolutionize stadium economics. However, not all markets will support New York prices for luxury seats; evidence suggests demand for tickets is elastic (Noll 1974); and the new tax laws promise to erode further the attractiveness of such seating to businesses. Still, new stadium revenue sources are being tapped, and improved stadium profitability appears destined to attract new private interest in stadiums.

However, while there is good news about some aspects of stadium revenue, this good news does not necessarily brighten the stadium outlook for cities. If a stadium is publicly owned, the city rents the facility back to the teams the city hosts. The rent that cities can command is jeopardized by several things relating to changing market conditions for stadiums and the teams they host. First, professional sports teams have provided evidence on shrinking profits. A study released by the Seattle Mariners Baseball Club indicated that in 1984 only eight professional baseball teams were profitable (cited in O'Grady 1987). The Mariners argued that, on average, professional baseball teams lost $2.2 million in 1984. Even with revenue sharing in the National Football League and their $2 billion plus television contract, some teams are claiming their operations are slipping into the red. Reduced profits for teams translate into reduced rents for municipalities.

In some cities, the rent the team pays the city is contingent upon team attendance. For example, according to the twenty-year lease agreement signed between the Chicago White Sox and the Illinois Sports Facilities Authority (ISFA), the White Sox will receive all ticket sales revenues, with the following exceptions: for the first ten years of the lease period, the White Sox will pay the ISFA $2.50 on every seat sold in excess of 1.2 million up to 2.0 million, and $1.50 on every seat sold in excess of 2 million. For the second ten years of the lease, the White Sox will pay ISFA $4.00 per ticket sold in excess of 1.5 million up to 2 million, and $1.50 for each ticket sold beyond 2 million. However, if during the second ten-year period the White Sox attendance is below 1.5 million, ISFA is required to purchase the difference from the Sox, up to a maximum of 300,000 tickets. Thus if the White Sox draw 1.2 million during the second ten years, IFSA will pay the White Sox in excess of $1 million per year, the exact number to be determined by an average White Sox ticket price (State of Illinois 1988). It should be noted that the White Sox have drawn two million or more fans only twice in their history, and in 1987 and 1988 they drew 1.208 million and 1.116 million, respectively.

A second factor that clouds the prospect for cities prospering through stadiums relates to unequal market power. Professional sports leagues have used their monopoly power to limit expansion. Thus, the number of cities seeking professional sports franchises outnumbers the supply of teams. In this seller's market, municipalities have been known to offer their facilities rent-free to teams they are courting or trying to retain. For example, Seattle agreed to give the American League Baseball Mariners free rent for the 1985–87 seasons. In addition, Seattle has agreed to pick up all game day expenses for this period. Other examples of municipal largess abound.

This municipal competition serves as a strong disincentive for private team involvement in stadium projects. James Quirk (1987) has identified a "Gresham's Law" for stadiums. Since league teams compete in publicly and privately financed facilities, the teams playing in publicly owned facilities have a clear economic advantage. Presumably to offset this advantage, disadvantaged teams will push harder for public support. The fact that only four of the twenty-nine stadiums built since 1960 have been constructed privately supports Quirk's application of Gresham's law to stadiums.

A third factor clouding stadium economic prospects for cities relates to stadium costs. While stadium revenues overall have increased, so have stadium costs. As the figures indicate, current stadium construction costs are enormous. Furthermore, the rate of increase in construction costs exceeds the overall rate of inflation. Increases in the construction cost index have been approximately 50 percent and 100 percent greater than increases for the consumer and wholesale price indices respectively for the 1965 to 1989 period. Note that the use of a composite construction cost index assumes no productivity gains from experience with building a particular type of structure and may obscure variations in costs across local areas or types of materials.

In addition, domes are the fashion in stadium design, and domes increase stadium costs substantially. Furthermore, all domed stadiums have been built with public funds.

The high cost of rigid-roof domed facilities has led municipalities to consider stadiums with flexible roofs. The 1989 cost of air-supported teflon-roofed domes ranged from 23 to 64 percent of the cost of the structures with rigid roofs. Lack of durability and energy inefficiency have been cited as disadvantages of the flexible-roof domes, but it seems unlikely that those disadvantages would be enough to favor building rigid-roof stadiums.

Of course, domes have some economic advantages. Climate is more easily controlled in a domed stadium, and for that reason domed facilities may be likely to attract more frequent near-capacity crowds than do open-air stadiums. In addition, domed stadiums can host conventions and exhibitions, while open-air stadiums are less likely to attract such non-sport events. The Alamo Dome in San Antonio, Texas, approved by voters in early 1989, has no professional sports tenant, but will be used for convention and trade show activities exclusively until a sports tenant can be secured.

Despite direct revenue and cost projections that do not argue for public subsidization of stadiums, municipalities are planning to build stadiums in record numbers. At least one-third of the sixty largest metropolitan statistical areas (MSAs) have plans for new stadiums (Baade and Dye 1988). Of course, planning does not guarantee construction, but the extent of planning indicates an optimism that belies market conditions.

In a survey conducted by one of the authors, city planners in the sixty largest MSAs were asked, "Do you believe that stadium construction or renovation can be justified on economic grounds?" Sixty percent of the twenty planning stadiums answered "yes," while only three of the twenty answered "no." Two city planners indicated they were "not sure," while one said he felt uncomfortable answering the question. Two did not answer the question. In a market in which professional sports team suitors already outnumber professional sports teams by a substantial amount, new stadiums seem destined only to intensify intercity competition for teams and to diminish further the prospect that cities can profit from building a stadium.

The survey revealed at least one other interesting fact. Nine MSAs ranking in the top twenty according to population have stadium plans and all of them already have at least one stadium. Rather than physical deterioration or obsolescence, new stadium construction is inspired by economic obsolescence. Cities in their desire to retain or attract a commercial sports franchise find they have to accommodate or provide for that which teams identify as critical sources of revenue. Luxury or preferred seating on a scale sufficient to keep franchises economically competitive cannot be engineered into existing facilities of even relatively recent vintages. The fact that Joe Robbie, owner of the NFL Miami Dolphins, was able to parlay revenues from preferred seating into funds sufficient to privately build a $120 million stadium has lent substance to the promise of enormous revenues through new stadium design and seating.

Three top-twenty cities, Atlanta, Baltimore, and Chicago, are seriously considering construction of two stadiums (Baade and Dye 1988). Furthermore, the survey indicated that officials in five of the top-twenty cities believe new stadium construction is essential to retain or reacquire at least one professional sports franchise they currently host or recently hosted. In the case of New York, stadium construction is contingent on bringing an NFL franchise back to the city. Only in Miami did circumstances suggest that the new stadium was not part of a defensive city action. After three referenda failed to produce public support for a new stadium, as noted earlier, the owner of the NFL Miami Dolphins decided to build his own.

The stadium referendum in Miami is not unique. Stadium operating deficits in Pontiac, Michigan (Silverdome) and New Orleans (Superdome) have galvanized taxpayer resistance across the country. For example, in Cleveland and in San Francisco taxpayers have voted down a number of proposals that would have cleared the way for public financial involvement. However, even in these cities as soon as one proposal is rejected, another appears. In attempting to elicit taxpayer support, stadium proponents have emphasized the indirect economic benefit that stadiums create. In fact much of the current debate on stadium economics is focused on the scope of indirect economic benefits.

INDIRECT BENEFITS AS THE KEY JUSTIFICATION FOR PUBLIC STADIUM SUBSIDIES

If public financial support for stadiums is to be economically justified, the paucity of direct economic benefit for the city suggests that substantial indirect benefits are perceived. Indeed, in most stadium feasibility studies, the indirect benefits (including multiplier effects) identified by stadium advocates greatly exceed direct benefits. For instance, a recent study by the City of Chicago (1986) indicated that the indirect and multiplier effects of a major league baseball team to the Illinois economy were approximately twice the direct impact. Indirect city benefits can be broadly or narrowly defined. They could include any increased economic activity in the area attributable to the stadium, or only the tax and other revenues to the local government collected from those activities. Indirect economic activity generally includes those sales outside the stadium which are attributable to stadium events, and the multiplier benefits from the respending of stadium incomes on local services. The existence of substantial indirect economic benefit is open to criticisms The fundamental issue is the extent to which the stadium causes a net increase in area activity rather than a mere reallocation or redistribution of the same level of activity—but with different beneficiaries of that activity. Indeed, any time there is a reallocation of economic activity, there exists the possibility that there will be a net decline in overall activity. Professional sports are just one kind of entertainment activity and as such compete for the local consumer's scarce disposable income and leisure time. Twenty dollars spent on football tickets may be merely twenty less dollars spent on theater tickets elsewhere in the city. The new restaurant across from the stadium may be offset by putting an old restaurant out of business in another neighborhood.

In the standard development models, local growth comes from increased export sales—net inflows of spending from outside the area. The multiplier then follows the new spending with expansion of locally produced secondary activities. The other way for a local area to grow is through import substitution—if the twenty dollars spent by a local resident on a sports ticket would have been used to buy goods outside the area, then net local spending will increase.

The size of the multiplier following any net increase in area spending depends similarly on the locus of the respending. If all of the new income is respent on locally produced goods, then the multiplier will be substantial. If, however, the highly paid athletes or executives maintain their residences outside the area or if the concessionaires import their semi-finished goods from outside, then the multiplier will be small.

The impact of a stadium on the local economy depends, therefore, on the details of where each dollar is spent and would be spent—on imports, on exports, or on local production. This information is extremely difficult to obtain (especially since it requires both the factual and the counterfactual) and the common technique is to proceed by making assumptions about the sources and uses of spending. Not surprisingly, those who get the greatest impact of stadiums on local economies assume that all the initial spending is a net increase in local spending (implicitly they are saying that all the spending is either export sales or import substitutions) and all the respending stays inside the area.

For example, a recent study by a University of Pennsylvania researcher estimated that Philadelphia's professional sports teams contributed more than $500 million to the city's economy in 1983 (Shils

1985). In a contrasting study, a Baltimore area researcher estimated the overall economic impact the NFL Colts had on the Baltimore area as merely $200,000 (Lancaster 1986). Sharply different assumptions can compel sharply different results. The leverage on alternative assumptions is particularly troublesome where the sponsor of the research has an identifiable economic interest or point of view. The Philadelphia study was funded by a consortium of the city's professional teams, while the Baltimore study was conducted just after the Colts had bolted for the greener pastures of Indianapolis. In any multiplier study the assumptions as to the locus of spending may simply be wrong. The usual new industry development impact study methodology is to assume new demand, at least at the first round.

Without direct knowledge of the locus of the spending, we prefer not to follow others in compelling the result by making assumptions. Instead, we present indirect, empirical evidence on the impact of stadiums on area income.

Since the issue is government subsidy of sports stadiums, substitutions at the policy level are also relevant. The question should not be whether a new stadium would have any net impact on area development, but rather if it has the largest impact on the area from a set of alternative development subsidy projects. The local development authority has limited time and budget: tax-exempt industrial development bonds are now restricted and rationed; the "political capital" to sell projects to those who pay the taxes or lose from the redistribution of economic activity is limited. Scarce development subsidy resources might better be targeted to industries which are more clearly engaged in export sales or import substitution. The attention of those who allocate development resources should also be devoted to the types of jobs which are being created in alternative development products (more on this later).

It may well be true that public support for high-visibility development products like stadiums does come easier than for some alternatives. If, however, such support comes only from the perception of substantial development flowing from the project—bolstered by the assumption-compelled impact studies—then this is not much of an argument.

Since a stadium or sports-based development strategy may change the structure of the local economy, the long-run impact is not necessarily amenable to prediction with the trade-multiplier approach.

We consider quite plausible one long-run scenario which could be detrimental to area income growth. The types of jobs induced by stadium activity are low-wage and seasonal: ticket takers, ushers, vendors, restaurant and bar workers, taxi drivers, etc. An area development strategy which concentrates on these types of jobs could lead to a situation where the city gains a comparative advantage in unskilled and seasonal labor. Compared to other areas (with their comparative advantage in high-wage, high-skilled labor) future growth here will then be concentrated in low-income jobs.

A very different long-run argument is made by advocates of sports-based development. They project that the "major league" image of the city is an intangible which will attract new unrelated businesses to the area. Assertions about the size of this effect are sometimes even used as input in multiplier models.

With such different possible outcomes in theory, the impact of stadiums and professional sports becomes an empirical question. To supplement the multiplier studies we present an alternative methodology which, in effect, offers an after-the-fact audit of whether a new stadium or team has a discernable impact on overall area development. We turn now to this empirical examination.

THE MODEL

Regression analysis is employed to evaluate the impact that stadiums and sports teams have on SMSA aggregate income, spending, and development. In considering the stadium and professional sports influence on these measures of aggregate economic activity, the analysis is straightforward. SMSA income statistics are regressed on independent variables which capture the character of the metropolitan area's economy before and after the establishment of sports stadiums and teams.

The FOOTball and BASEball variables are, of course, omitted from the individual SMSA equations when a pro team is either present or absent for the entire time period. One might expect that there is still a high correlation between the STADium and FOOTball or BASEball variables, but an analysis of the individual cases suggests that this is not the case—franchises are gained and lost without a change in the stadium, and stadiums are built for existing teams. We must acknowledge that one remaining concern with this method is the possibility of bias imparted by the correlation of unknown and omitted determinants of area growth with the stadium or franchise variables.

In an attempt to minimize this bias, the population (POP or POP/POPR) and time trend CTREND) variables are included as controls for general influences acting on metropolitan area personal income. Population can explain a large fraction of changes in income and has the advantage of being less colinear with the other explanatory variables than would, say, employment. The other problem with employment (or unemployment) measures is that they might be argued to be dependent on the outcome of the development strategies and thus determined simultaneously with income. The time trend variable is included as a proxy for omitted variables which exert a systematic influence on area income.

We choose not to include some other variables (such as race, education, percent poor or median income) which have been employed in studies of cross-metropolitan differences in income growth (see, for example, Burns 1982). There is too little year-to-year variation in these measures for individual metropolitan area regressions in the current study. Also, in the pooled regressions the separate shift variable for each individual area should capture these effects.

The time period for the regressions is 1965 to 1983. The decision to stop in 1983 was made because abrupt differences in the data series were encountered at the time reporting areas were changed from SMSA to MSA definitions.

RESULTS

The regression results for the impact of stadiums and professional football or baseball on the *level* of personal income for each of the nine metropolitan areas studied (Cincinnati, Denver, Detroit, Kansas City, New Orleans, Pittsburgh, San Diego, Seattle, and Tampa Bay): After controlling for the effect of population and time trend, the presence of a new or renovated stadium has an insignificant impact on area income for all but one of the metropolitan areas. The exception is Seattle, which shows a highly significant positive impact of a new stadium (combined with the contemporaneous effect of a newNFL franchise).

Section X: Sport Economics and Business

The impact of gaining a football franchise (Cincinnati or New Orleans) or a baseball franchise (Kansas City, Seattle, or San Diego) also shows up as insignificant.

In summary, the results are ambiguous but generally show that after controlling for population and trend, there is an insignificant impact of the stadium or sports variables on the level of metropolitan area income.

Looking at each metropolitan area relative to the multi-state region provides an additional set of controls for any unspecified forces acting on both the one metropolitan area and the larger region. One can expect that a metropolitan area's income, as a fraction of regional income, will be to a significant degree directly correlated with changes in the fraction of regional population represented by the metropolitan area. The relative population variable will in turn control for omitted influences acting on both population and income. Such controls plus the time trend variable leave a strong test for any residual impact of the stadium or pro sports variables.

The results are mixed, but a pattern emerges which suggests a potential negative impact of sports on area development. For four of the metropolitan areas analyzed (Cincinnati, Detroit, Kansas City, and Tampa Bay) stadium construction or renovation is significantly correlated with a reduction of that metropolitan area's share of regional income. For two of the metropolitan areas (New Orleans and Seattle) there was a significantly positive association. However, in the case of New Orleans, the positive effect of a stadium was offset by a significantly negative effect of professional football on share of income.

The impact of stadium construction or renovation on the metropolitan area's share of regional income is negative and significant. This result is consistent with the kind of economic activity that stadiums and professional sports spawn. Professional sports and stadiums divert economic development toward labor-intensive, relatively-unskilled labor (low-wage) activities. To the extent that this developmental path diverges from less labor-intensive, more highly skilled labor (high-wage) activities characteristic of other economies within the region, it would be expected that the sports-minded area would experience a falling share of regional income.

Table 1 presents results for the relationship between the sports variables and retail sales, a measure of economic activity often hypothesized to be significantly influenced by stadium and team activity. Among other things, retail sales include revenues generated at eating and drinking establishments. The same nine metropolitan areas are included as for the income regressions. Because retail sales data are published only at five-year intervals (*Census of Retail Trade*, various years), there are four years (1967, 1972, 1977, and 1982) for each of the nine metropolitan areas, yielding a total of thirty-six observations. Since there are not enough degrees of freedom to control for scale by using a separate dummy variable for each SMSA, an alternative technique is employed: a single scale variable is assigned the value estimated for the area dummy from the income regressions.

The first row of Table 1 has the estimated coefficients of the indicated variables in explaining the level of retail sales. All three sports variables show an insignificant impact on area sales. The second row is SMSA retail sales as a fraction of regional retail sales. As was the case in the pooled relative income regression, the impact of a new or renovated stadium shows up as significantly adverse to local economic activity. A new result here is the significantly positive impact of the presence of a pro football franchise on metropolitan retail sales compared to the region. Perhaps this result indicates not only the regional drawing of football, but also that football fans come to a metropolitan area for the weekend to view a Sunday game. However, since retail sales constitute only a fraction of an SMSA's personal income, the eight to ten weekends this football-generated spending occurs is apparently not substantial enough to positively influence a metropolitan area's share of regional income.

Table 1: The Impact of Stadiums and Professional Football and Baseball on the Level of SMSA Retail Sales and SMSA Retail Sales Relative to Regional Retail Sales for all Nine Cities (1967, 1972, 1977, 1982)

	POP	STAD	FOOT	BASE	TREND	R^2
$ Level	3.71 (10.98)	405.69 (.76)	-447.14 (-.88)	-269.56 (-.72)	63.21 (1.60)	.965
	POP/ POPR					
Relative to Region	.117 (.46)	-.0132 (-2.16)	.0150 (2.40)	.0067 (1.36)	.0006 (1.23)	.933

(t-statistics in parentheses)

CONCLUSION

More and more local and state governments are being encouraged to subsidize sports stadiums as an economic development tool. Previous attempts to estimate the impact of stadiums and pro sports on metropolitan area development have used trade-multiplier models, but those models are assumption-driven and based on the past structure of the local economy. Such models are not suitable for cases where long-run structural change is present. We, therefore, seek a different kind of empirical evidence on the effectiveness of sports-based development. The evidence presented here is that the presence of a new or renovated stadium has an uncertain impact on the levels of economic activity and possibly a negative impact on local development relative to the region. This result is consistent with the possibility that stadium subsidies might bias local development toward low-wage jobs. This should also serve as a strong caution to those who assume or assert a large positive stadium impact. We do not deny the possibility of "intangibles" or external benefits from "civic pride" or psychological identification with big-time sports, but stadium construction is often justified to the taxpaying public on tangible economic grounds. Therefore, we prefer to leave intangibles as a residual explanation after direct or indirect economic activities have been explored.

Section XI

Media and Sport

The Televised Sports Manhood Formula

Michael A. Messner, Michele Dunbar, & Darnell Hunt

A recent national survey found 8- to 17-year-old children to be avid consumers of sports media, with television most often named as the preferred medium (Amateur Athletic Foundation of Los Angeles, 1999). Although girls watch sports in great numbers, boys are markedly more likely to report that they are regular consumers of televised sports. The most popular televised sports with boys, in order, are pro football, men's pro basketball, pro baseball, pro wrestling, men's college basketball, college football, and Extreme sports. Although counted separately in the Amateur Athletic Foundation (AAF) study, televised sports highlights shows also were revealed to be tremendously popular with boys.

What are boys seeing and hearing when they watch these programs? What kinds of values concerning gender, race, aggression, violence, and consumerism are boys exposed to when they watch their favorite televised sports programs, with their accompanying commercials? This article, based on a textual analysis, presents the argument that televised sports, and their accompanying commercials, consistently present boys with a narrow portrait of masculinity, which we call the Televised Sports Manhood Formula.

SAMPLE AND METHOD

We analyzed a range of televised sports that were identified by the AAF study as those programs most often watched by boys. Most of the programs in our sample aired during a single week, May 23–29, 1999, with one exception. Because pro football is not in season in May, we acquired tapes of two randomly chosen National Football League (NFL) *Monday Night Football* games from the previous season to include in our sample. We analyzed televised coverage, including commercials and pregame, halftime, and postgame shows (when appropriate), for the following programs:

1. two broadcasts of *SportsCenter* on ESPN (2 hours of programming);
2. two broadcasts of Extreme sports, one on ESPN and one on Fox Sports West (approximately 90 minutes of programming);
3. two broadcasts of professional wrestling, including *Monday Night Nitro* on TNT and *WWF Superstars* on USA (approximately 2 hours of programming);
4. two broadcasts of National Basketball Association (NBA) play-off games, one on TNT and the other on NBC (approximately 7 hours of programming);
5. two broadcasts of NFL *Monday Night Football* on ABC (approximately 7 hours of programming); and
6. one broadcast of Major League Baseball (MLB) on TBS (approximately 3 hours of programming).

We conducted a textual analysis of the sports programming and the commercials. In all, we examined about 23 hours of sports programming, nearly one quarter of which was time taken up by commercials. We examined a total of 722 commercials, which spanned a large range of products and services. We collected both quantitative and qualitative data. Although we began with some sensitizing concepts that we knew we wanted to explore (e.g., themes of violence, images of gender and race, etc.), rather than starting with preset categories we used an inductive method that allowed the dominant themes to emerge from our reading of the tapes.

Each taped show was given a first reading by one of the investigators, who then constructed a preliminary analysis of the data. The tape was then given a second reading by another of the investigators. This second independent reading was then used to modify and sharpen the first reading. Data analysis proceeded along the lines of the categories that emerged in the data collection. The analyses of each separate sport were then put into play with each other and common themes and patterns were identified. In one case, the dramatic pseudosport of professional wrestling, we determined that much of the programming was different enough that it made little sense to directly compare it with the other sports shows; therefore, we only included data on wrestling in our comparisons when it seemed to make sense to do so.

DOMINANT THEMES IN TELEVISED SPORTS

Our analysis revealed that sports programming presents boys with narrow and stereotypical messages about race, gender, and violence. We identified 10 distinct themes that, together, make up the Televised Sports Manhood Formula.

Table 1 Race and Sex of Announcers

White Men	White Women	Black Men	Black Women
24	3	3	1

WHITE MALES ARE THE VOICE OF AUTHORITY

Although one of the two *SportsCenter* segments in the sample did feature a White woman coanchor, the play-by-play and ongoing color commentary in NFL, wrestling, NBA, Extreme sports, and MLB broadcasts were conducted exclusively by White, male play-by-play commentators.

With the exception of *SportsCenter*, women and Blacks never appeared as the main voices of authority in the booth conducting play-by-play or ongoing color commentary. The NFL broadcasts occasionally cut to field-level color commentary by a White woman but her commentary was very brief (about 3 1/2 minutes of the nearly 3 hours of actual game and pregame commentary). Similarly, one of the NBA broadcasts used a Black man for occasional on-court analysis and a Black man for pregame and halftime analysis, whereas the other NBA game used a White woman as host in the pregame show and a Black woman for occasional on-court analysis. Although viewers commonly see Black male athletes—especially on televised NBA games—they rarely hear or see Black men or women as voices of authority in the broadcast booth (Sabo & Jansen, 1994). In fact, the only Black commentators that appeared on the NBA shows that we examined were former star basketball players (Cheryl Miller, Doc Rivers, and Isaiah Thomas). A Black male briefly appeared to welcome the audience to open one of the Extreme sports shows but he did not do any play-by-play; in fact, he was used only to open the show with a stylish, street, hip-hop style for what turned out to be an almost totally White show.

SPORTS IS A MAN'S WORLD

Images or discussion of women athletes is almost entirely absent in the sports programs that boys watch most. SportsCenter's mere 2.9% of news time devoted to women's sports is slightly lower than the 5% to 6% of women's sports coverage commonly found in other sports news studies (Duncan & Messner, 1998). In addition, SportsCenter's rare discussion of a women's sport seemed to follow men's in newsworthiness (e.g., a report on a Professional Golfers' Association [PGA] tournament was followed by a more brief report on a Ladies Professional Golf Association [LPGA] tournament). The baseball, basketball, wrestling, and football programs we watched were men's contests so could not perhaps have been expected to cover or mention women athletes. However, Extreme sports are commonly viewed as "alternative" or "emerging" sports in which women are challenging masculine hegemony (Wheaton & Tomlinson, 1998). Despite this, the Extreme sports shows we watched devoted only a single 50-second interview segment to a woman athlete. This segment constituted about 1% of the total Extreme sports programming and, significantly, did not show this woman athlete in action. Perhaps this limited coverage of women athletes on the Extreme sports shows we examined is evidence of what Rinehart (1998) calls a "pecking order" in alternative sports, which develops when new sports are appropriated and commodified by the media.

Table 2 Sex Composition of 722 Commercials

Men Only	Women Only	Women and Men	No People
279 (38.6%)	28 (3.9%)	324 (44.9%)	91 (12.6%)

MEN ARE FOREGROUNDED IN COMMERCIALS

The idea that sports is a man's world is reinforced by the gender composition and imagery in commercials. Women almost never appear in commercials unless they are in the company of men, as Table 2 shows.

That 38.6% of all commercials portray only men actually understates the extent to which men dominate these commercials for two reasons. First, nearly every one of the 91 commercials that portrayed no visual portrayals of people included a male voice-over. When we include this number, we see that more than 50% of commercials provide men-only images and/or voice-overs, whereas only 3.9% portray only women. Moreover, when we combine men-only and women and men categories, we see that men are visible in 83.5% of all commercials and men are present (when we add in the commercials with male voice-overs) in 96.1% of all commercials. Second, in the commercials that portray both women and men, women are often (although not exclusively) portrayed in stereotypical, and often very minor, background roles.

WOMEN ARE SEXY PROPS OR PRIZES FOR MEN'S SUCCESSFUL SPORT PERFORMANCES OR CONSUMPTION CHOICES

Although women were mostly absent from sports commentary, when they did appear it was most often in stereotypical roles as sexy, masculinity-validating props, often cheering the men on. For instance, "X-sports" on Fox Sports West used a bikini-clad blonde woman as a hostess to welcome viewers back after each commercial break as the camera moved provocatively over her body. Although she mentioned the show's sponsors, she did not narrate the actual sporting event. The wrestling shows generously used scantily clad women (e.g., in pink miniskirts or tight Spandex and high heels) who overtly displayed the dominant cultural signs of heterosexy attractiveness to escort the male wrestlers to the ring, often with announcers discussing the women's provocative physical appearances. Women also appeared in the wrestling shows as sexually provocative dancers (e.g., the "Gorgeous Nitro Girls" on TNT).

Table 3 Instances of Women Being Depicted as Sexy Props or Prizes for Men

	SportsCenter	Extreme	Wrestling	NBA	MLB	NFL
Commercials	5	5	3	10	4	6
Sport programs	0	5	13	3	0	4
Total	5	10	16	13	4	10

Note: NBA = National Basketball Association, MLB = Major League Baseball, and NFL = National Football League.

In commercials, women are numerically more evident, and generally depicted in more varied roles, than in the sports programming. Still, women are underrepresented and rarely appear in commercials unless they are in the company of men. Moreover, as Table 3 illustrates, the commercials' common depiction of women as sexual objects and as "prizes" for men's successful consumption choices articulates with the sports programs' presentation of women primarily as sexualized, supportive props for men's athletic performances. For instance, a commercial for Keystone Light Beer that ran on *SportsCenter* depicted two White men at a baseball game. When one of the men appeared on the stadium big screen and made an ugly face after drinking an apparently bitter beer, women appeared to be grossed out by him. But then he drank a Keystone Light and reappeared on the big screen looking good with two young, conventionally beautiful (fashion-model-like) women adoring him. He says, "I hope my wife's not watching!" as the two women flirt with the camera.

As Table 3 shows, in 23 hours of sports programming, viewers were exposed to 58 incidents of women being portrayed as sexy props and/or sexual prizes for men's successful athletic performances or correct consumption choices. Put another way, a televised sports viewer is exposed to this message, either in commercials or in the sports program itself, on an average of twice an hour. The significance of this narrow image of women as heterosexualized commodities should be considered especially in light of the overall absence of a wider range of images of women, especially as athletes (Duncan & Messner, 1998; Kane & Lenskyj, 1998).

WHITES ARE FOREGROUNDED IN COMMERCIALS

The racial composition of the commercials is, if anything, more narrow and limited than the gender composition. As Table 4 shows, Black, Latino, or Asian American people almost never appear in commercials unless the commercial also has White people in it (the multiracial category below).

Table 4 Racial Composition of 722 Commercials

White Only	Black Only	Latino/a Only	Asian Only	Multiracial	Undetermined	No People
377 (52.2%)	28 (3.9%)	3 (0.4%)	2 (0.3%)	203 (28.1%)	18 (2.5%)	91 (12.6%)

Table 5 Statements Lauding Aggression or Criticizing Lack of Aggression

	SportsCenter	Extreme	NBA	MLB	NFL
	3	4	40	4	15

Note: NBA = National Basketball Association, MLB = Major League Baseball, and NFL = National Football League.

To say that 52.2% of the commercials portrayed only Whites actually understates the extent to which images of White people dominated the commercials for two reasons. First, if we subtract the 91 commercials that showed no actual people, then we see that the proportion of commercials that actually showed people was 59.7% White only. Second, when we examine the quality of the portrayals of Blacks, Latinos, and Asian Americans in the multiracial commercials, we see that people of color are far more often than not relegated to minor roles, literally in the background of scenes that feature Whites, and/or they are relegated to stereotypical or negative roles. For instance, a Wendy's commercial that appeared on several of the sports programs in our sample showed White customers enjoying a sandwich with the White owner while a barely perceptible Black male walked by in the background.

AGGRESSIVE PLAYERS GET THE PRIZE; NICE GUYS FINISH LAST

As Table 5 illustrates, viewers are continually immersed in images and commentary about the positive rewards that come to the most aggressive competitors and of the negative consequences of playing "soft" and lacking aggression.

Commentators consistently lauded athletes who most successfully employed physical and aggressive play and toughness. For instance, after having his toughness called into question, NBA player Brian Grant was awarded redemption by *SportsCenter* because he showed that he is "not afraid to take it to Karl Malone." *SportsCenter* also informed viewers that "the aggressor usually gets the calls [from the officials] and the Spurs were the ones getting them." In pro wrestling commentary, this is a constant theme (and was therefore not included in our tallies for Table 5 because the theme permeated the commentary, overtly and covertly). The World Wrestling Federation (WWF) announcers praised the "raw power" of wrestler "Shamrock" and approvingly dubbed "Hardcore Holly" as "the world's most dangerous man." NBA commentators suggested that it is okay to be a good guy off the court but one must be tough and aggressive on the court: Brian Grant and Jeff Hornacek are "true gentlemen of the NBA…as long as you don't have to play against them. You know they're great off the court; on the court, every single guy out there *should* be a killer."

When players were not doing well, they were often described as "hesitant" and lacking aggression, emotion, and desire (e.g., for a loose ball or rebound). For instance, commentators lamented that "the Jazz aren't going to the hoop, they're being pushed and shoved around," that Utah was responding to the Blazers' aggression "passively, in a reactive mode," and that "Utah's got to get Karl Malone toughened up." SportsCenter echoed this theme, opening one show with a depiction of Horace Grant elbowing Karl Malone and asking of Malone, "Is he feeble?" Similarly, NFL broadcasters waxed on about the virtues of aggression and domination. Big "hits"; ball carriers who got "buried," "stuffed," or "walloped" by the defense; and players who get "cleaned out" or "wiped out" by a blocker were often shown on replays, with announcers enthusiastically describing the plays. By contrast, they clearly declared that it is a very bad thing to be passive and to let yourself get pushed around and dominated at the line of scrimmage. Announcers also approvingly noted that going after an opposing player's injured body part is just smart strategy: In one NFL game, the Miami strategy to blitz the opposing quarterback was lauded as "brilliant"—"When you know your opposing quarterback is a bit nicked and something is wrong, Boomer, you got to come after him."

Previous research has pointed to this heroic framing of the male body-as-weapon as a key element in sports' role in the social construction of narrow conceptions of masculinity (Messner, 1992; Trujillo, 1995).

This injunction for boys and men to be aggressive, not passive, is reinforced in commercials, where a common formula is to play on the insecurities of young males (e.g., that they are not strong enough, tough enough, smart enough, rich enough, attractive enough, decisive enough, etc.) and then attempt to convince them to avoid, overcome, or mask their fears, embarrassments, and apparent shortcomings by buying a particular product. These commercials often portray men as potential or actual geeks, nerds, or passive schmucks who can overcome their geekiness (or avoid being a geek like the guy in the commercial) by becoming decisive and purchasing a particular product.

Table 6 Humorous or Sarcastic Discussion of Fights or Near-Fights

SportsCenter	Extreme	NBA	MLB	NFL
10	1	2	2	7

Note: NBA = National Basketball Association, MLB = Major League Baseball, and NFL = National Football League.

BOYS WILL BE (VIOLENT) BOYS

Announcers often took a humorous "boys will be boys" attitude in discussing fights or near-fights during contests, and they also commonly used a recent fight, altercation, or disagreement between two players as a "teaser" to build audience excitement.

Fights, near-fights, threats of fights, or other violent actions were over-emphasized in sports coverage and often verbally framed in sarcastic language that suggested that this kind of action, although reprehensible, is to be expected. For instance, as *SportsCenter* showed NBA centers Robinson and O'Neill exchanging forearm shoves, the commentators said, simply, "much love." Similarly, in an NFL game, a brief scuffle between players is met with a sarcastic comment by the broadcaster that the players are simply "making their acquaintance." This is, of course, a constant theme in pro wrestling (which, again, we found impossible and less than meaningful to count because this theme permeates the show). We found it noteworthy that the supposedly spontaneous fights outside the wrestling ring (what we call unofficial fights) were given more coverage time and focus than the supposedly official fights inside the ring. We speculate that wrestling producers know that viewers already watch fights inside the ring with some skepticism as to their authenticity so they stage the unofficial fights outside the ring to bring a feeling of spontaneity and authenticity to the show and to build excitement and a sense of anticipation for the fight that will later occur inside the ring.

GIVE UP YOUR BODY FOR THE TEAM

Athletes who are "playing with pain," "giving up their body for the team," or engaging in obviously highly dangerous plays or maneuvers were consistently framed as heroes; conversely, those who removed themselves from games due to injuries had questions raised about their character, their manhood.

Section XI: Media and Sport

Table 7 Comments on the Heroic Nature of Playing Hurt

SportsCenter	Extreme	NBA	MLB	NFL
9	12	6	4	15

Note: NBA = National Basketball Association, MLB = Major League Baseball, and NFL = National Football League.

This theme cut across all sports programming. For instance, *SportsCenter* asked, "Could the dominator be soft?" when a National Hockey League (NHL) star goalie decided to sit out a game due to a groin injury. Heroically taking risks while already hurt was a constant theme in Extreme sports commentary. For instance, one bike competitor was lauded for "over-coming his fear" and competing "with a busted up ankle" and another was applauded when he "popped his collarbone out in the street finals in Louisville but he's back on his bike here in Richmond, just 2 weeks later!" Athletes appear especially heroic when they go against doctors' wishes not to compete. For instance, an X Games interviewer adoringly told a competitor, "Doctors said don't ride but you went ahead and did it anyway and escaped serious injury." Similarly, NBA player Isaiah Rider was lauded for having "heart" for "playing with that knee injury." Injury discussions in NFL games often include speculation about whether the player will be able to return to this or future games. A focus on a star player in a pregame or halftime show, such as the feature on 49ers' Garrison Hearst, often contain commentary about heroic overcoming of serious injuries (in this case, a knee blowout, reconstructive surgery, and rehabilitation). As one game began, commentators noted that 37-year-old "Steve Young has remained a rock…not bad for a guy who a lotta people figured was, what, one big hit from ending his career." It's especially impressive when an injured player is able and willing to continue to play with aggressiveness and reckless abandon: "Kurt Scrafford at right guard—bad neck and all—is just out there wiping out guys." And announcers love the team leader who plays hurt:

> Drew Bledsoe gamely tried to play in loss to Rams yesterday; really admirable to try to play with that pin that was surgically implanted in his finger during the week; I don't know how a Q.B. could do that. You know, he broke his finger the time we had him on Monday night and he led his team to two come-from-behind victories, really gutted it out and I think he took that team on his shoulders and showed he could play and really elevated himself in my eyes, he really did.

SPORTS IS WAR

Commentators consistently (an average of nearly five times during each hour of sports commentary) used martial metaphors and language of war and weaponry to describe sports action (e.g., battle, kill, ammunition, weapons, professional sniper, depth charges, taking aim, fighting, shot in his arsenal, reloading, detonate, squeezes the trigger, attack mode, firing blanks, blast, explosion, blitz, point of attack, a lance through the heart, etc.).

Table 8 Martial Metaphors and Language of War and Weaponry

	SportsCenter	Extreme	Wrestling	NBA	MLB	NFL
	9	3	15	27	6	23

Note: NBA = National Basketball Association, MLB = Major League Baseball, and NFL = National Football League.

Table 9 Depictions of Guts in Face of Danger, Speed, Hits, Crashes

	SportsCenter	Extreme	NBA	MLB	NFL
	4	21	5	2	8

Note: NBA = National Basketball Association, MLB = Major League Baseball, and NFL = National Football League.

Some shows went beyond commentators' use of war terminology and actually framed the contests as wars. For instance, one of the wrestling shows offered a continual flow of images and commentary that reminded the viewers that "RAW is WAR!" Similarly, both NFL *Monday Night Football* broadcasts were introduced with explosive graphics and an opening song that included lyrics "Like a rocket burning through time and space, the NFL's best will rock this place…the battle lines are drawn." This sort of use of sport/war metaphors has been a common practice in televised sports commentary for many years, serving to fuse (and confuse) the distinctions between values of nationalism with team identity and athletic aggression with military destruction (Jansen & Sabo, 1994). In the shows examined for this study, war themes also were reinforced in many commercials, including commercials for movies, other sports programs, and in the occasional commercial for the U.S. military.

SHOW SOME GUTS!

Commentators continually depicted and replayed exciting incidents of athletes engaging in reckless acts of speed, showing guts in the face of danger, big hits, and violent crashes.

This theme was evident across all of the sports programs but was especially predominant in Extreme sports that continually depicted crashing vehicles or bikers in an exciting manner. For instance, when one race ended with a crash, it was showed again in slow-motion replay, with commentators approvingly dubbing it "unbelievable" and "original." Extreme sports commentators commonly raised excitement levels by saying "he's on fire" or "he's going huge!" when a competitor was obviously taking greater risks. An athlete's ability to deal with the fear of a possible crash, in fact, is the mark of an "outstanding run": "Watch out, Richmond," an X-games announcer shouted to the crowd, "He's gonna wreck this place!" A winning competitor laughingly said, "I do what I can to smash into [my opponents] as much as I can." Another competitor said, "If I crash, no big deal; I'm just gonna go for it." NFL commentators introduced the games with images of reckless collisions and during the game a "fearless" player was likely to be applauded:

"There's no chance that Barry Sanders won't take when he's running the football." In another game, the announcer noted that receiver "Tony Simmons plays big. And for those of you not in the NFL, playing big means you're not afraid to go across the middle and catch the ball and make a play out of it after you catch the ball." Men showing guts in the face of speed and danger was also a major theme in 40 of the commercials that we analyzed.

THE TELEVISED SPORTS MANHOOD FORMULA

Tens of millions of U.S. boys watch televised sports programs, with their accompanying commercial advertisements. This study sheds light on what these boys are seeing when they watch their favorite sports programs. What values and ideas about gender, race, aggression, and violence are being promoted? Although there are certainly differences across different kinds of sports, as well as across different commercials, when we looked at all of the programming together, we identified 10 recurrent themes, which we have outlined above. Taken together, these themes codify a consistent and (mostly) coherent message about what it means to be a man. We call this message the Televised Sports Manhood Formula:

> What is a Real Man? A Real Man is strong, tough, aggressive, and above all, a winner in what is still a Man's World. To be a winner he has to do what needs to be done. He must be willing to compromise his own long-term health by showing guts in the face of danger, by fighting other men when necessary, and by "playing hurt" when he's injured. He must avoid being soft; he must be the aggressor, both on the "battle fields" of sports and in his consumption choices. Whether he is playing sports or making choices about which snack food or auto products to purchase, his aggressiveness will net him the ultimate prize: the adoring attention of conventionally beautiful women. He will know if and when he has arrived as a Real Man when the Voices of Authority—White Males—say he is a Real Man. But even when he has finally managed to win the big one, has the good car, the right beer, and is surrounded by beautiful women, he will be reminded by these very same Voices of Authority just how fragile this Real Manhood really is: After all, he has to come out and prove himself all over again tomorrow. You're only as good as your last game (or your last purchase).

The major elements of the Televised Sports Manhood Formula are evident, in varying degrees, in the football, basketball, baseball, Extreme sports, and *SportsCenter* programs and in their accompanying commercials. But it is in the dramatic spectacle of professional wrestling that the Televised Sports Manhood Formula is most clearly codified and presented to audiences as an almost seamless package. Boys and young men are drawn to televised professional wrestling in great numbers. Consistently each week, from four to six pro wrestling shows rank among the top 10 rated shows on cable television. Professional wrestling is not a real sport in the way that baseball, basketball, football, or even Extreme sports are. In fact, it is a highly stylized and choreographed "sport as theatre" form of entertainment. Its producers have condensed—and then amplified—all of the themes that make up the Televised Sports Manhood Formula. For instance, where violence represents a thread in the football or basketball commentary, violence makes up the entire fabric of the theatrical narrative of televised pro wrestling. In short, professional wrestling presents viewers with a steady stream of images and commentary that represents a constant fusion of all of the themes that make up the Televised Sports Manhood Formula: This is a choreographed sport where all men (except losers) are Real Men, where women are present as sexy support objects for the men's violent, monumental "wars" against each other. Winners bravely display muscular strength, speed, power, and guts. Bodily harm is (supposedly) intentionally inflicted on opponents. The most ruthlessly aggressive men win, whereas the passive or weaker men lose, often shamefully. Heroically wrestling while injured, rehabilitating oneself from former injuries, and inflicting pain and injury on one's opponent are constant and central themes in the narrative.

GENDER AND THE SPORTS/MEDIA/COMMERCIAL COMPLEX

In 1984, media scholar Sut Jhally pointed to the commercial and ideological symbiosis between the institutions of sport and the mass media and called it the sports/media complex. Our examination of the ways that the Televised Sports Manhood Formula reflects and promotes hegemonic ideologies concerning race, gender, sexuality, aggression, violence, and consumerism suggests adding a third dimension to Jhally's analysis: the huge network of multi-billion-dollar automobile, snack food, alcohol, entertainment, and other corporate entities that sponsor sports events and broadcasts. In fact, examining the ways that the Televised Sports Manhood Formula cuts across sports programming and its accompanying commercials may provide important clues as to the ways that ideologies of hegemonic masculinity are both promoted by—and in turn serve to support and stabilize—this collection of interrelated institutions that make up the sports/media/commercial complex. The Televised Sports Manhood Formula is a master discourse that is produced at the nexus of the institutions of sport, mass media, and corporations who produce and hope to sell products and services to boys and men. As such, the Televised Sports Manhood Formula appears well suited to discipline boys' bodies, minds, and consumption choices within an ideological field that is conducive to the reproduction of the entrenched interests that profit from the sports/media/commercial complex. The perpetuation of the entrenched commercial interests of the sports/media/commercial complex appears to be predicated on boys accepting—indeed glorifying and celebrating—a set of bodily and relational practices that resist and oppose a view of women as fully human and place boys' and men's long-term health prospects in jeopardy.

At a historical moment when hegemonic masculinity has been destabilized by socioeconomic change, and by women's and gay liberation movements, the Televised Sports Manhood Formula provides a remarkably stable and concrete view of masculinity as grounded in bravery, risk taking, violence, bodily strength, and heterosexuality. And this view of masculinity is given coherence against views of women as sexual support objects or as invisible and thus irrelevant to men's public struggles for glory. Yet, perhaps to be successful in selling products, the commercials sometimes provide a less than seamless view of masculinity. The insecurities of masculinity in crisis are often tweaked in the commercials, as we see weak men, dumb men, and indecisive men being eclipsed by strong, smart, and decisive men and sometimes being humiliated by smarter and more decisive women. In short, this commercialized version of hegemonic masculinity is constructed partly in relation to images of men who don't measure up.

Section XI: Media and Sport

This analysis gives us hints at an answer to the commonly asked question of why so many boys and men continue to take seemingly irrational risks, submit to pain and injury, and risk long-term debility or even death by playing hurt. A critical examination of the Televised Sports Manhood Formula tells us why: The costs of masculinity (especially pain and injury), according to this formula, appear to be well worth the price; the boys and men who are willing to pay the price always seem to get the glory, the championships, the best consumer products, and the beautiful women. Those who don't—or can't—pay the price are humiliated or ignored by women and left in the dust by other men. In short, the Televised Sports Manhood Formula is a pedagogy through which boys are taught that paying the price, be it one's bodily health or one's money, gives one access to the privileges that have been historically linked to hegemonic masculinity—money, power, glory, and women. And the barrage of images of femininity as model-like beauty displayed for and in the service of successful men suggest that heterosexuality is a major lynchpin of the Televised Sports Manhood Formula, and on a larger scale serves as one of the major linking factors in the conservative gender regime of the sports/media/commercial complex.

On the other hand, we must be cautious in coming to definitive conclusions as to how the promotion of the values embedded in the Televised Sports Manhood Formula might fit into the worlds of young men. It is not possible, based merely on our textual analysis of sports programs, to explicate precisely what kind of impact these shows, and the Televised Sports Manhood Formula, have on their young male audiences. That sort of question is best approached through direct research with audiences. Most such research finds that audiences interpret, use, and draw meanings from media variously, based on factors such as social class, race/ethnicity, and gender (Hunt, 1999; Whannel, 1998). Research with various subgroups of boys that explores their interpretations of the sports programs that they watch would enhance and broaden this study.

Moreover, it is important to go beyond the preferred reading presented here that emphasizes the persistent themes in televised sports that appear to reinforce the hegemony of current race, gender, and commercial relations (Sabo & Jansen, 1992). In addition to these continuities, there are some identifiable discontinuities within and between the various sports programs and within and among the accompanying commercials. For instance, commercials are far more varied in the ways they present gender imagery than are sports programs themselves. Although the dominant tendency in commercials is either to erase women or to present them as stereotypical support or sex objects, a significant minority of commercials present themes that set up boys and men as insecure and/or obnoxious schmucks and women as secure, knowledgeable, and authoritative. Audience research with boys who watch sports would shed fascinating light on how they decode and interpret these more complex, mixed, and paradoxical gender images against the dominant, hegemonic image of the Televised Sports Manhood Formula.

Sports and the Media:
Synergy Is the Key to Winning Success

Jerry Colangelo & Len Sherman

The current buzz for the melding together of capabilities and interests is synergy, as anyone who has even glanced at a story about a giant merger in the paper or attended an introductory business school course knows.

The television and radio industries have a singularly strong symbiotic relationship to sports. The media devour product as the channels and stations transmit 24 hours a day, every day of the year. That means the media need the entertainment value that sports bring and the guaranteed endless supply of entertainment.

And so the networks have paid handsomely to obtain those many, many games from a multitude of sports.

At the same time, the sports business needs the media, needs the exposure and the excitement and the rights fees the networks pay. Thus, it might seem to make obvious sense for our organization to purchase our own media outlet.

Some of the smartest people in business, who control some exceptionally huge corporations, have embraced that position with a passion—a profitable passion, at that. Ted Turner has made his Atlanta Braves into a terrifically profitable and winning team by broadcasting their games on his national cable system, Turner Broadcasting System—simultaneously generating tremendous revenue for TBS. In this manner, each component—the team and the cable system—creates profits for the other, resulting in an entirely win-win situation for Turner.

Taking the same idea to another level is Rupert Murdoch and his Fox Network.

For years, Fox has delved deeper and deeper into the sports broadcasting business—buying the rights to the NFL's NFC games, televising MLB games, establishing a series of regional sports networks, which concentrate on local professional and other contests. Now Murdoch has purchased the Los Angeles Dodgers, one of the most fabled franchises in any sport.

Apart from owning this immensely successful franchise, Murdoch might very well be planning to bring the team to a global audience through Fox's worldwide television reach.

If that should happen (and I have no inside information, one way or the other), watch the synergy at work: Fox builds a new worldwide base of fans, perhaps broadcasting Dodger games not only in North America, but also to baseball hot spots such as Japan and Latin America, creating a new market not only for additional TV advertising revenue but also Dodger souvenirs. Can you imagine how many Dodger caps you can sell once the team goes planetary?

The more revenue the network earns, the more sports and games it can bid on for broadcast, producing more revenue.

The more revenue the team receives, the more aggressive it can be in signing high-priced stars, outbidding teams without national (let alone international) support. Thus, the cycle continues, with more revenue buying a better team, which in turn produces more revenue for the franchise, allowing it to buy more stellar athletes, the cycle spinning effortlessly round and round.

That is synergy on a grand scale. For both Turner and Murdoch, of course, sports might be regarded as a secondary business—maybe even tertiary. The same is true today for many of the owners of the professional franchises in any sport.

Whether, in the long run, having these corporate owners is the best for basketball or baseball or football remains an open question—though there is no question that the phenomenal costs associated with professional sports have rendered the individual owner virtually extinct. I believe that this will prove not only inevitable but beneficial for the sports industry.

This assumes that these conglomerates will prove to be intelligent, responsible stewards of the teams they purchase.

However, if it should turn out that the corporations care more about the bottom line than for the team and the players and the fans, then that clearly will not be a healthy situation. Once the game—any game—simply becomes a commodity, it ceases to be a game in any meaningful or even interesting sense. Why should any fan care what happens to its hometown team when it is apparent that the team itself, as embodied by the owners and management, and maybe its extremely well-paid players, too, only regard the team as another line on an accounting sheet.

We have seen that happen in Miami.

Although a very young franchise, the decision was made to spend great sums to sign all-star free agents, in order to garner fan support. Though the Marlins won the World Series, the fan support didn't materialize—at least not the amount of fan support required to pay those huge player paychecks. Dissatisfied with its return on investment, the ownership decided to cut its losses and rid itself of its high-priced stars, trading them away in return for young prospects. This rather shocking turn-about—from

World Series champions one year to a team with the worst record in baseball the next—left the fans disillusioned and disgusted, and they have stayed away in droves.

Of course, it need not be that way.

The rush to win on the field and profit off it pushed the Marlins into a problematic strategy. A more sensible strategy for long-term stability and growth, and one that the Diamondbacks have pursued, is to build a farm system which will develop the young talent that will provide the major-league club with a progression of trained, skilled players, year after year.

I believe, and have always believed, that owning a professional sports team is a privilege, not a right. And that same sense of privilege should be felt and honored at every level of pro sports, from the owners to the management to the players.

That, returning to the main point, is one reason we have stayed with the businesses we knew and enjoyed. Getting back to the media, we looked at buying into TV or radio, but decided the cost was prohibitive. Even if we raised the necessary funding, the effort and money expended would distract us from our prime business and eventually detract from that business.

Meanwhile, we feel we have as good a situation as we could without controlling a media outlet, because we can control the inventory, the games, the product. It comes down to what your play is, what your point is, what you want to do with your life and in what business you want to be.

With that in the forefront of our corporate consciousness, packaging our product is as important as anything we do. We maintain control of our destiny by controlling our rights. Additionally, by owning so many teams, so many products, so many assets, we have extra leverage with the media.

And the media is the gateway for the sponsors and advertisers. So by packaging all these rights into one bundle—entering into exclusive arrangements combining television, radio, signage, tickets and other promotional and marketing opportunities—you can maximize the value of those rights.

When you're in a small market, or even a relatively small market when compared to the majors, it is not possible to sell your rights for enough to compete with the bigger markets. You can only be competitive by being better—which translates into more creative and aggressive—at packaging than anyone else.

And in sports, marketing is not simply a matter of earning profits for the franchise; rather, marketing is a primary means by which you fund the salaries of your players and the improvements in your training and facilities. Thus, marketing helps ensure the competitiveness on the court of your team. And our marketing success has helped the Suns remain one of the NBA's better teams, year in, year out.

When America West Arena opened in 1992–93, the Phoenix Suns, located in what was then the 19th largest television market in the country, led the NBA in revenues. We did not accomplish this by having the highest ticket prices in the league. To the contrary: our tickets were somewhere near the middle of the pack in cost. So tickets didn't do it for us.

Marketing did. A potential sponsor couldn't buy signage in the arena or any association with the team in lone purchases, nor by consulting the advertising rate card. He had to buy the entire package, soup to nuts. We raised the marketing bar in this way and got more for both our sponsors and for the franchise.

This approach, which was so stunningly successful, had two significant results.

First, we transformed the many local and national companies who worked with us into more than just advertisers or sponsors—we made them part of our team, part of our experience, which resulted in them wanting to do more to support both their efforts and ours. Second, on the heels of our success, other people and franchises began to alter their business philosophies and adopted ours. Along with the many new buildings going up around the league, our revenue lead vanished very quickly. Today, the New York Knicks, for example, enjoy revenues that are twice that of the Suns.

So our challenge is to stay ahead of the curve and continue to be a little bit more creative and aggressive than anyone else.

All in all, when considering the direction of our operations, the structure of our investments, the course of our business, I am fairly well satisfied with the situation the way it is....We've grown from 25 employees to 500 full-time employees and a couple of thousand part-timers. We will surely continue to grow—the question is how and in what direction. Whatever we do, maintaining a synergistic relationship with our key businesses is paramount.